Death of the LEAPING HORSEMAN

Death of the LEAPING HORSEMAN

The 24th Panzer Division in Stalingrad

12th August – 20th November 1942

Jason D. Mark

STACKPOLE
BOOKS

Published in hardcover in the U.S. in 2014 by
STACKPOLE BOOKS
4501 Forbes Boulevard, Suite 200
Lanham, Maryland 20706
www.rowman.com

Maps and illustrations by Jason D. Mark

Printed in India

Distributed by NATIONAL BOOK NETWORK

Library of Congress Cataloging-in-Publication Data

Mark, Jason D.
Death of the leaping horseman : the 24. Panzer-Division in Stalingrad, 12th August–20th November 1942 / Jason D. Mark. — [First Stackpole Books edition].

pages cm
Originally published: 2002.
ISBN 978-0-8117-1404-4

1. Germany. Heer. Panzer-Division, 24. 2. Stalingrad, Battle of, Volgograd, Russia, 1942–1943. 3. World War, 1939–1945—Regimental histories—Germany. I. Title.

D757.5624th .M37 2014
940.54'21747—dc23

2014009957

This book is dedicated to all the proud veterans of 24. Panzer-Division

CONTENTS

ACKNOWLEDGMENTS

This book is far more than my sole contribution. Many people have given unstinting support and valuable assistance, even in the early days when it seemed as if this book would never be completed. I will try to list them all but if I have forgotten to name you, please accept my gratitude. First of all, I would like to thank Thomas Heitzer from Switzerland for his generous contributions and his trust in me by sending copious amounts of research material half way around the world. I was introduced to Thomas by Heinz Schlaefereit and after my initial letter, a stack of excellent unpublished photographs arrived at my home. Rare regimental histories, divisional newsletters, diaries and more photos continued to arrive over the next few months. Without his assistance, this book would be much the poorer. Thanks again Thomas.

My heartfelt thanks go to all the veterans who responded to my letters, queries and questions. Their effort in replying to a young Australian author is particularly admirable, especially when one considers that some of these octogenarians wrote page after page of anecdotes and recollections, and also sent their own private photographs. Special thanks go to Heinz Kolczyk, Dr. Horst Rocholl, Hans-Ludwig v. Stockhausen, Hasse v. Langenn-Steinkeller, Kuno von Meyer, Georg von Raison, Heinz Schlaefereit, Dr. Hans-Georg von Tiedemann, Hans Henning v. Christen, Dr. Hubertus Schulz, Richard Wildeus, Günter Koschorrek, Ernst Panse and Ferdinand Kusterer. Thanks also to Christian Keiler, Egbert v. Schmidt-Pauli, Konrad Freiherr von Woellwarth, Gerhard Uebach, Heinz Wippermann, Peter Leidner, Friedhelm Heuelmann, Dr. Thedel Freiherr von Cramm, Dr. Wolfgang Kuls, Horst Haubold, Egon Rudi Schwenger, Andreas Igor-Meyhoeffer, Horst von Bassewitz, Ina v. Knebel-Doeberitz, Annemarie v.d. Decken-Offen, the family of Friedrich Raaf, Isa-Karin Freifrau v. Eickstedt, Gabriele v. Sivers, and Anneli Rogge. My sympathy goes to André von Raison who had the sad duty of informing me of his fathers death.

I cannot neglect to mention the assistance given to me by veterans of other units, particularly Ansgar Pawelke of Panzer-Regiment 15, Karl Heinz Loschke of 11. Panzer-Division and Walter Rahn for excellent information about Karl v. Sivers. Walter Rahn was Ordonanzoffizier to Karl v. Sivers and was able to provide personal insights into his character. Thanks too to Albert Schick of 10. Panzer-Division for great information and fantastic photographs of Oberst von Broich.

I am grateful for the help and advice given to me by two fellow Stalingrad researchers, Geert Rottiers from Belgium and Hans Wijers from The Netherlands. Both men are conducting first-rate research and by their efforts, are casting a bright light into the dark corners of history.

Geert maintains an excellent Stalingrad website and Hans is in contact with hundreds of veterans, organises reunions and writes and edits many books. I would especially like to thank Hans for introducing me to the microfilms of the National Archives in Washington because it is the 24. Panzer-Division war diaries contained on one of them that provided the solid framework for this book. Thanks!

I would like to recognise the professionalism of the Bundesarchiv staff, in particular Frau Martina Caspars, for their prompt response to all my requests. Thanks to the ECPA in Paris and the National Archives in Washington for supplying me with great photographs.

Thanks to Paul Macarthur and Michael J. Pruett for the use of photos from their private collections, and Peter Fogg for helping me with other photographic needs.

My greatest respect goes to the patrons of Jason Pipes' Heer forum on the Web (www.feldgrau.net). No matter how difficult or obscure my question, there was always somebody there who could give me a lengthy but clear explanation. Many tricky and colloquial translations were also solved by the guys on this forum.

My gratitude goes to the staff of University of Sydney Library for helping me in the early stages of my research. I remember the looks on their faces when they saw me sitting in front of a microfilm printer churning out hundreds – perhaps thousands – of pages of war diaries. And their patience in repeatedly fulfiling my requests for more paper and more toner. I fondly remember the many eight hour days I spent there… but I hope I never have to do it again!

Although all of these people have contributed greatly to my book, all judgements and interpretations are my own and they bear no responsibility for any errors.

In a few instances, I have been unable to trace the copyright holder of works where the publisher has ceased trading. In these cases I apologise for any unintentional breach of copyright.

Any comments, criticism, corrections or additions will be greatly appreciated. Write to me at leapinghorseman@hotmail.com

Jason D. Mark
Sydney, Australia
July 2002

Approach to Stalingrad

Chapter One

12th August 1942:

The cool wind blowing across the steppe pushed puffy white clouds across the sunny sky and rustled the long steppe grass, but it no longer carried the sounds of explosions and gunfire. A peaceful intermission was granted to the men of 24. Panzer-Division. Together with the temporary cessation of combat, the troops were enjoying a break in the hot sweltering weather that had been their constant companion since the beginning of the offensive. With other units of 6. Armee, 24. Panzer-Division and its men had completed the destruction of Russian forces in the large Don bend west of Kalach and as a result, both man and machine were in urgent need of rest and repair. The panzergrenadiers and riflemen, billeted in the few isolated villages, caught up on their daily housekeeping, darned socks, had their hair cut, shaved, as well as performing more military pursuits such as cleaning rifles and overhauling machine-guns. Most caught up on sleep. The panzers, half-tracks and almost all types of vehicles were heavily worn and fatigued after a month and a half of operations. Mechanics inspected the vehicles, hoisted engines out, worked on transmissions and recalibrated cannon and machine-guns. It seemed like the Division was in for a long spell of rest and recovery.
After the urgent repair of vehicles had begun in the morning in the area of Blishne Melnichny, a small village south of Chir railway station, the Division received an order in the afternoon to immediately reach 4. Panzer-Armee in the area of Shutovo 2 via Potemkinskaya and Kotelnikovo. The future strategic advance of 4. Panzer-Armee required more divisions. Generalmajor von Hauenschild, Division Commander, transmitted an order terminating all non-essential maintenance, so vehicles that had not yet been stripped down for repairs received orders to stand by. The first march group set off on the same day.

The operations of 4. Panzer-Armee had begun on 21st July when XXXXVIII. Panzerkorps (General Werner Kempf), led by 14. Panzer-Division and 29. Infanterie-Division (mot.), set out from the bridgehead established over the Don near Zymlianskaya. Supported by IV. Armeekorps and VI. Romanian Armeekorps, the panzers and motorised infantry made steady progress along the railway line, always heading north-east to Stalingrad. The basic plan was for XXXXVIII. Panzerkorps to advance on Stalingrad from the south after swinging out far to the east in a concentrated movement along the Yergeni Hills. After passing through Kotelnikovo on 2nd August and Shutovo railway station on 3rd August, the panzers swiftly seized Abganerovo on 7th August before the front stalled north of Plodovitoye. And there the front stayed. Generaloberst Hermann Hoth, commander of 4. Panzer-Armee, finally came to terms with his drastically overextended supply lines and dwindling forces and called a temporary halt to

further operations. Husbanding his offensive forces, fuel and supplies was now his main priority.
With Hoth's advance faltering and the destruction of the Russian bridgehead around Kalach completed, Generaloberst Paulus had been ordered by Hitler on 12th August to release the formidable 24. Panzer-Division to Hoth. The Division would have to complete a lengthy march to join up with Hoth's other armoured divisions, the first units moving off from the Chir area toward the bridge thrown across the Don River near Potemkinskaya.

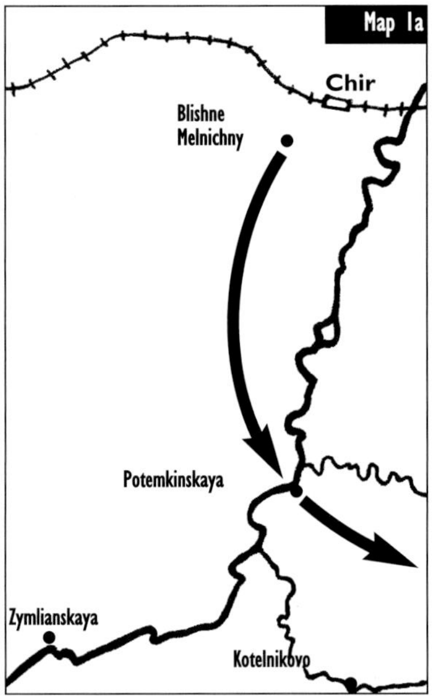

Casualties:

9 men killed

3 officers wounded (2 of those stayed with the troops)
- Oberleutnant Karl-Heinz Seufferheld; PGR26 (Wounded)
- Leutnant Müller (Zug Kdr); 1./PGR26 (Wounded but stayed with the troops)
- Hauptmann Erich Hicketier (Batterie Kdr); 2./PAR89 (Wounded but stayed with the troops)

22 men wounded (11 of those stayed with the troops)

13th August 1942:

The Division reached the Don River near Potemkinskaya in three march groups, their only battle being against the considerable traffic jams that developed due to 297. Infanterie-Division marching simultaneously on the same roads.

The sun shone down and bathed everything in a glorious light. A cool wind from the east blew into the faces of the panzer crewmen as they threaded their way toward the Don River. Immense log-jams of vehicles tried to funnel across the narrow pontoon bridges. Being the tip of the German lance allowed the panzers priority in crossing the bridge. The tracks of the panzers rattled the wooden

MARK

The Don! This is the view that greeted the German troops as they stood on the high western bank gazing to the east.

SPANNOCCHI

An engineer from a Brückenbau-Pionier-Bataillon (bridge construction battalion) takes a breather. The talc-like dust of Russian roads is clearly visible.

SPANNOCCHI

The first sections of the Potemkinskaya bridge are in place. More bridging ferries launched upstream carry some panzers across before being attached to the incomplete bridge.

SPANNOCCHI

A bridge is quickly assembled over the Don near Potemkinskaya. Seen in the background is one of the panzers being ferried across. These ferries later formed part of the bridge. By doing this, the panzers were delayed as little as possible while the bridge was being constructed.

KOLCZYK

Leutnant Freiherr von Maltzan's Panzer III '363' passes over the bridge spanning the Don River near Potemkinskaya. A few of the heavier vehicles had already been transported across the river by ferries.

planks on their metal stanchions, the midday sun's reflected light creating shimmering, watery patterns on the vehicles flanks and underbellies. The crews slumped in their hatches, eyeing the miserable landscape around them. The parched, treeless Kalmuck steppe stretched to all horizons before it disappeared into the distant glowing heat. Panzers and half-tracks shuddered and jolted through the roads, the dusty surface hiding an eroded base that was corrugated like a washboard. Stirred up by the pounding and whirring of tyres and tank tracks, massive clouds of dust developed, spreading out from the road. Fine yellow dust coated the black uniforms of the panzer crews. This hazy confusion was stressful and dangerous for the drivers; the massive walls of dust were honeycombed with shadows from which murky vehicles suddenly emerged. There were many near-misses – and many accidents.

Elements of 24. Panzer-Division stalled near the Don bridge around 1300 hours due to a lack of petrol and could not continue because no more had been obtained from 6. Armee. Now, 4. Panzer-Armee would supply it by dipping into its meagre reserves.

Late in the afternoon, Major i.G. Otto-Wilhelm von Menges, Ia (Chief-of-Staff) of 24. Panzer-Division, left his armoured units to continue their crossing. He'd been ordered to proceed to Korps HQ in Shutovo 2 for a meeting with General Kempf. It took quite a few hours of tortuous driving over bone-jarring, dusty roads before Major von Menges finally arrived at his destination at 2030 hours. With his arrival, the Division was formally subordinated to XXXXVIII. Panzerkorps. A conversation ensued between Korps' Chief-of-Staff Oberst i.G. Werner Friebe and Major von Menges. To begin with, the Division would be brought

MARK

Long-barrel Panzer IV '433' ploughs through powdery dust after crossing the river. With the front-line over a hundred kilometres distant, the crews were able to avoid their heated panzers' interiors by sitting outside.

forward to the area around Aksai where it would be held in reserve. Oberst Friebe discussed later operations of the Division and stressed that its arrival must not be discovered by the enemy, therefore, they were not allowed to reconnoitre to the east.

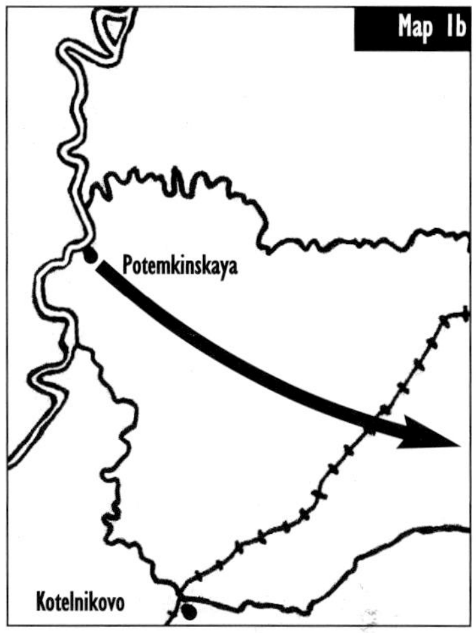

Casualties:
None

14th August 1942:

It would take days for the entire division to move into position. Out in front, heading the armoured procession, were the motorcycle and half-track reconnaissance platoons from Kradschützen-Abteilung 4. Keeping a diary was a young officer cadet, Fahnenjunker-Wachtmeister von Senger und Etterlin, leading the 1st platoon of Oberleutnant Heinz Kolczyk's 2. Schwadron: "After a short night's rest, we moved in a north-easterly direction into the steppe. A monstrous, whirling dust storm of such a kind arose that the man in front could not be seen. The salty ash dust got into everything. The weapons were smeared with dust. In our vehicles, we were up to our ankles in dust. We were black from the dirt which stuck to our sweat-moistened shirts and faces. I had two pairs of glasses on, one on top of the other, to prevent inflammation to my eyes. However, the advance continued unremittingly and we reached the railway line at Aksai."

The long, jostling column of panzers, half-tracks and armoured cars headed due east from Potemkinskaya into assembly areas on the other side of the Kotelnikovo-Stalingrad railway line, just south of Plodovitoye. One of the men remembers his first glimpse of this stretch of railway: "After several hours, we came to the single-tracked railway line from Rostov to Stalingrad. This railway line was unimaginably primitive, the sleepers simply placed on the sand without gravel so that an express train could not pass over it. The Russians did not ask much, however, the most important thing was that it fulfiled its purpose: sealed roads also weren't available. Rifle-pits were dug into the railway embankment. The Russians had defended themselves bitterly here."

WÄSCHLE

The division's vast armada of vehicles raises a huge cloud of dust as it heads east across the barren steppe. The temperature was well over 40 degrees C.

It was another warm day on the Russian steppe. Kilometre after kilometre of lifeless brown desert passed before the eyes of the panzer crews, the visual and spiritual monotony broken only by isolated settlements, small mud and wood houses surrounded by shady trees and lush gardens. From the dirty, noisy machines of war baking under the blazing sun, bleary eyes stared through dusty

SPANNOCCHI

The armoured spearhead is forced to halt to take on fuel. Shown here is Oberleutnant von Helldorff, platoon commander in 4./Panzer-Regiment 24, his face completely blackened by the choking black dust.

goggles at the inviting oases, full of vegetation, shade and tropical fruit. There were even reminders of the proximity to Asia: Bactrian camels, the two-humped relative of the well-known dromedary.

As the armoured vehicles trundled into the empty steppe east of the Don River, the grenadiers and riflemen of the two panzergrenadier regiments continued to slog their way south in their lorries from Nizhne-Chirskaya. Despite intense heat and unbelievable clouds of dust, they covered 90 – 110km on this day. Obergefreiter Walter Reddig, a driver in 1. Schwadron of Panzergrenadier-Regiment 21 wrote in his diary: "14th August: Continued along the Don, regular marshy areas, immense amount of dust. 1800 hours. Don crossed and spent the night on the open ground."

After they crossed the bridge, the grenadiers were given a short breather in a verdant forested depression west of the river before setting out through the parched steppe, first of all in a south-east direction, then later turning to the north-east toward Kotelnikovo. As on the previous day, petrol shortages delayed the march. The head of the Division – given the lion's share of the petrol – reached the Aksai area after a troublesome 250km march with oppressive heat and sandstorms. The first to arrive were elements of the Kradschützen-Abteilung 4 in the Aksai area and Division Stab, Panzer-Nachrichten Abteilung 86, Panzerjäger-Abteilung 40 and a light Artillerie Abteilung in Peregrusnyi.

Generalmajor von Hauenschild arrived at Korps headquarters at 1705 hours. General Kempf rose from his chair and walked to the entrance to greet him, Hauenschild saluted and both men shook hands. They then sat down and discussed various topics, concentrating on the arrival of the Division and its future assignments. Hauenschild departed an hour later. Hardly had he left when at 1830 hours General Ferdinand Heim, Commander of 14. Panzer-Division, called Oberst Friebe at Korps headquarters wanting the subordination of Kradschützen-Abteilung 4. Friebe told him that he would discuss it with General Kempf. After getting off the phone with Heim, Oberst Friebe then called Major von Menges at 24. Panzer-Division headquarters and informed him of the proposed subordination of Kradschützen-Abteilung 4 and that it was still being decided. It was not much of a decision for General Kempf. He saw that 14. Panzer-Division required the forces of Kradschützen-Abteilung 4 and he gave the go ahead for subordination. Oberst Friebe picked up the receiver and informed the appropriate parties that Kradschützen-Abteilung 4 was now officially subordinated to 14. Panzer-Division and would begin relieving the security forces of that division on the east flank.

The Division now had the duel role of serving as Korps-Reserve and taking over the security of the east flank of the Korps as part of 14. Panzer-Division. This last task was entrusted to the

SPANNOCCHI

The panzers and half-tracks refuel in the middle of the Aksai. Enormous quantities of fuel were required to fill the tanks of the thirsty panzers (note the rows of petrol drums). On the right (in front of the half-track) are Oberleutnant von Helldorff and Major von Winterfeld. In the background, Panzer II's 455, 454 and 453 (from the staff of 4. Panzer Schwadron) are in the process of refuelling, and behind them are Panzer 251 (Rittmeister Spannocchi's vehicle) and Panzer 252. In the distance, supply lorries head west after delivering the vital fuel.

SPANNOCCHI

The Sdkfz. 251 half-tracks of Oberleutnant von Dressler's I./Panzergrenadier-Regiment 26 also use the opportunity to replenish their vehicles' empty tanks.

SPANNOCCHI

The short refuelling stop is also utilised to check over the vehicles before the strenuous desert march is recommenced.

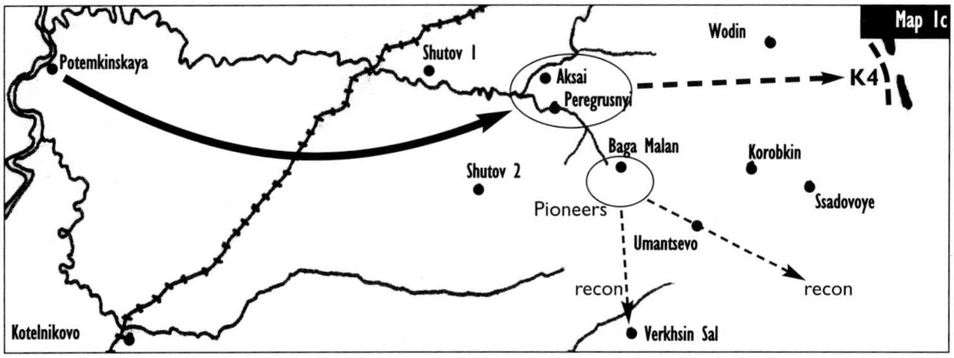

riflemen of Hellermann's Kradschützen-Abteilung, who climbed into their half-tracks and motorcycles and disappeared over the hills to the east.

Casualties:
None

15th August 1942:

The night passed quietly for the units of 24. Panzer-Division, scattered for hundreds of kilometres from the Aksai to the western shore of the Don. The day's effort would concentrate on bringing forward the bulk of the Division's forces and laagering them in the Aksai area. At 1225 hours, Generalmajor von Hauenschild called Oberst Friebe at Korps headquarters to outline the Division's plans for the day. Ritter von Hauenschild was in good cheer: the weather was comfortable with blue skies and a tepid breeze, there was no Russian interference and his units were moving into their rendezvous areas according to schedule. General von Hauenschild told Oberst Friebe that he would drop by at about 1400 hours after he had checked on the progress of his units.

Gruppe Hellermann (reinforced Kradschützen-Abteilung 4) took over a 25km front east of Plodovitoye, providing protection for the eastern flank of Korps whose front faced to the north, while the bulk of the Division pulled into the rest area around Aksai and repaired its vehicles. Fahnenjunker-Wachtmeister von Senger und Etterlin was with Gruppe Hellermann: "In 58 degree heat and continuous dust storms, we advanced further through the Kalmuck steppe toward the north-east. For days on end there are no human settlements, the earth is bare, burnt black and heatwaves rise into the air. There are no roads. We drive with the march compass over the hills. The Kalmuck steppe has swallowed us up."
Gruppe Hellermann took up positions behind the right flank of XXXXVIII. Panzerkorps where it was hanging in the air near Plodovitoye. Together with the rest of Kradschützen Abteilung 4, Fahnenjunker-Wachtmeister von Senger und Etterlin and his platoon moved into their assigned defensive sector: "Our Abteilung pushed up the slope of Yergeni Hill, which was in front like a straight chain crossing the Kalmuck steppe from north to south. Its east slope was as steep as that of the Don shore. We set up our defences here. In front of us, the salt-flats were completely flat and extended all the way to the Volga. At the foot of our hill, about four kilometres in the distance, lay the reedy shores of Lakes Tsatsa and Barmantsak. Through the scissors telescope we could see the bright silver glittering band of the Volga on the horizon.

WÄSCHLE

Oberleutnant Heinrich von Helldorff, commander of the Panzer IV long-barrel platoon of 4./Panzer-Regiment 24, sits atop the cupola of panzer '431'.

With that, we were the first German soldiers in the south to catch sight of Little Mother Volga."

To the men of 24. Panzer-Division, the bleak parched steppe was not the Russia they'd imagined. This was a barren desert. The blinding sun beat down mercilessly, huge clouds of dust billowed and swirled through the heated air, salt flats and endless expanses of lifeless, uninhabited dirt stretched from morning to night. This wasn't Russia, it was Africa! With these desert-like conditions, the men quickly adapted and they soon looked the part. After the panzer schwadrons of Oberst Gustav Riebel's Panzer-Regiment 24 had pulled into their assigned preparation areas near Peregrusnyi, the crews worked feverishly to bring the machines to the highest state of preparedness. Their new work fatigues: blue swimming trunks. Thus when the Regiment Commander drove past the laager area of 4. Schwadron, he was met by an incongruous sight. Oberleutnant Heinrich von Helldorff, a 24-year old platoon commander in the Schwadron, reported to Oberst Riebel complete with a bare-shaven head, Badoglio-style beard and wearing nothing but blue swimming trunks and jackboots. With a wry smile, Oberst Riebel registered this new style of 'desert attire'.

Oberleutnant Dietrich Micke, Abteilung Adjutant of I./Panzergrenadier-Regiment 21, also remembers the trying conditions: "The weather was unchanged for weeks. A merciless sun shone down on us from a mostly cloudless sky, the treeless steppe giving no protection from it. The loess soil was stone hard like a threshing floor and was run through with crevices, the grass was withered and frequent steppe fires – a ghostly sight at night – burned on the large plains. Where we or the panzers were advancing, one could not escape the yellow powdery dust. Uniforms, faces, vehicles, everything was constantly powdered with yellow dust, eyes were inflamed."

Although the conditions were tough, and memories of them occur with great frequency in veterans' eyewitness accounts, they did not really pose a major problem for the men. Rittmeister

Heinz Kolczyk recalls: "It was certainly dusty and hot, however, I cannot recall that soldiers of our age and professional training had particular difficulties."

As evening fell, most of 24. Panzer-Division had arrived in their accommodation areas with the exception of the supply services. Kradschützen-Abteilung 4 had taken over security on the east flank of 14. Panzer-Division south-east of Plodovitoye and so far, had only weak enemy contact. Pilots, however, reported large columns marching from north to south on the Tsatsa and Ssarpakin roads. Reconnaissance towards M. Derbety would be carried out as ordered with the beginning of the day on 16th August. There was only enough fuel for 50km, so rapid operations of large units on the east flank were not guaranteed.

Casualties:
None

16th August 1942:

The night passed quietly without enemy air activity. At 0745 hours, General Heim, Commander of 14. Panzer-Division, pressed Korps' Chief-of-Staff Oberst i.G. Friebe, saying that 24. Panzer-Division should take over the sector on the east flank of Korps. Oberst Friebe believed that the enemy should remain unaware of the arrival of 24. Panzer-Division for as long as possible. A small risk had already been taken by allowing Kradschützen-Abteilung 4 to take over a security sector but now, with more units of 24. Panzer-Division being proposed for security duty, it was less certain that the Russians would remain unaware of the presence of the Division. Oberst Friebe's misgivings were genuine but nevertheless, it was ordered. At 0900 hours, the corresponding order was issued to 24. Panzer-Division which requested to be allowed to employ several of its units side by side for this security assignment, in this way enabling part of the Division to carry out repairs. Oberst Friebe said that the Division, including Kradschützen-Abteilung 4, would be responsible for securing the eastern flank.

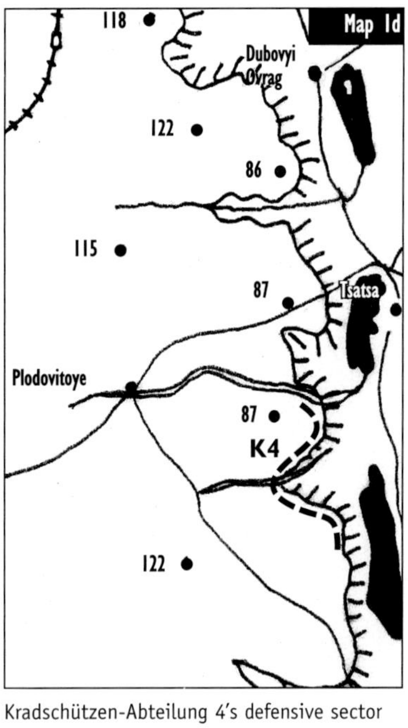

Kradschützen-Abteilung 4's defensive sector

At 0840 hours, Oberst Friebe called Hauptmann Roth, O1 of 24. Panzer-Division, and informed him that he wanted him, the Ordonanzoffizier of the Division, to come to Korps headquarters with maps showing the accommodation areas of the Division. At 0950 hours, Hauptmann Roth arrived at Korps command post in Schelestov with his numerous maps and oriented General Kempf and Oberst Friebe about the attained areas of the Division's units: "The pioneers are in Baga Mallan, the panzers in Peregrusnyi, and the supply services are still behind the Don. The brigade staff is in Aksai."

Friebe: "The Division must take over security on the east flank. Reconnoitre in the direction of Verkhsin Ssal and Umantsevo."

Oberst Friebe stressed that deep reconnaissance was

undesirable because there was a chance that the enemy still knew nothing about the arrival of the Division. This was to be taken into consideration, particularly during reconnaissance operations. Kradschützen-Abteilung 4 was re-subordinated to the Division. When Hauptmann Roth left Korps headquarters to head back to divisional headquarters, he took the latest Korpsbefehl with him.

At 1015 hours, Oberst Friebe reported to Major von Menges that a Kompanie of z.b.V. 800[1] was subordinated to 24. Panzer-Division for execution of special missions. This unit, with its innocuous designation, was in fact a unit of the famous Brandenburgers, their main task being infiltration behind Soviet lines in captured trucks and uniforms to seize important objectives, mostly bridges. The unit was filled with men that had a good knowledge of the Russian language and mentality but it is not exactly clear what their task was during their time with 24. Panzer-Division. The strength of the unit was 9 officers, 50 non-commissioned officers and 304 men, a total strength of 363 men.
In the meantime, the enemy displayed increased reconnaissance and movement activity in the deep east flank. This was probably the main reason why Heim wanted 24. Panzer-Division to shoulder more of the burden of protecting the lengthy eastern flank and the Division soon received the order to secure the deep east flank of Korps on an 80km front on the line Korobkin – Sakarov – hills 12km north-east of Plodovitoye. Reconnaissance troops based near Vassiliev secured further to the south, sending out patrols deep into the barren Volga lowlands. The most important hills, roads and villages were occupied as strongpoints but orientation was particularly difficult in the desert-like region without houses and roads. It was made more complicated by inadequate maps which often did not show the deeply-cut balkas – steep walled gullies washed out by rain and often kilometres long – making orientation so tricky that many units thoroughly lost their way. The only sign of human habitation were dusty roads that scoured their way through the scrubby steppe vegetation, heading over the horizon to one of the few small villages.

Small skirmishes occasionally flared during the week that the divisions were preparing themselves for the continued thrust to the north. Even at Kotelnikovo, now 70 kilometres behind the front, Soviet probes were a constant problem. The small Russian hamlet was base for one of 24. Panzer-Division's panzer workshop companies. Russian tanks rolled toward Kotelnikovo from the south-east out of the blazing Kalmuck steppe. There were no front-line forces available to repel the attack. KV-Rat[2] Reinhard Schönberger, commander of this company, hitched a damaged panzer to a powerful 18-tonne prime mover and dragged it out to the field of battle. Guiding the firefight through the radio on his prime mover, he was able to knock out several Russian tanks. The remaining tanks hadn't expected this fierce resistance. They turned around and utilised the shimmering heat mirages to scurry out of sight. A mechanic saved the day.

Barely 60 kilometres south of Stalingrad, the dusty panzers of Panzer-Regiment 24 were parked in hollows and gullies near Plodovitoye, waiting and preparing until they were to move out. The crews attempted to camouflage their vehicles with branches of green foliage but there wasn't nearly enough for the entire regiment. They needn't have worried; the Luftwaffe had complete aerial supremacy. During the daytime, anyway. At night, Russian biplanes would buzz

1. Zur besonderen Verwendung, or "at special employment."
2. KV-Rat, or Kriegsverwaltungsrat, was an administration official with the equivalent rank of Major.

overhead, toss flares overboard and circle the slowly descending parachutes, searching for signs of German activity. With the flares temporarily bathing the steppe in their false light, the German tank crews wouldn't move because they were safe in the trenches set in the ground below their tanks. A couple of 50 kilogram bombs scattered over the area and the planes would scarper back to their bases over the Volga.

On the security line along the Yergeni Hills, an enemy intrusion on the boundary between Kradschützen-Abteilung 4 and the right wing of I./Panzergrenadier-Regiment 103 of 14. Panzer-Division was repulsed by concentrated fire. Several attacks in battalion strength were repulsed under high enemy casualties by Gruppe Hellermann. The half-tracks of Kradschützen-Abteilung 4 were involved in one of these fiery little engagements. Fahnenjunker-Wachtmeister (Fhjwm.) von Senger und Etterlin reports:

> "It was Sunday and it was decided that we have a dance. The battalion was spread out 15 kilometres wide. Between us and 3. Schwadron on the right was a several kilometre wide gap and on the slope down to the east were unpleasant gullies. A reconnaissance troop discovered that strong Russian forces were approaching our hill position through these gullies. It was now best to attack the enemy before he struck back and before he realised how weak we were.
>
> "The 3rd platoon and I quickly drove to the enemy-occupied gully.
>
> "The 3rd platoon swung out far to the east to block the enemy's way back, while I attacked. We drove forward carefully with our right flank along the gully, ready to turn off at any time. All of a sudden we were halted by anti-tank rifle and machine-gun fire coming from a small hollow about 100 metres away. I received several hits but they bounced off. Both armoured glass blocks were shattered. The enemy could not be seen in the high weeds. As we slowly advanced, I suddenly glimpsed a Russian helmet through my optics. Because of the continuous, strong, anti-tank rifle fire I received an order requesting help. The hollow where the enemy was located extended to the right into the deep gully. In the gully, the enemy in company strength prepared to push past us and advance further towards the hill.
>
> "I decided to cut off the enemy's retreat on the right and therefore allow the group in the hollow to be passed in one swift bound, the enemy then being squeezed on two sides. We cautiously crept up to the edge of the hollow. The first, nevertheless, raised their heads above it and fell back with head wounds. We had hand grenades thrown at us by the enemy, whom we had not yet seen; however, they were stronger than we had thought, with several machine-guns, a small mortar and 2 anti-tank rifles firing ferociously out of the hollow.
>
> "We threw our hand grenades simultaneously and we then leapt out together. Suddenly we discovered that there were Russians on the hill behind us. The 3rd platoon had pushed too far to the east and was not yet in sight. The Commander ordered the foot assault to join up and to stay put. The 4th platoon was pulled back. (While the 2nd platoon remained in its positions, the empty vehicles of Leutnant Schulz, the commander of the Nachrichtenzug[3], counterattacked steadily, approaching the enemy who were threatening our positions. Every vehicle was occupied only by a driver and a machine-gunner to deceive the enemy about our full firepower).
>
> "At last the 3rd platoon also arrived and we concentrated the whole Schwadron to

3. Communications platoon.

> drive against the hollow. After a short, close-quarters battle, the enemy was destroyed. He then retired into a deep hole and fought to the last man. Even the badly wounded threw grenades, then we cleaned out the gully. About 30 men were destroyed here. We captured a heavy machine-gun, 3 anti-tank rifles and 1 mortar.
>
> "Unfortunately I also had two killed.
>
> "After this was finished, we then turned around and attacked the enemy placed in our rear; they had prepared the heights and were able to shoot into our vehicles from above. A projectile smacked near my seat, and a splinter penetrated my right hand, so that I could not use it. In a quick drive we pushed the group of Russians further back into the grass.
>
> "Twenty metres from me a Russian raised himself and threw a phosphorous-filled bottle (Molotov cocktail). My driver Anton, however, was alert and stepped on the gas pedal and drove through the Russians as the bottle went flying over my head. A lot of Russians with sub-machine guns were lying next to us; they all had Molotov cocktails and soon there were burning circles in the arid, dry steppe vegetation."

Wachtmeister von Senger und Etterlin's commander, Rittmeister Heinz Kolczyk, also recalls this fierce little encounter:[4]

> "I remember belonging to Kampfgruppe Edelsheim (who, by the way, was a genuine nobleman). My Schwadron was employed to secure a sector of the high ground up to Lake Tsatsa. Along this position, it came to combat action with a strong Russian reconnaissance troop (Stalin School) where I received an eye injury[5]. A combat-strength Russian reconnaissance troop in platoon strength (about 25 men) attacked our securing forces located in earth positions. In reaction, I launched an enveloping attack on the enemy with two platoons from my Schwadron. The enemy was quickly encircled and prepared himself for defence in a hollow, incessantly shooting at us. The hollow had a diameter of about 80 metres. Our armoured vehicles, 15 in number, positioned themselves around it.
>
> "My requests through a translator to give themselves up was answered with fire from submachine-guns and pistols. Repeated requests also led to no result! When almost all of them had been shot and two escapees moved toward us, one Russian came up through the heap of dead bodies and fired at us. We also had to use armed force on the two escapees so that they could not make use of their firearms in the current situation. From around 30 Russians, only these two were captured alive. The others were encircled by our half-tracks and, without heeding our request to surrender,

---

4. Herr Kolczyk prefaced this account with the following: "I thought about whether I should give you a report about a murderous event from this time. It isn't mentioned in any book and happened about a kilometre from the Abteilung command post. It verifies the fact that during war, men and commanders can be influenced to do the inhuman!!! (I'm still completely conscious of my terrible experiences during this war!!!) I will leave it up to you whether this genuine, dreadful history should suffice to serve as a warning for future generations!!!"
5. Herr Kolczyk said the following about his injury: "On 20th August, I sent myself to a doctor at the main hospital because I had a slight complaint with the sight in my right eye. The examination showed that there was a minute splinter in the cornea directly in front of the lens and the pinhead-sized splinter was immediately removed with a special instrument. This wound, entered into my Wehrpass on 16th August as 'Gr. Spl. Kopf.' (Mortar shrapnel in head), had not even registered to me as a wound because I was only away from my troops for an hour."

KOLCZYK

Rittmeister Heinz Kolczyk, Commander of 2. Schwadron of Kradschützen-Abteilung 4, equipped with half-tracks.

allowed themselves to be shot. The two prisoners later clarified the reason to us. Someone had told them that the German tanks were only dummies. After the interrogation, it appeared that this battle-strength reconnaissance troop consisted of 18-20 year old Stalin School cadets equipped with modern radio equipment."

In the divisional war diary, this savage little encounter only rated the following mention: "An enemy attack in company strength on 87.0 was repulsed."

While the bulk of Panzergrenadier-Regiment 21 would have 3 days rest in their assembly area, Major Wilhelm Schwanke's II. Abteilung already marched 40km further to the east in the afternoon. On the edge of the Yergeni hills, which extended from the large Volga bend near Krassnoarmeisk down to the south, the Abteilung secured the right flank of the Division in widely separated strongpoints with a front to the east. Further south, motorised reconnaissance troops reconnoitred into the steppe. North of II. Abteilung's sector were II./Panzergrenadier-Regiment 26 and Kradschützen-Abteilung 4. About nine to ten kilometres further east in front of these positions, extending from north to south through the endless lowlands parallel to the hills, was a chain of partially silted-up salt lakes and between them were several villages. At 2135 hours, 24. Panzer-Division reported to Korps that Tundutovo was enemy-free at 1900 hours. M. Derbety and the villages north of there in the chain of lakes were enemy-occupied. For the time being, it was still unclear whether the small-scale attacks were reconnaissance probes or whether the Russians wanted to produce a preparation area for later attacks. It seemed likely that new enemy forces were being brought in from the area of Astrakhan or from the north-east through the Kalmuck steppe.

Casualties:

10 men killed

1 officer wounded (he stayed with the troops)

- Oberarzt Dr. Twardy (Regiment Arzt); PAR89 (Wounded but stayed with the troops)

32 men wounded (17 of those stayed with the troops)

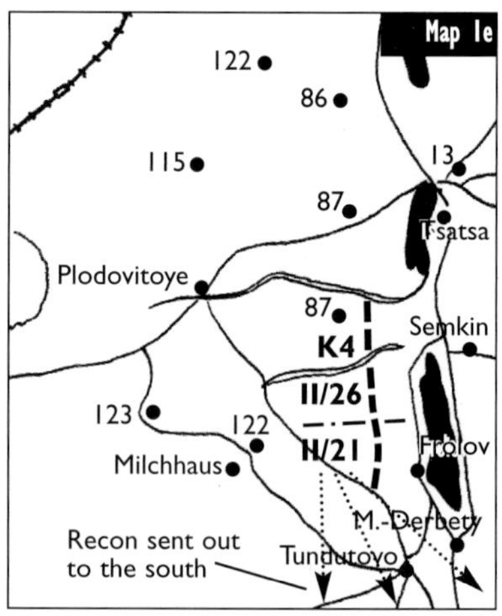

17th August 1942:

A generally quiet day for the Division. 24. Panzer-Division continued to secure the east flank of Korps, repelling small enemy probes. In the area of M. Derbety, two enemy companies and several tanks were identified. Air reconnaissance reported 15-20 enemy tanks 3km north-east of Tundutovo and vehicular traffic between M. Derbety – Tundutovo – Tsatsa.

At 2020 hours, General Kempf called 24. Panzer-Division. He wanted Generalmajor von Hauenschild to come with him for a meeting at 14. Panzer-Division HQ the next day to discuss details of the upcoming offensive. Hauenschild would make sure that his Division was used properly and not frittered away in some pointless offensive. That's how it had been since he assumed command. Generalmajor Bruno Ritter von Hauenschild was the experienced commander that this young panzer division needed. Born in Würzburg, Bavaria on 9th June 1896, 18-year old Bruno entered military service after matriculation as an officer candidate in the replacement battalion of 11. bayer. Feld.-Art.Rgt. (11th Bavarian Field Artillery Regiment). He was severely wounded in November 1914 and soon after, promoted to Leutnant in the field. He participated in the bloody battles along the Western Front, infamous battles that came to represent the futility of the Great War – the Somme, Artois, Cambrai. He suffered his fifth wound during defensive combat in August 1917, recovered, went back to the front and on 2nd September 1918, achieved the feat-of-arms that stamped him and all his later subordinates with the qualities of responsibility and individual initiative: in the battle near Bapaume with several batteries concentrated under his command, he steadfastly held out despite repeated counterorders and thus made it possible to parry the English penetration between Dury and Cagnicourt. For that, he was awarded the highest Bavarian medal for bravery, the Militär-Max-Joseph-Orden. The bestowal of this medal did not take place until after the war, on 2nd November 1921. During the war, he received the Iron Cross Second Class on 12th May 1915 and the First Class on 6th December 1917, as well as the Hausorden von Hohenzollern mit Schwerten, a rare decoration for a Leutnant.

During the critical years of 1918-1920, the course of Bruno von Hauenschild's life took a direction that led him straight into the Panzertruppe. From 1st October 1920, he was an officer in Kraftfahr-Kompanie 121. That was the beginning of his career in mobile warfare. As an Oberleutnant, he became Adjutant of Kraftfahr-Abteilung 7 in Munich on 13th October 1924, taking command of a similar unit in May 1928, now as a Hauptmann. After a transfer in October 1930, he came under the gaze of two of the 'pioneers of the Panzerwaffe', Generalmajor Lutz and Oberstleutnant Guderian, who confirmed that 'von Hauenschild has fundamentally advanced the formation of motorised reconnaissance battalions and the supplying of motorised combat troops with panzers and communications equipment'. High praise indeed! Von Hauenschild soon returned to his Kraftfahr-Abteilung in Munich and became its commander on 15th

Generalmajor Bruno Ritter von Hauenschild

September 1935, the unit receiving a new name exactly a month later: its new designation was Aufklärungs-Abteilung (mot.) 7. In August 1938, now an Oberstleutnant, he was called to Vienna to take command of Aufklärungs-Regiment 9, an experimental formation, and it was in this role that his commander said that he had 'boundless energy and devotion to troops subordinated to him'. This characteristic was shown again and again to the men of 24. Panzer-Division.

After winter training in 1938/39, operations in acquiring the Protectorates and intensive summer training in 1939, Hauenschild led his regiment over the Polish border on 1st September 1939 as the armoured spearhead of 4. leichte-Division, starting from the Carpathian Mountains and Beskiden, pushing through Radymno and in only two weeks, reaching the Bug. He received the Clasp to his Iron Cross Second Class on 24th September 1939 and for the First Class on 19th October. Upon conclusion of the Polish Campaign, he was named as commander of Panzer-Regiment 7 in October, leading this unit from success to success during the French Campaign. On 1st February 1941, he became commander of Panzer-Brigade 4, the formidable panzer unit of 10. Panzer-Division that pushed over the Russian border on 22nd June 1941 at the tip of XXXXVI. Panzerkorps. Leading a swift wedge of armoured vehicles, Hauenschild advanced from the Beresina up to the Dnepr where, on his own initiative, he seized several important bridges and formed a bridgehead that proved vital for the continuation of Korps' assault. Barely two months after the beginning of the Barbarossa, Oberst von Hauenschild was awarded the Knight's Cross on 25th August 1941 for his excellent leadership. This advance came to a standstill at Yelnya where for more than two months, the Division grimly fought back vicious Russian attacks, holding the line while other panzer units completed the massive encirclement of Kiev, an overwhelming tactical victory for the Germans but a massive strategic blunder. The advance towards Moscow was resumed on 1st October but two vital months had been lost. Oberst von Hauenschild and his panzers spearheaded the attack to the north-east and participated in the destruction of the enemy in the Vyazma pocket before continuing on to the main goal. The advance ground to a halt on 5th December just outside Moscow's western gate.

Hauenschild was called away from this icy hell and sent to France, arriving in early January 1942 at the embryonic division's command post in Georgenthal near Paris. His main task was to provide advice on motorisation and armoured combat tactics while also being in provisional command. Due to a tardy and inadequate allocation of panzers, the appropriate training of Panzer-Regiment 24 was made considerably more difficult and Hauenschild did not hesitate to make his feelings known in a report on the situation to OKH. The panzers arrived a couple of weeks later and on 26th February, training in panzer tactics began. Oberst von Hauenschild officially took command of 24. Panzer-Division on 15th April 1942 while it was forming near Rennes in France. A week later, he received a promotion to Generalmajor – backdated to 1st April – to reflect his new position as a division commander. Ritter von Hauenschild's 22 years of experience in motorisation, his knowledge of artillery from World War One and his acumen as a master panzer tactician all served to meld the Division – rich in cavalry traditions – into a formidable combination of strength, mobility and armoured might. This was proven from the beginning of the summer offensive when it pierced the enemy lines and reached Voronesh, swept through the large Don bend and now stood on Stalingrad's doorstep.

Casualties:

1 man killed

4 men wounded

18th August 1942:

The glorious sunshine gave way on this morning to overcast skies and cool winds and for the first time in three weeks, rain fell on the bone-dry steppe. At 0700 hours on the east flank, an enemy attack in the strength of two companies against Point 87.0, being held by Kradschützen-Abteilung 4, was smashed by artillery fire. Apart from this, the day passed quietly for 24. Panzer-Division. From the left came rolling thunder as XXXXVIII. Panzerkorps, with elements of 14. Panzer-Division and the entire 29. Infanterie-Division (mot.), attacked the enemy in the salient between Abganerovo village and Abganerovo railway station to straighten the front. This attack was launched at 0330 hours.

At 0850 hours, Major von Menges telephoned Oberst Friebe at Korps and asked whether known enemy batteries on the east flank could be suppressed. After a quick discussion with General Kempf, it was decided that this would still maintain secrecy about the arrival of 24. Panzer-Division and was therefore approved.

Towards midday Major Schwanke's II. Abteilung of Panzergrenadier-Regiment 21 was relieved by pioneers and shifted into a preparation area west of Lake Barmantsak, out of which at 0430 hours on the following day they were to attack the village of Vassiliev on the west shore of that same lake. It turned out that the enemy had evacuated it so the attack was not necessary. Mid-morning, General von Hauenschild jumped into his Kübelwagen and headed to Korps headquarters where he met General Kempf. Both of them drove to 14. Panzer-Division HQ north of Plodovitoye. There, a conference was convened with Generals Heim and von Hauenschild to discuss the proposed operation. The broad plan for the assault was firmly set but it still lacked the fine details and local objectives, many being set after the early attack of XXXXVIII. Panzerkorps had been taken into account. The three generals concluded the meeting and went back to their respective units. Once back at his HQ, General von Hauenschild immediately set his staff into action. He briefly outlined the plan of the assault and instructed his officers to draw up a preliminary order. The Division Quartermaster, Major i.G. Heinrich von Hobe, was set probably the most important task: calculating whether the Division's available fuel supplies would be sufficient. No-one was surprised when he confirmed that they weren't. He also reported a shortage of grease and lubricants. Therefore, at 1712 hours, Generalmajor von Hauenschild informed Korps that there wasn't sufficient fuel available for the planned attack and that an especially large deficiency of grease existed. Korps Chief-of-Staff Oberst Friebe replied: "It is known. We are also sending aerial photos for the sector of the lakes on the east flank." After getting off the phone with General von Hauenschild, Friebe and Kempf discussed this issue. Kempf knew that this matter with petrol supplies could jeopardise the timing of the offensive so at 1720 hours, Oberst Friebe informed the Chief-of-Staff of 4. Panzer-Armee, Oberst i.G. Friedrich Fangohr, about the petrol shortage and expressed Kempf's doubts about the success of the operation on these grounds.

An hour later, General Kempf was still concerned about the grease problem so he telephoned Oberst Fangohr at 1825 hours: "24. Panzer-Division reported that panzers are without grease."

Oberst Fangohr: "Today, 10cbm of oil and grease are en route to us from Zymlianskaya."

Kempf: "Perhaps the grease could come by air."

The shortage of grease was also worrying General von Hauenschild. He knew that his panzers could have difficulties because they relied on the grease to keep their tracks in running order. In this dry, dusty environment, it was more important than ever to keep the tracks and running wheels properly lubricated. General von Hauenschild thought that if sufficient quantities of

grease did not arrive in time, he might have to seek a postponement of the starting date. Upon his commander's instructions, Major von Menges called Oberst Friebe at 1910 hours and asked whether anything had changed the target date.
Friebe: "No, target date remains."
Menges: "Panzers have no grease, therefore they cannot be employed."
General von Hauenschild was standing behind Major von Menges as he talked. Hauenschild decided he had better try to convince Korps of the seriousness of his situation, so he took the phone off his chief-of-staff. General Kempf also came on the line at the other end.
Kempf said: "Nothing will change the target date and assault conditions are still favourable for 24. Panzer-Division."
General von Hauenschild once again pointed out the fuel and grease situation. The Division only had enough fuel for 60km.
Kempf: "I will once again report it to Armee."
Hauenschild then came straight to the point: "Perhaps a breathing space could be inserted…"
Kempf did not give a yes or no answer: "Immediately order what you are doing for tomorrow within the framework of the attack order."
Kempf then strengthened his answer. He pointed out that all preparations were to be met for the attack on 20th August. Hauenschild took this to mean 'no'.

While all this telephonic traffic was discussing important matters about the upcoming offensive, General von Hauenschild sent the following bland message to Oberst Friebe at Korps at 1925 hours: "It is pouring with rain here."
Friebe replied: "It has almost stopped here."
This is a strange little exchange. One wonders if it was an attempt by General von Hauenschild to force a cancellation by using the weather as an excuse. If it was, then Friebe's reply certainly expressed Korps' attitude. Or maybe it was an innocent report about weather conditions. Other entries in the war diaries of 24. Panzer-Division and XXXXVIII. Panzerkorps offer no further explanation.

At 1930 hours, following his conversation with General von Hauenschild, Kempf spoke by telephone with Oberst i.G. Fangohr at 4. Panzer-Armee. Fangohr reported that 300 cubic metres of fuel would be allocated tomorrow, 140 the day after, and that Armee would try everything to bring forward more petrol. Concerning the oil shortage, Fangohr reported that 10 cubic metres of oil and grease were on the way from Zymlianskaya.
At 2030 hours, General von Hauenschild reported to Oberst Friebe that the Division, after reaching the preparation areas, could still drive 30 kilometres with panzers, 50 kilometres with the armoured riflemen and a bit more with the Kradschützen. After the declaration of Armee, Oberst Friebe informed Division that grease would arrive near the troops in two days and transmitted the order to Division that tomorrow, all movements were to be implemented so that the Division could set off on 20th August. Written orders would follow.

The Division issued its Divisionsbefehl Nr. 47 at 2300 hours which ordered the preparations for the Division in the area north-west of Vassiliev for the assault on 20th August 1942. The task of XXXXVIII. Panzerkorps was to break through the enemy positions on its right wing early on the morning of 20th August and thrust as far to the north as possible. 24. Panzer-Division's instructions for this attack were as follows: Gruppe Sälzer (2./Pz.Jg.Abt. 40 and a company of pioneers from Pz.Pi.Btl. 40) would cover the flank that faced Tundutovo while the enemy in front of Gruppe Hellermann (Kradschützen-Abteilung 4) would be rolled up from south to

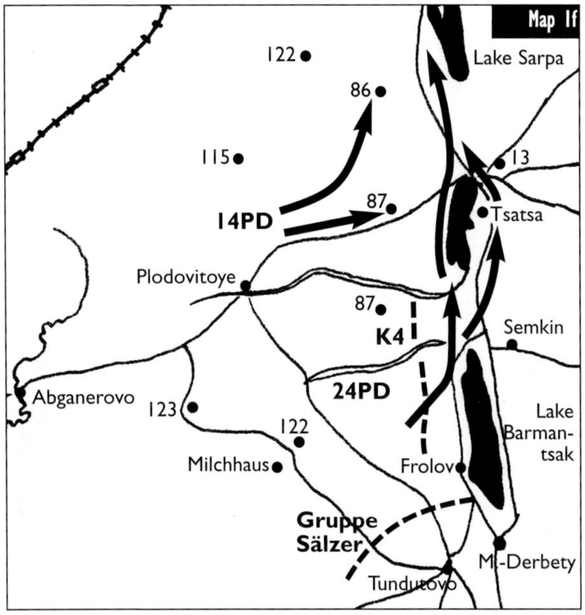

north by Angriffsgruppe Edelsheim (Panzergrenadier-Regiment 21, a schwadron of panzers and Panzerartillerie-Regiment 89 minus a battalion and a battery), which was aligned to the west of the chain of lakes. East of these lakes, a reinforced panzergrenadier battalion (II./PGR26 with regimental units and an artillery battery) would penetrate to the north and provide security to the east flank of the main attack. The armoured assault group (Panzer-Regiment 24 minus a schwadron, an armoured pioneer platoon and a flak platoon, the armoured elements of Panzergrenadier-Regiment 26 as well as I./Panzerartillerie-Regiment 89), commanded by Oberst von Broich, would lead the assault.

Panzer situation: 5 Befehlswagen (command panzers)
28 Panzer II
30 Panzer III short-barrels
23 Panzer III long-barrels
5 Panzer IV short-barrels
3 Panzer IV long-barrels

The 105mm and 150mm howitzers of Panzerartillerie-Regiment 89 would be brought into position so that they could support the defensive efforts of Gruppe Hellermann as well as be completely ready for the beginning of the assault. The artillery would also eliminate any flanking fire east of the chain of lakes.

All subordinated units were ordered to assemble in the appropriate preparation areas no later than 1700 hours on 19th August.

- Angriffsgruppe Edelsheim: in the area of Point 122 (12km SSE of Plodovitoye)
- Armoured Stoßgruppe: in the area of Point 123 (10km south of Plodovitoye)
- Division reserves: south of Angriffsgruppe Edelsheim in the area of the Milchhaus south of the road

Casualties:

2 men killed

2 men wounded (both stayed with the troops)

19th August 1942:

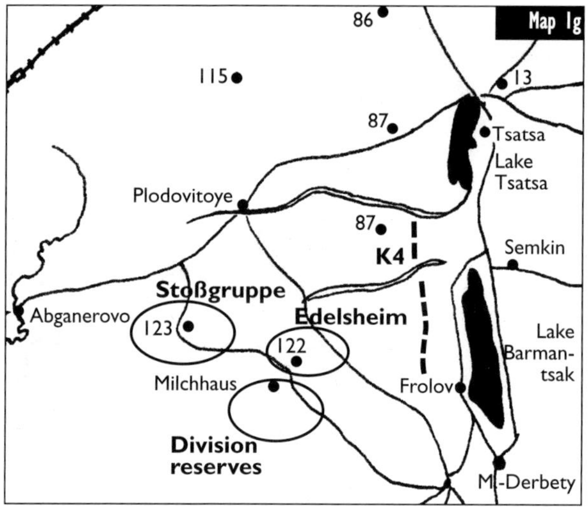

The night passed quietly in its entirety. At 0330 hours, 24. Panzer-Division started to march into the preparation areas, which they reached before 1400 hours. Division HQ was located 5km south of Point 122.0 near a dairy farm. The day was again overcast as dawn weakly illuminated the eastern horizon. Light flurries of rain swept across the steppe in the strong wind blowing from the east. In the faint light of pre-dawn, men in observation posts looked out far to the east, the dim mirror of the Volga arching northward in the distance, the leaden salt lakes pooled at the foot of the hills. The wind rushed up through gullies and swept over and around the many hills. The long grass bristled and swayed in the gusting eddies. This sullen weather provided perfect cover for the German formations moving into their starting positions, the grey skies preventing Russian pilots from observing any movements and the light rain soaking the ground, damping down the cement-like dust that usually acted like smoke signals to enemy observers. As the combat units headed toward their scheduled rendezvous areas, their commanders were involved in more conferences and inspections.

General von Hauenschild left his command post near the dairy farm for a meeting with Kempf. He arrived at Korps HQ at 1020 hours and spoke with Kempf about the conduct of the attack. According to that, the Division would employ an assault group of panzers out in front, followed by armoured riflemen and pioneers. The enemy front ahead of Kradschützen-Abteilung 4 would be dealt with, then it was planned to advance in the direction of Hill 118, 4km north of Morosov.

At 1300 hours, General von Hauenschild arrived at his new headquarters. He immediately picked up the phone and called Korps HQ. He told Oberst Friebe that the Kradschützen had been heavily attacked near Point 87 and a company might be surrounded. He requested 14. Panzer-Division to support them directly with artillery and also anything else. The Russian attack, conducted by Rifle-Regiment 50 of 15th Rifle Division, was smashed back by heavy artillery barrages and ferocious small-arms fire. Several prisoners were taken and their interrogation yielded extremely useful information about the defensive positions around Dubovyi Ovrag.

This was confirmed when aerial reconnaissance reported newly erected field fortifications in the Dubovyi Ovrag and Semkin areas, as well as in the tree-nursery in State Property Pryvolzhki and the marshy terrain east of there. Oberst Friebe drove forward to the command post of Kradschützen-Abteilung 4 near Point 87.0 to check out the situation. There had been attacks in company strength on the north wing of Kradschützen-Abteilung 4 north of Point 87.0 since 1045 hours. The attacks were repulsed but the Russians had dug themselves in there. Oberst Friebe drove forward with the Commander of Kradschützen-Abteilung 4, Oberstleutnant von Hellermann, to gain an insight into the terrain. Friebe saw that the terrain dropped down to the

lakes and was completely surveyable. The enemy occupants were weak on the previously recognised line, only the enemy artillery strengthening near Tsatsa.
On the basis of the prior telephonically transmitted orders and instructions, a Korpsbefehl was released at 1440 hours for the attack on 20th August. Aim of the Korps on 20th August 1942: XXXXVIII. Panzerkorps would set off at 0330 hours with the Schwerpunkt on the right to attack to the north, break through the enemy positions on the Tinguta Brook and then, in a north-west direction, gain the hills 10km west and north-west of Dubovyi Ovrag.

At 1730 hours, the Division issued Divisionsbefehl Nr. 48 for the attack out of the area west of Vassiliev towards the area of Dubovyi Ovrag and Hill 118. Within the framework of Korps' directive for the assault, Division command issued its plan. Advancing at 0345 hours, the armoured Stoßgruppe would roll up the enemy front ahead of Gruppe Hellermann from south to north and then, with the anti-tank guns of Gruppe Sälzer securing to the east, thrust east of the chain of salt lakes to the north, break through enemy positions both sides of the Tsatsa–Dubovyi Ovrag road in the area south-west of Lake Sarpa and then push north-west up to Hill 118 (11km north-west of Dubovyi Ovrag) into the enemy's rear. The layout of the landscape largely dictated the flow and direction of 24. Panzer-Division's assault. The Yergeni Hills extended north to south through the Kalmuck steppe, rising from the southern edge of Stalingrad. A broken chain of salt lakes – Sarpa, Tsatsa, Barmantsak and Almatin – stretched parallel to the range of hills, commanding the only road that led to Stalingrad. The panzergrenadiers and riflemen of Panzergrenadier Regiments 21 and 26, commanded by Knight's Cross holders Oberst von Lengerke and Oberst von Edelsheim respectively, would attack along this road and smash the Russian defences between Lake Tsatsa and the rugged hills to the west of it, while Oberst Riebel's Panzer-Regiment 24 moved along the high ground. 14. Panzer-Division would push through Pryvolzhki State Property, heading north with its left flank astride the railway line. Their initial target was Tinguta Station.

Oberst von Edelsheim inspected his troops and their preparations, driving from one schwadron to the next, conversing with the officers and men in informal gatherings. Everyone admired, respected and loved their commander, known by a few nicknames but the most common being 'Der Alte' (The Old Man), a standard nickname for a commander. Other nicknames, however, were even less flattering: 'Papa Grausig', 'der alte Isegrim' and 'König Etzel'[6], the last two being coined by Oberst von Nostitz-Wallwitz, Commander of Panzerartillerie-Regiment 89, during a champagne-filled stag evening at the Ohrdruf training ground in Thuringia prior to the 1942 summer offensive. Edelsheim was known to most for his excellent command skills and valour in the face of the enemy but he also had his own foibles and idiosyncrasies: he loved sweet things, having marmalade at every meal; he stamped his left foot and screamed 'Shit!' when he was angry; and he never wanted to write home to his wife Modeste during wartime, even though one of his adjutants repeatedly tried to persuade him, once even saying to Edelsheim: "Her Ladyship must think that Herr Oberst stands in front of the enemy day and night with primed hand grenades. Instead, he sits here and leisurely drinks his champagne." Edelsheim undoubtedly laughed his dry laugh. And during defensive situations, the men often heard the clear voice of Edelsheim yelling his well-known phrase: "Whoever does not dig, dies!" The men loved their commander's little quirks. They would do anything for him and he would look after them, as

6. 'Grausig' means horrible or terrible. 'Isegrim' is the name of the wolf in German animal fables (like Goethe's 'Reineke Fuchs'). 'König Etzel' is the name of King Attila the Hun in the Nibelungen saga. Some nicknames!

illustrated in the following account by Unteroffizier Karl-Heinz Möllers, who recalls a kindly gesture from the Oberst: "Enemy tanks had been reported. Everyone should dig in. I was therefore busy digging. The Commander was walking back and forth, back and forth. He came up to me and asked whether I could give him a cigarette. But I didn't have any cigarettes. If I'd have had one, I would've given it to him. The Commander continued to walk back and forth. And the Russian tanks had not yet come. Instead, a Hauptmann arrived. The Commander greeted him and also asked for a cigarette. The Hauptmann pulled out his cigarette case and offered the little sticks to the Commander. The Commander took one and pointed to me and said: 'And him there, he also has nothing to smoke!' The Hauptmann therefore had no choice. He also offered me a cigarette, which I gladly accepted. That was our Edelsheim."

At 1830 hours, barely nine hours before the assault was due to begin, the starting time for 24. Panzer-Division was altered. Major von Menges called Oberst Friebe at Korps headquarters. After discussing a few issues about the assault, Major von Menges talked about the starting time: "A favourable x-time is 0345 hours."

Friebe: "Alright, then it remains so, but 14. Panzer-Division will only attack at 0530 hours."

Menges had a short discussion with General von Hauenschild and both agreed that it was disadvantageous and would present the enemy with an opportunity to first parry the thrust of 24. Panzer-Division, then stop 14. Panzer-Division. It would be better if the starting times of both divisions were closer together. Menges picked up the receiver again and said: "Then the moment of surprise would not be kept, that is why 0430 hours is better. In doing so, it will be retained."

The Division moved up to its starting areas during the night. Flak-Bataillon 602 arrived near Division and was immediately sent to Gruppe Edelsheim. From 0430 hours, the advanced Division HQ would be located near Point 1.8, three kilometres north-west of Vassiliev.

The Division's current panzer situation was as follows:

5 Befehlswagen
27 Panzer II
29 Panzer III short-barrels
23 Panzer III long-barrels
5 Panzer IV short-barrels
2 Panzer IV long-barrels

The preparations for the assault on 20th August were met accordingly and the Division massed on the broad security line to attack. In the evening, Panzergrenadier-Regiment 21 had been pushed further north between Panzergrenadier-Regiment 26 and the chain of lakes, providing security for the preparations of the armoured Gruppe. The difficult night-time march and relief of the security posts went according to plan.

Casualties:

None

Struggle in the Hills

Chapter Two

20th August 1942:

The blackness of night gave way to the cold grey of pre-dawn, the horizon being faintly silhouetted against the pale sky. Fleets of panzers and half-tracks rolled over and around the hills north of Plodovitoye, deploying into battle formations. Once in position, the battalions of 14. and 24. Panzer-Divisions halted, waiting for the order to advance.

The early morning sun bathed the steppe in its radiant light, panzer crews and infantry enjoying the stark beauty of the Russian steppe. Leutnant Hans-Erdmann Schönbeck, a platoon commander in 6. Schwadron of Panzer-Regiment 24, recalls that morning: "We cannot take it in! This change on one particular morning. The Kalmuck steppe, this neverending, enormous grey-beige-brown expanse, was transformed overnight into a light-violet sea. Millions of meadow saffron converted the autumnal beauty of the landscape into a vivid picture. "Because everything which now followed in the steppe up to the great city on the Volga was no longer connected with the same thoughts of beauty, I have never forgotten this dreamlike spectacle of nature after fifty years."

The fresh morning air vibrated from the noise of the idling panzer engines and clouds of blue smoke coughed from their exhausts. From the rear came the booming of the artillery. Heavy calibre shells roared overhead as the reinforced Panzerartillerie-Regiments 4 and 89 – from 14. and 24. Panzer-Division respectively – laid down a massive barrage to cover the eastern flank of the panzer assault. Explosions rent the morning air and sent fountains of earths erupting into the sky, raising a dirty grey-brown curtain of smoke and dust that was dragged over the German formations by a light easterly breeze. On a given signal, engines were gunned and hundreds of armoured vehicles lurched forward simultaneously. It was an impressive spectacle. The first five objectives of the Division had been laid down in the Division's order:

1st objective:	Plodovitoye road – southern edge of Lake Tsatsa.
2nd objective:	Plodovitoye road – northern edge of Lake Tsatsa.
3rd objective:	Suspected enemy positions with tank defences on the level of southern edge of Lake Sarpa.
4th objective:	Northern edge Dubovyi Ovrag – Point 43.3.
5th objective:	Point 118.

Gruppe Broich's panzer spearhead reached the area 4km north of Semkin at 0555 hours. The two battalions of Panzer-Regiment 24 which formed part of Gruppe Broich, I. Bataillon commanded by Major von Winterfeld, and II. Bataillon led by Major Burgsthaler, rolled in echelon down the hills west of Lake Barmantsak. Violent enemy artillery fire lay on the assault spearheads of the Division, sending fountains of earth sailing into the air as Russian artillery shells fell on the advancing mass of armour. The two panzer battalions – side by side – passed across the foxholes that formed the front-line of Gruppe Hellermann, plunged into the Russian defences and proceeded to blast any opposition. They wheeled slightly to the left and started to roll up the enemy front from the south. Resistance was swiftly broken as the panzers trampled their way north and the armoured Stoßgruppe soon fulfiled its first task: rolling up the enemy front ahead of Gruppe Hellermann. The riflemen of Gruppe Hellermann headed into the trenches, gathered the numerous prisoners and cleaned up the last resistance nests. Once this was completed, the next stage of their mission was to tie down any other enemy forces that lay to the east.

The command panzers of Panzer-Regiment 24 closely followed the initial assault, Oberst Riebel in Panzer '371', Regiment Adjutant Rittmeister von Aulock in Panzer '372' and the Regiment Ordonanzoffizier Oberleutnant Weidemann in Panzer '373'. The first two panzers were Befehlswagen (command panzers) but Oberleutnant Weidemann's panzer was an ordinary Panzer III. The command panzers were kitted out with powerful radio equipment but to fit this in they'd had to sacrifice their main guns. They were therefore armed only with dummy cannon and machine-guns, only Oberleutnant Weidemann's panzer, still armed with a 50mm cannon, providing a modicum of protection for the Regiment staff. Oberleutnant Weidemann marvelled at the view that opened up below him as his panzer clambered over the top of a hill. The battlefield stretched out before him in an awe-inspiring panorama. Despite the great distances and dimensions of the area, the hill offered such a view that it would allow the course of the battle to be followed as if on a sand-table. Small clouds of fog still lay in the hollows. The Volga lowlands sprawled before him, the leaden surface of the salt lakes glistening in the marvellous morning light. Down to his right, he saw muzzle smoke from the panzers of Major von der Lancken's III. Abteilung, signifying that it had made contact with the enemy. Major von der Lancken's battalion had been subordinated to Gruppe von Edelsheim.

MARK

Major Dietrich von der Lancken, Commander of III./Panzer-Regiment 24.

Since 0510 hours, Gruppe Edelsheim found itself in the attack on Semkin and field positions east as well as north of there. The attack of the panzergrenadiers had started well: two reinforced schwadrons quickly occupied the village of Vassiliev in the pre-dawn darkness, securing a vital cornerstone for flank security[1]. With Gruppe Broich's successful destruction of the enemy front opposite Gruppe Hellermann, both wings of Gruppe Edelsheim were secured and they flowed

1. Later in the day, the bulk of the two schwadrons returned to Gruppe Edelsheim and Vassiliev was held by the weakest possible forces barring the way north. These security forces later came under the command of Gruppe Sälzer.

smoothly down the hills, into the area around the northern tip of Lake Barmantsak. III. Abteilung of Panzer-Regiment 24 had been subordinated to Oberst von Edelsheim to support the panzergrenadiers in their assault to the east to take the small village of Semkin. Major Dietrich von der Lancken, commander of these panzers, moved out at the head of his battalion. His command panzer '1161', conspicuous with its large frame aerial, nosed forward over the hills. His battalion's task was to support the grenadiers as they entered the open valley near the southern end of Lake Tsatsa.

Major Dietrich von der Lancken's panzers moved forward, trundling slowly into the valley that led between the treacherous salt lakes out on to the flat lowlands. The terrain provided perfect hiding places for the Russians: the lowlands were covered in long grass and the salt lakes were girdled by thick reeds. Interspersed among the panzers were squads of grenadiers but there were no visible signs of the Russians as bullets whipped through the masses of panzers, forcing the grenadiers to drop to the ground or leap behind the panzers. Shots from anti-tank rifles pinged off the armour plate, occasionally penetrating the observation slits and shattering the hardened blocks of glass. The panzer commanders kept their heads in the cupolas. Grenades landed near the tanks, the blinding white explosions showing that the Russians were using phosphorous grenades. The turrets of the panzers swung around, machine-guns and cannon blasting the Russian infantry. The panzers continued, pushing deeper into the Russian defences. Several panzers drove on to mines, a dull thud emanating from beneath the panzers as pieces of track and roadwheels went whirring through the air. "Mines! Mines!" The dreaded word crackled through the radio net of the battalion. The area around the hills and Lake Barmantsak was thickly sown with mines. Grenadiers crawled forward, hoisting grenades into fox-holes and shooting down Russian riflemen when they tried to run but the grenadiers were on their own: the panzers couldn't move until pioneers cleared a lane through the minefields and this was a laborious and dangerous job. Involved with the attack and the mine clearance was Fhjwm. von Senger und Etterlin: "The Panzer spearhead moved forward against the lake narrows and there we ran unexpectedly into mines. The whole narrows were mined. Strong enemy defence hindered further progress. We moved out and followed the attack. All of a sudden we were in the middle of a minefield. My pioneer squad cleared 52 mines with 5 men."

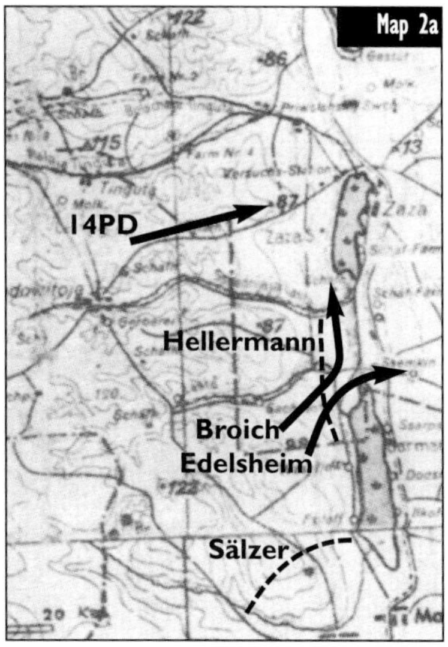

While 24. Panzer-Division was embroiled in tough combat, 14. Panzer-Division was making headway and at 0615 hours, reached Hill 87. This hill was vital, more so for 24. Panzer-Division than 14. Panzer-Division because this hill was probably the keystone for any continuing attack to the north. Whoever controlled this hill controlled all movement through the lowlands to the north and east. Within half an hour of reaching it, 14. Panzer-Division had it firmly under control after wiping out weak Russian resistance. Now that it was in German hands, 24. Panzer-Division was ensured entry between it and Lake Tsatsa to the north. At 0700 hours, the commander of 14. Panzer-Division reported to Korps: "Hill 87 taken at 0645 hours. Difficult situation because of strong fire out of Tsatsa and the gullies. Cannot go further to the north for the time being. 24. Panzer-Division should stand near Point 12.2. Main fire from the east out of northern and southern edges

SPANNOCCHI

A Sdkfz. 250 of Rittmeister Kolczyk's 2./Kradschützen-Abteilung 4 passes in front of a concentration of Panzer-Regiment 24's panzers located safely behind the forward line. Note the flag draped over the engine deck of the half-track.

SPANNOCCHI

A brief battlefield conference (from left): Oberst Riebel (Panzer '371'), Major von Winterfeld (Panzer '361') and Rittmeister Spannocchi (Panzer '251') discuss the course of the attack on the morning of 20th August 1942.

SPANNOCCHI

The panzers of Major von Winterfeld's I. Panzer Abteilung head east toward Semkin on the parched salt-flats. Grenadiers have dug foxholes to gain some protection in the totally exposed terrain. A 5cm anti-tank gun has been partially dug in, ready to support the assault. The openness of the ground is evident in this photo.

SPANNOCCHI

The panzers pause amongst the high grass of the steppe. On the left is one of the passenger vehicles (PKW - Personenkraftwagen) used by commanders (schwadron commander and up) of Panzer-Regiment 24. In combat, however, the commanders climbed into the cupolas of their panzers.

SPANNOCCHI

Panzers '212', '132' and '133' observe the vista below them. The Yergeni Hills ran through the steppe from south to north parallel to a chain of salt lakes. The eastern edge of the hills ended in a plateau overlooking the Volga lowlands.

SPANNOCCHI

The crew of Panzer '132' (a long-barrelled Panzer III) continue to observe the terrain. Directly in front of them is one of the many treacherous salt-lakes surrounded by high reeds. The panzers steered clear of these tank traps: the surface of the lakes looked firm with their solid crust of dried salt but it was only thin, covering a deep morass of stinking mud.

SPANNOCCHI

Panzer '252' approaches a destroyed farmstead. In the background, a burning Russian tank sends up a thick plume of smoke.

SPANNOCCHI

The panzers charge! Rittmeister Spannocchi in Panzer '251' and the heavy Panzer IV's of Rittmeister Thiel's 4. Panzer Schwadron rush north toward Lake Tsatsa.

SPANNOCCHI

Oberleutnant Freiherr von Maltzan (at right in black cap) and his crew of Panzer '363' inspect a destroyed Russian gun position. The Russian gun was hauled out of its shelter upon the approach of the Germans but did not have much success: the Russian gun crew lay dead to the right of the gun.

of Tsatsa, 4 batteries recognised. We must wait until 24. Panzer-Division moves up." Division-scale fire and movement tactics were needed for 14. Panzer-Division to advance because with Hill 87 firmly in hand, the next step was to eliminate flanking fire from the east and this basically came down to the capture of Tsatsa. At this moment, 24. Panzer-Division, in whose attack sector Tsatsa lay, was embroiled in violent combat south of Lake Tsatsa. At 0720 hours, 24. Panzer-Division was reported to be north-west of Semkin and in front of enemy positions near Semkin. 14. Panzer-Division would have to wait until 24. Panzer-Division moved up.

SPANNOCCHI

Oberst Riebel controls his panzer battalions from his command Panzer '371'.

At 0740 hours, 24. Panzer-Division reported that as a consequence of increasing enemy resistance in Semkin, the panzers were supporting the attack of the riflemen on Semkin and therefore still could not advance northward on the west side of the lake. The entire Division was halted, waiting for the grenadiers to crush Russian resistance and take Semkin because without a secure east flank, a northward advance was impractical. The bulk of the battle vehicles were forced to stand still, offering tempting targets to the Russians. With their vision restricted in the cupolas, panzer commanders popped their heads out of the hatches to survey the situation, and casualties resulted. Amongst them was Leutnant Horst von Poser, commander of 3rd platoon in 4. Schwadron, when he raised his head outside of his Panzer IV '431'. A bullet to the head promptly ended his life.

The panzers of Major von der Lancken's III. Abteilung of Panzer-Regiment 24 were not sitting idly by while the pioneers cleared mines and grenadiers cleared Russians. They had been subordinated to Gruppe Edelsheim to support the grenadiers and that was what they were going to do. They were frequently called upon to head into the hail of defensive fire and assist the struggling grenadiers, and Rittmeister Kuno von Meyer's 9. Schwadron performed this hazardous mission four times. Leading the way in Panzer '951', von Meyer and his Schwadron repeatedly dashed into the boiling cauldron, the panzer skilfully handled by its driver Unteroffizier Bartsch, a former cook who transferred to the panzers from a field-kitchen.

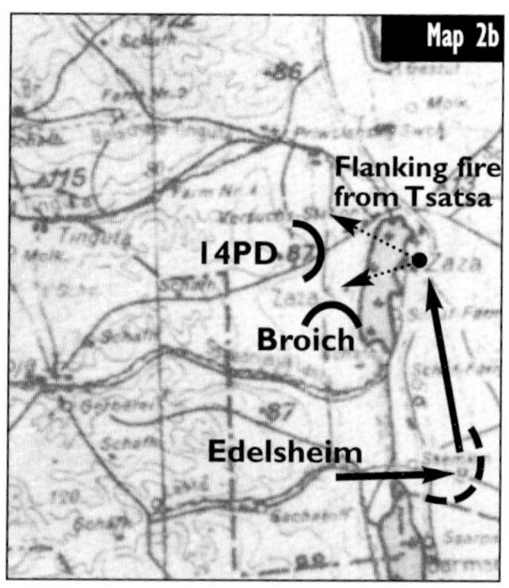

Edelsheim takes Semkin, forms defence to the south-east, then moves north to Tsatsa.

At 0745 hours, after violent combat, panzers and grenadiers pressed into Semkin. The grenadiers finally succeeded in penetrating the Russian positions, slowly inching forward and levering the Russian riflemen out of their holes, gradually grinding down the stiff opposition. In the village itself, the merciless hand-to-hand fighting conducted with grenade and bayonet ended with the Germans victorious.

Once Gruppe Edelsheim was able to anchor its right wing on Semkin, it was able to thrust up to Tsatsa from the south. At 0800 hours, a few minutes after they had set off, they were attacked by 12 Russian bombers protected by fighters. As the bombers swooped over the turrets of the

panzers, they opened their bomb-bay doors and scattered their deadly loads. Bombs exploded amongst the panzers as panzergrenadiers threw themselves to the ground. Clods of dirt and earth rained down, pattering the armoured roofs of the panzers. After dropping their bombs, the Russian bombers swung around and disappeared to the north. The grenadiers stood up, dusted themselves off and the advance continued. At 0815 hours, the panzer spearhead was located 2km north of Semkin. While Edelsheim and his troops headed up the east side of Lake Tsatsa, the panzers of Gruppe Broich planned to push up the west side after a short regrouping.
At 0825 hours, General Heim reported to Korps that there was an anti-tank front near State Property Pryvolzhki and that the bulk of 24. Panzer-Division was still located around Point 12.2. General Werner Kempf arrived at 14. Panzer-Division HQ shortly after 0900 hours where he was oriented about the situation: Point 87 was comparatively easily taken but positions near State Property Pryvolzhki were heavily occupied by the enemy. A breakthrough with an armoured assault group was attempted when Panzer-Regiment 36, together with the half-track battalion, started to attack a hill in the grounds near State Property Pryvolzhki. Enemy artillery operated on the northern slope with medium calibres and numerous mines were detected in the area around the State Property.

General Kempf was of the opinion that air support was needed, first of all for 24. Panzer-Division because their progress was decisive for the continuing assault of Korps. With Tsatsa still heavily occupied by the Russians and spitting fire at every German movement, its capture was absolutely vital. While at 14. Panzer-Division HQ, Kempf radioed his Chief-of-Staff back at Korps HQ: "How is 24. Panzer-Division?"
Friebe replied: "I believe that Luftwaffe support will be requested for Tsatsa by 24. Panzer-Division."
Kempf: "Luftwaffe must support 24. Panzer-Division. You will request support from VIII. Fliegerkorps. 14. Panzer-Division very strongly flanked from east."

With Gruppe Edelsheim now on the move to the north after the capture of Semkin, the panzers of Gruppe Broich, now advancing after having been forced to halt and assist the panzergrenadiers of Gruppe Edelsheim in their assault, were focused on their primary mission. They attacked to the north on the west side of Lake Tsatsa, Gruppe Edelsheim pushing north on the east side. The panzers battled hard, knocking out one Russian strongpoint after another. They suffered small but constant casualties, mainly due to the fire coming from the village of Tsatsa on the other side of the lake. This was in Gruppe Edelsheim's attack area and Oberst von Broich had no direct say in its capture. At around 1000 hours, Broich radioed HQ, informing them that his Gruppe had reached the road that led from the north edge of Tsatsa to Sukhaya Lasta. Here, however, they were finally forced to halt for the time being because of the strong flanking fire from Tsatsa village and the remaining tank defences to the front. Without Tsatsa village being under German control, the further course of the offensive was threatened.
At 1015 hours, Generalmajor von Hauenschild reported to Korps the loss of 10 panzers with track damage, apparently as a result of a shortage of grease. It seemed like General von Hauenschild was saying 'I told you so' to Korps. The track damage was mainly due to mines and it is unclear how many panzers suffered track damage due to a 'shortage of grease'[2].

2. When the author asked Heinz Kolczyk, Commander of the half-track schwadron of Kradschützen-Abteilung 4, whether his vehicles were damaged due to grease shortages, he replied: "Only our panzers had such problems with their tracks. Our light half-tracks were a production of the Henschel firm in Kassel and were technically excellent, having only one weakness: it was a half-tracked vehicle with

Gruppe von Edelsheim slogged its way north, crushing bitter Russian resistance which centred around the buildings of isolated sheep farms, and the closer they were to Tsatsa, the tougher the resistance became. Oberst von Edelsheim knew the critical nature of Tsatsa but he would not senselessly sacrifice his men. He halted the attack and radioed HQ, demanding Stuka attacks on the village and the defence lines east and south of it. At 1030, Russian bombers again swept in and bombed the spearheads of the Division before quickly turning around and disappearing to the north. At the same time, the forward elements also received heavy artillery and mortar fire out of the area east of the northern edge of Lake Tsatsa. The road from the southern edge of Lake Tsatsa to the west was mined and Tsatsa itself was strongly occupied by the enemy. German fighter-bombers plunged down on the village with bombs and onboard weapons, silencing two Russian artillery batteries that were firing from within the village. Edelsheim appreciated the efforts of the fighter-bombers but they were too few in number. They prowled the battlefield looking for targets of opportunity. What he really wanted now was the flying artillery: the Stukas, for only with their help would he be able to launch his attack. Oberst von Edelsheim was handicapped by the fact that the hills north-east of Semkin – located in his right rear – were still heavily occupied by the enemy and he was forced to weaken his main assault by leaving some units behind to deal with these small but toughly defended hills. They could more accurately have been described as pimples rather than hills because they rose barely more than a couple of metres above the surrounding lowlands.

General Kempf drove to 24. Panzer-Division HQ on Point 87.0[3] and quickly came to the point: he said that Panzergruppe Broich must again set out from the area east of Point 87.0. He also pointed out that everything must be done to close up to 14. Panzer-Division and move up to the same level. Having received messages from both Broich and Edelsheim requesting air support, General von Hauenschild requested air support on Tsatsa from 1130 hours.
One and a half panzergrenadier regiments and one panzer battalion were employed under Oberst von Edelsheim at 1130 hours to destroy the very strong and tough enemy in the area east of Lake Tsatsa. Two panzer battalions and the remaining panzergrenadiers were employed west of the northern edge of Lake Tsatsa under Oberst von Broich who'd ordered combat reconnaissance in a northerly and easterly direction, concentrating on the tank trench.
The Stukas were a few minutes late. They plunged down in front of 14. Panzer-Division at 1135 hours, and finally smothered Tsatsa village at 1140 hours. Still at 24. Panzer-Division HQ, Kempf observed the Stuka attack through binoculars. He then saw that the panzer regiments of 14. and 24. Panzer-Divisions were finally side by side. He radioed his Chief-of-Staff back at his Korps HQ at 1145 hours: "The panzer regiments of 24. Panzer-Division and 14. Panzer-Division were seen advancing together. Stuka attack on Tsatsa five minutes ago and Stuka attack on positions in front of 14. Panzer-Division ten minutes ago." Even with Stukas swarming over the attack spearheads and the enemy in front, enemy air attacks continued on 24. Panzer-Division. Like clockwork, the Russians bombed 24. Panzer-Division again at 1230 hours, exactly two hours after their previous attack. 24. Panzer-Division immediately sent off the following message to Korps: "Punctually every two hours at 0800, 1030 and 1230 hours, strong

wheels at the front end. These wheels were disadvantageous when it came to certain obstacles (trenches, etc.). When I was Commander of Aufklärungs-Abteilung 7 of 7. Panzer-Division, however, my vehicle lost the axle with both wheels due to the effect of a mine and despite that, we succeeded in driving back to a strongpoint. Closing opinion: fully-tracked vehicles are better."

3. There were two hills called Point 87.0, one in 24. Panzer-Division's area and the other in 14. Panzer-Division's area of operations.

bombing attacks on the Division. Request fighter support for 1430 hours." Oberst Friebe relayed this message to Armee HQ at 1350 hours.

At 1400 hours, Panzer-Regiment 24 received an order by radio from General Kempf that Panzer Abteilung Lancken would remain subordinated to Gruppe Edelsheim. Edelsheim would need all types of support to take Tsatsa village. It was certainly a tough nut. At 1530 hours, Major von Menges reported to Korps that the enemy east of the lakes was stronger than assumed. Kampfgruppe Edelsheim prepared itself for an attack, while Kampfgruppe Broich reconnoitred to the north for a possible advance in that direction.
After regrouping, Gruppe Broich attacked the north-west corner of Lake Tsatsa. Objective: Tsatsa village. The panzers struggled through difficult terrain and the assault of Gruppe Edelsheim east of Semkin proceeded slowly as a result of mines and enemy influence. Edelsheim realised that without first flattening the village with Stukas, any infantry and panzer attack would drown in the infantry and anti-tank fire coming from the village.
Oberst Friebe immediately set out to resolve this problem. At 1555 hours, he called General Fiebig, Commanding General of VIII. Fliegerkorps and informed him about the situation: "Tsatsa very strongly occupied, air support requested."
Fiebig: "Will attack Tsatsa at 1700 hours with Stukas."
Having attained air support, Friebe sent a radio message to 24. Panzer-Division at 1600 hours: "Schwerpunkt of air support 1700 hours area around Tsatsa, mark the forward line (Forward line will be pulled back at 1611 hours)."

The men of Gruppe Edelsheim crouched in their shallow foxholes or peeked out of the hatches of their panzers, watching the Stukas peel off and dive on the village of Tsatsa. The Stukas circled above the village like a flock of eagles waiting to pounce on their prey. One at a time, they dived down from the skies, accompanied by the banshee wailing of their Jericho sirens. For a second, they looked like they would spear themselves into the ground, but they would release their bombs and pull out of the dive, levelling off and ducking into the pall of smoke which hung over the village. As soon as the last bomb was dropped, the grenadiers clambered out of their foxholes and the panzers lurched forward. The Germans knew better than to think that all Russian opposition would be crushed but they were surprised and disappointed at the wall of fire into which they now advanced. Gruppe Broich continued to attack Tsatsa from the west. Towards evening, they were finally able to achieve freedom of movement and thrust to the north of Lake Tsatsa, enveloping up to the northern edge of the village. The enemy was thereby prevented from retreating from Tsatsa to the north.

The Division's left neighbour, 14. Panzer-Division, was having difficulties with its assault. They'd crossed over the Tinguta Brook but were delayed by numerous mines, and were only able to construct a bridgehead over the Tinguta. Point 86.0 north of State Property Pryvolzhki was taken, however, while 24. Panzer-Division would presumably just finish up near Tsatsa and would no longer move up to 14. Panzer-Division's level that evening. The chief-of-staff of 14. Panzer-Division placed the request to Major von Menges to push forward rifle elements in the direction of Tinguta Gully so that there was no hole in the east flank. This posed a minor problem because the few riflemen that belonged to Gruppe Broich were fully engaged in the encircling movement north of Tsatsa and were located 2 kilometres west of the northern edge of Tsatsa. After one and a half hours of vicious fighting, Edelsheim finally reached the southern edge of Tsatsa at 1830 hours against strong enemy resistance. Even though the result of the day was disappointing in that the attack objective had not been reached, the elimination of the unexpectedly strong enemy on the east flank produced the conditions for a further attack to the north.

The panzers hedgehogged in the rosy light of a summer sunset. Supplies were brought up to replenish the empty ammunition racks, 24. Panzer-Division's units consuming large quantities of shells during the day due to the unexpectedly tough Russian opposition. As the crewmen and grenadiers constructed positions, swarms of bombers hummed overhead on their flight to Stalingrad. White flashes and mushroom clouds stained the northern horizon. The command panzers of the Regiment staff huddled under the trees of the State Property. The evening air was warm. The day had not been as successful as was hoped but the intention of the command was to press on early to master the uncertain situation and assert dominance over the startled Russians. The situation around Lake Tsatsa was still confused with both sides manoeuvring, the Germans to crush the Russians, the Russians trying to break free. The starlit sky once again covered the steppe. Orange flashes flickered along the northern skyline, Stalingrad's fires serving as an admirable orientation point. The men bedded down in fox-holes or under their panzers and promptly fell into a coma-like sleep.

At 1955 hours, General Kempf congratulated General Heim by telephone for the day's success. General Heim informed Kempf that he was open to the east and that the enemy still occupied the tree-nursery and a couple of houses near State Property Pryvolzhki, besides the positions north of Bolshaya Tinguta, but a connection had been established with 29. Infanterie-Division (mot.). The crossing forged over the Tinguta by 14. Panzer-Division was very narrow. No water flowed in the river. Kempf feared flanking fire from an easterly direction, even if 24. Panzer-Division was to move up in tomorrow's attack: "24. Panzer-Division will surely move up tomorrow, when the orchards are free, then there will be no more flanking fire. Under cover towards Dubovyi Ovrag, Division must advance with elements on 115.7, then on Tinguta railway station. Dubovyi Ovrag must also be straightened out."

Oberst Friebe phoned 14. Panzer-Division and urged them to compile a list of aerial targets, whereupon the Division immediately replied that Stukas would be needed for the orchards and the last bomb should fall on the orchards at 0415 hours. At 2050 hours, Oberst Friebe gave the following aerial targets to VIII. Fliegerkorps:
1.) West part of orchards near State Property Pryvolzhki.
2.) Near 24. Panzer-Division, Point 13.0 and gullies east of Tsatsa and northern part of Tsatsa.
3.) Alternate target Dubovyi Ovrag and assistance near Lake Sarpa.
VIII. Fliegerkorps told Oberst Friebe that the divisional artillery would be required to direct smoke shells on to the targets. At 2058 hours, Kempf informed 24. Panzer-Division that they would rely on the display of yellow aerial recognition panels and marking fire with smoke on enemy artillery.

24. Panzer-Division reported that about 25 panzers had fallen out due to mines or technical defects but a precise panzer report could not be made because the Panzer Regiment was still on operations at 2045 hours. At 2115 hours, Division sent the following teletype to XXXXVIII. Panzerkorps: "M. Derbety still weakly occupied by the enemy. Residents state that an enemy battalion has abandoned Tundutovo to the south. In front of the centre and left strongpoints, there is no longer enemy contact with the security line."

Casualties:

2 officers killed

- Leutnant Horst von Poser und Groß-Naedlitz (Zug Kdr); 4./PR24 (Killed)
- Leutnant Leonhard Stählin (Zug Kdr); 4./PGR26 (Killed)

21 men killed

- Obergefreiter Alfred Buchwald; PGR26 (Killed)
- Obergefreiter Robert Hartung; PGR26 (Killed)
- Wachtmeister Fritz Reiter; PGR21 (Killed)
- Obergefreiter Hans Kattemeier; PGR21 (Killed)
- Obergefreiter Max Radtke; PGR21 (Killed)
- Unteroffizier Max Serapin; PGR21 (Killed)
- Gefreiter Bruno Eismann; PGR21 (Killed)
- Obergefreiter Reinhold Wagner; PGR21 (Killed)

7 officers wounded (4 of those stayed with the troops)

- Oberleutnant Heinrich Prinz von Reuß (Abteilung Adjutant); I./PGR26 (Wounded but stayed with the troops)
- Oberleutnant Grunau; PGR26 (Wounded but stayed with the troops)
- Hauptmann Walter Thom (Batterie Kdr); Regiment Stabs Batterie/PAR89 (Wounded)
- Leutnant Gornth; PAR89 (Wounded)
- Leutnant Horst Erdmann (Batterie Officer); 5./PAR89 (Wounded but stayed with the troops)
- Rittmeister Heinz Kolczyk (Schwadron Kdr); 2./K4 (Wounded but stayed with the troops)
- Oberleutnant Gerhard Schönfeld (Kompanie Kdr); 3./Pz.Pi.40 (Wounded)

70 men wounded (22 of those stayed with the troops)

4 men missing

21st August 1942:

The night passed quietly and the enemy situation in the south near Semkin was unchanged. At 0415 hours, Gruppe Edelsheim came up from the south and armoured Stoßgruppe Broich around the northern tip of Lake Tsatsa, breaking the last enemy resistance on the north edge of Tsatsa at 0445 hours. Among the prisoners taken in Tsatsa were 200 uniformed women. The Germans were not without casualties. As well as numerous wounded, the following men of Panzergrenadier-Regiment 21 were killed near Tsatsa: Gefreiter Rolf Meißner, Stabsschwadron, and Obergefreiter Edmund Seikowski, 2. Schwadron, who was severely wounded and died the next day in the Division's dressing station. There was still strong enemy resistance to the north-east. After clearing Tsatsa and leaving behind the weakest of elements near Semkin to secure against the enemy retreating to the east there, Gruppe Edelsheim assembled in the area north of that village for an attack to the north. Panzer-Abteilung Lancken was supplied to Gruppe

Combat and Ration strengths on 21st August 1942

Units	Combat strength				Ration strength				
	Offz.	Beamte	Uffz.	Men	Offz.	Beamte	Uffz.	Men	**Total**
Division Staff	17	12	41	138	37	12	60	253	**362**
Pz.Gren.Brigade 24	4	–	17	73	4	–	16	70	**90**
Pz.Rgt. 24	64	10	530	1358	69	14	596	1732	**2411**
Pz.Gren.Rgt. 21	37	–	335	1418	41	7	352	1475	**1875**
Pz.Gren.Rgt. 26	35	5	311	1531	40	5	325	1573	**1943**
Krad.Abt. 4	19	–	176	939	20	4	183	969	**1176**
Pz.Art.Rgt. 89	67	–	321	1671	75	11	405	2053	**2544**
Pz.Jg.Abt. 40	10	1	71	407	9	3	55	267	**334**
Pz.Pi.Btl. 40	13	–	73	575	14	4	88	608	**714**
Pz.Nach.Abt. 86	7	–	68	326	11	3	62	288	**364**
Dinafü. 40	–	–	–	–	31	18	189	1115	**1353**
San.Ko. 1./40	–	–	–	–	7	3	32	196	**238**
San.Ko. 2./40	–	–	–	–	9	3	26	157	**195**
Bäckerei Ko. 40	–	–	–	–	1	1	19	135	**156**
Schlächterei Ko. 40	–	–	–	–	2	1	8	68	**79**
Verpfl. Amt 40	–	–	–	–	–	7	12	69	**88**
Feldpostamt 40	–	–	–	–	–	18	–	9	**27**
Feldgend. Trupp 40	–	–	–	–	3	–	42	42	**87**
Sum:	**273**	**28**	**1943**	**8436**	**373**	**114**	**2470**	**11079**	**14036**
Subordinated Units									
I./Brandenburg 800	9	–	50	304	9	–	49	296	**354**
Flak-Bataillon 602	14	–	100	497	14	3	110	529	**656**
schw.Art.Abt. 800	4	–	67	445	16	4	70	454	**544**
Total:	**300**	**28**	**2160**	**9862**	**412**	**121**	**2699**	**12358**	**15590**

Broich, leaving Edelsheim without any panzers. After straightening out the north edge of Tsatsa and the small hills north-east of there, Gruppe von Broich advanced northward east of the large road, Major Burgsthaler's II. Panzer-Abteilung forming the spearhead of the assault. The command panzers of the Regiment staff followed close behind them. The commander of Schützen-Brigade 24, Oberst Fritz Freiherr von Broich, accompanied the attack in one of the Division's command panzers. The sight of the two commanders would provide one of the enduring images for veterans of 24. Panzer-Division: Oberst Riebel, his burnished face topped by a black forage cap, headphones clamped over his ears, black panzer jacket and German Cross in Gold coated in dust and slouching in his cupola, pleased to have his panzers rolling again: Oberst von Broich, handsome in his field-grey uniform, tobacco pipe clenched firmly in the corner of his mouth, vigilantly scanning the horizon for signs of the enemy. General von Hauenschild also liked to stay in close proximity to his spearheads so at 0630 hours, he shifted Division HQ from Hill 87.0 to the east slope of Hill 87.

From 0700 hours Gruppe Broich, containing most of the Division's armour, attacked the strongly fortified positions east of the Kastenwäld (Square Forest) near State Property Pryvolzhki whose defenders had been reinforced by artillery, anti-tank guns, flamethrowers and numerous mines. Division command kept Korps informed with a string of messages. At 0700 hours: "Panzergruppe still attacking the eastern edge of Square Forest and positions east of there. Already this morning, 100 prisoners taken, numerous enemy dead." At 0715 hours: "Very strong air attacks on the Division and Tsatsa village. Division once again requests heavy flak."[4] At 0735 hours: "Panzers in combat at the first tank trench east of Square Forest. Kradschützen-Abteilung 4 attacked south-east corner of Square Forest. Heavy mining north of Tsatsa village."

General Heim reported to Korps at 0905 hours that a detailed enemy plan of bunker construction and mine-laying had been found. From this, a strong occupation and a defensive field with great depth was identified. This discovery would greatly benefit future attacks by allowing the spearheads to target gaps in the minefields.

General Kempf began the day by visiting his division commanders and issuing orders that would assist 24. Panzer-Division. First of all, he drove to 29. Infanterie-Division (mot.) HQ and spoke with General Fremerey, commander of the division, about the relief of Korps' east flank. Several battalions of his division were to be sent to the east flank around Vassiliev, Tundutovo and Semkin, which at the moment was being held by Gruppe Sälzer of 24. Panzer-Division, and elements of Panzergrenadier-Regiment 26 left behind near Semkin by Edelsheim to cover his vulnerable east flank and rear. General Fremerey was informed that to maintain the assault forces of 24. Panzer-Division, the speedy release of their security forces on the east flank was necessary and in accordance with this, relieving elements of 29. Infanterie-Division (mot.) would immediately take over security of the east flank of Korps on the general line: south-east of Vodin – Vassiliev – Semkin – south corner of Lake Tsatsa. From the area around Vodin, strengthened combat reconnaissance would drive to the ordered security line Ssadovoye – M. Derbety. During both of the last days, Gruppe Sälzer (half of Panzerjäger-Abteilung 40, Pionier Kompanie and Flak-Zug) repeatedly repulsed enemy reconnaissance thrusts on a broad front

4. Obergefreiter Reddig, a driver from 1. Schwadron, wrote down in his diary: "21st August: 0730 and 0800 hours. Attack by Russian bombers and fighters." At 0915 hours, due to 24. Panzer-Division's request for anti-aircraft guns, Korps immediately ordered 29. Infanterie-Division (mot.) to supply I./Flak 5 to 24. Panzer-Division.

and besides that, still managed to take over the security of the narrows between Lakes Barmantsak and Tsatsa. The narrows lying north of there, between Lakes Tsatsa and Sarpa, were taken over by Gruppe Melchers with anti-tank and anti-aircraft forces. With the eastern flank securely held by the anti-tank guns of the Panzerjäger Bataillon, the assault forces of the Division were free to advance to the north, secure in the knowledge that their rear and flanks were covered. Kempf subsequently drove forward to Point 87.0, to the HQ of 14. Panzer-Division where General Heim informed him about the situation: the attack of the Division was progressing slowly through strong emplacements equipped with flamethrowers, and they were defended toughly and to the last bullet. General Heim had ordered regrouping and would renew his attack at 1300 hours on the area west of State Property Pryvolzhki. Kempf then drove to 24. Panzer-Division.

Throughout the morning, the attack of 24. Panzer-Division had only moved forward slowly due to enemy resistance with mine barriers and flamethrowers. Panzergrenadier-Regiment 21 attacked east of Broich's armoured assault group but numerous mines and anti-tank trenches there also delayed the continuous advance. Despite this, the armoured Stoßgruppe succeeded towards 1100 hours in taking the Kastenwäld east of State Property Pryvolzhki, together with elements of 14. Panzer-Division. The enemy positions west of there were cracked open with strong air support.

Obergefreiter Reddig, the driver in 1./Panzergrenadier-Regiment, wrote: "1100 hours: Vehicles to front to combat troops and march to Tsatsa." Reddig and the other drivers, together with their vehicles, were kept a safe distance from the immediate fighting. When the combat troops needed to be moved, the vehicles were called forward.

After the destruction of strong enemy groups in numerous bunkers, an armoured Stoßgruppe consisting of the panzers of the weakened Panzer-Regiment, under the leadership of Oberst von Broich, set out at midday to thrust to the high ground at Hill 118. This prominent hill was located east of Tundutov railway station and the Germans believed it to be the key to victory, as well as a first-class observation point. The panzers advanced, leaving the grenadiers and infantry to continue the difficult struggle with enemy field positions between the southern edge of Lake Sarpa and Point 32.5. Huge battlefleets of panzers, motorcycles and half-tracks rolled through the steppe under bright sunlight, swinging from hill to hill, clouds of billowing dust rising behind them. A cloudless sky covered the infinite steppe. As far as the eye could see, formations of panzers pushed through the grass, emerging from behind hills or dipping into depressions. The undulating terrain made a simultaneous observation of all vehicles impossible. Charging panzers rolled straight over the Russian defences, trampling trenches, anti-guns and artillery emplacements under their tracks. Resistance nests dug into the reverse slopes and the eroded gullies were shattered by cannon and machine-gun fire. Grenadiers disembarked from the half-tracks to mop up the survivors. Fahnenjunker-Wachtmeister von Senger und Etterlin reports: "After overrunning some positions we smoothly assaulted the enemy artillery positions, and in the smoking rubble we overwhelmed gun and mortar positions and our armoured group thrust along the high edge of the hills deep into the enemy hinterland. The attack objective was the Volga knee near Krassnoarmeisk."

Gruppe Broich continued northward, reaching Golodnoya Gully at 1315 hours. For two hours, the armoured Stoßgruppe stormed its way to the north-west, toward Hill 118. Several enemy motorised and horsedrawn columns fleeing after the breakthrough were destroyed, high bloody casualties being inflicted on the enemy. The Russian infantry, panicked by the sight of the rampaging panzers, scuttled into the gullies and long grass. They searched for an escape and

BÖKE

Panzer assault! Panzers and half-tracks of Gruppe Broich roar to the north at noon on 21st August 1942, heading toward their daily objective of Hill 118. Russian opposition was crushed under the tracks of the rampaging panzers.

headed north. When they neared the crown of the hill, they were silhouetted against the horizon. Turret machine-guns chased them over the hill, some being felled by the bullets, others dropping to the ground and slithering out of sight, their earth-coloured uniforms blending perfectly with the earth. At 1400 hours, after breaking through several deep enemy positions and rolling over more artillery batteries, the panzers drove over Hill 115.7 and took Morosov, a tiny hamlet south-east of the vital hill. The enemy in the village beat a hasty retreat. Finally, after many hours of fighting, the armoured Stoßgruppe pushed up the southern slope of Hill 118 at 1435 hours. This success was quickly radioed back to Division HQ. Oberst von Broich and his men stood in their vehicles atop the hill and admired the magnificent vista stretched out before them. Krassnoarmeisk, the most southerly of Stalingrad's suburbs, could be seen in the distance, its high-rises and factory buildings shining in the golden afternoon sun. Behind it was the silver ribbon of the Volga River. Having now gained the all-important Hill 118, the aim was for Gruppe Broich to hedgehog on the hill and allow the bulk of the Division to catch up from the south. The thankless task of 'clearing out' the traversed terrain fell to Panzergrenadier-Regiment 21 which entailed not only breaking the surviving resistance that had flared up everywhere in the overrun positions but also grappling with enemy forces brought out of the Volga lowlands.

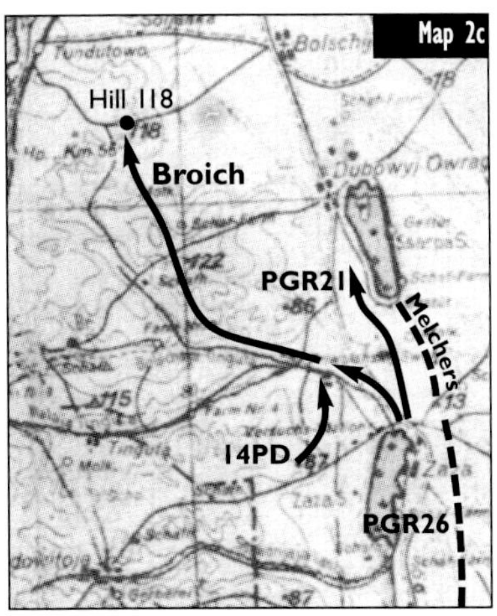

Rittmeister Heinz Kolczyk, Commander of 2./Kradschützen-Abteilung 4, recalls the victorious assault:

"With my Schwadron, I participated in the assault of Gruppe Broich, following directly behind the panzers. The Kampfgruppe (panzers and light half-tracks) marched along the contour line in the

> direction of 118. During the assault, the Commander von Hellermann came up to my side in his vehicle during the drive and called over the question, 'Kolczyk, have you at all practiced the Volga Song[5] with your Schwadron!'
> "At the beginning of the attack, we barely had any enemy resistance. Only on Hill 118 did we find earthen positions with weak Russian infantry forces who, upon the arrival of the first panzer, came out of their positions, surrendered and were marched away as prisoners. The panzers formed a hedgehog and my 2./K4 received the mission of securing the east flank towards Lake Tsatsa. We were in a melon field, echeloned to the right behind the panzers, protecting their flank. I was in a Sdkfz. 250/3 with a large frame antenna and powerful radio equipment. While securing on Hill 118, we were able to listen in to the radio conversation between the spotter aircraft and the artillery.
> "When we stopped, however, to allow a regrouping, I nearly became disobedient because I could not comprehend that a successful offensive operation, without any further enemy forces in front of it, could be called off. Naturally, as a 'small unit commander', I lacked the knowledge of the larger overall situation. It was a victorious assault and that's why I wanted to continue to push on. Over the entirely surveyable plains in the direction of Stalingrad, there was only one thing to be observed. At about 400 metres distance, we saw a horse-drawn 7.62cm gun gallop up and at about 300 metres, it went into position. Only two of our half-tracks would have sufficed to destroy this gun and its crew! But we were not allowed to do it!!! That's why I had thoughts of being disobedient!"

At 1445 hours, General von Hauenschild reported to Korps the breakthrough of the panzers under the command of Oberst von Broich in a northern direction and the capture of Hill 118. At the same time, Panzergrenadier-Regiment 26 attacked the fortified constructions hard north-east of State Property Pryvolzhki. The Regiment outflanked east of the State Property forest to partly negate the dangerous flamethrowers and flaming-oil mines placed along the entire sector. In the afternoon, they attacked east of the Kastenwäld (Square Forest), widening the gap smashed by Gruppe Broich and thrusting into the area of the Milchhaus 6km north of the Square Forest. After hard combat against bunker positions, the daily objective, the area of Hill 86, was reached.
General Kempf spoke with General von Hauenschild about the utilisation of the decisive breakthrough of Stoßgruppe Broich for the assault of Korps. Kempf drove back to the HQ of 14. Panzer-Division located on the embankment west of State Property Pryvolzhki only to discover that General Heim had already deployed his Division staggered rearward to the left to exploit the success of Gruppe Broich. The attack proceeded rapidly.

As preparations to exploit the successful penetration were being prepared far behind them, Gruppe Broich prepared to defend the hill itself. Waves of heat flickered over the battlefield. The mid-afternoon sun glowered from the bleached sky. Oberleutnant Weidemann sweltered in his turret, sweat drenching his back and trickling down his face. He leant out of his cupola and, being careful not to burn himself on the sun-heated metal, scanned the horizon. Objects appeared – and disappeared – in the shimmering heat mirages but he noticed black dots moving on the plains north-west of Tundutov railway station. Tanks. Most likely Russian.

5. The Volga Song (Wolgalied) is not the Song of the Volga Boatmen made famous during the Second World War by Glenn Miller but is the Ilya Song from the operetta by Franz Lehar, 'Der Tsarevitsch', which refers to the Volga and which most Germans could either sing or whistle.

Flashes rippled along the line of dots, followed by shells screeching past the German panzers. They were definitely Russian. The encounter caught both sides by surprise. Orders flew across the radios and battle formation was quickly assumed. The entire Panzer-Regiment 24, fanned out across the steppe, advanced towards the Russians. The right flank was held by a Schwadron with seven vehicles. The Regiment Staff, including Oberleutnant Weidemann, hovered behind this right wing, searching for favourable positions that had a wide field of fire. Weidemann's Panzer III '373' was the last vehicle on the extended line.

Still moving into position, Weidemann spotted a T-34 approaching, barely 400 metres separating the two machines. It was obvious that the Russian had spotted Weidemann. A shell left the T-34 but it rushed past '373', exploding far behind.

"Thank God," Weidemann mumbled to himself. He peered through his sight. The Russian tank was in a well-covered position, only half of its hull being visible.

"12 o' clock! 400 metres! Fire!"

The breech-block recoiled, the vehicle rocked and the brass shellcase ejected into the canvas shell receptacle. Cordite fumes filled the turret. Weidemann's glance never left the Russian tank. Missed. It went too high.

"Once again, calmly prepare!"

The T-34 fired again. Weidemann clearly heard the whistle as the shell raced past. "Thank goodness, too high!" he thought to himself.

The loader slammed another shell into the breech as the gunner adjusted his aim. He then fired. The second German shell dug into the ground in front of the T-34. It appeared to be unharmed. At that moment, Weidemann's gunner yelled out: "Blockage!"

Quickly assessing the situation, Weidemann knew that their exposed position offered the Russians a prime target, and with the main gun jammed, their situation was indeed perilous.

"Pull back!" he shouted to the driver over the intercom.

In the excitement, the driver throttled the engine and it refused to start. Weidemann expected a Russian shell to thud into their machine at any moment.

"All men out of the vehicle!"

Weidemann secretly hoped that their call for help would be heard by another panzer that could come to their rescue. The five men piled out of the hatches, landing on the hard ground beside their panzer. Hardly had they left their vehicle when the hatches of the T-34 flipped open and the crew of four similarly jumped clear, crouching next to their machine. Weidemann wondered whether they had actually struck the Russian vehicle. Not stopping to think too deeply about it, Weidemann ordered his driver back into the panzer. The motor rumbled back to life and the rest of the crew remounted. After clearing the blockage in the breech, Weidemann and a neighbouring panzer blasted the T-34 now standing no more than 100 metres away. It erupted into flames. The Russian crew was not to be seen.

This engagement lasted about 15 minutes, fifteen of the longest minutes of Weidemann's life.

For aiding in the further conduct of the attack of Korps by the decisive breakthrough of Gruppe Broich, Oberst Freiherr von Broich, Commander of Schützen-Brigade 24, was recommended for the Knight's Cross by Generalmajor von Hauenschild. Exploiting the thrust of the panzers were the unarmoured elements of the Division, in the attack on the tank trench to the north since 1600 hours. While the bulk of Gruppe Broich hedgehogged on Hill 118, some of its armoured units were called back to support the riflemen. At 1820 hours, General von Hauenschild said to Oberst Friebe that he expected the situation north of the tank trench to be settled by sundown.

Kradschützen-Abteilung 4 was part of the group that reached Hill 118 on this day. The battalion, subordinated to the armoured Stoßgruppe since the morning, was passed through with other unarmoured units by a system of panzer convoys and in the evening, again stood with the armoured Stoßgruppe. Fahnenjunker-Wachtmeister von Senger und Etterlin reports: "Towards nightfall we reached Hill 118 west of Chapurniki. From this commanding hill one had a marvellous view several kilometres into the distance, to the villages bordering the chain of lakes. Behind this stretched the shine of the setting sun, from glaring yellow to soft rose, blending into the glimmering heat of the steppe, and bordering the horizon was the band of the Volga.

"A reconnaissance vehicle skilfully drove down the hill to reconnoitre towards the chain of lakes, and it looked like a tiny bug, but in a quick journey it drove through wafting yellow clouds to the east.

"We were the northern spearhead of Korps and wanted to reach the Volga in the morning... The Panzergruppe formed a large round top, and after much toing and froing, a hedgehog was formed. I had to secure the eastern flank and from my vehicle observed the sinking sun pushing the shadow of Yergeni Hill quickly to the east, covering the lakes and finally enveloping the steppe in a new night."

Oberleutnant Ludwig Dittmar, Commander of 6. Schwadron in Panzergrenadier-Regiment 21, wrote the following in his diary: "21st August: The entire day, we advanced in fits and starts. In the evening, attack on a bunker-occupied hill, 8 men wounded. Subsequent 7km foot march." Luckily for the 8 wounded men, none of their wounds were fatal.

At 1925 hours, Oberst Friebe gave the order to Major von Menges that the south-west corner of Lake Sarpa must be straightened out. The units standing there must stay until relieved by elements of 29. Infanterie-Division (mot.). Two battalions of 29. Infanterie-Division (mot.) would secure from Semkin to the south-west, a third battalion between Tsatsa and Lake Sarpa. Dubovyi Ovrag would be straightened out as soon as possible, but only without heavy combat, otherwise it would be screened off.

Korps sent the following order to General von Hauenschild: "24. Panzer-Division will cover the north flank of Korps on the general line Dubovyi Ovrag – Hill 118 – railway near Point 105. In addition to this, battleworthy elements on Hill 118 will advance by thrusting with an armoured Kampfgruppe up to the railway line and there sealing off to the north. Capture of Dubovyi Ovrag is to be strived for."

In a communiqué sent at 2250 hours, the deeds of Oberst von Broich were described to Korps.

> "21/8/42 1840 hours. Gen. Kdo. XXXXVIII. Panzerkorps | Chef des Stabes.
> Proposal for Knight's Cross for Oberst Freiherr von Broich, Commander 24. Schützen-Brigade.
> As Commander of the armoured Stoßgruppe of the Division, Broich has, in 36 hours of hard combat 20km deep in enemy lines on 20.8.42 and in the morning of 21.8.42, taken hundreds of bunkers, consisting of toughly defended enemy positions between Vassiliev and State Property Pryvolzhki, whereby he himself is always leading in the front-line, often personally participating in close combat.[6] At midday on 21.8., Broich advanced to the north from Pryvolzhki on his own decision. He once again broke

6. When asked by the author whether he had seen Oberst von Broich fighting hand-to-hand with the enemy, Heinz Kolczyk said: "I did not personally witness Oberst von Broich during this fighting but I can confirm that panzer commanders must always be far to the front to immediately exploit a favourable situation. I also had this experience in 7. Panzer-Division where I sometimes commanded an armoured Kampfgruppe, always exploiting successfully."

through numerous enemy positions, destroyed several enemy batteries in their emplacements and after many hours of uninterrupted combat, took the dominating Hill 118 18km north-west of Pryvolzhki at 1435 hours. He destroyed numerous enemy columns and according to pilots' reports, after his penetration on this broad and deep sector, the entire Russian front was in turmoil. This was thanks to his daring and effective thrust.
In the afternoon of 21.8. and 22.8., 14. Panzer-Division and 24. Panzer-Division will gain the area to the north on the decisive eastern wing of the Panzer-Armee. With that, the conditions for the penetration of both of these divisions to the west and for the destruction of the enemy ahead of the Armee front in front of Stalingrad by rolling over them will be produced. Broich has particularly distinguished himself in all campaigns as a commander of troops by his personal bravery and art of command.

SCHICK

Oberst Fritz Freiherr von Broich, Commander of Schützen-Brigade 24, was awarded the Knight's Cross for his actions on 21st August 1942.

Oberst Freiherr von Broich, Fritz. Born 1.1.1896 in Strassburg. Peacetime troop units:
KR6 RDA 1.8.39.
EK2 17.9.39
EK1 4.6.40
DKiG 3.11.41
Home address – Darmstadt, Heidelbergstraße 91."

The proposal was quickly approved and Broich received the Knight's Cross on 29th August.

The breakthrough by Oberst von Broich was a great achievement, partly negated by 14. Panzer-Division lagging behind on the left flank as it struggled through bitter Russian resistance. It was vital to retain the conquered ground near Hill 118 if it was to be of value. A hedgehog extended from the hills near Tundutov railway station, around Hill 118, down into the lowlands east of Yergeni Hills where grenadiers of Panzergrenadier-Regiments 21 and 26 still skirmished in the burning villages. The troops consolidated their positions and awaited the dawning of a new day.

The booty of this day and the destroyed enemy war materiel couldn't be immediately surveyed. Several hundred mines were cleared in the very densely mined attack area. The number of prisoners – corresponding to the hardness of the fighting and the high casualties of the enemy – were very small, with only 350 being taken. Most of those were wounded.
Captured were seven guns, four of these being 10.5cm, three 12.6cm, 19 anti-tank guns, four mortars and 23 anti-tank rifles.

The position of XXXXVIII. Panzerkorps was summed up in a concise daily report to 4. Panzer-Armee: "In hard bunker fighting on 20.8. and 21.8., Korps has broken through the strong Russian defensive line Tinguta – south edge Lake Sarpa to a depth of 25km. 24. Panzer-Division, with a Kampfgruppe, won the Milchhaus 4km south-west of Dubovyi Ovrag, with another Kampfgruppe reached high ground 118.0 after the destruction of strong enemy."

Panzer situation: 3 Bfwg, 17 Panzer II, 35 Panzer III, 3 Panzer IV kz, 2 Panzer IV lg.

Fahnenjunker-Wachtmeister von Senger und Etterlin wrote: "At midnight the first of our supplies arrived from a panzer schwadron and the supply troops skilfully returned through the Russian-infested area. The usual shooting of tracers that we are used to in the hedgehogs gave warning to us. The soldiers' mess-tins rattle against the fuel containers that were carried together."

Casualties:

11 men killed

- Panzergrenadier Anton Klose; PGR21 (Killed)
- Gefreiter Rolf Meißner; PGR21 (Killed)

2 officers wounded (1 of those stayed with the troops)

- Leutnant Schenk; PGR26 (Wounded)
- Oberarzt Dr. Günter Spode; PAR89 (Wounded but stayed with the troops)

26 men wounded (7 of those stayed with the troops)

- Obergefreiter Edmund Seikowski; PGR21 (Wounded but died on 22nd August)

22nd August 1942:

On the entire Korps sector during the night, there was negligible enemy and friendly air activity. The enemy situation west of Lake Barmantsak was unchanged and no enemy forces were recognised in the deep east flank in front of Gruppe Edelsheim but it had been observed that the enemy was strengthening north of Hill 118. The Division planned to set off at 0400 hours towards the railway line from 118.0 with Gruppe Broich and from the dairy to the north and east with Gruppe Edelsheim. It was planned for the bulk of the Division to reach Hill 118 and the hills around Morosov in the rear of the enemy. At the same time, it was also planned to clean out the attack strips and destroy the enemy west of the southern part of Lake Sarpa, and further screen off the east flank. Generalmajor von Hauenschild and his Division staff advanced through the dairy to set up a new HQ in the area of Hill 86.1.

While all this planning was going on, the important Hill 118 was only being held by the advanced armoured Gruppe, and the Russians had been attacking the hill since the previous night. Strong Russian artillery and Stalin Organ barrages plastered the hill and its surrounds. The Russians knew the importance of the hill because from there, the main roads and railway

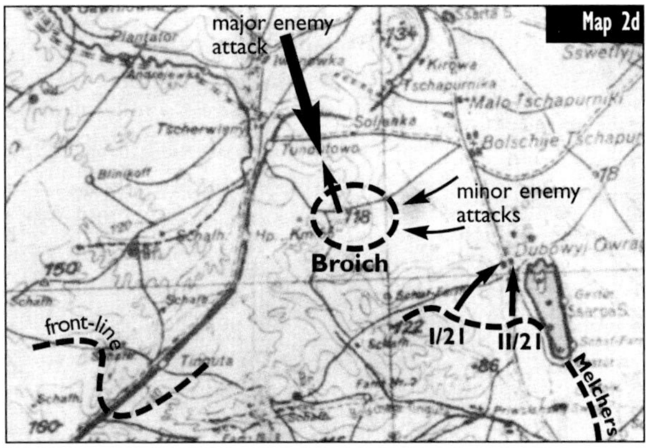

out of the Russian front, still placed 10km south of the Tinguta Railway Station, were dominated and menaced by the Germans on the hill. All nocturnal Russian attacks toward the hill had been repulsed. The Russian commander then shifted some of his armour behind the land-bridge, trying to strike the German spearhead in the flank. Before the eastern horizon had even begun to lighten, numerous clashes flared around the perimeter of the hedgehog. The panzer schwadrons of Oberst Riebel's Panzer-Regiment 24 passed through the outer defences of the hedgehog to engage the Russian tanks that had massed on the high plains north-west of the railway line. Each side fired, orange flashes strobing throughout the grey steppe. The clang of shell striking armour echoed through the pre-dawn stillness. Fahnenjunker-Wachtmeister von Senger und Etterlin observed the first clashes of the day: "While the first rays of the morning sun already shone over our faithful reconnaissance troops, an important announcement was heard over the radio, which I marked with a red pencil on my map that I carried.

"I was suddenly ordered: hard north-west of us, 15 enemy tanks are approaching. And in the same moment the stillness of the morning was broken by the shrill shooting of our long panzer cannon. Now there was also strong infantry appearing from behind the tanks. We were at once pulled back from the east, and the hedgehog position of the hill extended to another hill located 1km south-west of Hill 118."

Squads of Russian riflemen followed in the wake of the advancing tanks. The grenadiers of Panzergrenadier Regiments 21 and 26 in the Volga lowlands had extreme difficulties with the Russians penetrating their line through the gorges. As the sun cleared the horizon and climbed into a clear sky, the superior tactics of the German commanders began to tell; marauding squads of Russians were mown down and after a few hours, the initial crisis had been mastered. The hard fighting had only just begun however. The day promised to be hot, and so did the combat. It was reported at 0515 hours that Points 1.8 and 1.5, as well as terrain east of Vassiliev, were now free of the enemy. Security forces near Vassilievski had been fighting with enemy armoured reconnaissance vehicles since 0630 hours. Elements of 29. Infanterie-Division (mot.) arrived to relieve security forces in the lake narrows near Semkin. II./Infanterie-Regiment 15 of 29. Infanterie-Division (mot.) relieved Gruppe Sälzer in the Semkin area at 0500 hours.

At 0720 hours, 24. Panzer-Division requested air support on Hill 115.8 and the roads west of there, concentrating on infantry, artillery and 27 Russian tanks identified by aerial reconnaissance. Dubovyi Ovrag was heavily occupied by enemy units and three batteries were recognised near the village, as were strong enemy garrisons with tanks east of the railway line near 115.8 and 120.2. At 0930 hours, VIII. Fliegerkorps informed Korps that Stukas would attack Dubovyi Ovrag.

At 0925 hours, Major von Menges telephoned Oberst Friebe at Korps and informed him of the situation near the Division: "Gruppe Broich in combat with 27 tanks and 2 batteries. Enemy reinforcing himself. Connection with 14. Panzer-Division established. Edelsheim attacked Lake Sarpa and Milchhaus, prepared himself for an attack on Dubovyi Ovrag with

Panzergrenadier-Regiment 21. Known tank, anti-tank and artillery and airfield south-west of Dubovyi Ovrag. Sälzer reported relief by elements of 29. Infanterie-Division (mot.)."
Friebe: "Where there is heavy flak, move it to the front."
Menges: "Schwere Artillerie Abteilung 800 will only fire on profitable targets."
Friebe: "Where is Flak-Bataillon 602?"
Menges: "2. Kompanie near Edelsheim, 1. Kompanie near Division HQ."

After shifting to a new position, Wachtmeister von Senger and his men were immediately presented with a crisis: "My platoon was the foremost and accelerated to a shallow ridge where we defended to the north and to the west. Hardly had we arrived on the hill when the first Russian troops appeared opposite us. There were always more and more and soon the slope over there was covered with hundreds of advancing Russians. We worked feverishly to entrench ourselves. After 5 minutes, both of my hands were covered in blisters and I wrapped my handkerchief around them. The enemy came ever closer, however they were finally contained by the well-placed artillery fire of our faithful Panzer-Begleitabteilung (armoured escort detachment). The enemy kept low; he had apparently not expected such strong resistance here. Then finally there was the rumble in the air of our Stukas and the blasts on the enemy tank and infantry concentrations. A Stuka burst in the air."
"We stayed in these positions overnight and pulled our vehicles in between us."

With the perimeter firmly held by units such as von Senger's, the panzers were free to continue a furious duel that had developed mid-morning. Both sides slugged it out. Black pillars of smoke marked the funeral pyre of a panzer or a T-34. A heavy toll was taken on the Russian tanks but the Germans didn't escape lightly: Oberleutnant Hanno Rinke, Commander of 6. Schwadron, was severely wounded when his panzer was smashed by Russian shells, only he and his heavily wounded gunner managing to crawl out of the blazing vehicle. Leutnant Hans-Erdmann Schönbeck, a platoon commander in Rinke's Schwadron, was wounded by shrapnel but stayed with his panzer.

MARK

Rittmeister Kuno von Meyer, Commander of 9./Panzer-Regiment 24.

To assist their own forces, heavy Russian artillery fired into the burning battlefield. Volleys of shells bracketed the panzers, forcing the commanders to close their hatches and blinding the drivers with walls of dust and smoke. Shrapnel swept over the Germans, forcing everyone below ground or to seek cover in their vehicles. Effectively sightless by having their hatches closed, some commanders risked their safety by re-opening them so that they could properly survey the battlefield and, inevitably, this led to further casualties. Rittmeister Kuno von Meyer, Commander of 9. Panzer Schwadron, describes how he was wounded: "Looking out of my panzer, I was wounded in the head by an artillery splinter. I was lucky, however, because at that time, we still had rubber protectors over our headphones. The splinter in my head caused a speech impediment. The interchanging of vowels." Rittmeister von Meyer had the wound dressed and was then sent to hospital. "I was brought to the Sanitätskompanie in a

Kübelwagen and then to hospital in Stalino. From there, I came on convalescence leave to XXXXVIII. Panzerkorps as an Ordonanzoffizier."[7]
Kuno von Meyer can no longer remember who took command of his 9. Schwadron, but it may have been Oberleutnant Ernst Eichhorn who was commanding the Stabsschwadron of III. Abteilung.

Leutnant Walter Wiktorin, Ordonanzoffizier of III. Bataillon, was also a victim of this severe Russian fire. He was killed when he showed himself outside of his Panzer III '1163'. Surprise barrages smashed into German formations and searched out staff headquarters huddling in the gullies. With the enormous help of their artillery, the Russians contained the Germans in their current positions. The situation for the Germans in the lowlands was hampered by increasingly tough resistance. At 1040 hours, 24. Panzer-Division reported that after they had successfully defended against the enemy assaults on Hill 118 from the west and north-west, the thrust westward towards the railway line was still intended. A continued advance was not possible during the heavy Russian attacks. Gruppe Edelsheim, with the bulk of the Division, was employed in the assault on Dubovyi Ovrag, after the continuing cleansing of the southern edge of Lake Sarpa had ended. Elements of this Gruppe secured the north flank up to Hill 118.
Major Schwanke's II. Abteilung of Panzergrenadier-Regiment 21, thrusting along the highway from Tsatsa to the north, was firmly held in front of Dubovyi Ovrag, its strong field fortifications consisting of tripwires, mines and installed flamethrowers. The assault against Dubovyi Ovrag was also made very difficult because the enemy continuously reinforced himself there. The attack of the riflemen only made slow progress because of strong enemy artillery flanking fire from the north-east point of Lake Sarpa. General Kempf indicated to General von Hauenschild that the capture of Dubovyi Ovrag was of decisive importance. Later, General Kempf drove to the command post of Panzergrenadier-Regiment 21 to speak to its commander, Oberst Wilhelm von Lengerke.
Rittmeister Bechtold Graf von Bernstorff's I. Abteilung of Panzergrenadier-Regiment 21 was held up by the flooding around Pryvolzhki State Property. The enemy had blown the dam of Tinguta reservoir and energetically defended himself in field positions north of the flooded terrain. A crossing over the Tinguta Brook was finally obtained by the pioneers when the final nest of resistance was cleared up; a bunker from which a burst of flame spurted. It contained a flamethrower. Fortunately for the pioneers, a Russian trench allowed them to approach the bunker from its flank and knock it out. The way was now open! The riflemen of Bernstorff's battalion moved up. The exhausted pioneers, faces blackened by smoke and etched with fatigue, sat on both sides of the road, puffing cigarettes and gulping warm water from their canteens. White teeth were revealed in dirty faces as they smiled and waved at the passing columns of lorries. It was said that panzer crewmen had the greatest respect for the footslogging grenadiers, but the grenadiers felt the same about the pioneers.
The lorries roared through the battle area, heading for the Pryvolzhki State Property after traversing the Tinguta Brook. With its lush plantations, green vegetation and fruit orchards, it was a shady, green oasis in a sea of parched, brown prairie. Rittmeister Graf von Bernstorff's I./Panzergrenadier-Regiment 21 continued mounted up for a short distance, then the Abteilung attacked from the south-west, to the left of II. Abteilung over trenches that cut

7. His duties on Korps staff were not strenuous: "As an Ordonanzoffizier, I was more or less used as a messenger. At that time, I even had to build a bed for the chief-of-staff, which meant standing the four feet of the bed in water-filled jam tins, so that the bugs could not reach him..."

through the otherwise flat terrain of hard steppe earth. There, Rittmeister Hans-Heinrich Schlenther, Commander of 2. Schwadron, was severely wounded by a shot in the thigh. He was treated at the dressing station and immediately transported back to a hospital in Germany. Without panzers supporting, I. Abteilung likewise came to a standstill in the most violent enemy fire.

At 1430 hours, General von Hauenschild sent the following message to Korps: "Near 118.0, attack repulsed under our own panzer casualties. Edelsheim in attack on Dubovyi Ovrag. Panzerjäger 40 are moving up now."

Half an hour later, he sent another one to Oberst Friebe at Korps: "One Russian battalion attacked towards 118.0 from the north-east. All vehicles stand there unfortunately."

Friebe: "Employ panzers against it. Advance then does not come into question."

Hauenschild: "Heavy artillery fire lies on Sälzer's sector south of Lake Sarpa."

The goal set in the morning, to thrust through to the railway and road 2km south of Hill 115.8 with the armoured Stoßgruppe, had to be finally given up as a consequence of the changing enemy situation in the afternoon.

Reinforced Panzergrenadier-Regiment 21 pushed forward in a progressive attack on Dubovyi Ovrag reaching a point barely 1.5km south-west of the village. One battalion secured from Dubovyi Ovrag to Point 118.0 in strongpoints. Near Hill 118, Kampfgruppe Broich was in defensive combat the entire morning against enemy attacks with infantry and tanks from the north, north-west and west. The attacks were repulsed at 1100 hours. Nevertheless, strong enemy forces were still there. This was shown when an attack in battalion strength was thrown against Gruppe Broich from the north-east. The advance of this Kampfgruppe in the direction of the railway was not possible. All that Broich and his men on Hill 118 could do was observe how the enemy opposite them produced a deeply-echeloned defensive system out of thin air without being able to do much about it. For what use it was, 9./Panzerartillerie-Regiment 89 was able to fire up to the Volga with their guns. Panzerjäger-Abteilung 40 secured from Hill 118 to 86.3 to the west. In the territory taken in the previous days, the enemy again made himself noticeable, turning road signs in a false direction and capturing, among others, elements of the supply train of Panzerjäger-Abteilung 40 near the village of Vassiliev.

In a telephone conversation at 1825 hours, General von Hauenschild discussed his Division's situation with Oberst Friebe at Korps. He said that Edelsheim had not been making substantial headway and his attack had stalled 1000 metres south of the village of Dubovyi Ovrag. The attack had been carried forward to the hills south and west of Dubovyi Ovrag, the riflemen of Edelsheim's Kampfgruppe subsequently securing on this line to the north and the east. The enemy pushed new forces towards Dubovyi Ovrag so that the capture of the village was not able to be carried out with Edelsheim's own small forces. Russians still sat on the hills north-west of the village and strong attacks rolled in from the north-east. Moreover, the Russians had strong artillery and were continually bringing up fresh forces. Hill 118 was being attacked from the north and was covered by artillery and mortar fire. These conditions prompted General von Hauenschild to pose the following question to Korps: "Should we continue the attack tomorrow on Dubovyi Ovrag? Supply road negotiable. Should 118 be held or should we be content with 115.7? Supply not possible during the day. If 118 given up, how formation?" Friebe put down the receiver and talked to Kempf about the questions posed by Hauenschild. After a few moments, he came back on the line and gave Hauenschild his answer: "I have discussed with KG[8], and KG says he agrees with withdrawal from 118."

8. General Kempf

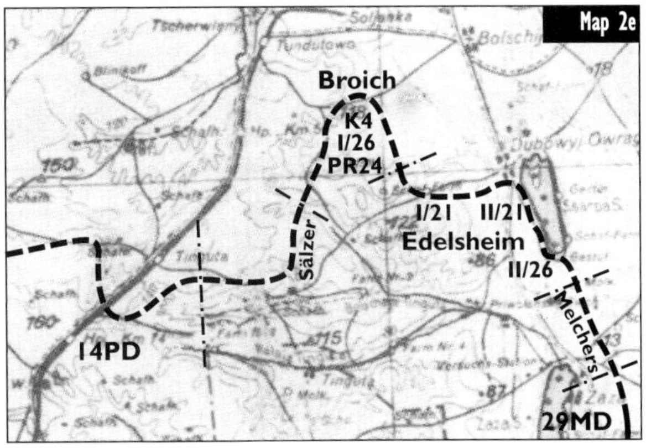

At 1832 hours, Edelsheim reported that the enemy had attacked both sides of the brook which ran from the north-west direction of Dubovyi Ovrag. It was brought to a standstill under heavy enemy casualties. The enemy was still observed supplying reinforcements on shuttling lorries from the north to Bolshiye Chapurniki.

As the sun slowly set, greasy smoke poured into the sky and artillery shells from both sides arched overhead, tearing up the burnt ground. The haze hanging over the steppe made the setting sun glow in lurid colours. The violet darkness enveloped the battlefield, covering the German retirement back into the hedgehog. The day's fighting had ended in a deadlock, a result that favoured the Russians. Late in the evening, 24. Panzer-Division submitted its daily report: "East flank of Division unchanged. Area hard west of Lake Sarpa straightened out. Attack on Dubovyi Ovrag brought close to village from south and west. Security line of II./PGR26 runs from Golodnoya Gully over 43.3, left wing hard south of Point 17.8. Strong attacks on 118.0 from north and west. Russian attacks from direction Bolshiye Chapurniki repulsed by a panzer battalion and artillery at 1800 hours. Gruppe Sälzer secures area 86.3.

"Aim for tomorrow reported by phone conversation with KG.

"It is not possible to exactly survey operational panzers, about 14 Panzer II, 25-30 Panzer III and IV, of those 1 Panzer IV long."

24. Panzer-Division continued to protect the east flank of Korps. The Division went over to the defensive as ordered, at the same time covering the northern flank of the Korps that wanted to continue to attack to the west and north-west. Hauenschild shifted his Division HQ again to a position 500 metres south of the Milchhaus near 115.7.

At 2230 hours, the Division issued Divisionsbefehl Nr. 49 incorporating Korps' directive for the Division to go over to the defensive and protect the northern flank of XXXXVIII. Panzerkorps. The line designated to be held against enemy attacks was as follows:

North edge of Tsatsa village – south-west corner of Lake Sarpa – west edge of Lake Sarpa – area of 10.5 – 14.5 (both south of Dubovyi Ovrag) – middle of Golodnoya Gully – 43.3 – 1km south of 17.8 – hard north and west of 118.0 – 86.3 – 1.5km south to the western slope of 115.7. The various combat groups of the Division took up defensive positions, as shown in the map to the right.

Casualties:

28 men killed

- Unteroffizier Karl Kätz; PR24 (Killed)
- Obergefreiter Ferdinand Then; PR24 (Killed)
- Obergefreiter Josef Förster; PGR21 (Killed)

13 officers wounded (7 of those stayed with the troops)

- Rittmeister Kuno von Meyer (Schwadron Kdr); 9./PR24 (Wounded but stayed with troops)
- KV-Rat Reinhard Schönberger (Kompanie Kdr); Werkstatt/PR24 (Wounded but stayed with the troops)
- Oberleutnant Freiherr von Schlichting (Zug Kdr); 9./PR24 (Wounded)
- Leutnant Cay-Lorenz Baron von Brockdorff (Zug Kdr); 1./PR24 (Wounded but stayed with the troops)
- Oberleutnant Heinrich von Helldorff (Zug Kdr); 4./PR24 (Wounded but stayed with troops)
- Stabsarzt Dr. Ernst Schumacher (Regiment Arzt); PR24 (Wounded but stayed with the troops)
- KV-Rat Otto Herold; PR24 (Wounded but stayed with the troops)
- Leutnant Hans-Erdmann Schönbeck (Zug Kdr); 6./PR24 (Wounded but stayed with troops)
- Oberleutnant Hanno Rinke (Schwadron Kdr); 6./PR24 (Wounded)
- Oberleutnant Walter Wiktorin (Abt OO); III./PR24 (Wounded but died of these wounds on 24th August 1942)
- Rittmeister Hans-Heinrich Schlenther (Schwadron Kdr); 2./PGR21 (Wounded but died of these wounds on 7th November 1942)
- Leutnant Gert-Dietrich Woelki (Batterie Offizier); 2./PAR89 (Wounded)
- Oberleutnant Martin Neßlinger (Abt Adjutant); I./PAR89 (Wounded but stayed with troops)

156 men wounded (66 of those stayed with the troops)

- Panzergrenadier Peter Wichary; PGR21 (Wounded but died on 23rd August in Feldlaz. 1./522)

23rd August 1942

The night passed relatively quietly near 24. Panzer-Division. Toward 2325 hours on 22nd August, a barrage of Stalin Organs and artillery pummelled Hill 118, followed by an attack of infantry forces, which was repulsed. The Ic (Enemy Intelligence Officer) of the Division, Rittmeister Adalbert Graf vom Hagen, submitted the following statement from a deserter to Korps: "Attack towards 1700 hours on Bolshiye Chapurniki by a newly organised motorised regiment (set up on 5th July) with 7.62cm guns. Mission: Attack Hill 115.7. Regiment thrown forward here from Stalingrad. Has not previously been in combat.
"Deserter from Rifle-Regiment 92 of 422nd Rifle Division from Vladivostok, arrived 20 days ago. "Mission: With strong artillery support and Stalin Organs, attack 118.0 (about 20 guns)."

Another clear sunny day was ushered in on the Kalmuck steppe. At 0545 hours, Gruppe Edelsheim began its day by facing a Russian attack of one to two battalions out of the Bolshiye Chapurniki area into the area north-west of Dubovyi Ovrag. The attack was smashed by the concentrated fire of two artillery battalions of Panzerartillerie-Regiment 89. Spotter planes buzzed overhead, directing the fire into the mass of charging Russians. Apart from controlling artillery fire, the pilots of these planes also identified eight Russian artillery batteries on this sector, three of which were successfully suppressed by schwere Artillerie Abteilung 800 with the help of these planes. Having easily withstood the Russian attack, Gruppe Edelsheim began its proper assignment: clearing out the area around Lake Sarpa. The starting time had been set for 0430 hours but the Russian attack had postponed it for a couple of hours. For his task, Oberst von Edelsheim's combat group had the following components at its disposal:

Panzergrenadier-Regiment 21
Panzergrenadier-Regiment 26 (without I. Abteilung)
II. and III./Panzerartillerie-Regiment 89 (each without one battery)
a light Nebelwerfer battery of schwere Werfer Regiment 53
Flak-Bataillon 602 (without one company)
two flak combat groups of 10./Panzerartillerie-Regiment 89
z.b.V. Kompanie 800

The assault squads moved forward, plunging into the thick masses of reed and rushes, the swampy ground trying to pull the boots off their feet. Bullets brushed through the long grass or thwacked into the soft ground, forcing the riflemen into the mud: a light machine-gun quickly brought into position sawed through the tall reeds, more often than not striking a Russian poised only a dozen or so metres from the Germans. And so it continued. It was dirty, tiring work but Gruppe Edelsheim steadily cleared the southern shore of Lake Sarpa.
As their footslogging comrades waded through knee-deep muck in the Lake Sarpa marsh, the men of Gruppe Broich were enjoying a respite in the punishing combat. The entire front-line in their sector was quiet. Oberst von Broich had been informed that in front of him was one Russian tank brigade and 422nd Rifle-Division but it emerged from monitored radio communications and observation that the Russian division was anxious about their south-east flank as a result of the advance of 14. Panzer-Division.

At 0800 hours Major von Menges spoke by phone with Oberst Friebe and reported that the situation was generally unchanged.
Friebe: "We are after possibilities to hold Hill 118 because it is a dominating hill. If, as it is hoped, everything comes into order today, then 14. Panzer-Division will immediately move up to the left next to your Division. Air support today only to a limited extent."
Thus Korps now gave the order to hold Hill 118 because of the possibility that 14. Panzer-Division would move up to the left of 24. Panzer-Division. At the moment, despite strengthening Russian attacks from three sides, Hill 118 was still being held. The command panzers of Panzer-Regiment 24 rolled up on to a hill south of Tundutov station as the sun peaked over the horizon. Oberst Riebel, Rittmeister von Aulock and Oberleutnant Weidemann surveyed the scene: circling around from their left was the railway line, dipping into a depression that lay in front of them, where it then continued on to the lowlands and swung north to Krassnoarmeisk. In the glorious morning light, the black shapes of German vehicles stood out from the dry yellow grass. Russian artillery shells landed here and there, throwing up grey veils of smoke and dust that drifted across the battlefield. It was not aimed fire. The Regiment staff could hear sounds of battle resounding through the valleys. To their left, combat groups of 14. Panzer-Division struggled against the obstinate Russian defence system; to their right, down in the lowlands, their comrades from the grenadier regiments launched repeated thrusts into the enemy. Riebel had been informed that these regiments would be regrouped to continue the thrust from a different direction. With their panzer units enjoying a temporary exhaustion-induced peace with the Russians, the Regiment staff decided to make the most of it. The constant strain of commanding the battle could dull the brain at a decisive moment. The three command panzers, together with the five Panzer II's of Leutnant Daschkey's Aufklarüngs Zug (reconnaissance platoon), rested on the slope of the hill, all hatches flung open to catch the sun and some air. Several crews performed essential maintenance. Others, engrossed in letters from home, lounged on the panzers. While Rittmeister von Aulock, Oberleutnant Weidemann and a few of the other commanders stood in their turrets swapping stories and jokes, Oberst

SPANNOCCHI

On the beautifully sunny morning of 23rd August 1942, there was a chance for the dirty panzer crews to wash up and shave after two days of fierce fighting. They were far enough behind the forward line to not worry about Russian interference.

SPANNOCCHI

Oberleutnant Falk-Eberhard Freiherr von Maltzan, Ordonanzoffizier of I./Panzer-Regiment 24, takes the opportunity to have a shave, resting his mirror on the opened engine cover of the battalion staff car.

SPANNOCCHI

After their morning ablutions, they move off. Major von Winterfeld is in the passenger seat of his staff car.

SPANNOCCHI

Oberleutnant von Maltzan and his crew of Panzer '363' pose for a souvenir photograph in the hills south of the fiercely-contested Hill 118.

Riebel's command tank '371' was always to be seen up front. On the left is Panzer '363', the mount of Oberleutnant von Maltzan, Ordonanzoffizier I./Panzer-Regiment 24.

Riebel sat in a folding chair on the engine-deck of his '371'. Everyone was enjoying this beautiful late summers morning. Nobody noticed the reports of artillery among the distant sounds of battle. There was a sickening whistle and shells crashed between the panzers, sending shrapnel whizzing through the air as smoke and dirt billowed from the impact. The cloud of dust and gunpowder slowly drifted away. A deathly stillness gripped the scene.
"Medic! Medic!" A frightened voice shattered the stunned silence. The full horror of the incident soon became clear. Oberst Riebel, struck by a splinter, had been killed instantly. Rittmeister von Aulock was seriously wounded. Other men had been killed and wounded, including the Regiment Ordonanzoffizier, Leutnant Klaus von der Decken, and Leutnant Hammer of Panzer-Nachrichten-Abteilung 86. The driver of one of this battalions armoured vehicles, Obergefreiter Hannes Speckner, was killed instantly, while Obergefreiter Exner[9] had one of his legs ripped off by shrapnel.

Word soon spread throughout 24. Panzer-Division, the news of Oberst Riebel's death producing a feeling of great loss amongst the officers and men. Gustav Adolf Riebel – known to his friends as Peter – was a battle-hardened panzer commander who'd led his regiment with a level head. He'd entered the armed forces in August 1914 as an officer candidate and it was not until January 1916 that he became a Leutnant while serving in Ulan-Regiment 4. Early in the 1920's, he served as a Leutnant in Reiter-Regiment 2 which in late 1941 was converted to form Panzer-Regiment 24. For a long time during the Reichsheer period, he'd been Guderian's trusted adjutant in his role as Chef der schnelle Truppen im OKH. Riebel's military career was thus closely linked with the development of the German Panzertruppe. He began the Second World War as a Korps Adjutant, first for XXII. Armeekorps during the Polish campaign, subsequently being transferred on 15th October 1939 to Guderian's XIX. Armeekorps where he stayed for exactly a year, once again enjoying his service under the man considered to be a military genius. He assumed command of Panzer-Regiment 15 of 11.

9. Exner survived his wounds – and the war – eventually passing away on 4th August 1983.

Panzer-Division on 23rd February 1941 in Megedia, Romania, after the previous commander, Oberst Johannes Streich, resigned his appointment on 9th February. He led his panzers into Serbia on 8th April 1942 through difficult terrain, the unit constricted to narrow winding mountain roads but on 13th April, his panzers stood on Belgrade's streets. Upon conclusion of the Balkans campaign, Riebel and his men recovered outside Vienna for a few weeks before being transported to Stalova Vola in eastern Poland – not far from the Soviet border. On the morning of 22nd June 1942, Riebel led his panzers through the border town of Sokal near the Bug River, crossing that river at exactly 1500 hours. It was the start of combat on an unprecedented scale and most men had no idea what was in store for them. The trials of the Eastern Front brought out the best in many officers and this was certainly the case with Riebel. Starting at a bunker line east of Sokal, Riebel fought through the first major armoured battle of the campaign on 23rd June near Radciekov, ending victorious with 46 Russian tanks – including T-34's – destroyed for the loss of only one of his own. Dubno and Ostrog were quickly captured but a blown bridge east of the last town proved a major obstacle, so a daring alternative was implemented: Riebel and his panzers carried out a hazardous mission to capture a railway bridge already wired with demolition charges and protected by heavy guns. The coup de main succeeded and the advance was renewed. On 3rd July, they passed through the Stalin Line near Karosten and advanced on Berdichev, Riebel always at the front, leaning out of the cupola of his command panzer '01'. On 21st July, while sealing off the eastern flank of the Uman Pocket, Riebel and his adjutant, both in command panzers equipped only with machine-guns, stood in line together with two other Panzer III's to repel a desperate enemy break-out attempt spearheaded by 20 heavy tanks. The attack was repulsed thanks mainly to two 88 Flak guns standing to the rear but the cold nerve of Riebel to remain at the front – defenceless against the onrushing tanks – impressed everyone, and the danger he was in was proven by the fact that the commanders of the cannon-equipped Panzer III's were both killed. The imposing figure of Riebel in his black panzer uniform, his cropped white hair unmistakable, was always seen at the front, wherever the action was hottest. On 22nd August, the mighty Dnepr River was reached near Gornistaipol. After a brief rest in Zhitomir in mid-September, they moved off once again, fording the Desna, marching through Malin before participating in the massive Vyazma encirclement on 8th October by holding the thin eastern wall of the pocket. Again Riebel was at the front, now clad in a greatcoat to ward off the increasingly colder weather, leading his panzers along the highway toward the ultimate goal of Moscow. The autumn rains turned all roads into bottomless quagmires, forcing a halt to offensive operations but on 16th November, after temperatures had turned sub-zero and frosts had hardened the ground, the advance was renewed. Day by day, the number of operational panzers kept shrinking but Riebel led his panzers to within 20 kilometres of the Soviet capital before being thrown back by the enemy winter counteroffensive. For his excellent command of these panzers, he earned the German Cross in Gold, presented to him on 24th December 1941. He was recalled from the depths of the Russian winter to take command of a newly formed panzer regiment: Panzer-Regiment 24. He officially took command on 3rd January 1942, arriving in Paris to set up his staff quarters in Chateau Vincennes on the eastern edge of the city. From that point on, his spirit, courage and methods left an indelible impression upon the conduct of Panzer-Regiment 24. He always felt a large responsibility for the men under his command, treating them with respect and consideration. The Division would miss him. He was buried the next day in the Pryvolzhki State Property, the site of 24. Panzer-Division's first graveyard in front of Stalingrad. Oberst Riebel was accorded full military honours and posthumously promoted to Generalmajor. General von Hauenschild, the regiment commanders and other members of the division provided his funeral train, as operations permitted. Major

SPANNOCCHI

Near Hill 118, a panzer crew uses a quiet moment to capture a photo for the family at home. It was during one of these calmer periods that Oberst Riebel and his staff, thinking they were safely away from the fighting, were struck by Russian artillery. Oberst Riebel was killed and his adjutant, Rittmeister von Aulock, was severely wounded.

SPANNOCCHI

The burial of Oberst Riebel on 24th August 1942 in Pryvolzhki State Property. Despite having only reached the Property on 22nd August, 24. Panzer-Division had already established a cemetery on the collective farm.

SPANNOCCHI

In attendance at Oberst Riebel's funeral was the Division Commander, Generalmajor von Hauenschild, several regiment and battalion commanders and many of the Panzer-Regiment's rank and file. Generalmajor von Hauenschild ended his eulogy with the words: "You now rest here in German soil, Kamerad Riebel."

SPANNOCCHI

Oberst Riebel's panzer schwadron commanders served as his pallbearers while the Division's protestant priest, Kriegspfarrer Arndt, conducted the service. Inset: Oberst Riebel as he will be remembered; a tough, nerveless panzer commander who led his regiment with great skill. His death greatly affected his officers and men.

MARK

Major Wilfried von Winterfeld, commander of I./Panzer-Regiment 24 (right) discusses orders with Rittmeister Emil Spannocchi, Chef 2./Panzer-Regiment 24.

von Winterfeld, commander of I. Abteilung, assumed temporary command of Panzer-Regiment 24. A search was initiated throughout the Wehrmacht for a new regiment commander.

At 1900 hours, General von Hauenschild reported the losses of the Division to General Kempf: "Panzer Regiment Commander killed, Adjutant wounded." Kempf expressed his sympathy but quickly turned back to military matters. "I am glad that 118.0 was held. Hauenschild: "Russians have concentrated around Tinguta railway station. Reinforced in Dubovyi Ovrag, above all by artillery (8 batteries). Three batteries observed east of Lake Sarpa."
Kempf: "Mission for 24. Panzer-Division remains the same. Near elevation line 140 are strong positions, flanking fire from there, hence 14. Panzer-Division avoiding it in forest direction."
During the course of the day, Panzer-Regiment 24 had lost its Commander, Adjutant and Ordonanzoffizier. There had been no progress made on 23rd August south of Stalingrad. The mission for 24th August remained the same. Reconnaissance was to be carried out on 24th August on the hill terrain between Krassnoarmeisk and Ivanovka, and Korps would continue the attack north early on 25th August. Position of 24. Panzer-Division at nightfall on 23rd August: north-east edge Lake Sarpa – 10.5 (2km south of Dubovyi Ovrag) – 14.5 – 30.4 – 43.3 – 118.0 – 1km east of 86.3. Panzer situation: 15 Panzer II, 10 Panzer III lg, 24 Panzer III kz, 2 Panzer IV lg, 3 Panzer IV kz, 2 Bfwg and 34 Pak 5cm.

Casualties:

1 officer killed

- Oberst Gustav Adolf Riebel (Regiment Kdr); PR24 (Killed)

8 men killed

- Obergefreiter Hannes Speckner; PNA86 (Killed)

5 officers wounded (1 of those stayed with the troops)

- Rittmeister Johannes von Aulock (Regiment Adjutant); PR24 (Wounded)
- Leutnant Klaus von der Decken (Regiment OO); PR24 (Wounded)
- Leutnant Fritz Binkow (Zug Kdr); 5./PGR26 (Wounded)
- Oberleutnant Hammer; PNA86 (Wounded)
- Leutnant Egon Reifner (Zug Kdr); 3./Pz.Pi.40 (Wounded but stayed with the troops)

48 men wounded (25 of those stayed with the troops)

- Obergefreiter Exner; PNA86 (Wounded)

5 men missing

Decorations bestowed from 17th August to 23rd August:

14 Iron Cross First Class
152 Iron Cross Second Class
54 Panzer Combat Badge in Bronze
1 Panzer Combat Badge in Silver
16 Assault Badge[10]

Prisoners and booty taken from 17th August to 23rd August:

660 prisoners
1 airplane
11 guns
6 batteries destroyed
3 tanks
24 anti-tank guns
2 anti-aircraft guns
18 mortars
25 anti-tank rifles

24th August 1942:

During the night, an Armeebefehl was issued in which it was stated that the Armee would start the assault on Stalingrad after regrouping its forces with the Schwerpunkt lying east of the railway line. XXXXVIII. Panzerkorps received the mission of destroying the enemy located east of this railway. After that, Korps would assemble its forces both sides and south of Tundutovo railway station and keep itself ready for the continuation of the attack on Stalingrad from 25th August.

The small Storch (stork) reconnaissance planes were out early, circling over the Russian rear area in the dazzling morning sun. Sunlight glinted off the planes' windows as they banked to the right or left. They reported that eight Russian tanks ahead of 24. Panzer-Division in the switch position (6km south of Tundutovo) were driving to the north-west.
When Oberst Friebe arrived at 24. Panzer-Division headquarters to discuss the upcoming attack, General von Hauenschild forcibly expressed his doubts, saying that 24. Panzer-Division could only set off when 14. Panzer-Division was on the same level. The Division now wanted

10. To qualify for this badge, the prospective recipient must have participated in a minimum of three assaults on three different occasions.

to support this thrust with flanking fire. Oberst Friebe approved this proposal and expressed his intention of sending the assault guns of 29. Infanterie-Division to support 24. Panzer-Division.

A connection with relieving elements of 29. Infanterie-Division (mot.) was established during the day. Relief was intended for the first half of the night to 25th August and it seemed like the situation would permit an easy handover: the enemy near Dubovyi Ovrag appeared to be becoming weaker, but the bunker positions on east edge of the village were still occupied. The area around Hills 146 and 13.5 were occupied by the enemy, as were Hills 84.5 and 111.4, both being covered in bunkers and strongly garrisoned.

At 1610 hours, General von Hauenschild spoke with Kempf about the attack the next day.
Kempf: "How is the conduct of the attack?"
Hauenschild: "I assume that 14. Panzer-Division is on the same level because the sector of the Division is too small."
Kempf: "I think it is enemy-free west of you?"
Hauenschild: "No!"
Kempf: "How could 14. Panzer-Division come up to the same level?"
Hauenschild: "Preparations on 118.0 not implemented during the day because the enemy is shooting here from the east."
Kempf: "Can't the riflemen prepare during the night?"
Hauenschild: "That can't be done. If 14. Panzer-Division cannot set out from 86.3, then it should advance from 84.6, but then that will delay my advance."
Kempf: "Can't the riflemen prepare in the gullies?"
Hauenschild: "No! If 14. Panzer-Division cannot advance from 86.3, preparations within the area of my Division near 84.6 are not possible."
As can be seen from the preceding conversation, Russian artillery fire was severely affecting German preparations to continue the attack. By tying up German forces around Hill 118 with constant attacks and pounding them with artillery, the Russians were preventing the German riflemen from safely regrouping. That was why Kempf suggested reforming at night or in the many gullies. And with 14. Panzer-Division lagging behind, Hauenschild's units were being fired on from the west, north and east. Until 14. Panzer-Division moved up and provided protection to the west, Hauenschild could not properly reassemble his units for an attack to the north.
Kempf called Hauenschild at 1705 hours: "14. Panzer-Division will ready itself with riflemen further west, only with panzers and half-tracks via Morosov. 14. Panzer-Division leaves Hill 76.4 and will advance from there at 0500 hours. We will be supported from the air at 0500 hours."

At 1810 hours, Leutnant Hubertus Freiherr von Eickstedt, O4 of 24. Panzer-Division reported the following to Korps: "At the moment, a company attacking part of Gruppe Melchers on the southern edge of Lake Sarpa, supported by mortars and artillery, will possibly delay the relief. At 1800, 7./PGR21 was attacked in the area of 0.6 south of Lake Sarpa in strength of one company with artillery and mortars. Attack was repulsed. Apart from that, near Point 16.4 east of Lake Sarpa at 1800 hours, two marching columns of two companies were observed marching to the south."
The mission for XXXXVIII. Panzerkorps was to break through the enemy both sides of Solianka and occupy the high ground north-east of Ivanovka. From there, Korps, without awaiting further orders, would adhere to the high ground and thrust through to Voroponovo

railway station – Novy Rogachik, searching for a connection there with 6. Armee. The industrial locality in the Volga valley would not be attacked. Under cover of the south-east and east flanks by 29. Infanterie-Division (mot.), 24. Panzer-Division and 14. Panzer-Division, assembled in the area around Morosov, would attack in a northern direction to gain the hills north-east of Ivanovka. The mission given to 24. Panzer-Division by Korps was as follows: "Attack over 84.5, break through the enemy positions both sides of Solianka and occupy the high ground 119.1 – 111.6. The swift capture of the massif 133.7 is to be strived for. If this is not possible, it should be screened off."
14. Panzer-Division would begin its attack at 0500 hours, while 24. Panzer-Division would only begin its attack when 14. Panzer-Division had taken Hill 107.4. In response to Korps' order, the Division issued Divisionsbefehl Nr. 50 at 2130 hours on 24th August, which called for a regrouping of the Division's forces and a renewed attack on 25th August in the direction of the Volga. The Division decided that as soon as the attack of 14. Panzer-Division was on the same level – as a prerequisite for its own advance – it would thrust to the north in two groups. There, they would outflank as far to the right as possible, then again towards Solianka, there to await a strong enemy attack with the united Division.

No battle actions occurred on the Division's sector during the whole day, apart from a Russian company-strength probe on Gruppe Melchers. That night, the men could see the searchlights of Stalingrad arcing back and forth in the dark sky. During the night, elements of 29. Infanterie-Division (mot.) relieved the bulk of Panzergrenadier-Regiment 21 in front of Dubovyi Ovrag. II. Abteilung of Infanterie-Regiment 71 (29. ID) relieved some units of 24. Panzer-Division near Hill 17.8. The Brigade staff again assumed command of both panzergrenadier regiments and made them available near Hill 118 for an attack to the north. Panzer situation for 24. Panzer-Division: 27 Panzer II, 30 Panzer III kz, 22 Panzer III lg, 2 Panzer IV kz, 2 Panzer IV lg, 2 Bfwg, 34 5cm Pak. Sturmgeschütz-Abteilung 243 was subordinated to the Division.
In the evening, Leutnant von Eickstedt submitted a report about the supply situation of the Division: "Ammunition stocks: infantry ammunition 94%, heavy mortars 65%, light infantry gun 60 %, heavy infantry gun 60%, light field howitzer 65%, heavy 10cm 50%, panzer ammunition 85%. Urgent requirements: 10,000 signal cartridges, 6,000 smoke signals (orange), 1500 heavy 10cm, 700 heavy field howitzer, 200 light field howitzer, 900 light infantry gun, 400 heavy infantry gun, 600 15cm shells. Continuing shortage of signal cartridges and heavy 10cm.
Urgently necessary: lubricant, grease, tyres, supply of panzer engines, general replacement parts for new type vehicles, suspension springs, bolts and nuts."

On the previous night, two squads of z.b.V. 800, in full camouflage, conducted reconnaissance in the Krassnoarmeisk area with good results.

Casualties:

1 man killed

- Obergefreiter Konrad Meier; PGR21 (Killed)

13 men wounded (10 of those stayed with the troops)

25th August 1942:

The advanced Division HQ was shifted north of Hill 115.7 into the area of Hill 118. From this vantage point, General von Hauenschild had a supreme view over his units. By 0430 hours, the Division advanced out of the rearward preparation area, deployed very narrowly and deeply echeloned. The Panzer Regiment was held back and would only advance after 14. Panzer-Division had reached its targeted hill but the impression seemed to be that the bulk of the enemy ground forces had retreated. This was more than compensated for by the ferocious artillery fire. From the beginning, the enemy overwhelmed the attacking Schwadrons with the heaviest fire from artillery, mortars, Stalin Organs and dug-in tanks which were transported only half-completed from Stalingrad without engines. The stone-hard ground caused the exploding shells to produce a particularly nasty shrapnel effect. The artillery and Stukas did their best to help the grenadiers move forward but despite that, the attack only slowly gained ground under disproportionately high casualties. At 0645 hours, the left wing of the panzergrenadiers was in connection to the right wing of 14. Panzer-Division. The panzers of Panzer-Regiment 36 were still in combat against T-34's at 0530 hours near Point 107.4.
The attack of 14. Panzer-Division only moved forward slowly and was constantly flanked by tanks from the west, especially since IV. Armeekorps standing further to the south-west was not able to launch its attack simultaneously. At 0805 hours, 14. Panzer-Division reported to Korps: "Heavy combat with enemy tanks at 107.4 – 115.8. All Panzer IV long knocked out, all panzers except 5 are knocked out. 24. Panzer-Division staying to cover the flank to the west. Advisable for 24. Panzer-Division to continue further to the north."
As a result, 24. Panzer-Division advanced to the north alone.

At 0830 hours, Kempf called Major von Menges wanting to know what was happening with the panzers of the Division.
Menges: "Panzers are still in position."
Kempf: "Impression that 14. Panzer-Division being strongly attacked on west flank. 24. Panzer-Division must advance now."
Menges: "Forwardmost riflemen lay in front of 111.4."
General Kempf drove to 14. Panzer-Division and after speaking with Heim, decided that 24. Panzer-Division should advance with panzers. Under these conditions, the Division was tightly concentrated and with their panzers and riflemen, set out towards Hill 111.4. At 0940 hours, Major von Menges transmitted a short message to Korps: "Riflemen advance on 111.4, then the panzers advance on Solianka. 14. Panzer-Division bends to the west. No tanks apparently in front of 24. Panzer-Division, but strong enemy forces."
At 1015 hours, General Kempf, still at 14. Panzer-Division HQ, sent the following report to Oberst Friebe back at Korps command post: "Very hard fighting on the left flank of 14. Panzer-Division. 24. Panzer-Division apparently making headway." Half an hour later, Point 111.4 was taken after hard fighting and good air support. At 1100 hours, Kempf again called Oberst Friebe: "It is going well near 24. Panzer-Division. It is not good near 14. Panzer-Division. Gruppe Scheven has met very strong resistance."

Oberleutnant Dittmar, Commander of 6./Panzergrenadier-Regiment 21, recalls the withdrawal from Dubovyi Ovrag and the attack the next morning, on 25th August: "At 0100 hours, we withdrew. (After relief in front of Dubovyi Ovrag, then still around 14km motorised march and preparations.) Large-scale attack. 6. Schwadron in forward line. 160 prisoners, 15 heavy, 5 light mortars, 17.5cm gun, 5 heavy machine-guns etc. were captured. Stukas and panzers supported us. A war correspondent is near us. 1 dead, 11 wounded…" The dead man was Gefreiter Albert Gaidies.

The panzers and riflemen of 24. Panzer-Division inched closer to the village of Schtschinin. At midday, pioneers produced a 100 metre wide gap through the deep belt of mines south of the village. Thrusting through the gap, the hills south of the village were taken. After the mine barrier was cleared by pioneers near 7. Schwadron of Panzergrenadier-Regiment 21, Unteroffizier Wessely and his 1st platoon set off to attack the strongly occupied trench system lying in front of them, barely 2.5km south of Solianka, when the panzer platoon of his brother, Oberwachtmeister Wessely of 5./Panzer-Regiment 24 rolled up. After a brief discussion, both brothers quickly came to an understanding. The 3 panzers headed up to the enemy position and worked over the garrison with hand grenades and machine-gun fire so that the grenadiers were only required to take the survivors prisoner with few of their own casualties[11]. Less fortunate was the neighbouring 3rd platoon under Leutnant Hans Freise. He did not want to wait for panzer support and was killed during the penetration into the enemy trenches, together with his messenger Gefreiter Erhard Mathes and Panzergrenadier Georg Pöhlmann. Several men were wounded, including Gefreiter Willi Fischer, who died on 31st August in a hospital in Kotelnikovo. Oberwachtmeister Kurt Prätzas, Commander of the heavy platoon that was supporting Freise with a heavy machine-gun squad, was fatally wounded. Unteroffizier Große Holz tried to help him: "I grasped his hand and said to him that he would soon receive help. He squeezed my hand convulsively and answered: 'This wound will not heal.' He died. It was dark and the Russians in the trench had either surrendered or disappeared."

At 1400 hours, the panzers proceeded northward along the passage cleared through the mines in front of Schtschinin while the riflemen advanced toward the strong field emplacements identified there. The right Kampfgruppe of 14. Panzer-Division advanced at 1337 hours from 107.4 to 106.5. More field positions were broken through north of Hill 111.4, several artillery and anti-tank positions being destroyed. Here, the narrow assault spearhead, strongly flanked from both sides, bogged down in front of fortified bunker positions and mine barriers, as well as under never-before-experienced artillery and mortar barrages. The panzer spearhead had been attacking since 1430 hours about 1km south of Schtschinin. The Panzergrenadier-Brigade followed closely behind. Strong artillery and mortar fire on the assault groups, as well as tough resistance in the field fortifications and gullies, strengthened the impression that the enemy was determined to hold the constructed defensive position near Schtschinin under all circumstances. The heavy Russian artillery fire continued to exact a heavy toll. Russian artillery hammered the hard ground, knocking out vehicles and men. The wounded crew of a battered panzer waited for help in the lee of their machine as the small Sanitätspanzer of Oberstabsarzt Dr. Schumacher, Regimental Surgeon of Panzer-Regiment 24, rolled toward them. He leapt from his hatch and started administering first aid to the wounded tankers when a salvo of Russian artillery caught him. He suffered shrapnel wounds to his lungs that proved fatal: he died two days later in a Stalino hospital. Thus ended the life of the doctor who'd been with the regiment since its earliest days.

---

11. A few hours later, Oberwachtmeister Wessely was wounded by night-time artillery fire. He was killed on 11th August 1944 on the Weichsel.

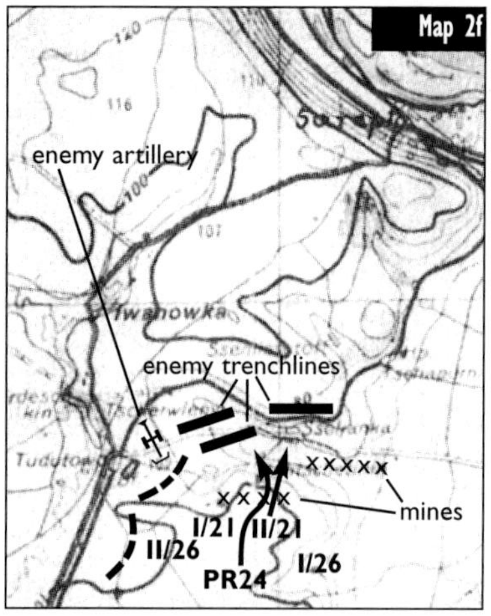

At 1410 hours, General von Hauenschild reported to Oberst Friebe: "Passage through the mines 100-150 metres wide. Also artillery and mortar fire. Enemy seems to want to hold there. Assault therefore progressing slowly. Nothing to be seen of 14. Panzer-Division. 260 prisoners. Bulk of the Division in hard fighting in area 115.8 – 120.2 – 107.4. Elements advanced and approached 106.5. This combat is extremely bitter and costly and will continue the entire day. Panzer Regiment still has 13 panzers. One Russian tank was hit 10 times without success, 3 were shot up, 2 others withdrew on fire."

Shortly after General von Hauenschild sent this message, the number of prisoners taken by the Division rose to 350. The prisoners were members of 422nd and 36th Rifle Divisions. The grenadiers were amazed to discover that some of the enemy units employed here wore First World War uniforms.

The assault was discontinued at 1700 hours in front of the well-constructed line of fortifications south of Solianka. The thick defensive belt consisted of continuous minefields, well-entrenched anti-tank guns and machine-guns, all covered by very strong enemy artillery. General von Hauenschild reported this to Kempf by phone at 1705 hours, saying the attack was stopped because the riflemen were caught in very strong artillery, mortar and Stalin Organ fire. The enemy artillery appeared to be far to the rear but was very strong. At that time, 12 enemy tanks attacked out of Solianka. General Kempf spoke to Hoth at 1750 hours and reported on the very difficult and costly fighting near the divisions: "Four Russian tanks and many of our own destroyed. The tanks stubbornly stand in position with a good view and unpleasantly outflank us from the west. Despite many hits, they have not moved. I have told 24. Panzer-Division that it must advance, despite 14. Panzer-Division. Heavy fighting around 111.4. Breakthrough succeeded with air support. 150 metre wide alley cleared through the mine belt south of Schtschinin. Panzers through and reached Schtschinin. Pilot reported: Solianka reached, infantry following, lying in the hill area. Hanging back on the right to 84.5 is the half-track battalion. Division was attacked at the time by heavy tanks which came from Sarepta and Solianka. Heaviest artillery fire out of the Tundutovo area from the north and from east. The division commander reported very bad casualties of about 200-250… Still only has 13 panzers… Division extraordinarily tied up and has suffered high casualties in men and equipment. Above all, 24. Panzer-Division suffered under artillery from three sides."

Hoth: "I don't want you to penetrate to the west too early."

Kempf: "Start roughly about 115.8. Strong flanking fire also to be expected there. Division wearing away very quickly. 29. Infanterie-Division (mot.) cannot occupy to the south-east."

The staff of II./Panzergrenadier-Regiment 21 had a rough time on this day. The Abteilung Adjutant Oberleutnant Curt von Burkersroda, Ordonanzoffizier Leutnant Gebhardt von Treuenfels and Ia-Schreiber Oberwachtmeister Babin fell out through wounds.

Oberwachtmeister Babin reports: "Sanitäts-Oberfeldwebel Rudolf Schneider was already fatally wounded at the beginning of the attack by shell splinters[12]. Shortly after we had set ourselves

12. Died in the dressing station of 2./40 Sanitäts-Kompanie.

up in the Russian trenches, the vehicles were drawn forward with the onset of twilight. An 8.8cm flak gun also came up with them. Major Schwanke criticised the presence of the flak in our immediate vicinity because it was visible from afar in the almost flat terrain. Major Schwanke would be proved right. Darkness had completely closed in when a barrage from Stalin Organs burst upon us. After it had passed and the sky was illuminated by burning vehicles, I saw that our Kübelwagen, in which our few belongings (topographic maps, war diary, regiment orders etc.) were located, was also burning.

"I first of all wanted to try to salvage these things, so I leapt out of the trench, ran up to the burning vehicle (about 40 metres from the command post), and had already ripped out the large leather briefcase when a second salvo from a Stalin Organ closed in above us. I flew backwards through the air, landed next to a panzer, must have been unconscious for a short time, then grasped my head first of all and found a large grazing wound, wanted to stand up and toppled forward.

"My left foot was pulp. Several comrades then brought me into the trenches, the only medic that was still there gave me some painkilling opiate (tetanus was no longer available). At the insistence of the battalion commander, I was taken to the Regiment command post on a panzer and from there to a hospital. Near the Regiment command post, I bid farewell to Oberst von Lengerke. Hours later, at the dressing station, I saw him dead on a stretcher. In the early morning, there was a low-level attack by the Russians on the dressing station. A few of the medical staff were wounded. Transport by ambulance to a small railway station. From there, in a freight car together with Romanian and Hungarian wounded to an airfield. We severely wounded men were flown by Ju-52 to Stalino. From there by hospital train to Kielce."

No less severe were the casualties already suffered by the badly decimated I. Abteilung of Panzergrenadier-Regiment 21. First Schwadron lost 17 wounded, while 3. Schwadron had 6 killed men killed on Hill 111.4. They were: Wachtmeister Josef Herden, Unteroffizier Bruno Schekelinski, Obergefreiter Herbert Petrikat and Gefreiters Albert Fiedler, Paul Friedrich and Willy Kujus. Among the wounded of 3. Schwadron was Oberwachtmeister Hütt, one of the most successful tournament riders of the Regiment in peacetime, who died two days later. Of the three rifle platoons of 2. Schwadron, there were only a couple of men remaining. Fourth Schwadron lost Gefreiter Helmut Langanke on Hill 118. Up until 26th August, the total losses of Panzergrenadier-Regiment 21 amounted to 36.4%, Panzergrenadier-Regiment 26 to 28%. With the onset of darkness, the regiments retracted their forward elements and set up defences with fronts to the east and north. In the centre was Panzergrenadier-Regiment 21, closing up to the left with a front to the west was II./PGR26, further right was I./PGR26.

On this day, the Schwerpunkt assault of 24. Panzer-Division indeed gained ground to the north but subsequently came to a standstill because of the flanking effect of the enemy. This gave the possibility, after regrouping, of taking Dubovyi Ovrag and after that, Bolshiye Chapurniki. General Kempf and his Chief-of-Staff Oberst Friebe favoured this solution. In the opinion of Generalmajor von Hauenschild, however, a further attack here with the available forces would only be possible under the heaviest casualties. The conquered hill terrain would be held for the night and secured to all sides, especially since 14. Panzer-Division was stuck 4km to the left rear. Generaloberst Hoth was inclined to agree with Hauenschild. The bloody casualties amongst his units and the stubborn Russian defence prompted him to rethink his strategy. This cool strategist refused to continue this slogging match, so he ordered the assaults to be stopped. In his command post in Plodovitoye, Hoth leant over his map, searching the symbols for clues as to his next step. His Chief-of-Staff, Oberst i.G. Fangohr, pencilled in the latest situation reports. With his panzer units deeply enmeshed in the Russian defences, his initial move would be to extricate them. Two hours earlier Hoth had visited General Kempf at his Korps headquarters and had driven with him to see General Ritter von Hauenschild, where he listened to a report on 24. Panzer-Division's situation. He had also visited Generalmajor Heim at the Tinguta railway station. In one of the deeply-eroded gullies, Heim had explained the 14. Panzer-Division's difficult situation. Here, too, they could go no further.

"We have to approach the matter in a different way, Fangohr," reasoned Hoth. "We're bleeding ourselves in front of these damned hills, it's no battlefield for panzer units. We must regroup and attack at a completely different spot far from here. Look here..."

As the Generaloberst developed his plan, Fangohr drew eagerly on the map, compared reconnaissance reports, measured distances. "That will work," he said repeatedly. But he wasn't entirely pleased by Hoth's plan because they would again lose time by regrouping. As well, the shifting of forces would consume a great deal of fuel, and the fuel simply wasn't there. And finally, those 'damned hills' would have to be taken one way or another, because they commanded the entire southern city and its approaches – the same argument raised by General Kempf against a regrouping. In the end, however, both Fangohr and Kempf were convinced by their Commander-in-Chief. Hoth phoned Armeegruppe B headquarters and spoke with Feldmarschall Maximilian Weichs for half an hour, and the latter gave his approval.

At 2015 hours, Kempf transmitted an inquiry by phone to Armee as to whether Korps could lead the assault with 94. Infanterie-Division because in the opinion of Korps, the spearhead, even if 94. Infanterie-Division were employed, would be too small. Kempf proposed that Korps stay in its present area and IV. Armeekorps gain the area to the left by attacking at the same time. Hoth then put forward his proposal to Kempf: "Proposal: Korps moves into the area of the Romanians and from there, thrusts to the north, IV. Armeekorps relieves us, but a lot of time is required for the basic relief."

Kempf: "Subordination of 94. Infanterie-Division will also not lead to success because the front is too small."

Hoth: "Korps will hold the attained area."

Hoth then set the ball rolling. Orderlies raced off with orders. The telephone wires were never cold. Every man in the headquarters was busy: regroup!

In accordance with the Armeebefehl, 24. Panzer-Division received the mission for 26th August at 2055 hours from Oberst Friebe: "Mission for tomorrow: Hold the attained line and dig in." An advanced order from Korps arrived soon afterwards, confirming that the Division would be pulled out in the night to 27th August for new employment in another position for a successful attack on Stalingrad. After relief in the State Property Pryvolzhki area – Farm 3 – Farm 2, Korps would assemble around Plodovitoye. For the later thrust of Korps out of the area both sides of Tebektenerovo, they were to immediately launch reconnaissance under the strictest camouflage measures. At 2330 hours, the following order was given to 24. Panzer-Division, 14. Panzer-Division and 94. Infanterie-Division regarding the relief: the relieved elements of 94. Infanterie-Division would be subordinated with the arrival of the panzer divisions up to the implementation of the relief. The delivery of orders was to be reported to Korps after the completion of the relief by 94. Infanterie-Division. 14. Panzer-Division and 24. Panzer-Division would each leave a heavy Flak battalion in the combat sectors, their withdrawal being ordered by Korps.

Positions at nightfall: I./PGR26 south of Schtschinin to the north, east and west.
Panzerjäger and Flak were on Hills 78 and 99, and then from north to east. Kradschützen-Abteilung 4 near Hill 118 secured to the east.
Division HQ was located on the approach road south of Hill 118.
Panzer situation: 12 Panzer II, 25 Panzer III kz, 15 Panzer III lg, 2 Panzer IV kz, 3 Panzer IV lg and 2 Bfwg.

Casualties:

1 officer killed

- Leutnant Hans Freise (Zug Kdr); 7./PGR21 (Killed 2.5km south of Solianka)

18 men killed

- Obergefreiter Anton Blaumauer; PGR21 (Fatally wounded on Hill 118)
- Oberwachtmeister Kurt Prätzas; PGR21 (Killed 2.5km south of Solianka)
- Gefreiter Erhard Mathes; PGR21 (Killed 2.5km south of Solianka)
- Panzergrenadier Georg Pöhlmann; PGR21 (Killed 2.5km south of Solianka)
- Gefreiter Albert Gaidies; PGR21 (Killed near Dubovyi Ovrag)
- Gefreiter Helmut Langanke; PGR21 (Killed on Hill 118)
- Gefreiter Paul Friedrich; PGR21 (Killed near Ssarpakin)
- Wachtmeister Josef Herden; PGR21 (Killed on Hill 111.4 south of Solianka)
- Unteroffizier Bruno Schekelinski; PGR21 (Killed on Hill 111.4 south of Solianka)
- Obergefreiter Herbert Petrikat; PGR21 (Killed on Hill 111.4 south of Solianka)
- Gefreiter Albert Fiedler; PGR21 (Killed on Hill 111.4 south of Solianka)
- Gefreiter Willy Kujus; PGR21 (Killed on Hill 111.4 south of Solianka)
- Gefreiter Walter Ehlers; PNA86 (Killed)

13 officers wounded (6 of those stayed with the troops)

- Major Wilhelm Schwanke (Abteilung Kdr); II./PGR21 (Wounded but stayed with troops)
- Oberleutnant Jürgen Pachnio (Abt Adjutant); I./PGR21 (Wounded but stayed with troops)
- Oberleutnant Curt von Burkersroda (Regiment Adjutant); PGR21 (Wounded)
- Oberleutnant Gebhardt von Treuenfels (Abt OO); I./PGR21 (Wounded)
- Leutnant Werner Tutein (Zug Kdr); 1./PGR21 (Wounded but stayed with the troops)
- Stabsarzt Dr. Ernst Schumacher (Regiment Arzt); PR24 (Wounded but died on 27th August)
- Hauptmann Nahler (Abteilung Kdr); I./PAR89 (Wounded but stayed with the troops)
- Hauptmann Hubert Platz (Abteilung Kdr); III./PAR89 (Wounded but stayed with troops)
- Oberleutnant d'Heureuse; 7./PAR89 (Wounded but stayed with the troops)
- Oberleutnant Waetjen (Batterie Kdr); Stabs III./PAR89 (Wounded)
- Leutnant Baaden; III./PAR89 (Wounded)
- Leutnant Edelmann (Wounded)
- Leutnant Aloisius Buchholz (Zug Kdr); Nachrichten Zug/K4 (Wounded)

191 men wounded (53 of those stayed with the troops)

- Knight's Cross winner Wachtmeister Otto Brakat; 2./K4 (Wounded but stayed with the troops)
- Gefreiter Willi Fischer; PGR21 (Wounded but died on 31st August in Kotelnikovo hospital)
- Oberwachtmeister Walter Hütt; PGR21 (Wounded on Hill 111.4 but died on 27th August)
- Sanitäts-Feldwebel Rudolf Schneider; PGR21 (Wounded 4km south of Tundutovo railway station but died near 2./40 San. Ko. later that day)

1 man missing

26th August 1942:

Apart from artillery fire during the night and early morning, there were no particular incidents and the Russian artillery fire did not interfere with 94. Infanterie-Division, whose Infanterie-Regiment 276 and IV./Artillerie-Regiment 194 were marching into the area around Morosov. The relief near Hill 115.8 was in full swing but the further replacement of the Division could only be carried out with the onset of darkness because of enemy observation. The relieving elements of 94. Infanterie-Division were subordinated to XXXXVIII. Panzerkorps until the completion of the withdrawal of 24. Panzer-Division and 14. Panzer-Division. At 1400 hours, the Division issued Divisionsbefehl Nr. 51 for the relief of the Division by elements of 94. Infanterie-Division during the night of 26th/27th August 1942 and the transfer of the Division's forces into a new accommodation area. Gruppe Broich and Abteilung Dressler of Gruppe Hellermann would be relieved by Infanterie-Regiment 267 during the night, as would Gruppe Sälzer by a pioneer company of 94. Infanterie-Division while the rest of Gruppe Hellermann would withdraw without being replaced by another unit. The divisional artillery would gradually be replaced by Artillerie-Regiment 194 starting in the afternoon. Preparations had already begun with all vehicles no longer immediately required being sent into the rest area in an effort to avoid congestion on the few roads during the vital nocturnal hours. Troops relieved before nightfall would also march into these rest areas south-west of Hill 115.7. The order for entry into the rest areas was set down as follows: Gruppe Hellermann, Gruppe Broich and finally Gruppe Sälzer. The later groups would only file into the area once the preceding group had completed its march. Gruppe Hellermann would be the first to move out the next morning.

During the day, the enemy continually covered the German positions with heavy artillery and Stalin Organ fire and in the morning scored a direct hit on a Regiment command post on the rear slope of Hill 118. Oberst von Lengerke, Commander of Panzergrenadier-Regiment 21, was sitting in a Kübelwagen writing a letter home when he was severely wounded by a shell splinter. Two members of Regiment staff, Wachtmeister Otto Papin and Obergefreiter Bruno Wölki, were also severely wounded in the same barrage. Oberleutnant Egbert von Schmidt-Pauli, Regiment Adjutant, came through it with a couple of scratches. Revered throughout the entire Regiment like a father, as a leader and the model of a highly reliable regiment commander, Oberst von Lengerke succumbed to his severe wounds at the main dressing station a short time later. 24. Panzer-Division mourned the loss of another valuable leader. Soon afterwards, Obergefreiter Wölki also died of his wounds and Wachtmeister Papin died in Reserve Hospital VI in Stettin on 6th February 1943, more than five months later.

At 1415 hours, Oberst Friebe sent out instructions to all Nachrichtenführer (communications chiefs) stating that radio silence was ordered in all areas north of Plodovitoye until the beginning of the new assault. Barely 45 minutes later, at 1500 hours, General Heim informed Korps that his Nachrichten Aufklärung Zug (listening post) had monitored the following text broadcast sent in the clear: "By order, the divisions should relieve all panzer units and replace them with infantry divisions. Assemble the panzers in the area north of Tinguta."
Whether the Russians heard the broadcast was uncertain. The possibility existed, however, that the enemy had listened in on this message and could draw conclusions about the coming assault actions. The incident was reported to Armee, who affected the appropriate countermeasures. A message sent by General von Hauenschild at 1530 hours assuaged fears that the Russians had monitored the broadcast: "Listening posts confirmed that the broadcast was not so dangerous because the Russians have already radioed that enemy tanks [meaning the German panzers] were preparing to attack near Tinguta."

In the late afternoon, elements of 94. Infanterie-Division relieved Panzergrenadier-Regiment 21 which was withdrawn about 20km and had one and a half days rest in the Tinguta sector. The bulk of the Division, however, was still employed. Unemployed elements of 24. Panzer-Division were already set in march to the south, among them 3./Panzerpionier-Bataillon 40. An unnamed soldier from that unit wrote the following account: "…Hell broke loose on Hill 118! Me and the main part of my pioneer platoon were badly hit. It was hot, red hot… and the minefields were marked and we were retreating when all hell broke loose – it seemed to 'come from nowhere'. 'Panzers march to the rear', that's what sounded in our ears. Then the impacts shattered and the Obergefreiter, who pulled me up on a self-propelled Vierlingsflak[13], said 'Herr Unteroffizier, that's a sin!' My face covered in blood, spitting blood and totally exhausted, I prepared my camera and said: 'Take a picture, this may be the last for my mother.' My mother received the photo but it was not the last one. For that, we thank the dear Lord!"
The relief would proceed during the night, as planned, being launched with the beginning of darkness. Elements of Kradschützen-Abteilung 4, artillery and pioneers were already marching into the new accommodation area. Division Staff would march back to the old headquarters at 0700 hours on 27th August.
At 1800 hours, Generals Kempf and Heim, Major von der Lancken and the chief-of-staff of 14. Panzer-Division came together for a conference about the new assignment. Kempf reported the aims of Armee and the view of the Romanians. The entire Luftflotte would be placed at their disposal.
Oberst i.G. Friebe spoke to Major von Menges about the impending relief by 94. Infanterie-Division. Menges said: "We'll hand over between 2300 and 0100 hours. Move off about 0700 hours."
Friebe: "Commander or Ia must be in Abganerovo tomorrow for a terrain discussion by division commanders. Time still to come through." A little while later, the details of the conference arrived: 1000 hours western edge of Abganerovo, entrance to railway station, commanders conference.
After reconnaissance for the coming attack, Oberst Friebe reported that an assault west of Tebektenerovo on Point 164.0 was possible. Sadnaya – Myschkova Gully was impassable. Only an assault between this gully and Tebektenerovo was possible. To improve the positions near

13. An anti-aircraft gun consisting of four 20mm guns

Tebektenerovo, the Romanian Armeekorps would carry out an assault on 27th August, supported by VIII. Fliegerkorps with strong forces.

Casualties:

1 officer killed

- Oberst Wilhelm von Lengerke (Regiment Kdr); PGR21 (Killed)

5 men killed

- Obergefreiter Otto Neuendorf; PGR21 (Killed)
- Obergefreiter Max Butterhof; PGR21 (Killed on Hill 111.4 south of Solianka)
- Unteroffizier Heinz Manglitz; PGR21 (Killed on Hill 111.4 south of Solianka)
- Obergefreiter Paul Mikoteit; PGR21 (Killed on Hill 118, 5km south of Solianka)
- Obergefreiter Bruno Wölki; PGR21 (Killed on Hill 118, 5km south of Solianka)

2 officers wounded (1 of those stayed with the troops)

- Oberleutnant August Böke (Abteilung Adjutant); III./PR24 (Wounded but stayed with the troops)
- Leutnant Wilhelm von der Trenck (Zug Kdr); 6./PR24 (Wounded)

19 men wounded (11 of those stayed with the troops)

- Gefreiter Gerhard Einicke; PGR21 (Wounded but died in hospital)
- Wachtmeister Otto Papin; PGR21 (Wounded but died on 6th February 1943 in Stettin)

The result of the fighting and the thrusts in the direction of Stalingrad since 12th August 1942 was as follows: by securing the east flank of the Korps in a broad formation to repel repeated enemy attacks, the Division made it possible for XXXXVIII. Panzerkorps to attack. The Division's thrust to the north further eliminated the enemy on the east flank and thereby produced the conditions for the quick and united thrust of Korps to the north. Through the capture of the decisive Hill 118, the way into the rear of the enemy was opened and the prerequisites produced by the destruction of the strong remaining enemy elements. In the end, through their thrust within the framework of the Panzerkorps, the Division had in 6 days ripped open the entire front for about 30km and with that, the ring around Stalingrad had been narrowed. The Division had considerably weakened the enemy front south of Stalingrad by inflicting extremely bloody casualties on the Russians as well as the taking large amounts of prisoners and captured equipment.

Casualties for the time from 12th – 26th August 1942:

	Offz.	Uffz. and men
killed	5	102
wounded	23 (a further 21 stayed w/ troops)	359 (a further 213 stayed w/ troops)
missing	–	8

Booty and prisoners in the time from 12th – 26th August 1942:

1,425 prisoners
11 aircraft
15 guns
36 guns destroyed by artillery
4 tanks
33 anti-tank guns
2 anti-aircraft guns
54 anti-tank rifles
53 mortars
1 automatic rifle
1 radio

SPANNOCCHI

Enormous quantities of captured Russian weaponry were assembled at Abganerovo railway station. Most of the guns shown here are undamaged.

Prisoners and total booty from 28th June –26th August 1942:

14,885 prisoners
69 aircraft
125 guns
36 guns destroyed by artillery
250 tanks
183 anti-tank guns
25 anti-aircraft guns
211 anti-tank rifles
192 mortars

Total casualties from 28th June (beginning of the campaign) – 26th August 1942:

	Offz.	Uffz. and men
killed	33	555
wounded	75 (a further 81 stayed w/ troops)	1,912 (a further 1,047 stayed w/ troops)
missing	–	26
total	108 Offz.	2,493 Uffz. and men

Percentage of troop casualties prior to 26th August 1942:

Pz.Gr.Rgt. 21	36.4%	San.Ko 2./40	9.9%
Pz.Gr.Brig	28.2%	Pz.Rgt.24	9.3%
Pz.Gr.Rgt. 26	28.0%	Pz.Nach.Abt.86	7.6%
Pz.Jg.Abt. 40	17.6%	San.Ko 3./40	7.3%
IV./Pz.Art.Rgt.89	17.0%	Stab 24.Pz.Div.	5.4%
Pz.Pi.Btl. 40	16.8%	San.Ko 1./40	1.2%
Krad.Abt. 4	15.1%	Dinafü. 40	1.0%
Pz.Art.Rgt.89	10.0%		

On 26th August, despite the casualties in officers, non-commissioned officers and men as well as vehicles and equipment, the Division was still fully mobile and able to fulfil every assault operation, even though the Panzer Regiment, as a consequence of shortages in replacement parts, still only consisted of a weak battalion.

27th August 1942:

In the night to 27th August, the Division started pulling out of the area south-east of Tundutovo. During the night, the enemy attacked west of Hill 106.0 with tanks and fired on Hill 118 with artillery and mortars. The sound of Russian planes reverberated throughout the night and three were shot down. At 0315 hours, 24. Panzer-Division handed over its area to 94. Infanterie-Division without any incidents. Two artillery battalions were only pulled out at 0530 hours after the situation had calmed down. The pause in fighting was appreciated by the men. Leutnant von Senger und Etterlin[14] made the following note in his diary: "A quiet day. We fooled about with some camels, gathered melons and serviced our vehicles."

His commander, Rittmeister Kolczyk, recalls that despite the ferocity of the last weeks fighting, his unit had come through it relatively unscathed: "All 37 armoured half-tracks[15] of my Schwadron were operational after the regrouping on Hill 118. We had no losses and also had no losses due to mines. The Schwadron had two men killed during a night-time securing operation. I no longer remember their names. They were killed before the main attack during a securing mission on the high ground near Lake Tsatsa during a nocturnal battle between Russian reconnaissance and our advanced listening posts."

14. He was promoted from Fahnenjunker-Wachtmeister to Leutnant on 24th August.
15. In one of his letters to the author, Heinz Kolczyk said: "My humble self grew up amongst machines and I am an avid motor fan!"

After a week of furious combat, the Panzer Regiment was finally able to take stock. As if casualties caused by Russian weapons were not enough, casualties of another sort inflicted a high toll, for in this part of Russia, there was a high incidence of infectious jaundice and it caused not only the Panzer Regiment, but the entire Division, a great deal of trouble, thinning out the ranks of the Schwadrons. Only as a result of high panzer casualties was there still enough crews to be able to man the battleready vehicles. Nevertheless, several of the sick men remained with their units and after becoming wounded, the jaundice made itself noticeable now and then, whereupon it was treated. The lightly wounded were also treated in the rearward supply area. Several gave up hospital treatment and arrived in the reserve hospital in the homeland. General von Hauenschild also finally clarified the command structure of Panzer-Regiment 24 after the death of Oberst Riebel on 23rd August. Major von Winterfeld had assumed temporary command of the Regiment after Oberst Riebel's death and led it for the remainder of the assault toward Krassnoarmeisk. Now with a chance to organise the command structure, General von Hauenschild made the following known:

1.) The command of supplies, repairs, IIa area (personnel matters) and replacements of the Panzer Regiment would be immediately taken over by the Regimentsführer, Major von Winterfeld.
2.) The tactical command of all operational panzers would be immediately taken over until further notice by Major von der Lancken, Stab III./Panzer-Regiment 24, who would constantly keep the Regimentsführer informed.
3.) All tactical orders during the operations of the Division and the Kampfgruppen were henceforth only to be directed to Major von der Lancken with the designation 'Panzer Abteilung Lancken', accordingly all orders about personnel to Major von Winterfeld with the designation 'Panzer-Regiment 24'.

At 1000 hours, the division commanders converged on the west entrance of Abganerovo. General Kempf drove with them first of all to the headquarters of 2. Romanian Division. Near BW 6km south-west of Abganerovo railway station, the commanders met with Commanding General of VI. Romanian Armeekorps and the Division Commander of 20. Romanian Division. According to reports about the enemy situation and reconnaissance of terrain, an assault between Sadnaya Myschkova Gully and Tebektenerovo appeared to be favourable. The sector, however, was too narrow to direct through the three divisions to guarantee a fluid advance after a successful breakthrough against the first enemy positions. Despite the

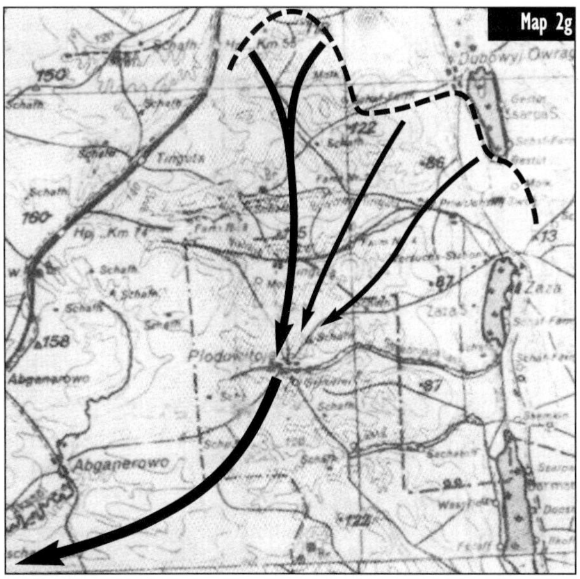

24. Panzer-Division withdraws from Yergeni Hills

gullies, the terrain for the attack west of Tebektenerovo was deemed to be passable and suitable for large-scale panzer operations. Because a dividing of Korps appeared unsuitable and an attack on the terrain in the sector west of Tebektenerovo was only immaterially unfavourable and wide enough for 3 divisions, the attack was set for this sector. Without exception, the enemy positions were weakly occupied without anti-tank guns and only a few artillery pieces, the focal point of the enemy defence lying near Farm Nr. 1 and State Property Yurkina. The commanders subsequently drove forward to Hill 124.0 to reconnoitre the preparation areas of the divisions. It turned out that the enemy on the hills north-west of Vassilievski had a view into the assigned starting areas, so preparations would have to be carried out at night to avoid a flanking effect from enemy weapons. They returned from reconnaissance at 1415 hours. After personally observing the proposed assault area, it was confirmed that the attack would be conducted west of Tebektenerovo. General Kempf reported this to Generaloberst Hoth. Kempf later informed Oberst Fangohr (Chief-of-Staff 4. Panzer-Armee) by telephone of the results of the conference and terrain reconnaissance. At the same time, Kempf indicated that Armee should take measures to unconditionally stop the roaming of Russian civilians from village to village, on the grounds of espionage.

As a consequence of the pressing situation, the proposed day of rest could not be afforded. Towards evening, the Division – now fully relieved by 94. Infanterie-Division – arrived in the accommodation area Plodovitoye – State Property Pryvolzhki – Farm Nr. 4.

Panzer situation: 17 Panzer II, 22 Panzer III kz, 18 Panzer III lg, 2 Panzer IV lg, 3 Bfwg.

Pak situation: 34 5cm Pak

BUNDESARCHIV, BILD 183/R64042 / PHOTO: UNKNOWN

Commander of Panzergrenadier-Regiment 21, Oberst Wilhelm von Lengerke, killed on 26th August 1942 on Hill 118.

Casualties:

1 officer wounded (he stayed with the troops)

- Hauptmann Hans-David von Engel (Batterie Kdr); 6./PAR89 (Wounded but stayed with the troops)

4 men wounded (3 of those stayed with the troops)

- Knight's Cross winner Wachtmeister Otto Brakat; 2./K4 (Wounded but stayed with the troops)

28th August 1942:

Initial movements were initiated at 0330 hours. After putting aside the march on 28th August, the Division had enough fuel for about 50km, on average, for an advance out of the preparation area, while Kradschützen-Abteilung 4 had enough on hand for about 100km.

At the Heroes Cemetery of the Division near Pryvolzhki State Property, 48-year old Oberst von Lengerke was honourably buried. Generalmajor von Hauenschild issued a Tagesbefehl on this day remembering the much-loved Oberst von Lengerke:

> "Today, the Commander of Panzergrenadier-Regiment 21, Oberst von Lengerke, was laid to rest.
> "A commander has left our ranks, a member of the Division for many years and who, as a cavalry commander and commander in our proud Panzer Division, has been wholeheartedly devoted to it.
> "He was a knightly example of noblest convictions and sense of responsibility, an officer who has effortlessly won the respect and the hearts of his comrades and subordinates through his superior knowledge and untiring care.
> "With hearts full of sadness but also gratitude, our Division says its goodbyes today.
> "And tomorrow, when we face battle again, we will attack filled with his spirit, until our flags finally flutter over this soil that is saturated with the blood of the best of German manhood.
>
> signed
> v. Hauenschild
> Generalmajor"

Oberst Wilhelm von Lengerke was an old-style officer who upheld the Prussian tradition and insisted that his soldiers did too. His obedience to the authorities, however, met its limit when orders violated the laws of decency and dignity, honour and humanity. And the biggest violation to Lengerke's moral code arrived soon after crossing the Russian border on 22nd June 1941: the infamous Commissar Order demanding that all captured commissars, and those already in German captivity, be immediately shot by the troops. The directive was not well-received by Lengerke. "That's an order to murder!" von Lengerke called out, "and incompatible with the honour of German soldiers. I will not allow us to give in to it!" And so it was. The order was not passed on to the troops under his command. His respect for his soldiers was unsurpassed and he was heard to say that he wore his Knight's Cross as recognition for the contributions and performance of his men. Thus one of the Division's most honourable men was interred in Russia's soil. The Knight's Cross that he wore so proudly, together with his other decorations, were sent to his widow Marianne[16]. Oberstleutnant Vollrath von Hellermann, commander of Kradschützen-Abteilung 4, took command of Panzergrenadier-Regiment 21. One of von Hellermann's subordinates, Oberleutnant Heinz Schlaefereit, remembers him as "an excellent strategist. I have witnessed him several times giving out orders

BUNDESARCHIV, BILD 146/III-500 / PHOTO: UNKNOWN

Oberstleutnant Vollrath von Hellermann, Commander of Kradschützen-Abteilung 4, took command of Panzergrenadier-Regiment 21 on 26th August 1942 after the death of Oberst von Lengerke.

16. Frau Marianne von Lengerke died on 4th March 1965 at the age of 61.

SCHLAEFEREIT

Rittmeister Otto von der Groeben (sixth from left) and the headquarters staff of 4. Schwadron of Kradschützen-Abteilung 4. Von der Groeben took command of the Abteilung on 26th August 1942.

while commanding the vanguard battalion: Clear, lucid, forward-thinking, a daredevil in action." Rittmeister von Langenn-Steinkeller, Commander of 3. Schwadron, has provided a longer recollection of his old commander and remembers him somewhat differently to Heinz Schlaefereit:

> "He originated from military origins – he was a cadet in the time of the Kaiser. He was a soldier in the First World War but I don't know anything more about that. He was, as we all were, a cavalryman, and among others, had served in Reiter-Regiment 5 in Stolp during the Reichswehr period – his family origins were Pomerania/Brandenburg, thus East German. When I met him he was adjutant of our 1. Kavallerie-Division, therefore from 1940 onwards. I came into closer contact with him when in March 1942, he took over Kradschützen-Abteilung 4 from the famous, very independent Oberstleutnant Baade, first in Ohrdruf, then trained in Bretagne in France and led it as Commander until August 1942. Then he took over Panzergrenadier-Regiment 21 and gave it up in November 1942, being transferred to OKW as Inspizient und General für den Führernachwuchs. I was thus under him from March to August 1942. I was the youngest schwadron commander in Kradschützen-Abteilung 4 and especially liked him. He was devoted to me and was very considerate toward me. In a self-selected change of name, he called me 'Steinkneller'[17] – Among intimate friends, he was called 'Hellermops'[18]. I would not describe him as a daredevil as someone else mentioned. He commanded sensibly but not daringly. He was always friendly toward me and very considerate but occasionally he could be gruff."

Taking Oberstleutnant von Hellermann's place as Commander of Kradschützen-Abteilung 4 was Rittmeister Otto von der Groeben, Commander of its 4. Schwadron. Oberleutnant Heinz Schlaefereit, a platoon commander in 4. Schwadron, describes him as a "very popular, humourous and well-liked officer, an experienced fighter." Born in Juckstein on 25th April 1913, Otto von der Groeben was an experienced combatant that had participated in the war from its very first day. In December 1939, he became part of Reiter-Regiment 21, taking command of its 4. (MG) Schwadron on 1st November 1940, then 2. Schwadron on 25th July 1941. He fought hard through the French and Russian campaigns and in November 1941, when 1. Kavallerie-Division was reformed to become 24. Panzer-Division, von der Groeben was transferred to the new Kradschützen-Abteilung 4 and assumed command of its 4. Schwadron, equipped with the swift and lethal combination of motorcycle sidecars. He was not

17. Literally meaning 'stone-presser' but more colloquially it would mean 'tough guy'.
18. 'Heller' being an old form of Austrian currency and 'mops' meaning 'a lot of money', the obvious implication being that he was rich.

Rittmeister Karl v. Sivers, Commander of 5./Panzer-Regiment 24, assumed command of II./Panzergrenadier-Regiment on 26th August after the previous commander, Major Schwanke, was sent back to Germany to recover from nervous exhaustion brought on by the loss of so many of his men.

the senior in age of the Abteilung's schwadron commanders[19] but he was the best choice to take command.
After the assumption of command by Oberstleutnant von Hellermann, there was also another change for Panzergrenadier-Regiment 21. The brave, universally popular Commander of II. Abteilung, Major Wilhelm Schwanke, was so exhausted through the continuous strain, together with the extremely heavy mental strain that arose from his feelings of responsibility for the lives of every individual subordinate – especially considering the severe casualties of his Schwadrons – that he was ordered home by doctors to completely recover. A few days later, on 25th August 1942, he suffered a light wound. Rittmeister Karl v. Sivers, a schwadron commander from Panzer-Regiment 24, was charged with the command of the Abteilung. The units were newly distributed, command positions newly occupied.

On the basis of the preliminary discussions and reconnaissance, a Korpsbefehl with the following objective was issued at 1100 hours: "XXXXVIII. Panzerkorps will break through the enemy positions west of Tebektenerovo on 29th August, occupy the high ground north-west of State Property Yurkina, from there thrusting forward over the line Farm Nr. 2 State Property Yurkina – Hill 150.0 – Sety on the high ground west of Blinikov."

Missions for the divisions were as follows:
"14. Panzer-Division will thrust with a strong left wing over 130.1, roll up the enemy front, destroy the enemy artillery suspected to be in the gullies west of State Property Yurkina and occupy the high ground north-west of there. Further direction of the attack: high ground around 140 (4km west of Farm Nr. 2 State Property Yurkina).
"29. Infanterie-Division (mot.) (without the elements employed on the east flank of Panzer-Armee) will attack past Farm Nr. 1 and occupy the western part of the high ground 180, from there thrusting out to Hill 150.0.
"24. Panzer-Division will attack with a strong right wing under cover of the left flank, occupy Farm Nr. 1 and gain the high ground south-west of Bolshaya Tatarskaya Gully, from there thrusting out with the left wing to Sety."

At 1230 hours, the Division commanders, General Stumpfeld (Arko 108, controlling all artillery in XXXXVIII. Panzerkorps) and General Fiebig, Commanding General of VIII. Fliegerkorps, arrived at Korps HQ for a conference. They first of all discussed the Korpsbefehl

19. He was born on 25th April 1913 (29 years old), Rittmeister Kolczyk was born on 20th November 1912 (29), Rittmeister von Langenn-Steinkeller was born on 7th December 1916 (25) and Rittmeister Wrede was born on 5th November 1912 (29).

in detail. A uniform time for the commencement of the attack was not fixed. When the beginning of the assault was set for 0500 hours, the division commanders reserved the right to launch appropriate local thrusts. Later, the division commanders made their wishes known to General Fiebig for the time and location of Luftwaffe support in their attack sectors.

The Division headed into the rendezvous area with huge delays caused by dust and traffic jams in Plodovitoye. General von Hauenschild temporarily installed his headquarters in a gully 2.5km north-west of Hill 145.0. At 1530 hours, General Heim requested at least one and a half hours to free up the bridge in Aksai for the panzers of 14. Panzer-Division. At the moment, the bridge was being used by 24. Panzer-Division, so this was discussed with and approved by General Hauenschild. So, in a troublesome dusty march, all three divisions marched into their assembly areas. As a result of other simultaneous march movements, 24. Panzer-Division marched into the new preparation area south-west of Tebektenerovo after swinging out far to the south. Unfavourable road conditions, only one available route of advance as well as an indescribable development of dust delayed and made the march movements more difficult. From the viewpoint of Armee, Korps and Division, the transfer of the armoured forces proceeded smoothly, apart from the inconveniences and traffic snarls caused by the deplorable condition of the roads.

At 1650 hours, Hoth arrived at Korps HQ. He was of the opinion that the enemy hard west of the railway line must be destroyed and at the moment, it was of no consequence to quickly thrust up to the Chervlenaya Gully. Kempf was of the same opinion. From this attack, the Armee expected Korps to surprise the enemy and destroy several divisions because the Russians located opposite the Romanian front only had weak forces.
At 2000 hours, the Division issued Divisionsbefehl Nr. 52 for the attack out of the Tebektenerovo area through the Romanian front. For the attack, the Division was concentrated into the following Kampfgruppen:

I. Kampfgruppe Lancken (also called the armoured Stoßgruppe):

Panzer Abteilung (without one light Panzer platoon),
armoured pioneers and Flak-Zug,
armoured elements of I./Panzergrenadier-Regiment 26 with subordinated 2./Kradschützen-Abteilung 4
Directed to co-operate were:
I./Panzerartillerie-Regiment 89 with subordinated I./Flak-Regiment 5 for tank defence and artillery missions.

II. Brigade:

Panzergrenadier-Regiment 21,
Panzergrenadier-Regiment 26 (without armoured elements),
1 light platoon of Panzer-Regiment 24,
Panzerartillerie-Regiment 89 (without I. Abteilung),
light Abteilung/schwere Werfer Regiment 53,
11./Panzerartillerie-Regiment 89
1. and 2./Panzerpionier-Bataillon 40 (assigned for co-operation),
3 flamethrower squads Panzerpionier-Bataillon 40,
1./Panzerjäger-Abteilung 40,
3./Flak-Bataillon 602,
Sturmgeschütz-Abteilung 243.

III. Flak:

I./Flak-Regiment 5 (without 1. Batterie),
IV./Panzerartillerie-Regiment 89 (without 11. Batterie).

IV. At disposal of Division:

a) Gruppe Edelsheim:
Panzerjäger-Abteilung 40 (without 1. Kompanie) with Flak-Zug,
Kradschützen-Abteilung 4 (without 2. Schwadron),
Flak-Bataillon 602 (without 3. Kompanie),
b) Panzerpionier-Bataillon 40 with 3. Kompanie and Brüko-K,
c) Division-Stab, Panzer-Nachrichten-Abteilung 86, Flak-Zug,
d) Kompanie z.b.V. 800 (Brandenburgers)

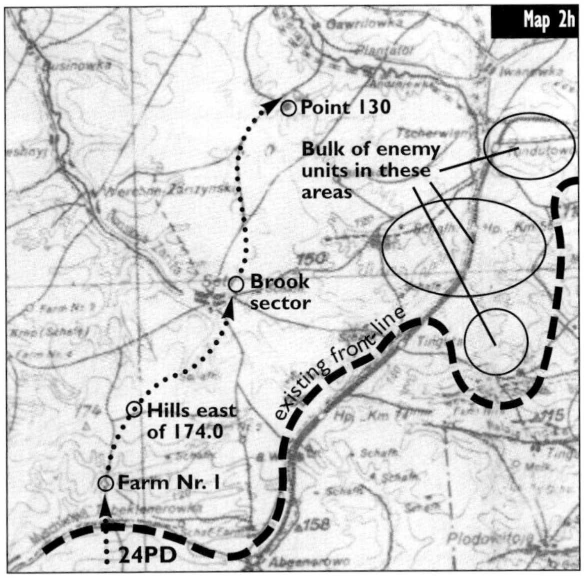

24. Panzer-Division's proposed assault and objectives

With the armoured Stoßgruppe at the front echeloned rearward to the left, the Division would break through the enemy front in the area 3km west of Tebektenerovo after artillery preparation, then gain Farm Nr. 1 as the first attack objective, the hills east of 174.0 as the second attack objective, the brook sector hard north-east of Sety as the third attack objective and Point 130 (6km north-west of Blinikov) as the fourth attack objective. The Division took a calculated risk and ordered its units to thrust through to the daily objective without regard to the open west flank. The 2. Romanian Division, partly employed in the defence, would secure Farm Nr. 1 after the successful attack and take over protection of the open west flank of Korps. Reconnaissance and preparations were made more difficult by the fact that the Romanian division and regiment commanders could not give faultless information about the course of the forward line and picture of the enemy.
The bulk of the Division arrived in the starting areas near Tebektenerovo without any major difficulties. Lagging behind were Kradschützen-Abteilung 4, Panzerjäger-Abteilung 40, 2./z.b.V. 800 and elements of Brigade. The arrival of these units was not reckoned on until early on 29th August, barely in time for the attack. Division HQ was located in a gully 1.5km north of Hill 145.0. Panzer situation: 13 Panzer II, 18 Panzer III kz, 16 Panzer III lg, 2 Panzer IV lg, 3 Bfwg.

Leutnant von Senger und Etterlin's describes the march of his unit:

> "After a long, extraordinarily quick march, we reached the region of northern Aksai in the night. We stopped there. After assembling the armoured group and a quick replenishment of fuel and ammunition, preparations were made to advance further into the night. After several kilometres I noticed that my platoon had lost the connection with the Schwadronstrupp. I frantically drove along to try and stop the spearhead. It was a pitch dark night. No stars could be seen in the sky, no tracers, no roads, no trees – nothing – only the burnt, black earth of the steppe. The rumble of

SPANNOCCHI

A reminder to 24. Panzer-Division members of their roots; a Romanian cavalry unit plods across the steppe on a cool August morning.

motors was audible far in the distance, but everyone asserted that it was coming from the other direction.

"We couldn't wait because it would soon be light and the preparations must be ended before daybreak. I had no idea where we were as I had no map and I only established that we were going in a northern direction. We only had two hours of darkness left, so we had to act quickly as soon as possible. I sent several people out to the right and left with pocket lamps to a distance of several hundred metres to search for panzer tracks in the soil. By good luck we were the last Schwadron of the armoured group, and behind us were only the baggage trains. Under all circumstances we had to be present for tomorrow's assault, otherwise the group would be too weak.

"At last we found panzer tracks and with half-covered lights, we followed these to the north-east. Suddenly, after we had been driving for a quarter of an hour, we found a bivouac in a hollow and a fortified position of 14. Panzer-Division that was to the right of us. I decided that we would now drive dead straight into the steppe to the north-west; some time or other we must find some of our troops. At last in the grey of the morning we found a Romanian artillery position in a deep gully. During the night they had heard a lot of panzers drive by and they showed us the tracks. They were correct; broad tank tracks and the smaller square pads of the half-tracks.

"I now drove behind the 30 Schützenpanzerwagens at a top speed of 35km per hour. At last we saw before us the groundswell of preparations, and just now the treads of the panzers. We followed the lonely vehicles of the Schwadronstrupp. I ordered the radio operator of the Schwadron to at once send out the order to attack."

Casualties:

3 men killed

3 officers wounded (all 3 stayed with the troops)

- Oberleutnant Egbert von Schmidt-Pauli (Regiment Adjutant); PGR21 (Wounded but stayed with the troops)
- Leutnant Heinz Lakenbrink (Zug Kdr); 3./PGR21 (Wounded but stayed with the troops)
- Oberleutnant Jürgen Pachnio (Abteilung Adjutant); I./PGR21 (Wounded but stayed with the troops)

46 men wounded (29 of those stayed with the troops)

Armoured Stampede!

Chapter Three

29th August 1942:

Leutnant von Senger und Etterlin arrived just in time for the beginning of the attack. Other units were not so punctual. At 0400 hours, Hauptmann Roth, O1 of 24. Panzer-Division, informed Korps that the following units had still not yet arrived: Sturmgeschütz-Abteilung 243, Flak-Bataillon 602, I./5. Flak, Panzerjäger-Abteilung 40, z.b.V. 800 and 4./PAR89.
As planned, the Division advanced at 0500 hours, 14. Panzer-Division and 29. Infanterie-Division (mot.) also setting off at the same time. All of the available panzers of Panzer-Regiment 24 were now concentrated into a Kampfgruppe under the command of Major Dietrich von der Lancken, starting the attack with 8 Panzer II, 13 Panzer III kz, 8 Panzer III lg, 1 Panzer IV lg and 2 Bfwg, a total of 32 panzers.
We follow the start of the assault with Zugtruppführer Herrmann in 3./Panzergrenadier-Regiment 21: "...Everyone dreamed of home leave. We only shifted back to the Aksai area, however. During the night at around 2400 hours, we marched into the preparation area. Near us lay our Romanian comrades-in-arms, lying in a dreadful spell of fire during the entire night. At dawn, we set off to attack, making good progress at first but later considerably slowed down by dreadful enemy infantry fire. We reached the first enemy position, well-camouflaged foxholes. From all sides, the enemy came out of the holes with white rags, so I was very careless. Suddenly, I felt a heavy blow that threatened to dismember me. My left shoulder was bent completely to the front and because I could no longer see my left arm, I thought it had been ripped off and awaited the stream of blood. Then I passed out. In a semi-conscious state, I noticed that I was being carried by a number of Russians. Still in my light coma, I thought that I was going into captivity. They turned out to be prisoners, however, who were carrying me under guard to the Abteilung first-aid post. What I had not noticed was that our excellent Sanitäts-Unteroffizier Grumpmann had dressed my wounds so expertly that the battalion doctor at the first-aid post was not required to redress it until I was transported to the Division dressing station."

Leutnant von Senger und Etterlin, having just arrived, immediately ordered his vehicles into action alongside the panzers. He again reports: "We broke into the enemy's prepared positions in a simultaneous movement with the panzergrenadiers, and we at once penetrated deeply. Heavy fire from the Romanian and German artillery covered the enemy who was well entrenched along the northern edge of a deep gully. The gully was boggy and only had a small ford. The spearhead schwadron of the Panzer Abteilung pushed through in a narrow shape and climbed the far side. The leading panzer was shot and it went up in flames. The others pushed

'The spearhead pushed through in a narrow shape and climbed the far side...' The armoured spearhead passes through a shallow gully on the morning of 29th August, as viewed from the troop compartment of a Sdkfz. 251/10 armed with a 37mm anti-tank gun. The half-track on the right (with the frame aerial) is the Sdkfz. 251/6 of Generalmajor Ritter von Hauenschild.

further on. Following behind them were the large half-tracks of the von Dressler Abteilung[1], the larger part of which remained stuck in the gully or could not climb up the slope. Our light vehicles easily negotiated this terrain. My platoon was again the spearhead platoon. I drove across the ford, ordered the first squad to the left, and the second squad to provide cover defence on the right, where a few hundred metres away the Russian anti-tank rifles were shooting from their foxholes. The Schwadronstrupp drove near me. After we had taken the hill, we pushed further through at full throttle behind the panzers. A raging flanking fire struck both sides. Several panzers were shot up. The commander's vehicle ahead of me was stopped by several anti-tank hits that passed cleanly through. The Commander[2] was wounded. I took over the Schwadron."

Rittmeister Heinz Kolczyk describes how he was wounded: "After regrouping and a night-time march from Hill 118 and an expanded assault in the direction of Stalingrad, I received – driving behind the panzers – a hit on the left side from a Russian anti-tank rifle. The small shell smashed through the armour plate of my light half-track and detonated in my back. None of the crew were wounded, and they brought me back in our half-track to a dressing station that was nearby. The shrapnel was immediately removed at the dressing station. Because the suspicion existed that a part of the projectile had also succeeded in going inside me, it was a so-called 'Heimatschuß'[3]. Lying on straw in a Ju-52, I landed 400km distant in a hospital in Artemovsk.

1. I./Panzergrenadier-Regiment 26
2. Rittmeister Heinz Kolczyk
3. Literally 'home wound', an injury that was serious enough for treatment in hospital back in Germany.

"Because my wounding occurred during the attack, I am not able to name my successor: my commander, Oberstleutnant von Hellermann, who happened to be at the dressing station, was able to speak with me and said he would discuss and arrange it. He also wished me all the best. "My wounds were not as severe as was first thought. Internal injuries laid me out for no more than four weeks of recovery."

Oberleutnant Weidemann, Ordonanzoffizier of Panzer-Regiment 24, describes the initial moves of the panzers: "We advanced further through the steppe ocean in the bright light of the morning sun, to be deployed in the distance; the lead panzer was only recognisable by the cloud of dust drawn behind it. Our panzers were struck by anti-tank fire coming from the banked enemy heights. The Soviet positions were immediately covered by the fire of the following panzer artillery. While the opposite slope was enveloped in fire and smoke, our panzers – the battle reconnaissance of the Kradschützen in front – thrust forward over the sector and won the hill terrain lying behind it. Were we going to advance further?"

With the rapid progress of the armoured units, Major von Menges made a change of HQ to Hill 124.0 at 0540 hours. At 0600 hours the Division was attacking Farm Nr. 1. Strong flanking fire from anti-tank guns and anti-tank rifles struck the armoured units from both sides. The panzers pushed on, the sound of anti-tank rifle bullets ringing throughout the vehicle, a projectile occasionally smashing through the reinforced glass blocks that protected the vision slits. Through their periscopes and sights, the commanders and gunners noticed a few Russian tanks ahead of them and this news was quickly passed by radio to Division HQ. At 0615 hours, 24. Panzer-Division reported to Korps that there were Russian tanks north of Hill 130.0. At 0642 hours, the panzers of Gruppe Lancken penetrated into Farm 1 under persistent strong flanking fire from the west. Once the farm had been hastily secured – and even though the

BUNDESARCHIV, BILD 101I/218/504/18 / PHOTO: DIECK

Conference at the advanced Division command post. From left to right are: Rittmeister vom Hagen (Division Ic – Enemy Intelligence Officer); unknown; Major von Menges (Division Chief-of-Staff); Generalmajor von Hauenschild (Division Commander); Oberst von Edelsheim (Commander Panzergrenadier-Regiment 26); Major Henrici (Commander Panzer-Nachrichten-Abteilung 86); and Rittmeister von Langenn-Steinkeller (Commander 3./Kradschützen-Abteilung 4).

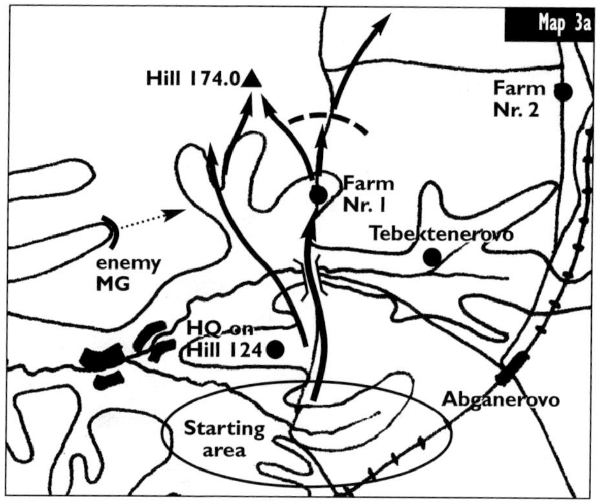

farm itself was still occupied by the enemy – the panzer crews took a short breather, forming a temporary defence line about 1km north of the farm. Major von der Lancken and his staff halted near the farm itself. Stukas were meant to arrive and eliminate some of the annoying enemy nests on both flanks, but shortly after halting around Farm 1, Major von der Lancken received a radio message informing him of a delay with the aerial attack. The panzer attack was therefore delayed because of tardy Stukas. The riflemen were strongly flanked from the gully 4km west of Farm 1. A request for assistance went out over the airwaves, and a schwadron of panzers was sent back to help the Schützen-Brigade, the panzergrenadiers only then succeeding in thrusting through to Farm Nr. 1. The west flank was still completely open, however, so the attack would only make slow progress as a consequence of strong flanking fire coming from that direction.

The small Storch reconnaissance planes flew over the battlefield and at 0710 hours reported that German panzers 1km north-west of Farm Nr. 1 were in tank combat against an enemy vehicle assembly. At 0715 hours, they also reported that the panzer spearhead was 3km west of Farm Nr. 1 and that three panzers were burning. At 0715 hours, Oberst Friebe sent a terse message to 24. Panzer-Division: "Why aren't the panzers advancing?" 24. Panzer-Division replied that the assault was only progressing slowly as a result of strong flanking fire from the west. Half an hour later, the hills west of Hill 180 were reached. At the same time, 14. Panzer-Division took Hill 162.0. Panzers of both divisions continued to advance at 0745 hours to the north-east. Fifteen minutes later, Leutnant von Eickstedt, O4 of 24. Panzer-Division, reported to Korps that 4 Panzer III, 1 Panzer IV long and 1 Panzer II had been knocked out by shelling. At 0805 hours, Major von Menges reported to Korps: "HQ 124.0, Commander on Myschkova bridge." While von Menges took care of matters at HQ, General von Hauenschild was amongst his troops in his Sdkfz. 251/6, a half-track equipped with powerful radios and an Enigma decoding machine, enabling him to lead his units from the front.

At 0815 hours, riflemen set out to renew the assault on Farm 1, supported by the panzer schwadron sent back to assist them. It would remain there as Division-Reserve. Even though the panzers had penetrated into the farm more than one and a half hours earlier, brave Russian soldiers continued to hold out. The panzers had orders to continue on so it was left to the riflemen and grenadiers to finish off the stubborn enemy. After more than an hour of tough fighting amongst the outbuildings, the riflemen of 24. Panzer-Division finally gained complete control of Farm 1. The panzers stood 4km north in the area of Hill 174.0, advancing in a north-east direction. At 1045 hours, Russians still sat in a tooth-shaped gully west of Farm 1 from where they fired on the bridging position across the Myschkova Gully. As pioneers strengthened the bridge, shells howled in, exploding on the banks and the muddy mess in between, sending up plumes of dirt and sludge. In transit with HQ staff, Menges reported to

Korps: "I am on Myschkova bridge. Going to Farm 1. Up to now, 8 panzers knocked out. So far, no tanks appearing. Strong anti-tank fire."

BUNDESARCHIV, BILD 101I/218/510/20 / PHOTO: THIEDE

Kampfgruppe von der Lancken advances northward. Major von der Lancken can be seen in the distance, standing in the cupola of his command panzer '1161' giving orders and directions to his spearhead. Panzer '373' is commanded by Oberleutnant Weidemann.

After the capture of Farm Nr. 1, the Division thrust forward to the north in a fluid advance without regard to the situation on the west flank. Some of the panzers took Hill 174.0 which was only weakly held by Russian defenders.
24. Panzer-Division reported to Korps: "Panzers and mounted riflemen 1110 hours west of Bolshaya Tatarskaya Gully. Left wing again stopped. Where are the Romanians?"
At 1115 hours, the spearhead was in the farmstead 5km north-east of Hill 174.0. Enemy horsedrawn vehicles were observed moving out of the forest 3km south of Sety in the direction of Sety. At 1150 hours, the small Storch planes that trailed like kites behind the armoured wedge reported that the panzer spearhead was 1km south of that village. There, they were halted by artillery fire. The panzer crews pulled their hatches shut and prepared to weather the storm. They sat tight as explosions hammered the hard ground, sending showers of dirt and red-hot shrapnel spattering against the armoured flanks of the panzers. Major von der Lancken realised he had to get the assault moving again. One of his Schwadron Commanders, the exotically named Rittmeister Guy-Bernhard von Le Tanneux von Saint-Paul[4], was wounded when he popped his head out of the cupola of his Panzer IV '1251'. Major von der Lancken yelled down to one of his radio operators to send out a message: 'Advance!' The vehicles of Kampfgruppe von der Lancken seized upon the order and charged through the storm of artillery fire. At 1200 hours, the panzer spearhead reached the southern edge of Sety.

Until midday, the enemy still held out on the west flank in well-constructed flanking positions opposite Gruppe Sälzer until they were destroyed by a thrust by Kradschützen-Abteilung 4 from the north-east. The fighting on the flanks was particularly tough and is shown by a

4. Rittmeister von Saint-Paul, whose ancestors had migrated from France 300 years earlier on religious grounds, was transported to a dressing station where his wounds were treated, then he was shuttled to an army hospital where he convalesced.

MARK/ROTTIERS

One of the Stalin Organs captured by Kampfgruppe von der Lancken.

message sent by 24. Panzer-Division at 1225 hours: "Entire Sturmgeschütz-Abteilung knocked out. The last gun of Sturmgeschütz-Abteilung 243[5] has been knocked out." The message does not indicate whether the assault guns were totally destroyed or, as is more likely, simply put out of action for an hour or so due to minor damage.

Sety was strongly occupied by enemy forces with artillery and anti-tank guns. The armoured assault group (the one available Panzer Abteilung, armoured elements of I./Panzergrenadier-Regiment 26 and I./Panzerartillerie-Regiment 89), further in front of the panzergrenadiers, had already thrust through Sety at 1230 hours with their spearhead. Three Stalin Organs and several batteries were captured. The panzers thrust through Sety to the north, standing about 200-500 metres north of this village. Before them retreated vehicles to the north, north-east and north-west.

Oberleutnant Weidemann reports on these events: "Our panzers struck the Soviet field emplacements with its tank trench on the land bridge east of Sety. Under the cover-fire of the panzers, a Panzerpionierzug under the command of Leutnant Reifner pressed forward and blew up part of the tank trench. Also installed here were the Soviet electrically-ignited flamethrowers, which cost the pioneers heavy casualties; their fighting spirit mastered this crisis. Utilising the smoke developing from the fires, the enemy accepted the sight and blew up their bunkers. Our courageous comrades gratefully signalled the crews of our advancing battle vehicles as they drove through the passage obtained by combat. Numerous anti-aircraft, anti-tank guns and Stalin Organs were captured. Our panzer raid once again pushed our further advance into the enemy's depths. Our panzer spearhead hit unsuspecting Soviet columns, which believed they were far behind the front, and they were surprised and quickly disarmed."

Leutnant Egon Reifner provides the following account for this same event. While the two accounts generally correspond, there are some differences:

> "In good spirits, we rolled behind the Panzer Regiment in the direction of Stalingrad. Suddenly, the radio crackled. Mission: 'Tank trench in front of us, produce a crossing, we will give cover fire.' The armoured Pionierzug rolled out. A long time ago, we had practiced with the panzers near Kursk when an explosive charge was dragged in a quick trip up to the tank trench, blown in and the mass of earth blasted away.
>
> "Here, our great hour had arrived. The panzers came to a standstill. The pioneers headed off.
>
> "No firing. We soon stood 200 metres in front of the construction. We literally heard

5. Assigned to support the grenadiers.

Leutnant Egon Reifner. Note the two badges on his right sleeve, both awarded for the destruction of an armoured train on 31st August 1942.

a lark trill towards the sky. With binoculars, I saw a crossing, solid and stable enough for our panzers. We must have that crossing, precious time would be saved. The silence was oppressive, the embrasures of the many bunkers looked out on us with their black dead eyes. The half-tracks stood still. Cover fire. Fingers on the triggers of the machine-guns behind the armoured shields, the reliable men stood there. The commander's vehicle now drove on alone, this time slowly, up to the trench. The tension was enormous but there were no movements there and no shots.

"Then the vehicle stood in front of the crossing. Furtive glances over the armoured side. Mines must be placed there. There were none to be seen. Further on to the earthen gangway – 1 metre – 3 metres – 5 metres. There, the half-track was in the middle of the crossing and to the right and left of it, on the road on the other side of the tank trench, was a bunker. Deathly silence. The nervous tension was almost unendurable.

"Just as we moved forward in one movement, there was a sinister howling. Twelve fixed flamethrowers, electrically ignited, sprayed from all sides on to the centre of the crossing. It was hell. The crew cried in terror. Skin burned under the pall of flames. No more air. The vehicle burned. Out and next to the vehicle on the ground. And then firing out of every bunker. A hellish din. All of the shooting was a metre too high. The ricocheting bullets sang and cracked. The crew overcame the terror and pain. They looked with relief as the thick oily smoke slowly drew back to the bunker. Now the enemy must close the embrasures. 'Now or never', someone cried.

"Someone extinguished the burning vehicle with sand. Concentrated charges out. The other pioneer half-tracks were already rolling up. With large strides, the men quietly advanced into the thick clouds of smoke and arrived behind the bunker with gasping lungs. Already sounds of crashing to the right and left. Explosives in the embrasures. One group of bunkers gave themselves up, 20, 25 Russians stood there with raised hands. Then the Panzer Regiment rolled up. Resistance was broken. Distraught

> prisoners received cigarettes from the pioneers and they couldn't believe it.
> "Standing on the crossing were the crew of the commander's vehicle, singed, black and weary, waving at the first panzer of Abteilung von Winterfeld. The turret hatch opened. 'The doctor is in the tenth panzer, I thank you.' The burns did not hurt at all. Proud and very lucky, they stood there as panzer after panzer rolled past. They advanced and in this operation, not one single man was killed."

Seeing the terrifying pall of flames spewing forth from the flamethrowers, it is easy to understand why Oberleutnant Weidemann thought the pioneers suffered large casualties. As Reifner confirms, not one of his men was killed.

At 1330 hours, Hauptmann Roth, O1 24. Panzer-Division, sent off the following report to Korps: "Panzers in combat near Sety rolled through the village. Several enemy batteries and Stalin Organs captured. Riflemen tightly closed ranks. Two enemy batteries north of Sety firing on Sety. II./PGR26 south-west of Farm 1 against toughly fighting enemy. Heavy casualties. On the other hand, Kradschützen-Abteilung 4 employed on the east, took over flank protection. Romanians with elements in Farm 1. Left flank hangs back, still like this morning. It should advance, with that, we fight freely on the flanks. Near Sety, right neighbour seemingly already close. Our panzers continue to thrust from Sety to the north-east."
"Not too far, however!" said Oberst Friebe in a schoolmasterly tone. Korps did not want any of the divisions to push too far ahead.

Leutnant von Senger und Etterlin: "We again drove stubbornly for 60 kilometres through drifting dust clouds thrown up 100 metres by our quick advance. The Russian anti-tank guns were pointing at us from the front and behind, and I was hit once with a loud crack by an anti-tank rifle. My Schwadron drove against the flank covered by the smoke-screen and only the last vehicle was stopped by a hit. The breakthrough was successful. In a swift drive the armoured group pushed through, over hills and gullies deep into the enemy's hinterland.
"Somewhere, the reviving resistance was again germinating. Villages were being overrun, unsuspecting Russian supply lines were cashiered. The armoured group irresistibly forced its way through and sometimes, when we were moving forward and drifted further apart, we attacked in force and came together to move forwards. My little half-track pushed further out, clearing up and covering the flanks.
"The General was driving in his command tank in the middle of the armoured wedge. Once, through the glassy glimmer lying over the steppe, I saw somewhere far to our right the other Panzergruppe likewise driving over the hill with us. That must be the spearhead of the 14. Panzer-Division. Following to the left behind us was the 29. Infanterie Division (mot)."

At 1340 hours, the hills 1km north of Sety were taken after fighting by the bulk of the Panzergrenadier Brigade, reinforced by some armoured vehicles. Reinforced Kradschützen-Abteilung 4 cleaned out the area south-west of Farm 1 and covered the west flank. Generalmajor von Hauenschild was pleased with the progress of his units, especially with his armoured spearhead slicing its way north. Mid-afternoon, Generalmajor von Hauenschild sent a radio message to Korps. "Are you agreed to the view reported at 1435 hours? Div.Kdr." Hauenschild had already asked the question but since he had not received an answer, he decided to ask again. He wanted Korps' opinion about his units thrusting forward to the Chervlenaya Gully and forming a bridgehead there. At 1540 hours, Oberst Friebe reported the intention of 24. Panzer-Division to Oberst Fangohr at Armee headquarters: "Division wants to

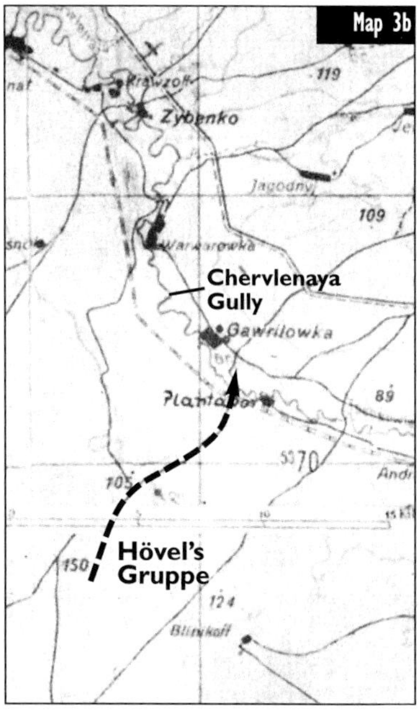

advance west of Blinikov and form a bridgehead over Chervlenaya Gully."

Fangohr: "24. Panzer-Division will advance on Blinikov but will not form a bridgehead."

While Korps and Armee were still deciding, General von Hauenschild took matters into his own hands. According to Oberleutnant Weidemann, riding in his panzer with the spearhead, the armoured Stoßgruppe received the order from General von Hauenschild to thrust towards the Chervlenaya Gully and form a bridgehead near Gavrilovka. Leutnant Heinz Hövel, with a small group of panzers, had the mission of taking the bridge over the gully in a surprise raid. Obergefreiter Ernst Panse, radio operator in Hövel's Panzer III '911' describes what happened:

> "Leutnant Hövel, renowned as an intrepid and daredevilish officer, was entrusted with the following mission: lead a Hussar strike to form a bridgehead over the bridge.
>
> "Two operational panzers of our platoon followed an old Russian Ford lorry occupied by 15 German soldiers in Russian uniforms along the street in the direction of the bridge. Their weapons consisted of submachine-guns, several hand grenades and a few Panzerfausten[6]. They sped down the road at full speed. With our two panzers, we followed the fleeing lorry at a distance of between 200 and 300 metres, firing several machine-gun bursts over or behind the lorry every now and then just for show whilst they on the other hand, also just for show, threw a few hand grenades at us from the lorry. Our panzers now drove off the road, that is, one drove 30 metres in front of us on the left side of the road and we followed him on the right side of the road. Operation 'Hövel', as the mission was named, had proceeded smoothly up until the moment the lorry with the camouflaged soldiers reached the bridge when, at that instant, there was an almighty explosion and the lorry disappeared. At the same time, the Panzer III driving in front of us received two direct hits and immediately went up in flames. Before we could accurately engage anything, we also received a direct hit on the left drivers side and shortly after that a second hit, placed a bit higher.
>
> "Both panzers were total losses, all five crew members in the first panzer were dead. With us, only Leutnant Hövel and I, Obergefreiter Panse, got out alive. Our driver had taken a direct hit that at the same time also killed the loader standing behind me. The second shot, striking between the body and turret of the panzer, hit our gunner; Leutnant Hövel was wounded in the feet by several splinters. From this operation therefore, only two men survived. I had the greatest luck but I was totally smeared in the blood of my dead comrades. Hövel's wounds were also very light but on the other

6. No doubt these are Brandenburgers of z.b.V. 800 temporarily assigned to 24. Panzer-Division. It is very interesting to see their use in the course of this operation. It is unknown what weapons Herr Panse is referring to when he says 'Panzerfausten' because the weapon of this name did not appear until late the following year.

> hand our driver, gunner and loader were totally pulped. Bailing out, we both went out of the right turret hatch and had to climb over our dead comrades. In this fear of death, however, there remained no feeling of compassion amongst the survivors, only to get out of the old heap and save our lives.
>
> "In the evening, as we once again talked about the experience, we were certain that the Russians had not been fooled by our bluff. We were struck by several anti-tank guns or dug-in T-34's which we concluded on the basis of the penetrative force of the shells.
>
> "After the failure of Operation Hövel, we were pulled out of the battle for several weeks. I arrived at the combat train the next day and after several days, received the task with two comrades of driving to Dnepreptretovsk to procure several wagons of panzer replacement parts for our workshop."

As Hauenschild saw several of his panzers go up in flames and jet black clouds of smoke pulse into the sky above them, he realised that his surprise attack had failed. The Russian tanks near Hill 130 had delayed the seizure of the bridge. Then a Korpsbefehl arrived. 24. Panzer-Division had its answer as to whether Korps agreed with the reported view to take Hill 130 and form a bridgehead. The order issued by Oberst Friebe was as follows: "Forward elements in daily objective of Blinikov will on no account try to reach Hill 130 and Chervlenaya Gully." Daily objective of Blinikov had already been taken by the forwardmost elements while the bulk of the Division was in the area of Hill 150.0 and Sety. The advanced elements of the Division were to pull back to the line Hill 150.0 – Sety and there secure the north flank of Korps. Even though it rankled to order a withdrawal, Korps was more aware of the situation than 24. Panzer-Division. Strong resistance in front of 14. Panzer-Division and 29. Infanterie-Division (mot.) caused both to lag and, as a result of this and the unclear enemy picture in the west, Korps and Armee were forced into this decision.

With a heavy heart, the spearheads of the Division pulled back for the night, forming secure positions around Hill 150.0 and Sety. The panzers hedgehogged under the clear, starry sky in the increasingly cool late summers night, and supplies were passed through to them. Major von Winterfeld and the staff of Panzer-Regiment 24 drew into Gromosslavka, a small village that offered favourable communications connections with Major von der Lancken's Kampfgruppe as well as the repair troops and supply services in Kotelnikovo. Long lines of retreating enemy columns were cut off to the north-east. Reinforced Kradschützen-Abteilung 4, which had been forced to stay behind to clear up the uncertain situation near Tebektenerovo, was freed up in the evening by the advance of the Romanians.

Preliminary booty of 24. Panzer-Division up to 1600 hours amounted to 350 prisoners, 10 guns and 3 rocket-launchers. At 1830 hours, General von Hauenschild reported to Korps: "Because of my request to thrust on Hill 130 with the bulk of the Division and from there form a bridgehead over the Chervlenaya was expressly forbidden by Korps at 1555 hours, we now find our armoured Stoßgruppe near Hill 150 and Sety as ordered. Because of darkness, changes are no longer possible. Div. Kdr." Contrary to what General von Hauenschild may have believed, the withdrawal from Hill 130 – because the armoured assault group was already there – was also not to the taste of General Kempf. At 1835 hours, 24. Panzer-Division received the radio message: "Remain on Hill 150, there conduct forcible reconnaissance on Gavrilovka." This at least allowed some latitude and even gave tacit approval for an approach toward Gavrilovka under the guise of 'forcible reconnaissance'.

For the major successes achieved on this day, General Kempf gave his appreciation to the divisions, and arriving with this was an order with the following mission for Korps:
"The enemy has been completely surprised by today's thrust by XXXXVIII. Panzerkorps. As far as enemy units that weren't destroyed or caught in the pursuit, they are evading to the north and north-west. The objectives fixed on this day were reached in their entirety. I express my utter appreciation to the command of the troops."
For 30th August, the division received the following combat mission: "24. Panzer-Division will gain a bridgehead near Gavrilovka under cover of the north-west flank."

Late in the evening, 24. Panzer-Division sent off its daily report to Korps: "After breaking through south of Farm 1, the Division took Sety at 1300 hours, Hill 130 at 1600 hours after fighting. Several enemy batteries destroyed, numerous prisoners.
At 1630 hours, by order of Korps, the assault toward Chervlenaya was postponed and groups on the line 130.0 were withdrawn to Sety for security. They secured: armoured Stoßgruppe 150.0, Panzergrenadier-Brigade joined up to Sety. Division HQ: Sety. Panzer situation will be reported later.
Amount of booty from 29th August: 700 prisoners, 5 tanks (2 of these heavy), 18 guns, 6 Stalin Organs, 6 anti-aircraft guns and over 50 anti-tank rifles. Numerous light and heavy mortars, 30 machine-guns."

Leutnant von Senger und Etterlin: "By night we hedgehogged somewhere. In no way did we actually know where we were, only the direction of the sky and, to some extent, driving kilometres, could we make our destination – like ships at sea.
"The supply troops follow our tracks through the penetration in darkness and then made contact with the hedgehogs through the regular firing of green tracers.
"The night was splendidly quiet. Nothing except millions of cicadas chirping in the high wormwood plants. There seemed to be no enemy, only the toing and the froing of the white tracers climbing into the sky and lighting up the steppe and the sinister black outlines of the heavy panzers, which again sank back into the darkness like primeval ghosts."

Casualties:

1 officer killed

- Leutnant Claus Heinrich von Barner; Dinafü 40 (Killed)

21 men killed

- Gefreiter Heinz Braun; PGR26 (Killed)
- Gefreiter Josef Güth; PGR26 (Killed)
- Unteroffizier Anton Schlüter; PGR21 (Killed near Farm 1 north-west of Tebektenerovo)
- Obergefreiter Otto Grenda; PGR21 (Killed near Farm 1 north-west of Tebektenerovo)
- Unteroffizier Otto Rieder; PGR21 (Killed 3km north-east of Kapinka)

10 officers wounded (3 of those stayed with the troops)

- Rittmeister Heinz Kolczyk (Schwadron Kdr); 2./K4 (Wounded)
- Leutnant Friedrich Sodemann; PAR89 (Wounded)

- Leutnant Kurt Masuhr; PGR26 (Wounded)
- Oberstleutnant Vollrath von Hellermann (Regiment Kdr); PGR21 (Wounded but stayed with the troops)
- Oberleutnant Peter Schmidt (Schwadron Kdr); 9./PGR21 (Wounded)
- Oberleutnant Korb (Wounded but stayed with the troops)
- Rittmeister Guy von Saint-Paul (Schwadron Kdr); 12./PR24 (Wounded)
- Oberleutnant Hans-Jürgen Liebe (Abteilung NO); I./PR24 (Wounded)
- Leutnant Wilhelm von der Trenck (Zug Kdr); 6./PR24 (Wounded)
- Leutnant Heinz Hövel (Zug Kdr); 9./PR24 (Wounded but stayed with the troops)

140 men wounded (21 of those stayed with the troops)
- Gefreiter Robert Kung; PGR21 (Wounded but died in hospital later in the day)

30th August 1942:

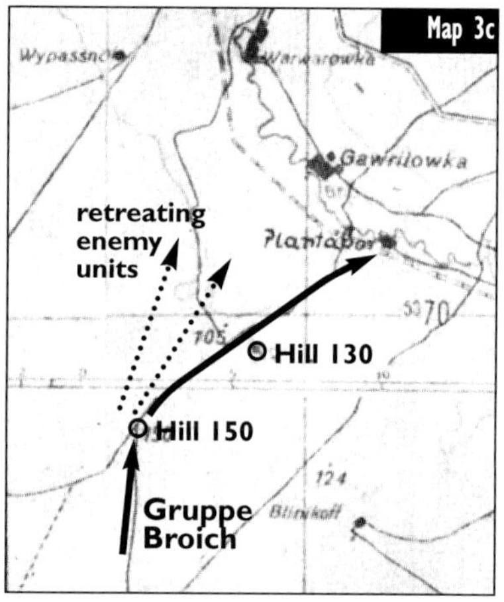

The glorious rising sun shone through the crisp morning air. Not a cloud blemished the clear blue sky. The armoured spearhead of 24. Panzer-Division set out at 0400 hours and, after cruising to the north for an hour without running into the enemy, reached Hill 130. Pushing further to the north, they struck strong enemy forces, including a few enemy tanks that were observed north of Hill 130. Oberleutnant Weidemann reports on how the enemy tanks were dealt with: "With the first sunlight, Stukas participated in the ground fighting. Enormous clouds of smoke rose upwards over the emplacement area of the Soviet tanks, which were partly thrown or flung into the craters by the shock waves of the bombs."
After the destruction of several tanks, the assault continued forward but despite the spectacular attack on the tanks, a strong enemy garrison holding out near Hill 150.0, in addition to enemy groups retreating to the north-east, continued to tie down the armoured Gruppe. After defending against Russian tanks, Oberst von Broich's Brigade resumed the advance at 0615 hours from Hill 130 to the north-east, the grenadiers being left behind to attack the strong enemy garrisons near Hill 150.0, the hill itself still being heavily occupied by enemy. At 0730 hours, Broich was 1.5km north of Hill 130 and numerous T-34's were seen opposite, scurrying around after being disturbed by the Stuka attack. Until about 0820 hours, the riflemen had taken about 1000 prisoners from trenches, foxholes and bunkers around Hill 150.0. The retreating enemy streamed to the north-east in numerous columns. Once Hill 150.0 had been overcome and secured, Kampfgruppe Broich reached the Chervlenaya Gully near Nariman (Plantator) without appreciable enemy resistance after about a 25km advance.

From his command post near Bodeno, General Kempf drove along the advance road of 24. Panzer-Division via Sety and Hill 130 to meet up with General von Hauenschild, who reported that the spearhead had just reached Chervlenaya Gully and was about to force the crossing with all available forces and create the bridgehead. The panzers, lagging because of petrol shortages, were filled up in the morning and brought forward. Kempf particularly stressed the ceaseless pursuit of the retreating enemy and, for Korps, the important objective of a bridgehead over the Chervlenaya Gully. Kempf then departed to visit General Fremerey at 29. Infanterie-Division (mot.) HQ.

Several T-34's still menaced the east flank. Every now and then, they would appear on the horizon, send a few shells into the assembled German units, and then disappear. After a short preparation, the Gully was assaulted and a crossing forced over it west of Plantator at 1010 hours by Panzergrenadier-Regiment 21, who formed a small bridgehead on the north shore. Numerous enemy movements were observed. An anti-tank trench on the south shore and extensive mining of villages, as well as energetic defence from strong positions constructed with trenches and bunkers on the partly banked north shore, hindered a broadening of the bridgehead for the time being. On the inquiry of 24. Panzer-Division about further objectives, the Division received the mission from XXXXVIII. Panzerkorps of thrusting northward "with all available forces on Gavrilovka". The panzers were pushed into the bridgehead in preparation for an advance to the north. Several enemy attacks from the north and north-west, supported by tanks, were repulsed. At the same time, Gruppe Edelsheim covered the west flank with weak forces but enemy resistance stiffened in front of the bridgehead. With the bulk of its forces, the Division launched an attack against the enemy retreating into Gavrilovka. At 1130 hours, General von Hauenschild shifted his Division HQ to a location 2km south-west of Plantator. At 1200 hours, General von Hauenschild's radio operators sent a quick sitrep back to Korps: "Forward elements in attack against weakly occupied bunker at present, 1000 metres north of Plantator. Plantator is still being cleared." Up to midday, the number of prisoners had risen to 1500.

While the panzers battled Russian tanks at the northern tip of the German penetration, Rittmeister von der Groeben's Kradschützen-Abteilung 4, together with other units of the Division, secured the lengthy and vulnerable western flank. Leutnant von Senger und Etterlin reports: "The night (of 29th/30th August) was again completely quiet, but early in the morning there was movement in the hedgehog. The sentries who scouted in panzers until the first dawning of the morning, still covered in their thick overcoats, pointed excitedly to the north. Were they ours or were they the Russians? Soon we knew exactly: separated by distance, something was marching through the steppe, several kilometres away from our hedgehog. Soldiers, vehicles, tractors. The Schwadron was ordered to halt, to scout and advance on a broad front to find what was actually there. It was like we had seen a ghost.

"We slowly drove forward and left our hedgehog further behind us. It was now made clear that the enemy was in no way preparing to flee or to fight, but stolidly marching in a distant direction. Slowly and cautiously we drove nearer, always prepared to turn around or to open fire. At last we were only a hundred metres away and weren't fired upon. It was inexplicable to us where these Russians were driving. Or was the whole thing a spectre?

"We now waved at the leading wagons and they stopped. The Russians approached, looked at our panzers with interest and were ordered to place their weapons together in a pile. Some were now right in front of the radiator, and we drove cautiously forward in the middle of a wide open form of marching Russian troops. Some vehicles were permitted to go back carrying prisoners and captured material. More and more Russians came together – called together by their own people – to lay down their weapons. A dozen Panje wagons, some tractors with attached heavy anti-tank guns and 30 anti-tank rifles were already collected.

"Then I saw a Tatschanke in a gallop and it was trying to flee. With full throttle I frantically chased him and then stopped him. After he stopped, he saw me, and a high-ranking officer

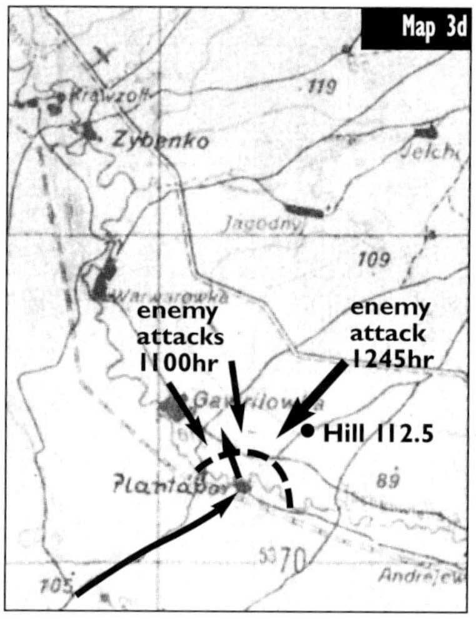

pulled out his revolver and shot himself three times through the head. He was a colonel and the commander of this rifle brigade, and here, he believed he was far behind the front, when he was shoved into another sector. 1,700 prisoners were steadily brought in with negligible casualties."

At 1245 hours, it was pointed out to 24. Panzer-Division by radio of the decisive significance of the broadening and retention of the bridgehead for further operations. At this moment, expansion of the bridgehead was out of the question, and even retaining it looked doubtful as several enemy tank attacks rolled in from the north-east. The largest and most threatening attack on the bridgehead was headed by 12 T-34's. Anti-tank shells from the fearsome 88's speared into the attackers and the Russian tanks turned back, four of them being left on the battlefield as blazing wrecks. At 1600 hours, an attack by one enemy battalion out of the Gavrilovka area was repulsed and enemy resistance stiffened significantly in the afternoon. Leutnant von Senger und Etterlin reports about the Russian tank attack:
"In the evening hours... the Russian 23rd Tank Brigade attempted to throw us back. A dozen heavy tanks appeared on the far side of the hill. They fired into our armoured wedge from a long range without damaging anything. In lightning quick time, an 88mm flak battery was driven up, a Stukagruppe and a Werferabteilung laid down bombs so thick that some of the enemy tanks fell into the craters, and in such a manner caused the remainder to retreat."

Strong resistance with newly appeared tanks and bunkers on the north shore slowed down further assaults. The crossing site also presented difficulties: the Russians had densely mined the gully and there was only one available bridge, so a ford was being consolidated. On the west flank, no enemy worth worrying about had been recognised so, apart from obstinate local resistance, the enemy seemed to be strongly surprised. According to statements from prisoners about the advance of the Division, 62nd Army had not been informed for several hours. Important secret material, including Russian situation maps, were captured. The enemy had concentrated his entire defence against the widely echeloned Division. Several enemy tank attacks in the evening hours were repulsed by operations of all available 8.8cm flak. Standing beyond the range of the flak guns were about 20 heavy Russian tanks on the dominating Hill 112.5, hindering every large-scale movement. At 1840 hours, General von Hauenschild informed Korps that enemy tanks had attacked from Hill 112.5 and tomorrow, the Division would position itself in the direction of Gavrilovka to eliminate flanking fire. He also said that the north shore of Chervlenaya Gully was steep and difficult to cross.
At 1315 hours, 14. Panzer-Division received an order by radio to form a bridgehead south of Hill 92.0. Six hours later, General Heim reported to General Kempf that the Division would probably not succeed in forming a bridgehead that night because the enemy took every movement under strong fire from tanks on the north shore.
Kempf: "We are placed favourably, so the crossing must succeed quickly."
Heim: "Propose to cross everything over 24. Panzer-Division's bridge."
General Kempf needed to discuss this with his staff and also get General von Hauenschild's opinion.

At nightfall, the bulk of 24. Panzer-Division secured the bridgehead and was deployed as follows: Schützen-Brigade secured the bridgehead, Kradschützen-Abteilung 4 and Gruppe Edelsheim (II./PGR26, Panzerjäger-Abteilung 40 and elements of Flak-Bataillon 602) secured the west flank, Point 81.5 as well as the deep west flank south-west of there near 105.2 and 130 in a strongpoint-style defence. Elements of the armoured Gruppe secured the east flank near 82.8 and 77.9 because 29. Infanterie-Division (mot.) had not yet been able to join up. Division HQ was located in a gully 2km south of Plantator. On this day, the Division succeeded in taking 2,100 prisoners, 4 tanks, 11 guns, 3 anti-tank guns and large amounts of booty.
Panzer situation: 11 Panzer II (of those, 2 Sanitätspanzer), 15 Panzer III kz, 12 Panzer III lg, 1 Panzer IV kz, 2 Panzer IV lg.
At 2130 hours, Kempf oriented Hoth by phone about the areas reached by the divisions.
Kempf: "24. Panzer-Division has a small bridgehead, 29. Infanterie-Division (mot.) still hopes to form one, 14. Panzer-Division has no bridgehead. Numerous tanks near 112.5. For tomorrow, ordered to advance at 0600 hours and widen the bridgehead. 7,000 prisoners, also Stalin Organs and guns. Four divisions smashed."
Hoth: "This success must be exploited."
Kempf: "Our operations will be decisive because tomorrow will be difficult due to the tanks. Machine-gun flanking fire from the north-west."

In the evening, the entire Division celebrated and congratulated one of their own. The Commander of Schützen-Brigade 24, Oberst Fritz Freiherr von Broich, received the Knight's Cross of the Iron Cross for his actions on the afternoon of 21st August. General von Hauenschild took the coveted award out of its case and placed it around von Broich's neck, Major von Menges standing behind him to tie the ends of the ribbon. General von Hauenschild and Oberst von Broich shook hands and then the General delivered a speech, extolling von Broich's leadership qualities, personal courage and daring tactics.

Casualties:

10 men killed

- Unteroffizier Erwin Haack; PGR21 (Killed near Nariman)
- Obergefreiter Erich von der Höh; PGR21 (Killed south-west of Plantator)
- Gefreiter Willi Leutbecker; PGR21 (Killed south-west of Plantator)
- Panzergrenadier Ernst Tischer; PGR21 (Killed near Nariman)
- Obergefreiter Ludwig Tobergte; PGR21 (Killed near Nariman)
- Obergefreiter Lorenz Zametzer; PGR21 (Killed near Nariman)
- Gefreiter Alfred Behrendt; PGR21 (Killed near Nariman)
- Obergefreiter Leopold Franek; PGR21 (Killed near Gavrilovka)
- Obergefreiter Otto Korte; PGR21 (Killed near Gavrilovka)
- Gefreiter Heinz Winkler; PGR21 (Killed near Gavrilovka)

2 officers wounded

- Assistenarzt Dr. Lang (Wounded)
- Leutnant Pickert (Wounded)

73 men wounded (29 of those stayed with the troops)

Decorations bestowed from 24th August to 30th August:

26 Iron Cross First Class
258 Iron Cross Second Class
24 Panzer Combat Badge in Silver

Prisoners and booty taken from 24th August to 30th August:

3500 prisoners
10 airplanes
39 guns
12 guns destroyed by artillery
10 tanks
17 anti-tank guns
6 anti-aircraft guns
78 mortars
100 anti-tank rifles
7 Stalin Organs

Results of 29th and 30th August 1942:

Through the swift, straight thrust of the Division to the north, the enemy front was broken through to a depth of 30km on the first day, making it impossible for the enemy to renew resistance south of the Chervlenaya, and making it difficult to supply coherent garrisons for the constructed positions on the Chervlenaya Gully. Through the depth of the thrust, all enemy elements standing further to the west were forced to retreat to the north. The divisions of Korps fighting further to the east kept the flanks and rear clear and on that point, had already partially opened the road to later successes.

31st August 1942:

During the entire night and with the onset of daylight, continuous enemy air attacks fell on the entire Korps sector but for all three divisions of XXXXVIII. Panzerkorps, the night passed quietly with no Russian ground actions. Aim of Korps on this morning was to advance at 0600 hours under strong Luftwaffe support, widen the bridgehead over the Chervlenaya Gully with 24. Panzer-Division and, together with the recently arrived 14. Panzer-Division and 29. Infanterie-Division (mot.), thrust through to the railway line eastwards of Bassargino in the area of Point 128.5.

After stabilising the situation on the flanks, Rittmeister von der Groeben's Kradschützen-Abteilung 4 (minus 2. Schwadron) was relieved by a Romanian unit and brought forward to participate in the attack from the embryonic bridgehead, joining the armoured element of this battalion – 2. Schwadron – which was already at the front. Leutnant von Senger und Etterlin reports: "Panzergrenadier-Regiment 21 formed a shallow bridgehead over the river near Plantator and Gavrilovka but could go no further due to the strong enemy in well-constructed positions lying on the hill. We moved over a very bad ford to the other shore and then attacked through the panzergrenadiers against the strong enemy positions."

Leutnant Hans-Ludwig von Stockhausen, Abteilung Ordonanzoffizier of Kradschützen-Abteilung 4, also reports on these events: "There was a traffic jam in crossing over the small dam. We stood in a command panzer[7] between the closely parked half-tracks. Suddenly, there was a loud roaring in the air. Stalin Organs? Many explosions between our vehicles! Thank God there were only light casualties. Standing in the panzer, I received a blow to the face. Blood dripped from my mouth. An incisor was missing. Behind the panzers, between the half-tracks of 2./Kradschützen-Abteilung 4, we overcame the small crossing and attacked through the positions of the panzergrenadiers." Despite his painful wound, Leutnant von Stockhausen stayed with his commander, Rittmeister von der Groeben, but when he had the wound looked at, it was apparent it was more serious. "I had been wounded in the upper jaw by Stalin Organ shrapnel and was sent to a jaw specialists clinic in Konstantinovka." The position of Abteilung Ordonanzoffizier was taken over by Leutnant Gert von Ulrici.

VON STOCKHAUSEN

Leutnant Hans-Ludwig von Stockhausen, Ordonanzoffizier Kradschützen-Abteilung 4.

Both 14. Panzer-Division and 24. Panzer-Division set off to attack as scheduled at 0600 hours to broaden the bridgehead against continuously strengthening enemy resistance. The Division advanced with Oberst von Broich's Schützen-Brigade and the Panzer Abteilung working in close co-operation. They attacked to the north and north-east over a distance of about 3km up to Hill 112.5 and, supported by fighter-bombers, proceeded to expand the bridgehead. Every now and then, a Russian tank would fire into the sides of the armoured wedge or stand directly in front and delay the advance. After a short telephone conversation with General von Hauenschild, Kempf sent off a radio message to VIII. Fliegerkorps at 0750 hours: "Strongest air support urgently requested in front of 24. Panzer-Division against individual tanks. Kempf."

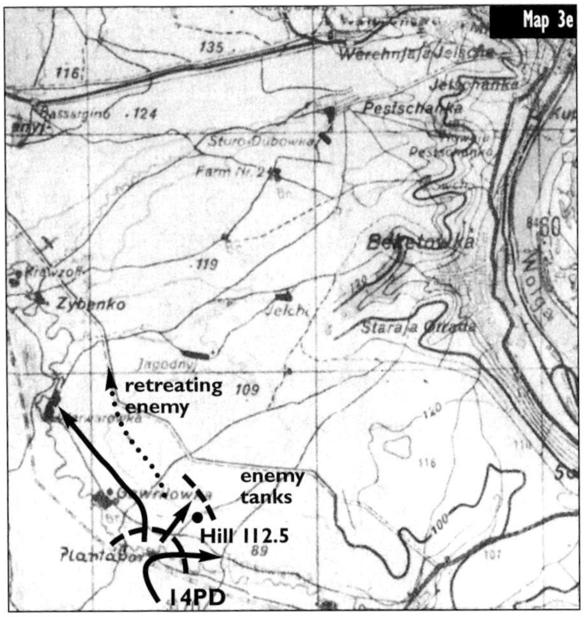

7. He is referring to the Sdkfz. 250/3 command half-track, fitted out with powerful radio equipment and armed with a machine-gun.

At 0848 hours, a radio message was sent to General Kempf by General Heim with a proposal that would have neutered 24. Panzer-Division. He proposed concentrating all panzers of Korps in the bridgehead of 24. Panzer-Division under the command of Oberst Theodor Kretschmar, commander of his Panzer-Regiment 36. This was an amazing piece of effrontery by Heim because not only had 24. Panzer-Division formed the bridgehead and pushed most of its forces into it, but Heim's own attempt at forming a bridgehead had failed and he planned on using 24. Panzer-Division's bridge to get to the north shore. When he put forward his proposal, none of his own forces were even in 24. Panzer-Division's bridgehead! Korps did not immediately turn it down, however. General Heim ordered his Chief-of-Staff to send off another message to Korps at 0900 hours: "Attack began at 0600 hours, considerable fire."

Friebe: "Request for concentrating the panzers is still not decided. Panzers of 24. Panzer-Division are already advancing on 112.5. Panzers of 14. Panzer-Division are directed over 24. Panzer-Division's bridge, to attack to the east." Therefore, due to difficulties in their own crossing attempts, elements of 14. Panzer-Division would use the crossing of 24. Panzer-Division, thrusting from there to the north-east.

Major von Menges phoned Korps at 0910 hours to report on the situation. He spoke with the Chief-of-Staff, Oberst i.G. Friebe: "Everything is rapidly advancing. At 0845 hours hill 1km west of 112.5 taken, panzers echeloned rearward to the left. Anti-aircraft guns on north shore." Friebe broke the news to Menges: "14. Panzer-Division wants to take over 24. Panzer-Division's panzers."

Menges took it in his stride. He simply replied: "Concentration of panzers is not necessary because panzers of 24. Panzer-Division have already approached 112.5." Exactly what General von Hauenschild's reaction was to this proposal has not been recorded but it would be safe to assume that he was not pleased.

Despite Major von Menges' confidence, the spearhead was held up. With 20 to 25 heavy tanks, the enemy on the east flank attempted to stop the attack. The enemy tanks were not advancing but were standing at great distances and shooting at the German panzers which simply did not have a tank cannon powerful enough to reply. The impasse continued for hours. The enemy tanks were unsuccessfully engaged with Rotkopf, the anti-tank shells[8] used by the short-barrel Panzer IV's. It was obvious that the Russian tanks could not be destroyed from the ground because the German panzers could not get close enough to engage them within the effective range of their guns. Therefore, a howitzer of 1./PAR89 was brought forward. Despite high expectations, it was unable to achieve a direct hit because of its curved trajectory in direct shooting over 1000 metres. An 8.8cm Flak battery quickly dashed forward and after firing a few rounds, forced the enemy to turn around, but not before one of the 8.8cm Flak received a hit while unlimbering. Stukas were then called to hunt down the fleeing Russian tanks. They appeared very quickly over the battlefield and proceeded to hammer the Russian giants and a short while later, three of the enemy tanks east of Hill 112.5 were burning, greasy plumes of sooty smoke climbing into the sky. Leutnant von Senger und Etterlin watched the air attack from his vehicle: "Close in front of us, a Stuka attack drummed in and stopped low. Then our panzers swept forward, overrunning the trenches and, after a short fight, we fetched hundreds of Russians from their foxholes. My small nimble vehicle was like hound chasing a hare." Leutnant von Senger und Etterlin's armoured reconnaissance troop, taking advantage of the confusion caused among the Russian tanks by the Stukas, pushed toward the north-west.

8. Kern Granate rot, an anti-tank shell used by 7.5cm L/24 guns, used on Stug. III Ausf. A–E and Pz IV Ausf. A – F1. KGr rot could penetrate: 41mm @ 100m, 38mm @ 500m, 35mm @ 1000m, 32mm @ 1500m.

REIFNER

A Russian T-70 reconnaissance tank burns after being destroyed by Panzerpionier-Bataillon 40 on 31st August. Notice that all the steppe grass has been burnt away, leaving only blackened stumps and scorched earth.

Enemy opposition was weak and the brickworks at Varvarovka were soon reached and cleaned out, the Russians offering little resistance. The aim was to reach and firmly hold the line 112.5 – 110.8 – 98.8 – 86.4 – Varvarovka. General von Hauenschild had the impression that good progress could be made to the north on this day but it would be questionable tomorrow. Combat activity was dying down on 112.5 after its capture at 1100 hours but fighting was still fierce against the Russian tanks, three of the valuable 8.8cm flak guns being lost to tank fire.

Despite a few of the Russian tanks being knocked out by Stukas, 24. Panzer-Division did not succeed in driving back the bulk of the enemy tanks or knocking them out of the battle. The presence of this Russian armoured formation meant tough fighting and high casualties if the attack continued in this direction. General von Hauenschild decided to swing out to the left, sidestepping the armoured roadblock, but the enemy tanks soon hindered a continued advance here. On the other hand, reconnaissance results from Gavrilovka reported by Leutnant von Senger und Etterlin showed what seemed to be only weak enemy forces: at 1245 hours, he reported that Stalin Organs were north of Gavrilovka, and at 1315 hours, enemy columns were seen retreating to the north-east. Upon inquiry by General von Hauenschild, Korps gave permission, under utilisation of the favourable situation, to thrust north to the railway line and gain Hill 128.5 and Hill 123.6. After breaking enemy resistance near Varvarovka and defending against an attack coming from the south-west through Zybenko, the dominating Hill 111.5 would be taken regardless of flanking fire, and subsequently, with the panzers in front and Panzergrenadier-Regiment 21 behind, they would thrust towards the Bassargino – Stalingrad railway line.

While several of the Division's units, such as II./Panzergrenadier-Regiment 21, remained in the positions facing the Russian tanks, the armoured Gruppe, excellently supported by fighter-bombers, thrust from Varvarovka north-west along the Chervlenaya Gully. Up to 1330 hours,

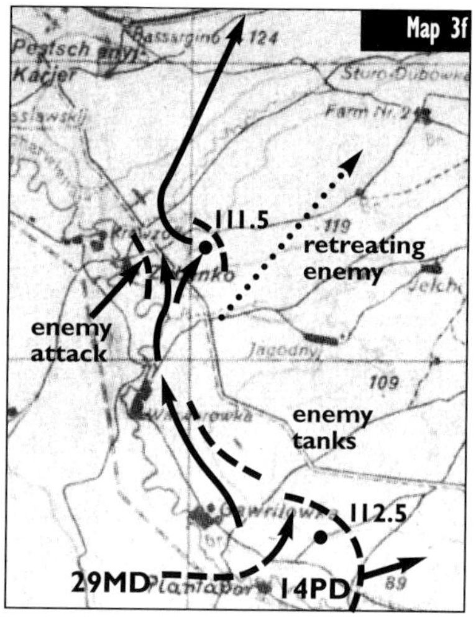

after advancing about 25km, the Division thrust through to Hills 93.7 – 111.5 against weak opposition. General von Hauenschild sent a message to Korps: "Division has reached 93.7 – 111.5. Question: What now?" The question for Korps was whether to exploit this success by a further thrust to the north against the railway line and with that, fulfil a major goal in the overall strategy: a union of 4. Panzer-Armee with 6. Armee for a decisive assault on Stalingrad. On the other hand, it was important from Korps point of view to first destroy the enemy on the north-east flank but by then however, the enemy would have re-established himself on the northern flank and in the fortified field emplacements north-east of the Chervlenaya Gully. The enemy had toughly defended the north shore of Chervlenaya Gully, probably with hastily formed ad hoc units, as well as numerous tanks of the heavy and heaviest types. The surprisingly successful thrust of 24. Panzer-Division had opened the possibility of still pushing forward to the railway line this day and if it was to be exploited, all available forces of Korps would need to be concentrated. Fifteen minutes after receiving the query from Hauenschild, Korps sent its response: "Under utilisation of this success, the Division will continue to thrust to the railway line…" The choice had been made: a union of 4. Panzer-Armee and 6. Armee at the temporary cost of local instability.

The evolving situation prompted Kempf to issue new directives and the corresponding orders were quickly radioed to the divisions:
"24. Panzer-Division will thrust up to the railway line east of Bassargino railway sidings."
"29. Infanterie-Division (mot.), under the exploitation of 24. Panzer-Division's success, will be drawn forth behind the division and reach the line 112.5 – 110.8 – 77.7 to protect the east flank of 24. Panzer-Division."
"14. Panzer-Division will facilitate the crossing of IV. Armeekorps over the Chervlenaya Gully by attacking 128.2 and will later attack through Yagodnyi."

At 1530 hours, Oberst Friebe took a phone call from Hauptmann Roth, O1 of 24. Panzer-Division. The Division requested air support.
Friebe: "VIII. Fliegerkorps has already promised the heaviest air support."
Roth: "Enemy bunkers on 111.5 and 119.7."

At 1615 hours, Gruppe Broich advanced from Hill 111.5 to the north. Forty-five minutes later, the armoured Stoßgruppe under the superb leadership of Oberst von Broich, including the half-tracks of Panzergrenadier-Regiment 26 and Kradschützen-Abteilung 4, broke through positions constructed with concrete and steel and topped with tank cupolas, capturing bunker positions south of the railway. The railway line – which was the daily objective – was reached near a linesman's hut 1km north-west of Hill 128.5, barely 10km west of Stalingrad. There, the railway line was blown up, an enemy transport company captured and several supply columns destroyed. Bunker positions along the railway line were taken. The Kampfgruppe destroyed an armoured train and the rear-area services of unsuspecting Russian units still standing further to the west were torn apart. The enemy was completely surprised.

REIFNER

Leutnant Egon Reifner inspects the armoured train destroyed by him and his men.

REIFNER

Russian prisoners from the train receive first aid from German Sanitäter (medics). Behind the medic is a Sonderführer supplied by Division to translate. All the other men are from 3./Panzerpionier-Bataillon 40.

Leutnant von Senger und Etterlin describes these happenings: "The armoured Gruppe thrust to the north-east despite the strong flanking and anti-tank fire coming from all directions and, towards evening, reached the Kalach – Stalingrad railway at Bassargino Station. Hardly had the panzer hedgehog been constructed when a monster, spitting fire to all sides, approached from the west. At first, we were fairly taken back by this novel attraction. The monster came closer and it looked like this huge armoured train was going to burst through and shoot it's way to Stalingrad. An 88mm Flak drove up and, firing direct at 400 metres, shot several shells into the body so that the monster of terror with a tail of three wagons stopped, and then withdrew snorting and spitting to the west."

This was one version of the armoured train story. The other has Leutnant Egon Reifner of Panzerpionier-Bataillon 40 destroying the train with explosives. This is the true version as can be seen by the accompanying photos. Seeing the train approaching, Reifner and a couple of his men ran up to the tracks, placed some demolition charges under the rails, detonated them and left a metre-wide gap in the tracks. The armoured train continued on, eventually reaching the spot where the tracks were destroyed. The wheels of the train came off the track and it eventually ground to a halt. Even though it was doomed, a tremendous volume of machine-gun fire emanated from the train as shell after shell from the 88mm flak gun crashed into it. Knowing their situation was hopeless, the crew gave themselves up and contrary to what the Russians thought would happen, the Germans treated them well and dressed their wounds. The pioneers stared at the train with fascination. It was painted a light sand colour and had a scruffy camouflage scheme. The armoured locomotive had large dark green, amoeba-like blotches of paint and a large slogan painted down its side: 'Death to Fascism'. Leutnant Reifner was awarded two Tank Destruction Badges for taking care of the train, which was added to the tally of 24. Panzer-Division.

Here is the day according to Obergefreiter Reddig, the driver from 1./Panzergrenadier-Regiment 21: "31.8.1942. 1200 hours. Schwadron was collected and drove to the west, then to the north up to the railway line to Stalingrad. En route, attacked by Russian tanks that were soon forced to turn away by us. Our Kradschützen had many casualties at midday due to Stalin Organs. Several Russian aerial attacks during the day. We hedgehogged in front of the railway line. Suddenly, we saw smoke rising along the tracks to the left (west), coming ever closer. With the vehicles, we moved up to about 200 metres from the stretch of railway and now established that it was a Russian armoured train taking us under fire. There was no more to think about, we drove backwards into a ploughed field. Our pioneers blew up the tracks and the armoured train was then shot up. Many prisoners were taken… During the night we heard loud engine noises. Russians continually fired with anti-tank guns and Stalin Organs."

More enemy groups were observed north and east of Zybenko, east of Varvarovka and Yagodnyi, where there were large concentrations of artillery. Tanks were everywhere but were particularly harassing Kampfgruppe Edelsheim which was securing the flanks and supply roads. At 1703 hours, General von Hauenschild reported from his new HQ in Varvarovka: "Prisoners rose from 1,000 to over 2,000, one battalion giving itself up without a shot." Four enemy tanks had also been destroyed. And at 1708 hours: "Enemy position Gavrilovka Varvarovka with three enemy battalions rolled over."

The Division was again successful with a deep breakthrough without regard to its open flanks. In the late evening, they were positioned in a roughly 20km long narrow tunnel in the middle of the enemy who were either evading the pursuing neighbouring German and Romanian units, or were trying to cut off the Division. The 20km deep west flank and the dominating

Hill 111.5 were secured in the evening by Gruppe Edelsheim. 24. Panzer-Division requested strong fighter protection and air support from daybreak to defend against expected enemy attacks. In the evening, the following mission was sent to the division: "On 1st September, 24. Panzer-Division will close up to the railway line in the area 128.5 – 123.6 and south of there under cover of the flanks until the arrival of the neighbouring divisions." The Division also received the order to push forward reconnaissance on to the high ground around Yezovka to ascertain whether the enemy was supplying forces out of Stalingrad and where further enemy positions and defensive installations were located.
The Division still had the following panzers: 9 Panzer II, 8 Panzer III lg, 12 Panzer III kz, 2 Panzer IV lg, 1 Panzer IV kz and 1 Bfwg. In addition to these panzers, the Division now had the 7.62mm self-propelled guns of Panzerjäger Abteilung 670 subordinated to it. The number of battleready vehicles kept shrinking.

There is an interesting directive from General Kempf, issued in the evening of 31st August to all his Division commanders. In it, he said: "I have ascertained that in the last few days, many combat vehicles (panzers, self-propelled guns etc.) have left the battlefield because they have either suffered some negligible damage (failure of radio equipment, loss of a running wheel), or have brought back wounded men. So long as the combat vehicles are mobile and battleworthy with their weapons, they will remain on the battlefield until the conclusion of fighting. It is an absurdity that intact combat vehicles bring back wounded men.
"I urgently request that appropriate instructions be issued immediately. It can be announced that a supervisory body will be appointed to superintend this directive from time to time."
There were also two other interesting points in Kempf's directive:
"Every intact enemy weapon that falls into our hands – particularly guns, anti-aircraft guns, Stalin Organs, anti-tank rifles etc. – are of the greatest use for the supply of our own armed forces. It is therefore extremely careless to make such weapons unusable by taking particular items, foolish play or senseless destruction.
"I request that every unit commanders inform his men about this. An especially obvious example that can be directed in front of the eyes of the soldiers is that captured anti-aircraft guns can be supplied to the homeland as quickly as possible… where they will be employed for air defence of our large cities, protecting women and children."
And this:
"The leading spearheads of our attacking troops must know that it is wrong to shoot with tracer ammunition into grain and hay stacks, as well as undefended small cottages, and set these on fire. All grain, etc. is urgently required by our troops for the nourishment of man and animal. All destroyed grain damages the supply situation of the German Reich. It is just as senseless to kill horses and other useful livestock (cattle, sheep etc.) because all of these animals are also urgently required for draught and nourishment purposes. An instruction about this will also be given by unit commanders."
It is unknown whether these directives reached the troops and if they did, whether they had any effect.

Casualties:

7 men killed

- Obergefreiter Rudolf Weiß; PR24 (Killed)
- Obergefreiter Willi Ebeling; PGR21 (Killed near Gavrilovka)

- Panzergrenadier Alois Anleitner; PGR21 (Killed near Plantator)
- Unteroffizier Georg Küffner; PGR21 (Killed 5km north-west of Nariman)
- Obergefreiter Herbert Rogowski; PGR21 (Killed 5km north-west of Nariman)
- Wachtmeister Heinz Steinau; PGR21 (Killed near Nariman)
- Obergefreiter Lorenz Rattelsdörfer; PGR21 (Killed near Nariman)

3 officers wounded

- Leutnant Scholz; PR24 (Wounded)
- Oberleutnant Hans Thylmann (Schwadron Kdr); 2./PGR26 (Wounded)
- Leutnant Hans-Ludwig von Stockhausen (Abt OO); K4 (Wounded)

56 men wounded (34 of those stayed with the troops)

- Obergefreiter Erwin Lohstroh; K4 (Wounded)
- Gefreiter Werner Barkowski; PGR21 (Wounded but died on 1st September in hospital)

1st September 1942:

During the night of 31st August/1st September, II./Panzergrenadier-Regiment 21 – still defending a flank far behind the spearhead – was to be relieved by elements of 29. Infanterie-Division (mot.) and catch up to the bulk of the Division. Oberleutnant Guercke, Commander of 8. Schwadron, was ordered to drive to the Division command post north of Varvarovka to receive instructions for reconnaissance of new positions for his battalion. He received the immediate order to reconnoitre a position about 3km further east with a front to the east so that the battalion could be inserted there that night. Together with a communications vehicle of the Stabsschwadron laying a line from the new battalion command post to Division, Guercke drove off in the specified direction. Terrain features could not be made out in the darkness. When they were approximately in the specified area according to the odometer, they bumped into a group of civilians who, upon questioning, said that no Russian soldiers were in the vicinity. Driving on, they soon ran into a large group of Red Army men, the glowing ends of their cigarettes visible in the darkness. The Russians gave themselves up without causing any trouble. While one of his men spoke to them to see if there were more Russians nearby, Guercke ordered the vehicles to turn around, as a precaution. One of his communications men spoke fair Russian and reported that the prisoners maintained there were no more Red Army troops in the area. In the meantime, several nearby houses began to burn and a bright moon rose on the horizon, its light illuminating the landscape. Guercke was suspicious and peered towards the bright light. He was able to clearly discern a large crowd that was on the point of outflanking him and his companions in a large semicircle and cutting them off.

The ten prisoners received directions to follow the vehicles and Guercke made sure that he got away with his men. The brave Red Army men actually reported themselves at Division headquarters during the course of the night. Guercke was sent back to speed up the insertion of the battalion. On the way, he captured a Russian lieutenant and a soldier that had been separated from their unit. After their relief, the battalion remained near the vehicles, only setting off at dawn. Guercke met them en route. In approaching the Division command post, a 2cm flak already fired and the battalion deployed for combat. The Abteilung Commander,

Combat and Ration strengths on 1st September 1942

	Combat strength				Ration strength				
Units	Offz.	Beamte	Uffz.	Men	Offz.	Beamte	Uffz.	Men	**Total**
Division Staff	18	11	36	132	35	11	58	248	**352**
Pz.Gren.Brigade 24	4	–	18	71	4	–	18	70	**92**
Pz.Rgt. 24	52	9	483	1266	57	15	576	1658	**2306**
Pz.Gren.Rgt. 21	34	–	307	1274	37	4	320	1301	**1662**
Pz.Gren.Rgt. 26	29	6	298	1575	34	6	312	1639	**1991**
Krad.Abt. 4	17	–	164	855	20	4	167	875	**1066**
Pz.Art.Rgt. 89	56	–	314	1596	65	13	396	1962	**2436**
Pz.Jg.Abt. 40	13	1	69	373	15	3	76	385	**479**
Pz.Pi.Btl. 40	14	–	70	592	14	4	83	626	**727**
Pz.Nach.Abt. 86	6	–	69	339	12	3	69	321	**405**
DiNaFü. 40	–	–	–	–	30	20	184	1138	**1372**
SanKo. 1./40	–	–	–	–	7	3	31	184	**225**
SanKo. 2./40	–	–	–	–	6	3	24	144	**177**
Bäckerei Ko. 40	–	–	–	–	1	1	19	126	**147**
Schlächterei Ko. 40	–	–	–	–	2	1	9	67	**79**
Verpfl. Amt 40	–	–	–	–	–	8	11	73	**92**
Feldpostamt 40	–	–	–	–	–	18	–	8	**26**
Feldgend. Trupp 40	–	–	–	–	3	–	45	41	**89**
Sum:	**243**	**27**	**1828**	**8073**	**342**	**117**	**2398**	**10866**	**13723**
Subordinated Units									
Flak-Bataillon 602	12	–	93	472	12	3	103	504	**622**
I.Abt.Werf.Rgt. 53	15	–	69	345	17	3	76	362	**458**
I./Brandenburg 800	8	–	46	292	8	–	47	296	**351**
I./Ersatz Bataillon I	1	–	21	128	1	–	21	128	**150**
I./Flak Regiment 5	24	5	158	904	24	5	148	1006	**1183**
RAD Gruppe K 22									**640**
Total:	**303**	**32**	**2215**	**10214**	**404**	**128**	**2793**	**13162**	**17127**

Rittmeister Karl v. Sivers, noticed Russians moving to the north-east, now clearly visible over the high ground and despite the direction, they wore overcoats and therefore could not be German. He allowed the Schwadrons to continue to advance on foot without firing and ran into a violent enemy barrage. As a result of this, 5. Schwadron lost numerous wounded and 5 dead, including three of its best squad commanders: Unteroffizier August Daszenies, Unteroffizier Georg Drees, Unteroffizier Artur Liedke, Gefreiter Kurt Höppel and Gefreiter Herbert Stritzke. The men of 7. Schwadron also did not escape lightly with three of its men being killed: Unteroffizier Georg Pfaffenberger, Panzergrenadier Heinz Weber and Obergefreiter Michael Badum, whose severe wounds proved fatal.

In other sectors of 24. Panzer-Division, the night generally passed without particular incidents, apart from the usual bombing, artillery fire and Stalin Organs. The troops were glad to see the Luftwaffe above their heads in the morning hours.
At 1055 hours, Major von Menges reported to Korps that Edelsheim had secured the east flank of Division and also mentioned the proposed change of HQ to a gully south of Point 123.6. A short while later, Major von Menges again spoke to Oberst Friebe: "Enemy situation near Gruppe Broich unchanged, artillery fire, 1000 prisoners. Edelsheim will be relieved."
Friebe: "Heavy fighting near 14. Panzer-Division and 29. Infanterie-Division (mot.)."
Menges: "Not much infantry at the top."
Friebe: "Division will prepare an assault group."

While visiting 14. Panzer-Division, General Kempf voiced his concern that the breakthrough of 24. Panzer-Division to the north hadn't destroyed the enemy in front of 14. Panzer-Division and in addition to that, IV. Armeekorps could not move forward, both of these problems causing Panzerkorps to become widely separated instead of concentrating its forces. The withdrawal of 24. Panzer-Division from its salient had to be considered. Generalmajor von Hauenschild emphasised that with concentrated forces, more penetrating power would be available and the objectives of Korps more easily reached. To exploit the success of 24. Panzer-Division, XXXXVIII. Panzerkorps must assemble its concentrated forces there, unite itself into wing-thrusts in conjunction with Panzer-Armee and then, together, thrust through both sides of Krutenkiy-Stalingrad railway up to the city.

At 1530 hours, 24. Panzer-Division sent the following interim report to Korps: "Enemy picture near railway unchanged. There, weak enemy artillery firing up to now. Position with tank trench near Hill 151.7 is heavily occupied.
"Overall impression: A quickly implemented assault in the direction of Stalingrad is promising, conditional on the elimination of enemy artillery. Gruppe Edelsheim was relieved near 111.5 when 29. Infanterie-Division (mot.) came up, took over security to the east up to and including Hill 111.5. The Romanians also approached from the south-west. After relief on 111.5, Gruppe von Edelsheim attacked the weakly enemy-occupied Hills 100.1 and 115.0, which were taken easily in the afternoon. Gruppe Edelsheim then secured there to cover the east flank."
This summary covers the Division's activity on this day. There were none of the spectacular penetrations and advances of the previous day, just consolidation of positions and defensive lines and a shifting of forces for a more advantageous disposition for the continuation of the assault. During the course of the day, II./PGR21 took over a position about 4.5km further south-west on and both sides of Hill 116.1, with a front to the west.

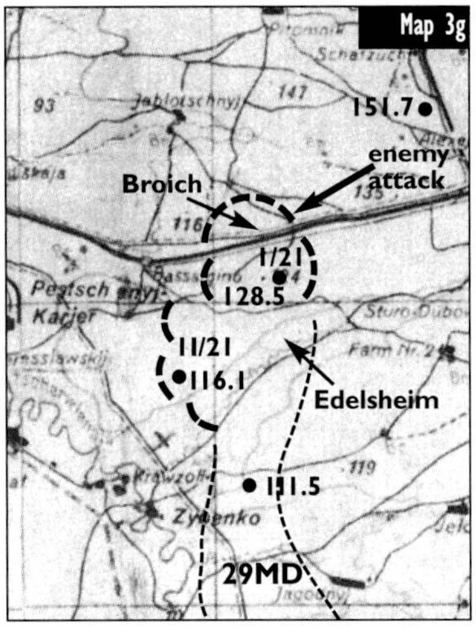

In the late afternoon, a change of weather moved across the steppe. A cool wind sprang up and thick banks of cloud drew over the sky and a short while later, lashed the dry ground with heavy rain. The moistened soil of the steppe turned into greasy clay, frustrating efforts at climbing slopes or crossing the numerous gullies that scored the area. It was only a minor inconvenience and did not greatly hinder movement. After a few hours, the rain eased and a watery sun showed through the grey skies. While 24. Panzer-Division sat at the end of its long salient, shuffling its units and completing preparations for an advance, the other divisions of Korps were experiencing difficulties. To the south-east of the Division, 14. Panzer-Division was still locked in heavy combat with enemy tanks and artillery, its conclusion not yet in sight. As long as 14. Panzer-Division was still tied up with this enemy, a thrust over the railway line by 24. Panzer-Division was not possible. It was even considered by Korps as to whether an armoured group of 24. Panzer-Division should thrust in a south-east direction together with 14. Panzer-Division to destroy this enemy. When this possibility was put to Oberst Fangohr at Armee HQ, he pointed out the decisive importance of the advance of Korps over the railway in a northern direction because 6. Armee was waiting for this. Long-term strategic objectives outweighed temporary local crises.

Near 24. Panzer-Division, an enemy assault – consisting of two battalions with four to six tanks in support – was launched against the railway line north of Hill 128.5. It was smashed back between 1800 and 1900 hours. It had now become noticeable that the enemy had strengthened himself in front of the Division, particularly with artillery. Reconnaissance established that the enemy had solidly occupied the constructed positions based around a tank trench both sides of Hill 151.7. After units had moved into their assigned sectors, Division secured as follows: Gruppe Broich in previous area along the railway line with a front to the east – north – west; Gruppe Edelsheim was on Hills 100.1 – 115.0 with a front to the east. Both hills had been taken in the afternoon. Division HQ was in Pestshanka Gully, 3km south of 123.6. The Division's panzer situation was as follows: 14 Panzer II, 36 Panzer III, 6 Panzer IV and 1 Bfwg. Booty: 1,300 prisoners, 1 aircraft, 2 anti-tank guns, 2 guns and 1 mortar. Korps took a total of 3,200 prisoners on this day.

I. Abteilung of Panzergrenadier-Regiment 21 was holding positions around Hill 128.5 just south of the railway line. Obergefreiter Reddig wrote the following in his diary: "Repeated Russian aerial attacks on us. In the evening, Russian anti-tank fire from both sides of the road. At night, rain and icy winds. Generally, the nights are already very cold."

At 2015 hours, Major von Menges spoke to both General Kempf and his chief-of-staff: "Russians attacked from the east (135.1) and north (125.0) with infantry and tanks. Weather so unfavourable at the moment that we cannot advance."
Kempf considered whether a battalion would be able to relieve elements of Kampfgruppe Edelsheim near 100.1 and 115.0. It did not take long for him to make up his mind. At 2035 hours, the chief-of-staff of 29. Infanterie-Division (mot.) was told by Oberst Friebe that the

Division would relieve elements of the security parties of 24. Panzer-Division near Hills 100.1 and 115.0.

At 2130 hours, Armee issued an order that Korps would set out on 2nd September at 0900 hours with 24. Panzer-Division and 20. Romanian-Division out of the area east and south of Bassargino and gain the area east of Pitomnik and seek a connection with 6. Armee. The enemy near Yagodnyi would be attacked from the rear by swinging out over 119.7. If possible, strong forces would be supplied to 24. Panzer-Division. On the basis of this, the following order was issued to 24. Panzer-Division: "At 0900 hours, 24. Panzer-Division will set out over the railway line and thrust forward via Hill 147.3 up to the Schafzucht area – BW 5km east of Pitomnik, there to reach forces of 6. Armee pushing down from the north-east. (20. Romanian Division will set out at the same time to cover 24. Panzer-Division's west flank)."

In the evening, the Division issued its very brief Divisionsbefehl Nr. 53, a preliminary order for regrouping and attacking on 2nd September to encircle Stalingrad. A re-allocation of forces was needed to bring to bear the most striking power so, in accordance with this, Gruppe Edelsheim would form a new defensive front while Gruppe Broich became the spearhead. The new deployment of forces was as follows:

Gruppe Broich:

- Brigade staff
- Panzergrenadier-Regiment 21
- Panzerartillerie-Regiment 89 (without II. Abteilung)
- An Abteilung of schwere-Werfer-Regiment 53
- III./Panzer-Regiment 24 with Pionier- and Flak-Zug
- Armoured elements of I./Panzergrenadier-Regiment 26
- Panzerjäger-Abteilung 670
- Staff of IV./Panzerartillerie-Regiment 89 with 10., 11. and 12. Batteries
- One heavy and one light battery of I./Flak-Bataillon 5
- 3./Flak-Bataillon 602
- Kompanie z.b.V. 800
- One pioneer company

Gruppe Edelsheim:

- Panzerjäger-Abteilung 40 with Flak-Zug
- II./Panzerartillerie-Regiment 89
- II./Panzergrenadier-Regiment 26
- Flak-Bataillon 602 (without 3. Kompanie)
- One pioneer company
- Commander of I./Flak-Bataillon 5 with two heavy batteries

Division reserves:

- Panzer-Nachrichten-Abteilung 86
- Kradschützen-Abteilung 4
- Panzerpionier-Abteilung 40 (without two companies)

The beginning of the attack was set for 0900 hours dependent upon the enemy situation and the weather.

Casualties:

1 officer killed

- Stabszahlmeister Hans-Georg Schneider (Mitarbeiter to IVa); 24. Panzer-Division Stab (Killed)

24 men killed

- Obergefreiter Walter Bringezu; PGR26 (Killed)
- Obergefreiter Kurt Bödrich; PGR21 (Killed near Zybenko)
- Panzergrenadier Heinz Weber; PGR21 (Killed near Varvarovka)
- Unteroffizier August Daszenies; PGR21 (Killed near Varvarovka)
- Unteroffizier Georg Drees; PGR21 (Killed near Varvarovka)
- Unteroffizier Artur Liedke; PGR21 (Killed near Varvarovka)
- Gefreiter Kurt Höppel; PGR21 (Killed near Varvarovka)
- Gefreiter Herbert Stritzke; PGR21 (Killed near Varvarovka)
- Gefreiter Otto-Victor Köhler; PGR21 (Killed 8km north of Bereslavski)
- Unteroffizier Georg Pfaffenberger; PGR21 (Killed near Varvarovka)

3 officers wounded (1 of those stayed with the troops)

- Oberarzt Dr. Günter Spode; PAR89 (Wounded)
- Leutnant Thuiske von Metzsch (Schwadron Kdr); 3./K4 (Wounded but stayed with the troops)
- Leutnant Stetzkowski (Zug Kdr); 5./PGR26 (Wounded)

80 men wounded (32 of those stayed with the troops)

- Obergefreiter Michaels Badum; PGR21 (Wounded near Varvarovka but died later in the day)
- Unteroffizier Heinrich Wessel; PGR21 (Wounded near Gavrilovka but died later in the day)

2 men missing

2nd September 1942:

Artillery and mortar harassment fire plagued the Division during the night but there was minimal damage to man and machine, the largest casualty being the loss of sleep. At 0400 hours, an enemy battalion supported by heavy tanks attacked the security line of I./PGR21. It was repulsed. Strong enemy preparations with tanks were also recognised in the area east of Hill 119.7. With the onset of daylight, very strong enemy air attacks focused on the advance road of the Division. Several soft-skin vehicles became casualties but it was noticed that the enemy airforce seemed to concentrate on the forward panzer spearheads of the Division. To compound the difficulties, the condition of the roads in the area of the Division were terrible due to the preceding rain and it made evasion from the swooping enemy aircraft particularly tricky. Obergefreiter Reddig of Panzergrenadier-Regiment 21 reports: "2.9.42. 0630 hours. Russian aerial attack, the tanker of 1. Schwadron and 3 vehicles of I. Abteilung burned. In the morning, the rain stopped."

General Heim called Korps and spoke to Oberst Friebe. Several of his units had been scheduled to replace a sector of 24. Panzer-Division but he said that relief was very difficult because every metre of ground was covered by tank and artillery fire. His anti-aircraft guns had been drawn forward to combat Russian tanks. His half-track battalion could immediately relieve elements of 24. Panzer-Division. At 0820 hours, Oberst Friebe called Oberst Fangohr at Armee HQ requesting a slight postponement of the attack, citing the reason that some units had not been able to complete reliefs due to difficult conditions.
Friebe: "Can attack be shifted to 0930 hours?"
Answer: "Yes. Armee agrees with the change."
Oberst Friebe reported this to Major von Menges at 0845 hours: "Beginning of attack 0930 hours. Relief by elements of 14. Panzer-Division in about 2 – 3 hours." Friebe oriented about the route to Armee from the north. Generalmajor von Hauenschild was confident and believed it would work.

Combat reconnaissance north of the railway in the early morning hours established that there was no longer any enemy in front of the armoured Gruppe so, while Gruppe Edelsheim (with II./PGR26, I./PAR89, Flak-Bataillon 602, Panzerjäger 40 and one pioneer company) took over security to the west and east, Gruppe Broich with the Panzer Abteilung and the bulk of the panzergrenadiers set off at 0930 hours to attack, pushing over the railway towards the Milchfarm. The plan was for them to advance to the north up to Hill 147.3 and establish a connection with elements of 6. Armee coming down from the north. Elements of the Gruppe also advanced in a north-east direction to Hill 151.7, on to the so-called ring railway north-west of Alexeyevka. Obergefreiter Reddig: "At 0930 hours, advance of mounted I. Abteilung over the tracks, then dismount and immediate assault, vehicles back into a gully. We are now 12km in front of Stalingrad. Throughout the day, continuing attacks by Russian low-level aircraft with fighter protection."

At 1035 hours, Major von Menges reported to Korps that the tank trench east of Hill 135.1 was free of the enemy, as well as the area 3km east of there, and there was also no enemy along the railway. Major von Menges asked whether the seemingly abandoned positions – including the tank trench – should be occupied. Hill 125.0 had already been taken. Oberst Friebe said he would speak to Armee about it. Half an hour later, Armee transmitted the order to Korps that 24. Panzer-Division should push forward up to the line Farm Nr. 2 – Hill 135.1. The tank trench was to be occupied if it was free of the enemy. There, the Division should prepare itself on this line for an eventual continued advance to the east, on to Stalingrad or to gain a connection to the north with 6. Armee. Oberst Friebe passed this information on to 24. Panzer-Division at 1117 hours. Barely an hour later, Armee gave another order for Korps to push to the east and north-east north of 119.7 with the left wing on the railway line and reach the mouth of the Tsaritsa and the area south of there in the city of Stalingrad. Half an hour later, Oberst Friebe informed 24. Panzer-Division about the mission of Korps with the order that the Division should push forward battle-strength reconnaissance with the left wing up to the Tsaritsa Gully. 14. Panzer-Division would only be able to advance the next morning so, while 24. Panzer-Division attacked with its left wing north of the railway, 14. Panzer-Division would advance in the general direction of Pestshanka. 29. Infanterie-Division (mot.), echeloned rearwards to the right, would take over the protection of the east flank.
In a spirited attack, the enemy positions north of the railway were broken through, Farm 2 being taken by Gruppe Edelsheim and the dominating Hill 151.7 and Schafhaus by Gruppe Broich. Riflemen constructed foxholes in the sloping sides of the tank trench. The daily

objective of the Schafzucht was reached at 1100 hours. Three enemy batteries and numerous war materiel was destroyed. General von Hauenschild reported this to General Kempf: "Russians running away everywhere. Hill 151.7 and Schafzucht reached. One battery and two anti-tank guns captured. I want to sound out up to 147.5 – 153.2 with an armoured Stoßgruppe. If enemy stronger, line 119.2 – Farm Nr. 2 – 147.5 – 151.7 held. Farm Nr. 2 just taken."
Kempf congratulated Oberst von Broich and Oberst von Nostitz for their successes. He then told Hauenschild that 14. Panzer-Division would relieve elements of the Division.

Looking out over a distant barren hill, the men of I./PGR21 glimpsed a tall water tower in the distance, the landmark of Voroponovo. Since 1430 hours, the armoured assault group had been advancing toward 153.2 as part of General von Hauenschild's reconnaissance-in-force, which in fact was just a continuation of the attack. The bulk of the Division secured the line 119.7 – Farm 2 – 147.5 – 151.7. It was still not completely clarified if enemy tanks were being held back south of Farm 2. The assault group of 6. Armee, which was also scheduled to thrust to the area of Schafzucht and join hands with 24. Panzer-Division, did not set out on this day. XXXXVIII. Panzerkorps had the following mission: "Using the favourable situation produced by the penetration of 24. Panzer-Division, thrust forward both sides of the railway line and gain the Volga south of the mouth of the Tsaritsa." The mission for 24. Panzer-Division said: "Capture the forests west of the city, with the later objective of thrusting through to the Volga north of Stalingrad-South railway station."

Up until evening 24. Panzer-Division, after reaching Hill 151.7, had thrust into strong enemy forces in field emplacements with tanks, artillery and anti-tank guns on the line Pestshanka – Alexeyevka. Increasing enemy resistance in the evening temporarily prohibited a further attack. With the attack halted, the Division sent its daily report to Korps: "After a successful thrust to the daily objective of Schaffarm, the Division pushed to the east at 1330 hours, taking Hill 151.7. Since then, the Division secured on the line Farm 2 – 113.7 – railway line west of 147.5 – 151.7. Six enemy batteries, including four heavy ones, were silenced by artillery directed by spotter planes.
"Strong enemy forces with artillery and tanks in Pestshanka. Tank trench and positions east of Alexeyevka heavily occupied by anti-tank guns and anti-tank rifles. The initial rearward movement of the enemy to the east during the day stopped in the afternoon.
"600 prisoners, 4 guns destroyed, 27 guns and 2 anti-tank guns silenced, 6 railway carriages with armoured turrets.
"Division HQ: gully Milchfarm 2km north of railway line.
"Panzer situation: 10 Panzer II, 15 Panzer III lg, 16 Panzer III kz, 5 Panzer IV lg, 1 Panzer IV kz and 1 Bfwg."

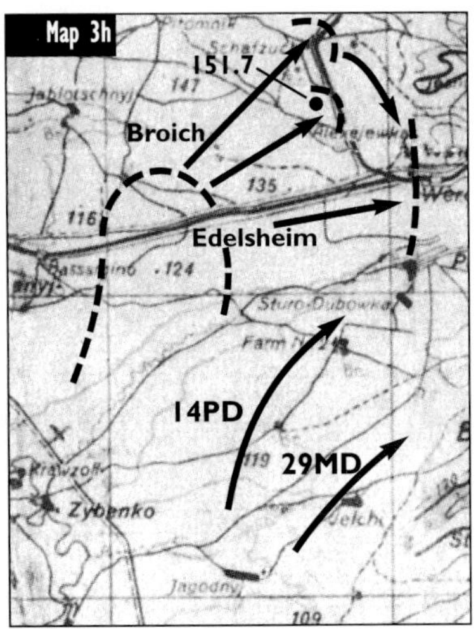

The result of the day was that the connection to 6. Armee was not established due to the non-appearance of the troops from the north but in lieu of that, the enemy picture near Stalingrad was clarified by the attack and, contrary to expectations, it seemed that the enemy had not yet completely occupied the forward positions west of Stalingrad. The only thing to do was to exploit the situation.

Oberst Friebe and Major von Menges held a telephone conference at 1955 hours. Oberst Friebe oriented about events at 6. Armee and then told Major von Menges that he had been selected to go to Berlin and speak about capture of Stalingrad. Menges' reaction was not recorded. He was all business, however, simply reporting his Division's status: "Enemy infantry not very strong, artillery negligible, anti-tank and anti-aircraft fire. Division wants to pull back from Pestshanka to make flanking fire ineffective. We are anxious because we still don't have a northern flank at the moment." Friebe replied: "Advance to come into line with 14. Panzer-Division."

At 2315 hours, the Division issued Divisionsbefehl Nr. 54 for the attack on Stalingrad on 3rd September. The plan was for reconnaissance to move out at 0330 hours to establish whether the enemy had been reinforced before the Division advanced at 0800 hours at the latest, after preparations and artillery bombardments, with the Schwerpunkt on the left out of the area of Hill 151.7 up to the Volga north of the railway station. First objective was Hill 153.2 and further objectives were Verkhne-Yelshanka or the small forests north of there. Defensive Gruppe Edelsheim would maintain a connection to 14. Panzer-Division to the south, using smoke and cover-fire to suppress flanking fire from Pestshanka and the southern flank while Gruppe Broich attacked out of the area of Hill 151.7 with armoured units and grenadiers with the aim of taking the tank trench north-west of Hill 153.2 as quickly as possible, preferably from the north. Panzerpioniers would bridge the trench and clear it of any mines, making it useable for a continued advance. Direction of the attack would be to the east either north or south of the road, dependent upon the enemy situation. Panzerartillerie-Regiment 89 would concentrate its fire on Voroponovo, Hill 153.2 and ahead of Gruppe Broich as well as screening

MARK

A Panzer IV long-barrel of 4. Schwadron ploughs through a dusty road on the western outskirts of Stalingrad.

FREIMANN

The forbidding skyline of Stalingrad. A massive cloud of smoke spews from burning oil tanks struck by the Luftwaffe. This photo was taken from one of the many wooded hills on Stalingrad's south-western outskirts.

off the northern edge of Pestshanka and suppressing Yelshanka and the forests north of there. The Luftwaffe would support the attack with Stukas and fighter-bombers controlled by radios amongst the assault groups. General von Hauenschild had set up his advanced command post on Hill 151.7 to observe and control the assault.

The number of prisoners taken on this day amounted to 1,400 prisoners, 6 heavy tanks and 31 tanks also being captured. The amount of booty since 29th August rose to 11,000 prisoners, 24 tanks, 11 Stalin Organs, 71 guns, 29 anti-aircraft guns, 4 aircraft, 1 armoured train, and further war material.

Casualties:

45 men killed

- Gefreiter Bruno Pallentin; Pz.Pi.40 (Killed)
- Oberpionier Hans Rudat; Pz.Pi.40 (Killed)
- Gefreiter Erich Jebramzyck; PGR26 (Killed)
- Unteroffizier Kurt Winter; PGR21 (Killed near Zybenko)
- Obergefreiter Heinrich Wingen; PGR21 (Killed near Zybenko)

12 officers wounded (5 of those stayed with the troops)

- Oberarzt Gulbin (Wounded)
- Leutnant Willi Bachler; PAR89 (Wounded but stayed with the troops)
- Oberleutnant Helmut von Amsberg; PAR89 (Wounded but stayed with the troops)
- Hauptmann Nahler (Abteilung Kdr); I./PAR89 (Wounded but stayed with the troops)
- Leutnant Fritz Reininghaus; IV./PAR89 (Wounded)

- Leutnant Wofram Wagner; IV./PAR89 (Wounded)
- Leutnant Alfred Bock; IV./PAR89 (Wounded)
- Leutnant Dinse (Wounded but stayed with the troops)
- Leutnant Marschner (Zug Kdr); 6./PGR21 (Wounded)
- Oberleutnant Heinz Longere (Abteilung Adjutant); Feldersatz Abt. 40 (Wounded)
- Leutnant Hans Jürgen Otte (Zug Kdr); 4./K4 (Wounded)
- Hauptmann i.G. Heinrich Siegfried Baron von Hobe (Division Ib); 24. Panzer-Division Stab (Wounded but stayed with the troops)

185 men wounded (79 of those stayed with the troops)

1 man missing

Piercing the Ourskirts

Chapter Four

3rd September 1942:

Apart from artillery fire, Stalin Organs and air attacks, the night passed quietly near all divisions without any special incidents and the enemy picture was unchanged: he still sat in constructed positions. Divisional reconnaissance troops – on foot and in panzers – were shot at shortly after crossing the railway line. A connection with infantry of 71. Infanterie-Division (Infanterie-Regiment 191) was established at 0700 hours north of Pitomnik. Edelsheim's southern wing was anchored on the so-called Five-Finger Gully, and previously reported Russian tanks seemed to have disappeared.

Heavy enemy artillery barrages groped their way to the shallow gullies where the half-tracks waited with the grenadiers for the start of the assault. There were barely any casualties and the men took this as a good omen for this day of attack. After regrouping, preparations and detailed orientation about the enemy, 24. Panzer-Division set out at 0800 hours from Hill 151.7 with a sharply concentrated attack led by Gruppe Broich. The right wing moved past the left of Pestshanka, holding themselves to the left of the railway line. Gruppe Edelsheim would only feint attack on a broad front for the time being, later to follow staggered rearwards to the right. Romanians covered the north flank. The first objective of Panzergrenadier-Regiment 21 was a hill on the ring railway, the second was the village of Alexeyevka. The attack progressed well, quickly reaching the hill in front of the circular railway of Stalingrad. The railway line stretched out into the distant naked steppe and joined up with tracks coming from the north and south. Rifle-pits studded the area. The armoured Gruppe pushed forward over this railway embankment. Around 0815 hours, the escorting Brigade Adjutant Rittmeister Rudolf von Knebel Doeberitz was severely wounded by shell splinters while in a half-track on the right of the attacking I./PGR21. The Division sent the following report to Korps at 0845 hours, reporting the status of the attack: "Assault south-east of Hill 151.7 at a standstill at the moment in strong artillery, mortar and anti-tank fire, tank fire from the direction of Krutenkiy, as well as flanking out of the area north of Tsaritsa Brook." And five minutes later: "Continue to advance after proposed Stuka operations and artillery preparation. Infantry opposition slight, apart from numerous mortars."

Then at 0855 hours, Division reported some bad news to Korps: "Division Commander lightly wounded, Brigade Adjutant wounded, Oberst von Nostitz [sic] severely wounded." General von Hauenschild was lightly wounded by shrapnel when he was visiting the forward line to watch the progress of his attacking units from a small hill overlooking the road. Together with his Chief-of-Staff Major von Menges, Hauenschild was sitting in a foxhole behind a wall of earth when several enemy shells exploded nearby, sending slivers of shrapnel whizzing past, a smaller piece striking the General in the head. Luckily, it was only a grazing wound which was quickly dressed by a medic and before long, Hauenschild had the telephone receiver in his hand, continuing to direct the assault of his units. On the other hand, Oberst Gustav von Nostitz-Wallwitz, Commander of Panzerartillerie-Regiment 89, was severely wounded by shrapnel. He suffered a dangerous wound in his upper thigh and one of his forearms was ripped to pieces. Even though his wounds were severe, an acute danger to his life did not exist at that moment. A possible proposal for the Knight's Cross was accelerated and a search for a replacement was immediately launched. Major Hans-Walter von Pawel, Commander of Panzerartillerie-Regiment 89's I. Abteilung, took temporary command of the Regiment. These searches took quite a while: since the death of Oberst Riebel on 23rd August, a search had been initiated to find a replacement commander of Panzer-Regiment 24. The name of Oberst von Lederer was suggested but Division did not think it was desirable because he was unknown to them. The Division had their eye on the very famous Oberstleutnant Hyazinth Graf von Strachwitz, currently fighting along the Volga north of Stalingrad at the head of his panzer battalion in 16. Panzer-Division.

During the morning, General Kempf arrived at the command post of 24. Panzer-Division where Major von Menges reported that combat was particularly difficult and costly under the very strong effect of enemy weapons. The wounding of Generalmajor von Hauenschild and Oberst von Nostitz was ample proof. The impression existed that in front of the Division the enemy had brought forward all his freed-up forces from the south for the defence of Stalingrad and its bridgehead.

Despite the loss of some of their commanders, the men of 24. Panzer-Division continued the assault. Reported at 0925 hours: "Panzergrenadiers making slow progress, beginning at gully 1.5km south-east of 151.7." At 0930 hours, the fighting was still very hard and costly. Dug-in Russian tanks, mortars and artillery forced the grenadiers to retreat. For an hour after that, an artillery bombardment pummelled the Russian emplacements, geysers of earth climbing into the air and creating a curtain of hazy dust along the eastern horizon. Occasionally, there was a particularly loud crack when a bunker or a Russian tank was annihilated. The riflemen pushed forward to a gully which was shown on the maps as a dotted outline. To the dirty grenadiers and the crewmen sweating in their panzers, the fighting seemed to be becoming a little easier. General von Hauenschild was informed by reconnaissance that the village of Yagodnyi was free of the enemy. At 1015 hours, Major von Menges informed Oberst Friebe at Korps that resistance was still very strong, above all by artillery and mortars. Grenadiers and riflemen that had advanced up to the Brook sector were forced to retreat a couple of hundred metres. After a short preparation by mortars and artillery, the advance was renewed down into the gully. At 1035 hours, there were definite signs that the Russians were slowly giving way and retreating eastwards. At 1200 hours, the panzers were ordered to roll forward and support the troops. The riflemen continued to make slow progress. The panzergrenadiers

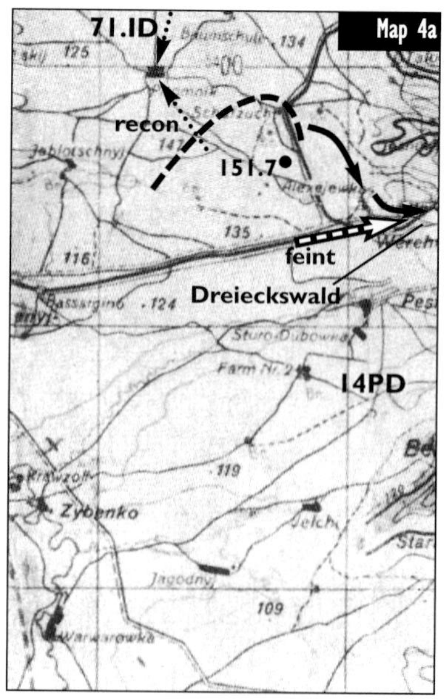

SPANNOCCHI

BUNDESARCHIV, BILD 101I/218/504/9 PHOTO: DIECK

Rittmeister Ernst Thiel, Commander of 4. Panzer Schwadron, consults a map while perched atop his Panzer IV. Inset: Oberleutnant Thiel, shown in 1941 as a company commander in Reiter-Regiment 2.

followed close behind in their half-tracks. Defending the southern sector was Major Hans-Wilhelm von Heyden's II./PGR26. Further south, 14. Panzer-Division took Dreihügelgrab (Three Knoll Trench). At 1345 hours, the area north of Alexeyevka and the enemy-infested slope 1km north-west of 153.2 were reached with the leading troops. Panzers advancing toward Hill 153.2 dragged along the riflemen and then turned to the west into occupied Alexeyevka. Kradschützen-Abteilung 4 was thrusting up to Hill 151.0 and Gruppe von Edelsheim reached the railway fork east of Krutenkiy. Enemy tanks were present in Pestshanka, Voroponovo and on Hill 145.8. Artillery was also located there. In contrast to the morning, enemy fire had decreased somewhat.

Oberst Friebe called Generalmajor von Hauenschild at 1350 hours and notified him that strong air support would take place at 1500 hours. At 1450 hours, Hill 153.2 was taken by Gruppe von Edelsheim after conducting a systematic attack, and toughly defended Alexeyevka was taken from the north-west. I. /Panzergrenadier-Regiment 21 cleaned out the deep gully lying close behind the village and dug themselves in for the night. To the left of them, II. Abteilung reached to the south of Yezovka. Here fell Leutnant Edgar Werther, the recently arrived Commander of 8. Schwadron. He did not live to see his promotion to Oberleutnant, which had only just been approved.

The Division also achieved another success further north at 1630 hours. Despite the strongest resistance, the armoured Stoßgruppe won the Dreieckswäld (Triangle Forest) 1.5km east-north-east of Hill 153.2 after the destruction of several enemy batteries and continued to advance toward 147.5 at 1800 hours. The results were not without sacrifices, however: Rittmeister Ernst Thiel, Commander of 4. Panzer Schwadron, was killed by a head shot by an enemy sniper while looking out of the cupola of his Panzer IV '451', while Oberleutnants Gerhard von Loesch and Gottfried von Dietze were wounded and transported to hospital. In the evening, Krutenkiy was also taken by the Division after tough combat. To hold the ground won at such cost to the

Division, the bulk of the two panzergrenadier regiments secured around Hill 153.2 while elements of Panzergrenadier-Regiment 21 also secured near the small village of Krutenkiy which, together with Voroponovo, was still partly occupied by the enemy. Because of the unfavourable terrain conditions however, the panzers were pulled back a little for the night. General von Hauenschild installed his HQ in a gully 2km north-west of Milchfarm. Available panzers were 8 Panzer II, 10 Panzer III kz, 12 Panzer III lg, 1 Panzer IV kz, 4 Panzer IV lg and 1 Bfwg.

During the day, Korps was again supported in an excellent manner by VIII. Fliegerkorps in the difficult fighting. The number of prisoners taken since 29 August rose to 14,000; 51 tanks, 128 guns, 13 Stalin Organs and a large amount of war material had also been captured. For the coming day, the aim of Korps was to first straighten out the flanks by advancing on Hill 145.8. Air support would be provided, the Schwerpunkt initially being placed near 14. Panzer-Division and 29. Infanterie-Division (mot.). To 24. Panzer-Division, the order from Korps was simple: "Push into the city." Therefore, at 2150 hours, the following combat assignment was issued to the Division: "24. Panzer-Division will attack east on 4th September, press into the city of Stalingrad and clear out the city sectors between the ordered dividing line to 14. Panzer-Division and the Tsaritsa Gully. Beginning of the assault will be reported."
The Division mourned the loss of another officer during the night. Panzergrenadier-Regiment 21 lost its excellent Nachrichtenoffizier[1], Oberleutnant Dieter Bömcke, when his vehicle drove over a mine near Alexeyevka. He was the only person in the vehicle killed; all the other men in the vehicle were wounded.

Casualties:

3 officers killed

- Rittmeister Ernst Thiel (Schwadron Kdr); 4./PR24 (Killed)
- Leutnant Edgar Werther (Schwadron Kdr); 8./PGR21 (Killed)
- Oberleutnant Dieter Bömcke (Regiment NO); PGR21 (Killed)

18 men killed

- Obergefreiter Johann Bonnekessel; PGR26 (Killed)
- Obergefreiter Leopold Zettl; PGR21 (Killed south of Yezovka)
- Obergefreiter Wilhelm Wedeking; PGR21 (Killed)
- Gefreiter Bernhard Lichtenberger; PGR21 (Killed)
- Obergefreiter Hermann Donnerberg; PGR21 (Killed)
- Obergefreiter Ernst Borrek; K4 (Killed)

7 officers wounded (2 of those stayed with the troops)

- Oberleutnant Gerhard von Loesch (Zug Kdr); 10./PR24 (Wounded)
- Oberarzt Dr. Kurt Pisselhoy (Abteilung Arzt); K4 (Wounded but stayed with the troops)
- Oberst Gustav Adolf von Nostitz-Wallwitz (Regiment Kdr); PAR89 (Wounded)
- Oberleutnant Helmet von Amsberg; PAR89 (Wounded)
- Oberleutnant Gottfried von Dietze; PR24 (Wounded)
- Rittmeister Rudolf von Knebel Doeberitz (Brigade Adjutant); SB24 (Wounded)

1. Communications officer

- Generalmajor Bruno Ritter von Hauenschild (Division Kdr) (Wounded but stayed with the troops)

114 men wounded (53 of those stayed with the troops)

- Obergefreiter Konrad Hofmann; 6./PGR21 (Wounded)
- Obergefreiter Gerhard Broschek; PGR21 (Wounded but died on 4th September in hospital)

1 man missing

4th September 1942:

The attack was going to be continued in the morning and it would be preceded by a Stuka attack on the enemy positions in and around the 'Wäldchen' and bush terrain that stretched both sides of the highway from Krutenkiy to Stalingrad, up to the edge of the city. During the Stuka attack, the ground troops would reach the starting positions for the actual attack on the 'Wäldchen' at 0500 hours. Later, a squadron of Henschel attack aircraft would support the attack of the ground troops. Their appearance was considered the signal for attack by the panzers and II./PGR21. Yet, before the Stukas appeared, several German fighters and Henschel doubledeckers flew over the battlefield so that the impression existed that this was the signal for the attack on the Wäldchen. Accordingly, 8. Schwadron of Panzergrenadier-Regiment 21 moved up with their vehicles into an area pre-determined as the starting position. During the advance, the Stukas suddenly appeared. Oberleutnant Guercke listened into the 'Gustav' radio as the pilots talked to each other on their radios as to whether the troops down there were Russian or their own troops.
Wachtmeister Wolf, anti-tank platoon commander in 8./Panzergrenadier-Regiment 21, remembers: "Everything was in motion when the Ju 87's suddenly appeared. The pilots made their 'circles' in the sky, trying to make out the front. I suppose that the flight-leader considered our forward movement as a Russian retreat. In any case, they deployed themselves, as far as I was able to judge, far behind us to dive-bomb. Yellow flares were fired, aerial recognition panels laid out in all haste to give the signal 'forward line'. It was bad luck that the Russians, probably with captured flares, fired these same signals so that the air crews were puzzled and could no longer distinguish between the enemy and our troops. Moreover, it was already too late for those still remaining under the roar and howling of the bombs to take complete cover. And then the impacts lay in front and amongst us, wounded cried out, parts of vehicles flew through the air. It was horrible."
The Schwadron lost 2 dead on this day, Obergefreiter Ambros Schuch and Panzergrenadier Marion Lempka. Among the wounded was Wachtmeister Wolf and an anti-tank gun of his platoon was knocked out by a bomb hit.

It was not a very auspicious beginning to the attack. The panic quickly subsided and the troops composed themselves before quickly beginning the assault. It proceeded smoothly. The last part of Krutenkiy and Voroponovo were taken by assault as well as Hill 145.8 as a widening of the basis of the assault. The attack pushed south of the highway. Hauptwachtmeister Louis Rubbel[2], a platoon commander in 7./Panzergrenadier-Regiment 21, reports:

2. Born 21st March 1912, died on 20th September 1999

> "Attacking together with panzers in the morning hours, II./PGR21 reached the forward (west) edge of a comparatively light mixed forest nursery – pines and shrubs – and went into cover there. Shortly after that, our Stukas bombed the nursery, several bombs landing damned close in front of us. Then at 0615 hours, the grenadiers attacked through the woods, the panzers following close behind.
>
> "Enemy resistance was not very strong, several heavy anti-tank guns were overrun, a few prisoners were taken. After passing through the 3km deep Wäldchen (Little Forest), we went into positions on the eastern edge. From here, one could clearly observe with the naked eye a valley leading out from the southern part of Stalingrad. High pillars of black smoke climbed into the sky.
>
> "After a few minutes, we set off out of the 'Wäldchen' to attack together with the panzers on a broad front, this time immediately behind the panzers. When we were about 100 metres past the edge of the forest, a violent Russian anti-tank fire set in, probably from entrenched T-34's. After the first salvo, two of our Panzer IV's burned. Because the enemy generally could not be made out, the panzers pulled back to the 'Wäldchen' and the grenadiers went to ground, then they also pulled back to the edge of the forest. Defence was set up here. The heavy platoon of our Schwadron had its positions immediately north of the broad unstrengthened street that led in the direction of Stalingrad. Firing direction: on the street and on the ground south of this. It did not last long, and out of the bushy area on the other side of the road in front of our positions resounded intense tank noises. Because our foxholes were still not very deep, it was not very agreeable.
>
> "A terrible detonation behind me relieved the tension. On the other side of the street, a tongue of flame climbed up out of the bushes, then a further detonation and a second burst of flame. About 10 metres behind me, a heavy self-propelled gun had gone into position, which I had not noticed in the zeal of combat, and had achieved two hits. The remaining enemy tanks immediately withdrew, the noise indicating that there was still 5 of them."

Seventh Schwadron of Panzergrenadier-Regiment 21, commanded by Rittmeister Otto Drews, had three men killed on this day: Obergefreiter Erich Wengler, Gefreiter Rudhardt Münch and Gefreiter Peter Meschenich who died of his severe wounds. Several men were also wounded. The self-propelled gun mentioned by Rubbel would undoubtedly have been a Marder III equipped with a Russian 7.62cm anti-tank gun belonging to Panzerjäger-Abteilung 670 that was subordinated to 24. Panzer-Division.

At 0600 hours, I./Panzergrenadier-Regiment 21 advanced to the south-east without thrusting into the enemy. Oberleutnant Dietrich Micke, Adjutant of I./Panzergrenadier-Regiment 21, reports:

> "We advanced through Krutenkiy and then on to the railway line where a long row of freight trains stood on the rails in the area of Voroponovo. Loud rumbling of tank engines allowed us to reconnoitre between the freight cars to the south, where we saw on a large field on the other side of the railway – apparently an airfield – an entire row of T-34's standing or driving about, several even standing close behind the freight cars not far from us. The neighbouring sector of 14. Panzer-Division had not advanced as quickly so we must therefore cover our open right flank to the south and advance in remaining areas further to the east, obtaining a further connection with

Oberst Maximilian Reichsfreiherr von Edelsheim, the revered and popular commander of Panzergrenadier-Regiment 26.

the Regiment. There, the order reached us to report to Oberst von Edelsheim, meeting him in a small forest close to the approach road.

"Thus Graf von Bernstorff, Funkmeister Classen and I mounted our Kfz. 15 and drove forward.

"The railway line to the right of us, leading to Stalingrad, passed into a flat basin that became deeper to the east. The undulating terrain climbed both sides of the railway line. We drove out of the area of Hill 153.2 in a north-east direction to the middle of the divisional sector. Over the empty terrain and in the distance, the edge of a forest was seen. The lengthy village of Verkhne-Yelshanka could be seen on the opposite slope south of the railway line. It was clear to us that it must still be occupied by the enemy, not a very comfortable feeling. We drove forward in a fairly dashing tempo and also noticed nothing of shelling, reached the edge of the forest, fairly thick bushy terrain, and to our relief spotted the Regiment command post submerged in the bushes, and also welcoming us there was von Hellermann and von Schmidt-Pauli. Both were completely amazed to see us driving here in our vehicle. They told us that the bush terrain was full of well-camouflaged T-34's, our men, who had not advanced very far here, were grappling with them in close combat and had already finished off a few of them. Besides that, there were barrages by mortars here at regular intervals. The command post of Edelsheim must be to the rear somewhere because it was not in the vicinity here. Therefore, drive on further! We did not delay long but drove back. After about 1.5km we fell into a mortar salvo on a hill, a shell exploding about 10 metres half left of our vehicle, several splinters smashing through the windshield. We instinctively leapt out of the vehicle and ran to the outskirts of a gully about 10 metres away, then we saw that Bernstorff was obviously wounded and remained lying next to the vehicle. The three of us hurried over to him and carried him into cover. Two splinters had struck him, one in the temple, another in the neck, and he was unconscious.

> "The driver was lightly wounded, both of us were as good as if nothing happened, the vehicle was still driveable. I therefore sent the driver back with the vehicle to fetch an ambulance. After a short time it appeared, escorted by a doctor, and we lay Bernstorff into it and drove back a little bit with him. On the way, we separated from this transport with complete sorrow, to search for Edelsheim. I soon found him, more in the centre of the divisional sector, reporting myself to him and from him received the order for our Abteilung for renewed operations on the southern edge of the 'Wäldchens'."

With the wounding of Graf von Bernstorff, the Regiment had lost not only its second Abteilung Commander in a week but at the same time also its oldest active officer that had belonged to it for almost 10 years, a true nobleman and brave soldier. A few hours after his wounding, he passed away and was one of the first to be buried at the Heroes Cemetery of the Division near Voroponovo.

Afterwards, the armoured Stoßgruppe with a Panzergrenadier Abteilung and Kradschützen-Abteilung 4 under the command of Major von der Lancken set off at 0800 hours, followed by Gruppe Hellermann (I./PGR21) to assault the edge of the city. At 0840 hours, 24. Panzer-Division reached the Barracks on the edge of the city. Infantry remained behind on the left flank, clearing out the Triangular Forest and Tsaritsa Forest. Strong flanking fire from Yelshanka lashed the advancing troops. Oberleutnant Jürgen Pachnio's 3./Panzergrenadier-Regiment 21 suffered from it as they advanced north of the railway line. The heavy infantry fire from Yelshanka, on the high ground south of the railway line, forced it to be left behind until the onset of darkness. Unteroffizier Wolfgang Lindenberg and Obergefreiter Wilhelm Janke were killed, Panzerobergrenadier Josef Schröder died of his wounds in a 1./40 Sanitäts-Abteilung's first aid post. Many other men were wounded.

The enemy had doubtlessly reinforced himself but despite this, and the unfavourable terrain, the panzers succeeded in pushing through the Square Forest north of Hill 147.5 and with panzers at the front, won the edge of the city east of the forest at 0945 hours. After weeks of the hardest combat, 24. Panzer-Division were the first German troops of two armies on the city edge of Stalingrad. Leutnant von Senger und Etterlin participated in this attack: "We moved further forward and reached the outskirts in the sector between the railway line and the Tsaritsa River. For several kilometres we passed through a large tree-nursery, the renowned Wäldchen. Several well-camouflaged Russian tanks were here and we couldn't get past. We shifted to the right flank of the Division and took up defensive positions on the edge of the forest facing to the south in the direction of a broad valley, the Minina, and a road into the city. Our right neighbour, 14. Panzer-Division, hadn't yet moved up far enough. The left flank of my Schwadron bent back into the thick pine forest where it joined with a Schwadron of the Dressler Abteilung. A PK[3] man joined our Schwadron in the forward trenches, where he got his first glimpse of the southern part of the city and produced a radio report about the fall of Stalingrad. Down below, only a few hundred metres away, lay the city, and behind that, very nearby, was the wide, bright blue band of the Volga, our objective for this week."

Toward 1200 hours, I./Panzergrenadier-Regiment 21 occupied their new positions to the left

3. Propaganda Kompanie

of Panzergrenadier-Regiment 26. The Abteilung was soon pulled out again and employed between the left wing of II./Panzergrenadier-Regiment 21 and the Tsaritsa in the northern stretches of the 'Wäldchen'. After the death of Rittmeister von Bernstorff, the command of I. Abteilung was taken over by the Commander of 1. Schwadron, Rittmeister Friedrich Graf zu Solms-Wildenfels. New commander of 1. Schwadron was Leutnant Werner Tutein.
Panzers of 24. Panzer-Division reached the edge of the city but as a consequence of very strong anti-tank, tank and infantry defence from the northern and western edge of the city – basically from all directions – they were withdrawn behind the eastern edge of the forest at 1200 hours. It was not possible for the panzergrenadiers to follow because of this strong flanking fire, especially since the neighbours to the south were not able to gain ground as quickly. There were also problems to the north. The neighbouring division, 71. Infanterie-Division, was informed that the panzers and panzergrenadiers of 24. Panzer-Division were pinned down on the east edge of Square Forest as a result of flanking from the north and south, and was asked by Korps when the division would move up to the same level and through that, eliminate the northern flanking fire on 24. Panzer-Division.

At 1420 hours, Generalmajor von Hauenschild received an order to hold the eastern edge of Square Forest with weak forces and with the bulk of the Division prepare to attack in a southern direction to eliminate the flanking fire out of Verkhne-Yelshanka. After regrouping, the attack was carried forward again. The assault broke down at 1630 hours in front of the eastern edge of the village. It finally had to be suspended because of the unfavourable terrain conditions and the strongest enemy defence, including flanking fire from both sides. Major von Menges reported to Korps: "Division has not gained the objective of Verkhne-Yelshanka because the artillery was not eliminated. Aim: hold, reconnoitre toward Verkhne-Yelshanka, if enemy weaker, then advance. Fighting very costly today." The armoured assault group secured in Square Forest facing to the east. Elements of the Division secured opposite Yelshanka, along the railway line. The Division was holding fronts to the south and east under simultaneous defence of enemy attacks against its flanks. Hauptwachtmeister Louis Rubbel, platoon commander in 7./Panzergrenadier-Regiment 21 recalls one of these attacks: "In the afternoon, the enemy attacked the eastern edge of the Wäldchen north of the road with strong infantry forces. At this moment, the commander of a battalion in our Artillerie Regiment fortuitously found himself at the front in his command half-track. In a few minutes, he placed the concentrated fire of his battalion on the attackers, bringing the attack to a standstill."

General von Hauenschild moved his Division HQ to Hill 153.7. The aim was to hold the attained line under the withdrawal of Gruppe Hellermann, still in the evening of 4th September, into the western part of Square Forest. In the evening report to Korps, this withdrawal was tactfully described as follows: "The positions of Gruppe Hellermann were shifted a little to the west." As a result of the day, the Division was the only one to succeed, with elements graduated far ahead, to fight through to the area of the city outskirts and with this spearhead wedge, lay the foundations for later assaults on Stalingrad. Here, the continuous multiple enemy defensive belts were deeply penetrated.

Casualties:

2 officers killed

- Hauptmann Ferdinand Mayer (Kompanie Kdr); 2./Pz.Pi.40 (Killed)

• Leutnant Friedrich Karsten (Killed)

29 men killed

• Gefreiter Gustav Preiß; Pz.Pi.40 (Killed)
• Gefreiter Rudolf Nedwed; PR24 (Killed)
• Obergefreiter Rudolf Bader; PGR26 (Killed)
• Obergefreiter Gerhard Konietzka; PGR21 (Killed)
• Obergefreiter Ambros Schuch; PGR21 (Killed)
• Panzergrenadier Marion Lempka; PGR21 (Killed)
• Obergefreiter Erich Wengler; PGR21 (Killed)
• Gefreiter Rudhardt Münch; PGR21 (Killed)
• Unteroffizier Ernst Szameitat; PGR21 (Killed)
• Gefreiter Werner Langer; PGR21 (Killed)
• Unteroffizier Wolfgang Lindenberg; PGR21 (Killed)
• Obergefreiter Wilhelm Janke; PGR21 (Killed)
• Gefreiter Fritz Behnke; PGR21 (Killed)
• Gefreiter Ernst Werker; PGR21 (Killed)

9 officers wounded (4 of those stayed with the troops)

• Oberleutnant Hans Wilhelm Willenberg (Batterie Kdr); 1./PAR89 (Wounded)
• Oberleutnant Herbert Oberbeck (Schwadron Kdr); 8./PGR26 (Wounded)
• Rittmeister Bechtold Graf von Bernstorff (Abt Kdr); I./PGR21 (Wounded but died late in the day at a first-aid post)
• Oberleutnant Arnold von Günther; PR24 (Wounded)
• Assistenarzt Dr. Martin Kuls (Abteilung Hilfsarzt); III./PR24 (Wounded)
• Leutnant Erdmann Graeve (Zug Kdr); 3./Pz.Jg.40 (Wounded but stayed with the troops)
• Oberleutnant Heinrich Krebs (Schwadron Kdr); 3./Pz.Jg.40 (Wounded but stayed with the troops)
• Oberleutnant von Sperber (Wounded but stayed with the troops)
• Leutnant Thuiske von Metzsch (Schwadron Kdr); 3./K4 (Wounded but stayed with the troops)

130 men wounded (24 of those stayed with the troops)

SPANNOCCHI
The much-feared Nebelwerfer; the German six-barrelled rocket-launcher.

• Hauptfeldwebel Konrad Mai; Div. Stab (Wounded)
• Gefreiter Peter Meschenich; PGR21 (Wounded but died later in the day)
• Panzerobergrenadier Josef Schröder; PGR21 (Wounded but later died in San.Kp 1./40)
• Gefreiter Heinz Schröter; PGR21 (Wounded but died on 5th September in hospital)

3 men missing

5th September 1942:

During the night, violent enemy artillery fire lay on the sector of the Division. Near 14. Panzer-Division and 24. Panzer-Division, there were barrages by Stalin Organs and enemy aircraft attacked with bombs and onboard weapons several times during the night. Enemy pressure was unchanged in front of 24. Panzer-Division but the enemy strengthened in the bushy terrain south of Square Forest. The momentary condition of 24. Panzer-Division's forces permitted no further attacks for the time being so all the Division could do was defend the attained positions. The enemy smothered the Wäldchen at irregular intervals with heavy barrages by artillery, Stalin Organs and above all by mortars in unheard-of concentrations. It caused high casualties, in many cases by direct hits on the foxholes. Strong enemy air attacks also followed. The schwadrons prepared for more trouble from the repeated enemy infantry assaults so, with the Division in precarious bulges thrust deep into the Russian lines, the other divisions of XXXXVIII. Panzerkorps were ordered to move up to the same level as 24. Panzer-Division and through this, the Division would at least have its southern flank covered. In accordance with Korps instructions, 29. Infanterie-Division (mot.) and 20. Romanian Division set off at 0400 hours, 14. Panzer-Division an hour later at 0500 hours.
There were dangerous signs that the Russians were considerably strengthening their defensive line. At 0700 hours, aerial reconnaissance reported 20 enemy tanks east and north-east of Elkhi in Elkhi Forest. The line was also strengthening in front of 24. Panzer-Division. At 0845 hours, Major von Menges reported to Korps that the enemy picture was basically unchanged except for the fact that he was apparently reinforcing in front of the village of Yelshanka.

The attack of 29. Infanterie-Division (mot.) and 14. Panzer-Division eventually broke down with only small gains of ground, stalling in front of considerable enemy resistance and strong flanking fire. Casualties were not inconsiderable for the minimal amount of territory gained. Kempf phoned Hoth at 0850 hours and reported the bad news. He then proposed the following plan to Hoth: 29. Infanterie-Division (mot.) and 14. Panzer-Division would be relieved by 20. Romanian Division and then both divisions shifted into the area gained by 24. Panzer-Division and the three divisions would then advance out of this area in a south-east direction. Hoth liked what he heard and immediately approved this plan. The attack of Korps was suspended and the relief of the divisions would follow that night. Regrouping was immediately initiated. Kempf also wanted confirmation that his plan had a good prospect of success. After a quick discussion with Oberst Friebe, Kempf had his chief-of-staff on the phone talking to the divisions about his plan. At 0942 hours, Friebe spoke to Major von Menges: "In the opinion of the Division, is a thrust to the south or south-east possible?"
Menges could not immediately answer. He needed to talk to General von Hauenschild, as well as the various unit commanders. Oberst Friebe gave him a little time to think about it. But not too long. He was about to head out to meet Major von Menges for a conference about the proposed operation.
Oberst Friebe arrived soon after and got straight down to business. He made the following statements about the conduct of the assault: the disadvantage of all previous attacks out of the conquered area was enemy flanking fire. On the left, 71. Infanterie-Division would move up to the same level as 24. Panzer-Division. Previously, two schwadrons had to be turned to the north for this open flank. Further flanking emanated from heavily occupied Pestshanka. The assaults to the south and south-east had to be started simultaneously and on a large attack frontage and with that, outflanking by the enemy from a frontal direction would be eliminated. The first phase of the attack would have to be carried out without panzers because of the terrain.

During the further course of the conference, the proposal of Oberst Friebe was held to be possible and favourable by Major von Menges, conditional on reconnaissance of the terrain and knowledge of the enemy situation. According to the proposal, 24. Panzer-Division would attack out of their attained area over Hill 147.5 on the eastern part of the larger piece of forest along the Pestshanka-Stalingrad road, while 14. Panzer-Division would attack out of the barracks area over the western part of Verkhne-Yelshanka, gain Hill 144.9 and thrust through to the Volga. Oberst Friebe later drove forward to a 24. Panzer-Division observation post on Hill 153.2 with Major von Menges to gain an impression of the terrain. In the opinion of the Brigade Commander, Oberst von Broich, and the temporary commander of Panzerartillerie-Regiment 89, Major von Pawel, the planned attack seemed possible if terrain conditions were practicable and promising. It was here that the proposal of the Brigade Commander was approved. He'd suggested that the riflemen break into the forward line during darkness after a short barrage by the rocket-launchers and artillery.

There was a welcome change during the morning hours for the men of 7./Panzergrenadier-Regiment 21 when single Soviet supply lorries appeared from the direction of Stalingrad and fell intact into their hands. Among them was an entire lorry full of vodka, its driver also being full. A light moment amongst the gruelling defensive combat.

An Armeebefehl was issued at 1630 hours in which the mission of XXXXVIII. Panzerkorps remained the destruction of enemy forces placed in the area around Pestshanka. After regrouping its forces, it would fulfil this by an enveloping attack from the north. 20. Romanian Division remained subordinated to Korps and would be employed to relieve the motorised units south of Pestshanka.

In the evening, Leutnant Freiherr von Eickstedt submitted the daily report of the Division to Korps: "Several enemy attacks with strong artillery support against Gruppe Hellermann on the

BUNDESARCHIV

Oberleutnant Heinz Endruweit, signals officers of Panzer-Regiment 24, scans the horizon from command panzer '372'.

northern wing in Square Forest were repulsed during the day, partly in hand-to-hand combat. Enemy continually reinforcing himself. Strengthening artillery activity. Forward positions of the Division unchanged.
"Relief PGR21 and PGR26 and elements of Gruppe Sälzer by Gruppe Scheven, K64, Pionier-Bataillon 651 and 635 initiated, being implemented early morning of 6th September.
"Our own strong air activity, negligible enemy air activity.
"24. Panzer-Division HQ: Crowfoot Gully 2.5km west of Yezovka.
"Panzer situation: 10 Panzer II, 20 Panzer III, 4 Panzer IV lg and 1 Bfwg.
"Destroyed: 2 T-34's, 1 anti-tank gun, 320 prisoners."
To ensure that the assault was tipped with a powerful armoured wedge, Oberst Friebe decided that every panzer still available to Korps must be concentrated in one group. He knew that this would disgruntle a few people but it had to be done. Playing the diplomat, Friebe came up with a solution that would satisfy Generals Heim and Hauenschild, both strong personalities who usually spoke their minds. At 1810 hours, he informed 14. Panzer-Division of his decision: "For the assault, all panzers of Korps will be concentrated under Major von der Lancken near 14. Panzer-Division." The panzers of the three armoured divisions would be under the command of Major von der Lancken from 24. Panzer-Division but located in 14. Panzer-Division's area of operations. General Heim would have tactical control of the panzers but General von Hauenschild knew that as long as one of his men was leading the Kampfgruppe, the interests of 24. Panzer-Division would be looked after. Most commanders feared that when one of their units was subordinated to another division, it would be used in ways that resulted in heavy casualties.

Since Korps intended launching the assault out of the area of 24. Panzer-Division, the Division sent out reconnaissance in the evening. Also in preparation for the assault, a section of the southern front was relieved by elements of 29. Infanterie-Division (mot.) and 14. Panzer-Division. Corresponding to reconnaissance and discussions in the area, the Korpsbefehl was issued at 1830 hours with the following combat assignments:
"Reinforced 14. Panzer-Division will attack over the railway line from the line 153.2 – Barracks over the western edge of Verkhne-Yelshanka and occupy Hill 144.9. With a progressive attack, an anti-tank defensive front will be constructed on the right flank facing the high ground east of Pestshanka.
"After the capture of Hill 144.9 by grenadiers, Panzer Abteilung von der Lancken containing all of Korps' panzers will immediately thrust through to the Volga bridge south of Kuperossnoye. For this attack, it is subordinated to 14. Panzer-Division.
"29. Infanterie-Division (mot.) (without panzers) will attack out of the area south-east of 145.8 through Dreieckswäldchen (small triangular forest) to Verkhne-Yelshanka and take it. After clearing this village, the division will next gain the Pestshanka–Stalingrad road.
"24. Panzer-Division (without panzers) – while holding their positions in Square Forest – will attack with the bulk of the Division over Hill 147.5, clean out the area from the southern slope of this hill up to the railway line and in the further course of the attack, cover the eastern flank of Korps and in addition to this, win the eastern edge of the forest south-east of Verkhne-Yelshanka."

While the commanders planned for the upcoming attack, the men of 24. Panzer-Division continued to hold out in their foxholes. Until nightfall, several enemy attacks with strong artillery support directed against the northern flank in the Square Forest were halted, partly in hand-to-hand fighting. That evening, 24. Panzer-Division reported: "Several enemy attacks in

'Viereckswald' against Gruppe Hellermann were repulsed." In the daily action reports, one line was sufficient to describe the actions on this sector but to the men at the front, the reality was different. The constant tension and danger to life from this defensive action in the small forest could not be conveyed in any official report. Leutnant von Senger und Etterlin summarised the day's fighting in a few terse lines in his diary: "A few dozen metres away from us, the Russians were lying in their fortified bunkers on the opposite slope. There were constant detonations in the Wäldchen. Mortar fire, artillery, Stalin Organs, anti-tank rifles came together in an undreamt-of degree. It gave us continuous casualties. Opposite the cutting for the railway line, 14. Panzer-Division attacked the radio station at Yelshanka. We supported them through flak and artillery fire."

Casualties:

1 officer killed

- Oberleutnant Dieter Bömcke (Schwadron Kdr); Stabsschwadron/PGR21 (Killed)

18 men killed

7 officers wounded (all of them stayed with the troops)

- Leutnant Heinz Lakenbrink (Zug Kdr); 3./PGR21 (Wounded but stayed with the troops)
- Oberleutnant Dietrich Micke (Abt Adj); I./PGR21 (Wounded but stayed with the troops)
- Oberleutnant Erich Guercke (Schwadron Kdr); 8./PGR21 (Wounded but stayed with troops)
- Rittmeister Fritz Schriewer (Schwadron Kdr); 5./PGR21 (Wounded but stayed with troops)
- Oberleutnant Ludwig Leopold (F.d.Trosse); II./PR24 (Wounded but stayed with the troops)
- Oberleutnant Ullrich Schwarz (Zug Kdr); 12./PR24 (Wounded but stayed with the troops)
- Assistenarzt Dr. Wilhelm Zieher; PR24 (Wounded but stayed with the troops)

208 men wounded (78 of those stayed with the troops)

6th September 1942:

In the early morning hours, 24. Panzer-Division repelled an enemy attack in battalion strength from an eastern direction against the Square Forest. During the night, bombing attacks and Stalin Organs. A usual night outside Stalingrad's city limits.

A conference took place near 24. Panzer-Division. Present were: Generaloberst Hoth – General Kempf – Oberst i.G. Friebe – Division Commanders Heim, von Hauenschild and Fremerey, as well as their chiefs-of-staff – Generalleutnant Fiebig. Hoth began the conference by thanking everyone for their attendance. He first of all talked about the previous successes of 4. Panzer-Armee but specifically XXXXVIII. Panzerkorps. The advance of Korps, beginning on 29th August from the sector of the Romanians Korps, had brought the following results:
1.) Strong enemy forces were smashed to pieces.
2.) The perfectly positioned infantry were ripped apart.
3.) The strongly constructed field emplacements on Gniloy Aksai – Donskaya-Tsaritsa and Chervlenaya Gully were broken through.

4.) The enemy infantry were pushed back close to Stalingrad.
Hoth said: "Wherever the panzer forces are employed closely compressed with concentrated strength, the attack is a success. The new regrouping of Korps will and must lead to success. That the enemy – pressed back into a narrow area – will offer considerable resistance, is certain."

General Kempf was next. He laid out his points clearly and precisely:

1.) The Schwerpunkt clearly lies near 14. Panzer-Division. All the panzers are there.
Mission: in the shortest possible time, push past Verkhne-Yelshanka with the Panzergruppe and gain the dominating high ground near the radio station.
Eliminate the menace to the flanks near the north-western part of Yelshanka by barrages from one heavy and one light Werfer battery.
When the hills are reached, the menace to the flanks will be ineffectual. Romanians will cover the flank of 14. Panzer-Division on the north-eastern part of Pestshanka through fire.
2.) For the entire attack to succeed, it is of decisive importance that 29. Infanterie-Division (mot.) push along the railway and occupy Yelshanka.
Mission: quickly push through, forward elements will continue on while following elements will clear the village.
3.) 24. Panzer-Division will cover the eastern flank. Difficulties will develop through flanking fire out of the city.
4.) Luftwaffe target I is Pestshanka, II is the hills along the double stretch of road, III is Verkhne-Yelshanka (if not taken), IV is the western edge of the city (Leather Factory), V is the eastern part of the right forest.
5.) Gruppe Sälzer is subordinated to 14. Panzer-Division at 1400 hours.

The men in the trenches were unaware of this conference and its far-reaching consequences. Obergefreiter Reddig from 1./Panzergrenadier-Regiment 21 wrote in his diary: "6.9.42: Mail delivery. The Schwadrons lie under heavy artillery bombardments, air attacks and Stalin Organs. From 1. Schwadron, Cunczorra was severely wounded, Benno Grabowski wounded in the head. The vehicles are parked in a very long, broad gully. Here was a Russian artillery position, in which the drivers had set themselves up." Obergefreiter Reddig was lucky because as a driver, he stayed with his vehicle in a comparatively safe area while the grenadiers hunkered down in their foxholes.

The assault of Korps scheduled for 7th September was postponed for a further day because the regrouping of the divisions required more time. The remaining reliefs were carried out. Gruppe Sälzer, securing the west flank towards Pestshanka, was temporarily subordinated to 14. Panzer-Division. Since Gruppe Sälzer was subordinated to 14. Panzer-Division, the new divisional boundary was strengthened. Regrouping for preparations to attack were initiated. A reconnaissance troop from Kradschützen-Abteilung 4 reported that near the left neighbour, 71. Infanterie-Division, the situation was still unchanged at the moment.
At 1545 hours, strengthening artillery and mortar fire fell on the sector of the Division in the area of Square Forest. Several enemy reconnaissance probes on Square Forest were repulsed. At 1925 hours, Major von Menges called Korps and reported the Division's situation: "Anxious about ammunition, particularly smoke and heavy field howitzer, also light field howitzer. Light field howitzers still 26% availability. Smoke shells entirely absent. Heavy field howitzers still 40%. Russians attacked Square Forest in reinforced regiment strength on a 3km wide front. 24. Panzer-Division repelled the attack, partly in hand-to-hand combat. Enemy came to a stop

100 metres in front of the Division's sector. Lively artillery and mortar fire, Stalin Organs. Monitored radio communications of the enemy allow us to conclude that he has recognised the regrouping.
"Gruppe Hellermann with Kradschützen and panzers in Square Forest, Gruppe Edelsheim in area west and north of 145.3."

As Major von Menges reported, the enemy in the forest lay 100 metres opposite, continually strengthening himself with infantry and heavy weapons. The strongest enemy attack took place in the evening after a thorough, well-placed preparatory barrage. Leutnant von Senger und Etterlin reported: "Several deserters were brought in but saying they were not new. They pretended they had caught a secret order, produced by the Soviets showing that they were going to completely pull all posts over the Volga tonight."

At 1930 hours, Oberst Fangohr, Chief-of-Staff of 4. Panzer-Armee, informed Oberst Friebe that panzer replacement parts had finally arrived in Kotelnikovo. Oberst Friebe raised the division's anxiety about ammunition shortages. Oberst Fangohr said he would personally ensure an improvement or a compromise. The ammunition situation was now so severely strained that without further supplies, the necessary strong bombardment on 7th September was hampered and the implementation of the attack on 8th September questionable.

Casualties:

13 men killed

- Gefreiter Karl-Heinz Hoffmann; PR24 (Killed)
- Obergefreiter Franz Katzer; PGR21 (Killed)
- Gefreiter Johann Kitzberger; PGR21 (Killed)
- Obergefreiter Willi Betke; PGR21 (Killed)

2 officers wounded (both stayed with the troops)

- Leutnant Friedrich Schröder (Zug Kdr); 3./Pz.Pi.40 (Wounded but stayed with the troops)
- Leutnant Heinz Lakenbrink (Zug Kdr); 3./PGR21 (Wounded but stayed with the troops)

124 men wounded (71 stayed with the troops)

- Obergefreiter Gerhard Himmeldirk; PGR21 (Fatally wounded)
- Gefreiter Adalbert Fritschka; PGR21 (Wounded near Yezovka but died on 12th September)
- Cunczorra; PGR21 (Wounded)
- Benno Grabowski; PGR21 (Wounded)

Decorations bestowed from 31st August to 6th September:

6 Iron Cross First Class
138 Iron Cross Second Class
131 Panzer Combat Badge in Bronze

Prisoners and booty taken from 31st August to 6th September:

4910 prisoners
10 airplanes
87 guns (40 of those captured on railway wagons)
27 guns destroyed by artillery and aircraft
46 tanks
54 anti-tank guns
21 anti-aircraft guns
36 mortars
86 anti-tank rifles
2 Stalin Organs
503 railway wagons with war materiel
25 locomotives (most were useless)

7th September 1942:

At 0230 hours, an enemy reconnaissance patrol – with a tank in support – attacked the line in front of Rittmeister Sivers' II. Abteilung of Panzergrenadier-Regiment 21. The enemy scouts were repulsed but the tank dug itself in. At the same time, the noise of battle could be heard coming from the area of the left neighbour. There was decreased night-time air activity compared to the previous day. Nevertheless, during one of those air attacks, General Kempf was lightly wounded. After having his wounds treated, General Kempf drove to a conference with his division commanders at the headquarters of 24. Panzer-Division. The division commanders reported that reconnaissance for preparations and insertions into the starting areas were progressing as scheduled. It worked out favourably that the preparations for the attack required 24 hours more than was originally planned. Kempf stressed that the armoured Kampfgruppe was not bound to divisional boundaries. First objective of the attack remained the destruction of the enemy near Pestshanka, a thrust to the Volga only being implemented in the second phase. The unfavourable ammunition situation was improved by a compromise with IV. Armeekorps who would supply sufficient ammunition during the course of the day up to the beginning of the attack.

Here again is a look into Obergefreiter Reddig's notebook: "7.9.42: The Russians fire artillery over at us (empty vehicles), Hans Müller being severely wounded in the head. In the positions, Jäckel II was killed, Unteroffizier Kabbeck and 1 man from the squad were wounded."
During the course of the day, the last reconnaissance and movements for the next days assault progressed according to schedule but harassing enemy artillery fire lay on the entire preparation areas of Korps. General von Hauenschild called Korps at 1550 hours and pointed out that tomorrows attack would be very difficult in the beginning because the starting positions of the Division lay under constant artillery and rocket-launcher fire. Oberst Friebe laconically replied that it was already known at Korps headquarters and had been taken into consideration. Leutnant von Hanstein, temporary commander of 4./Kradschützen-Abteilung 4 and described by a fellow commander as a "young, dashing and brave officer" was wounded by this fire but after having his wounds dressed, returned to his command post and resumed command of his unit.

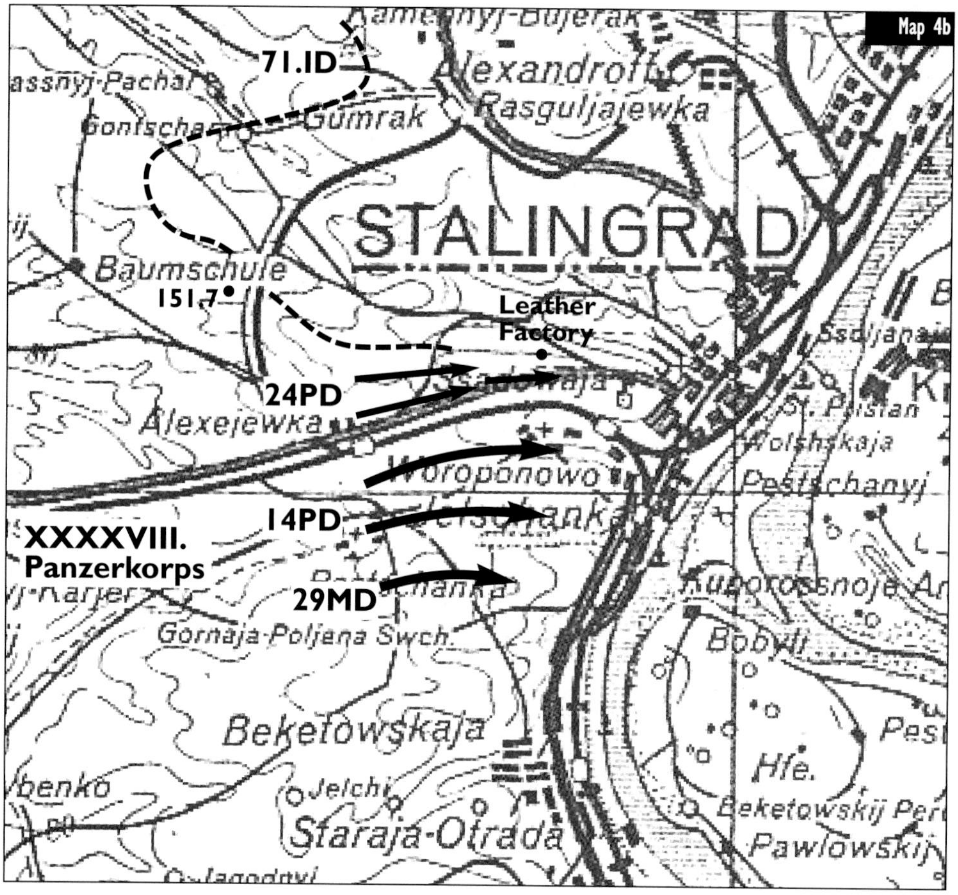

During the entire day, strong enemy artillery, mortar, anti-tank and tank fire lay on the Square Forest, as well as on the hills and gullies west of there. Enemy ground activity consisted of isolated enemy reconnaissance probes against Square Forest – all of which were repulsed. Other than that, the day passed relatively quietly for the Division. General von Hauenschild set up his advanced HQ on Hill 153.2. Panzer numbers: 14 Panzer II, 13 Panzer III kz, 14 Panzer III lg, 4 Panzer IV lg and 2 Bfwg. Fifty deserters and prisoners were taken during the day and the following artillery was silenced: 5 batteries, 2 anti-tank guns, 1 Stalin Organ and 1 anti-aircraft gun. Additionally, found in the Alexeyevka–Voroponovo railway station were 503 goods wagons with war materiel and forty 7.62cm guns. Booty taken since 29th August rose to 15,600 prisoners, 95 tanks, 261 guns, 15 Stalin Organs, 12 aircraft, an ammunition carrier for Stalin Organs, 503 railway wagons, 1 armoured train and numerous war material.

The Division issued Divisionsbefehl Nr. 58 for the attack on 8th September to screen the eastern flank of XXXXVIII. Panzerkorps during its advance towards Stalingrad. The plan was for Gruppe Broich and the southern wing of Gruppe Hellermann to attack to the east and south-east, the spearheads aiming to reach the railway line as the first objective and the double-laned road 2 kilometres south of the Leather Factory as the second objective and ultimately, by constantly pushing to the east, covering the deep flank of Korps attacking further to the south.

While these elements of the Division attacked, the bulk of Gruppe Hellermann would hold the current line. For the attack, the Division's forces were allocated as follows:

Angriffsgruppe Broich[4]:

Panzergrenadier-Regiment 26 (without I. Abteilung)
I./Panzergrenadier-Regiment 21
1./Panzerpionier-Bataillon 40
Panzerartillerie-Regiment 89 (without Stab II. Abteilung, 4. and 5. Batteries)
IV./Panzerartillerie-Regiment 89
Elements of Panzerjäger-Abteilung 670
1. and 3./Flak-Bataillon 602

Abwehrgruppe Hellermann[5]:

Panzergrenadier-Regiment 21 (without I. Abteilung)
Reinforced I./Panzergrenadier-Regiment 26
Pionier-Bataillon 635
2./Panzerpionier-Bataillon 40
Commander of Panzerartillerie-Regiment 89 with 4. and 5. Batteries
Elements of Panzerjäger-Abteilung 670 (3 guns)
One platoon of 1./Panzerjäger-Abteilung 40
3./Kradschützen-Abteilung 4 for the time being (withdrawn as soon as possible with the continuing assault of the northern neighbour, 71. Infanterie-Division.

Division Reserve led by Commander of Panzerpionier-Bataillon 40:

1./Kradschützen-Abteilung 4
Kradschützen-Abteilung 4 (after the beginning of the attack, also temporarily without 3. Schwadron)
I./Flak-Bataillon 5 for air defence
1./Panzerjäger-Abteilung 40 (without a platoon but with a subordinated Vierlingsflak[6])
Panzerpionier-Bataillon 40 (without 1. and 2. Kompanie)

Units of 24. Panzer-Division subordinated to 14. Panzer-Division:

1.) Sicherungsgruppe Sälzer[7]:
Commander of Panzerjäger-Abteilung 40 with 2. Kompanie and a Flak-Zug
2. and 4./Flak-Bataillon 602 (without one platoon)
1./Pionier-Bataillon 651

2.) III./Panzer-Regiment 24 with Panzerpionier Zug and Flak-Zug

---

4. Assault group Broich
5. Defensive group Hellermann
6. Quadruple barrel 20mm anti-aircraft gun
7. Security group Sälzer

Casualties:

5 men killed

- Gefreiter Wilhelm Postleb; PGR21 (Killed)
- Gefreiter Franz Riermeir; PGR21 (Killed)
- Obergefreiter Friedrich Busch; PGR21 (Killed)
- Obergefreiter Rudolf Jäckel; PGR21 (Killed)

1 officer wounded (he stayed with the troops)

- Leutnant Karl-Ludwig von Hanstein (Zug Kdr); 4./K4 (Wounded but stayed with the troops)

42 men wounded (19 of those stayed with the troops)

- Gefreiter Hans Müller; PGR21 (Wounded)
- Unteroffizier Kabbeck; PGR21 (Wounded)

PRELUDE

CHAPTER FIVE

8th September 1942:

After the night passed quietly, Korps set off at 0330 hours as scheduled with the aim of capturing Verkhne-Yelshanka and breaking through to the Volga at Kuperossnoye with 29. Infanterie-Division (mot.) and 14. Panzer-Division, all panzers of Korps being concentrated in Kampfgruppe Lancken near 14. Panzer-Division.
After a comparatively quiet night, 24. Panzer-Division reported that everything was prepared as planned. Gruppe Broich attacked at 0330 hours in a south-east direction, aiming to capture the enemy positions east of Yelshanka, then continuing to push to the east to cover the east flank of Korps, which was attacking to the south. They swiftly broke through the enemy field emplacements in difficult hand-to-hand combat under continued flanking fire. In the meantime, 14. Panzer-Division approached Hill 144.9 with panzers. Resistance and enemy fire was light to begin with. It was somewhat more difficult near 24. Panzer-Division with their spearhead on the railway line, the Russians still offering violent resistance there. Artillery fire also lay on the forest. Resistance and flanking fire was light. Overall, the enemy was surprised and relatively easily overrun. After a short, sharp tussle with a few stubborn Russian troops, 14. Panzer-Division won Hill 144.9 with Kampfgruppe Lancken. 29. Infanterie-Division (mot.) cut through to the southern edge of Verkhne-Yelshanka with forward elements at 0430 hours, thus positioning the division for a further attack in a south-east direction.
Under severe flanking fire out of the left neighbours sector, 24. Panzer-Division took the following area up to about 0600 hours: area 500 metres north of trapezoid-shaped forest, south-east of Verkhne-Yelshanka – bend in railway north of Ssadovoye – 700 metres east and north-east of Hill 147.5. Particularly troublesome flanking fire emanated from the left neighbours (71. Infanterie-Division) sector.

Since the beginning of Korps' assault, Kempf and his chief-of-staff Oberst Friebe had installed themselves at the advanced command post of 14. Panzer-Division where they received reports that the attack of 29. Infanterie-Division (mot.) was making good progress and that the village of Verkhne-Yelshanka was soon passed through. Major von der Lancken's panzers thrust past west of Hill 144.9 but as soon as the panzers moved on and the hill was only being held by weak elements, the Russians counterattacked strongly and retook it. At 0620 hours, General Heim reported to Korps that the fighting had become very hard. He mentioned the loss of Hill 144.9. Kempf ordered 29. Infanterie-Division (mot.) to participate in the attack to the east. In a telephone conversation at 0640 hours, the chief-of-staff of 29. Infanterie-Division (mot.) told Oberst Friebe that the enemy was surprised but strong flanking fire was coming from the direction of the Leather Factory. During the continued advance of 24. Panzer-Division, Kradschützen-Abteilung 29 would take over the security of the east flank.

To prevent the Stukas from bombing the advancing troops, Oberst Friebe informed General Fiebig, Commander of VIII. Fliegerkorps, about the attained line. Air support was needed, however, because the enemy was now very strong and fighting like the devil. The Stukas flying over the battlefield reported that the panzer spearhead was 1.5km west of Novo Pestshanka. Air support was repeatedly requested from VIII. Fliegerkorps on that village. At 0745 hours, Major von Menges informed Oberst Friebe that the spearhead of 24. Panzer-Division was pinned down in front of Trapezoid Forest.

Generaloberst Hoth arrived at Korps headquarters at 0650 hours and was informed that Kempf and Friebe were at the advanced command post. Hoth immediately jumped back into his vehicle and headed toward the advanced command post. Together with several aides, he drove along the street that ran alongside the Kalach–Stalingrad railway. The small Kübelwagen could hardly be seen. Yellow, whirling clouds gushed behind the light-green jeep with the Armee standard fluttering on the bonnet as it swept along the dead street. A pair of horse corpses were lying in a roadside ditch, a burnt-out tank stretched its gun in an empty threat towards the endless blue sky and a confused tangle of torn down telephone wires obstructed the roadway from time to time. The vehicle rolled through the ankle-deep dust, which was like a solid carpet between the dried-up grass.

To the right, on the other side of the low road embankment, was the village of Pestshanka, which the Russians still held with undiminished toughness despite numerous bombardments by the Stukas, fighter-bombers and violent artillery bombardments. The Russian observers in the small village controlled every movement on the road and it was not advisable for vehicles to present themselves as targets to their guns for too long.

Nothing betrayed the proximity of the city. Only rubble, mortar craters and increasing numbers of trenches. Concealed in the sharply-cut gullies stood the batteries whose fire had been drumming the enemy's emplacements since daybreak on this big day of fighting.

The waiting soldiers squatting in their fox-holes cast a quick glance across at the Kübelwagen bearing the flag of the Oberbefehlshaber (Commander-in-Chief) of the Panzer-Armee. There, on the road embankment, where the observation posts were dug into the slope, the vehicle stopped. It was 0800 hours. Generaloberst Hoth accepted the salutes from General Kempf, Oberst Friebe and the division commanders, and through binoculars he inspected the magnificent picture of war, the distant area being painted with gloomy colours. When it was not hazy, the white blocks of flats of Stalingrad could be seen, but hanging over the horizon was a grey veil of smog from the enormous blue-black clouds of smoke that climbed high over the burning huts from nearby villages and were blown by the wind over the battlefield.

The birds of prey constantly circled and the steeply diving Stukas climbed in salute and warning towards dozens of white signal flares with which the panzergrenadiers announced their forward line. Over there on Hill 144.9, where the buildings of the radio station stood, enemy resistance appeared to be the hardest. The mortars placed several salvoes there, raising fireworks of red flashes and a wall of oily smoke over the ridge.

The short barking reports of the guns, the hissing of the enemy's shells flying overhead, the droning of the aircraft engines and the hoarse roar of their onboard weapons mixed into an infernal noise that filled the sky and the earth. A foreign noise was suddenly heard in the din, a noise that allowed sharp hearing and senses to be wide awake: enemy artillery! Smashing into positions in the area, with the tired splinters slapping down on the road embankment, Generaloberst Hoth remained standing, discussing the progress of the attack and further measures with the commanders. The Soviet shells now howled in at regular intervals, the dust mushrooms moving close, then moving further away. A few steps away from Hoth, his Ordonanzoffizier, Rittmeister von Papen, was wounded by a piece of shrapnel flying about, the crew of a Panzerbefehlswagen had casualties and a lorry parked near Hoth's Kübelwagen suffered a direct hit.

The narrow foxholes in the slope of the road embankment were comfortable. Here ran the lines that kept the attack together, each telephone set connected to a Kampfgruppe, and maps and aerial photos spread over a raw wooden table, allowing the course of the attack to be followed almost as though looking through a scissors telescope.

The advance of the units appeared to be slowing down and even stopped under the strong flanking fire from Pestshanka. On no account should the assault break down in this victory-promising stage. Hoth sent a radio message to the sturdy Romanian division with the instruction that they were to take this resistance nest and through that eliminate the flanking fire and make the decisive thrust possible. The commander of the flak battalion[1] employed for ground fighting pointed out the location of the batteries on an aerial photograph. From this advanced command post, Hoth ordered the panzers to continue the advance to the south-east as soon as Hill 144.9 was solidly in German hands. Oberst Friebe passed this order on to the commander of the armoured Kampfgruppe, Major von der Lancken. There was not a moment of peace in the observation post. The Oberbefehlshaber himself held the threads of battle in his hands, tying up considerable masses of enemy strength south of Stalingrad and creating the requirements for an assault on the city itself. The instructions he gave were clear and concise. A few kilometres away were the outskirts of Stalingrad and in the middle of the battlefield, in an inconspicuous fox-hole, the brains working the large battle could be found.

Obergefreiter Walter Reddig wrote in his diary: "8.9.42: (Thursday) Large attack on Stalingrad. First Schwadron in third wave. Unteroffizier Steiner killed. Wachtmeister Kasimir fatally wounded. Scheumann and Jankowski wounded. Division Commander lodged shrapnel."

As noted by Obergefreiter Reddig, Generalmajor Ritter von Hauenschild was severely wounded. This happened shortly after 0900 hours when the General was at the front, reviewing the plans for the attack by Kradschützen-Abteilung 4 and is described by the commander of the communications platoon of that battalion, Leutnant Hubertus Schulz: "On hand was a spread out map, illustrating the planned attack to the Division Commander and the assembled officers of the battalion staff. Everyone was standing in a dug-out, where there was constant, calculated harassing fire from Russian artillery. Suddenly, a shell from a mortar – which as everyone knows cannot be heard approaching, in contrast to an artillery shell – detonated right in the middle of the map. The effect was devastating. Hardly anyone survived, the General was severely wounded and our commander, Rittmeister von der Groeben, was dead on the spot. Only I escaped the terror. When the shell exploded, I had just stooped down to pick up a pencil and was thrown against the dug-out wall by the shell splinters."

Apart from the wounding of the General and the death of Rittmeister Otto von der Groeben, two other officers were killed. They were Oberleutnant Heinz Gerlach and Leutnant Eckart von Schinckel. A further six officers were wounded. A gaping hole had been torn in the officer ranks of 24. Panzer-Division. The elimination of Generalmajor Bruno Ritter von Hauenschild after his severe wounding was a great loss for the Division. The Division lost a commander who

1. From 7th – 8th September at 1430 hours, I./Flak-Regiment 25 had destroyed 20 tanks, including 2 KV1.

was a cavalry genius and a master of large panzer commands, leading it from success to success in its first year after conversion from horses. Command of the Division was taken over by the Brigade Commander, Oberst Freiherr von Broich. After the death of Rittmeister von der Groeben – who'd taken command of the Abteilung barely two weeks earlier – the command of Kradschützen-Abteilung 4 was entrusted to Rittmeister von Langenn-Steinkeller, Commander of 3. Schwadron. The Abteilung Ordonanzoffizier, Leutnant von Ulrici, was also wounded alongside his commander. This position was taken over by Oberwachtmeister Pack from 4. Schwadron. He was soon promoted to Leutnant to reflect his new position. Oberleutnant Egbert von Schmidt-Pauli, Regiment Adjutant of Panzergrenadier-Regiment 21, was also wounded by shrapnel from the same shell. The position of Regiment Adjutant was taken by the Regiment Ordonanzoffizier, Oberleutnant Artur Ferno.

Panzergrenadier-Regiment 21, attacking on the left wing of the Division without panzer support, only gained ground slowly against strong enemy units with tanks in the totally unsurveyable bush terrain, under continuous casualties in massed mortar and Stalin Organ fire. Rittmeister Graf zu Solms' I. Abteilung, together with elements of Panzergrenadier-Regiment 26, took a large barracks-like trench, constructed with wood and straw and camouflaged with foliage. Until 1000 hours, the division took 250 prisoners, 9 tanks, 14 anti-tank guns and 9 guns (not including the tally from Panzer-Abteilung Lancken). Gruppe Broich generally succeeded in gaining the forest east of Yelshanka and the Leather Factory as well as the hill terrain and Kalkberge (lime mountain). The objective was reached. Strengthening artillery and mortar fire was concentrated on the Division, particularly on the north flank which was still being overlooked because 71. Infanterie-Division could not push forward here against the well-emplaced enemy. At 1015 hours the Division had reached the following line: north edge of forest east of Verkhne-Yelshanka – Kalkberge, opposite occupied enemy emplacements. From the north-east corner of this forest to the north ran a lime mountain (Kalkberge), weak enemy infantry but the strongest artillery and

SPANNOCCHI

Conference on the outskirts of Stalingrad (from left): Oblt. Liebe, Major von Winterfeld (seated), Oblt. Raben, Oblt. Schulte (behind Lt. Sylla), Lt. Sylla (back to camera) and Lt. Meya.

SPANNOCCHI

Battle-hardened soldiers of Panzer-Regiment 24 (from left): unknown, Lt. Meya, unknown and Lt. Sylla. Rittmeister Thiel is in the foreground.

mortar fire that operated from north, east and south, making itself particularly noticeable due to its flanking effect.

While Gruppe Broich attacked, Gruppe Hellermann held its positions. Leutnant von Senger und Etterlin watched the attack of his comrades from his trenches dug in between the small pine trees of the Wäldchen: "Panzergrenadier-Regiment 26 attacked early this morning with II. Abteilung through our positions to Minina in the south, and then turned north to the railway line to the east. The attack of this group under Oberst von Edelsheim reached the outskirts. We were pulled back and the following day (9th September) we were lying in reserve in the north-west part of the Wäldchen."

At 1045 hours, the following report of enemy losses from Kampfgruppe Lancken was sent to XXXXVIII. Panzerkorps: 10 T-34, 2 KV1, 1 KV1 damaged, 1 T-60, 14 anti-tank guns, 9 guns, 1 anti-aircraft battery.
The Kampfgruppe had not avoided its own casualties, however. Up until that time, it had suffered five total losses in panzers and a further 33 damaged. These results were fought for under generally heavy casualties. Of the knocked out panzers, 28 were from 24. Panzer-Division. There was also a heavy human toll in valuable panzer commanders: Leutnant Hövel, platoon commander in 9. Schwadron and Leutnant von Falkenhausen, platoon commander in 8. Schwadron, were both lightly wounded and stayed with their men, but Oberleutnants Koch and Schwarz, both platoon commanders in 12. Schwadron, were severely wounded. Forty-year old Oberleutnant Ullrich Schwarz, born in sunny Palermo in Italy, died of his wounds in hospital later in the day.

Gruppe Broich gained ground in Square Forest while the railway, Volga and the southern part of Stalingrad lay under observed fire from German artillery. According to prisoner statements, only weak infantry forces were in Stalingrad but there were masses of artillery. At 1250 hours, Major von Menges reported to Korps that the Leather Factory seemed to have been taken and the Trapezoid Forest reached. No traffic could be seen at the main railway station. Menges then lodged a request with Korps: "If possible, 71. Infanterie-Division should attack to the east to bring relief to our north flank."
Since 1330 hours, the enemy had been observed pushing new forces towards the Kalkberge. From the Kalkberge, the front-line veered back in a north-west direction to the northern half of the previous forest positions in the Square Forest. Division held this attained line, dominating Stalingrad and the Volga River, including the bridge, from the Kalkberge with observed fire. An artillery liaison officer from 71. Infanterie-Division operated from the Division's sector against the southern flank of the enemy in front of 71. Infanterie-Division. Due to the high expenditure of ammunition needed to support the infantry, a very noticeable shortage of ammunition, above all for the light and heavy howitzers, became apparent. The ammunition situation was so severely strained that if large quantities did not arrive for the strong preparatory barrages, the continuation of the assault was in doubt. Korps stressed the importance of ammunition supply to Armee. Later in the afternoon, Armee Chief-of-Staff Oberst Fangohr said that early the next day, 1200 rounds of light howitzer ammunition and 500 rounds each for the light infantry guns, 10cm and 8.8cm guns would be sent to the troops.
At 1452 hours, Major von Menges sent a message to Korps: "Russian artillery and infantry preparations on edge of the city. Impression that the Russians want to thrust toward the Leather Factory." At 1455 hours, Korps transmitted to VIII. Fliegerkorps the report of 24. Panzer-

Division that enemy artillery was overtly driving into open firing positions on the western edge of the city east of the Leather Factory. Intervention by the Luftwaffe was imperative.

As the sun slowly slipped below the western horizon and the sky glowed a lurid red, Major von Menges sent a report to Korps at 1815 hours: "Left neighbour proposes to reach Hill 76.8 tomorrow. It is necessary that something happen there. Russians appear to be planning an attack tomorrow on Square Forest. Right wing has front to the east in Trapezoid Forest." The flanking fire originating from 71. Infanterie-Division's sector was becoming a serious problem and severely hindered all forward movements by 24. Panzer-Division. Nevertheless, the Division's mission was fulfiled but as a consequence of the strong flanking fire from both sides, it was only won with high casualties. The remaining divisions of Korps made good ground but they could not thrust through to the Volga. Kampfgruppe Lancken performed well under the command of 14. Panzer-Division. After capturing the radio station on Hill 144.9 at 1600 hours and clearing weak enemy remnants out of the area, 14. Panzer-Division renewed the assault by thrusting into an enemy defensive front in the direction of Dreihügelgrab with Kampfgruppe Lancken south of the Pestshanka–Novo Pestshanka road. Up until the onset of darkness, despite strong flanking fire from Pestshanka, Dreihügelgrab was taken and several Russian tanks defending it were destroyed. Kampfgruppe Lancken again did not escape casualties – it was practically gutted by the loss of most of its panzers. Fortunately, most of those could be quickly repaired and sent back to the front.

Darkness covered the mangled battlefield, providing excellent cover for the small reconnaissance patrols sent out by all of the Division's front-line units. Their findings seemed promising for a continued assault: only weak enemy forces were located in front of the spearhead of 24. Panzer-Division. In the deep east flank and north-east corner of the large Square Forest, however, the enemy seemed to be steadily reinforcing himself. An enemy attack against defensive group Hellermann in the north was smashed back.

MARK

A panzer of II./Panzer-Regiment 24 leaves its assembly area and heads into the attack.

Once reports had been radioed in from all front-line commanders, Major von Menges compiled the following Tagesmeldung (daily report) and sent it to Korps: "Attained line at the end of the day: north part of Trapezoid Forest (east of Verkhne-Yelshanka) – Leather Factory area – Kalkberge – north-north-west to Tsaritsa Brook – south Tsaritsa Brook – north-west corner Square Forest. Connection to the left exists. It is established to the right. Weakest enemy in front of southern sector, increasingly stronger enemy in northern sector. Particularly strong enemy artillery and mortar activity. The day's casualties are particularly heavy: about 230 men, among them Division Commander wounded, one Abteilung Commander – Rittmeister von der Groeben – was killed, one Abteilung Commander wounded.
"Preliminary booty: 440 prisoners, 10 tanks (21 with Abteilung Lancken), 14 anti-tank guns, 9 guns, 3 aircraft.
"Acute ammunition shortage: s.F.H.[2] only 5%, l.F.H.[3] still only 38% (situation from 1700 hours today).
"Very heavy panzer losses with a total of 28 knocked-out panzers of 47 that began the attack. Panzer situation: 9 Panzer II, 5 Panzer III lg, 4 Panzer III kz, 1 Panzer IV lg and 0 Bfwg."
The figures for booty captured or destroyed by 14. Panzer-Division were 41 tanks, 43 guns and anti-tank guns, 20 motorised vehicles and 11 bunkers with armoured cupolas. The deadly 88mm guns of I./Flak-Regiment 25 shot 15 of the 41 tanks.

Issued at 2015 hours, an Armeebefehl stated that Korps should enclose Stalingrad from the south without itself engaging in local combat. The following missions for 9th September were issued to the divisions:
"29. Infanterie-Division (mot.), together with 14. Panzer-Division, will clear out the south-west corner of the forest east of Hill 144.9, then take over and relieve elements of 14. Panzer-Division to the south, including the radio station. Later missions for the division will be to follow up the attack of 14. Panzer-Division and seal off the southern edge of the city."
"24. Panzer-Division will hold the attained line and reconnoitre in the direction of Stalingrad. An advance of 71. Infanterie-Division in an easterly direction will be taken advantage of."
"14. Panzer-Division, together with 20. Romanian-Division, will occupy Pestshanka under cover of the eastern flank, destroy the enemy located there and clean out the village."
Beginning of the attack is set for 1000 hours.
For the days successful combat, the following acknowledgment from General Kempf is sent to 14. Panzer-Division, 24. Panzer-Division and 29. Infanterie-Division (mot.):
"In hard combat and exemplary fighting spirit, the divisions have attained their daily objectives and with that, produced the conditions required for the continuation of the assault. I express my thanks and complete recognition to the divisions for the achievements of the day."

This day was counted as a Sturmangriffe day for Panzer-Regiment 24:
8.9.42: attack on Verkhne-Yelshanka

2. schwere Feldhaubitze, or heavy howitzers
3. leichte Feldhaubitze, or light howitzers

Casualties:

3 officers killed

- Leutnant Eckart von Schinckel (Killed)
- Rittmeister Otto von der Groeben (Abteilung Kdr); K4 (Killed)
- Oberleutnant Heinz Karl Gerlach (Killed)

38 men killed

- Gefreiter Heinz Schlenther; Pz.Pi.40 (Killed)
- Obergefreiter Wilhelm Leszinski; PGR26 (Killed)
- Gefreiter Werner Günther; PGR21 (Killed)
- Obergefreiter Johann Pfändtner PGR21 (Killed)
- Obergefreiter Franz Stramp; PGR21 (Killed)
- Gefreiter Josef Ernst; PGR21 (Killed)
- Gefreiter Kurt Effta; PGR21 (Killed)
- Hauptwachtmeister Willi Lagies; PGR21 (Killed)
- Unteroffizier Herbert Steiner; PGR21 (Killed)
- Wachtmeister Richard Link; PR24 (Killed)

15 officers wounded (6 of those stayed with the troops)

- Hauptmann Hubert Platz (Abteilung Kdr); III./PAR89 (Wounded)
- Oberleutnant Ullrich Schwarz (Zug Kdr); 12./PR24 (Wounded but died later in the day)
- Oberleutnant Korb (Wounded)
- Leutnant Heinz Hövel (Zug Kdr); 9./PR24 (Wounded but stayed with the troops)
- Oberleutnant Horst Koch (Zug Kdr); 12./PR24 (Wounded)
- Oberleutnant Gerhard von Knobloch (Schwadron Kdr); 5./K4 (Wounded but died later in the day)
- Oberleutnant Hans Peters; Pz.Pi.40 (Wounded)
- Leutnant Egon Reifner (Zug Kdr); 3./Pz.Pi.40 (Wounded but stayed with the troops)
- Oberleutnant Haseroth (Wounded but stayed with the troops)
- Oberleutnant Weiß (Schwadron Kdr); Stab II./PR24 (Wounded but stayed with the troops)
- Oberleutnant Egbert von Schmidt-Pauli (Regiment Adjutant); PGR21 (Wounded)
- Oberstleutnant Fritz von Melchers (Abteilung Kdr); IV./PAR89 (Wounded but stayed with the troops)
- Generalmajor Bruno Ritter von Hauenschild (Division Kdr); 24. Panzer-Division (Wounded)
- Leutnant Alex Frhr. v. Falkenhausen (Zug Kdr); 8./PR24 (Wounded but stayed with the troops)
- Leutnant Gert von Ulrici (Abteilung OO); K4 (Wounded but died the next day)

206 men wounded (54 of those stayed with the troops)

- Wachtmeister Gustav Kasimir; PGR21 (Wounded but died later in the day)
- Scheumann; PGR21 (Wounded)
- Jankowski; PGR21 (Wounded)

9th September 1942:

Apart from the usual enemy artillery activity, the night passed quietly near 24. Panzer-Division. When Oberleutnant Ferno, who'd taken over the adjutancy of Panzergrenadier-Regiment 21 from Oberleutnant von Schmidt-Pauli, did not return during the night from a trip in a motorcycle-sidecar, Wachtmeister Schmah headed out in the morning to search for him. He eventually found him, together with the driver Gefreiter Hermann Lillig, dead near their machine on the road into the Wäldchen. There were several craters scattered around the wreck. They'd apparently driven into the middle of a Stalin Organ salvo. The new Regiment Adjutant was Oberleutnant Dietrich Micke, Abteilung Adjutant of I. Abteilung. His position was taken by Leutnant Dr. Theodor Penners, Commander of 2. Schwadron.

Obergefreiter Ferdinand Kusterer, going about his daily chores, witnessed the carnage of the constant offensives: "At half past four in the morning, I drove into a violet-red dawn with an ammunition lorry to the battery positions. In the vicinity there I found the main dressing station in a gully, known by the Stalingrad fighters as a 'Rachel'. Because vehicles were constantly arriving there, it was easy to find a vehicle that would take me further forward to the rifle schwadrons. At the dressing station, which consisted of a reception tent and operating theatre tent, intense activity dominated. New wounded men continually arrived, and the bandaged men were sent to the rear in ambulances or with the almost vertically taking-off light aircraft 'Fieseler Storch', with that, freeing up another space in the tent. The doctor, who occasionally came out of the front of the tent to smoke a cigarette, looked like a butcher with his blood-flecked rubber apron. He barely had time to eat during the day. When I arrived, two bodies were carried out of the tent. A Wachtmeister had completed his twelve years of service – a head shot. Once again, a family would suffer great sorrow. Here, however, there remained no time to grieve. The wedding ring was quickly slipped off – would his wife have a premonition of it? – the insignia, medals, wallet and valuables were placed into a handkerchief, the Soldbuch was taken and the dog-tags broken in half. One half of this tag remained with the body, then it was buried nearby by medics or, if the opportunity arose, at the divisional cemetery. A dying

MARK

Aid stations and hospitals were set up in gullies west of the city to care for the steady influx of wounded men.

MARK

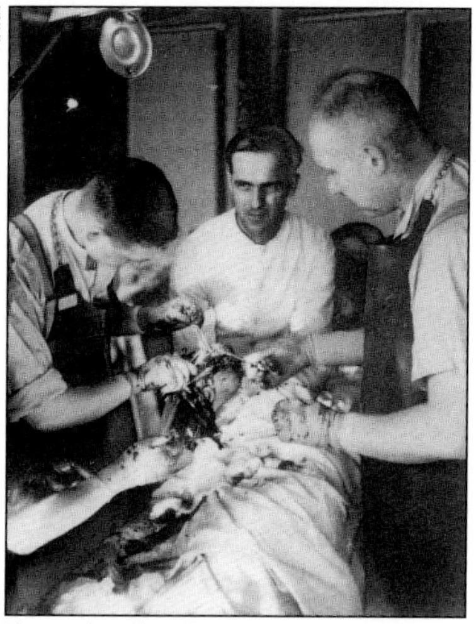

The stark reality of war: surgeons amputate the shattered leg of a wounded man, a procedure carried out innumerable times by the surgeons.

'Hitler Youth' called for his mother and did not want to die for 'Führer, Volk und Vaterland'. The bodies were wrapped in tent-quarters, cleared away and buried somewhere..."

Now lying in reserve in the north-western part of the Wäldchen, Leutnant von Senger und Etterlin and his men did not receive the peace and quiet they had been hoping for: "These reserve positions were very unpleasant, the constant artillery and mortar fire causing continuous casualties. It was again urgently necessary after long weeks of fighting and marching in the steppe, but at last we once again washed our black dirt-encrusted shirts. The tracks were greased, filters and gears were cleaned.

"A direct hit from a mortar struck my vehicle from above, in which the entire crew was having breakfast. The only thing left was a pulpy mass of vehicle innards. The poor men were honourably buried. This was the first vehicle of mine that had become a casualty. Our competent repair troops could put it in running order again. The 1st platoon was disbanded and the others were brought up to full strength. It was very beautiful in our copse when there was no shooting. We listened to the radio and were given canteen goods."

Early in the morning, Kempf arrived at 24. Panzer-Division HQ and spoke with the temporary Division Commander Oberst von Broich about the securing actions of the Division and reconnaissance towards Stalingrad, into the empty vacuum on the north and east flanks of Korps. Kempf also told Broich that 71. Infanterie-Division of the neighbouring Armee had temporarily advanced up to the edge of the forest near Experiment Station Nr. 6, where it remained. A further advance was not planned but was once again indicated. After concluding the brief conference, Kempf then drove to the advanced command post of 14. Panzer-Division to gain an insight into the terrain for further combat actions.

Major von der Lancken and his panzers were part of 14. Panzer-Division in its assault on the village of Pestshanka. Korps was kept informed about the course of the attack courtesy of a stream of radio messages:

"1100 hours. Pestshanka completely in flames. Riflemen apparently very close to the village."

"1110 hours. Our panzers have taken the small forest east of Farm Nr. 2 (south of Pestshanka)."

"1115 hours. Our troops in Pestshanka, several Russians in foxholes north-west of Pestshanka. Eight Russian bombers attacked our troops in Pestshanka."

Once the capture of Pestshanka had been confirmed, Oberst Friebe called Armee HQ at 1130 hours: "Pestshanka taken at 1120 hours, will go on to Dreihügelgrab and the bridge after straightening." 14. Panzer-Division had taken Pestshanka by attack from the east but was still involved in protracted fighting against the enemy in emplacements west of that village. The bulk of that division prepared itself until 1400 hours in the area around Hill 143.5 for an advance through Novo Pestshanka to the east. At 1315 hours, General Heim reported to Oberst Friebe that south of Pestshanka, strong enemy groups were still in the mill and also in the terrain up to Dreihügelgrab. These had to be cleared out first. It was questionable whether 14. Panzer-Division could still advance toward the Volga in large numbers. Even after clearing the enemy out of Pestshanka, 14. Panzer-Division wasn't able to wrap up the fighting around the emplacements west of Pestshanka. The division had until now destroyed 21 tanks, captured 46 guns and over 1000 prisoners.

SPANNOCCHI

Conference on Stalingrad's outskirts (from left): unknown, Oberleutnant Raben and Leutnant Otto, both from the staff of I. /Pz.Rgt. 24.

While 14. Panzer-Division was struggling in tough combat in the hills south-west of Stalingrad, 24. Panzer-Division was having a comparatively quiet day. At 1330 hours, Major von Menges reported a minor Russian attack to Korps: "At the moment, attack with strong artillery preparation on north-east corner of Square Forest. Request air support." During the course of the day, 24. Panzer-Division repelled several enemy attacks in battalion and regiment strength with strong artillery support against the positions in the Square Forest and south of the Division. Further offensive preparations from strong enemy forces east of Square Forest were recognised, so Division demanded Stukas to crush the massing Russian forces. Korps immediately contacted VIII. Fliegerkorps: "Air support on enemy attacking 24. Panzer-Division (with artillery on city edge) from north-east corner of Square Forest." VIII. Fliegerkorps' response: "Promised in about 1 – 1 ½ hours." Oberst von Broich knew that Stukas alone could not stop a large enemy assault so, to strengthen the defensive front, he urgently requested the re-subordination of Gruppe Sälzer[4] as soon as possible, recently freed up by the capture of Pestshanka. The request to have Gruppe Sälzer re-subordinated was answered from the aspect of Korps in an order at 1600 hours, with the following teletype message also being sent to 14. Panzer-Division: "After completion of fighting around Pestshanka, Gruppe Sälzer is to be returned to 24. Panzer-Division."

After threatening to attack the Division's lines throughout the day, the enemy finally launched an attack at dusk. At 1838 hours, Oberst von Broich reported the outcome to General Kempf: "Attack near 24. Panzer-Division smashed back. In general, artillery and mortar fire. How far 71. Infanterie-Division has advanced cannot be ascertained." Half an hour later, Division reported to Korps: "A little quieter this evening. Enemy has dug himself in. How far 71. Infanterie-Division has advanced is still not clear." The Division's daily report was also submitted to Korps: "Forward line unchanged: North edge Trapezoid Forest (in the centre) – Leather Factory (about on 'L') – to north-east on Kalkberge – edge of forest – then bent backwards to 37.0 – along Tsaritsa Brook.

"Connection on right wing with II./15 secured north edge of Trapezoid Forest.

"Booty: 600 prisoners. 10 guns silenced, several anti-tank guns and mortars destroyed by artillery.

"Panzer situation: 11 Panzer II, 6 Panzer III kz, 10 Panzer III lg, 1 Panzer IV lg, 2 Bfwg."

On this day, 2300 prisoners were taken by Korps.

4. Subordinated to 14. Panzer-Division.

At 1930 hours, an Armeebefehl was issued stating that Korps would clear the enemy out of the area south-west of Stalingrad and encircle the city from the south and west so that every enemy break-out attempt could be smothered. Apart from that, an attack on the actual city itself was to be prepared. 94. Infanterie-Division was subordinated to Korps, the chief-of-staff of the division reporting to Korps at 1710 hours. For 10th September, Division received the following mission: "24. Panzer-Division will hold the attained line and clear out the Tsaritsa Brook area, corresponding to the advance of 71. Infanterie-Division."
Toward 2000 hours, the enemy launched weak reconnaissance probes against Gruppen Dressler and Heyden. The enemy was repulsed and 15 prisoners were taken.

This day was counted as a Sturmangriffe day for Panzer-Regiment 24:
9.9.42: attack on Pestshanka

Casualties:

1 officer killed

- Oberleutnant Artur Ferno (Regiment Ordonanzoffizier); PGR21 (Killed)

9 men killed

- Unteroffizier Karl Kluwe; Pz.Pi.40 (Killed)
- Gefreiter Johann Hollubarsch; PGR26 (Killed)
- Unteroffizier Werner Hans Geissler; PGR21 (Killed
- Gefreiter Hermann Lillig; PGR21 (Killed)
- Gefreiter Herbert Bromand; K4 (Killed)

1 officer wounded (he stayed with the troops)

- Leutnant Prinz zu Oettingen (Zug Kdr); 6./PGR21 (Wounded but stayed with the troops)

104 men wounded (48 of those stayed with the troops)

- Obergefreiter Otto Meyhöfer; PGR21 (Wounded but died on 10th September in hospital)

1 man missing

10th September 1942:

The night passed quietly. Enemy reconnaissance probes against the Division's sector were repulsed. The constant menace of enemy patrols – not to mention the fear of being snatched – kept the grenadiers alert. In the Square Forest in front of Panzergrenadier-Regiment 21, the enemy appeared to have reinforced himself during the night.

The day started on a high for the entire Korps when 29. Infanterie-Division (mot.) reached the Volga. In one of its telegrams, Korps' reaction was summed up in five words: "Spearhead on the Volga, marvellous!" At 1045 hours, Hoth arrived at Korps HQ. Generaloberst Hoth, General

Kempf and Oberst Friebe discussed the further conduct of the attack on Stalingrad. Hoth wanted to conduct the attack from the south and was of the opinion that this attack would lead to success with few casualties. Upon the advice from Kempf that it was absolutely essential for the attack that 71. Infanterie-Division move up to the same level, Hoth said he would arrange for corresponding measures with the neighbours on the left. The target date of the assault was still to be decided but it was tentatively set for 12th September. At 1120 hours, General Pfeiffer, Division Commander of 94. Infanterie-Division, and his chief-of-staff also arrived at Korps HQ. On the basis of the new situation from the course of the morning, Oberst Friebe proposed that 94. Infanterie-Division be employed between 29. Infanterie-Division (mot.) and 24. Panzer-Division, beginning with the sector between Yelshanka and the Voroponovo-Stalingrad railway line. The bulk of 24. Panzer-Division was tied down and would therefore not be able to support the attack of 29. Infanterie-Division (mot.).

For 24. Panzer-Division, the entire morning passed quietly. Kradschützen-Abteilung 4 improved its positions by capturing a few enemy posts. The attained line was sturdily held by the Division but when an opportunity to attain better positions was presented, they took full advantage. On the southern wing, a thrust by 29. Infanterie-Division (mot.) was utilised and the right wing was shifted forward and with that, a straight line was established with 29. Infanterie-Division (mot.). This was reported by Major von Menges to Korps at 1235 hours: "Edelsheim conducted an attack from Leather Factory to the east, together with Kradschützen-Abteilung 4 and another battalion. Attack as planned only the day after tomorrow. One schwadron south of the railway line pushed into the first houses, a weak spot seemingly there." Weak enemy artillery fire harassed the forward lines of 24. Panzer-Division. The ordered relief by 94. Infanterie-Division was started and was scheduled to be completed on the morning of 11th September. The Division also received some other welcome relief. Gruppe Sälzer, re-subordinated to Division, arrived in the divisional sector in the area west of Yelshanka. The Gruppe was not complete, however: one Kompanie of Panzerjäger-Abteilung 40 would be set in march the next day to Sety for retraining on 7.62cm Panzerjäger Selbstfahrlafette.
Deserter statements and reconnaissance revealed that enemy casualties in Square Forest were extremely high. From attacking battalions, only 10-15 men were still available and these units had received no relief since first meeting 24. Panzer-Division. The backbone of the enemy defence was the countless batteries of artillery, built up over the past few weeks into tremendous concentrations. This massing of artillery resulted from the fact that numerous units had been compressed into the city with their backs against the Volga and was compounded when front-line infantry units melted away in the fierce fighting, leaving the artillery units in the rear. Heavier artillery units had also begun to be stationed on the east shore of the Volga, free to fire into the attacking Germans from behind their vast watery moat. An enemy armoured train was even observed firing south of Stalingrad railway station. It soon drew down a hail of artillery and was severely damaged but was apparently not destroyed. It is not known how it escaped the gaze of the German artillery observers.
Booty: 30 prisoners, several direct hits on batteries and an ammunition dump, 1 Stalin Organ destroyed, 3 damaged, 1 armoured train damaged. On this day, Korps took 2,400 prisoners. Kampfgruppe Lancken still contained 6 Panzer II, 7 Panzer III lg, 6 Panzer III kz, 3 Panzer IV lg and 2 Bfwg.
Division received its mission for 11th September from Korps: "The Division will hold its positions and regroup itself after the relief of divisional elements positioned south of the railway line by 94. Infanterie-Division, so that on 12th September they can join up on their

right wing with a Stoßgruppe for the attack of Korps on Stalingrad. The settlement of the north flank, together with 71. Infanterie-Division, is to be further strived for."

This day was counted as a Sturmangriffe day for Panzer-Regiment 24:
10.9.42: attack on Dreihügelgrab (Three Knoll Trench)

Casualties:

4 men killed

• Obergefreiter Laurenz Johnen; Pz.Jg.40 (Killed)

2 officers wounded (1 of those stayed with the troops)

• Assistenarzt Dr. Kleinjohann; II./PGR26 (Wounded but stayed with the troops)
• Leutnant Fritz Binkow (Zug Kdr); 5./PGR26 (Wounded)

28 men wounded (10 of those stayed with the troops)

11th September 1942:

The scheduled relief by elements of 94. Infanterie-Division was not carried out during the night because they didn't arrive. Messages and inquiries sent to 94. Infanterie-Division and Korps did not resolve the issue and with the rising of the sun, there was no possibility of relief taking place on this morning. During the night, an enemy tank caused a mild panic when it broke through the front-line, fired wildly and then withdrew, intact and well-satisfied with its surprise attack. Apart from a disturbed nights sleep, there was not much damage inflicted upon the Division. Most importantly, no lives were lost. Otherwise, the night passed quietly.

Obergefreiter Reddig noted the following in his diary: "11.9.42. At 0430 hours, I drove to Schwadron with coffee. Cook Augustin was organising pigs for the kitchen when he was severely wounded by a Stalin Organ. In the positions, Paul Tureck was lightly wounded in the neck, Oberwachtmeister Eisen came to the vehicles in the evening and drove to the dressing station for an eye operation. Coming out of the positions to the vehicles due to wounds or sickness were Oberwachtmeister Grannas, Unteroffizier Bettko, Unteroffizier Biernath (burst eardrum and suppurated ears)."

Under sunny morning skies, General Kempf turned up at the headquarters of 24. Panzer-Division, arriving around 0800 hours. Oberst von Broich, the Division Commander, oriented him about the situation. The Division's lines were steady and with every passing day, the fronts of the neighbouring units pushed eastward, aligning with 24. Panzer-Division and gradually eliminating the harmful flanking fire. The southern wing of the Division was covered but the northern flank was still open, and this was confirmed to Kempf when they both drove forward a short distance to the command post of Panzergrenadier-Regiment 21 where the Regiment Commander, Oberstleutnant von Hellermann, briefed Kempf about the forward line in his area and in particular pointed out that the enemy flanking fire was being caused by 71. Infanterie-Division lagging behind and that it was causing continuous casualties. Kempf said he would

Combat and Ration strengths on 11th September 1942

Units	Combat strength				Ration strength				
	Offz.	Beamte	Uffz.	Men	Offz.	Beamte	Uffz.	Men	**Total**
Division Staff	18	10	36	137	30	10	56	234	**330**
Pz.Gren.Brigade 24	2	–	7	26	2	–	18	69	**89**
Pz.Rgt. 24	41	8	437	1174	44	15	556	1687	**2302**
Pz.Gren.Rgt. 21	30	3	263	1125	33	4	271	1132	**1440**
Pz.Gren.Rgt. 26	28	5	264	1424	33	5	278	1481	**1797**
Krad.Abt. 4	14	–	156	763	16	2	167	787	**972**
Pz.Art.Rgt. 89	39	–	220	1163	43	9	283	1500	**1835**
Pz.Jg.Abt. 40	12	1	75	399	15	3	80	409	**507**
Pz.Pi.Btl. 40	13	–	64	527	14	3	82	568	**667**
Pz.Nach.Abt. 86	6	–	62	321	14	2	94	411	**521**
Dinafü. 40	–	–	–	–	29	16	174	1070	**1289**
SanKo. 1./40	–	–	–	–	7	3	31	178	**219**
SanKo. 2./40	–	–	–	–	6	3	25	151	**185**
Bäckerei Ko. 40	–	–	–	–	1	1	19	119	**140**
Schlächterei Ko. 40	–	–	–	–	2	1	9	64	**76**
Verpfl. Amt 40	–	–	–	–	–	9	13	86	**108**
Feldpostamt 40	–	–	–	–	–	18	–	8	**26**
Feldgend. Trupp 40	–	–	–	–	2	–	39	16	**57**
Sum:	**203**	**27**	**1584**	**7059**	**293**	**104**	**2195**	**9970**	**12560**
Subordinated Units									
Flak Bataillon 602	12	–	93	472	12	3	103	504	**622**
RAD Gruppe K 22									**640**
I./Ersatz Bataillon I	1	–	21	128	1	–	21	128	**150**
Pz.Jg.Abt. 670	9	–	44	125	11	4	82	252	**349**
I./Flak Regiment 5	17	5	120	930	20	5	156	899	**1080**
Total:	**242**	**32**	**1862**	**8714**	**337**	**116**	**2557**	**11753**	**15401**

talk to the neighbouring Korps commander again to see if this could be resolved. 24. Panzer-Division had been handicapped by its open north flank for a week.

The course of the morning passed quietly for 24. Panzer-Division. At 1420 hours, they reported to Korps that with the exception of artillery and mortar fire, the day had passed quietly and the forward line was unchanged. Relief by 94. Infanterie-Division would be carried out with the onset of darkness. Slowly, the Division was regaining its strength as certain sectors were relieved and units subordinated to other divisions were returned. There was still one very important component missing. Panzers. The Division had been without its panzers for four days. What use was a panzer division without panzers? Oberst von Broich decided to fix this situation. He had his chief-of-staff, the ever-reliable Major von Menges, telephone Korps HQ at 1500 hours. He spoke with Oberst Friebe and Menges came straight to the point: "Regarding the return of the panzers?"
Friebe: "Because of pressure to the north today and tomorrow, that cannot be reckoned on. We ourselves have the greatest interest in the panzers being withdrawn."
At 1630 hours, however, Oberst Friebe phoned back and reported that the panzers were being withdrawn from 14. Panzer-Division. The panzers, concentrated in Korps for the attack on 8th September, were finally being returned to the division. They would only arrive on the morning of 12th September. Kampfgruppe Lancken reported that it still had 4 Panzer II, 6 Panzer III kz, 2 Panzer III lg, 2 Panzer IV lg and 2 Bfwg.

At 1800 hours, the following Panzer-Armee-Tagesbefehl was issued by Hoth:

> "The battle around Stalingrad has reached its climax. Thanks to the extraordinary achievements of the troops, in three weeks of fighting we have succeeded in pushing up to the edge of the city and encircling it from the south and west. It is now vital to take Stalingrad together with the neighbours, and with that, complete the defeat of the enemy.
> "The enemy also knows what is now at stake. In the message to the Red Army which was broadcast on Moscow radio on 8th September, he said:
> "'The enemy advances towards the old Russian river, the Volga. Our continued existence now hangs on the results of the battles that are now being violently fought out. Not one step back! Stand until death! This is the proclamation of our nation. The Russians have always defeated the Prussians. The militaristic tradition of the Russian people lives in the heroic acts of the Soviet fighters.'
> "I know of your previous exertions and the privations imposed on us by this land, I know the sacrifices that this fighting has cost us, but I also know that your sense of duty, your soldierly courage and your conviction will get you through this battle until the end. That demands our honour, the soldiers' death of our best and the homeland watches us with bated breath. This gives me the certainty that 4. Panzer-Armee will succeed in wrenching Stalingrad, the city of Stalin, away from the Soviets.
> "The fame won will be unforgettable for you, the German Army and your descendants.
> "It comes down to each man. Everyone will double their strength. The weight of German weapons will break the last of the enemy's will to resist.
> "Long live the Führer!
>
> Der Oberbefehlshaber
> signed Hoth"

The preceding proclamation was immediately made known to the troops.

Preparations for the assault on 12th September in the direction of Stalingrad began. The plan was that XXXXVIII. Panzerkorps, with 14. Panzer-Division and 29. Infanterie-Division (mot.), would attack out of the Yelshanka area along the Volga to the north-east. In the Korpsbefehl issued at 1800 hours, 24. Panzer-Division received the following combat mission: "24. Panzer-Division will hold its positions and participate in the attack of Korps on Stalingrad with an assault group on the right wing and initially take into possession the group of houses east of the Leather Factory. Further advances into the city depend upon the development of the situation."

The Division issued Divisionsbefehl Nr. 59 which called for the attack on Stalingrad itself on 12th September. Gruppe Hellermann was weakened up to its limits to supply as many men as possible to Angriffsgruppe Edelsheim. A sign that ferocious enemy defence was expected is shown by the fact that all flamethrowers from Panzerpionier-Bataillon 40 were incorporated into Edelsheim's combat group, as well as 5 self-propelled 76.2mm guns from Panzerjäger-Abteilung 670 and two of the formidable 88mm anti-aircraft guns. Several 20mm anti-aircraft guns mounted on half-tracks were also attached, not for air defence but for use in sweeping away tough enemy resistance. Oberst von Broich and his staff were completely aware of the new type of fighting into which they were about to plunge and issued appropriate instructions to their troops about what would be needed for combat in the city. These included:

- Forming of assault groups and attaching flamethrowers, anti-aircraft and anti-tank guns, as well as individual artillery pieces, for house-to-house fighting. Explosives and hand grenades should be supplied in quantity to the assault spearheads.

- Thrusting in several deep columns along the streets with good radio communications.

- Leaping up to corner houses and eliminating them first of all. As far as was possible, they should not be broken in to frontally.

- Assaults being swiftly followed up by panzers and half-tracks.

- Reckoning that all public buildings and factories will be mined. It was advised that prisoners and the local population should be questioned as quickly as possible about mining. Translators with 1:20,000 city maps were on hand at the divisional command post. Immediate signposting of suspected mined areas should be carried out.

- Informing all members of the Division of the order regarding plundering and securing of available enemy supply dumps. This order forbade soldiers from plundering enemy stocks but ordered them to report it so they could be used to supplement the supply of German armed forces.

Near 24. Panzer-Division, the relief of the divisional elements employed south of the railway line began with the onset of darkness. 94. Infanterie-Division was inserted between 24. Panzer-Division and 29. Infanterie-Division (mot.) during the night. It had not been an eventful day for the Division. Prisoners and amount of booty: 80 prisoners and 1 tank.

This day was counted as a Sturmangriffe day for Panzer-Regiment 24:
11.9.42: attack on north Pestshanka and the hills south of there

Casualties:

4 men killed

- Gefreiter Erich Maczernies; PGR26 (Killed)

4 officers wounded (2 of those stayed with the troops)

- Oberleutnant Heinrich Prinz von Reuß (Abt Adjutant); I./PGR26 (Wounded)
- Oberarzt Lücke (Wounded but stayed with the troops)
- Rittmeister Emil Spannocchi (Schwadron Kdr); 2./PR24 (Wounded)
- Leutnant Horst Freiherr von Quadt (Zug Kdr); Aufklärung Zug, Stab/PR24 (Wounded but stayed with the troops)

84 men wounded (33 of those stayed with the troops)

- Cook Augustin; PGR21 (Wounded)
- Paul Tureck; PGR21 (Wounded)
- Oberwachtmeister Eisen; PGR21 (Wounded)
- Oberwachtmeister Grannas; PGR21 (Wounded)
- Unteroffizier Bettko; PGR21 (Wounded)
- Unteroffizier Biernath; PGR21 (Wounded)

12th September 1942:

During the night, Russian planes were once again active over the heads of German troops but at dawn, the fighters of the Luftwaffe appeared and quickly scared off the last Russian planes, which disappeared to the east into the dazzling morning sun that had just peaked over the horizon. The Russians had maintained light artillery harassment fire throughout the night and early morning. Elements of the Division in the sector south of the railway line were relieved by 94. Infanterie-Division, as scheduled. Panzer Abteilung Lancken, arriving in the divisional area early in the morning, was drawn forward.
With the Schwerpunkt concentrated on the right with Gruppe Edelsheim, the Division set off at 0700 hours after a short artillery barrage, attacking in the direction of Stalingrad with the limited objective of the projecting residential quarter on the western edge of the city. When I./Panzergrenadier-Regiment 21 advanced out of the forest toward the Leather Factory about 2700 metres west of the station, violent defensive fire forced the Schwadrons to ground for the time being. Obergefreiter Reddig reports the casualties sustained by his 1. Schwadron: "12.9.42. We attacked on entire sector. Bolz killed, Unteroffizier Döring, Obergefreiter Fleischer, Marewski, Sikorra, Karl Loehr wounded. Russians fired sporadically with artillery over to our vehicles."

At 0900 hours, the assault group was only slowly moving forward. Half an hour later, after costly combat in difficult terrain, the factory area north of the railway line – the first attack objective – was captured against heavy flanking fire from the north, a total of about 1km of ground being gained. Enemy tanks poised on the edge of the city slowly crawled forward. Even though the factory was captured, clearing actions and heavy fighting would continue deep into the afternoon as small nests of Russian resistance – phoenix-like – kept rising out of the ruins. An enemy counterattack collapsed after a few critical moments thanks to the excellently directed fire of Panzerartillerie-Regiment 89. At 0955 hours, there was strong artillery fire from the north and Russian tanks were seen moving about in the area. North of the so-called two-laned road, the enemy that seemed to be retreating was actually moving forward. The spearheads of Korps had come up against a very toughly defending enemy and only moved forward slowly due to heavy flanking fire, whose elimination was possible only to a limited extent because of severe ammunition shortages. A further hindrance was the strongly-constructed bunker positions.

At around 1215 hours, 24. Panzer-Division established a good connection with neighbouring units to the south, the enemy retreating slowly ahead of the advancing panzers and riflemen. Soon after, it was decided that to get the most benefit out of the available air assets, the Luftwaffe would now only be used to support 24. Panzer-Division and 94. Infanterie-Division because 29. Infanterie-Division (mot.) had been left behind. As the enemy tried to retreat in front of the southern wing of Gruppe Edelsheim, they were immediately followed up by another attack of the last reserves of the division at 1300 hours into the south-west corner of Objective 11, and the edge of the city won. This last reserve consisted of two schwadrons, including Leutnant von Senger und Etterlin's unit. After resting for a few days in the dangerous reserve positions in the Wäldchen, Leutnant von Senger und Etterlin and his men of 2./K4 – held in reserve as part of Gruppe Edelsheim – were again called to the front-line for this attack to exploit the initial success already won by Edelsheim: "We are pulled forward again today for the renewed assault to the river through the southern part of the city and are placed under the von Heyden Abteilung[5].

"We assembled in a hollow in the region of the Leather Factory, on the left flank of the Abteilung. From here, we had a steady assault with the objective 'Barracks Hill'; this was a large white building on a hill about 1 kilometre away from us. Towards midday, we attacked in deep formation. We moved forward over several hundred metres of good, clear terrain. We suddenly came under strong defensive fire and I knew that about 100 metres in front of me was a small cross gully and a small field but behind it were strong, well-camouflaged enemy positions. I decided to fire as quickly as possible and my platoon crept in and reached the small gully, where we first took a breather.

"I saw that 70 metres in front of us, within the enemy's defensive system, was a field howitzer now shooting directly at us with shrapnel. I called together my squad leaders and ordered the MG-34's to give covering fire. On my whistle we would make a sudden fire attack with 5 machine-guns on the gun and then after that, leap forward into the breach. Under cover-fire of one squad which remained in the gully, both of the other squads leapt out towards the enemy positions. We threw hand grenades while running and several Russians tried to flee. We leapt into the positions and the remaining Russians were overpowered with sub-machine guns and bayonets. I inspected the gun and counted 80 indentations on the gunshield from my machine-guns.

"I at once arranged for defence, then 100 metres from us where the bushy terrain began, several enemy tanks suddenly appeared, rumbled back and forth and before I knew it, they had gone."

---

5. Major Hans-Wilhelm von Heyden's II./Panzergrenadier-Regiment 26 forming part of Angriffsgruppe Edelsheim.

Rittmeister Ernst-Hasse von Langenn-Steinkeller, Commander of Kradschützen-Abteilung 4, narrowly escaped death while closely monitoring the attack: "As Commander of Kradschützen-Abteilung 4, I followed the attack of my schwadrons toward the outer districts of Stalingrad. Escorted by a messenger, I moved through a meandering gully to be able to better direct the fighting. Coming towards me was one of our wounded men who was still able to move by himself. I pointed out to him where he could find the dressing station and continued on. Already a short distance from him, it occurred to me that the wounded man would have difficulties climbing a half-metre high ledge at the foot of the gully. Therefore I turned around and went back to help him. When I returned to continue toward the enemy, a shell exploded exactly on the spot where I would've been had I not turned back to help the wounded man. Within the confines of the gully, the shellburst would have been fatal for my messenger and myself."

BUNDESARCHIV, BILD 146/III-499 PHOTO: UNKNOWN

Rittmeister Ernst-Hasse von Langenn-Steinkeller, former commander of 3./Kradschützen-Abteilung 4. He took command of the Abteilung on 8th September 1942 after the previous commander, Rittmeister von der Groeben, was killed.

Gruppe Hellermann and the northern half of Gruppe Edelsheim came to a standstill with fronts to the east and north-east. The front to the north-east was forced upon both Gruppen in an effort to negate the heavy flanking fire coming from that direction. The enemy holding opposite Gruppe Hellermann was unchanged but in front of Gruppe Edelsheim, the enemy again tried to position himself in the Barracks and around Objective 8 with tanks, infantry and artillery. In the afternoon, Division pushed into grid square 04 hard north of the railway line. There were numerous bunkers on the right along the railway line. The further aim was to push forward the southern wing of Gruppe Hellermann towards evening, if the situation permitted it, and form a bridgehead in Objective 11. The southern wing of Gruppe Hellermann participated in an attack to maintain a connection with Edelsheim. Besides that, they checked several enemy attacks which were well supported by tanks. Up to this time, the Division had suffered at least 80 wounded and taken 50 prisoners.

At 1700 hours, Oberst i.G. Clausius, Chief-of-Staff of LI. Armeekorps, talked to Oberst Friebe by phone: "We are only progressing very slowly."

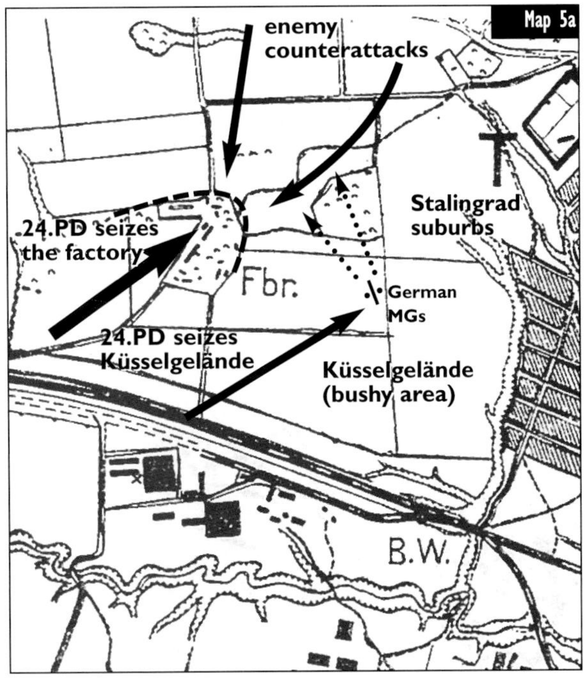

Friebe: "We are suffering considerably under flanking fire. It is somewhat better in the centre. It is our greatest wish that 71. Infanterie-Division advance, to create some room for us in the north."
LI. Armeekorps planned to press forward with 71. Infanterie-Division and help XXXXVIII. Panzerkorps eliminate flanking fire from the north: "We will at least reach the edge of the city everywhere tomorrow. Then continue to advance in the direction of the main railway station."

Towards 1800 hours, the area south-east of the factory was taken. This factory, located on open ground north of the Stalingrad-Voroponovo railway line and west of Stalingrad's sprawling mass of proletarian suburbs, would need to be taken if the attack were to continue to push freely into the city. The enemy defending the southern and western outskirts of the factory fought grimly and had to be destroyed in hand-to-hand fighting. The grenadiers then assumed temporary defensive positions in and around the factory. A few minutes after they settled into hastily excavated foxholes, several rapid enemy attacks with tanks washed towards them from the north and north-east. All attacks were repulsed. At this point, 24. Panzer-Division was deployed as follows: two schwadrons with forward edge in the first house with front to the east and north-east in grid square 04 south-west, two schwadrons in the factory area with fronts to the east and north. A connection between both groups was not available as a result of a shortage of reserves. The course of the front-line in front of Gruppe Hellermann remained unchanged.
At 1820 hours against stubborn enemy resistance, another assault group took the Küsselgelände (bush terrain), located hard east of the factory and between the factory and western edge of Stalingrad. Seeing that an enemy attack was heading towards the factory located to their west, the men of this group were able to set up their machine-guns and fire into the flank of the Russian attack. They also contributed to the repulsion of several more attacks before the Russians realised the futility. After the capture of the factory, the total number of enemy soldiers captured during the day rose to 80 prisoners and 100 deserters. The total amount of booty taken since 29th August rose to 16,800 prisoners, 239 tanks, 512 guns, 15 rocket-launchers and numerous other war materiel. Panzer situation: 8 Panzer II, 2 Panzer III kz, 7 Panzer III lg, 1 Panzer IV kz, 4 Panzer IV lg, 2 Bfwg.
The following combat mission for 13th September was issued to the Division: "24. Panzer-Division will hold the attained positions. By pushing forward the southern wing along the railway line, the north flank of 94. Infanterie-Division will be covered."

Casualties:

1 officer killed

- Leutnant Heinz Lakenbrink (Zug Kdr); 3./PGR21 (Killed)

26 men killed

- Obergefreiter Rudolf Schneider; PGR26 (Killed)
- Obergefreiter Gerd Heine; PGR26 (Killed)
- Obergefreiter Günter Schilling; PGR26 (Killed)
- Obergefreiter Wilhelm Kühn; PGR26 (Killed)
- Gefreiter Heinz Freudenthal; PGR26 (Killed)
- Obergefreiter Johann Unger; PGR26 (Killed)
- Obergefreiter Otto Busack; PGR26 (Killed)
- Obergefreiter Kurt Schiebeck; PGR26 (Killed)
- Obergefreiter Gerhard Rozewski; PGR21 (Killed)
- Gefreiter Werner Liebig; PGR21 (Killed)
- Obergefreiter Kurt Kühl; PGR21 (Killed)
- Panzergrenadier Heinrich Werlemann; PGR21 (Killed)
- Gefreiter Werner Bolz; PGR21 (Killed)
- Gefreiter Manfred Stoebe; PGR21 (Killed)

7 officers wounded (5 of those stayed with the troops)

- Leutnant Mangels (Wounded)
- Leutnant Segger (Zug Kdr); 10./PGR21 (Wounded but stayed with the troops)
- Leutnant Helwig Luz (Zug Kdr); 10./PR24 (Wounded but stayed with the troops)
- Leutnant Hellmuth Reymann (Zug Kdr); 3./PGR26 (Wounded but stayed with the troops)
- Rittmeister Arnold von Dressler (Abt Kdr); I./PGR26 (Wounded but stayed with the troops)
- Oberleutnant Eugen Weckesser (Schwadron Kdr); 4./PGR26 (Wounded but stayed with the troops)
- Hauptmann Rolf Weyer; IV./PAR89 (Wounded)

163 men wounded (120 of those stayed with the troops)

- Unteroffizier Döring; PGR21 (Wounded)
- Obergefreiter Hermann Fleischer; PGR21 (Wounded)
- Marewski; PGR21 (Wounded)
- Sikorra; PGR21 (Wounded)
- Karl Loehr; PGR21 (Wounded)

3 men missing

13th September 1942:

During the night, strong enemy bombing attacks began on the forward line and no longer ceased during the entire fighting in front of Stalingrad. Through rolling sorties, alternating between low-level and high-level enemy attacks, the troops received no rest during the night, watchful as they were of personal and material casualties. Despite every endeavour, an active defence was not completely successful. The available searchlights were too weak and numbers too small and night-fighters were not available in the entire Armee area. On the basis of the morning reports about enemy air activity, Kempf spoke to Hoth by phone and requested night-fighter support and more searchlights. At 0945 hours, Oberst Fangohr from Armee HQ called General Kempf and said that all searchlights of Romanian VI. Armeekorps and IV. Armeekorps were attached to XXXXVIII. Panzerkorps, effective immediately.

At 0855 hours, Hauptmann Roth, O1 of 24. Panzer-Division, reported to Korps that the north wing had advanced around 100 metres. At 1017 hours, however, he had to call Korps and tell them that the right wing was pinned down in front of bunkers. And there it remained, the situation and forward line unchanged. A connection with the right neighbour was available along the railway line. As before, the enemy fought toughly and grimly. Strong artillery and mortar fire, as well as air activity, covered the area of the Division. There were no appreciable changes during the further course of the day apart from positions being improved locally. The neighbouring division made headway in its assault on Stalingrad but had not been able to reach the same level as 24. Panzer-Division.
At 1930 hours, the situation and forward line was still unchanged. Enemy artillery and mortar fire became weaker at times but otherwise enemy behaviour was unchanged. About 50 deserters and prisoners were brought in during the day. The booty taken by Korps since 29th August rose to 17,100 prisoners, including 600 deserters, 246 tanks, 20 aircraft and further war materiel. Panzer situation: 7 Panzer II, 5 Panzer III kz, 6 Panzer III lg, 1 Panzer IV kz, 3 Panzer IV lg and 1 Bfwg.
The following mission was issued to 24. Panzer-Division at 2220 hours: "LI. Armeekorps will attack with its right wing early on 14th September from the direction of Abteilung 6 over 457 and 468 (map reference points). This attack will be supported by the Division's artillery. Any opportunities offered to exploit the advance of neighbouring Korps are to be used. A close connection remains for the southern part of the Division sector."

Towards evening, Generalmajor Arno von Lenski reached a small village on the edge of the Kalmuck steppe in which he reported to Hoth, the Commander-in-Chief of 4. Panzer-Armee, and where he finally learned some details about his Division, about its mission, what awaited him and about the changing condition of the forces that had made it impossible to capture the Volga city on the march.
General von Lenski recalls the moment he received news of his new assignment:
"On 11th September 1942, I received the order to take over the command of 24 Panzer Division from the severely wounded Generalmajor Ritter von Hauenschild. Until then, I was – apart from two short stints at the front – Commander of the School for Schnelltruppen in Krampnitz. While reporting to the Heerespersonalamt (Army Personnel Office) in Berlin, the Chef der I. Abteilung, Generalleutnant von Dräbich-Wächter, confidentially shared with me that OKW had scheduled 24. Panzer-Division to be pulled out of the fighting around Stalingrad as soon as possible and together with a motorised division, be employed in an advance on Baku."

Arno von Lenski was born in Czymochen, East Prussia, on 20th July 1893, the youngest of ten children. He spent a lot of his youth in the saddle and when he was fifteen, went off to cadet school near Berlin. In 1910, he passed his officer cadets exam and also had the high honour of serving as a court page to Kaiser Wilhelm II. On 22nd March 1912, he was assigned to Grenadier-Regiment zu Pferde Freiherr von Derfflinger Nr. 3, a dragoon regiment in Bromberg and a few months later, attended a nine-month course at the Kriegschule in Bad Hersfeld. He was commissioned as a Leutnant on 16th June 1913. Upon commencement of the First World War, Lenski's 3. Dragoon Schwadron was assigned to 3. Infanterie-Division. He first saw action on 18th August 1914 near a tiny village in Belgium called Aerschot, followed by battles near Mons before reaching the Somme. On 25th August, a mounted patrol led by von Lenski reached the Douai-Bapaume road, a mission typical of the next month. In early November 1914, von Lenski participated in the storming of the Spanbrockmolen. This was his last combat because on 2nd November, he became regimental adjutant. Just over two weeks later, von Lenski's entire division was transferred to the Eastern Front. He was promoted to Oberleutnant on 18th August 1916 and on 2nd November was assigned to Generalkommando 55, where he remained for the duration of the war, becoming an Ordonanzoffizier on 14th February 1918. For the next twenty years, he had assignments with various cavalry units, including a stint as commander of a cavalry school, and received several promotions: Rittmeister on 1st May 1923; Major on 1st July 1933, Oberstleutnant on 1st March 1936 and Oberst on 1st August 1938. While commanding Kavallerie-Regiment 6 in August 1937, he led it into the Rheinland after its demilitarisation. Barely a week before the beginning of the Second World War, this unit was disbanded and von Lenski was left without a cavalry command, instead being given command of Aufklärungs-Abteilung 33. This was only temporary for on 25th October 1939, he assumed command of the cavalry school in Krampnitz.

As head of the school, von Lenski was entitled to travel around and visit the few remaining cavalry units still in the Wehrmacht. One of his last stops was at Arachon in France, the headquarters of 1. Kavallerie-Division, the future 24. Panzer-Division. On 1st June 1941, von Lenski received a new assignment that had nothing to do with horses: he assumed command of Schützen-Brigade 2 (2. Panzer-Division) on 1st June 1941 shortly after its return from the Balkan's campaign. When the division headed east for Barbarossa, however, von Lenski was left behind and soon became acting commander of 11. Panzer-Division's Schützen-Brigade 11 after its commander, Oberst Günther Angern,[6] was seriously wounded. By the time he joined the division, it had already passed Zhitomir, crossed the Dnepr and advanced on Gomel. At the beginning of October 1941, von Lenski took temporary command of 11. Panzer-Division after its commander was admitted to hospital. He led it for approximately a month and performed adequately during the Vyazma Pocket battle. He then resumed command of the Schützen-Brigade and stayed with it until they stood at the gates of Moscow, whereupon he received an order to return to Germany and take command of the Schule für Schnelltruppen in Krampnitz. After his promotion to Generalmajor on 1st June 1942, von Lenski decided it was time for him to return to the action. Thus on 11th September 1942 he received news of his assumption of command of 24. Panzer-Division and arrived barely three days later to take up this new assignment.

6. Angern later commanded 16. Panzer-Division at Stalingrad.

Casualties:

26 men killed

- Unteroffizier Heinrich Boven; PGR21 (Killed)
- Obergefreiter Alfred Rehberg; PGR21 (Killed)
- Obergefreiter Bruno Hill; K4 (Killed)

2 officers wounded (1 of those stayed with the troops)

- Leutnant Heyl (Wounded)
- Leutnant Christian Keiler (Zug Kdr); 6./PGR26 (Wounded but stayed with the troops)

107 men wounded (23 of those stayed with the troops)

- Knight's Cross winner Wachtmeister Otto Brakat; 2./K4 (Wounded)

Decorations bestowed from 7th September to 13th September:

38 Iron Cross First Class
348 Iron Cross Second Class
11 Panzer Combat Badge in Bronze
83 Panzer Combat Badge in Silver
19 Assault Badge

Prisoners and booty taken from 7th September to 13th September:

1140 prisoners
10 airplanes
40 guns
20 guns destroyed by artillery
55 tanks
44 anti-tank guns
3 anti-aircraft guns
10 mortars
27 anti-tank rifles
1 locomotive, 6 wagons

14th September 1942:

Enemy air activity was negligible during the early part of the night, however, strong enemy bombing attacks took place later in the early morning hours. The Russians strengthened themselves in front of Gruppe Hellermann in the area of Kalkberge, also moving tanks there. Oberst Friebe drove to the headquarters of 24. Panzer-Division in the morning where Hauptmann Roth, the Division O1, pointed out to him that Major von Menges and Oberst von Broich had driven to the front to survey the units positions. Friebe headed back to Korps HQ. Korps placed particular worth in the fact that 24. Panzer-Division would set off the next day with a strong Kampfgruppe and advance to the railway station south of the Tsaritsa Gully. At 1220 hours, 71. Infanterie-Division of the neighbouring LI. Armeekorps reached Stalingrad's central railway station. At 1233 hours, Oberst Fangohr from Armee HQ called Oberst Friebe: "Establishment of connection with left neighbour advisable. When will 24. Panzer-Division advance with Edelsheim?"

Friebe: "They are too weak." Friebe told Oberst Fangohr that he would get details from 24. Panzer-Division. Once he got off the phone, he immediately called Major von Menges and asked for the Division's plans for tomorrow's attack. Major von Menges said he would call later with details.

In a Fieseler-Storch, Generalmajor von Lenski landed in Stalingrad-South, commissioned with the command of the Division. He soon arrived at the command post to take practical command of the Division. "I took command of 24. Panzer-Division in the afternoon of 14th September 1942. 24. Panzer-Division was subordinated to Generalkommando des XXXXVIII. Panzerkorps, which belonged to Hoth's 4. Panzer-Armee. At that moment, they still possessed fifty to sixty percent of their normal combat strength." Upon his arrival, General von Lenski issued a Tagesbefehl to the troops:

"From midday today, I have taken over command of the Division upon higher orders.

"I am proud that I have been entrusted with a Division that is particularly successful, whose courage is known throughout the entire army and is specially recognised by the Führer.
I offer my greetings to the Division and request trusting co-operation."

"Heil 24. Panzer-Division!
Generalmajor v. Lenski
Commissioned with command of the Division."

Leutnant Ernst-Wilhelm Nueske, Batterie Commander of 1./Panzerartillerie-Regiment 89, records his impression of the new Division Commander: "Towards midday, for the first time – I believe also for the last time – the new Division Commander, a Generalmajor von Lenski, drove to the front-line. Not exactly a very impressive personality. Quite small and ugly, he sat in his half-track and soon cleared off."[7]

A few days earlier, Oberst von Broich asked for his special home leave given to winners of the Knight's Cross. Approval had not been immediately granted because he was needed to command the Division but now that General von Lenski had arrived, there was no reason his request could be denied. At 1100 hours, Oberst Fangohr informed Korps: "No objection to the granting of leave to Oberst von Broich."

At 1645 hours, Major von Menges called Oberst Friebe at Korps headquarters and oriented him about the planned conduct of the attack with Gruppe Edelsheim. A battalion would be prepared as an assault group and the main objective was the southern railway station. Oberst Friebe seemed satisfied with the plan and told Menges that the starting time for the assault would be announced when everything was co-ordinated and cleared with 94. Infanterie-Division. At 1735 hours, Oberst Friebe called 94. Infanterie-Division and spoke to its chief-of-staff, Oberst i.G. Manitz: "24. Panzer-Division will go through along the railway line." Both men discussed various aspects of the attack and settled on a time: 0330 hours. Oberst Friebe called Major von Menges back at 1750 hours: "0330 hours agreed to! Dividing line railway line

7. This account was written well after the war and the veterans are not particularly fond of von Lenski, not for his actions as commander of the Division but more for his subsequent behaviour in captivity when he joined the various anti-Fascist groups set up by the Russians.

up to the Tsaritsa railway station for 24. Panzer-Division."
After the remaining divisions of Korps had gained further ground to the north, Korps gave the final mission to 24. Panzer-Division: "24. Panzer-Division will set off at 0330 hours on 15th September with tightly concentrated forces in one place in a surprise assault to break through the enemy defensive position, thrust with a Kampfgruppe at one stretch through the city sector west of the station and take that railway station into possession. By this swift penetration, the enemy will be denied the possibility of setting up new defences, as he has previously done. The destruction of the enemy and the clearing of the penetrated city sectors will follow after the successful breakthrough."

At 2000 hours, the Division issued Divisionsbefehl Nr. 60 which called for the continuation of the attack on Stalingrad on 15th September. Gruppe Edelsheim, substantially reinforced with heavy weapons, would capture the railway station while Gruppe Hellermann secured to the east and north. Forces were distributed as follows:

Gruppe Edelsheim:

Panzergrenadier-Regiment 26
I./Panzergrenadier-Regiment 21
Kradschützen-Abteilung 4 (without 1. Schwadron)
1. and 3./Panzerpionier-Bataillon 40
All flamethrowers of Panzerpionier-Bataillon 40
Panzerartillerie-Regiment 89 (without 4. Batterie)
Staff and elements of Panzerjäger-Abteilung 670 (five 76.2mm self-propelled guns)
2./Panzerjäger-Abteilung 40 (without one platoon)
10 panzers of Panzer-Abteilung Lancken[8]

Gruppe Hellermann:

Panzergrenadier-Regiment 21 (without I. Abteilung)
Pionier-Bataillon 635
4./Panzerartillerie-Regiment 89
Elements of Panzerjäger-Abteilung 670
One platoon of 2./Panzerjäger-Abteilung 40

The plan was for Gruppe Edelsheim to break through the enemy front-line in the western part of the city with two rifle battalions, penetrate into the railway station as quickly as possible and capture it.

First objective: the enemy front-line
Second objective: the railway station
Third objective: prospective penetration to the north

The northern flank of Gruppe Edelsheim outside the city was secured by the weakest possible forces but had half of Panzer-Abteilung Lancken ready to work in co-operation[9]. Individual operations by panzers would be avoided. They would be coupled with assault groups for a

8. The rest of the panzers stood at Division's disposal, ready to be switched to a favourable penetration point.
9. The Panzer-Abteilung had the dual role of supporting the securing forces and standing ready as Division reserve.

thrust in an eastern direction as soon as the front-line was broken. Gruppe Hellermann would hold the line but would be ready to follow up a successful penetration by Gruppe Edelsheim. So, for 14th September, the forward line of Division remained unaltered. The day passed relatively quietly with increasing artillery fire and local improvements of positions. Increasingly heavy artillery and mortar fire fell on the Square Forest area and south of there, as well as severe flanking fire out of the area of Objective 18. Twenty deserters were brought in and 3 tanks were destroyed. Panzer situation: 8 Panzer II, 6 Panzer III kz, 6 Panzer III lg, 1 Panzer IV kz, 4 Panzer IV lg and 2 Bfwg.

Casualties:

5 men killed

• Obergefreiter Paul Martens; PGR26 (Killed)

37 men wounded (22 of those stayed with the troops)

• Unteroffizier Willi Stuhlemmer; 2./PGR26 (Wounded)

Conquest of Stalin's City

Chapter Six

15th September 1942:

The Division attacked at 0330 hours with Gruppe Edelsheim, while Gruppe Hellermann, after having provided further forces for the assault groups, secured the previous sector. Gruppe Edelsheim advanced as planned to attack grid square 10 and was strongly flanked out of the factory area south of the railway line. They broke through the enemy front-line on the western edge of the city north of the west-east railway line and, in hand-to-hand fighting under cover of both open flanks, took the railway tracks in the early morning. Individual artillery pieces were drawn into the front-line to smash enemy strongpoints at close range. In hard combat under difficult terrain conditions, Gruppe Edelsheim succeeded in pushing along the railway tracks and taking the triangle of railways by mid-morning. As a further assault came to a standstill as a result of shortages in assault forces, the panzers were employed as support in local combat. Brave Russian infantrymen holding out in foxholes both sides of the tracks defended themselves bitterly but most of them, faced with being crushed or blasted by the panzers, gave themselves up.

After establishing a connection with 94. Infanterie-Division, flanking fire from the south was suppressed at 1135 hours when General Kempf ordered the blast-furnace area to be covered by artillery and heavy weapons of 94. Infanterie-Division. There was a noticeable decrease in machine-gun fire from that direction as shells burst among the factory's buildings and Gruppe Edelsheim, after more hard fighting until midday, was able to take the railway tracks south-west of orientation point 474 (south-west part of 16, middle and north part of grid square 15) and stood in the city sector west of the railway station. Toughly fighting enemy groups had to be individually

BÖKE

The panzer spearhead climbs over a railway embankment on the western outskirts of Stalingrad.

BÖKE

A Panzer II of the Regiment's reconnaissance platoon closely follows the armoured vanguard over the railway line.

thrown out of every street in hard hand-to-hand and close combat. Strong flanking fire now came from grid square 18 and tanks fired into the panzergrenadiers from out of the Barracks area. Strengthened covering fire toward there was necessary and Oberst von Edelsheim radioed a request to the supporting artillery. After a successful regrouping, with the panzers called forward for the attack, Gruppe Edelsheim was ready to penetrate into the heart of Stalingrad. General von Lenski wrote about the movement of the panzers in his memoirs: "A reconnaissance troop ascertained that a small track alongside the railway line was passable for a few panzers. Nevertheless, the deep balkas reached right up to the line on both sides. It was still also uncertain whether the wooden railway bridge hard west of the branch in the railway would fall into our hands intact because of a Soviet machine-gun nest that was located there. The bridge, however, was taken... by an assault group without a shot being fired. As a result of this, I ordered the attack on the northern wing of the Division to be suspended and... pulled a Panzer Abteilung in an independent march – partly on the rails – through the bottleneck."

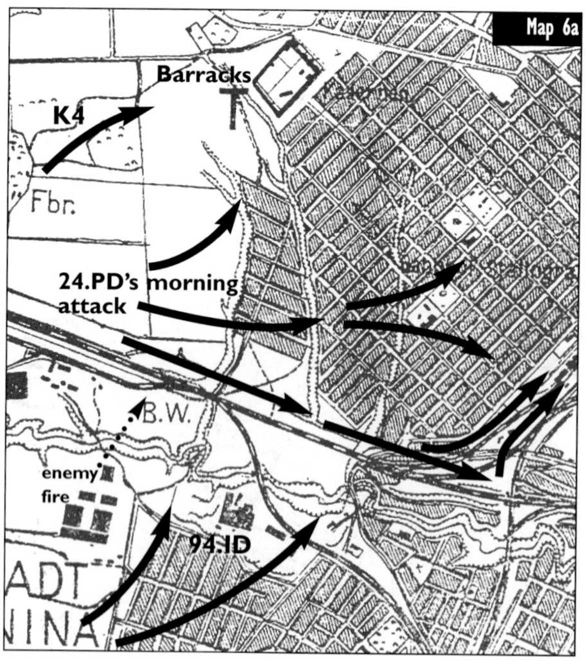

Leutnant von Senger und Etterlin, as part of Gruppe Hellermann, held his defensive positions. "Today I must spread out and relieve the schwadron that has been on our right. Panzer Abteilung Lancken is moving through the southern part of the city towards 'Barracks Hill' today but isn't making progress. The terrain over there, which we can't see from here, is full of bunkers, trenches and dug-in tanks."

Stukas had been called in to pummel these defences, together with other enemy obstructions ahead of the Division. The grenadiers, squatting in narrow washaways, gullies and behind bushes, enjoyed watching bombs ploughing up the defenders causing them grief, but things

BUNDESARCHIV, BILD 101I/218/528/3 / PHOTO: THIEDE

The Sdkfz. 251 half-tracks of I./Panzergrenadier-Regiment 26 straddle the tracks into the city, waiting for the order to advance. In the distance, a small cloud of smoke stains the horizon.

KOLCZYK

Southern Stalingrad. All that remains of one of the workers suburbs: chimneys, piles of ash and rubble, skeletal remains of shredded trees and the occasional intact masonry building.

BUNDESARCHIV, BILD 101I/218/528/9 / PHOTO: THIEDE

Major von der Lancken's panzers pass through an intact housing settlement. On 15th September, 27 panzers were available for the thrust into the city. Seen far in the background are several of Stalingrad's multi-storey buildings, one of which is on fire.

soon took a nasty turn: the bombs from the Stukas crept back toward them and started exploding among their own lines. Frantic radio messages were sent, demanding that the bombing be halted and a few minutes after it had begun, the bombing stopped as word of the error reached the pilots. Major von Menges reported this alarming development to Korps at 1210 hours: "Our pilots are bombing our troops. Armoured train in railway station." Friebe simply replied: "Forward group must reach the Tsaritsa Gully. Armoured train is targeted by Stukas."[1]

BÖKE

Oberleutnant Böke, Abteilung Adjutant of III./PR24, took this shot of the devastation from the cupola of his panzer.

Following repeated preparations by the Luftwaffe and after overcoming numerous terrain difficulties and mines, Gruppe Edelsheim, supported by panzers, pushed into the railway station at 1600 hours after suppressing a few field emplacements. The panzers drove carefully along the rails and dirt tracks that passed through the station, maintaining a steady pace. Squads of grenadiers and riflemen threaded their way through the warehouses, shacks and buildings along the line of advance,

1. The Soviets employed eight armoured trains during the first month and a half of the battle. The eight squadrons were: 24th, 25th, 28th, 30th, 40th, 51st, 59th and 377th AA

BUNDESARCHIV, BILD 101I/218/525/7 / PHOTO: SAUTTER

An Sdkfz.250/3 from a Luftwaffe unit attached to 24. Panzer-Division to provide liaison and help control the Stukas that were supporting the Division. Barely visible in the background is the omnipresent Grain Elevator.

BUNDESARCHIV, BILD 101I/218/528/20 / PHOTO: THIEDE

Grenadiers head north through the buildings of the Southern Railway Station under the constant gaze of the Grain Elevator. Fortunately for them, it was undefended at this time. Note the Hiwi carrying ammunition for the machine-gun.

The Grain Elevator after its eventual capture. On 15th September, 24. Panzer-Division could have seized it with little effort. By the time infantry units moved up, Russian defenders had occupied it and thereupon defended it to the death.

covering the panzers' flanks as well as looking for the enemy. The adamantine Grain Elevator stood in the east, menacing and grey, and no matter where the men were, the Elevator was always staring down at them. They wondered why such an impregnable strongpoint was not being defended by the Russians. A couple of minutes after entering the station, the panzers quickly reached its northern boundary, radioed their position and set up a temporary defence line while they awaited further orders. They did not have to wait long: an immediate response from Major von Menges ordered them to push up to the Tsaritsa. After a very swift regrouping, the panzers thrust alone to the north up to the Tsaritsa Gully. The terrain forced the panzers to proceed single-file. The railway line they were following ran atop an embankment that sometimes reached a height of ten metres, so the panzers advanced in the shadow of its western slope, avoiding the tops of gullies, wooden huts and abandoned Russian towing-tractors and guns. A few minutes after setting out, the panzers caught up to the retreating enemy units and scattered them, subsequently reaching the Tsaritsa at 1615 hours. The panzers then turned to the west and prepared to advance towards the dominating barracks terrain.

The grenadiers remained behind in the station area to thoroughly clear all Russian stragglers. The men were in a good mood: the radiant afternoon sun burst through a bank of cloud that straddled the western horizon and spread its golden light over the station as the men moved

NA/MARK

The route of Gruppe Edelsheim from the railway station to the Tsaritsa Gully on the afternoon of 15th September.

BUNDESARCHIV, BILD 101I/218/529/13 / PHOTO: THIEDE

A squad of grenadiers follows the path of the panzers who drove to the north under protection of the railway embankment.

along the rails, searching enemy foxholes dug among patches of trackside grass and weeds. Resistance was almost non-existent and the men smoked as they carried out their search.

Once the station area had been completely cleared of the few enemy stragglers, Division command staff moved in and set up their command post in a railway signal box. Hardly a majestic HQ for an East Prussian General and his staff but it served its purpose. At 1830 hours, Major von Menges sent a situation report to Oberst Friebe at Korps: "Enemy front-line removed, no more continuous defence after being broken through. Flanking fire from south very unpleasant. Connection still not completely available with 94. Infanterie-Division. Railway station not very heavily occupied. One enemy company flowing off to east. Tsaritsa no enemy. Our panzers push from Tsaritsa to the west. Precise report will follow." The available panzers advanced from the Tsaritsa Gully in a westerly direction towards the Barracks on the western edge of the city, still heavily occupied by the enemy. Surprised enemy troops were taken prisoner and overcome but the complete destruction of enemy forces and the exploitation of this success was hindered by the onset of darkness. The effect to morale in the rear areas of the strong Russian positions was nevertheless devastating.

Hauptmann Roth, O1 of 24. Panzer-Division, phoned Korps to report the latest: "Resistance north of Barracks has strengthened considerably. It was further reported that 3 of our panzers were shot up by the flak of 71. Infanterie-Division." This last sentence is very interesting because cases of 'friendly fire' are rarely reported in German war diaries. This is the only reference to this incident. The daily panzer figures of 24. Panzer-Division, however, seem to confirm this. Here are the figures for 14th September:
8 Panzer II,
6 Panzer III kz,
6 Panzer III lg,
1 Panzer IV kz,
4 Panzer IV lg,
2 Panzer Bfwg.

BUNDESARCHIV, BILD 101I/218/525/15 / PHOTO: SAUTTER

Grenadiers move north in the late afternoon, thoroughly investigating Russian foxholes dug along the railway line. The Grain Elevator is just out of frame to the right.

BUNDESARCHIV, BILD 101I/218/528/23 / PHOTO: THIEDE

The corpse of a Russian soldier lies between the rails in the southern station. The Kampfgruppen of 24. Panzer-Division experienced light resistance in its capture of the station.

BUNDESARCHIV, BILD 101I/218/528/31 / PHOTO: THIEDE

A radio post of Gruppe Edelsheim keeps in contact with Division. All binoculars are focused to the north-east, as is the gun of Panzer '525', but the man in the foreground is totally exposed and is not wearing a helmet, indicating that these men are not in immediate danger.

And 15th September:
7 Panzer II,
3 Panzer III kz,
7 Panzer III lg,
1 Panzer IV kz,
3 Panzer IV lg,
2 Bfwg.

It can be seen from these figures that on 15th September, 24. Panzer-Division had a shortfall of 1 Panzer II, 3 Panzer III kz and 1 Panzer IV kz compared to the previous day. It is simply not possible to tell from German panzer figures how many panzers were knocked out because at the same time as panzers were being knocked out, repaired panzers became active and were included in the number of operational panzers.
For the night, Gruppe Hellermann secured its previous positions while Gruppe Edelsheim tried to defend the line from the railway bridge at Voroponovo – Stalingrad – Stalingrad West – to the north edge of the railway station with fronts to the south, east and north. The panzers were withdrawn to Gruppe Edelsheim for the night into hedgehog positions around the railway station. Amongst the ghastly glow of burning buildings in the devastated city, the grenadiers, riflemen and panzer crewmen of Gruppe Edelsheim secured to all sides.

The mission of the day was fulfiled, the penetration of the Division into the southern sector of the city smashing the backbone of the enemy defence. This successful attack was attributed to the fact that the breakthrough was swift and in one bound without regard to the threats on the flanks and through that, had taken away the possibility for the enemy to set up new defences. Local crises developed during the attack and in the following night but these were tolerated. Preliminary booty: 630 prisoners, 2 guns, 6 anti-tank guns, 13 mortars, 27 submachine-guns and 3 tanks. Towards evening, Infanterie-Regiment 274 won the railway bridge south of the station area and established contact with 24. Panzer-Division.

At 1935 hours, Oberst Friebe talked to Major von Menges: "Mission, one Gruppe to gain crossing over the Tsaritsa and there seek contact with LI. Armeekorps, then clean out the city from east to west, covering the Volga." Menges replied: "Panzers penetrated into the Barracks.

Connection available with 94. Infanterie-Division." After getting off the phone, Menges discussed the course of tomorrow's attack with General von Lenski. It was decided that Gruppe Edelsheim would lead the attack. At 2010 hours, Major von Menges called Oberst Friebe and reported: "Gruppe Edelsheim will advance to Tsaritsa at 0600 hours." The following order was issued to the Division at 2050 hours: "Early on 16th September, 24. Panzer-Division will thrust forward west of the railway line up to the Tsaritsa Gully, form a bridgehead there and take up a connection with 71. Infanterie-Division. Besides that, the task of the Division is still to destroy the enemy groups holding out in the western part of Stalingrad and on the hills west of the city and clear out this entire area up to the Tsaritsa. A close connection will be maintained with 94. Infanterie-Division thrusting up the eastern side of the railway line."

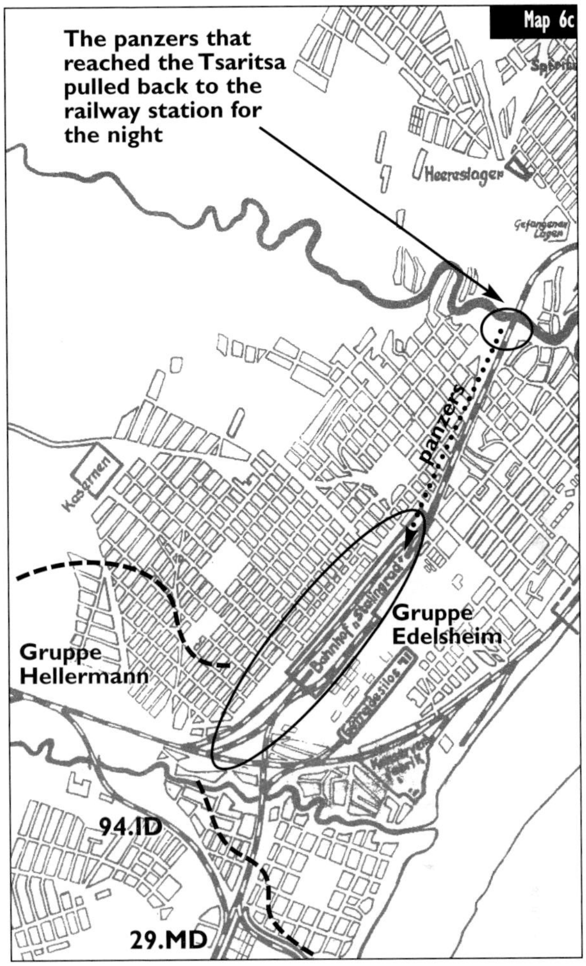

Positions of 24. Panzer-Division at the end of the day.

At 1810 hours, in accordance with an OKH order, a Panzer-Armeebefehl was issued stating that all forces advancing towards the city of Stalingrad be concentrated under 6. Armee. For that reason, XXXXVIII. Panzerkorps was subordinated to 6. Armee from 0000 hours on 16th September. The subordination under 6. Armee was only of a tactical nature: for supplies and troop services, Korps remained dependent upon 4. Panzer-Armee.

Casualties:

18 men killed

- Obergefreiter Alfred Scheithauer; PGR26 (Killed)
- Gefreiter Willy Schirrweit; PGR26 (Killed)
- Unteroffizier Paul Duille; PGR26 (Killed)
- Gefreiter Hubert Dölle; PGR26 (Killed)
- Gefreiter Bruno Obst; K4 (Killed)

4 officers wounded (2 of those stayed with the troops)

- Oberleutnant Alfred Dannebaum (Abt Adjutant); K4 (Wounded but stayed with the troops)
- Leutnant Christian Keiler (Zug Kdr); 6./PGR26 (Wounded)
- Rittmeister Wilhelm Rogge (Schwadron Kdr); 10./PGR26 (Wounded)
- Leutnant Erdmann Graeve (Zug Kdr); 3./Pz.Jg.40 (Wounded but stayed with the troops)

74 men wounded (17 of those stayed with the troops)

1 man missing

16th September 1942:

Reconnaissance carried out during the night reconfirmed that enemy resistance on a large scale had decreased but that the enemy still defended himself locally as obstinately as before, partly with operations by tanks. The enemy had considerably strengthened himself in the triangle bounded by the Volga – Tsaritsa Gully – railway station.

The twin objectives for this day, according to the Korpsbefehl, were focused upon the Tsaritsa sector where a connection would be established with 71. Infanterie-Division, and the enemy groups still entrenched in the western part of Stalingrad would be destroyed. In view of the small forces at its disposal, the Division decided to solve this by performing the missions sequentially. Gruppe Edelsheim set the ball rolling by attacking to the north at 0600 hours, capturing the railway bridge on the Tsaritsa after breaking weak enemy resistance with Panzer Abteilung Lancken and the armoured Grenadier Bataillon and forming a small bridgehead on the north bank in unfavourable terrain under strong enemy opposition. Now that 24. Panzer-Division and 71. Infanterie-Division were only separated by a short distance, it was decided that 71. Infanterie-Division could benefit from having an artillery observer placed in 24. Panzer-Division's sector. At 0800 hours, however, Hauptmann Roth reported to Korps: "A.V. Ko.[2] was not as scheduled, merely an officer with a radio connection to Division staff of 71. Infanterie-Division." 71. Infanterie-Division was supposed to send a highly-qualified artillery observer but instead simply sent an officer with a radio who had no experience at directing and correcting massed artillery fire.

The enemy north-east of the railway station – in the area east of the railway embankment but north of the Grain Elevator – had reinforced himself with artillery and tanks. This area belonged to 94. Infanterie-Division and it only made slow progress but as long as that division lagged behind, 24. Panzer-Division's lengthy eastern flank was uncovered. It was not a problem at the moment because the railway embankment largely protected the sector but if the enemy started to build up his strength and recover his offensive capability, he'd be able to penetrate any section of this thin defensive line. After clearing out the areas north-west of the railway station, a Kampfgruppe consisting of panzers and one rifle battalion would set out from the south and east to attack the Barracks area on the western edge of the city at 1130 hours. The city sector between the railway station and the railway bridge was cleaned out but the implementation had only been possible by greatly weakening the remaining sectors.

2. Artillerie Verbindungs Kommandeur, or artillery liaison officer

BUNDESARCHIV, BILD 101I/218/525/2 / PHOTO: SAUTTER

One of the Division's command panzers '24/2' trundles into the southern suburbs. Note that Russian prisoners have been collected in a hollow to the right of the chimneys.

Obergefreiter Ferdinand Kusterer of Panzergrenadier-Regiment 21 vividly remembers this day: "On 16th September, I saw the actual city and the Volga for the first time, as we were still deployed in its southern section. On a hill covered by low pines, we occupied a Russian camp, almost an underground barracks, and from there thrust forward to the railway station. As an Essenholer[3] I should go to the grenadiers in the forward line but the midday meal was already cold because the connection had been broken by violent artillery fire. A house in which the Russians had settled down was ablaze. On a flat hill lay a workers suburb where only the chimneys still loomed out of the smoke-blackened rubble.

"From a pine-forested hill, I saw through the scissors-telescope a tugboat with five barges swimming over the Volga. They moved over there without being disturbed by our artillery. The ferry traffic over the Volga must indeed be massive to satisfactorily cope with the vast amounts of supplies the Russians were throwing into the fighting: along the entire length of the city, there was not one single bridge over the river. We can barely get an idea of the size of this enormous river. The Rhine and Elbe are streams compared to it.

"The impression was still greater when all the water was visible, constantly dividing the different armies. On the opposite flat shore, nothing could be discerned except low swampy forests. That, however, was only an island, another arm of the river flowing behind it. Further north on the other shore were several installations, settlements and dairies but behind that was the almost uninhabited steppe and Kazakstani desert. Europe came to an end here."

3. Food carrier

FREIMANN

The chimneys of the incinerated workers suburbs reminded many German soldiers of gravestones.

To prevent any further accidental bombing of German troops by the Luftwaffe, as had happened yesterday, Oberst Friebe called General Fiebig at VIII. Fliegerkorps headquarters at 1135 hours and said: "Everything south of the Brook sector is handled." He then proceeded to orientate Fiebig about the positions of the spearheads.

After the penetration of panzers and armoured riflemen to the Tsaritsa Gully and the forming of a bridgehead over the railway bridge, the Division regrouped. Gruppe Edelsheim had fulfiled its mission so Panzer Abteilung Lancken and further elements of Gruppe Edelsheim were subsequently subordinated to Gruppe Hellermann, which advanced at 1145 hours to attack the Barracks area. The eastern half of Gruppe Hellermann set off from the south and east to attack towards the dominant high ground in the vicinity of the Barracks on the western edge of the city. On account of the success of the assault into the city and the continuing stubborn enemy resistance on the west slope leading up to Barracks Hill, Rittmeister von Langenn-Steinkeller's Kradschützen-Abteilung 4 was shifted to a more favourable position to launch an attack. Leutnant von Senger und Etterlin reports:

> "We are being pulled out here too, in order to attack the city with tanks again and finally wipe out this nest of resistance. We moved in marching order along the tracks into the city where the von Heyden Abteilung had just reached the southern railway station and pushed on to the Volga shore. We then turned around and moved westward towards 'Barracks Hill'. The city here was completely burned out, the streets peppered with shell craters. After a short preparation, the assault moved off.
>
> "We stopped at the edge of the city and, supported by fire from the panzers, set out to establish a system of strong positions on a north-south line rising to the heights. We pushed up to the first trenches and over them in tough, hand-to-hand combat. Thirty metres in front of us was the second trench and behind it was scrub dotted with bunkers and tanks. In one concerted plunge we took the second trench and mopped it up. Strong artillery fire now met us; it was impossible to tell whether it was ours or the enemy's. After the second trench was firmly

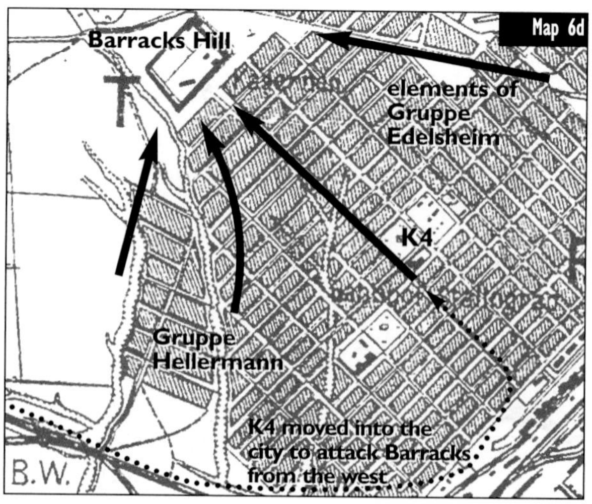

in our hands and the last Russians hauled out or shot down with pistols, we pushed into the bush like shock troops.

"In front of us was a small group of houses; a road led to the left and there was thick bush to the right in which numerous T-34's could be seen at a distance of 50 to 100 metres, however, the main thing was that our following panzers were in a firefight some distance to our rear. We cautiously forced our way through toward the group of houses and cleaned them out. My platoon already had 3 machine-guns' operations melt together. On the other side of the group of houses was an open expanse about 80 metres wide, standing under the trees on the right, well-camouflaged, were 2 or 3 T-34's, on the other side of the road to the left were bushes, and I knew from yesterday that behind them was a shot-up, burnt-out tank.

"We'd been instructed to push through to the western edge of Barracks Hill and to completely clean out the enemy. Straight ahead there was a well-camouflaged T-34 sitting under a tree, shooting in a westerly direction. I arranged for a squad to give cover-fire from the houses and with the other squad next to me, leapt out and ran 50 metres to a small hollow. When we jumped breathlessly into the hollow, a T-60 was standing there. An Unteroffizier leapt up from beside me and after performing several leaps, threw a hand-grenade through the hatch.

"Thirty metres from us stood the T-34 which had turned its attention to us, and slowly its cannon turned towards us. With my best MG-Schütze (machine-gunner), Obergefreiter Westermann, I leapt forward to destroy him before he could shoot at us. We plunged straight into some bushes and the Russians were 30 metres half to the left in front of us. I had no weapons at all except a concentrated charge and I threw myself behind a small mound, which offered no cover. The Russians were moving up only 15 metres away and the leading Russian aimed his sub-machine gun at me. I saw him pull the trigger and thought that my last hour had come. He raised it and it apparently jammed. Now Westermann's machine-gun rattled near me and the Russians rushed headlong back into the bushes.

"I at once leapt on to the tank while Westermann kept the Russians in check. I placed the concentrated charge on the engine deck but the screw fuse would not come undone. It did not help that the entire fuse was screwed down tight. Suddenly, the 500 horsepower diesel engine of the heavy tank howled and it drove in the direction of my other squad. I turned the screw fuse with my teeth, chased after the increasingly quick moving tank, screwed it down and pulled the fuse. I then threw myself flat against the ground, where there was no cover of any sort at hand. The tank rolled 10 metres, then a strong explosion resounded and the tank was instantly ablaze.

"The Russians now attacked again from out of the bush. Westermann had no more ammunition. A T-60 broke out of the trees – and we leapt back into the hollow – as it crawled along and reached our breathless squad. I immediately arranged everything here for the defence. A T-60 and a platoon of Russians came under fire from our machine-guns. Strong artillery fire continuously swept the area. All of a sudden, I received a blow to the head and sunk back into my hole."

That was the end of Leutnant von Senger und Etterlin's adventures in Stalingrad.

At around 1230 hours, the Barracks on the western edge of the city were taken after hard combat against strong enemy forces with anti-tank guns, anti-aircraft guns and 20 tanks. The Division then attacked the toughly fighting enemy groups west and north of the Barracks area.

WÄSCHLE

The command tank '1161' of Major Dietrich von der Lancken (commander of III./Panzer-Regiment 24) stands watch over the southern part of the city. With tactical command of all the regiment's panzers since 27 August, von der Lancken fulfilled every mission and earned himself the Knight's Cross.

WÄSCHLE

While Lancken's '1161' sits in the open, a half-track of 2./Panzerartillerie-Regiment 89 lurks in the shadows. This high ground was seized on 15 September.

WÄSCHLE

A northward view from the high ground, towards central Stalingrad. Observers from several units directed artillery fire from this vantage point.

WÄSCHLE

Six members of 2./ Panzerartillerie-Regiment 89, none of whom survived the war. The battery's casualties during the 1942 campaign (16 dead and 54 MIA) are representative of losses suffered by all units at Stalingrad.

With tanks, the enemy continually attacked with strong forces against the bridgehead near the railway bridgehead. The riflemen were defending a precarious position: to their right, the Tsaritsa split into two arms with the consequence that they were defending the isthmus between them and the only access to this was either by crossing the exposed wooden railway bridge high above the valley floor or by descending into the valley itself. This was also a dangerous prospect with numerous Russian soldiers fleeing through the valley towards the Volga. The semicircular defensive line consisted of scattered foxholes in which the riflemen hunkered down, backed by mortars and heavy machine-guns entrenched in the centre of the bridgehead.

The western half of Gruppe Hellermann entered into the attack in the early afternoon. After extremely tough fighting against a well dug-in enemy, they succeeded in taking a couple of dominating hills and tightly compressed the enemy that had previously stood opposite them. With the onset of darkness, the right wing and centre of Gruppe Hellermann, after heavy combat against a numerically superior force of tanks and numerous bunkers, took the hills 400 metres north and 800 metres north-west of the Barracks, then won the two-laned road south of Square Forest. The north shore of the Tsaritsa Brook had not been able to be reached everywhere by the northern neighbours, enabling a few enemy remnants to make their way to the east.

Obergefreiter Reddig jotted in his diary: "16.9.42. Mail delivery. Dry weather, cold wind. The Russians are encircled to the left of us. Our Schwadron in attack on the Kessel. Desperate Russian break-out attempts. Bartkowski killed, Wachtmeister Wippich, Obergefreiter Heichster[4], Fritz Schmielewski, Müller (2. Zug), Erich Schaffiamski (4. Zug) wounded. At night, active Russian air activity."

The Tsaritsa bridgehead was to be abandoned soon after sunset, according to plan, due to strong attacks from the north shore of the Tsaritsa and flanking fire from east and west, and also because 71. Infanterie-Division would not be moving up in the foreseeable future and the casualties of the riflemen defending there would

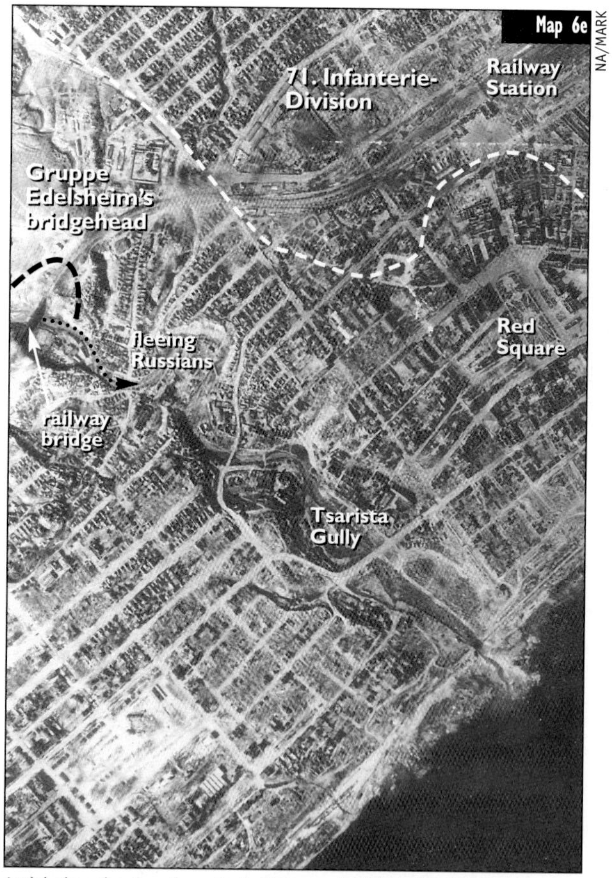

Aerial view showing the extent of Gruppe Edelsheim's bridgehead over the Tsaritsa and the proximity of 71. Infanterie-Division.

4. Reddig is referring to Obergefreiter Fritz Heigster.

bear no proportion to the result. After night had fallen and the threat of being smashed by Russian artillery was negated, the grenadiers and riflemen in the bridgehead abandoned their positions and lugged ammunition crates, weapons and casualties back across the railway bridge. Security posts were dug amongst the southern footings of the bridge and along the lip of the gully to stem the flow of Russian escapees that were sure to push eastwards along the valley floor during the course of the night.

In the evening, the Division secured along the following line: armoured riflemen were on the southern end of the railway bridge over the Tsaritsa Gully, a Kampfgruppe held a strongpoint 600 metres west-north-west of the northern edge of railway station; a Kampfgruppe with panzers was on the west edge of the city 400 metres north of the Barracks on the edge of the city and from there to the south-west was a connection to Gruppe Hellermann. Strong enemy aerial attacks and artillery fire still fell on the area of the Division. For the night, the moving up of searchlights and flak over the city was requested. During the day, the Division captured 470 prisoners and destroyed 4 tanks, 13 guns, 2 anti-tank guns, 1 anti-aircraft gun and 12 mortars. Current panzer strength was 7 Panzer II, 3 Panzer III kz, 4 Panzer III lg, 1 Panzer IV kz, 4 Panzer III lg and 2 Bfwg.

At 1855 hours, General von Lenski oriented General Kempf about the current forward line of the Division. Kempf then said: "The main wish of 24. Panzer-Division, that 94. Infanterie-Division should cordon off, was not performable." General von Lenski summed up the day for Kempf: "Bridgehead will not be held for the night, as during the day. A Gruppe will stand on the southern edge of the bridge for the night. Gruppe Hellermann fights very hard. Three (3) panzers lost. Aim: reach the Tsaritsa Gully and form the Kessel."

This day was counted as a Sturmangriffe day for Panzer-Regiment 24 and PGR21: 16.9.42: attack on Barracks Hill west of Stalingrad

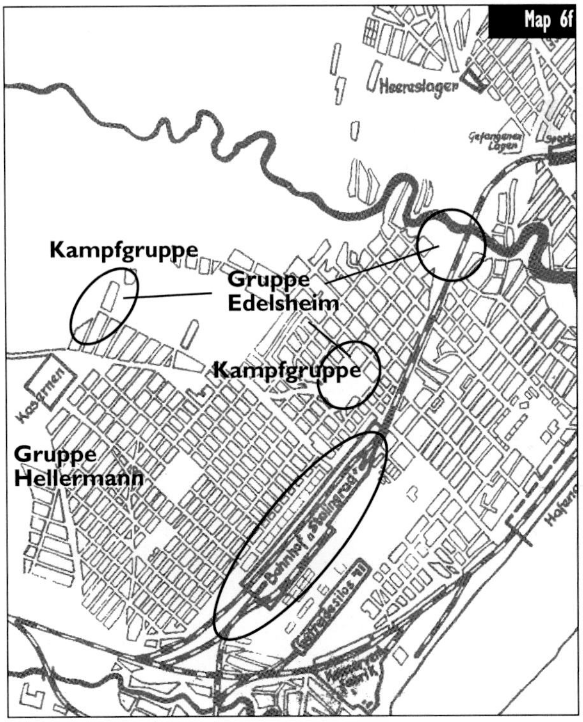

Casualties:

2 officers killed

- Leutnant Helwig Luz (Zug Kdr); 10./PR24 (Killed)
- Leutnant Karl Wolf (Zug Kdr); 6./PGR21 (Killed)

17 men killed

- Obergefreiter Johann Mildner; PGR21 (Killed)
- Obergefreiter Franz Niederleitner; PGR21 (Killed)
- Obergefreiter Karl Müller; PGR21 (Killed)

- Obergefreiter Bruno Bartkowski; PGR21 (Killed)

2 officers wounded

- Stabszahlmeister Gerhard Achmann (Abteilung Zahlmeister); I./PGR26 (Wounded but died on 17th September 1942 from these wounds)
- Leutnant Ferdinand von Senger und Etterlin (Zug Kdr); 2./K4 (Wounded)

87 men wounded (9 of those stayed with the troops)

- Wachtmeister Wippich; PGR21 (Wounded)
- Obergefreiter Fritz Heigster; PGR21 (Wounded)
- Obergefreiter Fritz Schmielewski; PGR21 (Wounded but died later in the day)
- Gefreiter Richard Müller; PGR21 (Wounded but stayed with the troops)
- Obergefreiter Erich Schafframski; PGR21 (Wounded)

1 man missing

17th September 1942:

During the night, the Division experienced heavy enemy air attacks, otherwise, there were no special incidents. On the sector of 24. Panzer-Division occurred a barrage from several enemy batteries located on the east shore of the Volga but this did not affect the days plan: 29. Infanterie-Division (mot.) and 94. Infanterie-Division set off to attack as scheduled. The Division commenced its operations a short time later, the main goal being the complete clearance of the city up to the Tsaritsa.

Rittmeister von Dressler's I. Abteilung of Panzergrenadier-Regiment 26 still held the railway bridge and awaited the appearance of a vanguard from 71. Infanterie-Division. The grenadiers could tell that 71. Infanterie-Division was close because the sound of small-arms fire echoed from the massive buildings that formed the centre of Stalingrad. For the past two days, pillars of smoke rose into the sky and Stukas plunged down along the riverbank. Rittmeister von Dressler also noticed that the Stukas were attacking a different sector today. Stuka after Stuka dove down on the buildings around Red Square and heavy artillery steadily pumped in shells, a boiling mass of dust and smoke emanating from the area. This did not bode well: with this sector still in enemy hands, the prospect of a link-up was greatly reduced. At 0935 hours, Rittmeister von Dressler reported that he still had no connection with the northern neighbour on the railway line. The rest of the Division was making good progress toward the Tsaritsa Gully.
After the destruction of several enemy armoured vehicles, Gruppe Hellermann made excellent northward progress, above all north of the Barracks area. The Russian defensive line, ably assisted by the last remaining tanks of a burnt-out tank brigade, was only able to temporarily restrain Hellermann's advance. Backed by anti-tank guns from Panzerjäger-Bataillon 40, Gruppe Hellermann knocked out the tanks in quick succession: five Russian tanks were destroyed while one was captured intact and put into service. Gefreiter Freimann of 2./Panzerjäger-Abteilung 40 was on hand with his camera to take a photo of the occasion. The remnants of the Soviet defenders resisted bitterly in rough terrain on the edge of the city. The terrain consisted of

uneven, hilly ground riven by numerous gullies, and the whole area was covered by long grass, low thick bushes and small trees. Russian trenches and dug-outs were tucked among the bushes, mortars and artillery being sited in deep gullies to the rear. The Tsaritsa Gully snaked past the rear of this position and served as an escape route to the Volga, although word had reached the Russian defenders that it was practically cut off by German troops positioned along its southern edge. A close connection was also established between Gruppe Hellermann and Gruppe Edelsheim. Gruppe Hellermann continued to make good progress into the gullies north of the two-laned road. One reconnaissance troop penetrated from the Barracks into the second gully west of the city. There were still enemy garrisons in the gullies leading north off the Tsaritsa, the strongest being east of the railway bridge, firing with infantry and individual heavy weapons occurring at the shortest distances, but most were busy fending off attacks from 71. Infanterie-Division.

FREIMANN

The T-34 captured intact by Gruppe Hellermann and elements of Panzerjäger-Abteilung 40.

At 1120 hours, Stalingrad was almost cleared out in the area of the Division. With Panzergrenadier-Regiment 26, the Division had cleared the city sector west of the railway line south of the Tsaritsa and stood along the Tsaritsa with I./Panzergrenadier-Regiment 26 on the railway bridge on the right and II./Panzergrenadier-Regiment 26 to their left, while Kradschützen-Abteilung 4 was on the west edge of the city. In a speedy advance shortly after midday, Gruppe Hellermann sliced through the confused enemy and took the hills south of the Tsaritsa Gully but the advance was then stopped by Division. Elements of Rittmeister v. Sivers' Abteilung of Panzergrenadier-Regiment 21, which lay with its front to the east, advanced together with the left neighbour and pressed down the Tsaritsa Valley from west to east, hoping to clear the entire valley. The desperate enemy resisted in small side gullies and rifts in the steep sides of the Tsaritsa Gully itself until the futility of their situation set in and they slipped off in ones and twos to try their luck in reaching the Volga. The brave enemy who had resisted for three full days was now caught in a pocket with one extremely narrow exit: 71. Infanterie-Division pressed down from the north, elements of Panzergrenadier-Regiment 21 squeezed the pocket from the west while Panzergrenadier-Regiment 26 held the southern edge and sat at the railway bridge, guardians of the enemy's only chance for safety.

HALEY

The T-34 was rebranded and put into German service.

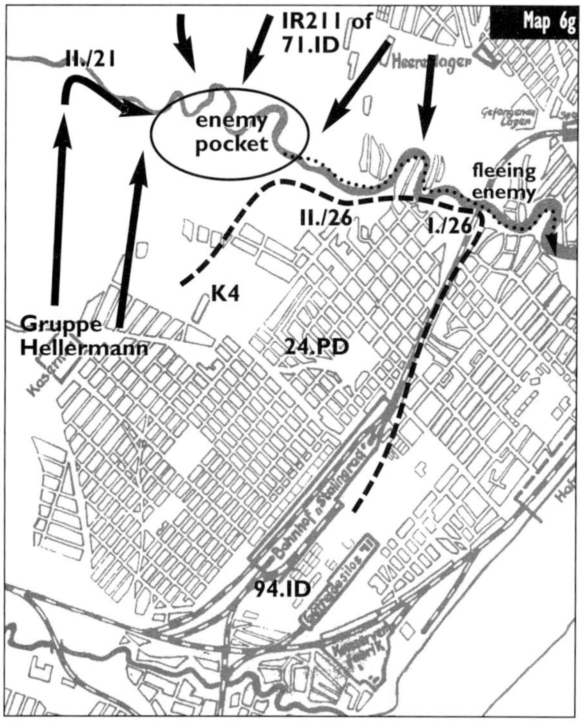

The straightening of this Kessel was reckoned upon toward evening. Obergefreiter Reddig's 1. Schwadron of Panzergrenadier-Regiment 21 was also involved in this operation: "17.9.42. Schwadron still attacking the Kessel. At midday, I was up front. In the meantime, they had changed positions three times and were making very good progress. In the evening, I brought coffee to the front. During this time, several bombs hit on the position of the Schwadronstrupp. Vehicle of Schwarz severely damaged, mine 10 metres next to it was intact. In the morning, the vehicle of Süß was severely damaged."

Now that there was no artillery activity from the Russians caught in the pocket, the Division's artillery was wheeled around to combat targets recognised on the east shore of the Volga. Barrages from this direction were increasing in ferocity and intensity and Major von Pawel[5] decided to eradicate some of these new batteries. Enemy targets were recognised on the island as well as on the east shore in Krasnaya Sloboda. Two batteries of Panzerartillerie-Regiment 89 fired on the shoreline and 2km south of Krasnaya Sloboda, as well as on anti-aircraft batteries, with effective results. Individual Volga ships and boats also came under fire. There were very good operational possibilities for heavy artillery.
In the early afternoon, a connection on the east wing, to the right, was established east of the railway bridge with Infanterie-Regiment 267[6] which left one of its battalions on the Tsaritsa Gully to secure to the north and maintain a connection with 24. Panzer-Division on the railway bridge. Thrusting up from the south, 94. Infanterie-Division was still in combat against the enemy bridgehead at the mouth of the Tsaritsa and the stubborn Grain Silo at the southern railway station. If General Kempf had known the trouble this Silo was to cause him, he would have ordered 24. Panzer-Division to take it on the afternoon of 15th September when it was undefended.

At 1755 hours, Major von Menges reported to Korps that the Tsaritsa had been reached everywhere – including west of the city and the entire gully was cleaned out. Gruppe Hellermann was in the gully itself with a connection to Edelsheim on the right but also having a connection available to the infantry on the left. These infantrymen belonged to Oberst Barnbeck's Infanterie-Regiment 211 of 71. Infanterie-Division. There was still an enemy

5. Commander of Panzerartillerie-Regiment 89.
6. An infantry regiment belonging to 94. Infanterie-Division

pocket ahead of the north front of the Division, however. Oberst Friebe said that now some of its forces were freed up, 24. Panzer-Division should prepare its unemployed units for a thrust through to the Volga. Korps' plan was to concentrate 94. Infanterie-Division in the north, 24. Panzer-Division would relieve a part of 94. Infanterie-Division and then they would advance together. If 94. Infanterie-Division succeeded in taking more ground on this day, then this plan would be negated. Menges also told Oberst Friebe that the missions remained the same for Gruppe Edelsheim and Gruppe Hellermann.

It had been a successful few days for the Division: 400 prisoners taken the previous day, 300 on this day. Two planes had been shot down and 8 tanks, 2 anti-tank guns, 55 anti-tank rifles and 12 mortars were destroyed. The only negative was that the enemy could still retreat to the north-north-east and this was through no fault of the Division. It had done all that was asked of it. In the evening, all enemy forces in the attack strips of the Division west of the railway and south of the Tsaritsa sector had been completely destroyed. Found in the Barracks area of Gruppe Hellermann and Viereckswald alone were 46 Russian tanks, among them 23 T-34's, all destroyed by German weapons. The Division's operational panzer strength at the end of the day was 7 Panzer II, 3 Panzer III kz, 6 Panzer III lg, 1 Panzer IV kz, 4 Panzer IV lg and 2 Bfwg. The Division had only suffered light casualties: two dead and 37 wounded, fourteen of these wounded men remaining with their units. A severe ammunition shortage caused concern amongst supply officers of all divisions of XXXXVIII. Panzerkorps. Near 24. Panzer-Division, the critical shortage was in light infantry gun ammunition at 15% availability, light howitzers at 25% and anti-tank shells for the 20mm flak guns, which currently stood at 0%. This last figure shows the severity of the fighting. These 20mm anti-aircraft guns, mounted on the flatbeds of half-tracks, were attached to combat groups to support the grenadiers and often formed the only anti-tank capability in emergency situations.
Since breaking through the front near Tebektenerovo on 29th August until the capture of Stalingrad on 17th September, the following were taken prisoner or captured by the Division:

10,500 prisoners
26 planes shot down
181 guns
47 guns silenced
130 tanks
120 anti-tank guns
36 anti-aircraft guns
269 anti-tank rifles
130 mortars
Immense quantities of infantry weapons, vehicles and equipment of all types.

Until the onset of darkness, 24. Panzer-Division had taken the Tsaritsa Gully north of the Barracks area on a broad sector after the destruction of the enemy tanks. A connection with the right neighbour existed near the railway bridge and with the left neighbour hard north-west of Objective Area 1 but there were still weak enemy groups located north of the Tsaritsa. Elements of Rittmeister Drews' 7./Panzergrenadier-Regiment 21 established themselves during the night in several wooden houses on the edge of the Tsaritsa Gully, right next to the massive railway bridge that spanned the broad gully. During the night, a group of Red Army men on foot tried to push past the steep slope to the east. A few of the enemy crawled up the slope and threw

MARK

One of the many destroyed or abandoned T-34s lying in 24. Panzer-Division's area of operations.

hand grenades as more groups appeared from the darkness and scurried through the gully to the east. The bulk of Russians succeeded in breaking through in the direction of the Volga.

At 1930 hours, Oberst i.G. Clausius, Chief-of-Staff of LI. Armeekorps, reported his Korps' current situation to XXXXVIII. Panzerkorps: "Gully south of MTS being cleared from west up to 600 metres south of MTS near 457. There is still an enemy group between the edge of the city and the west edge of the railway station. Still a very strong garrison near the Army Camp. From the centre of the railway station to the Waterworks.
"Aim: clear the western part of the city. First of all the Army Camp. Then, in the afternoon, thrust to south-west up to the railway line."

Casualties:

2 men killed

• Oberpanzergrenadier Kurt Kaukjalko; PGR26 (Killed)

1 officer wounded

• Leutnant Albrecht Köhne (Zug Kdr); 2./PGR26 (Wounded)

36 men wounded (14 of those stayed with the troops)

Result of the fighting in Stalingrad from 12th – 17th September 1942:

NA/MARK

Attempted Russian breakout attempt on the evening of 17th September.

On 17th September 1942, the Division was the first to take its allotted city sector of Stalingrad while violent fighting still raged in the other sectors of the city. This success was attributed to the excellent spirit and level of training of the troops, the close co-operation between panzers, armoured riflemen and panzergrenadiers in local combat, as well as the daring quick breakthrough of the armoured elements to the objective whereby it was made impossible for the Russians to construct further defensive positions. The clearance of the city sector usually followed soon after. Through the quick execution of its missions, the Division was freed up for further assignments.

While the success of 24. Panzer-Division in the fighting around Stalingrad was evident, in the opinion of the Division, those successes did not stand a favourable comparison to the casualties suffered. Formerly occupied by first-class personnel and excellently equipped, the Division had been involved in heavy city fighting for the second time in the 1942 summer campaign, conducted mainly by the numerically weak panzergrenadiers, and the uniqueness of the Division – being the only panzer division converted from a cavalry division and retaining its strong traditions – was not taken into consideration. After breaking through the strongly constructed winter positions east of Schchigry, the capture of Voronesh, the breakthrough fighting on the lower Don, the cauldron of Kalach and conquest of the fortified rings of Stalingrad, the Division, as a consequence of the mostly favourable spacious terrain, had gained all of these successes with comparatively small personnel and material losses. Only the fighting in Stalingrad raised the casualties, particularly amongst the panzergrenadiers, to such a degree that after only 14 days in the fortified area of the city, the bulk of the commanders had been eliminated by death or wounding. The casualties in men was also high.

Notwithstanding this, the morale of the troops was so excellent and confident that after a speedy resupply of sufficient replacements, the reconstruction of the Panzergrenadier Brigade was begun with a solid nucleus of hardened veterans.

18th September 1942:

The night passed quietly and there were no particular occurrences. The Russians along the Tsaritsa valley were too busy saving their lives by fleeing toward the Volga. Even their commander, General Vasili Ivanovich Chuikov, had abandoned his bunker in the northern wall of the Tsaritsa during the night. Together with his entire staff, he walked along the gully floor and embarked on a boat for the eastern shore.

German artillery placed harassment fire on positions in Krasnaya Sloboda on the east shore of the Volga. At 0810 hours, Major von Menges lodged the morning report with Korps: "Night quiet. Russians retreated north of Tsaritsa. Freed I./71, II./71, Pionier-Bataillon 635, panzers were repaired on the west edge of the city." The previously attained line was firmly held. By the approach of 71. Infanterie-Division north of the Tsaritsa sector from the west to east, elements of Panzergrenadier-Regiment 21 on the west wing were able to be pulled out. A connection to 71. Infanterie-Division was also taken up at the railway bridge over the Tsaritsa. When the enemy tried to filter through to the railway bridge from the west, he was caught in a savage crossfire and thrown back in a counterthrust.

At 1315 hours, General Kempf called Major von Menges with a simple request: "I immediately want 50 shots of 88mm flak fired into the Grain Elevator."

The heavy-punching fire of the 88mm flak guns was meant to help 94. Infanterie-Division in their assault on the concrete fortress but the staff of that division were apprehensive, as is evident in a three-way radio conversation between Major von Menges, the Chief-of-Staff of 94. Infanterie-Division, Oberst i.G. Manitz, and Oberst Friebe at 1340 hours.

Friebe: "24. Panzer-Division has offered to take over the sector up to the gully 1.5km south of the railway bridge with the elements of Gruppe Hellermann."

Manitz: "We are glad that we will free up some forces."

Friebe: "I will speak with 24. Panzer-Division."

Manitz: "Kempf has ordered that flak of 24. Panzer-Division fire on the Elevator from the Barracks area."

Menges: "We have notified 94. Infanterie-Division that they must take care because we are now beginning with the flak fire."

Friebe: "Do not shoot until further orders."

Menges: "I hope the order will still be passed by radio because there is no telephone communication."

Manitz: "Flak is very close there. Will once more ask definitely not to shoot."

Kempf's simple request for fire support had become diplomatic parleying between the three chiefs-of-staff. Oberst Friebe got up from the radio set and went off to talk to Kempf about the concerns of 94. Infanterie-Division. Kempf stuck to his guns. Previous tactics had failed to dislodge the Russians so it was now time to try something else and he insisted upon the use of the 88's. At 1400 hours, Oberst Friebe informed Manitz that General Kempf had finally ordered that 24. Panzer-Division open fire. Manitz replied: "We have great hesitation. Our people ought to dig themselves in. It is also still unclear who has overall control of the Elevator operation."

At 1430 hours, Oberst Friebe talked to Major von Menges again:

Friebe: "What has happened with the proposal of Oberst von Edelsheim to take over the sector up to the gully south of the railway bridge?"

Menges: "I don't know. Will clarify."

Friebe: "We are naturally right about freeing up forces of 94. Infanterie-Division. Kempf insists upon the opening of fire on the Silo by the flak of the Division."

Menges: "Opening fire has been ordered."

Soon after, Major von Menges reported to Korps:

"Flak firing since 1500 hours. 50 shells fired, shooting discontinued. 44 hits have been reported. 71. Infanterie-Division, pushing from west to east, is on the railway bridge. Connection with 94. Infanterie-Division established. Have spoken with Ia 94. Infanterie-Division, wants to leave the boundary as before on the railway line. Edelsheim has the relief."

After an hour and a half of conversations and negotiations by radio, Kempf got his wish of 88mm fire on the Grain Elevator. The guns fired on the Elevator from positions only 800 metres away. It did not have much of an effect. Apart from 44 circular two-foot holes over the facade and storage area, there was no tangible result, and Russian resistance did not ease. The

MARK

The result of fifty 88mm shells: numerous two-foot wide holes punched in the Grain Elevator's facade.

Grain Elevator was also fired on by 4./Panzerartillerie-Regiment 89 but with better results. A section of the lower floors collapsed under the steady pounding of the battery's 105mm guns.

The Division's current panzer strength was 7 Panzer II, 4 Panzer III kz, 6 Panzer III lg, 1 Panzer IV kz, 4 Panzer IV lg and 2 Bfwg. It also had 9 heavy and 32 medium anti-tank guns operational. A total of 250 prisoners had been brought in during the course of the day.
At 1815 hours, General Arthur Schmidt, Chief-of-Staff of 6. Armee, called Oberst Friebe at XXXXVIII. Panzerkorps HQ: "94. Infanterie-Division and 24. Panzer-Division will be subordinated to LI. Armeekorps. I will report it to KG[7]. Elements of 24. Panzer-Division will soon be pulled out and employed." At 2025 hours, this decision was confirmed. In the business-like message, it simply said: "24. Panzer-Division subordinated to LI. Armeekorps from 0800 hours on 19th September." Half an hour later, Oberst Friebe reported this to Generalmajor von Lenski. LI. Armeekorps planned to use 24. Panzer-Division to straighten out the northern part of Stalingrad. An hour later, the order went to 24. Panzer-Division that they would relinquish control of Pionier-Bataillon 635 and Flak-Bataillon 602 on 19th September. A short time later, another order was sent to 24. Panzer-Division stating that it would also give up Panzerjäger-Abteilung 670[8] which would remain in the present area at the disposal of Korps.

7. General Kempf
8. See Appendix 7 (page 481)

MARK

A 20mm gun on a half-track in position on Komitetskaya Street. The gun is aimed at the Grain Elevator.

MARK

A Vierlingsflak (four barrel 20mm AA gun) provides air cover for the ground troops. In Stalingrad-South, the eastern skyline was constantly dominated by the massive Grain Elevator.

Casualties:

4 men killed

• Unteroffizier Erich Dangeleit; PGR21 (Killed)
• Gefreiter Paul Schiwan; K4 (Killed)

20 men wounded (5 of those stayed with the troops)

The Flak did not have everything their own way: the threat of Russian air attacks was still sufficient to force all of these guns to adopt some sort of camouflage.

19th September 1942:

The night passed quietly for the Division. The morning dawned grey and overcast with a strong wind blowing from the east. 24. Panzer-Division was withdrawn from XXXXVIII. Panzerkorps and at 0800 hours, formally subordinated to LI. Armeekorps. Units of the Division had already begun to pull out during the night and were assembling in the Yezovka – Voroponovo – 'Schafzucht' areas for a few days of rest. Obergefreiter Reddig reports: "19.9.42: We collected the Schwadron with vehicles and drove them into a gully. Here for the first time, the Schwadron had a couple days of rest and could recover from the heavy combat. Canteen goods were given, a half bottle of sparkling wine per man and a bottle of alcohol for 11 men. Russian planes very active, only individual bombers heard during the night."
The last order from XXXXVIII. Panzerkorps arrived at 0845 hours. "To Panzerjäger-Abteilung 670 via 24. Panzer-Division: available guns will be subordinated to 94. Infanterie-Division, supply them to west part of Theatre Square, 500 metres south-west of Tsaritsa mouth." And with that, the Division departed from XXXXVIII. Panzerkorps under whose capable control they had been for more than a month.
On this day, the doctor of III./Panzer-Regiment 24, Stabsarzt Dr. Baatz, was transporting wounded back along the supply road when he became lost in the darkness. He continued too far south and drove right into the Russians. His name appeared on the list of missing men.

Casualties:

5 men killed

• Obergefreiter Johann Körver; PGR26 (Killed)
• Unteroffizier Wilhelm Knackstedt; PGR26 (Killed)

1 officer wounded (he stayed with the troops)

- Leutnant Werner Tutein (Zug Kdr); 1./PGR26 (Wounded but stayed with the troops)

25 men wounded (6 of those stayed with the troops)

1 officer missing

- Oberarzt Dr. Baatz (Abteilung Hilfsarzt); III./PR24 (Missing in action)

Casualties in the time from 27th August – 19th September 1942:

	Offz.	Uffz. u Mann.
Killed	13	346
Wounded	51 (a further 47 stayed with the troops)	1290 (a further 835 stayed with the troops)
Missing	1	13
Total	65 Offz.	1649 Uffz. U. Men.

Booty and prisoners in the time from 27th August – 19th September 1942:

10,750 prisoners
26 aircraft
184 guns (including 40 guns captured on freight trains)
47 guns silenced
133 tanks
122 anti-tank guns
36 anti-aircraft guns
271 anti-tank rifles
146 mortars
9 Stalin Organs
1 armoured train with 12 guns (7.62cm), 2 cannon (2cm) and 12 machine-guns
25 locomotives
510 freight wagons with war material
257 horsedrawn vehicles with 615 horses
Several hundred kilograms of flour, wheat and salt.

Intermission

Chapter Seven

20th September 1942:

Obergefreiter Reddig wrote in his diary: "20.9.42: Rest day, beautiful weather. Schwadron received wine. After a long time, pay rollcall. Rain at night."

The panzergrenadier schwadrons, miserably denuded after the costly fighting on the approaches to Stalingrad, were only roughly replenished with newly-arrived young replacements. The opportunity was also taken to reorganise the schwadrons. No time remained, however, to accustom the new replacements to the conditions at the front: they'd been trained in the homeland but it was only brief, so they were assigned to their schwadrons and allowed to feel at home in their new units. They would receive on-the-job training.

As a result of the strained situation around Mamayev Kurgan, Panzergrenadier-Regiment 26 had to move off at 0330 hours after an alarm to relieve elements of 295. Infanterie-Division which had endured strong attacks since the previous day. They marched from the Schafzucht area along the railway line to Gumrak, then from there along the double-laned road to the east into the area west of the Pilot's School. What followed in the northern part of Stalingrad was without doubt some of the fiercest fighting the Division would ever experience.

In the meantime, General von Seydlitz-Kurzbach, Commander of LI. Armeekorps, decided that 24. Panzer-Division would take over a large portion of 295. Infanterie-Division's sector, freeing up that division for an assault south-east of Hill 102.0 in the direction of the Volga shore. Accordingly at 1230 hours, Divisionsbefehl Nr. 62 was issued which ordered the Division to take over a sector from 295. Infanterie-Division and to defend it. This takeover was scheduled for the nights of 20th/21st September and 21st/22nd September with the aim of occupying the largest part of 295. Infanterie-Division's sector with Kradschützen-Abteilung 4, Panzergrenadier-Regiment 26 and Gruppe Sälzer. Panzergrenadier-Regiment 26 had already moved forward to take over its assigned sector and was given 2./Panzerjäger-Abteilung 40 and II./Panzerartillerie-Regiment 89 for support, but only until 1700

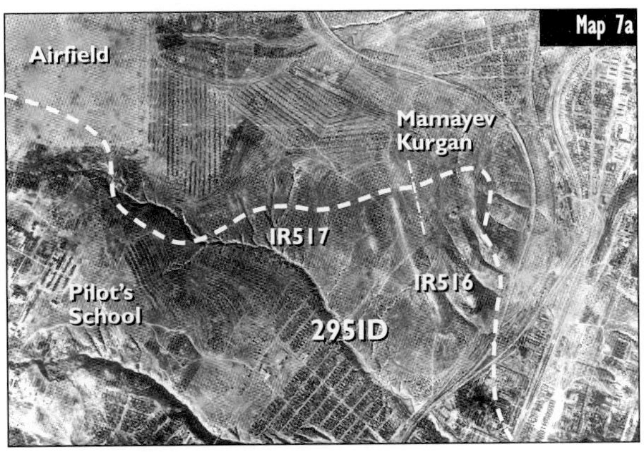

KOLCZYK

Under glorious autumn skies, a trooper of 1./K4 catches up on some rest, recuperation and paperwork. Even here at Gumrak, many kilometres from the city, camouflage against Russian aircraft was necessary.

hours the next day. During 21st September, Panzerartillerie-Regiment 89 would move up and dig in to provide coverfire for the defending grenadiers. The anti-aircraft guns of IV./Panzerartillerie-Regiment 89 would also be pulled forward in the afternoon of 21st September. On the night of 21st/22nd September, Kradschützen-Abteilung 4 (minus 1. Schwadron) would occupy the sector of the left battalion of Infanterie-Regiment 516 on the east slope of Hill 102, while Gruppe Sälzer would haul its anti-tank guns forward and dig them in along the northern edge of the airfield. During the night, Panzergrenadier-Regiment 26 took over the sector of Infanterie-Regiment 517 on the western half of Hill 102.0 down to and including the airfield. On the airfield lay a panzerjäger kompanie of 295. Infanterie-Division subordinated to Gruppe Edelsheim for the time being. Positions were taken from the notorious Hill 102 (Mamayev Kurgan) on the right across to the north-west part of the runway of the airfield, connecting there to 389. Infanterie-Division. The grenadiers of Panzergrenadier-Regiment 26 were given a helpful hint by their comrades in their sister regiment: Panzergrenadier-Regiment 21 had had very good experiences with orange smoke-grenades during bunker fighting. While the Russians for the most part tried to throw out hand grenades tossed into their bunkers, it was discovered that they did not venture to immediately handle the smouldering smoke-grenades. To begin with, a smoke-grenade was thrown into the bunker, quickly followed by a regular hand-grenade. General von Lenski, however, added a cautious note to this piece of advice: sufficient smoke-grenades should be available for their proper use of warning pilots during an attack.

Casualties:

5 men killed

3 officers wounded (2 of those stayed with the troops)

- Oberleutnant Herbert Oberbeck (Schwadron Kdr); 8./PGR26 (Wounded but stayed with the troops)
- Leutnant Karrasch (Zug Kdr); 1./Pz.Pi.40 (Wounded)
- Leutnant Friedrich Schröder (Zug Kdr); 3./Pz.Pi.40 (Wounded but stayed with the troops)

26 men wounded (8 of those stayed with the troops)

Decorations bestowed from 14th September to 20th September:

25 Iron Cross First Class

329 Iron Cross Second Class

50 Panzer Combat Badge in Bronze
26 Panzer Combat Badge in Silver
60 Assault Badge

Prisoners and booty taken from 14th September to 20th September:

1600 prisoners
4 airplanes
22 guns
23 tanks
16 anti-tank guns
6 anti-aircraft guns
57 mortars
87 anti-tank rifles

21st September 1942:

During the night, several enemy attacks against Hill 102.0 were repulsed by Panzergrenadier-Regiment 26. The enemy assaults were partly smashed in their starting positions by the Division's artillery. Throughout the day, the Regiment received welcome support in the form of the divisional artillery shifting into new positions. Hauptmann Gach of Panzerpionier-Bataillon 40 received the important task of reconnoitring crossing possibilities for panzers and heavy weapons over the gullies south-east and north-east of the Pilot's School and establishing improvements to roads and descriptions of the crossing possibilities. He was to report his findings to Division as soon as possible.

In the evening, once the sun had disappeared below the horizon and not a trace of its light was left in the sky, the relief of 295. Infanterie-Division commenced. Kradschützen-Abteilung 4 was employed east of Panzergrenadier-Regiment 26 in the fearful trenches and foxholes atop Mamayev Kurgan, and further west on the airfield was Gruppe Sälzer (Panzerjäger-Abteilung staff with 2./Panzerjäger-Abteilung 40 and 3./Panzerpionier-Bataillon 40). Now that the divisional artillery was safely emplaced, its guns were trained on the most dangerous areas, concentrating mainly on Hill 102 or, as it was better known, Mamayev Kurgan. Blocking fire could be called down by any officer simply by firing a red flare. Once the relief was completed, the call-sign 'Seydlitz' was transmitted to Division, signalling a successful takeover.

A panzer schwadron was made available close behind the front-line as a counterattack reserve, parking in a gully west of the Pilot's School. Panzerpionier-Bataillon 40, 1./Kradschützen-Abteilung 4 and the few men of Brigade-Staff were kept at the new Division command post near Abteilung Nr. 6, ready to intervene in any emergency. The remaining unemployed elements of the Division – Panzer-Abteilung Lancken and Panzergrenadier-Regiment 21 – stayed in the Schafzucht area to allow them the longest possible rest and time for repairs. One company of Panzerjäger-Abteilung 40 (1. Kompanie) was training on new guns near Sety.

The panzer schwadron assigned as a reserve was commanded by Oberleutnant Gert-Axel Weidemann:

> "I had the mission of reconnoitring for an operation by the panzers and for this, I had to establish a connection with the advanced command post of Panzergrenadier-Regiment 26. This lay in terrain overlooked by the enemy.
> "I drove to the front in my Kübelwagen; I'd taken command of 5. Schwadron and the

Combat and Ration strength on 21st September 1942

	Combat strength				Ration strength				
Units	Offz.	Beamte	Uffz.	Men	Offz.	Beamte	Uffz.	Men	**Total**
Division Staff	18	10	36	137	30	10	57	235	**332**
Pz.Gren.Brigade 24	2	–	7	27	1	–	12	67	**80**
Pz.Rgt. 24	35	8	445	1171	42	14	564	1678	**2298**
Pz.Gren.Rgt. 21	30	3	256	1049	33	4	265	1073	**1375**
Pz.Gren.Rgt. 26	26	4	208	1095	31	4	232	1197	**1464**
Krad.Abt. 4	13	–	159	690	14	2	172	723	**911**
Pz.Art.Rgt. 89	41	–	214	1184	45	9	280	1481	**1815**
Pz.Jg.Abt. 40	10	1	75	394	14	3	80	404	**501**
Pz.Pi.Btl. 40	13	–	58	492	14	3	76	526	**619**
Pz.Nach.Abt. 86	6	–	69	318	15	2	87	380	**484**
Dinafü. 40	–	–	–	–	23	17	139	894	**1073**
SanKo. 1./40	–	–	–	–	7	3	32	176	**218**
SanKo. 2./40	–	–	–	–	6	3	24	146	**179**
Bäckerei Ko. 40	–	–	–	–	2	1	19	125	**147**
Schlächterei Ko. 40	–	–	–	–	2	1	8	62	**73**
Verpfl. Amt 40	–	–	–	–	–	8	14	82	**104**
Feldpostamt 40	–	–	–	–	–	5	13	10	**28**
Feldgend. Trupp 40	–	–	–	–	3	–	39	13	**55**
Sum:	**194**	**26**	**1527**	**6557**	**282**	**89**	**2113**	**9272**	**11756**
Subordinated Units									
Pz.Jg.Abt. 670	9	–	44	125	11	4	82	252	**349**
Flak-Bataillon 602	15	–	90	427	16	2	104	495	**617**
IV./PAR89	13	–	72	369	14	4	89	444	**551**
1./Ersatz Bataillon 1	1	–	21	128	1	–	21	128	**150**
I./Flak Regiment 5	17	5	120	930	20	5	156	899	**1080**
RAD Gruppe K 22									**640**
Total:	**249**	**31**	**1874**	**8536**	**344**	**104**	**2565**	**11490**	**15143**

NA/MARK

Panzergrenadier-Regiment 26's defensive line between the airfield and Mamayev Kurgan. Kradschützen-Abteilung 4 took over the dangerous positions on and around the summit of Mamayev Kurgan.

panzers in front of Stalingrad were ordered to support the further attacks of the Panzergrenadier-Regiment 26 in the direction of 'Red October'. We drove forward alongside the railway line to Gumrak railway station, which was a welcome orientation point in this desert where the original roads were barely recognisable under the numerous crossings of tracks and wheel ruts. It was midday, the sun was shining in the cloudless sky. After a month of continuing dryness, almost all the sand of the steppe had become dust, whirled about by the wind and by the vehicles, the meagre vegetation transformed into a monotonous grey. Driving past, one could barely recognise the vehicle formations of the staffs and supply equipment through their camouflage nets. If their paperwork had been covered in dust, they would have blended perfectly with their surroundings. The mapboard on my knees, and in my panzer jacket, over the folded down windscreen I recognised the buildings of Gumrak railway station in the distance. My thoughts were of the forthcoming operation in co-operation with our riflemen; fire support, it was decided to keep us back from the house-to-house fighting, a factory area was to be taken; there were many others that had rolled up earlier for the attack! – Gumrak moved closer, in its environs was a well camouflaged vehicle assembly, tents, and the red cross of the medical equipment. After crossing the railway tracks on which stood misshapen, big-as-houses Russian freight cars, we found the road to Alexandrovka. Everywhere, where the road was crossed or branched off, the monotony of the landscape was broken by many pointers fastened to poles or anything that was available, like telephone masts; the various, stylised divisional symbols allied with the tactical signs were recognised by those who knew, and everyone had turned up for this 'rendezvous'; among these was the 'Springende Reiter' and the sign of the sought-after Panzergrenadier Regiment. I smiled when I saw an inscription on a sign on the solitary railway line near Voroponovo that said 'zur Stadtkommandantur'[1], while the tank battle raged on the edge of the city; perhaps this was wit or developed according to the instructions of 'our Führer to take far-sighted measures'. We continued on. The road now went over a flat hill, on the right and left were several Russian airplane wrecks, now and then there were the well-known circular, grey hollows with their star-like splinter paths of the artillery impacts. On the horizon in the march direction were the outlines of barracks-like buildings, Alexandrovka! The wheels were grinding through the sand, the Kübel was skipping over the washboard of this so-called street – In front of us was the web of roads, and again outlined behind them was the high plain with its blocks of houses. 'Halt' – a short orientation. Suddenly, we heard a clear howling – we lay down flat like postage stamps – shortly before the impact – like a cloudburst – the usual dirt, powder, screaming splinters – a surprise barrage by a Stalin Organ, the battlefield – which was cursed – had caught us again. – The driver came out frightened, the vehicle remained intact – 'Start up!' Quickly over the crossing into the covered view of the skeletons looming against the sky, the large, destroyed, abandoned buildings in front of us. Nevertheless! We looked in the cellar to see if 'our people' were here. Everywhere, there was only the yawning emptiness, destroyed staircases and rubbish. Continue on! Nearby was a wide hollow into which the inhabitants had moved after abandoning their rural settlements. I rendezvoused with my panzer here, which was covered against planes by being placed in the lee of the houses.

"Co-operation with our panzergrenadiers not only demanded that we establish contact while we were fighting but to also search for the command posts. Quickly out

1. 'To the city commandant'

of the panzer and – with haversack horizontal – we hurried from cover to cover, and in a moment, we were challenged. Good, our people had learned of us. This time we were searching for the command post of Panzergrenadier-Regiment 26, which had already been mentioned as lying in the airport south-west of the 'Red October'. The approach that way offered cover up to and deep inside Stalingrad; the last piece over the open field will be described. A glance at the map confirmed our information. Our Kübelwagen made use of a canal to swiftly move forward. The outskirts of the canal extended into the preparation area of the panzers. These canals were oversize tank trenches with both sides rising to steep, overgrown slopes: crossing high above this gully, for the time being anyway, was a railway and then a street bridge. Perhaps an industrialist had built this kilometre long, arrow straight supply track under cover from enemy sight and bombardment. Innumerable inhabitants of the city searched for security here and dug their makeshift accommodation into the slopes. Oven-pipes were smoking, washing was drying, it was like a large gypsy camp. Our vehicles only slowly moved forward. And then the floor was empty. We immediately passed an entrenched mortar position and we recognised the entrenching work of the prepared positions of our panzergrenadiers, and we also recognised the yellow Waffenfarbe[2], which indicated that they were 'one of us'. After driving about 8km, signs indicated that Panzergrenadier-Regiment 26 was in the direction of the airfield and to advance further, we would have to abandon our cover. I crept up the slope with my messenger, forewarned and instructed by the grenadiers lying there that the upper edge of the slope was under enemy fire and that the Regiment command post, with earth and groups of bushes thrown on, was about 300 metres away. Thus we crept slowly forward, there seemed to be 'sportsman-like defence' at the beginning of this part of the operation. There were similar moments in the battle during the periods of the mission of our Reiter Regiment; correct conduct was put in during our 'infantry movements'. I gradually advanced forward and I could see in front of me

The long search for a new regiment commander eventually settled upon Oberstleutnant Barthhold von Bassewitz, commander of II./Panzer-Regiment 2 deployed north of Stalingrad. He assumed command of Panzer-Regiment 24 in mid-October.

2. Waffenfarbe = branch colour. Each arm of the German Army had a different colour for use on piping, etc.

a sandy, grass-covered plain and behind that I could see the menacing walls of the 'Red October' rising through the sparse wood that bordered the plain. About 350 metres away, I discerned – as described – the Regiment command post, and there were positions here in the direction of the enemy where it would not be impossible to deploy our panzergrenadiers. The situation corresponded on the opposite enemy-occupied edge of the woods. At the moment the front was quiet here. I called to my messenger that with several more bounds, we would reach the command post over there. After one deep breath of air, we rushed forward almost horizontally. There were already detonations and we did not look forward at all. An anti-tank gun was shooting at us from the enemy's direction. Bangs from there, catch some breath. There was an impact somewhere close by. There was movement at the command post in front of us, people were watching us from the cover of the trench. We went forward. There was again a discharge from over there, and we were entirely under cover; a shell whizzed past. Go on, go! Panting, we reached the edge of the trenches and leapt into cover. Oberst von Edelsheim, the old war-horse, welcomed his 'panzer people' with a laugh and said with a shout 'Yes, there's shooting here'.

"This was his roguish, dry humour, his radiant and positive attitude to life that allowed us to forget the strains of the battlefield."

The Commander of II./Panzergrenadier-Regiment 21, Rittmeister Karl v. Sivers, was transferred back to the homeland for OKH training as a Panzer Abteilung commander. Into his position came Rittmeister Otto Drews, Commander of 7. Schwadron. Command of 7. Schwadron went to Leutnant Hans-Heino Freiherr von Eller-Eberstein.

While the panzer schwadron of Oberleutnant Weidemann was poised as a reserve behind the defensive line, the rest of the panzers were assembled in the area north-west of Voroponovo for urgently required maintenance and repair. The battle strength of the panzer schwadrons, which had an authorised combat strength of 22 battle vehicles, had melted away to the strength of a platoon. Major von Winterfeld, with the staff of his I. Abteilung, took over command of the battle units and this made it possible for Major von der Lancken and his staff to get a well-deserved rest.

Casualties:

7 men killed

3 officers wounded (all 3 stayed with the troops)

- Leutnant Werner Fähnrich (Abt Adjutant); I./PAR89 (Wounded but stayed with the troops)
- Major Hans-Wilhelm von Heyden (Abt Kdr); II./PGR26 (Wounded but stayed with troops)
- Leutnant Erwin Krämer (Abt OO); II./PGR26 (Wounded but stayed with the troops)

31 men wounded (7 of those stayed with the troops)

22nd September 1942:

The enemy brought new forces over to the west shore of the Volga in ferrying operations. Several enemy attacks against Hill 102.0 were repulsed. The enemy air force now attacked German positions with strong forces during daylight. Leutnant Hubertus Schulz, Commander of the Nachrichten Zug[3] of Kradschützen-Abteilung

3. Communications platoon

MARK

The panzers and their crews were withdrawn to Stalingrad's western outskirts for rest and minor repairs. This is the laager of I./Panzer-Regiment 24.

MARK

Vehicles requiring major repairs were shipped to workshops further in the rear. Mechanics worked under primitive conditions. Due to overburdened supply lines, replacement parts, especially engines, were lacking.

4, reports on his narrow escape during one of these aerial attacks: "I was caught. An aerial bomb broke into the earth bunker and collapsed the command post of the communication platoon, which I was in. Of the three survivors buried alive, only I was blessed to see the light again." Leutnant Schulz suffered serious wounds and was evacuated to the homeland for treatment.

SPANNOCCHI

The howitzers of Panzerartillerie-Regiment 89 are set up on the steppe outside Stalingrad to support the grenadiers on Mamayev Kurgan.

Perched on the battered slopes of Mamayev Kurgan, the men of Kradschützen-Abteilung 4 watched the sun creep over the horizon and cast its light on the hill. Stukas droned in from the west and plunged down over their heads, dropping their bombs south-east of the Kurgan. A few men peered through binoculars to watch the attack unfold. This attack by 295. Infanterie-Division was a prerequisite for the continued attack of Korps to the north: General von Seydlitz wanted the Russians pushed away from Mamayev Kurgan so that they presented no threat to his future lengthy eastern flank. After operations by the squadrons of VIII. Fliegerkorps and heavy preparatory artillery fire that had begun at 0500 hours, 295. Infanterie-Division launched its attack at 0620 hours under clear, sunny skies. The impact of the Luftwaffe bombardment did not have the expected effect on the enemy. From barricaded houses and numerous earth bunkers, the enemy offered very tough resistance with mortars, artillery and rocket-launchers, in part from the east shore of the Volga, not to mention violent counterthrusts. In costly combat with flamethrowers and concentrated charges, well supported by assault guns and pioneers, the infantry gained ground but their low strengths prevented a large gain of ground. They did have a measure of success because prior to midday, three weak assault spearheads from Infanterie-Regiments 517 and 518 pushed through to the railway running along the shore of the Volga at several points after difficult fighting. The clearance of enemy remnants from the blocks of houses continued for hours. On the left wing, Infanterie-Regiment 516 could not crack the enemy defences in front of it. The attack showed that the Division, with its eroded infantry forces, was no longer equal to the difficult task of house-to-house combat[4]. This northern wing, together with Kradschützen-Abteilung 4, successfully repulsed several battalion-strength attacks on Mamayev Kurgan.

Casualties:

1 officer killed

- Leutnant Heinrich Raeschke (Zug Kdr); 6./PGR26 (Killed)

18 men killed

- Obergefreiter Hans Schiemann; K4 (Killed)
- Gefreiter Boleslaus Kwasny; K4 (Killed)

4. 295. Infanterie-Division suffered serious losses on this day: 46 men killed, 7 officers and 164 men wounded, 4 men missing.

BUNDESARCHIV, BILD 101I/218/524/32 / PHOTO: SEIBOLD

There is even time for music. A gramophone retrieved from one of the huts delights a battleweary panzer crew. Sitting in the middle is Unteroffizier Heinrich Warzun, a panzer driver from 2./Panzer-Regiment 24. The man in the sweater, Obergefreiter Ossadnik, was a gunner in the same schwadron.

• Oberwachtmeister Ernst Horn; K4 (Killed)

2 officers wounded

• Oberleutnant Fichtenau (Schwadron Kdr); 1./Pz.Pi.40 (Wounded)
• Leutnant Hubertus Schulz (Zug Kdr); Nachrichten Zug/K4 (Wounded)

23 men wounded (8 of those stayed with the troops)

• Obergefreiter Otto Gades; I./PGR26 (Wounded)

23rd September 1942:

Several day and night-attacks of the Russians against Hill 102.0 were repulsed. The irritable enemy air attacks continued during the night. The reserve panzer schwadron, still in its laager position, was subjected to one of these attacks and is described by the Commander of 5. Schwadron, Oberleutnant Weidemann:

> "Here were the usual rural wooden houses in the shadows of the barracks-like, hideous mass quarters in the outskirts of the mighty factory halls. Our panzers were beneath these wooden houses; overhanging roofs and the side walls were utilised for camouflage. The air situation made this necessary. While our Luftwaffe sorties during the day did not allow Soviet reconnaissance to fly over, the 'Maxim Gorki' bombers came during the night; from time to time they were caught in the searchlights of our flak emplacements. With their enormous dimensions, they caused the already cold, dark sky to echo with the roar of their multiple engines; the flaming light of the detonating bombs was everywhere, the Soviets dropping them where they recognised

or suspected targets. Our 'friend', the 'Leukoplastbomber'[5], tried again and again every night to sail over us with their engines switched off and 'find some takers' for their bombs. Also here was every one of our battle vehicles, lined up, camouflaged and entrenched in a rectangular hole, and our crews were stretched out here to, if possible, get some sleep. As usual, the excavated earth was thrown towards the front and under the bowplate as protection against shrapnel. Again in the night, the roaring of the 'Maxim Gorki' grew louder in the sky. The crews, wrapped in their blankets, were already sleeping in foxholes under their battle vehicles, and the commanders were also near the assembled panzers. Messengers and Kübelwagen drivers were placed in the neighbouring houses near the foxholes. The cellars were avoided as there was the risk of fire or being buried alive under the rickety houses. My crew was awake, the 'shit bomber' grinding over us. Bombs poured down nearby, the ground shaking from their detonations. Everyone waited, and someone said scornfully that the bomber missions have '1000 for a Mark', and everyone was glad to have something to sneer at. The repulsive whistling came nearer. A thunderstorm! For a split second, it was as bright as lightning under the armoured hulk. The blast flung us up, I flew with my back towards the underbelly. Thick powdery smoke was over us, dirt and dust. The panzer remained intact. The bomb must have exploded right next to us. Did it affect the messengers? Out of the hole. There was smoke everywhere; the neighbouring house was burning. I shouted to my messenger; thank God!; he answered. I felt a warm moistness in my pants. I clutched there with my hand and in the dim light of a pocket lamp, I could see red ink. The loyal Sanitäts-Feldwebel Piesche, who was standing nearby, quickly approached in the first-aid half-track to bandage me. This marvellous Silesian gave me the unfortunate diagnosis by the light of a pocket lamp: 'Herr Oberleutnant, your arse is torn open and only the doctor can help here'. When I was hurled against the panzer, a bomb splinter came flying through the rollers and wounded me, a greeting from the 'Maxim Gorki'."

Leutnant Nueske, Commander of 1./Panzerartillerie-Regiment 89, wrote down the day's events in his diary: "Back to operations. We reconnoitred in the morning and moved into the positions in the afternoon. It appeared to be a fairly windy corner here in the area of the Pilot's Barracks and Hill 102. Both were shoved between the actual city centre, lying further to the south, and the large industrial factories drawn out for kilometres along the Volga to the north. My observation post on Hill 102 proved to be extremely dangerous from the beginning. From there, one had magnificent views of the industrial area, the Volga and the opposite shore, but at the closest distance was an unsurveyable, gully-ridden terrain where the enemy lay within hand-grenade range and one had to be very careful of well-concealed enemy snipers. Our infantry had high daily casualties through head wounds. My predecessor twice had his scissors-telescope shot away."

At 2200 hours, the Division issued Divisionsbefehl Nr. 63 ordering the relief of Panzergrenadier-Regiment 26 by Panzergrenadier-Regiment 21 on 24th September. Oberstleutnant von Hellermann, Commander of Panzergrenadier-Regiment 21, was ordered to report to the main entrance on the western edge of the Pilot's School at 1200 hours the next day, together with his advanced relief party, where a guide from Panzergrenadier-Regiment 26

5. Leukoplast is a trademarked sticking plaster. The nickname implies that the bombers did not cause any damage apart from cuts and bruises. Its psychological effect, however, more than compensated for its negligible military value.

would await him. Hellermann's men would be brought forward to the western entrance of the Pilot's School before 1700 hours and the vehicles that had transported them would immediately retire to a position roughly one kilometre from the School. The takeover would be hastened so that it was completed before 1900 hours, before the beginning of the enemy's night-time aerial attacks.

Casualties:

32 men killed

- Obergefreiter Günther Denecke; PGR26 (Killed)
- Obergefreiter Josef Kapp; PGR26 (Killed)
- Gefreiter Rudolf Suchy; PGR26 (Killed)
- Gefreiter Otto Barkowski; PGR26 (Killed)
- Gefreiter Bruno Borowski; PGR26 (Killed)

1 officer wounded

- Oberleutnant Gert-Axel Weidemann (Schwadron Kdr); 5./PR24 (Wounded)

121 men wounded (82 of those stayed with the troops)

24th September 1942:

In the early morning hours, the Russians attacked Kradschützen-Abteilung 4 in regiment strength on Hill 102.0 after a heavy artillery and air force preparation. Defence was extremely difficult because Germans and Russians lay face to face on the high crest and as a consequence of this, only a small field of fire was available. The attack was repulsed in vicious hand-to-hand combat.
Leutnant Nueske reports the happenings with his artillery unit: "The night passed quietly apart from several hand-grenade duels. In the afternoon, an attack was shot apart. Schwarzer[6] positioned himself further to the right for additional observation. Throughout the night, the enemy bombarded the entire area with brisk harassing fire. All approach roads lay under artillery shelling and Stalin Organ fire. To mend the wire connections proved to be a pointless exercise."

Throughout the day, Panzerartillerie-Regiment 89 succeeded in silencing 6 enemy batteries and an anti-aircraft battery with the aid of artillery observers, men such as Leutnant Nueske and Oberwachtmeister Schwarzer.

Because the planned assault on the northern part of Stalingrad was not to take place in the next three days due to an order from Korps, the Division decided to allow Panzergrenadier-Regiment 26 to be relieved by Panzergrenadier-Regiment 21 in the coming night. Panzergrenadier-Regiment 21 relieved Panzergrenadier-Regiment 26 with I. Abteilung on the right and II. Abteilung on the left in its positions between Kradschützen-Abteilung 4 (Hill 102) and Gruppe Sälzer on the left. It was a windy corner. The enemy not only strongly covered the positions and all approach roads with fire from artillery and Stalin Organs, but his snipers also made themselves unpleasantly noticeable. Thus they already made the briefing of the unit commanders difficult in their sectors in the late afternoon. Soon after the insertion into the positions near darkness, the telephone cable from the command post of I. Abteilung of

6. Oberwachtmeister Johann Schwarzer, German Cross in Gold on 9th October 1942.

FREIMANN

Anti-tank guns of 3./Panzerjäger-Abteilung 40 dug into the exposed ground of the airstrip. The men appear to be in good spirits.

Panzergrenadier-Regiment 21 to its 2. and 3. Schwadrons on the right was already shot to pieces and Gefreiter Vennemann had to repeatedly go out to check the line. The takeover was successfully ended and the grenadiers safely in foxholes before any Russian bombers moved overhead. The codeword 'Hellermann' was sent to Division, signifying the completion of the relief. The exhausted and bleary-eyed men of Edelsheim's Panzergrenadier-Regiment 26, after gathering in the Pilot's School, climbed into lorries that arrived after 1800 hours and drove to the west, into rest areas around Gumrak. One unlucky schwadron remained behind to serve as a reserve behind Panzergrenadier-Regiment 21.

During the relief, the Russians attacked hard west of Hill 102.0 in regiment strength at 2230 hours. The enemy succeeded with a roughly 400 metre deep penetration near 1./Panzergrenadier-Regiment 21 on the boundary to II. Abteilung. Obergefreiter Reddig, from the particularly hard hit 1./Panzergrenadier-Regiment 21, reports:

"24.9.42: Strong enemy fire at the front. Wachtmeister Kabbeck and Unteroffizier Rattey severely wounded, Harras lightly wounded. In the evening, I drove with Unteroffizier Winkler, Obergefreiter Schweinsberg, Roß, Gruppel and Gefreiter Elsässer with lunch to the Schwadron. Russians strongly covered the sector with anti-tank fire. We loaded up with the food containers and crept through a very deep and narrow Rachel to the front. At 2100 hours, we were finished with the delivery. The Russians must have noticed something…

"At 2200 hours, he attacked. It came down to hand-to-hand combat. Killed were Oberwachtmeister Hartkopf, Wachtmeister Wank, Unteroffizier Krüp, Obergefreiter Willi Galinke, Kühn, Weber I, Hugo Marquadt, Justus Jäckel, severely wounded Obergefreiter Schweinhorst, Gronau, Wessels, Kirsten, Unteroffizier Döring, Gefreiter Ulonska, Obergefreiter Knoblauch and Paul Krakau. This was by far the blackest day for the Schwadron near Stalingrad."

Following is a report from a direct participant in the defence against the Russian intrusion, Unteroffizier Hopp, also from 1./Panzergrenadier-Regiment 21:

> "After taking over the position and a lot of ammunition on 24.9., no more time remained to establish connections to the right or left, or for a thorough reconnaissance of the new locality.
>
> "Near our left wing platoon, both listening posts failed so that the enemy, strongly influenced by alcohol, succeeded in the darkness in noiselessly penetrating the position.
>
> "This time, he'd caught a particularly favourable moment because all squads had food-fetchers in transit. The return of the food-fetchers and the intrusion of the enemy resulted in confusion that was difficult to sort out. Obergefreiter Freimuth, an old experienced MG-Schütze 1, had sent his Schütze 2, Gefreiter Hugo Marquadt to fetch food from behind. When Marquadt returned and wanted to get to Freimuth in the position, several enemy soldiers suddenly appeared. Freimuth succeeded in

suppressing them with his machine-gun but he unfortunately could not avert the fatal bullet that struck Marquadt.

"We on the right wing suddenly found ourselves alone. We had no connection to the right. A hole had already existed there since the relief.

"As we were clear about the situation, it presented only one thing in the darkness: comrades from right and left were very sensible and came into my command post, an oversized machine-gun position. We were six men, my newly attached deputy Unteroffizier Eiben, Obergefreiter Alfred Fromme, MG-Schütze 1 Gefreiter Schmischke, Schütze 2 Kutz, my messenger Weber and my humble self. Now we were stronger, or at least it felt like it to us.

"The machine-gun had a shooting direction to the front, we others always in twos to the other sides. Whatever came could only be perceived at the shortest distance, the enemy that was working his way up repeatedly repelled with hand grenades that our relieved comrades had left in generous quantities.

"After many hours, the stressful listening and staring into the darkness, and the lightning-like reactions to suddenly appearing enemy, threatened to cause our strength to fail. When I saw a favourable time in the morning hours, I wanted to have a connection to Schwadron. Unteroffizier Eiben and Weber reported themselves for this task. They would report about the course of the night and bring up ammunition. Eiben came through, Weber was shot by Russians still wandering about behind us."

The penetration was sealed off for the time being with the help of 2./Pz.Pi.40 and a reserve Schwadron. Through a counterattack the following morning, the enemy penetration was sealed off and straightened out by elements of Panzergrenadier-Regiment 26 at 1000 hours. Sixth Schwadron of Panzergrenadier-Regiment 21 lost one of its best platoon commanders here when Oberwachtmeister Arnold was severely wounded in the morning hours by a Soviet sniper.

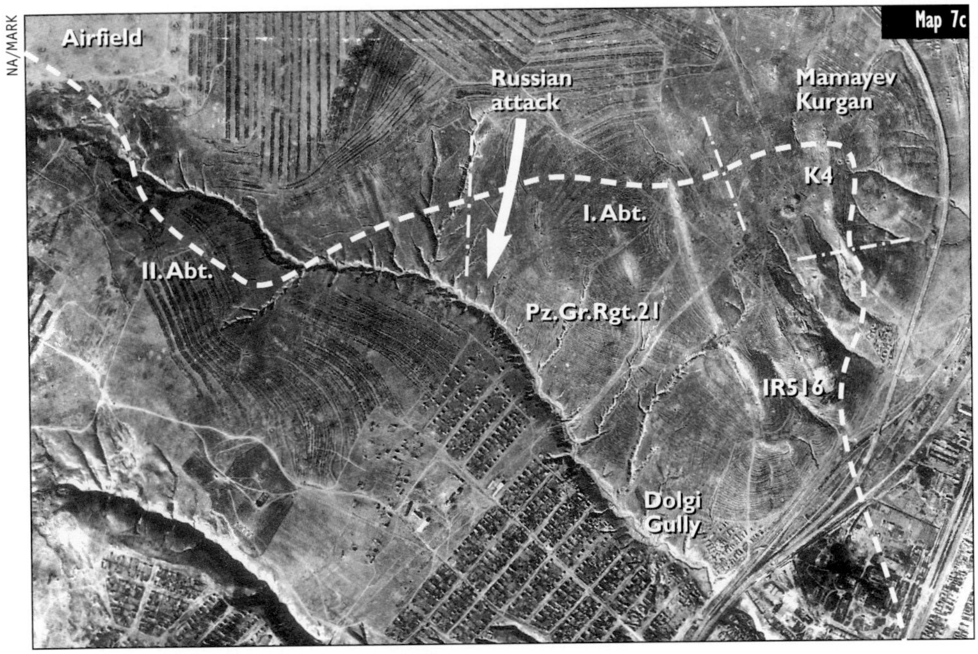

Russian attack on the night of 24th/25th September.

At 2100 hours, the Division issued Divisionsbefehl Nr. 64 ordering the relief of Kradschützen-Abteilung 4 and elements of Panzergrenadier-Regiment 21 on 25th September by the newly arrived 100. Jäger-Division. This meant the right half of the Division's sector, including the perilous foxholes burrowed into Mamayev Kurgan, would be handed over to the Jäger. The new divisional boundary on the right went from the north end of the gully in grid square 40c to the western edge of the shooting range. Rittmeister von Langenn-Steinkeller's Kradschützen-Abteilung 4 was to be relieved by II./Jäger-Regiment 227, as would elements of Panzergrenadier-Regiment 21. Advanced parties from the Jäger battalion had already arrived at Rittmeister von Langenn-Steinkeller's command post while the rest of the battalion would move into waiting positions in the Pilot's School at 1630 hours the next day. Once again, the order was for the relief to be completed by 1900 hours, prior to the enemy's now customary nocturnal bombing attacks.

Casualties:

25 men killed

- Oberwachtmeister Willi Hartkopf; PGR21 (Killed)
- Unteroffizier Johann Krüp; PGR21 (Killed)
- Sanitäts-Unteroffizier Willi Korsch; PGR21 (Killed)
- Gefreiter Hugo Marquadt; PGR21 (Killed)
- Obergefreiter Josef Hanke; PGR21 (Killed)
- Obergefreiter Heinrich Schaf; PGR21 (Killed)
- Wachtmeister Franz Kasparek; PR24 (Killed)

3 officers wounded (2 of those stayed with the troops)

- Leutnant Hans Warlimont (Zug Kdr); 3./K4 (Wounded)
- Leutnant Friedrich Buschinsky (Zug Kdr); 6./PGR26 (Wounded but stayed with the troops)
- Leutnant Horst Erdmann (Batterie Officer); 5./PAR89 (Wounded but stayed with the troops)

73 men wounded (12 of those stayed with the troops)

- Wachtmeister Fritz Kabbeck; PGR21 (Wounded but died on 25th September in hospital)
- Unteroffizier Rattey; PGR21 (Severely wounded)
- Harras; PGR21 (Wounded but stayed with the troops)
- Obergefreiter Schweinhorst; PGR21 (Severely wounded)
- Gronau; PGR21 (Wounded)
- Wessels; PGR21 (Wounded)
- Kirsten; PGR21 (Wounded)
- Unteroffizier Döring; PGR21 (Wounded)
- Gefreiter Ulonska; PGR21 (Wounded)
- Obergefreiter Knoblauch; PGR21 (Wounded)
- Paul Krakau; PGR21 (Wounded)

1 man missing

25th September 1942:

The enemy who had broken through the previous night were thrown back by a counterattack by panzergrenadiers and pioneers. Unteroffizier Hopp and his men were still besieged in their dug-out: "The breaking day was bright and clear. We could no longer shoot with the machine-gun because ammunition was too scarce. Whoever had a dangerous target was allowed to draw a cartridge out of the machine-gun belt and fire with the rifle. Every shot must count because we wanted to hold out during the day and try to reach our Schwadron in darkness.

"In the course of the morning, the enemy assembled without interruption in a hollow about 300 metres in front of us. Singly with 15 to 20 paces, the Red Army men worked their way forward.

"For us, time could not pass quickly enough. Nevertheless, carefully selected individual targets were combatted with rifles, if possible figures who we supposed could be the commander.

"After a couple of hours, we experienced a spectacle as I had never seen on a training ground – neither in Arys nor anywhere else. Under exemplary artillery fire precisely in the hollow and in front of it, our attacking units made 100 metres – and still some leapt. Our fear of being hit by our own artillery was not trifling. We continually fired white and green signal flares in the direction of the enemy. In any case, the observer of the artillery actually delivered precision work. We returned intact to our Schwadron, which had lost 8 killed and 20 wounded."

What achievements were behind this 'precision work' is illustrated in the diary notebook of Leutnant Ernst-Wilhelm Nueske, Commander of 1./Panzerartillerie-Regiment 89: "Schwarzer shot an attack to pieces. Several Panjes were captured. Towards midday, I had a duel with an enemy artillery observer. We tried to shoot each other out of our foxholes. The matter ended in a draw because we both sat on a narrow ridge that could only be reached with a fluke shot. We began to rake known nests with gunfire from our snipers and in this way, at least kept the Russian snipers at bay. Our barrels were fairly worn out and ammunition was inadequate. It now frequently showed itself by short shooting."

Obergefreiter Reddig: "25.9.42: Unteroffizier Willi Korsch and Obergefreiter Otto Chmilewski bandaged a Russian commissar. They had barely gone a couple of steps when they were shot at by him. Gefreiter Kath and Grenda were severely wounded.

"At 2300 hours, the Schwadron was pulled out of position and taken by us into the accommodation areas. They should be able to recover a little from the severe fighting."

A high-level conference to finalise details of the assault was held at LI. Armeekorps' command post in a brick building near Gumrak railway station. In attendance were many of the highest-ranking officers at Stalingrad, including the Commander of 6. Armee (Generaloberst Paulus), the Commanding General and Chief-of-Staff of LI. Armeekorps (von Seydlitz and Clausius respectively), the Commanding General of XIV. Panzerkorps (Hube), the Commander of 24. Panzer-Division (von Lenski) and the Commander of 389. Infanterie-Division (Jaenecke). Also present were the commanders of various artillery and flak units, such as the Commander of 9. Flak-Division (Generalmajor Pickert), the Commander of Artillerie-Regiment 389 (Oberst Schuster-Woldan), and the temporary commander of Panzerartillerie-Regiment 89 (Major von Pawel). The discussions began at 1045 hours with Generaloberst Paulus' arrival and ended at 1300 hours when Paulus and the others visited the advanced command post of LI. Armeekorps on the Tartar Wall east of Hill 154.8 to view the attack area.

Once night had fallen, II./Jäger-Regiment 227 started to relieve Kradschützen-Abteilung 4 and elements of Panzergrenadier-Regiment 21 on the eastern part of Hill 102.0. The guns of Panzerartillerie-Regiment 89 placed a protective barrage around the relief areas to prevent a recurrence of the previous night's disaster. Thankfully for the newly-arrived Jäger, the takeover proceeded smoothly and they were in position by the next morning, the codeword 'Tanne' being transmitted to both 24. Panzer-Division and 100. Jäger-Division Headquarters.

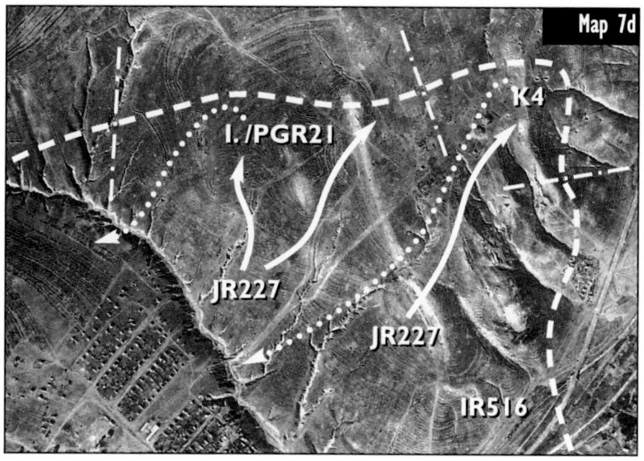

Casualties:

14 men killed

- Unteroffizier Johann Tröger; PR24 (Killed)
- Gefreiter Hubert Bappert; PGR26 (Killed)
- Obergefreiter Otto Arocker; PGR21 (Killed)
- Panzergrenadier Fritz Kluckert; PGR21 (Killed)
- Wachtmeister Hermann Wank; PGR21 (Killed)
- Obergefreiter Otto Chmilewski; PGR21 (Killed)
- Sanitäts-Obergefreiter Wilhelm Galinke PGR21 (Killed)
- Obergefreiter Justus Jäckel; PGR21 (Killed)
- Obergefreiter Herbert Kühn; PGR21 (Killed)
- Panzergrenadier Fedor Oeser; PGR21 (Killed)
- Gefreiter Georg Chrzon; K4 (Killed)
- Obergefreiter Reinhard Dörksen; K4 (Killed)

5 officers wounded (3 of those stayed with the troops)

- Oberleutnant Kurt Hoffmann (Schwadron Kdr); 5./PGR26 (Wounded but stayed with troops)
- Oberleutnant Wolfgang Dietrich Mack (Zug Kdr); 5./K4 (Wounded but stayed with troops)
- Oberleutnant Norbert Hermes (Zug Kdr); Stab II./PR24 (Wounded)
- Oberleutnant Martin Neßlinger (Batterie Kdr); 3./PAR89 (Wounded)
- Oberleutnant Hans-Jochen Kolbe (Zug Kdr); 40 Werkstatt (Wounded but stayed with troops)

53 men wounded (24 of those stayed with the troops)

- Oberwachtmeister Arnold; PGR21 (Wounded)
- Gefreiter Kath; PGR21 (Wounded)
- Gefreiter Grenda; PGR21 (Wounded)
- Gefreiter Nikolaus Schütz; PGR21 (Wounded but died later in the day)

Result of the fighting from 20th September – 25th September 1942:

The Division had completely fulfiled the set mission of holding the defensive positions. Every enemy attack was repulsed. This was difficult as the position in no way aided the defence but resulted in the attacks coming to a standstill. Every step backwards, however, would mean a deterioration in the starting positions for the forthcoming assault. The defence prevailed with the available small combat forces. The troops from the preceding fighting in the central and southern parts of Stalingrad were heavily fatigued and instead of receiving the promised rest, were again immediately committed in the northern part of Stalingrad.

Melee in the Suburbs

Chapter Eight

26th September 1942:

The nightly, strong enemy air attacks continued. Enemy reconnaissance probes were repulsed. Leutnant Ernst-Wilhelm Nueske wrote the following in his diary: "Strong mortar fire since dawn on the entire hill. Our riflemen were relieved during the night. Ivan noticed something and suspected the preparations. Direct hit on the bunker of Hauptmann Hicketier. We were relieved and would pull back to the Barracks. Shell splinter in the right upper arm. Luckily, the joint was undamaged. Nevertheless, it is a strange feeling to establish after several years of war that one is in no way bulletproof. Despite plenty of iron, we arrived safe and well at the Barracks. It was no stay at a resort here but in comparison to Hill 102[1], the new observation post, which I installed in a house ruin that looked like a stage-set, was agreeably quiet. Everyone who was not observing was able to be accommodated a bit further back in almost bombproof cellars."

The instructions of Korps for 24. Panzer-Division ran: "Destruction of the enemy south of and on the railway, gaining of Hill 107.5 as well as clearing out the city sectors lying north-east and north of there. If the situation allows it, gain the narrows on the north-west edge of the gully in grid square 74c and hold it open for a further attack.
"On the right, 100 Jäger-Division will follow, staggered, and win the south-east part of Krasny Oktyabr. To the left is 389. Infanterie-Division as flank protection with a strong right wing, to later roll up the enemy positions from the east."

At 1830 hours the previous night, the Division issued Divisionsbefehl Nr. 65 for the attack on Krasny Oktyabr on 27th September. The Division would advance at X-hour with the unarmoured assault group on the right under Oberst Reichsfreiherr von Edelsheim and at the same time with the armoured assault group on the left under the command of Major von Winterfeld, and destroy the enemy south of and on the railway line. Then, after crossing the railway in a totally concentrated mass, gain Hill 107.5 under cover of the east flank and take the city sectors lying east, north-east and north of there (grid squares 62a, 63c, 63a, 54d)[2], and clean these out.
Gruppe Edelsheim's mission was as follows: "With the Schwerpunkt on the right, break through the enemy positions in the bush terrain and as 1st attack objective win the railway line, and the

---

1. Mamayev Kurgan
2. A map of Stalingrad-North with grid square references is located at the back of the book (page 550).

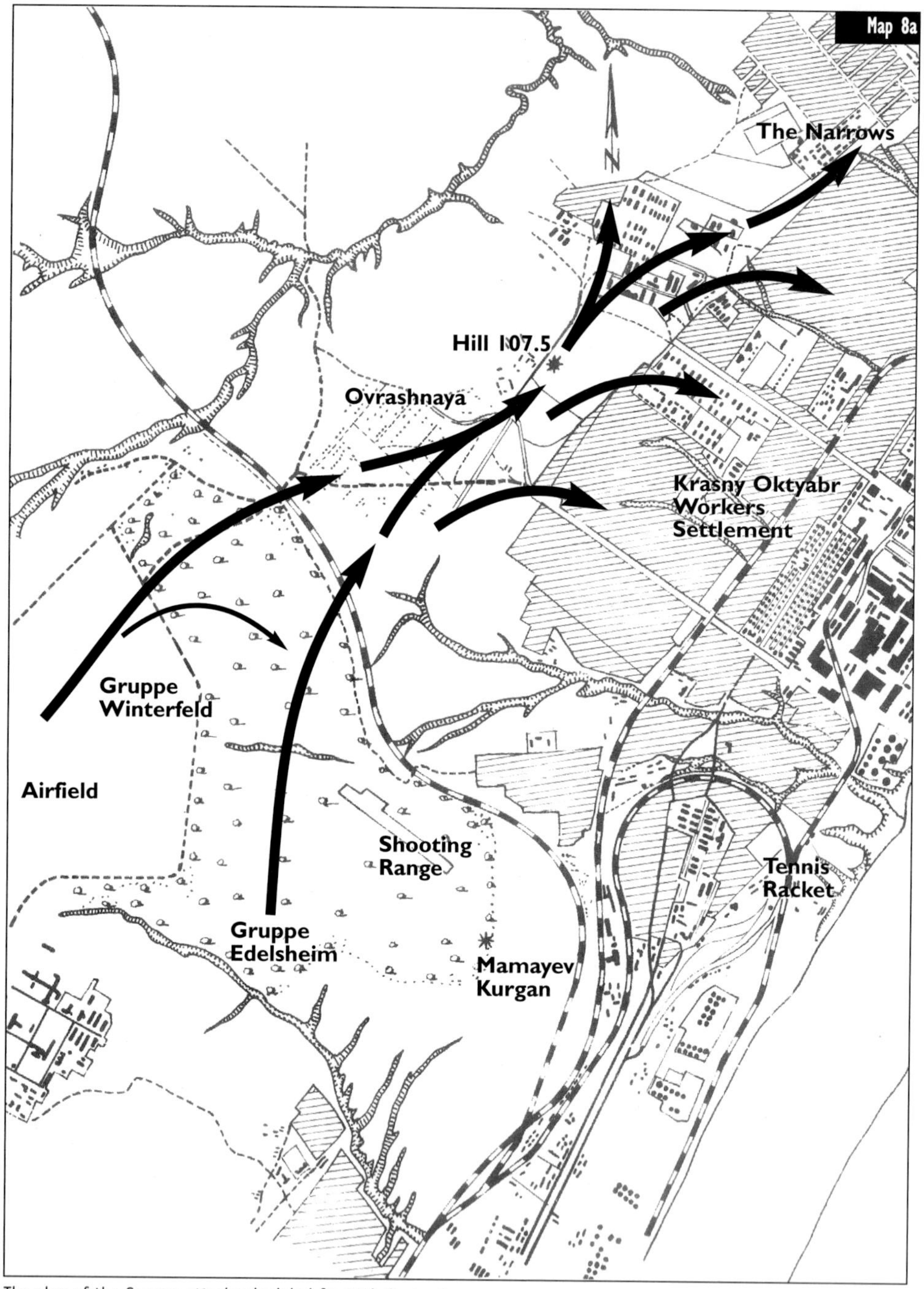

The plan of the German attack scheduled for 27th September.

2nd attack objective of Ovrashnaya utilising the advance of Gruppe Winterfeld. The 3rd objective depends upon the situation: advance on to Hill 107.5 with the bulk of the Gruppe under cover of the east flank, or if Hill 107.5 is already solidly in the hands of Gruppe Winterfeld, penetrate into the ordered city sectors (grid squares 62a, 63c, 63a, 54d) as the 3rd objective. These sectors will be cleared of the enemy."

Gruppe Winterfeld's mission was as follows: "Destroy the enemy in the forest south of the railway line and by that, open the way for Gruppe Edelsheim to the railway line. As 1st attack objective, win the railway line east of Point 735, whereupon a panzer schwadron will veer off to the east and from this point in time will be subordinated to Gruppe Edelsheim. Then, if possible, thrust through Ovrashnaya to Hill 107.5, the 2nd attack objective. The hill is to be taken, the enemy there destroyed. If the situation is favourable, advance up to the group of houses north of Hill 107.5 (53b, 63a) and later, if it comes in to question, up to the narrows on the north-west end of the gully in 74c."

There was also a contingency plan in Divisionsbefehl Nr. 65 if the railway line proved to be a greater obstacle than was thought. If the panzers could not move over the railway embankment, a bridgehead would be formed north of the line by Gruppe Edelsheim on the right and the armoured riflemen on the left. Wooden beams and other material were ordered to be made available for the crossing of the railway embankment. After making a practicable crossing, the armoured assault group would then advance out of the bridgehead.

Several heavy artillery battalions as well as elements of VIII. Fliegerkorps would support the attack. The firepower of the artillery units was formidable. Available for the assault were the following units (in addition to divisional artillery regiments):

- schwere Artillerie Abteilung (Mörser) 616 — 3 batteries of 21cm mortars
- schwere Artillerie Abteilung 851 — 2 batteries of 10cm howitzers
- schwere Artillerie Abteilung 101 — 3 batteries of 15cm howitzers
- schwere Artillerie Abteilung II./59 — 3 batteries of 15cm howitzers
- schwere Artillerie Abteilung 430 — 3 batteries of 10cm cannon
- schwere Artillerie Abteilung II./64 — 3 batteries of 10cm cannon (only from 28.9.)
- Beobachtung Abteilung 29 (Artillery observation detachment)

All of the artillery, concentrated under Artillerie Kommandeur 153, Oberst Hans-Joachim Meix, was already in position and had several objectives to fulfil on this day, the eve of the assault. They combatted known enemy batteries in certain target areas but more importantly for 24. Panzer-Division and Gruppe Edelsheim in particular, they suppressed numerous mortar positions in the bush terrain south of the railway line. Each of the independent Artillerie Abteilungen detached an artillery liaison officer to Gruppe Edelsheim. They reported to the command post of Panzerartillerie-Regiment 89 at 1500 hours.

A comprehensive artillery fire schedule was in place for the assault. From X -12 to X -8, there would be 4 minutes of destructive fire from all the artillery on the identified enemy artillery, the focal point being on and eastwards of Hill 107.5. A special assignment for the artillery was to make the railway wagons west of Point 735 immovable so that these could not be used as a mobile tank barrier. Subsequently, from X -6 until X -4, a bombardment of 2 minutes on the forward line at the breakthrough positions of the right and left assault groups, a 2 minute pause from X -4 to X -2, then the barrage was continued from X -2 until X-hour. At X-hour, a barrage would be placed on the heavy anti-aircraft guns on Hill 107.5. The strongpoint constructed in the small forest on the northern edge of the airfield (32c) would be suppressed

and in addition to this, Hill 107.5 and Ovrashnaya would also be constantly suppressed until the armoured assault group had taken them. As soon as the hill was taken, the focal point of the artillery would be shifted to combat targets in the city sectors east of the hill, as well as covering the flanks. At all times, enemy reserves and headquarters staffs in the Steel Factory would be fired on. Artillery spotter planes were available and, as always, elements of the artillery would be on standby to await calls for help coming from the hard-pressed infantry.
The Luftwaffe was also scheduled to play a large role in the attack. On this day, 26th September, they pounded the bush terrain opposite Gruppe Edelsheim, as well as Ovrashnaya and above all the strongpoints around Hill 107.5. The plan was to wear the enemy down by attrition.

General von Lenski had ordered some special safety measures for this attack with regards to Luftwaffe support: "The Division was promised support by bomber units of the Luftwaffe. Because the Division had already had a bad experience with the accuracy of our bombers during our thrust to the Tsaritsa on 16th September, I ordered the vehicles to be distinguished with flags for this attack. Apart from that, it was arranged with the Luftflotte commanders that our troops would let off lilac flares during the approach of our machines."

The preparations for the assault on Hill 107.5 and the Krasny Oktyabr settlement were completed. General von Lenski had already set up his advanced command post on the second floor of the furthest eastward lying building of the former Pilots School. For half a day, I./PGR21 was allowed to rest near their vehicles in the Gnussina Balka about 2km south of Gumrak. II. Abteilung remained in the positions and the Soviet snipers continued to make their lives difficult. Obergefreiter Reddig: "26.9.42: At 1500 hours, the Schwadron was driven to the front again. The Spießfahrer and I with my vehicle brought back 10 dead comrades for burial at the Division Cemetery on the highway."
While Rittmeister Graf Solms, Commander of I./Panzergrenadier-Regiment 21, walked ahead to get instructions for the attack scheduled for 27th September, the battalion waited in the vicinity of the artillery positions and were only brought up at the onset of darkness by the Abteilung Adjutant, Leutnant Dr. Penners. The messengers of Graf Solms – who had gone forward with the battalion commander in the afternoon – showed the way along a telephone cable. The terrain again lay under strong Soviet sweeping fire and before reaching the preparations area, he and Leutnant Penners were wounded by Stalin Organs, with them also Stabsarzt Dr. Walsdorfer, the generally loved and valued Abteilung and Regiment doctor known to all as 'Uncle Franz'.

Leutnant Nueske from 1./Panzerartillerie-Regiment 89: "Because the day passed quietly and there was no further developments to speak of, I drove to the main dressing station in the afternoon where Dr. Schuh removed the small piece of shrapnel from my arm. I was able to remain with the troops, however, I was after possibilities to take care of myself. For tomorrow's planned attack, I would therefore get a lift with Schwarzer. Still during the night, however, I drove to my observation post and went past the infantry units moving into position, and from there, I would at least be able to watch over the first phase of the assault."

Casualties:

3 men killed

- Gefreiter Josef Glück; PGR21 (Killed)
- Obergefreiter Heinrich Fine; PGR21 (Killed)
- Obergefreiter Kurt Spell; PGR21 (Killed)

6 officers wounded (3 of those stayed with the troops)

- Rittmeister Friedrich Graf zu Solms-Wildenfels (Abteilung Kdr); I./PGR21 (Wounded but stayed with the troops)
- Leutnant Dr. Theo Penners (Abteilung Adjutant); I./PGR21 (Wounded)
- Stabsarzt Dr. Franz Walsdorfer (Abteilung Arzt); I./PGR21 (Wounded)
- Leutnant Bauchspieß (Kolonne Kdr); 3. Kw.Kol. (Wounded but stayed with the troops)
- Hauptmann Erich Hicketier (Batterie Kdr); 2./PAR89 (Wounded but stayed with the troops)
- Leutnant Ernst-Wilhelm Nueske (Batterie Kdr); 1./PAR89 (Wounded but stayed with troops)

15 men wounded (9 of those stayed with the troops)

- Gefreiter Alfons Klapuch; PGR21 (Wounded but died on 28th September in Novy Rogachik hospital)
- Panzergrenadier Andreas Kallas; PGR21 (Wounded but died on 7th October in Kalach hospital)

27th September 1942:

From the dawn in the east rose a cloudless crimson and emerald sky. The German assault troops had completed their final preparations and awaited the beginning of the attack. The preparations of Angriffsgruppe Edelsheim had been constricted and made more difficult by the numerous gullies, so two companies of pioneers had been allotted to the Gruppe with orders to arrange crossings over the gullies, as well as to mark routes into the starting areas. On top of that, the Russians attacked with 137th Tank Brigade and 9th Motorised Brigade on and eastwards of the airfield at 0600 hours, deploying themselves on a

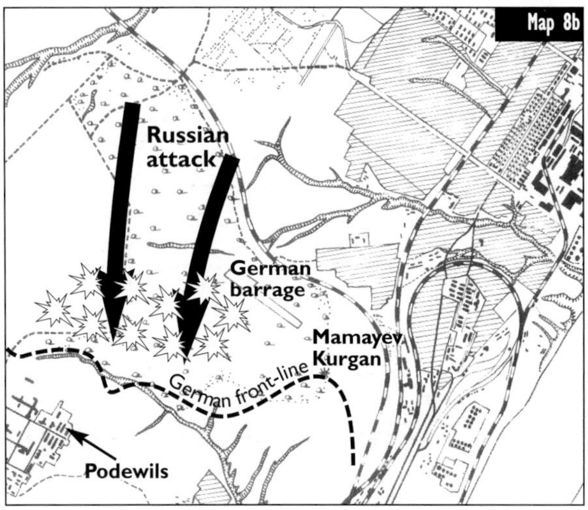

Russian attack in the early hours of 27th September.

broad front to occupy Hill 102.0. A war correspondent, Clemens Podewils, witnessed the Russian attack: "...we approached the Pilot's School. As the hour of the attack, preceded by an artillery barrage and Stuka operations, moved closer, we looked at our watches – instead of that, the fire of the enemy all of a sudden increased to such an unheard-of vehemence that we were down from our vehicle in no time and into a trench beside the paved road. Shells and Stalin Organ salvos hailed down everywhere. The assault guns waited, humming, on the street. It continued, again and again with interruptions, until I dashed into one of the buildings in which an observation post was installed and which offered a good all-round view of the battlefield. The buildings stood on a hill, broad sides to the east and west, small side facing to the north. From here was a view over an undeveloped plain which sank and on the other side rose to a gentle hill. There, the northern quarter of the city in its long narrow shape was pushed together into a staggered backdrop, a single industrial district. Out of the haze, fires and pillars of smoke rose the numerous tall chimneys, like a pine forest in the sky. But who was attacking – it was the enemy.

"Tank shells whistled along the front of the building and smashed into the walls. Infantry and anti-tank rifles, as well as machine-guns, fired at our lines. Should an accidental encounter with our intentions be seen in this attack? It was probable that the enemy anticipated the German attack, known to him at this day and hour. (No wonder when one knows the thoughtlessness with which German command posts telephone one another!)

"Now our artillery was employed, bombers diving on the enemy positions. It produced frightful devastation on the attacking and rear-area troops flowing over the terrain. This time it was a complete success. The survivors surrendered in droves to the storming German infantry..."

As noted by Podewils, the preparatory artillery fire crushed the attacking Russians. The Russian artillery barrage began at 0300 hours and the infantry attacked at 0400 hours. Podewils was correct when he said that the enemy had anticipated the attack. In his memoirs, the Commander-in-Chief of 62nd Army, General Vasili Ivanovich Chuikov, writes: "Everybody knew, felt and could see that the enemy was preparing for new active operations. To sit back and wait for the attack to begin was tantamount to suicide. The area occupied by 62nd Army on the west bank of the Volga was as narrow as could be – there was no room to retreat." German artillery smothered the front-line with obliterating fire, scything down the attacking Russian troops. The fire plan of the artillery was implemented according to schedule. The artillerymen of Panzerartillerie-Regiment 89 were using some unusual guns in this bombardment. As replacements for several heavy howitzers lost in earlier fighting, three Russian 122mm guns were incorporated into the Regiment's strength after the fighting in Stalingrad-South. These powerful guns had a range of about 13,000 metres. Captured with the guns were about 300 rounds and these were now being put to good effect, firing on their former owners[3].

3. All 300 rounds were used on this day. Four weeks later, the guns were still without ammunition, none being captured in any of the attacks in Stalingrad-North. Without ammunition, the guns were worthless and had become an encumbrance. The Panzerartillerie-Regiment told Division that unless some suitable ammunition was found soon, they would give these guns up. The Regiment also had three 76.2mm guns that were used in the bombardment on 27th September. All the captured ammunition was fired but fortunately for Panzerartillerie-Regiment 89, the guns weren't silent for long. Shells from various areas were found and sent up to the guns so that by the end of October, these three guns had fired a total of 3,100 shells. These guns also had a range of 13,000 metres.

With German shells hammering the Russian lines, the Stukas also swept in, peeling off one by one and with sirens screaming, bombed the forward line. Ju 88's droned overhead and unloaded their bombs on Hill 107.5. The attack area was enveloped in a murky haze of gunpowder, wafting dust and choking smoke, the flashes of explosions illuminating the fog. To the ground troops ready to push off, it looked and sounded like a storm cloud with cracking thunder and flashing lightning. As hands of watches ticked over to X-hour, another sound was added to the murderous symphony: the dry crack of 88mm flak guns. These powerful guns of 9. Flak-Division placed a barrage on the group of houses on Hill 107.5, their armour-piercing and high-explosive shells proving very effective against the brick buildings.

After the short preparatory barrage, the attack commenced with 100. Jäger-Division on the right and 389. Infanterie-Division on the left. Gruppe Edelsheim, consisting of Panzergrenadier-Regiment 21, Panzergrenadier-Regiment 26 (without its I. Abteilung), two companies of Panzerpionier-Bataillon 40 and 1./Panzerjäger-Abteilung 40, had to break obstinate resistance in the bush terrain and eliminate unpleasant flanking fire from both sides. From the composition of Gruppe Edelsheim, which actually contained the bulk of the Division's infantry, it would seem that Oberst von Edelsheim had ample forces under his command to carry out his mission. It was exactly the opposite. Panzergrenadier-Regiment 21 had 456 front-line troops, Panzergrenadier-Regiment 26 had 479 and Panzerpionier-Bataillon 40 had 156. That meant Gruppe Edelsheim had less than 1000 active front-line troops and because of this shortage of forces, it was only able to attack on a very small sector.
Oberstleutnant von Hellermann's Panzergrenadier-Regiment 21 attacked over a training ground overgrown with low scrub, in the vicinity of the shooting range. To the right was the rear slope of the menacing Mamayev Kurgan, its bald crown boiling and seething as shell after shell ripped up the ground, sending clods of earth, bits of wood and smoke high into the air. This was the unpleasant sight to their right as the men plunged into the bushes and pushed towards the shooting range. Encounters came at close range. A burst of fire from the bushes, a man would be hit and then crumple to the ground, his comrades also diving to the ground and opening fire on the suspected area. Grenades were thrown and the bushes stormed, usually ending in the death of the Russian. Then they moved on until fired on again. In this nightmarish terrain which provided excellent cover and camouflage for the Russians, 3. Schwadron under Oberleutnant Jürgen Pachnio quickly suffered 11 casualties, including Oberleutnant Pachnio himself who was severely wounded by a shot to the lungs. He succumbed to his severe wounds in a Leipzig hospital on 5th March 1943. Also killed were Obergefreiter Friedrich Symanzik, Obergefreiter Bruno Zimmermann and Gefreiter Franz Harder. Seven other men of 3. Schwadron were wounded.
Unteroffizier Hopp: "First Schwadron, together with the 2nd and 3rd, could still employ about 60 to 70 men. Oberwachtmeister Rogowski, as the only remaining Portepee (sword knot) bearer, fell out through wounding with the entire Schwadronstrupp, including the radio operator, when the hole in which they had taken cover almost received a direct artillery hit. "The good Kurt Schmischke fell, his Schütze 2 Kutz lost an arm. Schütze 3, Alfred Fromme, very bravely carried on the machine-gun alone and took up a very favourable position between the machine-gun posts of the Russian shooting range."
Obergefreiter Reddig, from the same Schwadron as Unteroffizier Hopp, also reports: "Again a heavy day for the Schwadron. Large attack. We conquered the strong positions of the Russians. Killed: Obergefreiter Schmischke, severely wounded: Oberwachtmeister Rogowski, Funk-Unteroffizier Heim, Obergefreiter Kutz, Karl Amsel, Paul Krakau, Wilhelm Blome, Gefreiter Heinz Wolf, Karl Schmidt, Leuchner, Obergefreiter Siegrits (hurled through the air by the

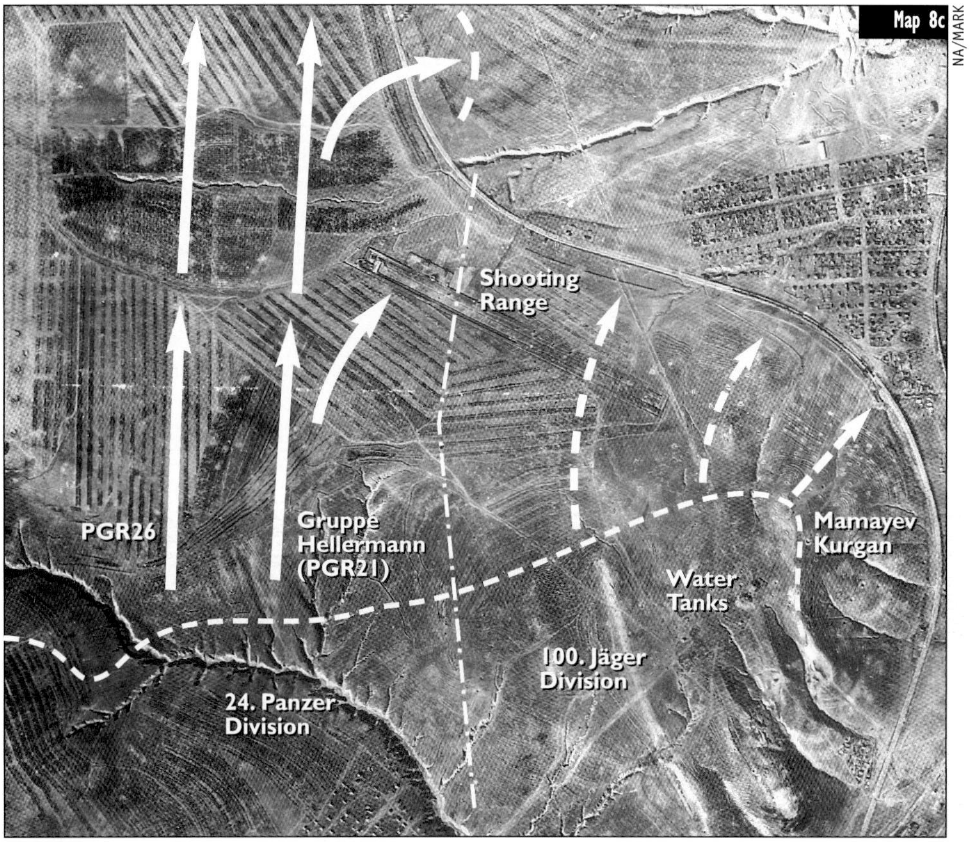

Gruppe Edelsheim's attack west of Mamayev Kurgan.

pressure of an aerial bomb), lightly wounded: Obergefreiter Heinrich Breuker, Alfred Fromme (remained at the vehicles). Strong fighting at the front during the night. We brought the wounded to the main dressing station with three vehicles."

While the grenadiers slugged it out in the bushy terrain west of Mamayev Kurgan, the armoured Stoßgruppe (Panzer Abteilung Winterfeld, the half-tracks of I./Panzergrenadier-Regiment 26, 2./Kradschützen-Abteilung 4 and I./Panzerartillerie-Regiment 89) rolled over the airfield. General von Lenski was concerned that "the airfield over which the panzers must roll was as flat as a plate which was overlooked from Hill 102." Nevertheless, the panzers headed on to the airfield as their General observed the attack: "The panzers, from the starting area hard west of the Tartar Wall, succeeded in overcoming the plain of the airfield under the employment of artificial fog without casualties. These only first occurred when they fell into a minefield on the eastern edge of the landing strip."

Major von Winterfeld's panzers dashed across the barren expanse of the airfield and they immediately saw that coming toward them were small groups of Russians, weaponless, hands in the air. The grenadiers would collect them. The panzers pressed on, scarcely noticing that a few of them had abruptly stopped after a dull thud and a small explosion. As they continued, the mines started to take a larger toll. The panzer of Wachtmeister Schrabeck was split open by a large mine which ignited the ammunition sitting in the racks. The panzer – and its entire crew

NA/MARK

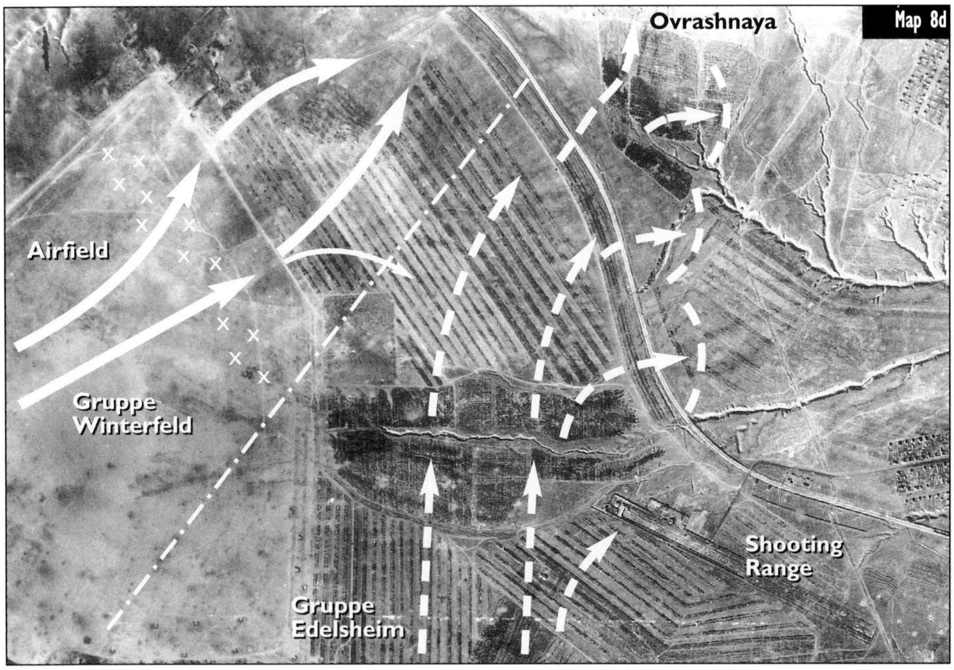

The assault of Gruppe Winterfeld. After crossing the airfield, a panzer schwadron veers off to the east to join Edelsheim.

– were rapidly engulfed in deadly flames. Killed were Wachtmeister Franz-Josef Schrabeck, Unteroffizier Wilhelm Zang, Obergefreiter Walter Krell, Obergefreiter Karl Wimmer and Oberschütze Martin Rehbein. Major von Winterfeld's panzer '361' also became a casualty but was lucky only to lose a couple of roadwheels and a small section of tread. About 100 metres ahead of '361', another two panzers came to grief on the mines. Half-tracks rushed forward and gathered the casualties while pioneers moved into the minefield, prodding the ground with mine probes (wooden poles with metal tips) and formed two narrow alleys through the danger area. The panzers filed along the passages, leaving behind the several victims of the mines. These were not total losses; the trusty Werkstattkompanien (workshop companies) would get them back in working order. Von Winterfeld's '361' was back in action a few days later.

Along the north-eastern edge of the airfield stretched messy woodland consisting of low trees and tangled scrub. It was not thick, the trees being widely spaced, but it still offered good defensive attributes to the Russians. Intelligence indicated that strong resistance could be expected here so Major von Winterfeld was ready for it. The panzers started taking fire from Russian tanks dug in along this edge and Stukas circling overhead to assist the armoured spearhead were immediately called in, diving on the enemy tanks. The panzers took advantage of the confusion, accelerating over the relatively level airfield into positions for accurate fire. The T-34's, often only their turrets being visible, were repeatedly struck and set on fire. The panzers suffered negligible casualties.

After overcoming the enemy tanks, a strong enemy flanking strongpoint was also taken by the panzers on the left divisional boundary. The armoured spearhead then broke into the forest and opened the way to the railway line to Gruppe Edelsheim from the west. A few of the panzers fell out through mines as they headed along dusty tracks through the woods toward the railway line. This line, perched along the top of an embankment but also levelling out and heading through a cutting, had caused a lot of headaches for the Division during the planning stages. In itself, the embankment was a formidable anti-tank obstacle, especially if it was incorporated into a defensive line, but it was made tougher – and more unpredictable – by a continuous line of 50 railway wagons standing on it. There had been concerns that the Russians could move the wagons along the track, in effect producing a movable anti-tank barrier. This had been remedied by the wagons being blasted by artillery. Now they were just a mess of shattered wood and steel but nevertheless, they were still an obstacle – albeit now an immobile one. There were two level-crossings, one hard north of the shooting range (in Gruppe Edelsheim's area of operations) and the other north of the airfield. Both were reported to be free of obstacles. The terrain appeared to be flat to the south-east but according to prisoner statements, on the other side of the line was a drop of about 2–3 metres. Division command could not confirm this on aerial photographs. The troops would only find out when they got there.

The panzers pushed toward the northern crossing, the panzer schwadron assigned to support Gruppe Edelsheim veering off at this point, heading east toward the shooting range. The armoured assault group soon reached the railway line. The row of railway wagons was still on the tracks barely 100 metres north of the crossing. The main problem now was the heavy defensive fire coming from Ovrashnaya and the area south of Hill 107.5, as well as the numerous mines buried around the level-crossing. The pioneers got to work, prodding the ground and checking for mines. A safe area was rapidly navigated through the mines both sides of the level-crossing. Under the strongest fire, the panzers pushed across the railway line at 1010 hours. The first attack objective of Gruppe Winterfeld was achieved. Once the panzers were on the other side of the railway line, a battle developed with the tanks of 23rd Russian Tank Corps in the suburb of Ovrashnaya, a ramshackle collection of widely-spaced wooden huts along a web of dirt roads. The panzers overpowered the Russian tanks and pushed up Hill 107.5 at 1100 hours. That was the second objective. On this dominating hill and its surrounding area, a hard battle subsequently developed for the armoured Stoßgruppe with fronts to the north-east and west.

After very tough fighting and early operations of the Division reserves, Gruppe Edelsheim succeeded at 1100 hours in breaking through the enemy position in its entire depth. The supporting panzer schwadron soon arrived and helped the struggling grenadiers forward and, under utilisation of the successful thrust of Gruppe Winterfeld, the bulk of Gruppe Edelsheim gained the railway line at 1200 hours. Not all units of the Gruppe managed to reach this objective however. Unteroffizier Hopp and his 1./Panzergrenadier-Regiment 21 moved over a former Russian training area, now overgrown by weeds and long grass: "Toward 1200 hours, the attack was interrupted for the time being. The enemy knew his training ground accurately and constantly allowed us to approach to the shortest distance before he opened fire with submachine-guns and rifles. In this way, we again already had numerous wounded."

After overcoming strong anti-tank and anti-aircraft guns, the large blocks of houses in 53b and 54d were taken at 1200 hours by Gruppe Winterfeld. Leutnant Hans-Erdmann Schönbeck of Panzer-Regiment 24 recalls the attack of his panzers after they had crossed the railway line:

NA/MARK

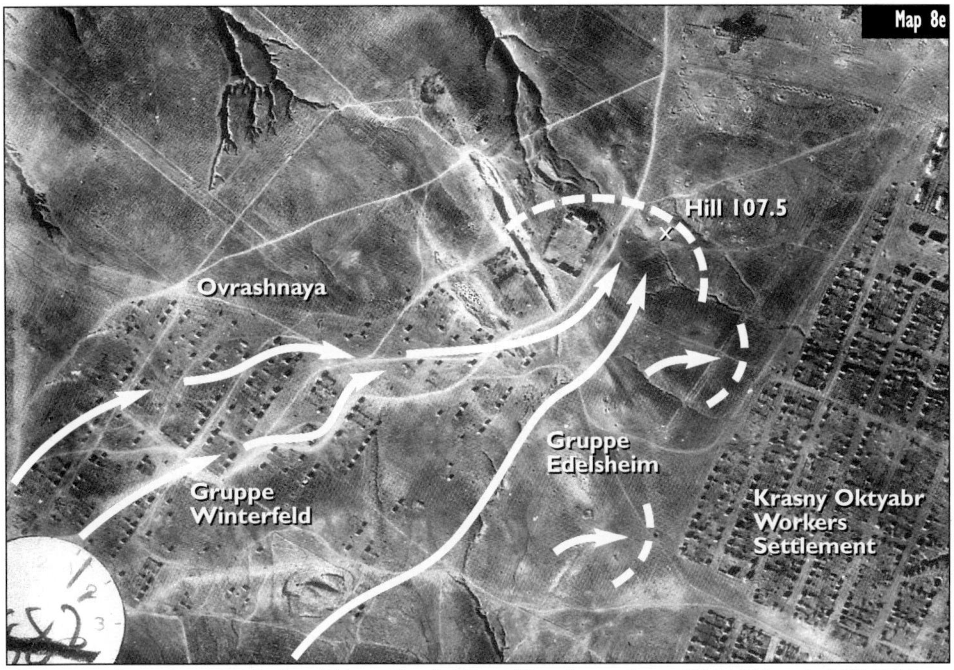

After overcoming enemy tanks in the widely-scattered village of Ovrashnaya, Gruppe Winterfeld reached Hill 107.5. Gruppe Edelsheim arrived later, dropping off units on its right to protect the ever-lengthening east flank.

SPANNOCCHI

Gruppe Winterfeld's panzers move across the exposed airstrip. Surrendering Russians walk forward with their hands up.

SPANNOCCHI

As the advance continues across the airfield, a panzer on the left flank suddenly stops and then begins to smoulder. It is the panzer of Wachtmeister Schrabeck.

SPANNOCCHI

A few seconds later, the ammunition within the tank ignites and turns the panzer into a fiery coffin. Wachtmeister Schrabeck and his entire crew died in this fire.

SPANNOCCHI

Russian prisoners, including these two women, give themselves up to the panzers.

SPANNOCCHI

Major von Winterfeld's Panzer '361' became a casualty in the minefields, losing a track and some roadwheels on the front left side. In the background, casualties are loaded into half-tracks.

SPANNOCCHI

Pioneers probe the airfield for mines. The advance continued while the mine casualties were left behind. Major von Winterfeld's panzer is on the left. Russian defences were located in the bush on the edge of the airfield.

"During our thrust into the northern part of the city, I received the order to conduct reconnaissance in front of our actual spearhead with two platoons (six panzers). I was surprisingly quick and far ahead, making progress against weak resistance when I was detected by our Stukas. They thought that it would have been impossible for German panzers to be able to penetrate so far and they unloaded their bombs on us in twice-repeated approach flights and dive bombings. All of our smoke signals were in vain. It was true that we were barely struck but with shredded tracks, we were unable to move. Because one of our strengths at that time was the radio and radio telegraphy, our Regiment knew our position very precisely. A great consolation for us. The night quickly set in so that we remained alone in the middle of the Russian infantry lines. Through our own constant covering fire, time and again we succeeded in repulsing all Russian attempts to finally blow us up with Molotov cocktails or magnetic mines. At the first break of dawn, the restarted assaulted wave of our Regiment reached us."
General von Lenski witnessed this attack on Schönbeck's platoon: "On the morning of 27th September, as the Division overcame a flat hollow filled with man-sized trees in a widely-spaced march column and the leading panzers had just reached the northern point of the cemetery, a Stukagruppe flew in from the east. I found myself in my Befehlswagen on the steeply sloping northern edge of a row of houses about five hundred metres further south. I suddenly saw that the leading Stuka tipped over and dove on the panzer column. Four or five machines followed, and the bombs were already exploding between our panzers. I immediately ordered flares to be fired – signifying our forward line – and succeeded, so that at least the remaining Stukas (about ten) no longer participated in this abortive operation. No casualties arose because all the bombs were next to the panzers. In future, however, the Division dispensed with the immediate co-operation of the bombers."

In the meantime, unarmoured Gruppe Edelsheim had also moved on to Hill 107.5 in an attack under the cover of the constantly threatened east flank, supported by the detached panzer schwadron. While the left neighbour division, 389. Infanterie-Division, was able to accompany the attack of 24. Panzer-Division on the same level with its right wing, 100. Jäger-Division could only move forward a little due to the strongest opposition. As a result, the deep east flank of 24. Panzer-Division was uncovered facing the complex city sectors, and to unconditionally reach the attack objective with the weak combat forces, the flank could only be covered for the time being with the smallest forces. When it was discovered that there was only a weak enemy presence on the east flank, it was immediately followed up with the smallest available elements. After hard fighting against enemy resistance that was gradually becoming stronger, two sectors of the city were taken before evening set in.

Unteroffizier Hopp of 1./Panzergrenadier-Regiment 21 reports: "In the late afternoon, the attack was continued. When we all had a break, I received from Graf Solms two shoulder-boards each with a star upon it and the words: 'A small acknowledgment for the heavy hours'. That was my promotion to Wachtmeister. Now I was the only Wachtmeister of the Schwadron at the front. In the evening, we reached the railway line, along which we dug foxholes for the night that must soon stand the test.
"For the enemy, it was simple during the night to fly along the railway line with his aircraft and unload everything he had on our side."
The mission was fulfiled, the objective reached and the enemy position penetrated to a depth of 4km despite constant strong flanking fire and weak forces. For the Russians, the assault came from a surprising direction and delivered a stunning blow and for the Division, the result was

Grenadiers assume defensive positions while Stukas deal with obstinate resistance near Hill 107.5.

rated higher because it only had low combat strengths and was heavily fatigued by the preceding assaults and defensive combat around Stalingrad. Captured by the Division on this day were 550 prisoners, 15 tanks were destroyed and 22 mortars were captured.
In the evening, the enemy still held out in grid squares 60, 51, 52c & d. Areas 52b and 63c appeared to be free of the enemy, while areas 63a, 64c, 54d and 53a1 still contained individual Russian tanks and infantry. The result of the day was tarnished by repeated attacks of the Luftwaffe on the Division's lines, whereby it was ascertained that the blame unquestionably lay with the Luftwaffe alone. This was sad as previous co-operation with the Luftwaffe was excellent.
Towards midnight, Gefreiter Robert Henning from the anti-tank platoon of 4./Panzergrenadier-Regiment 21 was directed by his platoon commander to take an order to another platoon, which lay about 300 or 400 metres away. He did not arrive with the order. A search conducted through the sector and an investigation were unsuccessful. It was assumed that Gefreiter Henning suffered a fatal injury en route, was buried alive, or was severely wounded and handed over to the hospital of another unit.

This day was counted as a Sturmangriffe day for Panzer-Regiment 24 and Panzergrenadier-Regiment 21:
27.9.42 (for PR24): attack on the airfield near Stalingrad
27.9.42 (for PGR21): attack on Hill 107.0

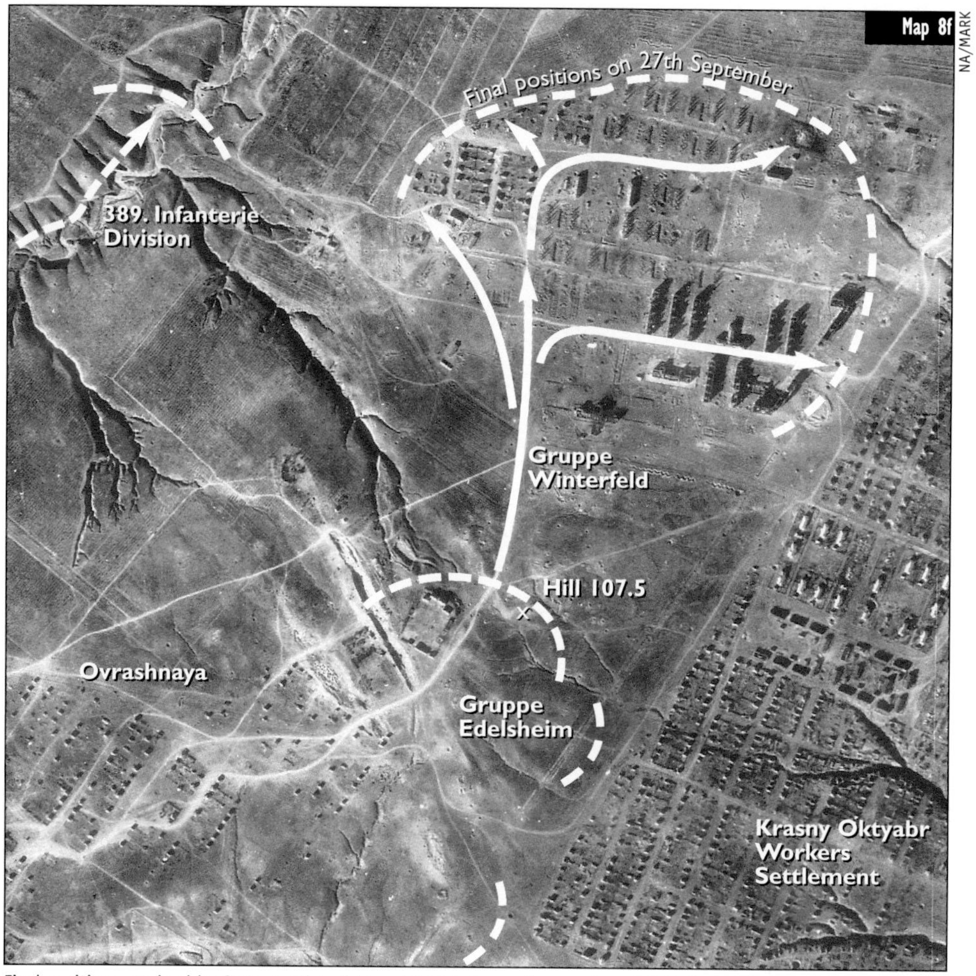

Final positions attained by Gruppen Winterfeld and Edelsheim on the evening of 27th September 1942.

Casualties:

1 officer killed

- Oberleutnant Reinhard Viertel (Schwadron Kdr); 2./Pz.Pi.40 (Killed)

36 men killed

- Gefreiter Heinrich Pankewitz; Pz.Pi.40 (Killed)
- Wachtmeister Franz-Josef Schrabeck; PR24 (Killed)
- Unteroffizier Wilhelm Zang; PR24 (Killed)
- Obergefreiter Walter Krell; PR24 (Killed)
- Obergefreiter Karl Wimmer; PR24 (Killed)
- Gefreiter Martin Rehbein; PR24 (Killed)
- Gefreiter Harry Oltersdorff; PGR21 (Killed)
- Obergefreiter Friedrich Symanzik; PGR21 (Killed)
- Obergefreiter Bruno Zimmermann; PGR21 (Killed)
- Gefreiter Franz Harder; PGR21 (Killed)
- Obergefreiter Kurt Schmischke; PGR21 (Killed)
- Gefreiter Walter Giese; K4 (Killed)
- Unteroffizier Claus Schröder; PNA86 (Killed)
- Obergefreiter Reinhard Kämpfe; PNA86 (Killed)

9 officers wounded (1 of those stayed with the troops)

- Leutnant Richard Gündel (Zug Kdr); 4./PGR21 (Wounded but stayed with the troops)
- Oberleutnant Jürgen Pachnio (Schwadron Kdr); 3./PGR21 (Wounded but died on 5th March 1943 in a Leipzig hospital)
- Leutnant Erhard Belli von Pino (Abteilung Adjutant); II./PGR21 (Wounded)
- Leutnant Harald Balser (Zug Kdr); 5./PGR21 (Wounded)
- Leutnant Hellmuth Reymann (Zug Kdr); 3./PGR26 (Wounded)
- Major Hans-Wilhelm von Heyden (Abteilung Kdr); II./PGR26 (Wounded)
- Rittmeister Hans Jankowski (Schwadron Kdr); Stab/K4 (Wounded)
- Assistenarzt Dr. Martin Kuls (Abteilung Hilfsarzt); III./PR24 (Wounded)
- Leutnant Dr. Helmut Exner (Zug Kdr); 2./PNA86 (Wounded)

212 men wounded (66 of those stayed with the troops)

- Feldwebel Oskar Mirwald; 3./Pz.Pi.40 (Wounded but stayed with the troops)
- Obergefreiter Werner Grünegras; PGR21 (Wounded but died later in the day)
- Unteroffizier Hans Hell; PGR21 (Wounded but died on 30th September in Novy Rogachik hospital)
- Oberwachtmeister Rogowski; PGR21 (Wounded)
- Funk-Unteroffizier Heim; PGR21 (Wounded)
- Obergefreiter Kutz; PGR21 (Wounded)
- Karl Amsel; PGR21 (Wounded)
- Paul Krakau; PGR21 (Wounded)
- Obergefreiter Wilhelm Blome; PGR21 (Wounded but died later in the day)

- Gefreiter Heinz Wolf; PGR21 (Wounded)
- Karl Schmidt; PGR21 (Wounded)
- Leuchner; PGR21 (Wounded)
- Obergefreiter Siegrits (hurled through the air by the pressure of an aerial bomb)
- Obergefreiter Heinrich Breuker; PGR21 (Wounded but stayed with the troops)
- Alfred Fromme; PGR21 (Wounded but stayed with the troops)

1 man missing

- Obergefreiter Robert Hennig; PGR21 (Missing in action)

Decorations bestowed from 21st September to 27th September:

19 Iron Cross First Class
264 Iron Cross Second Class
318 Panzer Combat Badge in Bronze
32 Panzer Combat Badge in Silver
11 Assault Badge

Prisoners and booty taken from 21st September to 27th September:

620 prisoners
6 airplanes
15 tanks
23 anti-tank rifles

28th September 1942:

According to the Korpsbefehl, the attack would continue to the north-east to gain the city sector of Barrikady. At 0100 hours, the Division issued Divisionsbefehl Nr. 66 which passed on the instructions of Korps that called for the continuation of the attack on 28th September on the north-west section of Krasny Oktyabr and Barrikady. Gruppe Edelsheim would attack to the north-east at 0630 hours while Gruppe Winterfeld would first of all hold the attained line and later follow up the attack. They would also support the attack of Gruppe

SPANNOCCHI

A T-34 shot up in the village of Ovrashnaya by Rittmeister Gerhard Thiel and Oberleutnant von Messerschmidt. The Panzer IV long-barrel of Oberleutnant von Messerschmidt is on the far left of the photo.

The route of Albrecht's reconnaissance troop.

Edelsheim through flanking fire. The left wing of 100. Jäger-Division was shifted to the north but despite that, it still remained for 24. Panzer-Division to protect the deep flank. A night-time Russian thrust against the weakly held eastern flank was repulsed.

In the early morning hours, a panzer schwadron from Panzer Abteilung Winterfeld arrived at the kholkoz in 53c to replace the schwadron that supported Gruppe Edelsheim the previous day. They arrived before the scheduled time of 0615 hours. The Luftwaffe prepared the attack by bombing the residential area around 64b & d, as well as attacking the 'Red Barricades' Gun Factory. The last bomb fell shortly before 0630 hours. Oberst von Edelsheim sent out reconnaissance at 0630 hours to determine the extent of the Russian defences. One of the reconnaissance teams ran into trouble. A troop from 3./Kradschützen-Abteilung 4 crept up to the crossing over the gully 500 metres west of the Bread Factory and there, Gefreiter Artur Albrecht was struck in the right side of the head and

REIFNER

Pioneers from Reifner's 3./Panzerpionier-Bataillon 40 move out. Despite being equipped with half-tracks, Reifner and his men fought on foot in Stalingrad-North. In the background is Panzer IV short-barrel '1221'.

chest by several Russian bullets. He died instantly. His comrades dived into cover and defended themselves. They had to leave the body of Gefreiter Albrecht in its exposed position. Any attempt to retrieve the body immediately drew enemy fire. The Russians forced them back and they lost sight of the body. It was not until the onset of darkness, however, that several men were sent out to bring back the body. It could not be found. It was not known exactly what happened but it was likely that the Russians seized the body in the hope of gaining valuable information.

Despite a few minor shoot-outs and the death and wounding of a couple of men, it was found that the enemy was still groggy from yesterdays fighting, so the bulk of Gruppe Edelsheim moved out soon after from their night-time positions around and to the south of Hill 107.5. Russian fire peppered the attacking troops but after hard fighting, they pushed into the houses on the city edge. The Gruppe continued to fight against obstinate resistance in the north-western area of the city fringe. From large white apartment buildings west of Hill 107.5, enemy snipers dominated the coverless 300 metre south-west slope of the lengthy rear of the hill. Five Hiwis that tried to bring ammunition to the hard fighting grenadiers of II./Panzergrenadier-Regiment 21 ran in frantic zig-zags across the ground between gardens and wooden houses and despite their desperate manoeuvres, three were shot. The Division's 150mm heavy infantry guns could do nothing against the apartment block because of the small firing distance, so a battery from an Armee artillery unit finally silenced the snipers.

The grenadiers of Gruppe Edelsheim sprinted from cover to cover, smashed their way through paling fences that surrounded small gardens and stormed the wooden huts. Grenades thrown into the small huts blew out the window panes and shattered the interiors. The supporting panzers remaining a healthy distance behind the grenadiers, demolishing stubborn resistance nests with a few rounds of high explosive. Nevertheless, the Russians defenders took a steady toll on the grenadiers. After a few hours, Gruppe Edelsheim reached one of the steep gullies. The gully branched into a fork about 100 metres east of the spearhead with the result that directly in the path of the grenadiers were two gullies, both of which needed to be crossed. The sweat-soaked grenadiers slid down the steep slope of the first gully, clambered up the other side and dashed across relatively open terrain. They went into cover behind a few huts that lined the street bisecting this isthmus of land between the two gullies. The midday sun glowered in the cloudless sky, baking the grassless ground and making the grenadiers extremely uncomfortable. With hearts pounding in their chests, they quickly recovered their breath and stormed forward, plunging into the second gully and capturing a few surprised Russians. They climbed the loamy slope and secured a few huts sited along the edge of the gully. After a quick regrouping, the grenadiers speared their way north-east through the drab wooden huts and dirt streets. At 1330 hours, with Gruppe Edelsheim reaching the area 63b, armoured Gruppe Winterfeld began their attack into the empty terrain between the two westernmost suburbs. The terrain consisted of coverless steppe pockmarked with shell craters and lines of Russian trenches. Their objective was to take the neck of land that lay between the steep-sided gully in 64d and the Barrikady housing estate north-west of there. This was seen as a vital objective because it would allow the panzers easy access to the northern area of the city without the need of passing through congested suburbs or crossing easily defensible gullies.

The armoured Gruppe was divided into two spearheads, the first swinging out to the north and taking the Barrikady housing estate from the west, the second heading straight through the cemetery on the estate's south-western side. After traversing the cemetery, the panzers bulldozed their way through the huts and seized the valuable narrows from the north-west, a totally

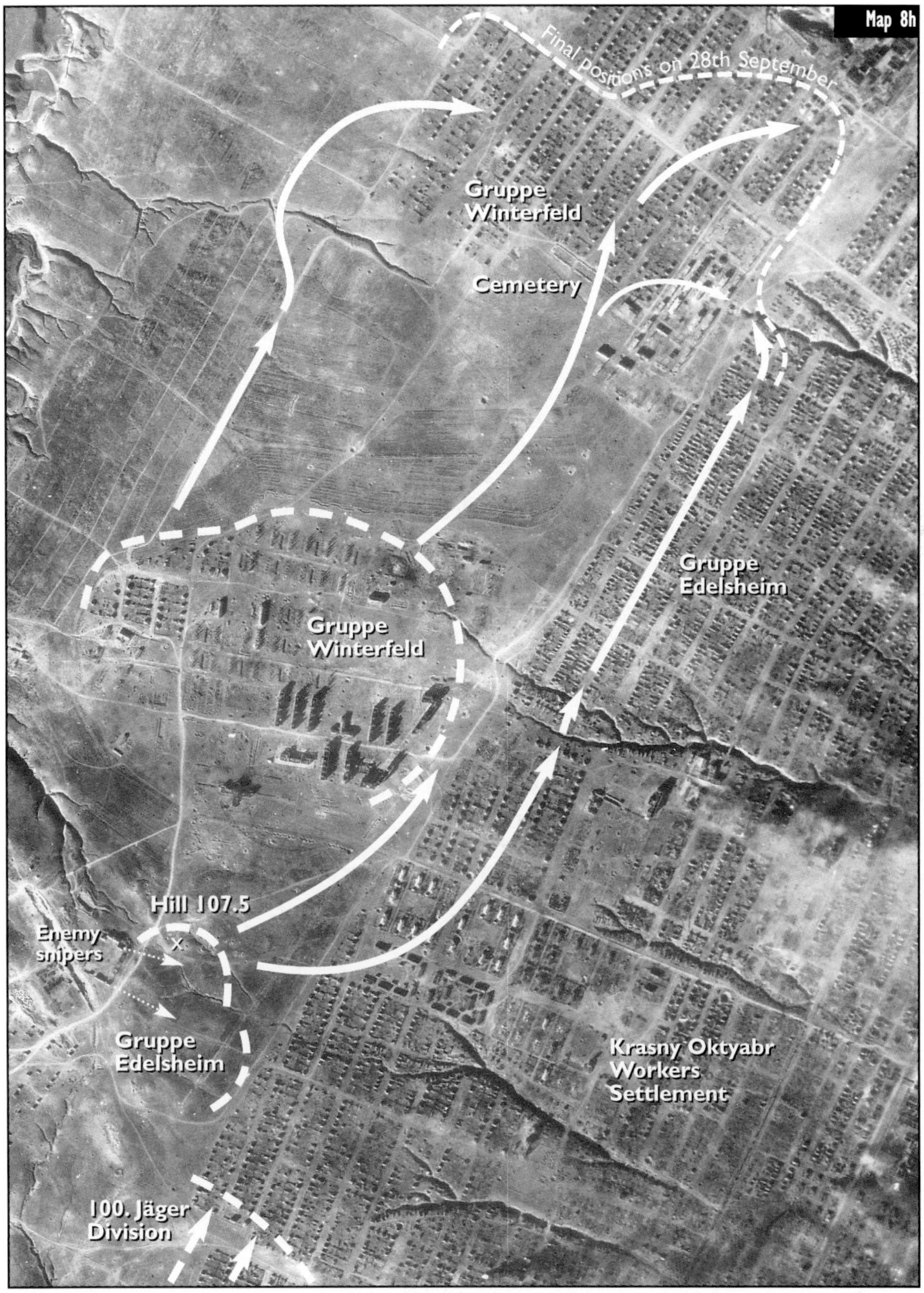

The assaults of Gruppe Edelsheim and Winterfeld's armoured Gruppe.

unsuspected direction to the Russian defenders. Towards evening, Gruppe Edelsheim pressed forward up to their daily attack objective, the southern bank of the cross gully that ran from 73b to 74c. Therefore, the grenadiers held the eastern end of the narrows while the panzers secured the west. With that, the objective was reached and securely held. During the day, the Division captured 280 prisoners and destroyed or captured 5 tanks, 9 anti-tanks guns, 32 anti-tank rifles, 7 mortars, 2 flamethrowers and 4 mine-dogs.
Obergefreiter Reddig reports on his 1./Panzergrenadier-Regiment 21: "28.9.42: Heavy fighting on the front. Wyjczinski, who had fetched the dead Obergefreiter Schmischke out of the fire position, had both of his legs ripped off by a bomb. – He soon died in hospital.
"Obergefreiter Stibhysen tipped over his motorcycle-sidecar during the evening and suffered severe bruising."
Obergefreiter Franz Scholz, 2./Panzergrenadier-Regiment 21, disappeared in the morning. A messenger from the Schwadron said that Obergefreiter Scholz had become very ill in the morning and wanted to go to the Schwadron's empty vehicles in the rear area to recover. He did not arrive at the Schwadron's vehicles or at the dressing station.

At 1315 hours, Major von Menges was in the advanced divisional command post when he received a short visit from Generaloberst Paulus and his small entourage. After being briefed on 24. Panzer-Division's situation and discussing the subjects of casualties, attainment of objectives and artillery support, Paulus thanked von Menges and headed off to visit the next unit.

During the day, the commander of Panzerpionier-Abteilung 40, Hauptmann James de Boer, together with his 3. Kompanie and a subordinated company from Pionier-Bataillon 41, removed mines along the railway line near Point 735, as well as from the airfield. Oberst von Edelsheim had his command post near Point 735 so it was vital that the mines be cleared quickly. The advanced Division command post was also supposed to move to Point 735 but with the area still thick with mines, it remained where it was. On the airfield, the mines were so dense that the pioneers were obliged to first produce two alleys through the belt of mines. These alleys were marked with lines of white tape suspended on steel rods, allowing vehicles and troops a safe passage while the pioneers continued to cleanse the other areas. Another company of pioneers, 2. Schwadron, was also busy removing mines. The previous day, it had been part of Gruppe Edelsheim and its duty as mine-removers was temporary because it was ordered to be returned to Gruppe Edelsheim as quickly as possible.
The enemy recognised the long east flank and attacked at 1830 hours from the south-east, penetrating the positions of Gruppe Edelsheim. At 2220 hours, an order reached Oberst von Edelsheim ordering him to seal of the enemy penetration by using his Gruppe's last reserves. After completing this, he was then to win back the old front line. By a supreme effort, a blocking position was formed by the last reserves and contained the enemy.

On this day, the Division received a communiqué that the wounded Division Commander, Generalmajor Ritter von Hauenschild, had become the 129th soldier of the German Wehrmacht to be awarded the Oakleaves to the Knight's Cross of the Iron Cross on 27th September 1942. On the occasion of receiving such a high decoration, Generalmajor von Hauenschild sent a message to his old division from his hospital bed:

"My comrades!

"The Führer has awarded me the Oakleaves to the Knight's Cross of the Iron Cross. Besides that, he has ordered my transport to the homeland on a special flight that shall take place tomorrow.
"The general physical and spiritual weakness following my seventh wound is still very great. I am therefore only in the position to thank you and our fallen and wounded comrades from the bottom of my heart for your courage, toughness and tenacity, your skill and your comradeship! I thank you alone that I have been allowed to lead the Division from success to success! I thank you alone for this high distinction!
"I have two requests:
"1.) See to it that the connection with our wounded comrades is maintained or looked for by any means so that after their recovery, they can return to the ranks of the Division and through this, the Division, also in regards to personnel, will remain the best German panzer division.
"2.) See to it, as soon as quiet times arrive, that all comrades eliminated as a result of wounds since 28th June and through changes in platoon commander, company commander and adjutant positions, know of their well-deserved decoration.

"My thoughts during my recovery naturally often go to you and your further path.
"I wish you continued luck, success and health and, so that our Führer may succeed, that you soon obtain the total victory that we require.

"Heil dem Führer! Heil 24. Panzer-Division!

signed Ritter von Hauenschild"

This day was counted as a Sturmangriffe day for Panzer-Regiment 24 and Panzergrenadier-Regiment 21:
28.9.42 (for PR24): attack on Barrikady
28.9.42 (for PGR21): attack on the edge of the city (northern part of Stalingrad)

Casualties:

3 officers killed

- Oberleutnant Wilhelm Urbons (Schwadron Kdr); Stab/K4 (Killed)
- Oberleutnant Alfred Franz Emil Theilig (Zug Kdr); 1./PR24 (Killed)
- Leutnant Karl-Heinz Horst; Pz.Pi.40 (Killed)

22 men killed

- Obergefreiter Gerhard Brauer; Pz.Pi.40 (Killed)
- Unteroffizier Albert Elsner; PR24 (Killed)
- Obergefreiter Engelbert Hoster; PGR26 (Killed)
- Panzergrenadier Otto Holzmann; PGR21 (Killed)
- Unteroffizier Edmund Wiederer; PGR21 (Killed)
- Gefreiter Kurt Sraga; PGR21 (Killed)
- Panzergrenadier Erich Köhler; PGR21 (Killed)

- Wachtmeister Otto Burgschat; PGR21 (Killed)
- Obergefreiter Otto Barkschat; K4 (Killed)
- Gefreiter Heinz Schäfer; K4 (Killed)
- Gefreiter Horst Klitsch K4 (Killed)
- Gefreiter Gerhard Goerke; K4 (Killed)

5 officers wounded (3 of those stayed with the troops)

- Leutnant Otto (Zug Kdr); 10./PGR26 (Wounded but stayed with the troops)
- Oberleutnant Thuiske von Metzsch (Schwadron Kdr); 3./K4 (Wounded)
- Hauptmann Hermann Heemsoth (Abt. Kdr); III./PAR89 (Wounded but stayed with troops)
- Leutnant Hans-Wilhelm Hilgenberg (Schw. Kdr); 2./PGR21 (Wounded but stayed with troops)
- Oberleutnant Segger (Zug Kdr); 10./PGR21 (Wounded)

159 men wounded (57 of those stayed with the troops)

- Gefreiter Alwin Wyzgowski; PGR21 (Wounded but died later in the day)
- Obergefreiter Edmund Wujozinski; PGR21 (Wounded but died later in the day)
- Obergefreiter Stibhysen; PGR21 (Wounded but stayed with the troops)

29th September 1942:

At 0430 hours, the Russians attacked the east front of Gruppe Edelsheim with strong artillery support and tanks. The main weight of the enemy attack fell upon Major von Heyden's II./Panzergrenadier-Regiment 26. The grenadiers had established their positions in overgrown vegetable patches, behind paling fences and in half-demolished wooden huts, but because the line ran through gardens and huts, there was no clear field of fire. In the split-second flash of bursting shells, the grenadiers caught fleeting glimpses of figures flitting through the gardens on the other side of the street. A few even saw the menacing silhouettes of T-34's. Machine-guns hammered and beads of tracers smashed into the huts standing opposite or splashed off remnants of crumbling masonry chimneys. Fires flared and cast a ghastly orange light over the battlefield. The Russians infiltrated the German line and killed several men in their foxholes. The thump of exploding grenades and hoarse Russian voices rang out and the deep rumbling of diesel engines caused the air to vibrate. Staunch resistance nests held on and prevented the defensive line from collapsing. Calls for help reached Division HQ and they responded immediately: orders were sent to Major von Winterfeld to dispatch some panzers to the hard-pressed grenadiers and these arrived a short time later. Officers of the besieged battalion quickly organised a counterattack constructed around the panzers and soon, they pushed into the surprised enemy and swiftly restored the situation. The attack was repulsed and the local crisis remedied by the intervention of panzers. A total of eight men were missing after the Russian attack, including Obergefreiter Will Hoppe and Panzergrenadier Johannes Laukötter, both from 6./Panzergrenadier-Regiment 26. Laukötter was only 19-years old. Their platoon commander, Leutnant Friedrich Buschinsky, was killed leading the defence.

Obergefreiter Reddig reports: "29.9.42: We attacked early in the morning. Heavy fighting over the entire day. Stukas bombed Russian positions on the other side of the Volga. Very cold and severe storms. I drove with 7 severely wounded men to the main dressing station."

A further advance by the Division to the north-east with the small forces and the deep east flank was not possible until 100. Jäger-Division had moved up. Later in the morning, however, one of 100. Jäger-Division's units, continuing the assault from the west in an eastern direction over the southern wing of 24. Panzer-Division, only came into the foremost edge of the city as a consequence of strong opposition but nevertheless brought relief to the Division and made it possible to free up some forces.
With 100. Jäger-Division now shouldering more of the burden for defending the lengthy, vulnerable eastern flank, 24. Panzer-Division was able to withdraw some of its forces and implement a speedy regrouping. Armoured Gruppe Winterfeld launched an attack to the north and managed to take into occupation the north-east half of Barrikady housing estate (74a).

Paulus was again inspecting units and visiting commanders, and shortly before noon he paid a visit to the Division command post. This time he was accompanied by the Commander of Heeresgruppe B, Generaloberst Freiherr von Weichs. Generalmajor von Lenski greeted his high-ranking visitors and talked about the success of the offensive and the major role played by his division. After discussions of tactics and further objectives, Weichs and Paulus departed.

It is interesting to note that on this day – in which the Division was occupied mostly with holding the line – 39 men were killed. This was the highest total so far for the assault on Stalingrad-North.

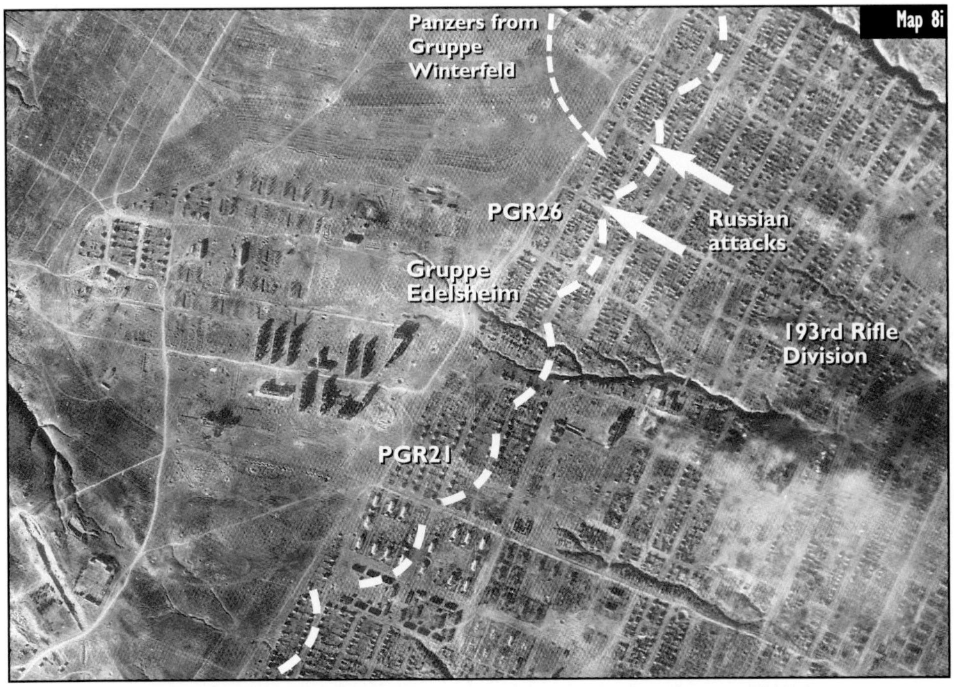

Russian attack on the morning of 29th September against the thin defensive line of Gruppe Edelsheim.

Casualties:

2 officers killed

- Leutnant Friedrich Buschinsky (Zug Kdr); 6./PGR26 (Killed)
- Leutnant Oskar König (Schwadron Kdr); 9./PGR26 (Killed)

37 men killed

- Obergefreiter Wilhelm Lücke; PGR21 (Killed)
- Obergefreiter Oscar Welsch; PGR21 (Killed)
- Obergefreiter Peter Wirtz; PGR21 (Killed)
- Gefreiter Edmund Blaszyck; PGR21 (Killed)
- Gefreiter Helmut Kretzchmar; PGR21 (Killed)
- Obergefreiter Franz Mey; PGR21 (Killed)
- Obergefreiter Kurt Wassermann; PGR21 (Killed)
- Obergefreiter Kurt Riemann; PGR21 (Killed)
- Gefreiter Fritz Remmert; PGR21 (Killed)
- Panzergrenadier Robert Kessler; PGR21 (Killed)
- Panzergrenadier Wolfgang Knosalla; PGR21 (Killed)
- Panzergrenadier Kurt Schröder; PGR21 (Killed)
- Obergefreiter Hermann Kremming; PGR21 (Killed)
- Gefreiter Otto Schwermer; Pz.Pi.40 (Killed)
- Gefreiter Otto Blaamann; 9./PGR26 (Killed)
- Obergefreiter Karl Holthusen; PGR26 (Killed)
- Obergefreiter Karl Dorsche; PGR26 (Killed)
- Gefreiter Paul Bönig; PGR26 (Killed)
- Wachtmeister Fritz Hahne; PGR26 (Killed)
- Obergefreiter Martin Redweik; K4 (Killed)
- Unteroffizier Hugo Grimm; Pz.Jg.40 (Killed)

3 officers wounded (all 3 stayed with the troops)

- Oberleutnant Herbert Oberbeck (Schwadron Kdr); 8./PGR26 (Wounded but stayed with the troops)
- Oberleutnant Kurt Hoffmann (Schwadron Kdr); 5./PGR26 (Wounded but stayed with the troops)
- Oberleutnant Rost (Schwadron Kdr); 3./Pz.Pi.40 (Wounded but stayed with the troops)

91 men wounded (26 of those stayed with the troops)

- Gefreiter Walter Sabrowski; PGR21 (Wounded but died in hospital later in the day)

8 men missing

- Obergefreiter Will Hoppe; PGR26 (Missing in action)
- Panzergrenadier Johannes Laukötter; PGR26 (Missing in action)

30th September 1942:

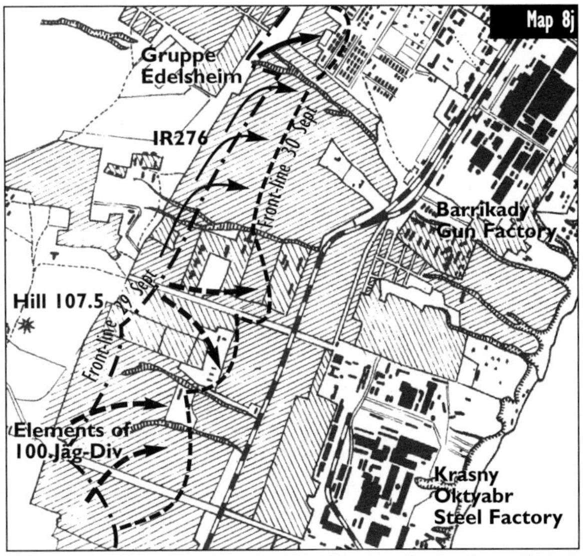

Infanterie-Regiment 276 moves into position, freeing up the southern wing of Gruppe Edelsheim. Elements of 100. Jäger-Division also occupy a large portion of the lengthy eastern flank.

The Korpsbefehl for 30th September ran: "Hold and improve the attained positions." To bolster the dwindling trench strength, the Division received a welcome addition to its manpower: Infanterie-Regiment 276 of 94. Infanterie-Division was supplied in the night and subordinated, freeing up forces of the Division for the further attack in a north-east direction. The southern half of Gruppe Edelsheim's eastern front was relieved by Infanterie-Regiment 276. Having gained an increase in men, Oberst von Edelsheim concentrated his grenadiers and attacked to the north, forming a bridgehead over the narrows in 74c in conjunction with the newly-arrived infantry of Oberst Müller's Infanterie-Regiment 276 as preparation for the further assault by Panzergrenadier-Regiment 21 and Kradschützen-Abteilung 4. Several enemy attacks, above all against the east flank, were repulsed during the course of the day.

REIFNER

Defensive positions of 3./Panzerpionier-Bataillon 40 in northern Stalingrad. The men can be seen in the shadows in the centre of the photo.

REIFNER

Leutnant Egon Reifner says a few final words over the bodies of his dead comrades. Over months of hard fighting. 3./Panzerpionier-Bataillon 40 melted away to the few men in this photo. Note that most of them are hardened veterans with many medals.

REIFNER

Men of 3.Panzerpionier-Bataillon 40 get some nourishment, in this case chicken and what looks like a block of cheese, or possibly a chunk of sugar. Surely almost delicacies in Stalingrad! The man on the left has a badge on his right sleeve for the single-handed destruction of a tank.

At 1615 hours, the Division issued Divisionsbefehl Nr. 67 which called for an attack to the north on 1st October to gain the hills on the north-east edge of Barrikady. The Division would advance at X-hour on 1st October with Gruppe Edelsheim on the right and Gruppe Winterfeld on the left, occupying the ridge in grid square 84a, 85c, 75d & c, working toward the units of XIV. Panzerkorps pushing down from the north and dominating the resulting bottleneck between the Germans pincers. Protection for the southern flank of the assault would be provided by the newly arrived Infanterie-Regiment 276.

In the afternoon, Infanterie-Regiment 276 re-established the connection to the right neighbouring division against the infiltrating enemy. Even though the Regiment with its two available battalions only had a trench strength of 160 riflemen in total (without crews of the heavy machine-guns, anti-tank or infantry guns), it was still welcome help.

The loss of so many experienced officers since the beginning of the attack on Stalingrad was a great concern for the Division. Replacements were slow in coming, so the return of familiar faces was always welcome. Leutnant Hans-Ludwig von Stockhausen, Ordonanzoffizier of Kradschützen-Abteilung 4, had been wounded on 31st August during the tough battles on the outskirts of the city. After weeks of recovery, he was able to return to the Division: "On 30th September, after a four-week hospital stay in a jaw specialists clinic, I was ordered to return to the Division, which in the interval had been in heavy, costly fighting. I was glad that, after seven landing attempts in a bomb-laden Ju-52 – I was allowed to fly as a gunner – I at last felt the solid ground under my feet in the bustling airfield at Stalingrad. Oberfeldarzt Dr. Schulz, who sent me the order, had wanted my upper jaw to heal in four to six-weeks of convalescence leave. It was to be six years before I saw my home again.
"With a motorcycle messenger I drove to the command post of the battalion in a gully from where a messenger brought me through the shell and bomb crater-studded suburb district under strong artillery fire. On the way there the messenger often pulled me under protective shelter, and here was the 'pungent air' that I was not used to.
"Leaping from cover to cover, in about an hour I was able to report back to Abteilungsführer[4] Rittmeister von Langenn-Steinkeller in an earth bunker in the 'Schnellhefter'. After my four-week absence, I was able to see the traces of the hard weeks of operations and clearly see his bad state of health. After weeks of heavy casualties the battalion was, as always, glad that officers reported back for duty to be near comrades. Many were no longer there.
"I took over the job as Adjutant from the jaundice-inflicted Oberleutnant Dannebaum and also – in a union of personnel – the command of the communications platoon from the wounded Leutnant Schulz. The co-ordination of the supplies applied just as much to the extensive paper war for the missions of the schwadron commanders."

The fighting over the previous two months had torn huge holes in all ranks but the shortage was noticeably felt when it came to commanders. Many older experienced officers had fallen out due to death, wounds or illness and their places taken by junior officers. The Division relied on officers returning after they had recovered from their wounds – such as Leutnant von Stockhausen – but they also placed a lot of worth in very young officers and experienced non-commissioned officers. Such was German training that if an officer became a casualty, there was always a subordinate ready to take command and lead the men forward. On this day, 2.

4. Temporary battalion commander

Leutnant Hans-Georg von Tiedemann who, at only 19 years of age, commanded a schwadron of Panzergrenadier-Regiment 21 in Stalingrad.

Schwadron of Panzergrenadier-Regiment 21, leaderless since 8th September, received a new commander, 19-year old Leutnant Hans-Georg von Tiedemann. Born in Danzig on 11th July 1923, von Tiedemann entered the service in September 1940 as an officer candidate in Reiter-Ersatz-Regiment 1 stationed in Insterburg, East Prussia. He was barely 17-years old. Promotions were swift for the eager young cadet: Gefreiter on 1st May 1941, Unteroffizier three months later on 1st August 1941, Wachtmeister four months later on 1st January 1942 and finally, only one month later, Leutnant on 1st February. He had progressed from Gefreiter to Leutnant in 8 months. He was still stationed in Germany but on 15th July he received a transfer to a front-line unit: Panzergrenadier-Regiment 21, where he assumed the role of Ordonanzoffizier for I. Abteilung. On 25th August, he received a dangerous new assignment: platoon commander in 2. Schwadron. He participated in the tough fighting around Hill 118 on his first day in the line, felt the heady rush of a successful assault when the Russian line was broken on 29th August and struggled through the Stalingrad's obstinate outer defences. On 8th September, the Schwadron Commander, Leutnant Dr. Penners, was transferred to the staff of I. Abteilung to take over the adjutancy, thus leaving the Schwadron without a commander. From the time Leutnant von Tiedemann became a platoon commander until he received command of the Schwadron, 13 of the Schwadron's men had been killed[5]. That was an alarmingly high death rate – and the number of wounded men was many times higher. Leutnant von Tiedemann advanced through the southern railway station with his platoon and on 27th September, was embroiled in the tough combat amongst the shrubs west of Mamayev Kurgan. The promotion of such a young officer showed that he had proven himself as a platoon commander and was ready for the responsibilities of leading a larger group of men.

5. They were Hauptwachtmeister Willi Lagies, Wachtmeister Otto Burgschat, Unteroffizier Heinrich Wessel, Obergefreiters Kurt Kühl, Karl Müller, Wilhelm Lücke, Oscar Welsch and Peter Wirtz, Gefreiters Otto-Victor Köhler, Fritz Behnke, Ernst Werker and Josef Ernst, and Panzergrenadier Heinrich Werlemann.

Casualties:

14 men killed

- Panzergrenadier Arthur Wiedenberg; PGR21 (Killed)
- Panzergrenadier Theodor Busche; PGR21 (Killed)

2 officers wounded (1 of those stayed with the troops)

- Oberarzt Dr. Horst Rocholl (Abteilung Arzt); I./PR24 (Wounded)
- Assistenarzt Dr. Heinemann (Abteilung Arzt); III./PAR89 (Wounded but stayed with troops)

55 men wounded (7 of those stayed with the troops)

1st October 1942:

The enemy attacked the defensive line of the Division on a broad front with strong forces, above all on the sector boundaries. They were thrown back everywhere. The Division continued to hold the attained line, under local improvements.
The major assault scheduled for this day was postponed until the northern neighbour, 389. Infanterie-Division, had begun their attack. At 2125 hours, the Division issued Divisionsbefehl Nr. 69 which simply changed the date from 2nd October to 3rd October.

Casualties:

14 men killed

- Wachtmeister Wilhelm Mäck; PGR21 (Killed)
- Unteroffizier Rudolf Hoheisel; Pz.Jg.40 (Killed)

1 officer wounded (he stayed with the troops)

- Oberarzt Dr. Kurt Donner (Abteilung Arzt); II./PGR21 (Wounded but stayed with the troops)

100 men wounded (63 of those stayed with the troops)

2 men missing

- Gefreiter Walter Jenkies; K4 (Missing in action)

2nd October 1942:

Several enemy reconnaissance probes were repelled. It came out from enemy statements that the Russians were continually bringing reinforcements over the Volga. If the Division was still strong, a quick thrust to the Volga could still be successful.
In preparation for the assault, the Luftwaffe bombed selected targets, mainly concentrating

Combat and Ration strength on 1st October 1942

Units	Combat strength Offz.	Beamte	Uffz.	Men	Ration strength Offz.	Beamte	Uffz.	Men	Total
Division Staff	18	–	39	131	25	10	54	201	**290**
Pz.Gren.Brigade 24	2	–	7	25	1	–	10	62	**73**
Pz.Rgt. 24	37	8	438	1089	40	14	508	1502	**2064**
Pz.Gren.Rgt. 21	26	3	216	896	30	4	249	930	**1213**
Pz.Gren.Rgt. 26	23	5	194	923	27	5	217	1044	**1293**
Krad.Abt. 4	9	–	142	586	10	2	154	618	**784**
Pz.Art.Rgt. 89	40	–	212	1169	43	9	265	1471	**1788**
Pz.Jg.Abt. 40	11	1	81	368	14	3	87	386	**490**
Pz.Pi.Btl. 40	11	–	32	264	11	2	70	470	**553**
Pz.Nach.Abt. 86	5	–	58	293	12	2	79	339	**432**
Dinafü. 40	–	–	–	–	22	15	124	842	**1003**
SanKo. 1./40	–	–	–	–	5	3	32	177	**217**
SanKo. 2./40	–	–	–	–	6	3	26	140	**175**
Bäckerei Ko. 40	–	–	–	–	2	1	18	148	**169**
Schlächterei Ko. 40	–	–	–	–	3	1	8	62	**74**
Verpfl. Amt 40	–	–	–	–	–	8	14	75	**97**
Feldpostamt 40	–	–	–	–	–	5	13	10	**28**
Feldgend. Trupp 40	–	–	–	–	3	–	37	13	**53**
IV./PAR89	14	–	65	353	15	4	83	425	**527**
Sum:	**196**	**17**	**1484**	**6097**	**269**	**91**	**2048**	**8915**	**11323**
Subordinated Units									
Pi.Abt. 635	9	2	53	341	10	2	66	363	**441**
Flak-Bataillon 602	11	–	56	382	11	–	56	382	**449**
1./Ersatz Bataillon 1	1	–	21	123	1	–	21	123	**145**
RAD Gruppe K 22*	–	–	–	–	–	–	–	–	**390**
SanKo. 696*	–	–	–	–	–	–	–	–	**150**
Armee Feldlaz. 613*	–	–	–	–	–	–	–	–	**200**
Total:	**217**	**19**	**1614**	**6943**	**291**	**93**	**2191**	**9783**	**13098**

*) Of these units, only the total ration strength is known

along the Volga and without knowing it, almost leaving the Russian 62nd Army leaderless after they struck an oil reservoir situated above the headquarters of General Chuikov, who had been told that the oil tanks were empty. A huge plume of oily black smoke rose up to the sky, met a westerly wind and spread to the east, forming a huge black blanket covering the eastern steppe for a distance of 25km. This pillar of smoke remained for several days, providing a perfect orientation point for the attacking troops.

From a post dug into Hill 107.5, General von Richthofen, Commander of VIII. Fliegerkorps, watches his Stukas pummel the Barrikady Gun Factory. General Chuikov, Commander-in-Chief of all Russian forces in the city, had his dugout on the riverbank below the factory.

The assault originally scheduled for 1st October was postponed until 3rd October. Early in the day, the Division issued a preliminary order for this attack. It was presumed that during the day, 389. Infanterie-Division would move up to the same level as 24. Panzer-Division and place its front to the east. The Division would set out at X-hour (still undetermined at this point), under cover of the flank by Infanterie-Regiment 276, and gain the areas 74d, 74b and 84a with a front to the north-east, then later turn to the south-east. Gruppe Edelsheim, attacking in a north-east direction, would capture the symmetrical group of houses in 74b2 & 4, later wheeling the entire front to the south-east. The favourable defensive positions in 74d and 84a South would be held. Gruppe Winterfeld would gain the dispersed group of houses in 84a under cover to the north. After reaching the objective, a front to the south-east would be taken up and then elements would turn into the rear of the enemy in front of Gruppe Edelsheim.

The result of the Stukas: Chuikov is almost incinerated after a bomb struck an oil reservoir above his command post. The resulting pillar of smoke was visible for many days and served as an excellent orientation point for the Germans.

The utter chaos caused by all-out bombing and shelling is shown in this workers settlement on the western outskirts of the factory district.

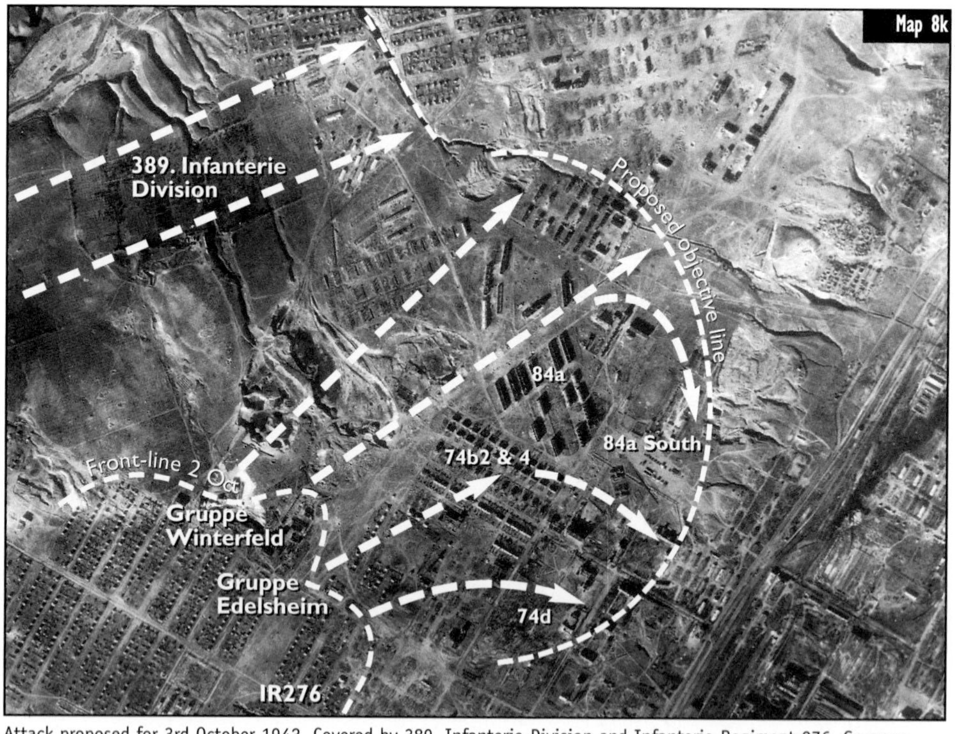

Attack proposed for 3rd October 1942. Covered by 389. Infanterie-Division and Infanterie-Regiment 276, Gruppen Winterfeld and Edelsheim would take 84a (Schnellhefter Block) and push a large bulge into the enemy defences.

Final details about the assault were announced at 2200 hours in Divisionsbefehl Nr. 70 which called for a limited assault on 3rd October in a north-east direction into the Barrikady settlement with Kampfgruppen Edelsheim and Winterfeld. Even at this late hour, the starting time was still not set. The left neighbour, 389. Infanterie-Division, was starting at 0800 hours from area 55, moving up to the same level as the Division on the north-south gully in 75a & c. Division would determine its own starting time based upon reports by Gruppe Winterfeld or Gruppe Edelsheim about the progress of the neighbours.
On this day, a soldier of the Division received a decoration: the Iron Cross Second Class. Panzergrenadier Fedor Oeser was awarded the Spange[6] to the Iron Cross. What this meant was that Oeser had already been awarded the Iron Cross Second Class – in the First World War! Fedor Oeser was born on 19th June 1890 in Lauterbach, making him 52 years old. He was one of the oldest men in the Division, if not the oldest. He was older than von Lenski, von Edelsheim and von Hellermann but what made Oeser so extraordinary was that he was fighting among 17-year old baby-faced recruits in hellish front-line conditions. Unfortunately, the decoration was a posthumous one: Fedor Oeser had been killed on 25th September 1942 and buried in one of the Division's Heroes Cemeterys[7].

Casualties:

20 men killed

- Obergefreiter Gerhard Neysters; PGR21 (Killed)
- Obergefreiter Kurt Leicksenring; K4 (Killed)
- Gefreiter Otto Hochmann; K4 (Killed)

6 officers wounded (5 of those stayed with the troops)

- Hauptmann Axel von Schack (Batterie Kdr); 4./PAR89 (Wounded but stayed with the troops)
- Oberarzt Dr. Kurt Pisselhoy (Abteilung Arzt); K4 (Wounded)
- Leutnant Walter Meya (Zug Kdr); Stab I./PR24 (Wounded but stayed with the troops)
- Kriegs Ingenieur Both; IV./PAR89 (Wounded but stayed with the troops)
- Leutnant Wilhelm Deuer (Batterie Kdr); 12./PAR89 (Wounded but stayed with the troops)
- Leutnant Herbert Sylla (Zug Kdr); 1./PR24 (Wounded but stayed with the troops)

132 men wounded (81 of those stayed with the troops)

- Konrad Dreibus; PGR21 (Wounded but died later in the day)

4 men missing

---

6. Clasp
7. There is some confusion about what rank Oeser actually held: one source says he was a Panzergrenadier when he received his Spange, but another source says he was a Leutnant when he was killed. Whatever the case, Oeser's story is certainly one of the most courageous that has come out of the dreadful battle for Stalingrad.

3rd October 1942:

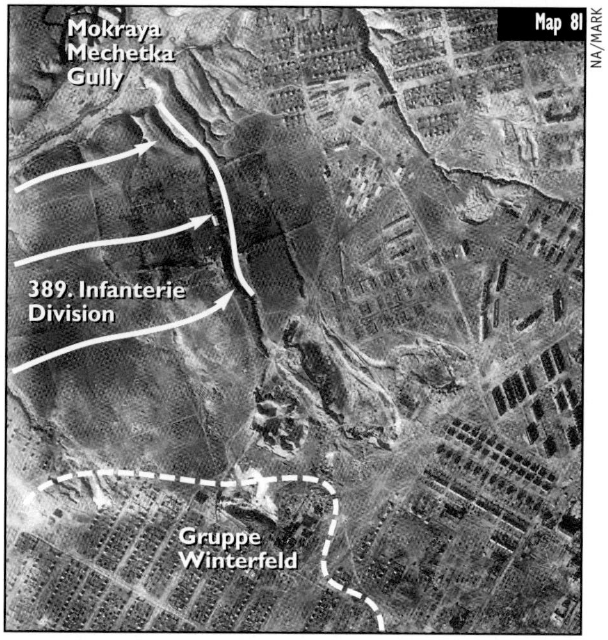

389. Infanterie-Division's attack on the morning of 3rd October.

Once again, nightly enemy reconnaissance thrusts were repulsed and strong enemy air attacks also occurred, neither of which hindered the preparations for the assault. **Gruppe Edelsheim** consisted of the following troops:

Panzergrenadier-Regiment 21
Panzergrenadier-Regiment 26 (without the half-tracks of I. Abteilung)
Kradschützen-Abteilung 4 (without 1. and 2. Schwadron)
1. and 2./Panzerpionier-Bataillon 40
1./Panzerjäger-Abteilung 40

III./Panzerartillerie-Regiment 89 would provide direct support to the Gruppe. The heavy rocket-launchers of II./schwere Werfer Regiment 2 would also add their firepower to the Gruppe.

On the left, **Gruppe Winterfeld** was as follows:

Panzer Abteilung Winterfeld with Panzerpionier Zug, Flak Zug and the Pionier Zug of the Panzer Regiment
the half-tracks of I./Panzergrenadier-Regiment 26
2./Kradschützen-Abteilung 4

I./Panzerartillerie-Regiment 89 would back up the assault with its 10.5cm howitzers. Two independent artillery units were assigned for the assault: schwere Artillerie Abteilung 851 with 2 batteries of 10.5cm howitzers; and schwere Artillerie Abteilung 733 with its 2 batteries of fearsome 21cm mortars.

At 0800 hours, the infantry of 389. Infanterie-Division, preceded by an artillery barrage, left their foxholes and advanced to the north-east. They skirted the westernmost suburb of the Barrikady settlement, their left flank bordering the Mokraya Mechetka Gully. The terrain was basically coverless dry ground with several small orchards scattered throughout the attack area, but the axis of the advance was intersected by several gullies. Resistance was stronger than expected and it was not until after midday that 389. Infanterie-Division finally reached their objective: a gully branching off the Mokraya Mechetka. Their casualties: 2 officers and 3 men killed, 3 officers and 40 men wounded[8]. Gruppe Winterfeld supplied a running commentary to Division about the progress of their neighbours and at one point, General von Lenski thought that he might have to postpone the offensive if 389. Infanterie-Division did not make faster progress. A postponement was not necessary.

8. Killed were Leutnant Beuttler, Kdr. 10./545 and Oberleutnant Gass, Kdr. 9./545. Wounded were Leutnant Bernhard, Kdr. 9./544, Major Gombel, Kdr. III./545 and Leutnant Mengel, Kdr. 1./544

NA/MARK

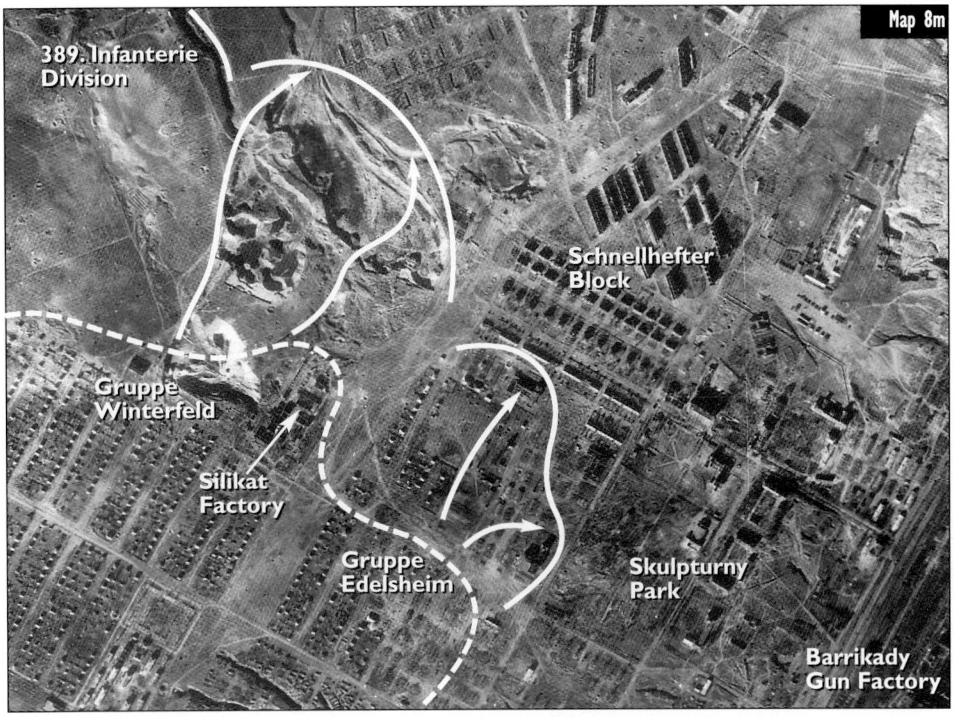

After 389. Infanterie-Division secured the northern flank, Gruppen Winterfeld and Edelsheim attack in the afternoon of 3rd October.

With the basic prerequisite met, the Division was ready to move out. At 1358 hours, a two-minute barrage from all heavy weapons was placed on known enemy positions and on the breakthrough positions. Artillery liaison officers supplied to the assault groups ensured precision placement in front of the troops. The Stukas also plunged down directly in front of the spearheads, concentrating mainly in front of Gruppe Edelsheim. The panzers and grenadiers advanced at 1400 hours. The grenadiers of Gruppe Edelsheim worked their way through the shattered streets, creeping through destroyed huts, buildings and gardens up to the western edge of Skulpturny Park, an overgrown area west of the dreaded Gun Factory. A defence line was quickly established here, the cornerstone being a solidly-constructed building on the right wing. The left wing of Gruppe Edelsheim pushed up to the south-western edge of the Schnellhefter Block but was unable to take this. They did, however, take a large building that overlooked the Schnellhefter.

The panzers, setting out from the north-eastern edge of the Barrikady suburb, pushed across terrain that had no buildings on it but the ground was an undulating mish-mash of hollows, hills and steep-edged depressions. The panzers avoided the worst by adhering to a couple of dirt roads that passed through the area, advancing up to the edge of a suburb totally devastated by fire and bombs. All that remained were dozens of chimneys and piles of ash, charred wood and shattered masonry. Even here, the Russians defended themselves from the cellars and trenches dug among the rubble.

So, after hard hand-to-hand fighting, the Division succeeded in gaining the houses in 74b and the terrain around 75d despite the assault forces becoming even weaker. The enemy was pushed back to the line 74d3 & 4 – b4 – b2 – 75d3.

The Silikat Factory, a small industrial complex set amongst the workers settlements.

In the evening, Gruppe Winterfeld on the north wing was involved in heavy combat deep into the night. It was stressful and draining work for the panzer crewmen. The battlefield around the destroyed workers huts and hollows was illuminated by burning buildings, the flickering flames causing shadows to move and dance, making it almost impossible to determine if Russian tank-killers were sneaking up with Molotov cocktails. Engagements would flare up with frightening speed: someone would notice a movement in the shadows, a flare would be fired, climbing a hundred metres into the dark sky with a trail like a rocket, bursting into a brilliant white star which then fell gracefully earthward, brilliantly illuminating everything within a circle of several hundred metres. As soon as the flare burst, walls of huts, small trees and naked chimneys instantly flashed up, glaring white against pitch black shadows. As the flare descended, the rising and lengthening of the shadows made the whole landscape appear to move and it was not easy to distinguish deadly Russians from harmless shadows. The panzers would fire their cannons, the muzzle-blasts momentarily intensely lighting up the area. Figures would be seen running in the staccato flashes, causing machine-guns and rifles to fire, the bullets flitting low over the ground. Tracers weaved intricate patterns as both sides let loose, occasional ricochets striking a chunk of masonry and whizzing into the sky.

General von Seydlitz issued a Korpsbefehl which called for the "Gaining of the dominating heights on the western edge of the northern part of Stalingrad by 24. Panzer-Division and 389. Infanterie-Division." In the evening, the Division issued Divisionsbefehl Nr. 71 which called for a limited attack on 4th October in a north-east direction to gain the plateau on the northern edge of the Barrikady settlement. This line would then be held. Infanterie-Regiment

REIFNER

Night combat. Panzers combat Russian intruders in the night of 3rd October.

FREIMANN

As a result of the fighting, many huts were set ablaze, providing an eerie light to the battlefield.

276's mission was unchanged. Gruppe Edelsheim and Gruppe Winterfeld would move out at 0900 in close co-operation, Edelsheim gaining the south-eastern section of the Schnellhefter while Winterfeld took the north-western part. After capturing their allotted target, Gruppe Edelsheim would turn to the south-east and form a defensive front ready to repel the expected counterattacks. Before the attack began, however, southern elements of Gruppe Winterfeld would relieve some of Edelsheim's units placed in front of the north edge of Schnellhefter. This would happen before 0630 hours.

Casualties:

11 men killed

- Gefreiter Heinz Pfennig; Pz.Pi.40 (Killed)
- Oberpionier Josef Deißenroth; Pz.Pi.40 (Killed)
- Obergefreiter Karl Malburg; PGR26 (Killed)
- Unteroffizier Heinrich Arand; PGR21 (Killed)
- Unteroffizier Wilhelm Dohrn; K4 (Killed)
- Obergefreiter Gerhard Müller; K4 (Killed)
- Gefreiter Adolf Böttcher; K4 (Killed)

2 officers wounded (1 of those stayed with the troops)

- Oberleutnant Alfred Dannebaum (Abt Adjutant); K4 (Wounded but stayed with the troops)
- Leutnant Karl Fassbender (Schwadron Kdr); 3./K4 (Wounded)

61 men wounded (32 of those stayed with the troops)

4th October 1942:

During the early morning hours, the relief of the northern sector of Gruppe Edelsheim was carried out according to plan. Several units of Kradschützen-Abteilung 4, forming part of Gruppe Winterfeld, shifted to the south and replaced their comrades from Gruppe Edelsheim. This move provided a clean boundary between the two assault groups and everything was completed before 0630 hours. At 0815 hours, Generalmajor von Lenski and Major von Menges moved into the advanced command post to monitor the attack. All units reported in that preparations were proceeding as scheduled.
To pave the way for the attack, the Russian defence lines were softened up by the Luftwaffe. The panzer commanders, leaning in the cupolas and silently watching the Stukas plunge down in front of them, kept looking at their watches. The last bomb was scheduled to fall at 0900 hours, the beginning of the attack. Great pillars of smoke billowed upwards. The Stukas concentrated on the massive block of houses in 84a, sending huge chunks of masonry spinning through the air. They also targeted Skulpturny Park in front of Gruppe Edelsheim. Ten minutes before the attack started, the howitzers of Panzerartillerie-Regiment 89 chimed in, placing a heavy preparatory fire on the same massive buildings that the Stukas were bombing. Artillery observers were assigned to each assault group. As hands of watches ticked over the hour, the panzers of Gruppe Winterfeld lurched forward. Available on this day were 9 Panzer III short-barrels and 17 Panzer III long-barrels, 5 Panzer IV short-barrels and 5 Panzer IV long-barrels, as well as 2 Panzer Befehlswagen (command panzers).

At 0900 hours, the Stukas stopped bombing as the assault troops pushed forward. The attackers set off, spearheaded by Major von Winterfeld's 38 panzers and Oberst von Edelsheim's vanguard of grenadiers. After a few hundred metres, anti-tank shells whizzed past the panzers, mortar shells exploded in random patterns and machine-guns, invisible amongst the dusty backdrop, sent long strings of bullets towards the grenadiers. This was to be expected. Artillery observers attached to the spearheads quickly established contact with their guns and soon,

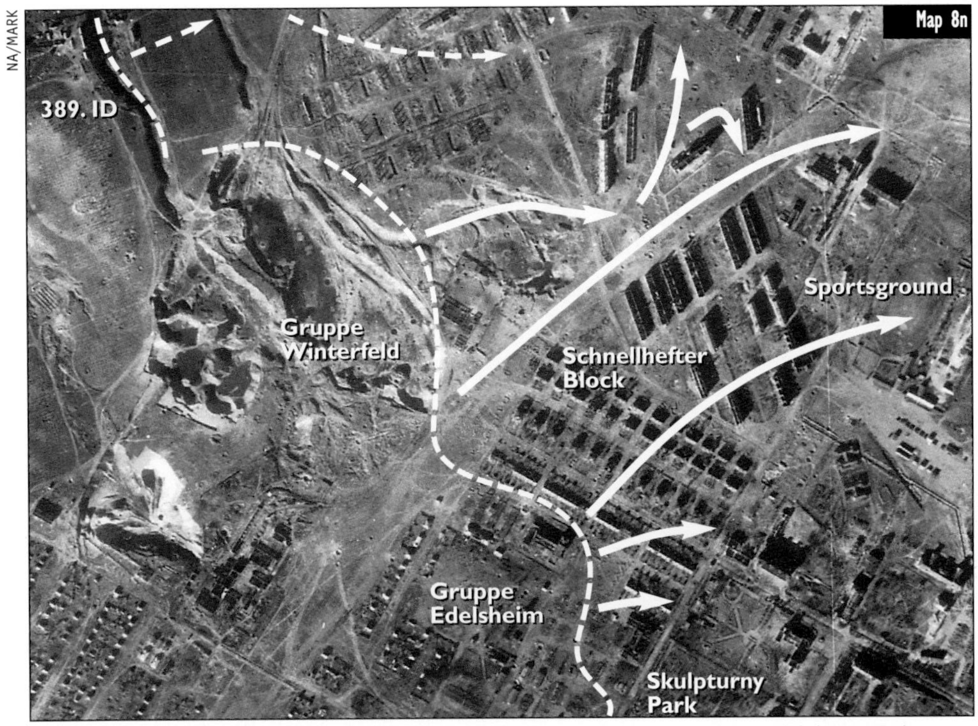

Gruppe Winterfeld's attack into the Schnellhefter Block and Gruppe Edelsheim's assault toward Skulpturny Park.

under their watchful eyes, volley after volley of heavy artillery fell on the Russian lines. Distracted by the barrage exploding around their ears, the Russians didn't notice the panzers sneaking forward behind the massive buildings and in quick succession, several of the T-34's were struck and destroyed by the long-barrel Panzer III's and IV's. Leutnant Sylla, positioning his long-barrel Panzer III at the southern end of a three-storey building, took out a T-34 at barely 30 metres distance. The panzers pressed home their advantage, overpowering the remaining tanks and rolling into the Schnellhefter Block. It was an uneasy feeling. The buildings were huge – up to six stories tall – and dozens of blank windows stared down on the German panzers, any of which could contain an enemy sniper.

The grenadiers were also gaining the upper hand: they approached the Russian lines during the artillery bombardment and took out a few important machine-gun nests, thus allowing the breach to be widened. They quickly cleaned up the rest of the defenders and headed to their daily objective of the Sportsground, which consisted of a playing field surrounded by a couple of small wooden spectator stands and a few buildings.

After a couple of hours, the attack objective of the Schnellhefter Block and the adjacent Sportsground was won, above all by the energetic thrust of Gruppe Winterfeld after hard combat with tanks and anti-tank guns. The panzers came out on top with 9 Russian tanks being destroyed, among them 7 T-34's. The 'Schnellhefter' was a block of houses that had this name because of the appearance of its outline on the city plan.[9]

9. 'Schnellhefter' being the German word for 'folder'.

The Schnellhefter Block, a vast area of open ground covered by multi-storey buildings. The panzers were able to use the large buildings to their advantage by crawling under cover to an extremely close range and knocking out the T-34's.

After a short breather, the Schnellhefter was thrust through in house-to-house fighting from west to east, the Division then deciding to thrust further to the east with the panzers up to the railway line and there destroying the stationary, surprised enemy. The railway was nevertheless a tank obstacle and hindered a further advance. The panzers were pulled back to the Schnellhefter. At the completion of the attack, the enemy had been thrown out of the Schnellhefter Block and Gruppe Winterfeld, with the support of Gruppe Edelsheim, had succeeded beyond the ordered objective by capturing the locality 84a (north-west corner) up to the crossroads 85c4. The left neighbour, 389. Infanterie-Division, also had a successful day, gaining the following line: block of houses 85c and a, east part and west edge of b (the so-called Burg).

After the initial weak resistance, the enemy strengthened himself in front of the entire divisional sector. New enemy concentrations were identified in front of the right wing of Panzergrenadier-Regiment 21. The severely dwindling battle forces of the panzergrenadiers prohibited the utilisation of this success. Because the left neighbour in the attack was not able to come up to the same level, the north wing of the Division was bent back a little.

This day was counted as a Sturmangriffe day for Panzer-Regiment 24:
4.10.: attack north of Barrikady

SPANNOCCHI

Leutnant Sylla in position, firing at the T-34, while another Panzer III faces in the other direction, protecting Sylla's rear.

MARK

A mixed Kampfgruppe of panzers and half-tracks, dwarfed by the massive buildings, pause during their advance.

SPANNOCCHI

The shattered Krasny Oktyabr workers settlement. At this stage of the battle, there were still many intact houses but this changed as the fighting wore on.

SPANNOCCHI

A Panzer III and a half-track take shelter next to the buildings on the right.

SPANNOCCHI

Hauptmann Hermann Koch, Commander of I./Panzerartillerie-Regiment 89, next to one of his armoured observation vehicles parked in the suburb of Krasny Oktyabr. In the background, several panzers are parked next to the houses.

SPANNOCCHI

Behind the half-destroyed wooden shacks of the workers settlements loomed the massive brick buildings of the Schnellhefter Block.

SPANNOCCHI

The Schnellhefter Block. This is the view looking north from Major von Winterfeld's command post. Buried under the churned-up earth in the foreground is a large bunker.

SPANNOCCHI

A Panzer III of Gruppe Winterfeld, camouflaged with wavy lines, awaits in the Badewanne for the order to attack.

SPANNOCCHI

The command post of Major von Winterfeld, known to the men of 24. Panzer-Division as "der Heldenkeller" (the Cellar of Heroes). Panzers are parked in the shadows.

SPANNOCCHI

Oberleutnant Endruweit, the communications officer of the Panzer-Regiment, stands at the entrance of the stairwell that leads down to the command post.

SPANNOCCHI

From left: unknown, Oberleutnant Hans Messerschmidt, Leutnant Paul-Heinz Pehl, and Oberleutnant Paul Schulte.

SPANNOCCHI

From left: unknown, Oberleutnant Messerschmidt and Leutnant Pehl. In the background, camouflaged by planks of wood, are a Panzer IV and two Sdkfz. 250/3.

SPANNOCCHI

Oberleutnant Nordmann (third from right) and several other officers and men from Gruppe Winterfeld gather outside the entrance to the command post.

SPANNOCCHI

Oberleutnant Nordmann (right) chats informally with some Panzer crewmen and a Luftwaffe liaison officer (second from left).

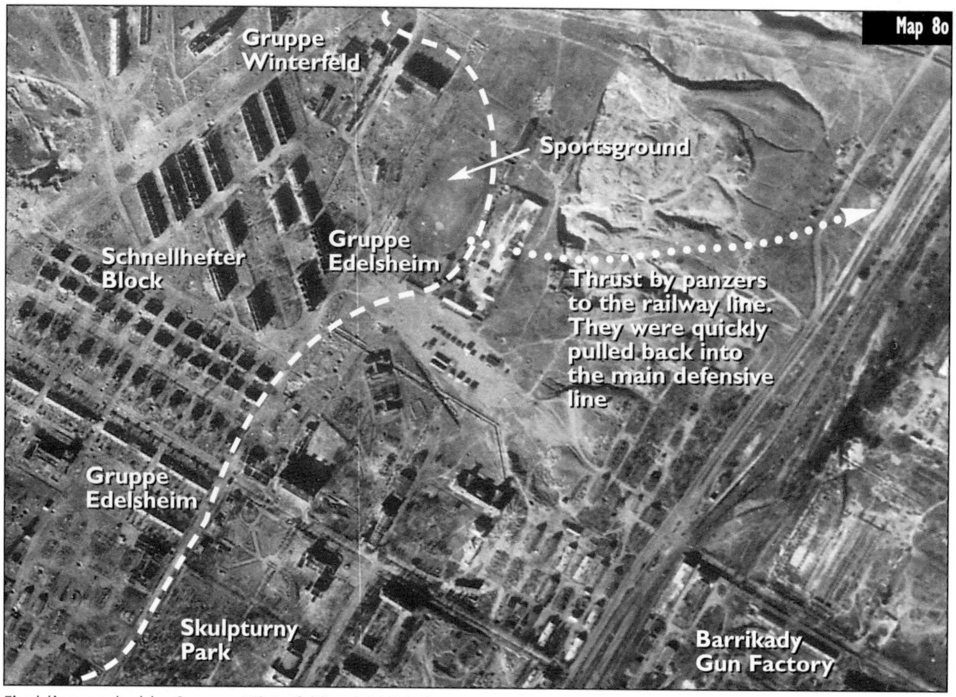

Final line reached by Gruppen Winterfeld and Edelsheim.

Casualties:

23 men killed

- Oberpionier Kurt Ludwig; Pz.Pi.40 (Killed)
- Gefreiter Walter Pantel; Pz.Pi.40 (Killed)
- Obergefreiter Heinrich Mertens; PGR26 (Killed)
- Gefreiter Georg Krause; PGR26 (Killed)
- Gefreiter Alois Prokupek; PGR26 (Killed)
- Unteroffizier Emil Brauner; K4 (Killed)
- Obergefreiter Josef Hermann; K4 (Killed)

4 officers wounded (3 of those stayed with the troops)

- Oberleutnant Holtz (Batterie Kdr); 3./PAR89 (Wounded)
- Hauptmann Hermann Heemsoth (Abt Kdr); III./PAR89 (Wounded but stayed with the troops)
- Stabsarzt Dr. Ernst Grübner (Abteilung Arzt); Pz.Jg.40 (Wounded but stayed with the troops)
- Leutnant Fritz Stegel (Zug Kdr); 3./Pz.Jg.40 (Wounded but stayed with the troops)

85 men wounded (24 of those stayed with the troops)

Decorations bestowed from 28th September to 4th October:

28 Iron Cross First Class
248 Iron Cross Second Class
23 Panzer Combat Badge in Bronze
2 Panzer Combat Badge in Silver
147 Assault Badge

Prisoners and booty taken from 28th September to 4th October:

785 prisoners
9 airplanes
3 guns
23 tanks
19 anti-tank guns
13 mortars
43 anti-tank rifles
2 flamethrowers
4 mine-dogs
1 reconnaissance vehicle

REIFNER

A half-track of 3./Panzerpionier-Bataillon 40, towing an anti-tank gun, passes through the Schnellhefter Block.

Result of the fighting from 27th September – 4th October 1942:

In eight days, the Division had completely fulfiled its daily objectives in constant assaults, thrusting to the north and establishing a connection with XIV. Panzerkorps. 389. Infanterie-Division was decisively helped forward up to the Gorodishche Brook and the decisive heights on the northern part of Stalingrad, essential for the continuation of the assault. The success was rated higher because 100. Jäger-Division wasn't able to accompany the attack on the flank and as a consequence, 24. Panzer-Division had to itself cover the ever-lengthening east flank against continuous enemy attacks during the assault in a north and north-east direction in the most difficult city terrain. The ever-shrinking assault forces unfortunately no longer permitted a swift exploitation of this developing success.

Trench strength of the Division on 27th September – 5th October 1942:

(Trench strength = combat strength without drivers)

	27.9.42	5.10.42
PGR21	456	265
PGR26	479	319
K4	290	160
Pz.Pi.40	156	94

Booty from 27th September – 4th October 1942:

1,305 prisoners
9 aircraft
3 guns
38 tanks destroyed
19 anti-tanks guns
43 anti-tank rifles
35 mortars captured
2 flamethrowers
4 mine-dogs

STALEMATE

CHAPTER NINE

5th October 1942:

In front of the Division lay the mighty complex of the 'Red Barricades' Gun Factory. Here, Panzergrenadier-Regiment 21 lost one of its last active officers that had belonged to it before the outbreak of war. The Commander of II. Abteilung, Rittmeister Otto Drews, was fatally wounded on a reconnaissance mission in a motorcycle-sidecar. He found the strength to write on a message pad to Regiment: "I am leaving", before he died. Everybody that had known him grieved for 'Butzer'. He was constantly cheerful and in the last years of peace was one of the most successful riders in the Regiment.

Continuation of the attack by Korps with the available forces did not seem possible, so Korps decided that it would defend the attained line. At 1245 hours, the Division issued Divisionsbefehl Nr. 72 for the defence of the attained positions in Barrikady-North. They would defend the line gained on 4th October until further notice and consolidate this line by any means according to instructions from battle group commanders. This order signalled the end of offensive operations for the next week but at that time, the commanders and men did not know how long they would be in these positions, so preparations were very comprehensive. These lines would later serve as support positions for the winter positions constructed on the shore of the Volga. The units had the following orders: Infanterie-Regiment 276 would hold the line, with particular emphasis on the right and left boundaries. A close connection would be maintained with the right neighbour, I./Jäger-Regiment 54 (100. Jäger-Division), whose front-line was unclear to the Division. Commander of Infanterie-Regiment 276, Oberstleutnant Julius Müller, was ordered to transfer his command post behind the centre of his Regiment. Gruppe Edelsheim would also hold the previous line. A close connection would be maintained with Gruppe Winterfeld on the

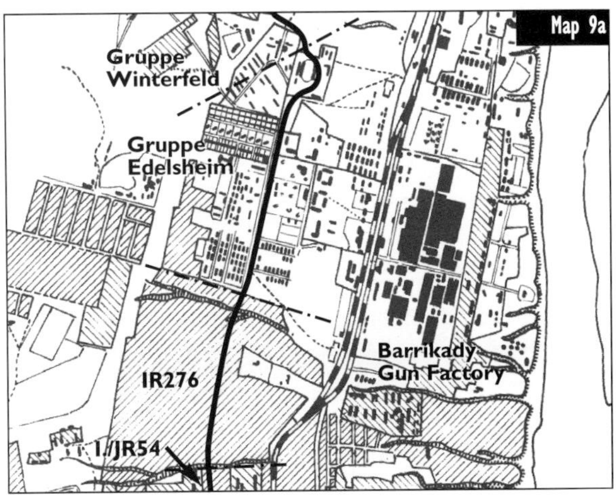

left and the focal point of the defence would be on a gully on the right wing, as well as in front of the Schnellhefter Block. Heavy rocket-launchers of Mörser-Abteilung 616 were to be brought into positions for defence so that the front-lines of Infanterie-Regiment 276 and Gruppe Winterfeld would each be within range of a battalion of the rocket-launchers.
Gruppe Winterfeld would hold the attained line, focusing their defence on the right boundary and the northern wing. Reserves were to be withdrawn from the open north wing.
The artillery was also ready for defence. Any officer, from platoon commander upwards, could request blocking fire from the artillery by firing a red flare. The artillery was also allotted targets in the continuing attack on enemy concentrations. The targets included the Gun Factory, enemy artillery on the east bank, ferries and bridging sites. The artillery would also place harassing fire during the night.
In Divisionsbefehl Nr. 72, there were also 16 helpful hints for organising the defence. Some of these were:

- dig and keep on digging;
- the best defence is to smash enemy preparations with artillery and the Luftwaffe;
- make extensive use of deeply constructed obstacles, street barriers, barricades, concrete- and armoured cupolas. The cupolas and obstacles left in the battle area of the last weeks should be used as much as possible;
- where fields of fire are absent, produce them by demolition;
- reconnoitre and fix operational roads for the panzers and half-tracks;
- constant close connection between the artillery and the panzergrenadiers;
- reconnaissance of blocking positions in case of an enemy breakthrough.

The remnants of Panzerpionier-Bataillon 40 came to a strength of two platoons but fortunately for the Division, it gained some engineering strength when Pionier-Bataillon 635 (combat strength 95 men) was supplied to it. The battalion was kept as Division reserve and was sequestered in a gully near 54a. It also received the task of reconnoitring approach routes, blocking- and counterattack possibilities near all three defensive groups. It would only be used if the enemy broke into the positions.

Hard though it was to believe, there were still many civilians in the battle area. They huddled in cellars, ravines and gullies, waiting for the fighting to pass them by. For some time, the entire population of Stalingrad was being evacuated and they'd received instructions from German authorities to leave Stalingrad in the direction of Kalach. In addition to this, the troops were urged that all civilians behind the front be set in motion towards Kalach. On 5th and 6th October, an action was carried out by the Feldgendarmerie (field police) with the objective of clearing civilians out of the Division's sector east of the Tartar Wall. The supply vehicles of the regiments were directed, as far as was practicable, to take women with children along the road to Kalach. The field police saw to it that this order was implemented. It was a different story for male civilians. All able-bodied men between the ages of 18 and 45 would be seized and brought to a prisoner collection point. From there, the civilian prisoners would be taken to Dulag 205[1], 2km north of the Voroponovo railway station. The Division received a report which stated that civilians that were passing through were plundered by German soldiers in a degrading way. With the harshest means, drastic steps were taken against all the soldiers, and also against members of another division.

1. Durchgangslager or transit camp

At the command post of 3./Panzergrenadier-Regiment 26, Obergefreiter Friedrich-Karl Lerche was ordered to go to the divisional dressing station. He hopped on to motorcycle/sidecar WH 900578 and headed off. He was seen speeding through the Schnellhefter Block and this was the last time he was seen. No trace of either him or the motorcycle was ever found. He was not reported missing until two days later.

The tension and strain produced by the fighting affected men in different ways. During the day, Obergefreiter Karl Rannow of 8./Panzer-Regiment 24 threatened a superior officer. The officer was not named and no further details are known except that on 9th October, Obergefreiter Rannow was charged and sentenced to six weeks of harsh arrest.

Casualties:

1 officer killed

- Rittmeister Otto Johann Drews (Abteilung Kdr); I./PGR21 (Killed)

24 men killed

- Gefreiter Herbert Ermer; Pz.Pi.40 (Killed)
- Gefreiter Walter Jacobs; K4 (Killed)

95 men wounded (31 of those stayed with the troops)

6th October 1942:

The irritating enemy night-time air attacks on the forward line and on the artillery positions continued and several enemy reconnaissance probes were repulsed. From sun-up, strengthening enemy artillery and rocket fire lay on the front line for the entire day. Panzerartillerie-Regiment 89 suffered casualties in men and weapons, as witnessed in Leutnant Ernst-Wilhelm Nueske's diary: "6th October. A black day. The fire emplacements have been recognised in the clear weather by enemy observers and were bombarded. Only in the afternoon had Lindenberg made one gun ready to fire in the new position. Three dead, Leutnant Punge and 12 men more or less severely wounded.
"An ammunition lorry flew into the air and three guns were damaged. I blamed myself for the Batterie not being pulled back the previous day even though Abteilung had declined my request."

For the next few days, the Division remained in its positions opposite the Gun Factory. The units of both panzergrenadier regiments were alarmingly worn down and apart from the continual casualties through enemy actions, jaundice and dysentery decimated the Schwadrons. The regiment commanders, Oberst von Edelsheim and Oberstleutnant von Hellermann, consolidated their command posts. Together, they sat in a narrow earth bunker on the edge of 'Barrikady' suburb. Often, there were very sharp telephone conversations between Oberst von Edelsheim and Division on the basis of several barely reasonable operational orders. Oberst von Edelsheim felt like Division was ignoring the real situation by issuing orders that befitted a full-strength regiment and he had no hesitation in arguing the point with General von Lenski.

Twenty-year old Gefreiter Lothar Abromeit, Panzerpionier-Bataillon 40, who had been awarded an Iron Cross Second Class on 27 September 1942, was killed on this day. It was another casualty that Panzerpionier-Bataillon 40 could not afford.

Casualties:

6 men killed

- Gefreiter Lothar Abromeit; Pz.Pi.40 (Killed)
- Panzergrenadier Reinhold Kersandt; PGR21 (Killed)
- Panzergrenadier Walter Rohr; PGR21 (Killed)
- Unteroffizier Bruno Bessing; PGR21 (Killed)
- Obergefreiter Siegfried Springer; PGR21 (Killed)
- Obergefreiter Franz Rautenberg; PGR21 (Killed)

1 officer wounded

- Leutnant Friedrich Punge (Batterie Offizier); 1./PAR89 (Wounded)

53 men wounded (28 of those stayed with the troops)

7th October 1942:

Night-time enemy air attacks struck the Division, and enemy reconnaissance probes were repulsed. A panzer schwadron detached to 389. Infanterie-Division on 5th October was able to decisively contribute to the elimination of an enemy penetration on this day.
The large scale attrition shooting, scheduled as preparation for the later continuation of the assault, had to be restricted on the evening of the first day and discontinued after the third day. As a result of petrol shortages, the necessary ammunition was not brought forward.

Casualties:

8 men killed

- Obergefreiter Karl Huhn; PR24 (Killed)
- Gefreiter Reinhard Krogmann; PGR26 (Killed)
- Obergefreiter Alfred Wiesner; K4 (Killed)

25 men wounded (12 of those stayed with the troops)

- Obergefreiter Paul Weishahn; PGR26 (Wounded but died on 8th October in Tazinskaya hospital)

2 men missing

- Obergefreiter Friedrich-Karl Lerche; PGR26 (Missing in action)

8th October 1942:

The site of Panzerbefehlswagen '361'.

It was a gorgeous autumn day. There was not a cloud in the sky and the men basked in the dazzling sun, the offensive at a halt and a defensive posture assumed. Major von Winterfeld's command panzer '361' was parked in the lee of a two-storey building, out of sight of enemy observers and well behind the forward line. Major von Winterfeld was not present – he was off at a conference – and the only occupants of the panzer were Oberleutnant Liebe, Abteilung Nachrichtenoffizier (Battalion communications officer), and Unteroffizier Brüdern, while outside, gathered around the panzer, were a few other men, messengers mainly, from other units of the Division. Unteroffizier Brüdern had to leave the safety of the panzer for a few moments to attend to other matters. Russian artillery shells howled in and exploded throughout the area, the echoes resounding through the tall buildings until the next volley rushed in. This had been happening all day so the men paid no heed as they knew it was totally unaimed fire. Another shell whistled in but this time, it plunged straight into the engine deck of Panzer '361', and the effect was catastrophic. The large-calibre shell exploded in the engine compartment and ripped the panzer apart, tearing off the superstructure and turret, flinging them a couple of metres. The vehicle was totally disembowelled. Oberleutnant Liebe, alone inside the vehicle, was killed instantly and four men next to the panzer were also killed, while several others were wounded. Oberleutnant Liebe was buried the next day.

Casualties:

1 officer killed

- Oberleutnant Günther Hans-Jürgen Liebe (Abt NO); I./PR24 (Killed)

5 men killed

- Gefreiter Waldemar Ueblacker; Pz.Jg.40 (Killed)
- Obergefreiter Helmut Pahlke; PGR21 (Killed)

27 men wounded (9 of those stayed with the troops)

- Obergefreiter Günther Klar; PGR21 (Wounded but died at Kalach hospital later in the day)

9th October 1942:

The nerve-straining combat around individual ruins or bunkers in the massive fields of rubble was now contested by the heavy weapons of the panzergrenadier regiments, artillery and Luftwaffe. Therefore an observer from the artillery and a ground observer from VIII. Fliegerkorps had installed themselves in the command post of 8./Panzergrenadier-Regiment 21, a former Russian bunker opposite the Gun Factory. In contrast to previous operations, above all south of the Tsaritsa, the co-operation now worked better between the Luftwaffe and Army units although, in the complex desert of rubble, the fact could not be avoided that the grenadiers still suffered under shortly placed artillery fire or mistaken bombing by the Luftwaffe.

The Commander of 6./Panzergrenadier-Regiment 21, Oberleutnant Dittmar, had installed himself in another bunker and christened it the 'Blaue Maus' in memory of a remark by Oberstleutnant von Hellermann on the occasion of a briefing of commanders before the beginning of the attack on the city. Now Dittmar invited people for coffee and cake (from fieldpost parcels) in the 'Blaue Maus'. Although the path to the bunker lay under constant enemy fire, none of the invitees allowed themselves to escape the enticing goodies.

In the afternoon, the Russians attacked on the entire front and were thrown back everywhere.

Casualties:

1 officer killed

- Sonderführer Werner Julius Karl Meyer (Dolmetscher); Stab 24. Panzer-Division (Killed)

6 men killed

- Gefreiter Franz Pribitzer; K4 (Killed)

36 men wounded (20 of those stayed with the troops)

- Gefreiter Willi Boy; PGR21 (Wounded but died later in the day in hospital)

10th, 11th, 12th and 13th October 1942:

The usual strong enemy artillery fire continued to fall on the Division's sector. The Division's artillery successfully combatted the enemy artillery, as well as the shipping traffic on the Volga. Better, more thorough, results could have been obtained but the continuous shortages of petrol made the supply of ammunition more difficult. On 10th October, strong enemy attacks on the northern neighbour, 389. Infanterie-Division, were repulsed by the intervention of the panzer schwadron.

On 10th October, Leutnant von Tiedemann, the 19-year old Schwadron Commander, received a reprieve from his dangerous front-line duties: he was called back to Abteilung headquarters to become adjutant to the very capable, experienced and well-liked Rittmeister Graf Solms[2] and retained this position for more than two months.[3]

Leutnant Georg Köhler, Commander of 3./Panzergrenadier-Regiment 26, became famous for an almost unbelievable deed performed in early October, the only official recognition of which is a tantalising reference in his Knight's Cross recommendation: "Leutnant Köhler, who has already excellently distinguished himself in Poland, Holland, France and during the Russian campaign in which the feat of blowing up a high-rise building in Stalingrad-North behind the enemy lines with 250 captured mines was mentioned in the Wehrmachtsbericht on 10th October[4], is alone worthy of the bestowal of the Knight's Cross of the Iron Cross because of this decisive defensive act.[5]" The story about this amazing deed is that equipped with a captured Russian lorry stacked with 250 mines and accompanied by ten men from his Schwadron, Leutnant Köhler drove through no-mans-land, talked his way past several Russian sentries[6] and managed to reach a massive building located behind the Barrikady Gun Factory that was reputed to be the headquarters of a senior Soviet General. After some more fast talking and the overpowering of a few enemy soldiers, the mines were planted throughout the basement and foundations of the building and, just as the mines were about to be blown, Köhler and his men were forced to use their weapons to repel some suspicious enemy sentries. Once that was done, they detonated the mines and headed back to their lorry. The building disintegrated behind them in a massive fireball, all walls collapsing and leaving nothing but a pile of smoking rubble. The lorry managed to reach friendly lines with everyone who had set out but a few of them were now wounded. Leutnant Köhler had successfully completed his suicidal mission.[7]

On 11th October Oberstleutnant von Hellermann, after receiving a transfer back to Germany to become a department chief in the Heerespersonalamt (Army Personnel Office), handed over the Regiment to Oberst von Below who had already belonged to it 15 years earlier in peacetime as a platoon commander, adjutant and schwadron commander. During the First World War, von Below fought on the Eastern Front from 1915 onwards, finally returning home from the Ukraine in 1919. He was then accepted into the newly raised Reiter-Regiment 1 which, just over 20 years later, would be converted to Panzergrenadier-Regiment 21. By 1931, he was a Rittmeister and commanded 5. Eskadron of the Regiment. After various transfers in higher staffs and promotions, the wheel turned full circle and he returned to his old Regiment. Throughout the Regiment, everyone was glad that 'one of their own' would lead them.

Regiment Adjutant Oberleutnant Dietrich Micke remembers: "I brought Oberst von Below straight to the new Regiment command post in the vicinity of 'Schnellhefter' because Oberleutnant Guercke appeared to have suffered severely from jaundice and had checked

2. His full name was Friedrich Graf zu Solms-Wildenfels but everyone referred to him simply as Graf Solms. He was a man of few words, sparing with his speech, but when he did speak, everyone listened.
3. On 20th December, Leutnant von Tiedemann was wounded in the head by shrapnel and flown out of the Kessel, spending the next two months recovering from his wounds in a hospital in Tübingen.
4. This mention in the Wehrmacht's daily report was as follows: 'Leutnant Köhler, Schwadron Commander in a Panzergrenadier-Regiment in central Stalingrad, has blown up a high-rise building in the enemy's rear, a centre for Soviet resistance, with 250 captured mines.'.
5. This defensive act – the reason for the recommendation for the Knight's Cross – was performed in late November/early December after the encirclement of Stalingrad by the Russians.
6. Köhler was born in Nizhne-Petropavlovsk, near Chelyabinsk in Siberia, and thus had a good understanding of the Russian language.
7. The story is difficult to confirm. Not one mention of this incident appears in the divisional war diary. In fact, the only mentions are in the Wehrmachtsbericht and Köhler's Knight's Cross recommendation. When the author tried to confirm the authenticity of this story with a fellow researcher who is in intimate contact with Köhler, he was told that this story is untrue.

himself into hospital. Then I celebrated the departure with Hellermann in a rearward regimental bunker. The banquet consisted of potatoes in their jackets, butter and onions, a delicacy after the long weeks of dried vegetables."

In appreciation of the success of the Regiment during the last weeks, Oberstleutnant von Hellermann received the Knight's Cross of the Iron Cross on 21st November 1942. Not all of Hellermann's subordinates were sad to see him go: "At the Staff Schwadron, the Regiment Commander again packed his bag. He asked for a tailor to sew on a button but he was already dead because the Oberstleutnant[8] as a fierce 'heroic attacker' had sent everyone to the front to alleviate the dwindling 'combat strengths'. From 150 men of the proud Schwadron, only 14 still remained."

On the morning of 10th October, Oberst von Edelsheim received a transfer and left Stalingrad a week later. His replacement, Oberst Alexander von Scheele, arrived soon afterwards.

For the three days of 11th–13th October, Obergefreiter Reddig wrote the following in his diary: "11.10.42: I went with Pasch to the front near the Schwadron. The Russians attacked strongly the entire night. During the day, our Stukas bombed heavily. The Russians now ceased their fire and we can again drive in our vehicle positions. At midday, I drove up with rations. Adelhelm was wounded carrying the food and got on the old Ju.[9]

"12.10.42: Russian artillery fires over to us to the Gumrak railway station."

"13.10.42: Obergefreiter Jansen wounded in the head as he brought lunch to the Schwadronstrupp as it lay under strong fire."

The above entry demonstrates the danger of supplying food to the front-line troops but it was essential not only to maintain their physical strength but also to sustain morale. The fewer warm meals, the quicker morale dropped. As it took longer and longer to comprehensively subdue the stubborn Russian defenders, the quality of food supplied to the troops declined. Obergefreiter Kusterer reports: "We hadn't eaten potatoes, vegetables or fruit for many weeks. A supply column that we sent to the Ukraine had not returned. The perpetually scarce petrol was so rare that we Essenholer[10] only brought warm food and 'coffee', known as Negerschweiß[11], into the forward positions once a day, and that meant during the night."

In the meantime, new divisions were brought forward for the assault to destroy the enemy in the northern part of Stalingrad. Endless columns of lorries and horse-drawn vehicles marched in from the south and south-west, over the airfield into preparation areas located in the large gullies west of the factory district. The weather was warm, the skies cloudless and the radiant autumn sun shone down as the small horses plodded through the deep dusty roads, overtaken by noisy lorries hauling ammunition or carrying troops. Swathes of dust floated over the road. Throughout 13th October, light rain had fallen during most of the day, softening the powdery roads. A glorious red sunset painted the western horizon before a clear and cold evening set in.

At 2300 hours on 12th October, the Division issued Divisionsbefehl Nr. 73 which clarified the Division's role in the large-scale attack on northern Stalingrad on 14th October by Gruppe Jaenecke. While Oberstleutnant Müller's Infanterie-Regiment 276 and Panzergrenadier-Regiment 21 held the previous positions, the newly formed Gruppe Edelsheim would attack

8. ie. Oberstleutnant von Hellermann
9. A kindly reference to the Ju 52, the reliable supply plane that formed the backbone of the German aerial transport and supply system.
10. Food-fetchers or ration-bearers.
11. Literally nigger-sweat

LUCIEN/ROTTIERS

Reinforcements and new units pour into northern Stalingrad. Panzers and lorries of 14. Panzer-Division move toward Stalingrad for a new offensive on 14th October.

and push forward the front-line to the southern and south-eastern edge of the Sportsground area. Gruppe Edelsheim consisted of Panzergrenadier-Regiment 26, Kradschützen-Abteilung 4 (without 1. Schwadron), Panzer Abteilung Winterfeld (without a Schwadron) with Pionier and Flak Zug, and 1./Panzerjäger-Abteilung 40, while I. and III./Panzerartillerie-Regiment 89 were to support this Gruppe. A troop of armoured cars from 1./Kradschützen-Abteilung 4 would also arrive one hour before the attack began. The Gruppe's mission was to follow up the attack of Infanterie-Regiment 576 and advance the front to the line shown on the map on the next page. The attained line was then to be held. A close connection would be maintained with Infanterie-Regiment 577. After the assault, the bulk of the panzers would be pulled out of the forward line and assembled at the disposal of the Division.

Infanterie-Regiment 276, without its I. Bataillon, would hold the line, the focus being on defence and maintaining connections to the right and left. The 10.5cm howitzers of II./Panzerartillerie-Regiment 89 could be called upon for support. In the centre, Oberst von Below's Panzergrenadier-Regiment 21, corseted by the 5cm anti-tank guns of 2./Panzerjäger-Abteilung 40, would also hold the line but they had the additional missions of supporting Gruppe Edelsheim's assault through flanking fire and moving forward the left wing as Edelsheim advanced, thereby keeping a solid connection. They could also rely on the guns of I. and III./Panzerartillerie-Regiment 89.

To provide some armoured support for the infantrymen of the neighbouring Infanterie-Regiment 577, panzers from the Division were supplied. Panzer Schwadron Schulte, consisting of 10 panzers and commanded by 27-year old Oberleutnant Paul August Schulte, was subordinated to Infanterie-Regiment 577 from 1200 hours on 13th October. Oberleutnant Schulte's task was to support the infantry but he was under strict instructions that individual missions by single panzers were to be refused. This guideline was also stipulated to the commander of Infanterie-Regiment 577, Oberstleutnant Hans-Georg Brandt. Oberleutnant

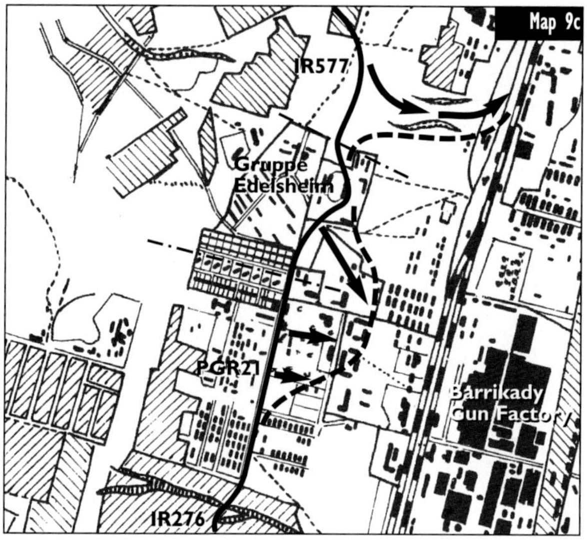

Schulte was also ordered to submit situation reports every three hours to Major von Winterfeld who would then forward them to Division. Generalmajor von Lenski knew that infantry divisions had a habit of using panzers as de facto assault guns and this had to be avoided at all costs. They were much too valuable to be wasted in house-to-house fighting.

Punctually at 1200 hours on 13th October, Oberleutnant Schulte arrived at the command post of Oberstleutnant Brandt who had to make do by sharing the command post of Major Wilhelm Knetsch, Commander of Infanterie-Regiment 545 of 389. Infanterie-Division.

On the eve of the new assault on Stalingrad-North, a report was compiled by the Division highlighting a few important issues. The first was weapons. The report stated that the trust of the troops in German weapons had suffered due to exploding barrels.[12] This had occurred to two leichte Feldhaubitze 18 and one schwere Feldhaubitze 18 since 20 September 1942 and since the beginning of the summer offensive on 28th June, seven of 24. Panzer-Division's artillery pieces had been destroyed by barrel-bursts. It was also reported that due to defective 20mm ammunition, 13 20mm flak barrels had been destroyed by barrel-bursts.

The second issue was ammunition, specifically flares. Division believed that fighting in Stalingrad had been detrimentally affected by the shortage of flares and signal cartridges. Orange smoke signals were not recognised by pilots in the smoke-filled streets, so flares served as the only recognisable indication of the front-line during air attacks. On account of the totally insufficient supply of green flares and signal cartridges, the illumination of the foreground as well as the identification of the forward line opposite 24. Panzer-Division's troops was very unsatisfactory and obstructed battle actions.

Casualties for 10th October:

8 men killed

20 men wounded (7 of those stayed with the troops)

12. When a shell explodes in the chamber of a gun, the barrel blows apart and sometimes causes casualties.

Casualties for 11th October:

7 men killed

- Gefreiter Albin Börner; PR24 (Killed)
- Gefreiter Werner Sprange; PR24 (Killed)

12 men wounded (9 of those stayed with the troops)

- Adelhelm: PGR21 (Wounded)

Casualties for 12th October:

15 men killed

- Obergefreiter Heinrich Tersteegen; PR24 (Killed)
- Obergefreiter Hans-Joachim Rasmus; PGR21 (Killed)
- Obergefreiter Alfred Richter; PGR21 (Killed)
- Obergefreiter Leonhard Steinmetz; PGR21 (Killed)

33 men wounded (16 of those stayed with the troops)

- Knight's Cross winner Wachtmeister Siegfried Freyer; 4./PR24 (Wounded but stayed with the troops)
- Gefreiter Rudolf Schmitz; PGR21 (Wounded but died on 13th October)

Casualties for 13th October:

4 men killed

- Obergefreiter Erich Pagels; PGR21 (Killed)
- Gefreiter Friedrich Döbler; PGR21 (Killed)
- Gefreiter Horst Bendler; PGR21 (Killed)
- Gefreiter Robert Dehmichen; PGR21 (Killed)

17 men wounded (11 of those stayed with the troops)

- Obergefreiter Jansen; PGR21 (Wounded)

1 man missing

Decorations bestowed from 5th October to 11th October:

4 Iron Cross First Class
31 Iron Cross Second Class
16 Panzer Combat Badge in Bronze
5 Panzer Combat Badge in Silver
61 Assault Badge

Prisoners and booty taken from 5th October to 11th October:

127 prisoners
1 gun
3 tanks
1 anti-tank gun

Fight for the Factories

Chapter Ten

14th October 1942:

After a heavy preparatory bombardment by VIII. Fliegerkorps and artillery, the assault of Gruppe Jaenecke with two newly supplied divisions moved off at 0730 hours against the Tractor Factory and the bridgehead there that lay north of the Division's sector. Obergefreiter Ferdinand Kusterer of Panzergrenadier-Regiment 21 vividly remembers this day:

> "At dawn, there was a mighty rumbling in the air and machine-guns rattled above us. We stormed out of the bunker and across the steel blue sky was squadron upon squadron of our Stukas and heavy bombers rushing north to the city while a stiff cold steppe wind made our bones shake... The Russians were there at the same time and a couple of 'Iron Gustavs' (armoured bombers) dropped bombs on Gumrak railway station located nearby while Soviet fighters flew around them like swallows. The Stukas, however, continued on their course unconcerned for without that, the fighters would have attacked. Before our Messerschmidts arrived, the Russians had disappeared because during daylight, the Russians could not match our air superiority. This was so conspicuous that they called forth a calm feeling. From early morning until late in the evening, the Stukas rushed over us... We would not advance on this day but would hold the positions and repulse any counterattacks. In front of us, over the northern part of the city, the howling Stukas dived down three, four, five times, circling around and dropping their bombs in the ruins of the armaments factory where the Russians had dug themselves in. The Russian anti-aircraft guns fired at them like crazy but the Stukas did not

The mighty Dzerhezinsky Tractor Factory, one of the main objectives of LI. Armeekorps' assault on Stalingrad-North.

MARK

Panzer Schwadron Schulte, assigned to support Infanterie-Regiment 577, arrives near the infantry.

MARK

Panzer '123' belches out exhaust smoke while awaiting the order to attack.

concern themselves about it. After they had released their cargo, they assembled in low-level flights and, not being able to be reached by the anti-aircraft fire, rushed past over our heads. As far as I could count and follow them, most of them returned, which was downright amazing considering the anti-aircraft fire. At the same time, the artillery also raised its voice until the pillars of smoke merged together over the city to form one massive cloud."

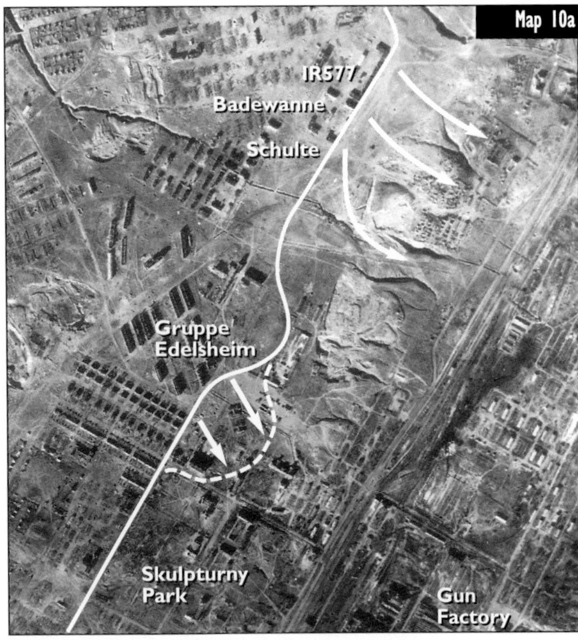

NA/MARK

Attack of Infanterie-Regiment 577 and Panzer Schwadron Schulte.

The mission of 24. Panzer-Division was this: "Through a limited attack on the northern wing, maintain a connection to the Angriffsgruppe while a panzer schwadron is detached to support Infanterie-Regiment 577 on the southern wing of Gruppe Jaenecke." The objectives of Oberst von Edelsheim's Gruppe were limited compared to Gruppe Jaenecke but just as much care and attention to detail was required. If Gruppe Edelsheim failed

MARK

Schwadron Schulte, consisting of 10 panzers, was attached to Infanterie-Regiment 577 for armoured support. On 14 October it overwhelmed an anti-aircraft battery, knocked out several tanks and helped the infantry reach the railway line.

to capture and hold its objective, flanking fire from this direction could jeopardise the progress of Gruppe Jaenecke. After a thunderous barrage from artillery and Stukas that extended from the front-line to the Volga, the grenadiers and riflemen scurried over the churned earth, closely trailed by the supporting panzers. The slightest enemy resistance was smothered in mortar shells, followed soon after by hand grenades and rifle bullets. The advance progressed quickly, facilitated by the powerful thrust of Gruppe Jaenecke to the left that cleared any flanking fire from the north. After a few hours and with low casualties, Gruppe Edelsheim won the Sportsground area 84a3 and repulsed two enemy counterattacks.

After coordinating actions with the commander of '634', an infantry NCO and his men move out.

In early mid-morning, the assault of Gruppe Edelsheim reached the ordered objective and secured a connection to Infanterie-Regiment 577 attacking from the north. Obergefreiter Reddig recorded in his diary: "14.10.42: At the front, Obergefreiter Karl Helmig was wounded. Our troops attacked on a broad front, Stukas continued operations. 25 Russian bombers attacked with strong fighter protection."

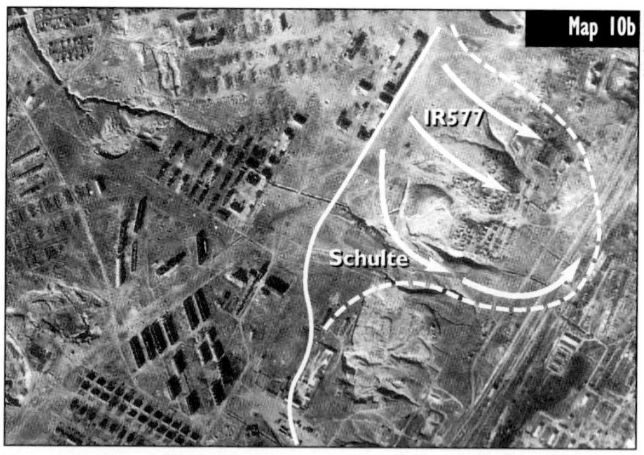

Line reached by Infanterie-Regiment 577 and the attached panzers.

The panzer schwadron attached to Infanterie-Regiment 577 succeeded in overpowering an anti-aircraft battery and destroyed several enemy tanks, eventually reaching the railway line in 94a. They were not without casualties, however. One of the panzers was struck by a 7.62cm Russian shell and Obergefreiter Peter Liebermann of Panzer-Regiment 24 was killed. He had been awarded the Iron Cross Second Class barely two weeks earlier, on 2nd October 1942. Several other panzer crewmen were wounded.

MARK

Assault guns and infantry of 305. Infanterie-Division pause under the protection of a large building in Stalingrad-North.

Once darkness had fallen, Obergefreiter Kusterer saw one of the most feared German weapons at work: "In the evening, I distinctly saw the 'Do-Werfer' firing… The Do-Werfer was the German rocket-launcher that tore lungs to pieces by a shockwave and caused huge casualties amongst the Russians. The dead were practically untouched on the outside and only a small stream of blood came out of the mouth.

"On both sides, new weapons were employed that made the war still more frightful: the 'Nebelwerfer' with us and the 'Stalin Organ' with them. Both were rocket-launchers that could fire a dozen shells in a few seconds, the Nebelwerfer relying on air pressure to kill while the Stalin Organ relied on shrapnel. Whoever was caught in a salvo was lost unless he immediately disappeared into the ground so that the shrapnel flew over him. Every Russian counteroffensive began before sun-up with the rumbling of the Stalin Organs."

This offensive was the first time in the history of 24. Panzer-Division that the bulk of the Division had not completely participated in the attack of Korps. The heaviest casualties from the past six weeks in the hardest street-fighting, attacking almost daily, was the reason.

This day was counted as a Sturmangriffe day for Panzer-Regiment 24:
14.10.: attack on the Brickworks and the southern part of the Tractor Factory

Casualties:

1 officer killed

- Oberleutnant Wolfgang Dietrich Mack (Zug Kdr); 5./K4 (Killed)

26 men killed

- Obergefreiter Peter Liebermann; PR24 (Killed)
- Obergefreiter Kurt Meyer; PGR26 (Killed)
- Obergefreiter Felix Maslowski; PGR26 (Killed)

2 officers wounded (1 of those stayed with the troops)

- Rittmeister Arnold von Dressler (Abteilung Kdr); I./PGR26 (Wounded)
- Leutnant Rohde (Abteilung OO); I./PAR89 (Wounded but stayed with the troops)

57 men wounded (16 of those stayed with the troops)

- Obergefreiter Karl Helmig; PGR21 (Wounded)

15th October 1942:

The attained line was held. The Division supported the assault of Gruppe Jaenecke through barrages and destructive fire from artillery and panzers. In the evening, Gruppe Jaenecke reached the Volga shore north of 24. Panzer-Division along its entire breadth.

During the day, the Intelligence Department of the Division ascertained that the enemy had developed a continuous front-line in front of the Division by connecting bunkers and constructing trenches. The enemy facing the Division were from 193rd and 308th Rifle Division, as well as 42nd Rifle Brigade and Rifle-Regiment 113 of 37th Guards Rifle Division. The Ic (Enemy Intelligence Officer) of the Division, Rittmeister Graf vom Hagen, believed that most of the enemy troops consisted of men from rear area services without sufficient training. Exploiting the present weakness of the enemy, Korps ordered the attack of Gruppe Jaenecke in a south-west direction between the front-line of 24. Panzer-Division and the Volga to roll up and destroy the enemy in front of 24. Panzer-Division. At 2345 hours, the Division issued Divisionsbefehl Nr. 74 which called for the enemy front ahead of 24. Panzer-Division to be rolled up on 16th October. While 14. Panzer-Division and 305. Infanterie-Division of LI. Armeekorps pushed south to roll up the Russian front, 24. Panzer-Division would hold its previous line, tie down the enemy in front of them from 0800 hours by firing and simulate an attack, facilitating the attack of 14. Panzer-Division. A second barrage would be fired upon the approach of 14. Panzer-Division, their forward spearhead indicated by firing green flares. Elements of Gruppe Winterfeld were held in readiness to destroy any enemy remnants left in front of the Division after 14. Panzer-Division had passed. If everything went to plan, the next step of the order would be initiated: after the destruction of the enemy in front of them, the Division would take over a defensive front along the Volga between the fuel installation and the Brickworks.

MARK

A German radioman observes the fierce fighting from his trench.

Casualties:

5 men killed

- Obergefreiter Heinz Schönemann; PGR26 (Killed)
- Obergefreiter Engelbert Walleser; PGR21 (Killed)

2 officers wounded (both of those stayed with the troops)

- Leutnant Axel Feldt (Schwadron Kdr); 5./PGR26 (Wounded but stayed with the troops)
- Leutnant Fritz Stegel (Schwadron Kdr); 3./Pz.Jg.40 (Wounded but stayed with the troops)

43 men wounded (20 of those stayed with the troops)

- Obergefreiter Ernst Wiechmann; PGR21 (Wounded but died later in the day)

16th October 1942:

Shortly before 0800 hours, the artillerymen stood next to their guns, a shell in the breech, the next round in hand. Upon a signal from the gun commanders, gunners pulled the lanyards and sent the first volley of shells into the Russian positions. The landscape erupted into a seething cauldron as barrages from the other divisions howled in from the north. Shell after shell ripped up the ground, shredding the trees in Skulpturny Park and leaving gaping holes in the large buildings. Stukas plunged into the thick haze and fighter-bombers swept low over the ground, clearing a path with their machine-guns. The Luftwaffe had been attacking various targets from 0700 hours but it was only now that they concentrated on the Russian front-line positions. The gunners of Panzerartillerie-Regiment 89 quickly broke into a lather of sweat as

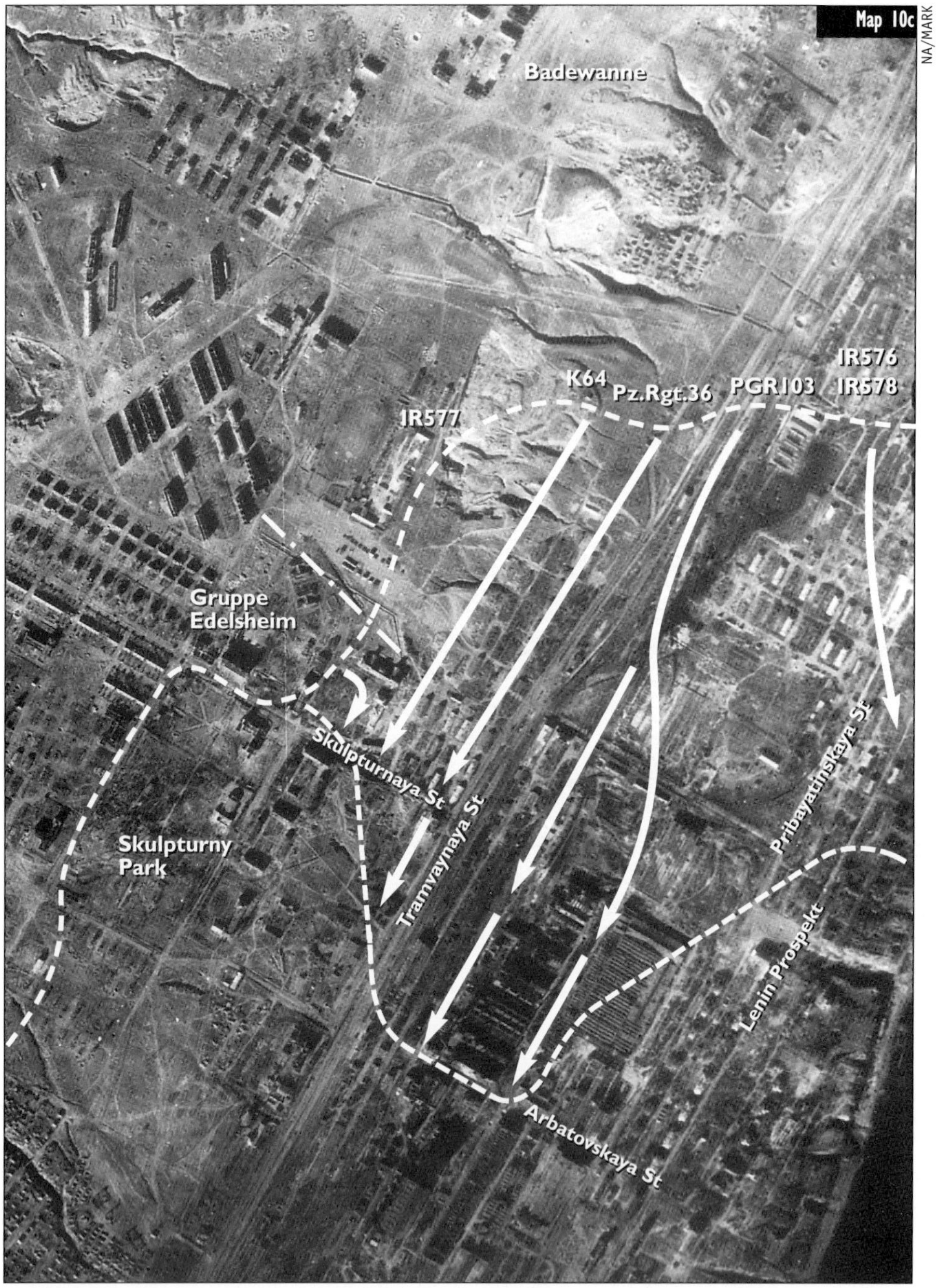

Assault of LI. Armeekorps on 16th October. Half of the Barrikady Gun Factory was taken by nightfall.

they threw round after round into the breech. When the artillery started to fire, Gruppe Jaenecke set off, heading south toward the Gun Factory and Skulpturny Park. Gruppe Edelsheim maintained a tight connection to the west wing of Gruppe Jaenecke during the initial stage of the attack. As the panzers, grenadiers and infantry of 14. Panzer-Division and 305. Infanterie-Division pushed south in front of them, the men on the left wing of Gruppe Edelsheim would pivot slightly to the east, keeping a solid line. A single panzer from Gruppe Edelsheim was attached to Gruppe Jaenecke to provide constant reports to Division about the location of the attack spearheads of 14. Panzer-Division.

Despite the thorough preparation by the artillery and the Luftwaffe, Gruppe Jaenecke ran into very tough resistance, contrary to expectations. Russian tanks dug in along Skulpturnaya and Tramvaynaya Streets survived the bombardment in fairly good shape and now awaited the onslaught of the panzers. A tank battle developed at close range, the Russian tanks not firing until the German panzers were large in their sights. Several panzers immediately erupted into flames and confusion reigned when salvoes of Katyusha rockets poured down on the stalled assault. The crewmen of 14. Panzer-Division toughed it out for the next few hours, trading blows with the Russian tanks which presented only their turrets as a consequence of being in hull-down positions. When the ferocity of the fighting caused a temporary halt towards midday, the casualties were surveyed: the Russians lost a total of 16 tanks[1], while 14. Panzer-Division suffered 17 panzer casualties.

General Chuikov, Commander-in-Chief of 62nd Army, wrote about this day: "…on 16th October, masses of enemy infantry, supported by tanks, swooped along the road from the Tractor Factory to the Barrikady factory. This large-scale, determined attack came up against the 84th Tank Brigade's tanks, which had been dug in. At and to the west of Tramvaynaya Street our tank crews met an enemy attack with concentrated fire from a distance of 100-200 metres. Ten or more enemy tanks immediately went up in flames. The German attack petered out. At that moment our artillery on the east bank opened up blistering fire on the enemy's halted infantry and tanks.

"Being a long way from the field of battle, and not seeing what was happening on the sector of the main attack, the German generals sent up more and more fresh units, which rolled up to our lines in waves. Here they were stopped and were pulverised by powerful salvos from our 'Katyusha'. The German tanks, coming under fire from our well-camouflaged T-34's and anti-tank guns, turned back and abandoned the infantry."

Apart from Chuikov's usual exaggerations[2], this account is fairly accurate. After a quick regrouping, the attack was relaunched again in the afternoon and, with the bulk of Russian armour now destroyed, the renewed assault led to success, half of the Gun Factory being taken before nightfall. The Division fulfiled its assignment, swinging the northern wing to the east and maintaining a solid with the neighbours.

The men of Panzergrenadier-Regiment 21 spent most of the day destroying or removing enemy mines from in front of their sector. A squad of pioneers from 3./Panzerpionier-Bataillon 40, supplied to the Regiment at 0700 hours, had performed most of the hazardous work. The removal of the mines was in preparation for an advance to the east.

1. 1 KV1, 7 T-34's and 8 T-60's, all from 84th Tank Brigade.
2. The Germans simply did not have 'more and more fresh units' to send forward and German tactical command was usually superior to the Russians, so the line about the 'German generals' is a typical comment that downplays the skills of the German command.

At 2400 hours, the Division issued Divisionsbefehl Nr. 75 which called for an attack in the direction of the Bread Factory and to roll up the enemy front ahead of 24. Panzer-Division on 17th October. At 0430 hours the next morning, Oberst Schmid's Panzergrenadier-Regiment 108 of 14. Panzer-Division would be subordinated to the Division and at 0800 hours, would attack from the sector of Infanterie-Regiment 276. Their objective was the railway bend in 73c where they would join hands with their divisional comrades pushing down from the north-east. Once a connection had been effected, the Russians would be trapped in a small pocket west of the Gun Factory and Panzergrenadier-Regiment 108 would again come under the command of its parent division. While the grenadiers of Panzergrenadier-Regiment 108 launched a real attack, the rest of 24. Panzer-Division had the same mission as yesterday: simulate an attack to tie down the enemy, as well as smothering him with gunfire and, if 14. Panzer-Division was successful in rolling up the enemy front, be prepared to take over a defensive front along the Volga with freed-up forces.

Casualties:

7 men killed

22 men wounded (9 of those stayed with the troops)

17th October 1942:

Throughout the night and early morning, harassing fire from German artillery covered the Russian positions, concentrating on the Russian landing-stage and on 24. Panzer-Division's sector, particularly in front of Infanterie-Regiment 276. The relatively light harassment fire was interspersed with heavy barrages. This continued until dawn. Under cover of the artillery umbrella, the grenadiers of Panzergrenadier-Regiment 108 moved into the positions in the shattered wooden huts. Guided by men from local units, the grenadiers silently filed through the dirt streets and overgrown gardens. Explosions and flashes strobed along the eastern horizon. An occasional flare arched high in the sky. The grenadiers crept into shallow trenches and smashed huts to await the beginning of the assault. On their southernmost boundary, along a gully, they established contact with their southern neighbours, Major Franz Weller's I./Jäger-Regiment 54, who would accompany them in the eastward advance. The gully served as a natural dividing line but it could also be a weak point: the responsibility of occupying it belonged to the Jäger.

To support Panzergrenadier-Regiment 108, Panzer Schwadron Messerschmidt of Panzer-Regiment 24 was assigned to provide some hard-hitting firepower. In the cold morning hours, the crewmen performed last minute duties, checked radios and ammunition stores, and toward 0530 hours, they mounted up and headed to the rendezvous. Up front was the Panzer IV of the Schwadron Commander: Oberleutnant Hans W. Messerschmidt leaned out of the cupola, looking at the fireworks display in the east. Twenty-three year old Messerschmidt wore the Iron Cross First Class and the Panzer Assault Badge on his left breast, and was a very capable panzer commander. He had led his platoon of Panzer IV's throughout the summer campaign and after the death of his Schwadron Commander, Rittmeister Thiel[3] on 3rd September, he had taken

3. There were two Rittmeister Thiel's in Panzer-Regiment 24: the first – Rittmeister Ernst Thiel – commanded 4. Schwadron and was killed on 3rd September 1942; the other, Rittmeister Gerhard Thiel, commanded 10. Schwadron. See Appendix 1 for full career details.

command of the Schwadron. Not that there was much left to command: the Schwadron normally had ten Panzer IV's and five Panzer II's. Now, most of those were sitting in workshops, waiting for spare parts to arrive. Very few of the panzers had been totally destroyed, however.

Oberleutnant Messerschmidt's five panzers crawled through the milky mists that pooled in the valleys and hollows, climbing a shallow rise up into the devastated Barrikady workers settlement. They drove along a ploughed-up street between crumbling and charred wooden huts, arriving at their destination, a block of concrete houses in 64d4, a few minutes before the scheduled time of 0600 hours.

At 0700 hours, the intensity of the artillery noticeably increased. The shells chewed up the ground very close in front of Infanterie-Regiment 276 and Gruppe Edelsheim. The men peeked over the parapets as the barrage ripped apart the Russian front-line. Forty-five minutes later, Stukas droned in from the west and promptly tipped into a dive over the heads of the grenadiers, plummeting down and placing their bombs squarely on target. The din was deafening. Sensing that something was afoot, Russian artillery fired into the German areas. Oberleutnant Messerschmidt's panzers started their engines and headed down a street that led straight into the rear of Infanterie-Regiment 276's positions. At 0755 hours, the artillery strengthened yet again, shell after shell pummelling the churned earth, concentrating on the breakthrough positions. Punctually at 0800 hours, the artillery curtain lifted in front of Panzergrenadier-Regiment 108, but continued to fall in front of Panzergrenadier-Regiment 21 and Gruppe Edelsheim. Oberst Schmid's grenadiers vaulted out of the foxholes and trenches and crouched low as they dashed across the open street toward the Russian positions, rifles and grenades in hand, ready to crush any opposition. The panzers crunched over splintered wood, masonry and sods of dried loam thrown about by the bombardment. The grenadiers of Panzergrenadier-Regiment 108 fought their way through the mesh of streets and

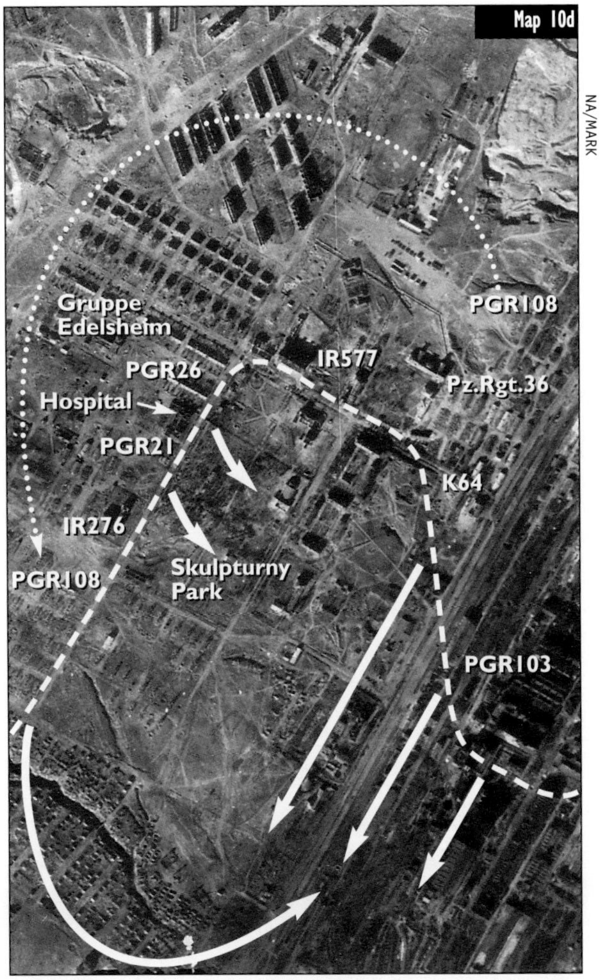

Assault of Oberst Schmid's Panzergrenadier-Regiment 108 and Panzer Schwadron Messerschmidt on 17th October.

shabby wooden huts, blasting the Russians out of their hiding places, but Russian resistance was desperate, especially when they realised they were being caught in an encirclement. Oberleutnant Messerschmidt's panzers operated in perfect unison with the grenadiers. With the grenadiers always in front, forming a protective cordon against Russian tank-killing teams, the panzers blotted out resistance nests indicated to them. The panzer crewmen were very comfortable working with Oberst Schmid's men as they had co-operated with their own panzers many times. The grenadiers casualties were low and so were the panzers: not one was lost or even temporarily put out of action. After the excellent support of the panzers and artillery, Panzergrenadier-Regiment 108 succeeded towards midday in reaching the first attack objective, the railway line west of the Barrikady, there establishing a connection on the south-west corner of the Gun Factory to units of 14. Panzer-Division attacking from the north-east.

Even though none of Oberleutnant Messerschmidt's panzers were knocked out, one of his men was not so lucky. In the chaos of ruins, many men simply disappeared. Whether they were killed by bullet or shrapnel and their bodies never found, or snatched by the Russians, the letters MIA appeared next to their names. Such was the case with 22-year old Unteroffizier Wilhelm Haase, not surprisingly known to his comrades as Willi. He was a panzer driver in 4. Schwadron of Panzer-Regiment 24, participating in the attack of Panzer-Schwadron Messerschmidt in the direction of the railway line. When his panzer stalled in a housing settlement west of the Bread Factory, Haase offered to fetch a handcrank for his Panzer IV from another panzer. That is when he went missing. His comrades never saw him again. Unteroffizier Wilhelm Haase: missing in action 17th October 1942.

NA/MARK

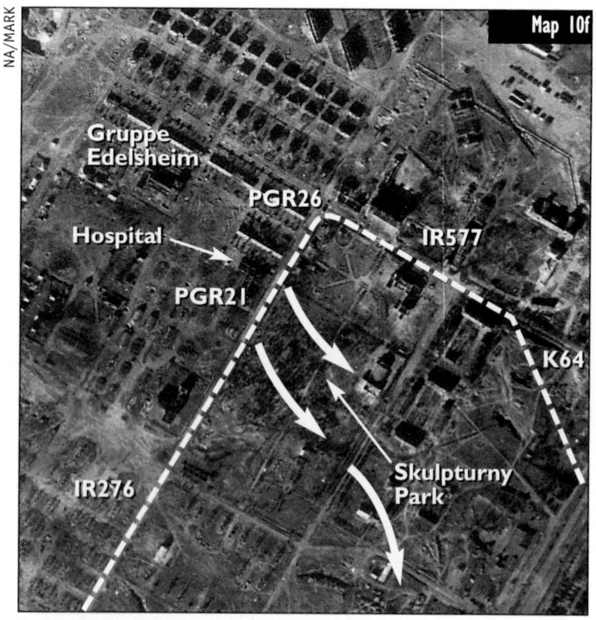

Gruppe Edelsheim's sector east of Skulpturny Park.

Because the advance of 14. Panzer-Division had not been led sufficiently far to the west to strike the enemy in front of 24. Panzer-Division, the enemy was rolled up by the Division itself in close and skilful co-operation with panzers. The assault groups set out from the defensive line that had been established along the western edge of Skulpturny Park for the past two weeks. A few solid buildings, including a hospital that was totally gutted, formed the basis of the defence. Now, they were convenient launching points for the attack. Observers sitting in the second floor of the hospital kept close watch over the park as it was being pounded by artillery and Stuka bombs. At the scheduled time, the bombardment ceased and the stormtroops ran out of cover, crossed the road and plunged into the parkland. The trees in the park had been stripped of all their leaves, many of them splintered and uprooted by the barrage. Huge craters studded the area. The grenadiers stole up to Russian trenches and lobbed stick-grenades into them. Those Russians not killed outright either fought on stubbornly or surrendered meekly, coming out of bunkers with hands over their heads and stunned looks on their faces. Any particularly obstinate strongpoint was dealt with by mortars and artillery. Through successful stormtroop methods, the Russian positions amongst the trees of Skulpturny Park were overwhelmed. Until afternoon, the enemy in front of Panzergrenadier-Regiment 26 and in front of the northern half of Panzergrenadier-Regiment 21 was destroyed. Killed in this assault was Obergefreiter Clemens Kanthak from Stabsschwadron of Panzergrenadier-Regiment 21.

Rear view of the Hospital

A machine-gun post in the Hospital watches over Skulpturny Park.

Oberleutnant Adalbert Holl,

Left: interior view of the destroyed Hospital.

ALL PHOTOS: FREIMANN

Right: all roofs of the Hospital were destroyed by bombs.

Commander of 7. Kompanie in Infanterie-Regiment 276, reports:

"I had been ordered to the battalion command post tonight. I should be there at 1700 hours.

Shortly before 1700 hours, I reported to my commander, Major Weigert. The welcome by our 'Papa Weigert' was – as always – warm, earnest and dignified. We had not seen each other for days. The commanders of the other companies of the battalion were likewise punctually to their places.

"The commander came straight to the point. 'Meine Herren, the positional warfare is ending here tomorrow. We are attacking! Look at the map here: the pocket in the northern part of the city has a large bulge towards us. At both the large factories, 'Red October' and 'Barrikady', the distance of our comrades fighting there from the shore of the Volga amounts to about 1000 metres. Here, to the north-west, up to us, is still about a good three kilometres to the shore of the Volga. It is the 24. Panzer-Division who succeeded in pushing a wedge into the enemy from the south to the north. These are now encircled in our sector, and that up to the Bread Factory. The Kessel will be straightened out tomorrow. 24. Panzer-Division, who we are subordinated to for the time being, will support us there with five panzers. Their commander knows about our low combat strengths, that is why the five panzers. Located to the right of us is III. Bataillon under Hauptmann Rittner. The panzers will drive along the street out of the sector of III. Bataillon at dawn, still within our front-line. They have the mission of removing these nests of resistance. As well, the panzers will go past us, over the street into the enemy trench system. They will then clean up the Kessel – from the south – in a generally northern direction. Our

FREIMANN

Interior of the Hospital

FREIMANN

Bombs exploding in Skulpturny Park.

FREIMANN

Skulpturny Park, shattered by artillery and bombs. The Hospital is in the background. Russian corpses lie in the foreground.

> heavy weapons remain in their old positions as they can reach all points of the Kessel. We must reach our objective tomorrow, with that, freeing up our troops occupied here for other tasks. The deployment of the battalions stay as they are now, the men knowing the terrain exactly in front of their command posts and nests. Have you any questions, meine Herren? That is not the case, so allow me to offer you some genuine French cognac… And now Prost to good successes for tomorrow!"

Hard though it was to believe, there were some light-hearted moments during the fighting. A few of the units carried pets with them, mainly dogs, which acted as unit mascots. One such animal was 'Meyer', a small wire-haired terrier that belonged to Oberleutnant Gerhard von Knobloch of 5./Kradschützen-Abteilung 4. Meyer was a proud member of the unit and the men were quite amused when he was issued with his own set of 'dog-tags' that hung on his collar! Oberleutnant von Knobloch was fatally wounded on 8th September and Meyer was left without an owner. For the past month however, other men of 5. Schwadron had cared for him. Then, one night, someone noticed that Meyer was not around. He had run off. There was such concern for him that a notice was placed in the Division's activity report for the period 12th to 18th October. There was a brief description of his appearance, plus details were given about his dog-tags: on one side it side 'Meyer', and on the other 'Oblt. v. Knobloch, F.P.Nr. 22639'.[4] It is not known what became of Meyer.

The freed-up Panzergrenadier-Regiment 26 was kept ready to take over a defensive sector from 305. Infanterie-Division on the Volga shore south of the Brickworks, which was still being fought for at the moment. At 2215 hours, the Division issued Divisionsbefehl Nr. 76 which called for the areas already won to be cleared of any enemy remnants and also ordered a sector of the Volga north-east of the Gun Factory to be taken over. Infanterie-Regiment 276 and Panzergrenadier-Regiment 21 would comb the areas conquered on 17th October and eliminate any enemy resistance and the enemy remnants still holding out in front would be destroyed. Major Weigert's Infanterie-Regiment 276, in close co-operation with Panzergrenadier-Regiment 108 and a few panzers, would clear the sector bounded by the railway line, the gully in 73 b & a, and the present front-line of Infanterie-Regiment 276. Oberst von Below's Panzergrenadier-Regiment 21, in tight partnership with I./Panzergrenadier-Regiment 103 of 14. Panzer-Division, would clear the sector in front of Panzergrenadier-Regiment 21. Panzer Abteilung Winterfeld would supply a schwadron of panzers which was ordered to arrive at Oberst von Below's command post before 0600 hours. The battalion of grenadiers from 14. Panzer-Division would attack

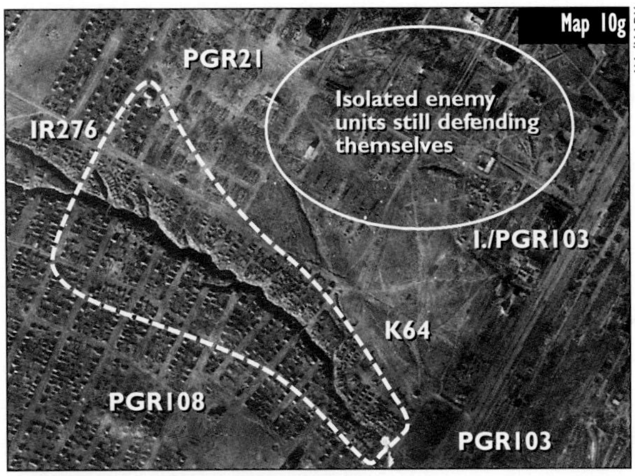

Enemy pocket west of the Bread Factory.

4. F.P.Nr. means Feldpostnummer, or field-post number, which was a postcode for a soldiers unit.

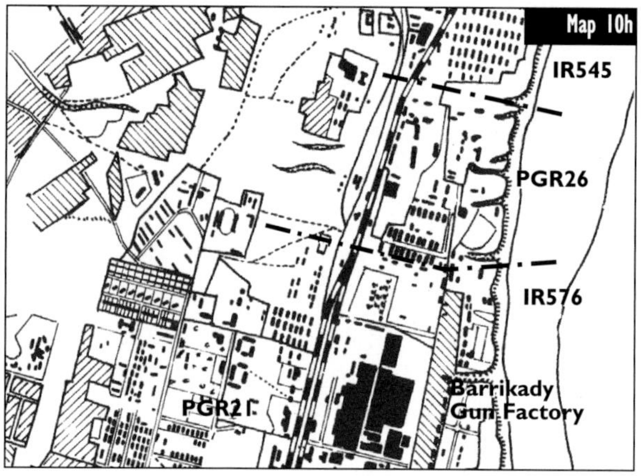

first, setting out at 0600 hours. All of these clearing attacks were ordered to be completed by 0800 hours at the latest.

The Volga sector north-east of the Gun Factory would be occupied by Panzergrenadier-Regiment 26 and, after completing its earlier assignment, Panzergrenadier-Regiment 21. Panzergrenadier-Regiment 26's allotted sector along the Volga was as follows: the right boundary was the south-west edge of the apartment block 84d East – 94c3 – gully (inclusive) in 94c South; left boundary was the Brickworks (exclusive). The Brickworks was held by units of Infanterie-Regiment 545 (389. Infanterie-Division). Upon the arrival of the Regiment, the unit currently holding this sector, Hauptmann Denz's I./Infanterie-Regiment 576 of 305. Infanterie-Division, would be subordinated to capture and clean out Russians still holding out in the deep gullies that emanated from the Volga. At dawn, grenadiers from Panzergrenadier-Regiment 21 and panzers from Panzer Abteilung Winterfeld would reconnoitre to see whether or not the Brickworks in 94c was still occupied by the enemy. Whatever the results of the reconnaissance, Panzergrenadier-Regiment 21 with subordinated units of Panzer Abteilung Winterfeld would start cleaning out the Brickworks from midday at the latest and after this was completed, take up positions along the Volga, north of their sister regiment. After the panzers had completed their tasks, they would withdraw to an assembly area in grid square 65.

Casualties:

4 men killed

• Obergefreiter Clemens Kanthak; PGR21 (Killed)

1 officer wounded

• Oberleutnant Kurt von Schütz (Batterie Kdr); 1./PAR89 (Wounded)

26 men wounded (10 of those stayed with the troops)

1 man missing

• Unteroffizier Wilhelm Haase; PR24 (Missing in action)

18th October 1942:

In the early morning, the assault of 14. Panzer-Division and the panzergrenadiers of 24. Panzer-Division supported by panzers continued. The objective was the destruction of the enemy in front of Panzergrenadier-Regiment 21 and the previously unconquered city sector in front of Infanterie-Regiment 276. Above all, the latter developed into extremely bitter house-to-house fighting against the Russians who fought doggedly until the last moment.

Oberleutnant Holl of 7./Infanterie-Regiment 276 reports the events of that morning:

> "I was already awake early. Sleep was restless. The responsibility and the uncertainty about success and failure made me somewhat nervous. I had to go through the waiting period. In such hours, time seems to stand still.
>
> All preparations were covered. Had anything been forgotten? Had I overlooked anything?
>
> To pass the time, I shaved particularly carefully, had breakfast in appropriately good conditions and, after that, waited for the day to dawn.
>
> It appeared to have begun. Battle noises could be heard from the right. Panzers shooting, machine-gun fire set in, rifle shots resounding between them. We watched from our observation post. The impacts of panzer cannon came closer; they engaged the recognised targets along the other side of the street with aimed fire. Several Russians tried to get behind them. Our men took them under fire.
>
> The first panzer could now be seen. III. Bataillon was already over the street, pressing into the enemy trench system. The defensive fire of the enemy now strengthened. Our infantry guns and heavy mortars also now joined in. Two panzers drove over our sector up the street, continuing along to the north. The three others turned to the east, into the Kessel. My right flank had also now crossed the street. We were in a row. Gruppe Dittner was already over there, I followed with the Kompanietrupp. At present, we tried to win the area straight ahead of us, that is, in the direction of the Volga. After the first hundred metres – of resistance of which there was hardly any trace – we abruptly ran into defensive fire. We were shot at with machine-guns, struck with mortars and also with well-aimed rifle fire. Our panzers achieved a good performance but they couldn't manage alone: the spadework was left to us infantrymen. Seen to the right of us was a windowless rear wall of a long, elongated building. From this direction, our progress was hindered by flanking machine-gun fire. We found cover in a communication trench. Juschko called to me: "Herr Leitnant, there is a hole in the wall over there. The fire is coming from there!"
>
> I looked through my binoculars in the given direction, saw the hole and believed I recognised some movement in the darkness.
>
> "Nemetz, I need the anti-tank rifle!"
>
> After a short time, I had it brought into position and waited. When a burst of fire came out of the hole, I squeezed. The machine-gun fell silent. My comrades on the right side had also come up to our level in the meantime. The obstinate resistance had caused us our first casualties. We worked our way forward with mutual fire support and engaged nest after nest. That also added to our casualties... The enemy defended himself to the last, none of them giving themselves up."

As the infantry of Regiment 276 struggled through tough enemy resistance, the first element of 24. Panzer-Division took over defence of the Volga sector at the Brickworks. Looking into the

NA/MARK

Defensive sector in the Brickworks.

watery morning sun, the advance parties of grenadiers and panzers pushed through the low buildings of the Brickworks, hunting down the remaining enemy defenders. After short struggles with a few desperate defenders, the factory was declared secure. The mixed units of panzers and grenadiers crept up to the edge of the riverbank and marvelled at the view in front of them. The riverbank was more like a cliff, standing about 20 metres above the Volga River and below this was a stretch of beach, about 20 metres wide, which basically stopped the waters of the river lapping at the base of the cliffs. The Russians had carved numerous caves and foxholes into the near-vertical sides. The men of 24. Panzer-Division stared to the east, deep into the heart of Asia. In front of them, Zaitsevskii Island bisected the impressively wide Volga, it and the eastern shore being covered by low scrub and trees. A slight haze hanging over the river, combined with strong winds that pushed low-lying clouds across the overcast sky, made for a dismal scene. Squalls of rain swept over the shattered factory, drenching the grenadiers and infantrymen. It was miserable on the front-line but the men felt like they had achieved one of the grand aims of the war: reach the Volga[5]. The crack of gunshots in the distance and a few bullets whining overhead reminded the men of the danger that still existed all around them. Nevertheless, the grenadiers of Panzergrenadier-Regiment 21 had fulfiled their mission by assuming defensive positions along the Volga.

Hauptwachtmeister Louis Rubbel, who had taken command of 7./Panzergrenadier-Regiment 21 on 10th October, reports:

> "In the early morning hours of 18th October, II./Panzergrenadier-Regiment 21 – without the heavy platoon of 7. Schwadron – was pulled out of the position opposite the 'Red Barricades' Gun Factory to participate in the attack on the 'Brickworks'. The heavy platoon of 7./Panzergrenadier-Regiment 21 remained in the previous positions for the time being and would be replaced by infantry during the course of the morning. The platoon had at its disposal a princely air raid bunker in a zig-zag shape, covered with a layer of beams and heaped earth and fitted out with double bunks, the heavy machine-gun being brought into position in the entrance. In possession of a few Russian trench periscopes, we were able to leisurely observe the foreground without the danger of snipers.
> "Toward 1000 hours, violent Russian artillery fire came into action. To begin with, we

5. In the directive for Operation Barbarossa, an eastern line had been drawn, from Archangel in the north to the Volga in the south, along which a defensive position would be constructed. Barbarossa of course failed and during the entire eastern campaign, only at one spot was this eastern position actually reached – Stalingrad.

> presumed it was a forthcoming enemy attack. Nevertheless, any of the other usual signs (Russian soldiers in helmets, fixed bayonets, etc.) failed to appear. Therefore, because an enemy attack was not expected, the soldiers not on watch lay on the bunk beds. I was just dozing off when there was a fearful cracking and the bunker was full of dust. The comrades on the bunk beds grumbled to me about their disturbed rest and spat out the inhaled sand. I leapt up from my bed and stumbled over something hard which upon closer examination – at first sight I felt a warm glow – turned out to be an artillery shell, shiny like a polished bit. I notified the comrades located in the positions outside about the unwelcome guest and ran to the other end of the bunker to fetch a piece of wire with which I could drag the dud (about 170mm calibre) outside. When I came back into the bunker a few minutes later, the shell had disappeared. Upon my question about its whereabouts, Obergefreiter Hermann X from the Memel district answered: 'I've already thrown it out, and it was still warm.'!"

Just south of Panzergrenadier-Regiment 26's sector, the Russians were more firmly entrenched and formed the beginning of the stubborn Russian bridgehead. Panzergrenadier-Regiment 26 would gain the northernmost part of this bridgehead by attacking together with the subordinated I./Infanterie-Regiment 576. On the slope down to the Volga, completely overlooked by the enemy, the assault had to be discontinued as a result of the very strong, concentrated enemy fire from the island lying opposite, especially since the right neighbouring division could not follow. The Russians very skilfully held out on this Volga shore in gullies and in constructed bunker positions on the steep slope which could only be reached with steep fire weapons. This would be proven the next day by Hauptwachtmeister Rubbel.

In the meantime, the men of Infanterie-Regiment 276 continued their assault. Oberleutnant Holl continues his report:

> "Located in front of us was a dug-out, apparently a command position. We worked our way up to it. Hand grenades were thrown. Willmann received a couple of splinters, nevertheless, he could go to the first-aid post by himself.
> "Juschko called: 'Herr Leitnant, there's a commissar!'
> "'Call to him that he should give himself up!'
> "With the shout from Pawellek, he took cover and opened fire on us with his submachine-gun. We returned fire. Dittner, to the left of us, had recognised the situation. With a leap, he was within 10 metres of the Russian. With this move, he recognised his helplessness, took out his Nagan pistol and shot himself. We continued on. To the right and left, one could hear the noise of battle. In this small Kessel of approximately 2 x 2 kilometres, one subsequently scarcely knew who was shooting. The Russians in the higher places naturally knew long ago what was happening here. Enemy artillery covered the sector with shells. The 'Stalin Organs' also sent their salvoes into the small pocket without consideration for their comrades who were still fighting there.
> "My Upper Silesians only saw red. Every time our casualties were large, they fought doggedly and pulled our young men along with them. The Kessel steadily shrunk, one sensing the absolute will of the fighters to reach the set objective.
> "We were leaping forward when Juschko yelled out to me: "Achtung, Herr Leitnant, the 'Organs'!"

"Like lightning, my comrades disappeared from the earth's surface. Everyone had thrown themselves into the nearest hole or mortar crater. With a leap, I landed in a fox-hole as they were already thundering and crashing. A shock wave on the left half of my face made me dizzy for a second. The 'stove-pipes' of the salvo were striking around the edge of the hole. The splinters, as well as a large part of the air pressure developed by the explosions, were blown into the air above. A part of this mighty pressure, however, came down into my hole. None of the 15 centimetre shells continued on to me – that would have been the 'finish'! My head buzzed and I felt as if I'd been hammered. As my comrades looked at me, I saw their lips move but I couldn't understand them. It felt like a steam valve letting off steam without interruption.

I was unable to hear any other sounds. I still had my voice however, and I told my Kompanietruppführer that he should substitute for me. Without hearing, I was like a 'deaf nut' here.

"By way of the old command post, I would go to Bataillon and file my report with my commander. Unteroffizier Paul and his Sanitäter (medics) had their hands full. Several of my men who could move by themselves came along with me. We had to take cover several times because of shells landing nearby.

"When I arrived at Bataillon, I learned from my friend Leutnant Schüler that Major Dr. Weigert had to leave the battalion on the suggestion of the Bataillon-Arzt. He had – like his predecessor, Major Dr. Zimmermann – fallen completely ill with jaundice. Shit!

"The Adjutant now commanded the Bataillon. My company, or better said, the miserable remnants, were being led by my Kompanietruppführer.

"It was curious that we understood each other. Jochen wrote the answers to my questions on a message pad. He had questions, so he wrote them down, and I then answered them.

"The day was over in an hour. Hopefully, the action of 'Kessel straightening' had been successfully concluded! How does our combat strength look then? First, the daily report was given over to us for a close inspection.

"I said to Jochen that I would spend the night near the combat train and my Hauptfeldwebel would take me along when he started back from the delivery of rations. Until then, I would lie down and try to get some sleep.

"A shake on my shoulders woke me up. It was Jochen. Near him stood my Hauptfeldwebel.

"I had to first collect myself as to where I was, then everything was clear to me. The whistling in my ears told me that I hadn't been dreaming. I'd been fast asleep for four hours and was removed from the world around me. Now I'd returned to the present, hard and pitiless.

"To my question of how it looked at the front, Jochen wrote: 'Kessel straightened out, the 5th, 6th and 7th Kompanie together have a combat strength of 23 men, of those, 7 Kompanie has seven men. III Bataillon has a total of 21 men in its rifle companies. Our battalion had 8 killed, 14 severely wounded, the rest medium and lightly wounded. Leutnant Weingärtner and Leutnant Fuchs are wounded.'

"I felt as if I was struck on the head and could not speak for the time being. What was to become of our Regiment!? What remains of the replacements? If no experienced and battle-hardened ones arrive – what use was the framework of staff and supply units, as well as units of heavy weapons? We infantrymen were in constant close touch with the enemy. This days high casualties proved that once again!

> "Jochen wrote again: 'Order from Regiment Commander. You will report to him tomorrow at 1000 hours to file your report.'
> "I nodded, offered my friend my hand and followed my Hauptfeldwebel. After I arrived at the combat train, I had something to eat and had only one wish: sleep, sleep."

As can be seen from the casualty figures in Oberleutnant Holl's report, high casualties were sustained by Infanterie-Regiment 276. Nevertheless, a stunning blow had been dealt to the Russians and the removal of this Russian pocket had freed up all the forces of 24. Panzer-Division, which now received new assignments. Substantial elements of 14. Panzer-Division were also released.

Obergefreiter Ferdinand Kusterer, a member of Panzergrenadier-Regiment 21, recalls Sunday 18th October when two men in his Schwadron were killed:

> "In the early morning as everyone left the bunker, a direct hit smashed into it and buried one man under the rubble. Someone dug him out with a smoke-blackened face and his body torn to pieces. As Sunday approached with cold rain showers, the second one was hit: a shell exploded directly behind him and tore away the back of his head. When one saw young comrades lying there, then totally different thoughts arise that cannot simply be put down in writing. Wrapped up in their Zeltbahnen[6], they stayed with us until the opportunity arose to take them to the rear and bury them in the divisional cemetery…
> "For four days the attack rolled on, which should be the final fighting for Stalingrad. Since then hundreds of dive-bombers have ceaselessly dived on the six kilometre long 'Red Barricades' Gun Factory under whose rubble the Bolshevists still hold out. Until midday, newly arrived anti-aircraft batteries brought forward on the other side of the Volga were constantly silenced so that the Stukas could 'work' undisturbed. Every morning, however, they again received hellish anti-aircraft fire because overnight, the Russians had thrown more guns into the insatiable abyss of the chaos that was Stalingrad. Today, the weather dampened the enthusiasm of deploying our dominating aerial weapon and one now only heard the grumble of the Stalin Organs and the thunder of the guns. Yesterday, accompanied by a rumbling noise, a smoke cloud climbed into the air that was so gigantic that it was hard to visualise. I thought the whole of Stalingrad had flown into the air. The Bolshevists had probably been dealt with by explosives. In addition to that, mixed into it was black

KUSTERER

Obergefreiter Ferdinand Kusterer sits atop his bunker on Stalingrad's western outskirts.

6. A tent-quarter that every soldier carried to protect himself from the elements and when combined with three others it would form a small tent.Its saddest use was to wrap up its owners lifeless body.

> smoke from a tanker shot in flames on the Volga. One can scarcely believe that men can still hold out in this."

Oberleutnant Paul Markgraf's Panzerjäger-Abteilung 40 was pulled back as Armee-Reserve behind the northern front (XIV. Panzerkorps) because there, strong enemy preparations and attacks were in progress. At the moment, they were laagered around Gumrak. They were later employed there with elements further to the front.

In the close confines of the destroyed city, it was essential to distinguish between friend and foe, especially at night, so in the interests of increased security, the Division issued passwords for the coming days which were changed daily at 1200 hours. They were:

'Adria' for 21st October
'Salonika' for 22nd October
'Capri' for 23rd October
'Palermo' for 24th October, and
'Pilsen' for 25th October.

The Division also notified the panzer troops about a new traffic regulation. It was repeatedly established that panzers stubbornly continued to use the available roads that were in good condition and by doing so, destroyed the surface. All panzer drivers and commanders were informed that everywhere that the terrain permitted, they would drive alongside the streets and roads.

Casualties:

4 men killed

- Oberwachtmeister Hans Witt; PR24 (Killed)
- Obergefreiter Wilhelm Höche; PGR26 (Killed)
- Obergefreiter Franz Kuklan; PGR26 (Killed)
- Gefreiter Friedrich Küppers; K4 (Killed)

11 men wounded (3 of those stayed with the troops)

- Gefreiter Wolfgang Jakob; PGR21 (Wounded but died in hospital later in the day)

Decorations bestowed from 12th October to 18th October:

57 Iron Cross First Class
369 Iron Cross Second Class
73 Panzer Combat Badge in Bronze
12 Assault Badge

Prisoners and booty taken from 12th October to 18th October:

326 prisoners (of those, 94 were deserters)
2 airplanes
2 tanks
1 anti-tank gun
2 mortars
12 anti-tank rifles
1 Volga boat

19th October 1942:

For this day, 305. Infanterie-Division proposed to take the northern half of the Gun Factory and then thrust through to the Volga with 24. Panzer-Division on the entire front. At 2245 hours the previous night, the Division issued Divisionsbefehl Nr. 77 which called for an attack in the direction of the Volga on 19th October. At daybreak, 305. Infanterie-Division would begin their attack with the aim of clearing the northern part of the Gun Factory and then, between 0800 and 0900 hours, attack in conjunction with 24. Panzer-Division from the north-east corner of the Gun Factory in the direction of the Volga shore. The areas of 94c and 94b3 would be cleared. General von Lenski and his staff were informed that the starting time was set for 0900 at the earliest. The assault troops of 24. Panzer-Division were concentrated into Gruppe Below under the command of Oberst von Below. The Gruppe consisted of the following:

Panzergrenadier-Regiment 21
Panzergrenadier-Regiment 26
a battalion of Infanterie-Regiment 576
5./Kradschützen-Abteilung 4
Panzer Abteilung Winterfeld (without one Schwadron)
two squads of pioneers from Panzerpionier-Bataillon 40.

This sounds like a formidable force but it must be remembered that the units had been bled white in the previous months of fighting and the replacements that had arrived were like a drop of water on a hot stone. The remaining men were battle-hardened and had fully adjusted to fighting in the tortured streets and shattered buildings of Stalingrad. The Panzer Abteilung still had quite a few panzers available:

6 Panzer II
3 Panzer III short-barrels
16 Panzer III long-barrels
1 Panzer IV short-barrel
1 Panzer IV long-barrel
2 Panzerbefehlswagens

In total, 29 panzers were available for action.

The pale sun struggled over the horizon, lighting the dismal grey morning. A cold mist enveloped the city. The artillery of both sides had long been at their murderous work. The guns of Panzerartillerie-Regiment 89 prepared the attack by placing barrages on known enemy positions from 0600 hours, as well as selective bombardments directed by forward observers on the intended breakthrough positions. The artillery of 305. Infanterie-Division hammered the northern sector of the Gun Factory. All steep-angle weapons, such as mortars and the 150mm infantry guns, had been ordered to lob shell after shell on to the largely hidden beach area along

REIFNER

Leutnant Egon Reifner conducts reconnaissance in the shattered city.

the Volga. All that could be seen by most men were small mushroom clouds from the exploding shells, showers of dirt that were sifted by gravity and the light breeze, then a pall of smoke: it looked like the Volga was steaming.

SPANNOCCHI

Russian prisoners are brought to 'Gefechtstand Theater', one of the Division's command posts located in the north of the city.

The drab, skeletal framework of the factory buildings stood menacingly over the attacking infantry. Violent explosions from artillery shells shattered the sheet-metals roofs and pulverised the foot-thick masonry walls. Choking clouds of smoke and gunpowder spread out from the impacts and then lingered over the miserable battlefield. The infantry of Infanterie-Regiment 576 ran through the pouring rain, splashing through pools of water and charging from rubble-mound to smoking crater as bullets whizzed past and ripped up the sloppy ground next to them. The brief stabs of fire from Russian muzzles showed the infantry where their adversaries lay. A volley of stick-grenades rained down around the resistance nest, which disappeared in a blinding cloud of fire and smoke. Up! Go, go!!! The infantry charged into the murky depths of the workhalls but Russian rifle fire felled a few of the rushing men. Mortar shells rained down. More and more men became casualties. It was clear to the commander of Infanterie-Regiment 576 that the cleansing of Hall 6 (Manufacturing Hall) and Hall 4 (Assembly Hall)[7] was going to be a bloody and protracted affair. There was no possibility that the sector could be cleared before the suggested time of 0800 hours.

A liaison officer of 24. Panzer-Division, equipped with a radio team, had been attached to Infanterie-Regiment 576 since 0630 hours and provided reports about the course of the attack. He informed Oberst von Below that the complete capture of the Gun Factory had not succeeded. As a consequence, the assault of 24. Panzer-Division was now also postponed. Most officers of the Division breathed a sigh of relief for the Division had been spared the casualties that usually resulted from an attack of this kind. General von Lenski was duly notified about the postponement by Oberst von Below. Another reason that Division was thankful for the postponement was the weather: for the past two days, a thick blanket of clouds had covered the city, strong winds had whistled through the ruins while heavy rain had lashed the city and the surrounding steppe. As a consequence of the continuous rain and ground run-off, many of the deep gullies on the western outskirts of the city had turned into greasy quagmires. The supply road of the Division passed through one of these gullies, in area 54c, and was now totally impassable to all wheeled vehicles. Everyone was informed that from 20th October, the old march route over the airfield and Hill 107.5 would be used. Obergefreiter Ferdinand Kusterer from Panzergrenadier-Regiment 21 remembers the atrocious condition of the roads: "The flying weather was past and the vehicles slid from one side of the road to the other, until the use of roads was forbidden so that the 'Stalin asphalt' was not totally destroyed. The clay built

7. This workhall consisted of gun construction and completion on conveyor belts.

up between the wheels and the mudguards and on boots, hanging off our feet like lumps of lead."

Some old familiar faces returned to the Division. Restored to health from his wounds suffered on 8th September, Oberleutnant von Schmidt-Pauli returned to Panzergrenadier-Regiment 21, only to report his departure for the commencement of his home leave:

Defensive line of II./Panzergrenadier-Regiment 21.

"At the Regiment command post, Oberst von Below said to me, 'Solms and Heyking sit about 200 metres in front of us'. In a bunker with a view over the river which flowed not far away, I found both of them. While they reported to me about the last costly fighting, Heyking's heavy Schwadron still having about 20 men with 2 light infantry guns and a 5cm Pak, of the three combined panzergrenadier Schwadrons of I. Abteilung, about 25 men were still operational, this slipped out of me: 'Now a direct hit on the bunker and the last three active officers available in the Regiment prior to the outbreak of war will be gone'."

Now that they were no longer required to attack, the men of II./Panzergrenadier-Regiment 21 sat in their positions right on the Volga River. Hauptwachtmeister Rubbel reports an interesting operation:

> "Sixth Schwadron, numerically still the strongest, lay with its left wing on the Volga. Then the forward line bent back to the west, on the right next to 6. Schwadron lay 5. Schwadron and to the right of them was 7. Schwadron. The right wing of the battalion was about 100 metres from the Volga, the ground climbing steeply up to there. In front of the sector of 7./Panzergrenadier-Regiment 21 was a gully that ran up from the Volga to about 50 metres in front of the positions of the schwadron. The gully was full of Russians and they brought the attack of the right wing to a standstill. On the evening of 18th October, the attack was to be continued, the Volga also being reached with the right wing, but it was postponed for the time being because with the available forces, the prospect of success was almost zero.
>
> "In the dawn of 19th October, Wachtmeister Ziegner, commander of a light infantry gun of 8. Schwadron, and I, taking along a telephone, climbed a long, fairly tall building from which one could excellently see the gully lying about 100 metres distant. As it became light, a connection was established to the fire emplacements of the light infantry guns and mortars. The gully was occupied on its entire length by at least 250 Russians. We had the captured Russian trench periscope and could thoroughly and safely observe. In a short time, 4 well-camouflaged heavy anti-tank rifles were spotted. The bulk of the comrades from the other fieldpost number were still snoozing in their foxholes constructed on the sides. A few early risers beat out their blankets. We made target distributions. Wachtmeister Ziegner would deal with the anti-tank rifles because the comparatively negligible straying of his guns' aiming points could combat them well. I roused the infantry with greetings from mortars. By

NA/MARK

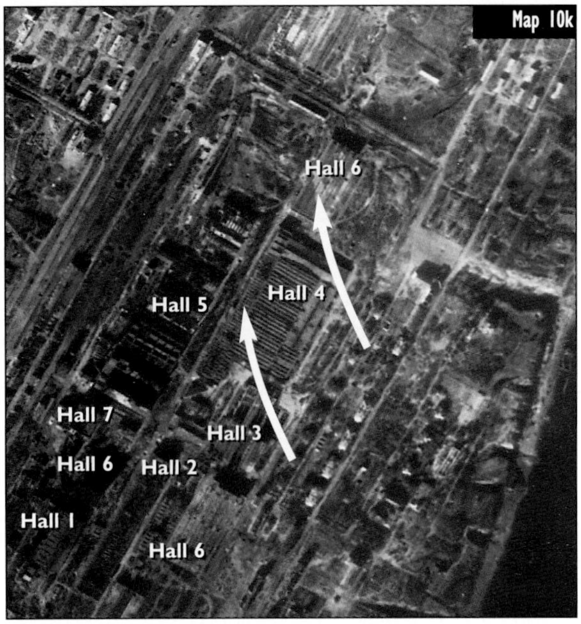

Russian counterattack in the Barrikady Gun Factory.

chance, there was abundant ammunition available, including S-Granaten, that detonated like a ricochet about 2 metres above the ground. By midday, the gully was clean."

"Somehow, my predilection for fun with mortars was spoken about. The commander of 6. Schwadron, Oberleutnant Dittmar, called me and offered an allegedly extremely worthwhile target. I crawled over to him and was led further to his extreme left combat post. This had its position immediately on the Volga in an old wooden hut, a telephone connection already existing to it.

"From this position, the Volga made a slight bend to the west so that several hundred metres of shoreline could be seen. From the water up to the 15-20 metre high steep shoreline was a flat stretch of sand about 20 metres wide. This visible length was populated by at least 200 Russian soldiers. I bet they were advanced supply units because several were armed with water buckets and besides that, smoke rose up from several holes in the steep wall. In this steep wall, more trenches were located, looking out for the appearance of aircraft. The soldiers generally took no notice of artillery fire because the entire stretch of sand lay in the dead angle. Over the telephone connection, I carefully fired on the steep sloping crest, moved it 50 metres and made a barrage of 10 shots from each mortar with S-Granaten. The effect was tremendous. After about 3 hours, when those on the Russian side believed that it had been pure coincidence and the beach was again populated, I carried out the next barrage.

"On the next day, the combat posts of 6. Schwadron transmitted to me by phone that only individual soldiers – always running – were observed on the beach. In the following nights, at totally irregular times, I then placed harassing fire, at times with the light and heavy infantry guns on the stretch of shoreline with lateral shifting. Unfortunately, only a little ammunition was available for that."

In the morning attack, the enemy fought bitterly and doggedly defended himself from numerous bunkers in the remaining bridgehead in and south of the Gun Factory. After the attack of 305. Infanterie-Division had been called off, the Russian troops went on the offensive and in a surprise attack, enemy stormtroops recaptured the northern part of the Gun Factory and broadened the bridgehead opposite 305. Infanterie-Division. The men of 24. Panzer-Division were warned to expect further enemy attacks out of the northern part of the Gun Factory as well as on the right wing. At 2200 hours, the Division issued Divisionsbefehl Nr. 78 which called for defence of the attained positions in and south of the Brickworks until the continuation of the attack some time in the future. The responsibility of holding the front was borne by the Gruppe of Oberst von Below, which would also maintain a tight connection to the neighbouring divisions. The focal point of Gruppe Below was concentrated on the right wing and flank. The heavy weapons of the Gruppe would place harassing fire along the shore of the Volga in front of the Division's sector, as well as on enemy reinforcements, supplies and movements. It was important that this fire be maintained, especially throughout the night. The men of Gruppe Below would also strive to erect obstacles and barricades as quickly as possible. By 1800 hours the next day, Oberst von Below had to supply sketches of the course of the front-line, deployments of the employed troops and positions of the heavy weapons, as well as locations of reserves and command posts down to battalion level.

The artillery received the task of suppressing the enemy with barrages on the shore in front of Gruppe Below and on Zaitsevskii Island, by this hindering any enemy movements toward the divisional sector. Panzerartillerie-Regiment 89 would work in close co-operation with the artillery of 305. and 389. Infanterie-Division's. Front-line officers in positions from platoon commander upwards could request a barrage by firing a green signal flare. Comprehensive plans for harassing fire and areas allocated for barrages were to be entered on to maps and drawn up into sketches, and lodged with Division headquarters before 1800 hours the next day.

Casualties:

1 man killed

- Obergefreiter Alfons Frieling; K4 (Killed)

18 men wounded (9 of those stayed with the troops)

20th October 1942:

The line was held while the right neighbouring division continued to fight in the Gun Factory. The only real activity during the day was from the artillery which succeeded in destroying 4 enemy batteries on the east shore of the Volga and sinking a barge on the Volga.

In Divisionsbefehl Nr. 78 that had been released the previous night, Infanterie-Regiment 276 had been ordered to immediately reconnoitre operational possibilities for counterattacks in the divisional sector, particularly on the right wing of Gruppe Below. It was proposed that these attacks be carried out together with Kradschützen-Abteilung 4, which lay in reserve. During the course of the day, however, Infanterie-Regiment 276 received orders from Korps to return to its parent unit so, in the evening, Infanterie-Regiment 276 separated from the Division and headed back to 94. Infanterie-Division. It had performed three weeks of valuable duty and there had been excellent co-operation with this Regiment which had apparently felt very comfortable within the framework of the Division. General von Lenski issued a Tagesbefehl that was made known to all men of the Regiment:

> "Soldiers of Infanterie-Regiment 276!
> "For three weeks, you have fought side by side with the men of 24. Panzer-Division. Day and night, you have fulfiled your duty in the heaviest fire of a fanatically defending enemy and repulsed numerous enemy attacks. You have protected the flank

of the Division day after day as it fought further through the centre of the city of Stalingrad.
"It is thanks to your heroic deeds that the Division was able to completely fulfil all of its missions and has stood on the shore of the Volga for the past few days.
"Now, you again return to the ranks of your division. Before your withdrawal from the Division during the day, I would like to offer you my and the Division's deepest thanks for your valour, your bravery, your comradeship and for your exemplary battle spirit that, particularly in the last few days, has contributed to the destruction of the enemy standing on your front.
"Deeply affected, we today remember all the fallen comrades of your Regiment that in the highest fulfilment of their duty have given up their lives for Führer and Volk in the fighting around Stalingrad.
"Their sacrifice obliges us to keep fighting until the final victory for our people."

"Heil our Führer!
signed von Lenski"

Casualties:

6 men killed

- Gefreiter Albert Elfert; PGR21 (Killed)
- Gefreiter Herbert Theophil; PGR21 (Killed)
- Obergefreiter Ernst Schwarzin; PGR21 (Killed)

15 men wounded (6 of those stayed with the troops)

ATTRITION

CHAPTER ELEVEN

21st October 1942:

For a local attack, Panzer Abteilung Winterfeld was ordered to detach a Panzer Schwadron to Jäger-Regiment 54 by order of Korps, despite previously reported objections. Here is an excerpt from General von Seydlitz's Korpsbefehl Nr. 92 , issued at 1315 hours 20th October:
"Attack of reinforced Jäger-Regiment 54 on 21.10.
As a prerequisite for the assault on X-day (23.10), 79. Infanterie Division on 21.10., with reinforced Jäger-Regiment 54, will break the strongpoint factory area in grid square 63d4 out of the enemy position and gain a connection with 14. Panzer-Division on the railway line.
For this, the Division will have a subordinated Panzer Schwadron of 24. Panzer-Division."

Following is the order issued by Kampfgruppe Weber (Jäger-Regiment 54) of 100. Jäger-Division for the assault on 21st October. This minor operation will be covered in some detail to illustrate the type of operations in which 24. Panzer-Division was increasingly ordered to perform:

Kampfgruppe Weber — Rgt.HQ, 20.10.1942
Abt. Ia

Der
79. Infanterie-Division, Ia.

Op.: Proposed continuation of the assault of reinforced Jäger-Regiment 54 on 21.10.1942.

It is planned to conduct an attack by reinforced Jäger-Regiment 54 on 21.10.1942 with the Schwerpunkt on the left in close co-operation with 2./Pz.Rgt.24 against the factory area and field emplacements north of there in grid square 63d4, left flank on both sides of the gully (63d2).

1st assault objective: factory and field emplacements north of there
2nd assault objective: railway bridge
The thrust will be led by three assault groups (each of a reinforced company). (I./54 with subordinated elements of II./54).

> The elements of the Regiment employed in the right sector positions will follow up the attack on their left and together with the right assault group, gain the railway line and the railway underpass in 62b2.
> The assault will be supported by a short preceding barrage on the factory area and the enemy emplacements up to the railway line, guided by forward observers connected to the batteries, and by a barrage of the remaining artillery on the area south-east of the railway line.
> Simultaneous smokescreens in the area of the railway underpass (62b2).
> Luftwaffe support with the beginning of the assault is desired on the Steel Factory, in particular on the northern section (tunnel) 72a3 and c1, as well as on the residential quarter north-east of there (72a2-4).
> Beginning of the attack: 0730 hours.
>
> Oberst and Regiment
>
> Commander
>
> (signed Weber)

The morning of 21st October was bleak and miserable. A heavy blanket of grey clouds covered the sky, rain pelted down and a brisk wind blew from the east, all three combining to make it bitterly cold. The artillery started laying down its fire at 0710 hours, plastering the small factory and the surrounding areas covered mainly by the wooden shacks of the factory workers. The assault squads moved out twenty minutes later. The panzers of Oberleutnant Schulte's schwadron were on the left wing of the assault, moving into terrain wholly unsuited for armoured vehicles. On the left was a gully that cut deeply into the earth and was therefore a barrier to any movement in that direction, and on the right was the strongly defended factory, definitely no place for vulnerable panzers. This left only a narrow passage for the panzers between these two obstacles.

The attackers gained ground despite tough Russian resistance. A block of wooden shacks and two small streets[1] were overcome before the left spearhead moved into the relatively open ground between the factory and the gully. As they crawled into the open area, the panzers were rocked by explosions under their tracks: they'd rolled straight into a minefield. In quick succession, several panzers were disabled by mines, becoming sitting targets for Russian anti-tank guns which now fired at the stationary panzers. Oberleutnant Schulte, commander of the Panzer Schwadron, was killed. The tragedy about this was that Kampfgruppe Weber had known about the minefields before the beginning of the attack and no special precautions had been taken to protect the panzers against them. The Jäger were unconcerned about letting the panzers spearhead the assault while they followed behind instead of moving ahead of the panzers, checking for mines and neutralising Russian defenders.

With the panzers mired in the minefield, the momentum of the attack ebbed away. Orders went out for a quick regrouping. To compound Kampfgruppe Weber's problems, a 150-metre wide hole, occupied by Russians, had developed between its left wing and the neighbour on the left (Panzergrenadier-Regiment 108 of 14. Panzer-Division, which had been verbally ordered to support Weber's attack with its heavy weapons). The flanking fire from these Russians was severely hampering his attack. At 1615 hours, Oberst Armin Weber requested that the hole be closed by his neighbour.

---

1. These were Demokratischeskaya and Anselaya Streets

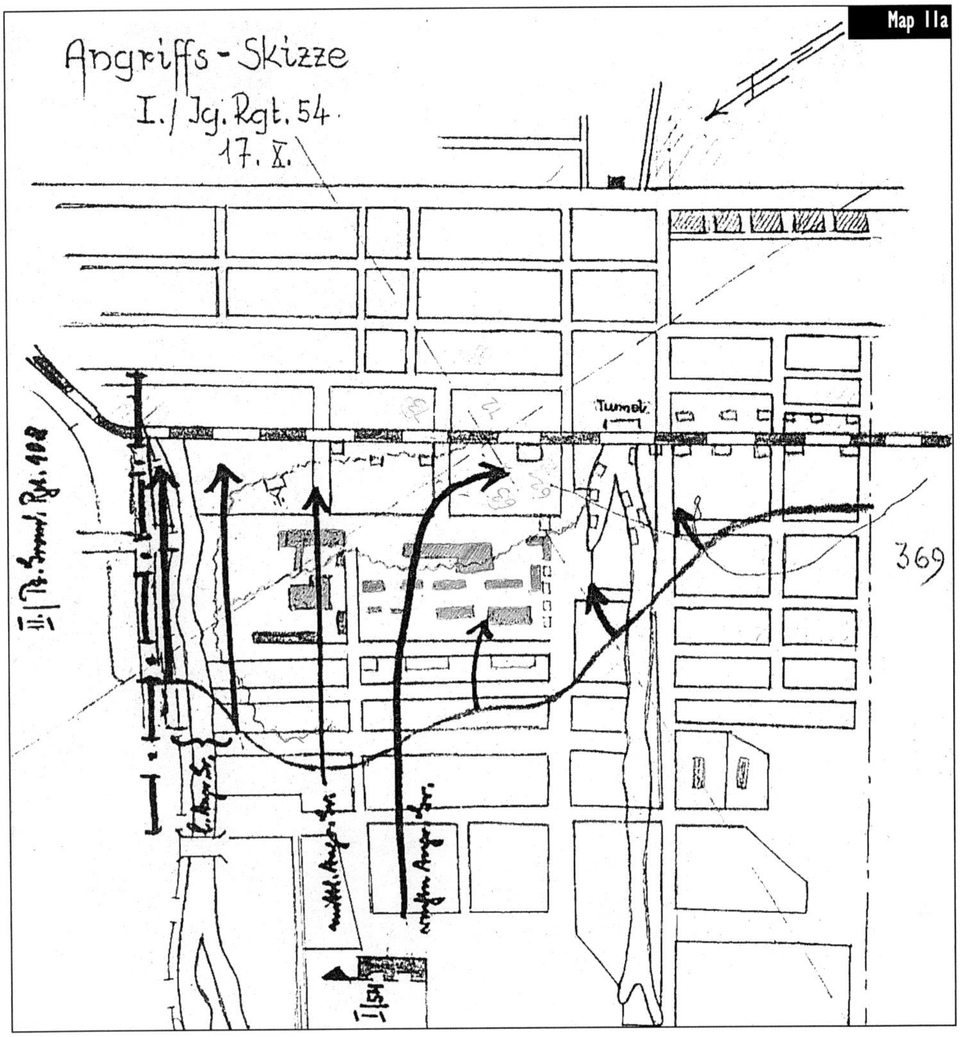

A sketch of the proposed attack, as put forward by Jäger-Regiment 54, dated 17th October 1942. Although the actual assault took place four days later, the objectives and routes did not change. There were three main spearheads (left, middle and right), while the front-line on the right, held by Kroat Infanterie-Regiment 369, would move forward to maintain a solid connection with the attackers. Panzer Schwadron Schulte was assigned to the left assault spearhead, between the gully on the left and the factory on the right.

A few hours after the initial attack had stalled, the assault groups renewed the push to the east at 1440 hours. The assault group on the left, now with only 2 panzers in support, succeeded in thrusting along the gully to reach the railway embankment, which they then crossed. Defence positions were quickly established to protect the newly won ground. Jäger-Regiment 54 reported 80 casualties up to this point in time. At 1800 hours, it was reported that the objective had been reached with the exception of the north-east section of the factory and the area east of the railway line, but Jäger-Regiment 54 would still be clearing enemy remnants out of the factory area (63d4) twenty-four hours later.

The enemy had defended himself with extreme obstinacy, apart from the right wing, where he was relatively easily overpowered. At then end of the day, 35 prisoners were brought in as well as numerous weapons and equipment but Jäger Regiment 54 payed a large tithe in blood for this result.

Casualties for Jäger-Regiment 54 on 21st October 1942:

1 officer killed

- Leutnant Hans Josef Boltersdorf (Zug Kdr); 9./JR54 (Killed)

19 men killed

2 officers wounded

- Leutnant Kaupke (Zug Kdr); 6./JR54 (Wounded)
- Leutnant Rost (Zug Kdr); 3./JR54 (Wounded)

129 men wounded

8 men missing in action

As a result of inexpert orders and operations by Jäger-Regiment 54 in the house-to-house fighting and against previously known mine barriers, the subordinated Panzer Schwadron lost its Commander, Oberleutnant Schulte, one other man killed and several others wounded, and 7 of the 10 employed panzers were knocked out by mines and anti-tank guns[2]. Even though all the disabled panzers were recovered and repaired, the loss of experienced panzer crewmen and the manner of use of his valuable panzers was a serious concern for General von Lenski. In his post-war memoir, General von Lenski wrote the following: "While the Division had only small total casualties in panzers during the past fighting, they climbed in this period up to fifty percent. These developed from the fact that we repeatedly had to supply a few panzers to the infantry, employed in stormtroop operations in place of the absent assault guns. My objection, that this type of use of panzers contradicted the regulations and every experience, and that improper missions by the regiment and battalion commanders of the infantry had only seldom led to the desired result, was also acknowledged by LI. Armeekorps. It remained with this unintelligible practice, however, leading to completely useless casualties."

It is not known whether the complaint lodged by General von Lenski to LI. Armeekorps about the use of his panzers had any effect, but on this day, Korps sent out an order that required the divisions subordinated to it to submit a report about their experiences in the fighting in Stalingrad. The order said: "It is important for the future that experiences in city-fighting in Stalingrad be interpreted to close an undoubted hole existing in our training. The divisions... are therefore requested to put down their experiences in writing while impressions are still fresh..." On behalf of the Division, Major von Menges forwarded this order to its units on 23rd October with the following addition: "The Division wants to avoid needlessly long reports by

2. 24. Panzer-Division reported 7 panzers knocked out, while Jäger-Regiment 54 reported 8.

all means. During the present defensive period, experiences are to be written down in point-form and with that, the Division will be able to submit them at short notice with the withdrawal from Stalingrad.[3]

"Participation by Schwadron and Abteilung commanders is necessary."

Division wanted attention paid to the following areas:

1.) Panzergrenadiers: in house-to-house fighting, with or without armoured vehicles, desired attachment of other weapons, strength requirements, objectives.
2.) Panzers: guidelines for compulsory employment of panzers in local combat. Instructions for co-operation with infantry and panzergrenadiers. Supplies.
3.) Artillery: artillery liaison commandos, forward observers, preparatory barrages, artillery suppression, the question of ammunition supplies, detachment of individual guns to the grenadiers.
4.) Pioneers: attachment to other weapons. Co-operation with panzers. Supply of weapons.
5.) Panzerjäger: experiences with self-propelled guns.
6.) Communications: peculiarities during attack and defence in a large city.
7.) Luftwaffe: co-operation."[4]

Casualties:

1 officer killed

- Oberleutnant Paul August Schulte (Schwadron Kdr); 2./PR24 (Killed)

2 men killed

- Gefreiter Nikolaus Weber; K4 (Killed)

14 men wounded (7 of those stayed with the troops)

22nd October 1942:

The situation and forward line were unchanged, the enemy still holding out in front of the Division. The hard combat of the right neighbouring divisions continued in the Gun Factory, particularly in the north-east section of Workhall Nr. 4 of the Gun Factory.

At 2030 hours, the Division issued Divisionsbefehl Nr. 79 which called for the support of 305. Infanterie-Division during its assault on 23rd October and for the relief of I./Infanterie-Regiment 576 in the evening of 23rd/24th October. For the assault of 305. Infanterie-Division, 24. Panzer-Division would provide support with all available weapons, especially steep-angle weapons like mortars and heavy infantry guns, while the grenadiers continued to hold the forward line. General von Seydlitz-Kurzbach, Commanding General of LI. Armeekorps, had ordered the Division to detach a schwadron of panzers to Infanterie-Regiment 578 of 305. Infanterie-Division. General von Lenski immediately phoned Major von Winterfeld and gave

3. 24. Panzer-Division had received several communiqués informing them of their impending transfer from Stalingrad for other duties with Armeegruppe A in the Caucasus.
4. The results of this survey were released on 31st October and can be seen on page 323

him warning that another of his panzer schwadrons would be used to support an infantry unit from another division. In Divisionsbefehl Nr. 79, this mission ran as follows:

"Panzer-Abteilung Winterfeld will detach 6 panzers, according to the verbal advanced order, to Infanterie-Regiment 578 on the express order of Korps. The panzers will only rely on co-operation with the forward battalion and will not be employed in front of the infantry, but will do small tasks and then withdraw behind the forward line.

"Pioneers will be supplied by Infanterie-Regiment 578. Self-contained operations as a panzer schwadron are out of the question. The difference between panzers and assault guns are indicated.

"A further operation is to be declined by the leader of the panzers."

There are a few interesting points in this order. The Division was angry that its valuable armoured assets, mainly the panzers, were being frittered away in useless attacks with infantry units inexperienced in panzer/infantry co-operation. After the debacle on 21st October, General von Lenski had taken some steps to rectify the reckless use of his panzers. He once again registered his displeasure with General von Seydlitz, who nevertheless chose to ignore his advice. If General von Lenski could not influence the use of panzers on a strategic level, he certainly could take matters into his own hands concerning their tactical employment. This is evident in the above order. Panzers would stay behind the infantry instead of spearheading attacks as had been done on 21st October; once they had completed their mission, they would be pulled back from the main fighting line; the panzer schwadron would not be used as an individual entity but would be accompanied by infantry at all times; and finally, but probably most importantly, it was pointed out to the infantry commanders that the panzers were not assault guns and should not be used as such. Assault guns had larger guns, thicker armour and possessed a smaller silhouette, all important factors when assaulting an enemy strongpoint. It would be seen the next day whether these measures had any effect.

Casualties:

3 men killed

12 men wounded (4 of those stayed with the troops)

23rd October 1942:

It was not quiet and peaceful for the men in the trenches. Throughout the night, Russian artillery pounded German positions, both at the front and in the rear. The night was clear with few clouds in the sky, the almost full moon sitting proudly in the sky, spreading its pale blue light over the shattered rubble, illuminating some areas and throwing others into total darkness. A steady breeze blew through the rubble. It was a nightmare world for the grenadiers: was that movement a piece of sheet-iron swaying in the wind or a stealthy Russian just waiting for his opportunity to cut some throats? The grenadiers definitely preferred full moon to no moon at all but it was still a mixed blessing. Strange and fantastic shapes were created by moonlight shining on twisted girders and shattered bricks; a macabre form of shadow puppets. The tension was slightly relieved when an artillery shell howled in, its explosion momentarily tearing away the dark mantle of night before everything was again thrown into darkness. The grenadiers were safe as long as they stayed in their foxholes. Russian artillery harassed the Germans throughout the night. Several bombers also flew overhead and scattered their bombs on the Gun Factory to

NA/MARK

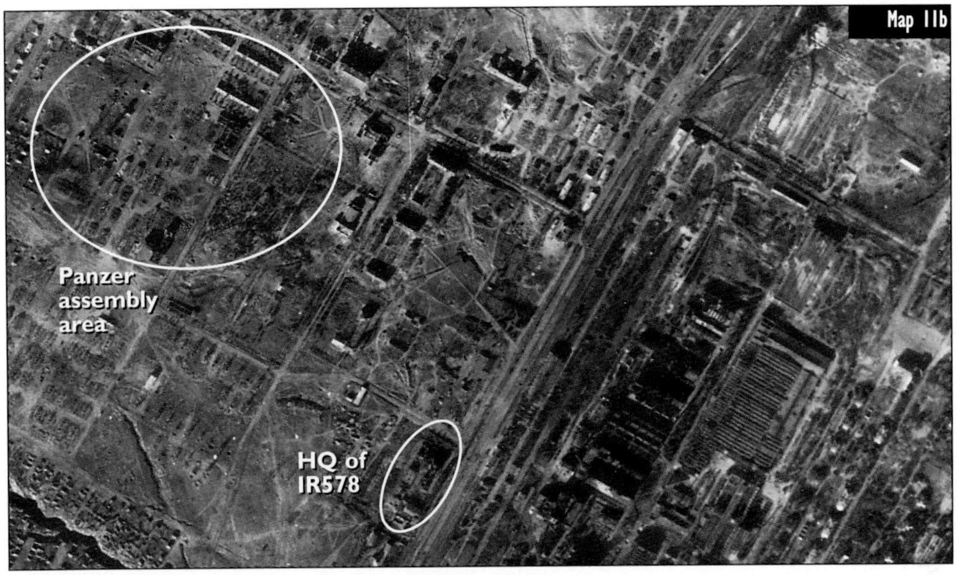

Headquarters of Infanterie-Regiment 578 of 305. Infanterie-Division.

the south. The Tractor Factory to the north was also targeted but fortunately for the men of Gruppe Below, they seemed to have escaped the worst of the artillery and aerial bombardments. Russian stormgroups also operated against German outposts and front-line positions but once again, Gruppe Below did not have to face many of these. In any case, these were spotted fairly easily in the bright moonlight and repulsed.

In the early morning, the commander of the panzer schwadron assigned to support Infanterie-Regiment 578 arrived at that regiment's command post a few minutes before 0600 hours. The headquarters was located in a large building – in grid square 73b – that stood on the bluff west of the Gun Factory. From the windows of this building, there was a marvellous panorama over the entire factory as well as the Volga and beyond. The commander of Infanterie-Regiment 578, however, did not have this view because his command post was down below, in the dank cellar. The panzer schwadron commander reported himself to the regiment commander, handed over the order and informed the commander that his panzers would soon move into position. They had been ordered to move into grid square 74, camouflage themselves and be ready to move out at a moment's notice. Everything seemed to be in order. The panzer commander called back to 24. Panzer-Division to report his arrival.

On this morning, the panzer strength of 24. Panzer-Division amounted to the following:

2 Panzer III short-barrels,
10 Panzer III long-barrels,
1 Panzer IV long-barrel, and
2 command panzers.

No Panzer II's or Panzer IV short-barrels were available.

The sun peaked over the eastern horizon and spread its glorious light over the hazy steppe east of the Volga River. The grenadiers positioned along the high edge of the Volga were glad to see the sun again after four miserable days of inclement weather. The day promised to be a good one for offensive operations. South of the sector of 24. Panzer-Division, an attack of several divisions against the Steel Factory began. The aim of this attack was to thrust through the Steel

Factory, Bread Factory and Gun Factory and reach the Volga. The Stukas arrived over the city shortly before 0700 hours and proceeded to blast Russian defences located in and west of the Steel Factory. At 0710 hours, the artillery opened fire, smothering targets in well-planned barrages. This massive bombardment lasted an hour before the infantry and assault guns moved off at 0810 hours. The men of Gruppe Below could feel the ground vibrating and saw huge clouds of dust and smoke rising out of the factories to the south. The thunderous noise of explosions rolled up the river and echoed throughout the city.

The southern neighbour of 24. Panzer-Division, 305. Infanterie-Division, would join up with the attack of 14. Panzer-Division to its south and push through to the Volga with its right wing, whereupon it would turn to the north and advance along the high cliff of the Volga shore until it reached its northern wing. In the night, the steep slope and crevices of the shore would be cleared by assault groups. That was the plan for 305. Infanterie-Division. The plan for 24. Panzer-Division was for Gruppe Below to hold the previous line and, if a favourable opportunity arose during the attack of 305. Infanterie-Division's northern wing, exploit this by advancing its right wing.

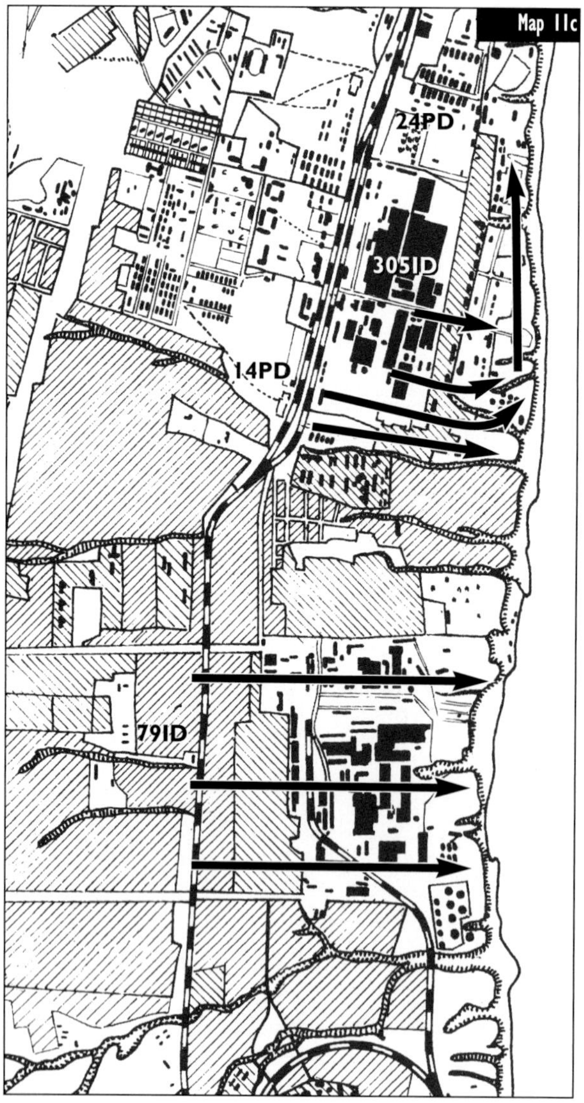

The grenadiers crouched in the foxholes, trenches and bunkers, waiting for information or any further orders. They kept an eye to the south, watching the enormous clouds of smoke billowing from the Steel Factory. Their assignment for the time being was to hold the line upon which they were entrenched. The grenadiers of Panzergrenadier-Regiment 26, located on Gruppe Below's right – or southern – wing, supported 305. Infanterie-Division with all available weapons. Forward observers from I. and II./Panzerartillerie-Regiment 89 moved forward with the assault groups of 305. Infanterie-Division, calling down a heavy and accurate fire whenever needed. A proviso for supporting 305. Infanterie-Division was that a rapid concentration of artillery fire must be able to be provided at any moment along the front of Gruppe Below, in the event of a Russian attack.

The panzer schwadron assigned to 305. Infanterie-Division crawled forward behind the assault groups, hammering Russian strongpoints indicated to them by infantrymen. General von Lenski's cautions had proven effective: the infantry still received the benefits of panzer support and the panzers themselves were relatively safe behind the infantry cordon.

Despite the auspicious beginning with beautiful autumn sunshine in the morning, a heavy cover of low-lying clouds formed over the city at 1030 hours, cancelling all Luftwaffe operations. The Russians capitalised on this opportunity by launching a strong counterattack in the Gun Factory and wresting Hall 4 from 305. Infanterie-Division. The strong flanking fire provided by Gruppe Below could not prevent its loss. With Hall 4 now in enemy hands, the men of Panzergrenadier-Regiment 26 now formed a salient which would greatly assist in the eventual recapture of the hall and their fire would hinder Russian movements between the hall and the Volga.

The Russian counterattack and capture of Hall 4 had dealt a severe blow to the men of 305. Infanterie-Division. During a visit to his division commanders, Generaloberst Paulus was informed at 1230 hours that 305. Infanterie-Division was no longer in a position for large-scale assault. This meant that the right wing of Gruppe Below was not moving forward.

Throughout the day, the heavier weapons of 24. Panzer-Division had fired on Zaitsevskii Island lying directly below them. Russian supply depots, mortars positions and reinforcements were scattered across the island, so its suppression was very helpful in retarding Russian offensive intentions. Any visible movement on the island was met by German mortar fire: an anti-aircraft battery that revealed itself while firing on Stukas was destroyed by well-placed artillery fire.

The low-lying clouds that had moved in at 1030 hours cleared up at 1300 hours and soon after, the Stukas reappeared in Stalingrad's skies. Hall 4 in the Gun Factory was attacked by Stukas and bombers, as well as by the artillery of 305. Infanterie-Division and Panzerartillerie-Regiment 89. For the remainder of the day, both sides crouched in foxholes and cellars while the artillery battled it out around them.

Not all units remained inactive, however. After the onset of darkness, 7./Panzergrenadier-Regiment 21 set out to capture a bothersome Russian strongpoint that lay immediately on the steep slope of the gully in front of their sector. Moving silently and stealthily across the rubble-strewn ground, the grenadiers led by Wachtmeister Wessely crept up to the strongpoint – a large bunker. When they were a dozen metres away, they rushed the bunker, surprised and overpowered the occupants and then occupied the bunker with their last 7 riflemen.

Night-time assault of 7./Panzergrenadier-Regiment 21.

The raid had been a complete success. Not one man was killed or wounded in the initial assault. Later in the night, however, Unteroffizier Ludwig Hopf was killed during the defence of the bunker and Obergefreiter Franzen was wounded. Three days later, on 26th October, Gefreiter Kurt Reinhardt was killed.
In the evening, I./Infanterie-Regiment 576 was relieved by the last Division-reserve, Kradschützen-Abteilung 4 (without 1. and 2. Schwadron). Upon its arrival, Kradschützen-Abteilung 4 was subordinated to Gruppe Below. The artillerymen of Panzerartillerie-Regiment 89 stood by their guns, ready to bring down a wall of fire if the Russians showed any signs of disturbing the relief. Luckily for all involved, the relief went undetected and the relieved battalion was returned to 305. Infanterie-Division.

Casualties:

3 men killed

- Obergefreiter Ludwig Fröchtenicht; PGR21 (Killed)
- Unteroffizier Ludwig Hopf; PGR21 (Killed)
- Gefreiter Herbert Lackner; PGR21 (Killed)

4 men wounded (2 of those stayed with the troops)

- Obergefreiter Franzen; PGR21 (Wounded)

24th October 1942:

The situation and forward line remained unchanged. During the entire day, the Artillerie Regiment supported the fighting of the neighbouring divisions and reported the destruction of three enemy batteries. The attack of the neighbouring divisions only moved slowly forward.
Unteroffizier Karl Ketelsen, commander of a gun in the II. leichte Infanterie Geschütz Zug (2nd light infantry gun platoon) of 4./Panzergrenadier-Regiment 26, wrote in his diary: "24.10. During the night, Russian planes were over us and dropped single bombs. In the morning, light artillery activity on both sides. Today, there is lively air activity near us. One can barely tell the difference between German and Russian planes. But the Stukas completely fulfiled their work near us. The gully in front of us is still not ready to be assaulted. Despite the artillery fire and hail of bombs, the Russians did not weaken."

The commander of Panzergrenadier-Brigade 24, Oberst Freiherr von Broich, received a new assignment on this day. Due to the size of the combat units employed at the front, the services of a Brigade Commander were not required in the gruelling combat in Stalingrad's factories. Instead, he was sent to the rear to immediately assume a supervisory role in the training of the march battalions. Two days earlier, on 22nd October, a march battalion had arrived at Chir railway station, west of the Don river. The Division had been awaiting the arrival of these replacements for many weeks. In total, the battalion numbered about 1000 men. According to a communiqué from OKH, a second march battalion should arrive on 15th November. Even the arrival of this second battalion would still not suffice to make up the losses suffered by the Division: since the beginning of the summer campaign, the Division had lost over 4000 men

due to casualties and other losses. Division staff believed that at least 4 march battalions were required to bring the Division back up to full manpower levels.
In his post-war memoir, General von Lenski wrote: "The casualties of the panzergrenadier regiments were substantial on account of the Soviet snipers and the increasingly unpleasant Stalin Organs. These caused casualties, on average, of ten men a day. It was thus calculated when the Division would be at the end of its tether with its strength in infantry combatants. To prevent this wear and tear, the General Kommando had suggested that the Division be pulled out of the battle line, replenish themselves again and hold themselves in preparation further to the rear as a mobile reserve. This proposal was not authorised because OKH had ordered that Stalingrad be taken more quickly with all available forces. On 19th November, it was proven that the renunciation of the armoured reserve was a mistake.
"A further weakening of the infantry combat forces was caused by the fact that the Division had to give up two of its three pioneer companies, which would be combined with the companies of other divisions into a pioneer regiment and employed in another position. Of these experienced specialists, the Division did not see one of these men again.
"To again strengthen the combat strengths of the panzergrenadier regiments, all dispensable soldiers from the offices and the rear services were pulled out and allocated to the units after brief training. In general, they were not full value reinforcements."
The names of men transferred from non-combat jobs to front-line duties are scattered throughout the Divisional war diary: on 20th October, Soldat Horrmann was transferred from Bäckerei-Kompanie 40[5] to Panzergrenadier-Regiment 26; on 24th October, Obergefreiter Nieslony was transferred from Bäckerei-Kompanie 40 to Panzergrenadier-Regiment 26; and on 25th October, Obergefreiter Luka and Gefreiter Zeidler were transferred from Nachschub-Kompanie 40[6] to Panzer-Regiment 24.
With all Germans being sent to the front-line, the rear area jobs were largely being taken over by Hiwis, who now formed a large part of the Division.

Casualties:

4 men wounded (1 of those stayed with the troops)

25th, 26th and 27th October 1942:

Unteroffizier Ketelsen wrote in his diary: "25.10. During the night, only single planes were above us. The Russians covered the observation posts with phosphorous bombs! …During the day, light artillery activity on both sides. Our bombers and fighter-bombers bombard in continuous sorties. The Gun Factory is taken today by our infantry. Russian fighters fly low over our positions. In the evening, his machine-guns rattle when he wants to attack."

From early on the morning of 25th October, the Division supported the attack of the neighbouring division with all available weapons. Enemy concentrations in front of the Division were smashed to pieces. With visible results, 9 batteries and 2 anti-aircraft batteries were combatted on the east shore of the Volga. Rittmeister Georg-Wilhelm von Raison, Commander of 8. Batterie of Panzerartillerie-Regiment 89, remembers this time: "I myself

5. Bakery company
6. Supply company

fought in Stalingrad as a battery commander with a heavy 15cm howitzer battery and indeed, from the beginning of the fighting until the middle of October, shortly before the encirclement. We were employed at focal points with the aim of suppressing enemy artillery aided by aerial observers. I had the unheard-of luck of being sent home shortly before the encirclement because of severe jaundice. I left Stalingrad on 25th October. The trip in the ambulance went to the other side of the Don, then to the airport. From there, together with two other battery commanders, we were flown to Berlin-Tempelhof within five days by aerial hitchhiking. In my Soldbuch, my admission into Reserve Hospital 137 in Berlin is confirmed as 3rd November. After my discharge I had convalescence leave, in which I married, but I again landed in the same hospital on 8th December with a severe relapse."

Jaundice, or infectious hepatitis, wreaked havoc on the German forces investing Stalingrad and 24. Panzer-Division was not spared the ravages of this disease. Obergefreiter Ferdinand Kusterer describes his introduction to the disease and the scene that met him at a dressing station:

> "I took wounded men to the main hospital, including an Unteroffizier with jaundice. A short time after that I reported sick to my platoon commander and said I felt so miserable that I could not perform sentry duty. He sent for a medic: 37.8 degrees Celsius. 'There is nothing wrong', the Leutnant responded. 'But I feel so bad and I cannot eat anything!' There was still only dry black-bread, canned meat and dried vegetables with barley. 'Go to the company command post!' The Spieß had already spotted my illness at ten metres distance: 'Jaundice. Hand in your rifle!' At the main hospital, where the illness was confirmed by the doctor, someone hung a sign around my neck that entitled wounded and sick men to ride along in empty vehicles. I believe this infectious jaundice was transmitted by the local population. Because more and more were struck down by it, a Führerbefehl ordered the transport into a homeland hospital because the illness did not heal in Russia and medication for it did not exist. This liver disease gradually led to death if it continued for too long. Thus I stood by the road and waited until I caught a ride with a panzer of 14. Panzer-Division. Numerous shot-up enemy tanks lay in the area where we had our positions. In Karpovka was the first dressing station where I tried to find accommodation. It was completely overcrowded however, and only received non-transportable cases. It was good that I didn't remain there because the misery of this hospital was indescribable. When I entered, a body was carried out and buried at a cemetery lying right next to it while at the same time, new graves were being dug by Russian prisoners. In the aisles and rooms, the severely wounded men were packed close together on straw. Many could not move themselves, while flies crawled around on their faces. The bearded faces were emaciated and filthy and mostly, through the loss of blood, were white as a sheet, and several of them were delirious with fever. In the dressing-station, however,

KUSTERER

Obergefreiter Kusterer and his comrades construct improved bunkers in the steppe outside Stalingrad.

> there were still no German sisters to alleviate distress. A panzer driver with severe burns was so well bound that only his mouth remained free; the man next to him had lost both his eyes, another had a stomach wound, a man with one leg already in plaster was taken to the operating theatre moaning: 'I'm going to die, I'm going to die!' Most of them had head-, stomach- or lung-wounds, but above all they had burns."[7]

On 26th October, the situation and forward line was unchanged. Assaults by the neighbouring division only moved forward very slowly against increasingly strengthening resistance. In his diary for this day, Unteroffizier Ketelsen wrote: "26.10. Already toward 1900 hours, Russian bombers are over us. They bombed when close above us. During the day, lively artillery activity. Our bombers again draw over us in continuous missions. Towards evening the Gun Factory is taken from us, up to a hall. The Russians sit above and we sit below in the cellar. But no-one gives themselves up. The entire night there is shooting near us. We can barely wait until it becomes light."

Continuation of the assaults of the neighbouring divisions on 27th October gained the Volga shore after hard combat. With the onset of darkness, the remnants of II./Panzergrenadier-Regiment 21 were relieved in the Brickworks by elements of 389. Infanterie-Division. On this same night, they made a change of position, taking over a smaller sector further to the right, up to the north-east edge of the Gun Factory, in conjunction with Kradschützen-Abteilung 4. It would remain here until 30th October when it was relieved in the night by 389. Infanterie-Division.
Unteroffizier Ketelsen reports: "27.10. The Russian planes also now bomb in continuous sorties. Must be obtained by fighting step by step. Despite that, however, Stalingrad is lost. During the day, he once again employed his planes in masses. 20-30 fighters, but also those that benefit nothing to him. Our fighters and flak shoot at them individually. Whoever got away was lucky. In the evening, he once again used his artillery."

Casualties for 25th October:

5 men killed

5 men wounded (all 5 stayed with the troops)

Casualties for 26th October:

3 men killed

- Obergefreiter Reinhold Schwomer; PGR21 (Killed)
- Gefreiter Kurt Reinhardt; PGR21 (Killed)

5 men wounded (3 of those stayed with the troops)

7. Obergefreiter Kusterer spent the night in a tent with other lightly wounded men. The next morning, he managed to get a ride on a lorry over the Don to a dressing station near Kalach. A short time later, he was put on a hospital train waiting at Chirskaya, then via Stalino, across the Dnepr and back to Germany for proper medical treatment.

Casualties for 27th October:

None

Decorations bestowed from 19th October to 25th October:

20 Iron Cross First Class
91 Iron Cross Second Class

Prisoners and booty taken from 19th October to 25th October:

8 deserters
1 airplane
2 anti-tank guns

28th October 1942:

Unteroffizier Ketelsen noted in his diary: "28.10. During the night, the Russian planes strengthened near us so that they made the night hell for us. Everyone longed for it to become day. Toward morning, our artillery is employed, then all hell broke loose. Stukas and dive-bombers were used at the same time. Our fighters dominated the airspace. Isolated Russian fighters attacked us. Toward evening, he employed his artillery and plastered us. But this also passed overhead."

During the day, Panzerartillerie-Regiment 89 silenced 3 heavy, 1 medium, 3 light, 2 anti-aircraft batteries and 1 rocket launcher, and a panzer schwadron was subordinated to 305. Infanterie-Division. Just a normal day in Stalingrad.

As the draining combat dragged on in the twisted wreck of Stalingrad-North, another march battalion was approaching Stalingrad. Among the men was 19 year-old Günter Koschorrek. For the past week and a half, he had been sitting on a transport train as it crossed Russia, heading deeper to the east. On 17th October, the commander of the training battalion at Insterburg[8] had bid them farewell with a rousing speech about operations on the Eastern Front. The next day, they boarded the train. In his wagon were one experienced Obergefreiter and sixteen recruits, six of whom were from his training company. Obergefreiter Marzog, being the oldest man in the wagon, was placed in charge of the men. In total, the train carried over 300 men. Koschorrek and his comrades passed the time by talking, playing cards, and listening to a comrade who excelled on the mouth-harmonica. They had been told that their destination was Stalingrad. Koschorrek recalls a conversation on the train.
'How far is it to Stalingrad?' asked Grommel, who in the meantime had made himself comfortable between myself and Obergefreiter Marzog.
Marzog shrugged his shoulders: 'No idea, but as I heard, we should reach our objective tomorrow.'

8. Panzergrenadier-Ersatz und Ausbildung Bataillon 413 in Insterburg commanded by Oberstleutnant von Busse.

As if to answer, we hear in the distance a dull rumble and rolling thunder. Then, when it was dark, we saw far to the front a red-coloured sky.
'That's Stalingrad!' someone said. "[9]

In the evening, the Division received the order to prepare for relief by 389. Infanterie-Division in the night of 30th/31st October. The verbal instructions of Korps for the operation ran as follows: "Withdrawal of the Division out of the front-line."

Casualties:

3 men killed

- Obergefreiter Karl Schmidt; PGR21 (Killed)
- Gefreiter Werner Viehäuser; PGR21 (Killed)

4 men wounded (1 of those stayed with the troops)

1 man missing

- Gefreiter Konrad Schröder; PGR21 (Missing in action)

29th October 1942:

Unteroffizier Ketelsen from 4./Panzergrenadier-Regiment 26 jotted in his diary: "29.10. Already around 0600 hours, the Russian bombers draw over us. The searchlights beamed and the bombs rattled over us. The earth bunkers trembled under our arses! Thus it went until daybreak. The Russian fighters are again in their best form over us. Today, we counted 4 Russian fighters shot down. To the right of us, our Stukas bombed continuously from morning to night. We had harassing fire the entire night. 65 shells!"

The Division Commander, General von Lenski, received instructions from Commander-in-Chief of 6. Armee[10] that contrary to the Korpsbefehl of the day, a relief for refreshment would only be implemented after the complete capture of Stalingrad. Until then, the Division would take over an extended defensive sector, freeing up additional forces of the infantry divisions for further assaults. If the Division was unable to take over the sector as a consequence of its low combat strengths, panzer crews (without drivers) would be pulled out. On the basis of this instruction, the Division ordered the immediate assembly of Alarmeinheit Panzer Regiment-24, an ad hoc Kampfgruppe formed from extraneous members of that regiment. The Alarmeinheit consisted of a platoon formed from each of the three panzer battalions. Each platoon had a strength of 1 officer and 40 men, therefore the Alarmeinheit, commanded by Rittmeister Weiß, totalled 4 officers and 120 men. It is not clear what men were assigned to this unit: they could have been mechanics, panzer crews without vehicles or clerks from the Regiment offices. General von Lenski wrote the following: "One suggestion of the Commander-in-Chief of

9. From the book 'Vergiß die Zeit der Dornen nicht' by Günter K. Koschorrek; v. Hase & Koehler Verlag 1998.
10. Generaloberst Paulus

6. Armee was to employ panzer crews, who had become surplus, as infantrymen, which I didn't understand. According to Dräbich-Wächter's words[11], 24. Panzer-Division would later be supplied to the Caucasus Army. Therefore, I had a great interest in keeping the technically trained personnel. It was allotted to the Werkstattkompanien who succeeded in untiring labour until 19th November in making about fifty to sixty panzers again completely useable."

Günter Koschorrek and his comrades, part of the march battalion being sent to 24. Panzer-Division in Stalingrad, continued their lengthy journey. They disembarked from the comfortable troop train and proceeded to march in an easterly direction. During the train trip across Russia, they experienced beautiful autumn sunshine and blue skies but it was a different story when they started marching. Koschorrek reports:

> "The rain was gradually getting stronger and then the wind sprang up. Lousy weather for the first time and in a form that we hadn't expected. The wind squalls were stronger because the empty plains offered no protection. The rain prickled my face like fine needles, it drummed on helmets that we had put on for protection. The gusts of wind pulled at the tent-quarters that only roughly protected our bodies. They flapped around the dampened legs of our pants and the gusts almost pulled them off us. We trudged and staggered on and on, until we simply could not go on.
> We rested in a hollow that lay out of the wind a bit. What muck!
> Fatigued, we lay on the soaked, greasy clay soil. Everything was wet and sticky, I was soaked through to my underwear and I didn't know whether it was from sweat or rain. We slowly recovered. Up! – Go on, go on! How far is it still? – We should reach the objective today.
> It continued for hours until at last we saw a village. The rain had stopped...
> It was said that we would be picked up from there in vehicles. They were still not there. Again we waited! They arrived in the darkness. We drove on in the darkness, then over a long bridge with many other vehicles.
> 'The Don', someone said behind me.
> After a few hours, we stopped somewhere between several Panje huts. We were directed into the huts for the night. Out of the distance, we heard rumbling, the sky was blood red – there was Stalingrad!"[12]

In the evening, the Division received Korpsbefehl Nr. 101, the last point of the order relating directly to the Division. It said: "In the night of 30./31.10. 389. Infanterie-Division will take over the sector of front from 24. Panzer-Division. 24. Panzer-Division will prepare to take over the southern front of 79. Infanterie-Division from the south-west corner of the Steel Factory up to the mouth of the gully on the Volga in 71b1 (exclusive). The earliest timing for the

11. General von Lenski recalls what General Dräbich-Wächter said to him: "On 11th September 1942, I received the order to take over the command of 24. Panzer-Division from the severely wounded Generalmajor Ritter von Hauenschild. Until then, I was – apart from two short periods of employment at the front – Commander of the School for Schnelltruppen in Krampnitz. While reporting to the Heerespersonalamt in Berlin, the Chef der I. Abteilung, Generalleutnant von Dräbich-Wächter, confidentially shared with me that OKW had scheduled 24. Panzer-Division to be pulled out of the fighting around Stalingrad as soon as possible and, together with a motorised division, be employed in an advance on Baku."

12. From the book 'Vergiß die Zeit der Dornen nicht' by Günter K. Koschorrek; v. Hase & Koehler Verlag 1998.

takeover of this sector is the night of 1.11./2.11."
Officers at Division headquarters were shocked that instead of being pulled out for a rest in a rear area, the Division was going to be shifted to another sector of the city. There was some discussion amongst some of the senior officers about the misuse of a valuable panzer division but this dissent was more a private matter between individual men rather than between officers. No protests were passed up the chain of command. It is not clear what General von Lenski thought about the continuing decay of his division due to the gruelling combat but barely three hours after receiving the Korpsbefehl, the Division issued Divisionsbefehl Nr. 80 at 2330 hours which ordered the withdrawal of the bulk of the Division out of the defensive front on the Volga and the later assumption of a defensive sector in the Steel Factory.

Casualties:

3 men killed

• Obergefreiter Rudolf Petschel; PR24 (Killed)

5 men wounded (1 of those stayed with the troops)

• Knight's Cross winner Wachtmeister Siegfried Freyer; 4./PR24 (Wounded)

30th October 1942:

In the war diary of the Division, it was noted that the day passed quietly but it was still life or death for the men in the front-line. Unteroffizier Ketelsen reports: "30.10. The night was once again made into hell for us. A light bomb was put down close between our guns, but without effect. Already around 0430 hours, he employed his long-barrel guns and plastered us when he wanted to attack. At 1000 hours, we received the order to pull out towards evening. Everyone is glad, but who knows for how long? Close behind us, 4 bombs burst through, in which 4 men are wounded (only lightly)."
Gruppe Below reached the reserve area near Gumrak railway station, where the empty vehicles were located. There was now home leave for a lucky few. Already in the previous weeks, several granting of leaves had continually taken place. In the first place, the married men were taken into consideration.
While some lucky men went home on leave, other men were just arriving. Günter Koschorrek reports his arrival, together with other replacements: "Awake at 0600 hours, it was still dark outside. Hot coffee and rations were given. Nobody knows anything concrete… Someone says that we're still not at our objective, but only near a regiment of the Division. From here, we would finally go to a unit that was located in Stalingrad.
The combat strengths have completely shrivelled, therefore we would fill the gaps. Someone said that the entire regiment was no more than two companies strong. Such 'latrine rumours' are often the only source of information for the simple Landser…
The entire group was ninety men strong. 'To first Abteilung, Regiment 21' a young Oberleutnant said to us."[13]

13. From the book 'Vergiß die Zeit der Dornen nicht' by Günter K. Koschorrek; v. Hase & Koehler Verlag 1998.

Günter Koschorrek and the other men were picked up at noon by several lorries and 4 Mercedes personnel vehicles and driven to the supply train that was located far to the west of Stalingrad.

With the arrival of fresh recruits, General von Lenski issued an order for the training of the replacements. In the opening paragraph of the order, General von Lenski said: "The combat strength of the troops can be substantially raised only if the replacements supplied from the march battalions have passed through intensive combat training..."
The focus of training for the new arrivals lay in the review of every single man to see whether he had completely mastered the weapon on which he had been trained. Where a shortcoming was established, the men concerned would concentrate on particularly intensive instruction. In addition to that, the second part would be thorough instruction on machine-guns, throwing of hand grenades and combat drill. General von Lenski had also arranged some rather novel – yet sensible – initiatives to accustom the recruits to military hardware. After securing close liaison with the Panzer-Regiment, General von Lenski had arranged for each man to inspect a panzer inside and out, and if possible, he wanted the men to allow a panzer to roll over them while they were in foxholes.
Each of the new recruits would also receive 3 egg hand grenades from the ammunition dumps near Businovka. This was no doubt in preparation for the next stage of the training. All efforts were to be made to get the replacements fully adjusted to the front as quickly as possible. General von Lenski also added: "Education will harden and strengthen their combat morale by emphasising our feelings of superiority over the Russians."

With the beginning of darkness, the relief of Gruppe Below by 389. Infanterie-Division was started and continued until dawn without any special incidents.

Casualties:

1 man killed

4 men wounded (2 of those stayed with the troops)

- Obergefreiter Werner Witt; PGR26 (Wounded but died on 31st October)

31st October 1942:

The artillery, remaining in their positions, combatted four enemy batteries on the east shore of the Volga with visible results. The men of 24. Panzer-Division were successfully pulled back from the front and their sector occupied by 389. Infanterie-Division. The Korpsbefehl for 1st November ran: "In the night of 1./2.11. 24. Panzer-Division will replace the employed forces on the south front of 79. Infanterie-Division from the border of 100. Jäger-Division up to and including the southern workhall."
Thus the Division was employed for a third time in Stalingrad. The desired and bitterly necessary rest and replenishment with following employment that was more in keeping with the character of a panzer division again came to nothing. Nevertheless, the men knew nothing of this and enjoyed the peace in the rear area. Unteroffizier Ketelsen of 4./Panzergrenadier-Regiment 26 wrote in his diary: "31.10. At the rear, it is quiet and we sleep in bunkers. In the

morning, the guns are cleaned. Now they are washed from top to bottom. The dirt is now removed. The vehicles are also seen to. "We slept in the afternoon. One can now breathe deeply again."

Günter Koschorrek reports: "A Hauptwachtmeister greeted us. He informed us that we now belonged to a Division rich in tradition that had ridden in the Polish and French campaigns, and whose vehicles carried the leaping horseman as its tactical symbol." The Hauptwachtmeister went on to explain that in this Division, a Feldwebel was a Wachtmeister, a Hauptmann was a Rittmeister. "'Jawohl, Herr Hauptwachtmeister!' we roared to his question as to whether we had understood."
Together with 30 men, Koschorrek was allocated to 1. Schwadron of Panzergrenadier-Regiment 21 while the other men were distributed to the other Schwadrons.
"Someone informed us that our Schwadron still only had a combat strength of 26 men. The Regiment was also heavily decimated..."[14]

24. Panzer-Division moves from the Brickworks to Krasny Oktyabr.

In the afternoon, General von Lenski issued a 13-page memo titled 'Command and training tips to heed', a collection of insights and experiences gained during the preceding months of hard combat. It was intended for distribution to every officer in the Division. Orders from higher offices, as well as the Division's own observations, were concentrated into the following principles:
1.) The most valuable asset are the men, therefore, mobile assault forces should be conserved. Men can be compensated for by using weapons and ammunition, for instance, attacks should be preceded by the heaviest bombardments by concentrating all weapons, including those of the reserve units, and by this, reducing casualties amongst the men. The same applies for defence: heavy defensive weapons should batter any enemy attack. In addition to this, half-tracks must be

14. From the book 'Vergiß die Zeit der Dornen nicht' by Günter K. Koschorrek; v. Hase & Koehler Verlag 1998.

on standby, ready to drive forward close behind the front to counterattack any enemy penetration.
Men could be spared if more of the troops consider their own protection. General von Lenski stressed the following: "I order the wearing of helmets from the command posts of battalion staffs to the front. Every officer and messenger that goes forward in this area must set a good example by wearing his helmet. Only by this can we reduce casualties due to head wounds." In addition to this, there should be an increase in entrenching, for which each commander is responsible. The aversion of Germans to digging in must be sharply opposed.
2.) Defence:
Defence calls for holding unconditionally. At the conclusion of fighting, the front-line must be in our possession. Defence is easiest when enemy preparations are spotted early and can immediately be smashed by artillery, heavy weapons and, when possible, by the Luftwaffe. Up to this point in time, this is also the easiest way of smashing the preparations of enemy tanks. Enemy penetrations cannot be straightened out by sealing them off but only by counterattacks. The counterattack must be swiftly implemented before the enemy is completely ready for defence and it must be conducted against the flanks while units either side of the breakthrough position hold at all costs. Reserves should immediately be brought up to the threatened position. Should a withdrawal be necessary due to the overall situation, this will only happen upon an order from Division. If this happens, on no account should any heavy weapons fall into enemy hands undestroyed. Irrespective of that, the gun crews will as a matter of course defend their battery with firearms. Sufficient rifle ammunition must be on hand. Masses of wire, tank traps and minefields will protect each battery. The choice of battery position will therefore be behind a tank obstacle. A gun from each battery must be able to be pulled out of its concealed position for tank defence.
3.) Utilisation of all weapons, particularly new specialists weapons:
It has often been established that attached weapons are not fully employed or brought completely to bear. Instead, these weapons stand inactive near command posts as attacks are carried out. By this, first of all think of the Flak combat groups, panzers and half-tracks, the new 7.5cm gun on a half-track, Wurfrahmen 40[15] on a half-track, the smoke-generating equipment of the pioneers. Accordingly, requests for attachments will be welcomed every time by the Division.
With the breakdown of every weapon (panzers, self-propelled anti-tank guns, half-tracks, armoured cars, all heavy weapons of the grenadiers, etc.), it is the duty of the commander to secure the fastest repair and supervise its speedy supply back to the front-line. When crews become casualties, it should be investigated as to whether remaining crew members can man weapons lacking their crews.
Snipers should be enlisted in every unit, be employed at focal points and must continually receive special assignments.
4.) Maintaining the mobility of the reserves at all times, despite every difficulty such as petrol shortages, mud or snow, should be the constant endeavour of every commander. Only necessary vehicles should be employed. Marching on foot, as well as the use of horses, if the need arises, should never be forgotten. Reports of units not being able to defend against an enemy attack due to the immobility of its reserves are not valid.
5.) Panzers:
Panzers are slower than panzergrenadiers, establishing battle-readiness requires more time,

15. Six 32cm rocket-launcher frames attached to the sides of an Sdkfz. 251 half-track.

therefore, time for distribution of orders is restricted to a minimum. Panzer units should be set in march by preliminary orders.
United operations by the Regiment, in exceptional cases the Abteilung, have constantly proved themselves.
Indispensable combat-ready, far-reaching reconnaissance and terrain evaluation is needed because a panzer unit is entirely dependent upon the terrain. No support without an immediate start of reconnaissance and terrain evaluation.
A panzer unit will never advance without fire control. In areas searched for mines, panzer units will be deeply echeloned. Close co-operation is required with pioneers and panzergrenadiers. Panzers will only advance once mines have been cleared. A simultaneous loss of 10 panzers by mine damage in a minefield is intolerable.[16]
Panzer Support Schwadrons are not 'maids-for-all-work'. When panzer numbers have sunk below 4, the Schwadron must be withdrawn as quickly as possible and not 'fight to the last panzer'. They then lack mutual fire support. The Panzer Support Schwadron will complete its assignments according to the principles of co-operation between panzers and riflemen.
Should a panzer schwadron fight with an infantry unit, the Division will constantly propose that the panzers are not subordinated but are working in co-operation. The commander of the panzer schwadron attached to the infantry unit will constantly procure an assignment. The resolution of the assignment is then his concern! Panzers are not assault guns. Operations of such a kind are always refused. Thorough discussions with the infantry and pioneers, careful preparations and systematic implementation are indispensable for success. No assault lust!
6.) Artillery:
The artillery has supported the panzergrenadiers in an excellent manner. A few ideas, however, should be clarified to eliminate misunderstandings between the grenadiers and the artillery.
First of all, the artillery, in addition to reconnaissance, needs the longest time requirements up to the first shot. That requires early operational orders for the artillery. Therefore, the following sequence should be adhered to:
1. Orders for reconnaissance,
2. Orders to the artillery
3. Orders to the panzergrenadier regiments.
Secondly, the artillery commander will go where he can see something and can best conduct his units operation. For this, the command post of the artillery commander should strive to be located in the vicinity of the panzergrenadiers' command post. If this is not possible, a connection between the two should be secured. As with everyone, the artillery should only carry out the task allotted to it.
The artillery observers attached to the panzergrenadiers should ensure that they fulfil their mission by not being coupled too closely to a grenadier schwadron. The danger exists that if the observer is restricted to the attack area of one schwadron, he will indeed have a good connection with the grenadiers but he will not be able to carry out his artillery duties.
The basic unit of artillery is an Abteilung and they will strive to concentrate their supporting fire into the form of barrages. The artillery cannot always fire close in front of the panzergrenadiers without endangering them and they should not do so because the responsibility of placing fire along the front-line belongs to the grenadiers heavy weapons, above all the heavy mortars, the light and heavy infantry guns.
7.) The pioneers are a valuable, difficult-to-replace specialist weapon. Their infantry operations

16. General von Lenski is obviously referring to the disastrous attack on 21st October when 10 panzers supporting Jäger-Regiment 54 fell into a minefield and quickly lost the bulk of them.

are only allowed in emergencies with approval by Division or in assault groups for house-to-house or bunker fighting. During infantry operations, the pioneers will have other heavy weapons attached to them, including some necessary tank defence.
During minelaying in the firing line, pioneer squads must be protected by panzergrenadiers.

There were several more points about organisation of communications, ammunition and petrol requirements, supplies and street signs, but the bulk of the memorandum was taken by the above seven points. Through tough combat, high casualties and the bitter realisation that the Division was embroiled in deadly street-fighting, General von Lenski and his Division now conducted their operations in methods entirely suited to the rigours of mortal combat in a destroyed modern city.

Casualties:

None

Retrospective View

Chapter Twelve

Since 4th September 1942, the date they first reached the edge of the city, the Division had been involved in tough combat in and around Stalingrad. After they had decisively participated during three weeks of combat in the capture of the centre of Stalingrad under the control of XXXXVIII. Panzerkorps, without a days rest they were then employed for the following six weeks within the units of LI. Armeekorps in infantry operations in the northern part of Stalingrad. The panzergrenadiers and Kradschützen (motorcycle riflemen) bore the main burden of the fighting and were excellently supported by panzers, pioneers, panzer-artillery, panzerjägers and Heeres Flak[1] as well as communications- and supply-troops. Despite the heaviest casualties, continuous physical over-exertion, ceaseless enemy artillery fire and draining night-time air attacks, the men of 24. Panzer-Division performed almost superhumanly.

The heavily eroded forces of the Division were forced to go over to the defensive in the last period to maintain a very small nucleus for replenishment. Despite this, during this time, the Division provided almost daily support for the neighbours in every possible way, either by offensive missions of the panzer units and panzerjägers, or by the fire of the very active Panzerartillerie-Regiment 89. Unfortunately, the panzer casualties were considerable because the bulk of the infantry had not learned to work together successfully with panzers.
In the time from 5th–31st October, Panzer Abteilung Winterfeld had participated in 22 attacks with 8 different units not belonging to the Division. In those operations, they destroyed 18 tanks and 15 heavy anti-tank and anti-aircraft guns. Their human casualties amounted to 11 dead[2], 18 wounded, 1 missing[3] and in panzers 2 total losses[4] and 20 repairable vehicles.

The results and casualties of Panzerartillerie-Regiment 89 in the period from 13th September to 30th October were as follows:

1. Army-level anti-aircraft units
2. Obergefreiter Karl Huhn on 7th October, Oberleutnant Günther Liebe on 8th October, Gefreiters Albin Börner and Werner Sprange on 11th October, Obergefreiter Heinrich Tersteegen on 12th October, Obergefreiter Peter Liebermann on 14th October, Oberwachtmeister Hans Witt on 18th October, Oberleutnant Paul Schulte on 21st October, Obergefreiter Rudolf Petschel on 29th October, plus two other unknown men.
3. Unteroffizier Wilhelm Haase on 17th October 1942.
4. Panzerbefehlswagen '361' and a Panzer IV short-barrel

Eliminated or destroyed enemy batteries:

137 light batteries
6 light anti-aircraft batteries
131 heavy batteries
11 heavy anti-aircraft batteries
109 individual guns

Number and type of eliminated or destroyed enemy infantry weapons:

7 infantry guns
85 mortars
64 anti-tank guns
50 Stalin Organs
2 anti-tank rifles
100 machine-guns

Captured guns in use, amount of captured ammunition fired:

6 guns
3400 shells

Number of enemy tanks destroyed:

7 tanks

Other enemy weapons destroyed:

3 ferries
5 bridges
1 raft
7 barges
3 tugboats
2 armoured trains
5 trains
3 field-kitchens

Length of telephone cables laid:

1164 kilometres

Number of disruptions repaired:

5569

Casualties from Panzerartillerie-Regiment 89:

79 killed
236 wounded in hospital
165 wounded remained with the troops

On the basis of its excellent shooting performance, Panzerartillerie-Regiment 89 was constantly the first to be called on for artillery missions by different artillery commanders. Considerably greater success would have been possible with better ammunition supply and ample supplies of petrol. The shortage of artillery ammunition was as follows:

Ammunition for the leichte Feldhaubitze (light howitzer):
In the time from 29th August to 5th October, too many shells with double fuses were supplied, sometimes more than shells with single fuses. The Regiment was therefore forced to fire double-fused shells rather than single-fused shells. In doing so, a conspicuously large amount of duds were observed. Bouncing shots are not possible with double-fuses because the fuse has no delay. Besides, double-fuses are complicated in their construction, their manufacture is more difficult, and they are more expensive.
In the time from 14th October to 21st October, H.L. were fired because of a shortage of single-fuse shells. A bouncing shot is also not possible with this shell. The shrapnel effect of this shell on impact is about 20 metres wider to the sides than the normal shell because the H.L. has a thinner casing. They drop back considerably behind the normal shells, over 20 metres. The reason lies in the directed detonation wave that takes affect on the longitudinal axis. This shell is technically difficult and expensive to make.

Ammunition for the 10cm Kanone 18:
At times, there were gaps in the supply of special cartridges. The suppression of enemy batteries standing far in the hinterland could not succeed. On 20th October, 10cm Granate 19 FES shells were supplied for the first time unannounced. These shells could not be fired to begin with because the necessary shooting tables for them were missing. After telephonic consultations with all reachable posts, the Regiment learned that a regulation shooting table was available at I./Artillerie-Regiment 430, the only one in the entire 6. Armee. After copying the modified values from this shooting table, the FES shells were able to be fired.

Ammunition for the schwere Feldhaubitze 18 (heavy howitzer):
A shortage of special ammunition for the heavy howitzers also occurred at times. Firing distance was therefore limited to 9775 metres. Distant enemy batteries could not be suppressed. 15cm Granate 19 with the marking o.M. only allowed up to five discharges (barrel bursts). With that, the firing distance was restricted to 8500 metres. Because the heavy howitzers mostly combatted enemy artillery at the greatest distances, such shells were pointless. It was better when they were completely drawn out of the supply system because they were only a burden. On 2nd September 1942, 15cm Granate 36 were delivered. Nothing was known about using the shells in the heavy howitzers. Higher offices also couldn't give any information about it. The shells were stopped. On 10th October, the Regiment finally learned the fixed values for using them. At times, the heavy howitzers had to fire these shells with double-fuses rather than single-fuses because of a shortage in the latter.

Ammunition for the 12.2cm Russian howitzers:
As replacements for knocked out schwere Feldhaubitze, three Russian 12.2cm calibre guns were enlisted in the middle of September. These had a firing distance of 12,800 metres. To begin with, the 300 available shells were fired with good results. Additional ammunition was not found or supplied. For 4 weeks, these guns have been without ammunition and with that, are worthless and only a burden. If the supply of 12.2cm ammunition seems hopeless, the Regiment will be forced to give up these guns.

Ammunition for 7.62cm guns:
In the Regiment, three 7.62cm guns are available. All available captured ammunition has been fired. For a short time, ammunition for these has regularly been supplied. This should be available in sufficient quantities. The guns possess a firing distance of 13,000 metres.

The experience of individual types of weapons in city fighting was contained in a report entitled *"Experiences in the fighting around Stalingrad"* and was divided into the following categories:

General:

The employment of an armoured assault group consisting of panzers, armoured riflemen, self-propelled anti-tank guns, a panzerpionier platoon and an artillery battalion has proved excellent in the spacious city areas.
All infantry combat forces must be concentrated under one commander. Sufficient allocation of pioneers (only for pioneer tasks, however) is required from the outset.

Panzergrenadiers:

Formation and equipment: Decisive for operations and objectives for panzergrenadiers is the number of well-equipped assault groups. Only one light machine-gun but many riflemen. Assigning of snipers. Outfitting with submachine-guns, hand grenades, concentrated charges, explosives and smoke-generating equipment is necessary. Ample attachment of assault guns, artillery pieces, self-propelled 2cm Flak guns, 3.7cm anti-tank guns (5cm is too large for attacks but very good in defence). The explosives squad is for clearing mines and tank obstacles. A squad of flamethrowers is incorporated into a platoon. Light infantry guns and mortars with a lot of ammunition supplied. Rifle grenades are desired[5]. For observing enemy snipers, Russian trench periscopes have proved very useful[6]. Assault troops sufficiently equipped with radios because the necessary messengers and use of linesmen is often impossible or too costly.
Implementation: The complete clearing of all enemy resistance nests during the attack is ordered. Supplying of forces to cover the flanks and repeated conscientious clearing of streets where the fighting has already passed through, above all in the cellars, is necessary.
Conquering of empty areas, crossroads, factory courtyards and railway installations only under cover of artificial fog. Against bunkers, smoke and smoke-grenades (when sufficiently available) are often better than hand grenades.[7]
Caution of mines at crossroads.
Continual distinguishing of the forward line by smoke signals and flares is required to facilitate co-operation with the Luftwaffe.
Fighting from half-tracks: Only in the open areas of the city and in city sectors with low, small and partially destroyed wooden houses has fighting from armoured vehicles proven itself. By

---

5. In an appendix attached to a later memorandum, it is apparent how infrequently rifle-grenades were used. Under the heading of Schießbecher (rifle discharge cup), it says: "There are only 7 discharge cups available in the Division, proving themselves excellently during the fighting in Stalingrad. In accordance with A.H.M. 42, the planned provision of rifle cups for a division – for 24. Panzer-Division it is a total of 219 – has still not been carried out because allocations have not yet occurred." The Schießbecher was a rifled, 3cm calibre discharge cup which came with a special sight, and this cup could be clamped to most types of rifles. The grenades it fired were wide and varied: explosives, anti-tank, smoke, parachute flares, anti-personal etc.
6. There was a lack of telescopic sights and sniper rifles in the Division. When they were available they were put to good use and it was noted many times that when camouflaged snipers covered the advance of the riflemen, picking off any enemy soldier who showed himself, casualties amongst 24. Panzer-Division's infantry were reduced.
7. Division seems to have taken notice of the advice that Panzergrenadier-Regiment 21 passed on to the grenadiers of Regiment 26 on 24th September (see page 194).

attaching heavy panzers, enemy bunkers being suppressed by panzers can be destroyed from the vehicles with smoke-grenades and explosives.
Surprise assaults in the early morning are only possible on foot because the noise of the motors is too loud and surprise is therefore not guaranteed.
For bunker fighting, attachment of small flamethrower squads and a large supply of pioneers explosives is desired. Twelve men in a half-track is too much because each soldier has little freedom of movement. A squad strength of 1:9 (1:10 at the most) is advantageous.
Armoured cars have proven themselves in the city only as liaison vehicles behind the front-line.
Co-operation with panzers: Co-operation with panzers has proven itself.
A prerequisite, however, is accurate preparations for the operation, systematic reconnaissance of the terrain and attachment of pioneers for mine removal. The plan of attack must be laid down and discussed in detail. Mission of panzers in platoon- or squad strength as a mixed unit of Panzer III and IV in or behind the panzergrenadiers as protection is to be strived for. The elimination of enemy tanks and tank-destroying weapons by individual Panzer IV long-barrels from covered fire positions before the beginning of the attack has proven itself.
Co-operation with artillery: Direct support of the assault groups by artillery is only possible by well-advanced individual guns. These would be employed to strengthen the grenadiers own heavy weapons close behind the forward line. Due to restricted observation possibilities during the attack, concentrated artillery fire would mostly be employed to eliminate enemy artillery and to eliminate flanking fire.
Ammunition requirements: Plenty of ammunition for the light and heavy infantry guns (for heavy infantry guns = 1 ammunition provision[8], for mortars and light infantry guns = 2 provisions per day kept ready). Requirement for 20mm explosive shells = 3 provisions.

Panzers[9]:

Terrain difficulties such as house ruins, bomb craters, narrow streets, minefields, tank barriers and obstacles largely limit the manoeuvrability and observation possibilities of panzers so that in principle, operations of panzer units in city combat must be avoided. The casualties received bear no comparison to the success of this most valuable weapon of the army. The main weapon of the panzers, 'fire and movement', cannot be used properly. They present a target and see very little.
The panzer is not suited for city fighting when operating in units such as a Panzer Regiment or Abteilung. On the edge of the city and in completely disintegrated sectors of the city, panzer operations are often useful, especially when the enemy has no time to set up his defence.
To support weak and battleweary panzergrenadiers and infantry units, a Panzer Support Schwadron (as the largest command unit) can be employed as an exception.
Their employment should adhere to the following guidelines:
A departure from these too easily exposes the few employed panzers to destruction by dug in, well camouflaged enemy tank-killing weapons.
Attack: While the panzers will support the experienced panzergrenadiers, they will only be employed to co-operate with foreign infantry because the bulk of infantry in the German Army are unschooled and unaccustomed to fighting alongside panzers.

8. An 'ammunition provision' was a standard quantity of ammunition expected to be fired per gun per day. Because the fighting was so fierce at Stalingrad, the artillery often had the ammunition provisions doubled or trebled.
9. The following points also later appeared in a memorandum under the heading 'Guidelines for Co-operation between Panzers and Grenadiers'.

Before the beginning of an attack, a precise reconnaissance of the attack area and the enemy situation (enemy tanks, anti-tank guns, mines, etc.) must be carried out.
Exact establishment of the plan of attack and implementation of this attack is to be discussed together with all of the employed commanders.
The operations of panzers will be in platoons and squads, Panzer III and IV mixed, on specific streets. Operations by single panzers are refused because as a rule, mutual support by cover-fire is not guaranteed. Prior to the beginning of the attack, enemy tanks and anti-tank guns will be eliminated by a Panzer IV long-barrel directed on foot into a concealed position.
The panzer platoons and squads will not fight in front of the panzergrenadiers, only in or behind them because only then is mutual communication possible.
Contact with panzergrenadiers will only take place through side hatches on the enemy-free side, not out of the cupola hatch.
The panzers will be used for covering fire and not as assault guns.
The infantry will not be allowed to advance bunched up behind the panzer but must comb through the terrain on a broad front under the cover-fire of the panzers. In the city, panzers attract all types of fire.
When mines are encountered, under no circumstances should panzers continue before the attached pioneers have cleared the minefield or made a gap through it.
If a panzer falls out due to a mine, by a hit or because of terrain difficulties, the panzer must be defended by panzergrenadiers or the other panzers against close quarter attacks and further enemy action because otherwise, the immobilised, usually lightly damaged panzers will be destroyed by further enemy activity.
Operations of panzers without grenadiers in the city is only expected to succeed against a very demoralised enemy with no anti-tank defences. Employment in limited local flanking attacks is recommended as being successful.
Defence: Only as a local reserve close behind the forward line for counterattacks do operations promise success.
Employment of panzers in the forward line is not desired. In difficult situations, however, well-camouflaged single panzers located directly behind the main battle line have proved useful. They provide moral support!
Using Panzer II's to guard supply columns through city sectors that haven't been cleared has proven successful.

Weapons:

7.5cm long-barrel only against armoured targets, the long gun being too easily damaged.
7.5cm short-barrel is the best weapon. Delayed-fuse shells have an excellent effect against bunkers and houses.
Smoke shells have been proven against totally obstinate enemy resistance and to blind enemy snipers.
Armour-piercing shells are good against masonry walls.

The most dangerous enemy weapons:

Anti-tank rifles mostly appear only at close ranges and are always difficult to recognise and to suppress.
Snipers.

Summary:

Operations by panzers in known and uncleared minefields, as well as in impassable terrain, destroyed factories and city sectors in Stalingrad churned by bomb craters has led to exceptionally high losses of employed panzers. The successes in no way offset the losses sustained, especially when co-operating with untrained infantry. The latter place impossible demands on the panzers.
After the experiences in fighting in Stalingrad, employment of panzers for city combat must in principle be avoided and only be viewed as an emergency measure.
An enforced operation in a critical situation with experienced panzergrenadiers can succeed in exceptional cases when following the guidelines shown above.
The infantry must learn to co-operate better with panzers and the infantry commander must recognise the limitations of the panzers. They are not assault guns with double armour protection!

Artillery:

In city fighting, the operation of artillery immediately ahead of the front-line is difficult to carry out as a result of poor possibilities for observation and the danger of short-shooting by the tall ruins of houses. Fire support of the grenadiers is therefore increased by using their own heavy weapons. Forward observers from the artillery attempt to superimpose their fire on the forward line.
Firing: The fire unit of artillery is the battalion. Concentrating in battalion units has proven itself in previous firing. Through thorough preparation and briefings, a concentration of fire by the entire regiment can also be implemented.
Also, firing by foreign army artillery units by the radio posts of the armoured observation vehicles has proven effective. For unarmoured observation posts, enemy activity is too considerable and the cable required for telephones to cover the distance is too great. Therefore, firing can mostly succeed only with the armoured observation vehicles. A further outfitting with the proper armoured observation vehicles is therefore urgently required.
As a result of shorter targets, the command and swift concentration of fire in regiment units is very feasible. The material and moral effect of barrages by the entire regiment is particularly severe according to statements by prisoners.
Artillery liaison officer: The employment of artillery liaison officers near the panzergrenadiers has proven itself. It is desirable to equip the liaison officer with an armoured observation vehicle and that way, he will be able to escort the regiment commander of the grenadiers, who most of the time is located in an armoured command vehicle. Because pack radios do not work reliably, the liaison officer will connect by line to the panzergrenadier battalion commander, when a break in the fire allows it.
Forward observers: The employment of forward observers near the panzergrenadiers is good as a consequence of personal, years-long mutual knowledge. They are generally alone in the situation, helping in the city fighting. Often, they see better from elevated positions behind the forward line rather than immediately out of the front-line.
Artillery reconnaissance: It is necessary that reconnaissance be equipped with a lot of communications equipment so that under normal weather conditions, almost every enemy battery can be caught. In contrast to this, the armoured observation battery, for use by the Division, is only equipped with radios. That suffices for continuous operations but not for reconnaissance of the entire enemy concentrations of artillery. For that, all surveying posts[10] must be connected by cables.

10. Used to monitor enemy artillery

Employment of the Lichtstaffel[11] was effective from tall buildings during the day.
Because of a strong echoing phenomenon, all sound-ranging systems[12] erected must be removed as soon as possible from the city.
Losses of guns: Since 1st July 1942, the Artillerie-Regiment has lost 7 guns due to barrel bursts. A considerable reduction of firepower and an especially unfavourable effect on the gun crews was the result.
Summary: To summarise, one can say that the principles of artillery in mass have provided many successes but as a consequence of ammunition and petrol shortages, they could not be exploited.

Pioneers:

Previous principles for employment in city fighting have proven themselves.
Before leaving their vehicles, the pioneers must be told what mission lies ahead. Only by this can the respective equipment be brought into position in time.
During employment of pioneer assault groups against bunkers and resistance nests, sufficient support by heavy weapons, anti-tank guns and machine-guns is necessary. If possible, pioneer forces will only be employed in company or, at the most, platoon strength, achieving a united employment of pioneers at the focal point. Distribution of pioneer squads is refused.
The Pionier-Bataillon's current mine-detection equipment has not proven effective on the Russian wooden mines. Outfitting with mine-detection equipment for wooden mines is urgently required.

Panzerjäger:

Pak 40 (Sfl.)[13] has proven effective as a result of its greater firing height, making it possible for it to fire over remnants of walls, fences and the like. Its mobility makes quick changes of position possible in city combat and with that, the hunting of enemy tanks. Employment behind the forwardmost line of infantry and drawing forward of platoons on certain sectors has proven advantageous because the panzerjäger have been able to go into cover most of the time.
Employment in the forward line is unsuitable because the guns with their open compartments can be easily knocked out of the fighting by explosives, hand grenades and snipers.
During defence, these anti-tank guns belong further back behind cover while observers lie further forward. Proving very disadvantageous are the unarmoured ammunition vehicles so that many times, a quick resupply is not guaranteed and the anti-guns themselves must drive back to rearm.
The chassis and construction of the machines seem too weak.
The 5cm Pak is not very suitable for combatting tanks in the city. They require too much time to get into position and are then immobile. They also don't seem to be very suitable to escort an infantry attack. Their employment is only suitable to combat bunkers and only after thorough reconnaissance. For this, the captured 7.62cm anti-tank guns have also proven themselves particularly suitable.
During defence, the 5cm anti-tank gun is an excellent defensive weapon when dug in and well-camouflaged.

---

11. Used to spot the muzzle-flashes of enemy artillery
12. Used to locate enemy artillery positions by triangulating the sounds from their discharges.
13. Selbstfahrlafette or self-propelled gun carriage

Co-operation with the Luftwaffe:

Co-operation with Stukas and fighter-bombers through a Flivo[14] attached to the Division has proven extremely effective. Effective support is often possible barely 100 metres in front of the forward line. The Flivo is in an armoured vehicle far to the front.
Employment of bomber units ahead of the attack spearheads has not proven itself because the course of the front-line frequently changes within a short time and a radio connection by the Division with the bomber units in the air does not exist. As a result of the quickly shifting situation, short-bombing by the bomber units arose several times. The Division therefore requests that in future, bomber units only be employed for suppression in the enemy's rear area, in any case preventing the demoralising effect of short-bombing on the troops.
Furthermore, the Division requests continuous orientation by Fliegerkorps as to what time and on what targets the aerial units will be employed. Because our own troops are extremely insufficiently supplied with flares and signals, it is particularly important that Division receive the additional information of when our planes will be employed to directly support the Division's own troops.
White signal flares, also fired by Russians, should not be used as the designation for 'forward line'.

Command and tactical control were made particularly difficult by the fact that during the period from the beginning of September until the end of October, besides the Division Commander, all Regiment and almost all Abteilung commanders were killed or wounded. The remaining commanders were transferred at this moment by the Heeres-Personalamt (Army Personal Office). For instance, of the 1 Brigade-, 4 Regiment- and 15 Abteilung commanders that set out on the attack with the beginning of the campaign on 28th June 1942, still available on 30th October were: no Brigade- and Regiment commanders and 4 Abteilung commanders.

Casualties in the time from 20th September – 31st October 1942:

	Offz.	Uffz. &. Men.
Killed	12	440
Wounded	27 (a further 34 stayed with the troops)	1056 (a further 748 stayed with the troops)
Missing	–	21
Total	39 Offz.	1515 Uffz. &. Men.

Booty and prisoners in the time from 20th September – 31st October 1942:

1,835 prisoners
20 aircraft
3 guns
51 tanks destroyed (2 KV1, 36 T-34, 6 T-70, 7 T-60)
1 armoured car

14. Flivo, or Flieger Verbindungs Offizier, was an officer from the Luftwaffe sent to a ground unit to control and guide the planes on to the assigned targets. This function became more important when the fighting moved into congested areas, such as cities, where the front-line could not be easily distinguished.

26 anti-tank guns
56 anti-tank rifles
38 mortars
122 machine-guns
2 flamethrowers
4 mine-dogs
5 submachine-guns
1 Volga barge

Booty and prisoners in the time from 28th June – 31st October 1942:

27,270 prisoners
115 aircraft
272 guns
431 tanks destroyed (of those, 273 by the Panzer Regiment)
328 anti-tank guns
61 anti-aircraft guns
548 anti-tank rifles
478 mortars

The 273 enemy tanks destroyed by Panzer-Regiment 24 were:

KV2 = 1
KV1 = 31
T-34 = 169
T-70 = 12
T-60 = 60

Losses in weapons and equipment in the time from 28th June – 31st October 1942:

92 MG-34
3 anti-tank rifles (schwere Panzerbüchse 41)
11 2cm Flak
1 2cm Kwk
6 heavy mortars (schwere Granatwerfer 34 – 8cm mortar)
3 light infantry guns (leichte Infanteriegeschütze 18 – 7.5cm)
1 heavy infantry gun (schwere Infanteriegeschütze 33 – 15cm)
1 light howitzer (leichte Feldhaubitze 18 – 10.5cm)
2 heavy howitzers (schwere Feldhaubitze 18 – 15cm)
3 8.8cm Flak
3 Pak 38 (5cm anti-tank gun)
2 half-tracks equipped with 3.7cm anti-tank guns
6 large rubber boats (große Floßsäcke)
2 small rubber boats (kleine Floßsäcke)
3 power saws
5 entire pontoons
3 assault boats
1 special trailer for the boats
1 large air compressor
1 sound survey vehicle (Schallaufnahmewagen 40)
1 set of sound survey equipment

Total losses in vehicles in the time from 28th June – 31st October 1942 [15]***:***

	Total	Repairs in homeland	Total amount
Panzerbefehlswagens	1		
Panzer II	3		
Panzer III	25		
Panzer IV	5		
Armoured cars	3		
Motorcycles	146	35	181
Cars	85	27	112
Lorries	151	13	164
Towing tractors	29		
Trailers	37		

Total casualties from 28th June 1942 (beginning of campaign) to 31st October 1942:

	Offz.	Uffz. U. Men.
Killed	58	1341
Wounded	153 (a further 162 stayed with the troops)	4258 (a further 2631 stayed with the troops)
Missing	1	59
Total	212 Offz.	5658 Uffz. U. Men.

Replacements that arrived in the same period: 73 Officers, 2225 Unteroffiziere and men

Percentage of casualties up to 31st October 1942: (Including losses to jaundice).

	Casualties	Jaundice
PGR 26	72.9%	1.4%
PGR 21	67.9%	1.0%
K4	48.6%	2.6%
Pz.Jg.Abt. 40	43.3%	4.7%
Pz.Pi.Btl. 40	41.0%	1.3%
Pz.Gr.Brig. 24	36.9%	4.3%
IV./PAR89	25.9%	5.4%
Pz.A.R.89	24.5%	3.5%
Pz.Rgt.24	20.4%	4.0%
Feldgend. Tr. 40	13.2%	5.5%
Pz.N.A.86	11.0%	7.4%
San.Ko. 2/40	10.9%	7.2%
Div. Stab	8.3%	7.3%
Bäck. Ko. 40	7.3%	5.3%
Dinafü 40	1.7%	4.4%
San.Ko. 1./40	1.1%	4.7%

15. See Appendix 10 (page 515) for more detailed lists of vehicle and equipment losses during Operation Blau.

Trench strengths:

	Offz.	Uffz. und Men.
After the position of 20th September		
PGR21	23	724
PGR26	18	615
K4	13	365
Pz.Pi.40	13	350
After the position of 31st October		
PGR21	16	401
PGR26	10	299
K4	5	129
Pz.Pi.40	10	131

The Division tried all methods to raise combat strengths. Numerous Hiwis[16] were employed as craftsmen, drivers, cooks and ammunition carriers, and some individuals had even proven themselves as machine-gunners. In a few rare instances, entire rifle squads were formed from Russians, but most Hiwis were employed in non-combat roles. In this way, around 700 additional German combatants were released. For instance, from Bäckerei (Bakery)-Kompanie 40, the following men were assigned to combat duties:

To Panzergrenadier-Regiment 21
Unteroffizier Barkowski
Obergefreiter Klarnetzki
Obergefreiter Schäfer
Obergefreiter Krömer
Gefreiter Kanert
Gefreiter Stier

To Panzergrenadier-Regiment 26
Unteroffizier Ahrendt
Obergefreiter Hartmann
Gefreiter Wilk
Gefreiter Huntenburg
Gefreiter Rohde
Gefreiter Wiezorek

16. Hiwis, or Hilfsfreiwillige, were Soviet ex-prisoners of war that volunteered to help the German Wehrmacht. They were used mainly in non-combat roles such as ammunition- and food-carriers, stretcher-bearers and various construction and road-building projects. In a few isolated cases, the Hiwis were issued with weapons and participated in combat.

Krasny Oktyabr

Chapter Thirteen

1st November 1942:

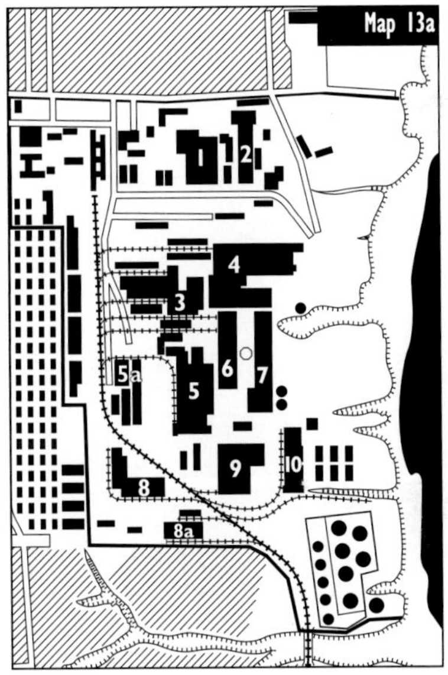

In the morning, General von Lenski received confirmation of a new assignment for his depleted units. In Korpsbefehl Nr. 103, General von Seydlitz ordered 24. Panzer-Division to relieve the forces of 79. Infanterie-Division in the southern part of the Steel Factory and take over the defensive positions there, which stretched from 100. Jäger-Division on the right to the southern building of Hall 4. This was not what the Division wanted: instead of receiving some well-deserved rest, they were now to relocate to another area of Stalingrad, this time to the grim Krasny Oktyabr Steel Factory. The factory was an immense area of slag-heaps, railway sidings, workshops and huge buildings that were now no more than shattered steel skeletons. Shells of the largest calibres – from both sides – had worked over the factory, ripping up the ground, tearing huge chunks out of the buildings and creating an indescribable mess of tangled girders, sheet-metal and rubble. The terrible atmosphere of the factory is best captured in a passage from Vassili Grossman's 'The Line of the Main Drive': "There had always been something grim and severe about the factory, but nowhere in the world could a grimmer sight have been seen than that which met the gaze of the men… The dark towering bulk of the workshops, the wet glistening rails already touched in spots with rust, the chaos of the shattered goods trucks, the piles of steel girders scattered in confusion over a yard as spacious as a city square, the heaps of coal and reddish slag, the mighty smoke stacks pierced in many places by shells – this was what met their gaze… "

Nevertheless, orders were orders. At 1230 hours, the Division issued Divisionsbefehl Nr. 81 which called for the relief of the southern front of 79. Infanterie-Division during the night of 1st/2nd November and defence of the southern area of the Steel Factory. The order made mention of a few events that had occurred in the factory over the past days. The previous day, on 31st October, the Russians had launched an attack in the northern part of the factory

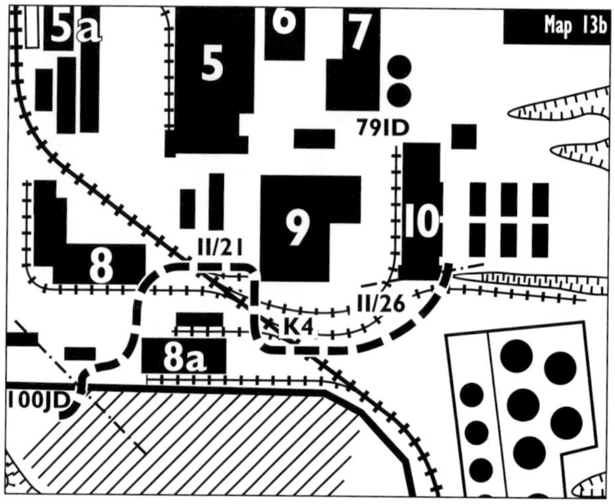

supported by tanks. The appearance of the Russian tanks shocked the Germans for they believed that there was no possibility of Russian armour existing on the west bank. Also in the past few days, the Russians had repeatedly thrown themselves against the German line on the southern front of the Steel Factory, the spearheads of the attacks moving both sides of the railway line there. This was in the sector assigned to 24. Panzer-Division. Also in this sector was the fuel installation, a cluster of 7 large and 5 small oil tanks that served as an orientation point for Russian reserves and also as a concentration point for artillery barrages and infantry attacks. The troops were also told that the area behind the front-line had still not been completely cleared of enemy remnants.

The task of fulfiling the order fell to Oberst von Below and his Kampfgruppe consisting of II./Panzergrenadier-Regiment 21 and II./Panzergrenadier-Regiment 26, as well as Kradschützen-Abteilung 4 (without Abteilung Staff, 1. and 2. Schwadron). The units were no more than tough groups of battle-hardened veterans leavened with a few fresh-faced youngsters. To compensate for the low combat strengths, Panzerartillerie-Regiment 89 would stand completely at the Kampfgruppe's disposal. Panzer-Abteilung Winterfeld had been

MARK

Deadly Stukas cruise the skies over Stalingrad. Directly below them is the Tennis Racket and in the background is the Krasny Oktyabr Steel Factory. The oil tanks on the south-east corner of the factory have been hit.

designated Division reserve and the bulk of its panzers (about 20) stood ready in grid square 75, while individual panzers would be sent into the Steel Factory behind the grenadiers as support. While their comrades were about to be sent to another windy corner in Stalingrad, I./Panzergrenadier-Regiment 21 and I./Panzergrenadier-Regiment 26 were in the rear areas, resting, integrating replacements and retraining.

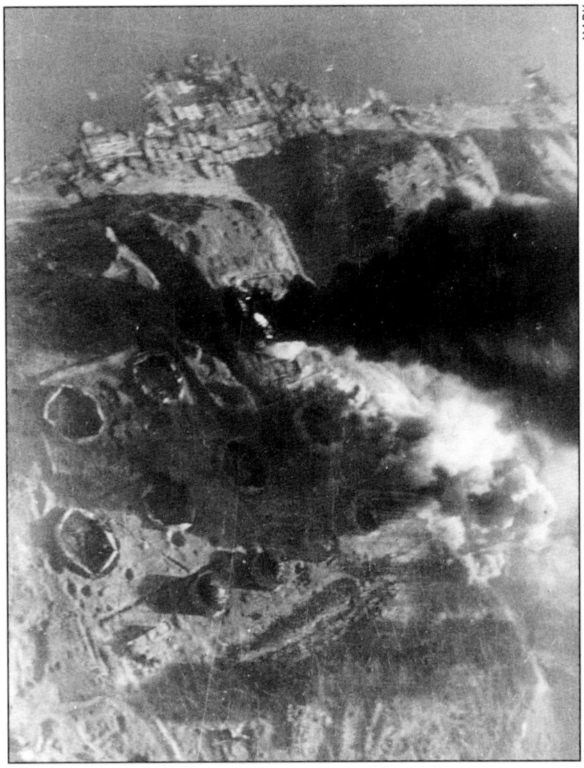

Close-up of the burning oil tanks just north of Banny Gully.

During the night, the troops of Kampfgruppe Below snaked their way into the dark menacing factory, relieving elements of Grenadier-Regiment 212 and the remnants of Oberst Victor Pavicic's Kroat Infanterie-Regiment 369, taking over defensive positions in the southern part of the Steel Factory. Shell after shell from the howitzers of Panzerartillerie-Regiment 89 arched overhead, exploding amongst the crumpled tanks of the fuel installation. The curvy forward line had a length of about 800 metres with fronts to the south-east and south. Panzergrenadier-Regiment 21 took over the right half of the sector, Kradschützen-Abteilung 4 was in the centre while Panzergrenadier-Regiment 26 held the left end. As in the previous positions, a connected front with continuous lines of trenches was out of the question. The forward line was formed by machine-gun and rifle nests, mostly in captured Russian trenches and bunkers, so the men quickly got to work strengthening the positions by extending trenches, deepening foxholes and providing better cover for the existing bunkers and dug-outs. Opposite them, the Russians still held a large bridgehead based around the Chemical Factory 'Lazur' (Tennis Racket) into which they constantly fed fresh forces from over the Volga.

Once all his men were in place, Oberst von Below sent the codeword 'Metall' back to Division headquarters, signifying a successful relief. All in all, the operation proceeded smoothly but as with any night-time manoeuvre, there were mishaps. When the weary men of II./Grenadier-Regiment 212 were trudging back through the ruins, one of the men stepped on a mine. Two men were killed and four were severely wounded. Gruppe Below, however, escaped lightly with only one man missing: his name was Unteroffizier Rudolf Josef Mühlbauer from 7./Panzergrenadier-Regiment 21.

Once night had fallen, the sky was filled with the familiar sounds of the enemy's nocturnal airforce which consisted mainly of wooden biplanes whose engines sounded like sewing-machines. The German troops had many names for these planes such as 'Duty Sergeant',

'Sewing-machine', 'Coffee-grinder' and 'Leukoplastbomber'. All the nicknames were disparaging yet these small aircraft – often piloted by women – caused a lot of grief amongst the Germans, and their nightly appearance denied much needed rest, not to mention inflicting some damage. And on this night, they wounded the two top brains of Division staff: General von Lenski and Major von Menges. The biplanes, searching out bunkers and staffs located in the gullies and plains west of the city, managed to drop a few small bombs around the command post of 24. Panzer-Division. General von Lenski and Major von Menges were standing outside when the bombs exploded and suffered a few light shrapnel wounds, which were quickly bound. Both men resumed their duties soon after.

Casualties:

2 officers wounded

- Generalmajor Arno von Lenski (Division Kdr); (Wounded but stayed with the troops)
- Major i.G. Otto-Wilhelm von Menges (Division Ia); (Wounded but stayed with the troops)

2 men wounded

1 man missing

- Unteroffizier Rudolf Mühlbauer; PGR21 (Missing in action)

Decorations bestowed from 26th October to 1st November:

22 Iron Cross First Class
209 Iron Cross Second Class

Prisoners and booty taken from 26th October to 1st November:

2 airplanes
3 tanks
10 anti-tank rifles

2nd November 1942:

At first light, the complete misery and indescribable chaos of the shattered factory was revealed to the grenadiers of Gruppe Below. Their defensive line began immediately south of Hall 10, a relatively small workhall that consisted of a large, single-storey work area with vast glass windows and skylights that ran the length of the roof, buttressed on its southern end by a three-storey brick construction[1] that contained offices, lunchrooms and stairwells. After months of protracted bombing and shelling, all windows had been shattered, the corrugated iron roof had been shredded and in many places, the masonry walls bore gaping wounds from shells. The interior was a tangled mess of twisted girders, derelict machinery, shards of glass and smoke-blackened walls, and through all this ran the German defensive line currently held by Kompanie Roth of 79. Infanterie-Division. The men of Panzergrenadier-Regiment 26 held the northern end of Gruppe Below's line, crouching in foxholes beneath the shadow of Hall 10. As long as 79. Infanterie-Division held the hall, they were secure, but if the Russians retook it, they were in immediate danger of being outflanked, cut off and captured. Close in front of them were the huge oil-tanks used as a staging area for many enemy attacks. The line then turned to the west, the backbone of this sector being based on a single railway line that ran into Hall 10. The line then crossed four railway tracks – the main artery of the factory – turned back to the north to avoid the enemy-occupied Hall 8a, and curved to the west to the strongpoint formed by Hall 8 before veering to the south-west.

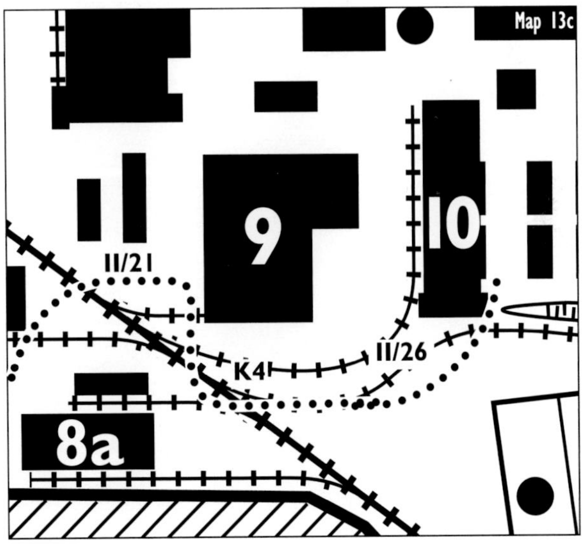

So, apart from a lucky few who maintained positions in the relative safety of Halls 8 and 9, the bulk of Gruppe Below held defensive positions out in the open. Foxholes and trenches were dug in the undulating terrain, utilising whatever cover was available: a stretch of railway line, shattered railway wagons, piles of unfinished gun barrels, a crater. They had been able to improve their positions during the night but they were still not satisfactory. Most of the men were unable to move during daylight hours for fear of being picked off by a sniper and until a continuous line of trenches – with communication trenches to the rear – was completed, it would remain so. Nevertheless, the men sat in their positions and watched the dawn break over the depressing, bleak battlefield, their breath visible in the crisp morning air, but they were thankful that there was no rain. The bitter cold that clung to foxholes and trenches among the mangled workhalls was hard enough to bear.

1. The single-storey work area and the three-storey office were the same height.

MARK

Hall 8, part of the defensive positions of Panzergrenadier-Regiment 21 in the Krasny Oktyabr factory.

The war diary of the Division laconically noted the following about the new sector: "The sector, with extremely tangled factory ruins, giant craters, frequent Russian activity, small distances between both opposing fronts and our own negligible combat strengths, proves to be difficult."

In the morning, another schwadron of Panzer-Abteilung Winterfeld was subordinated to a foreign unit. This time, a panzer schwadron consisting of 7 panzers was sent to 305. Infanterie-Division to support the infantry in local attacks. The abuse of valuable armoured assets continued.

In the afternoon, a Russian reconnaissance patrol crept out of the fuel installation and managed to get within twenty metres of Gruppe Below's front-line, on the south-west corner of the factory near Hall 10. A hail of grenades was the first sign of the Russian intruders. Fortunately for the Germans, they were able to react and launched their own barrage of hand-grenades, both sides then opening up with their submachine-guns. With their heavier MG-34's, the men of Gruppe Below held the upper hand and after throwing a few more grenades, the Russian patrol withdrew.

Casualties:

2 men killed

- Unteroffizier Josef Endres; PGR21 (Killed)
- Obergefreiter Paul Gentzig; PGR21 (Killed)

1 man missing

- Gefreiter Erich Schnick; PGR21 (Missing in action)

3rd November 1942:

The command of the employed Panzergrenadier Abteilungen, led by Oberst von Below, would be taken over on 4th November by Oberst von Scheele, Commander of Panzergrenadier-Regiment 26.

At 1300 hours, the Division issued Divisionsbefehl Nr. 82, a supplement for the defence of the southern area of the Steel Factory. The bulk of the order consisted of mundane issues, such as protocol for submitting morning and evening reports, lines of communication and the use of correct maps. There were a couple of important points relating directly to the defensive positions, the most relevant to the grenadier in the trenches also being the most self-evident: where possibilities existed, the positions must be bolstered by mines. There was also some heartening information for the men of Gruppe Below: the strengthening of defensive forces had already been ordered by moving mortars to firing-pits close behind the forward positions. A further reinforcement of heavy mortars was to be strived for. The grenadiers at the front needed all the assistance they could get. Further help came from I./Grenadier-Regiment 212 (without its 3. Kompanie), subordinated during the day to Gruppe Below.

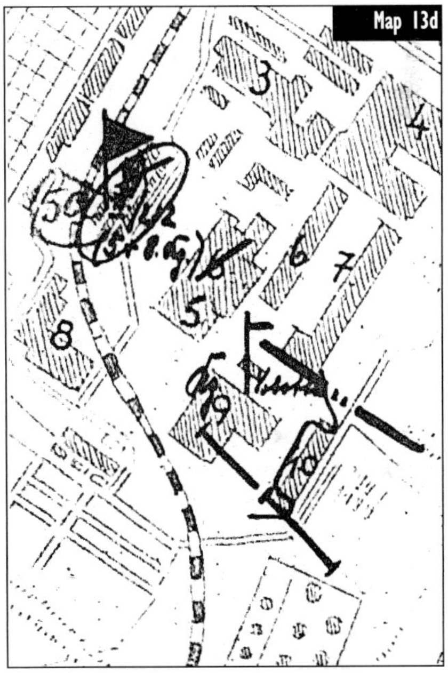

A 79. Infanterie-Division situation map clearly shows the Russian capture of most of Hall 10. Gruppe Scheele's sector began just south of there. Luckily for the grenadiers of Gruppe Scheele, the Russians were quickly pushed out of the hall by Gruppe Sobottka from 79. Infanterie-Division.

One point raised in Divisionsbefehl Nr. 82 was to ensure that enemy tanks knocked out directly in front of the main fighting line must be completely destroyed, otherwise the Russians would cart them off during the night, repair them and then redeploy them. It had been noticed over the past few days that Russian tanks involved in the vicious little probes and counterattacks were machines that had already been knocked out in previous encounters.

General von Lenski also issued another order during the day. It began: "On the basis of reports received, the use of gas by the Russians is possible. Therefore, all units are to implement an inspection as soon as possible on every unit with gas defence equipment."
It is unclear what reports General von Lenski received that caused him to issue this alarming order but it is interesting to see that after more than a year of savage combat on the Eastern Front – in which both sides had ample opportunities for an advantageous use of gas – the possibility of gas being used was still feared by the Germans.

Casualties:

2 men killed

8 men wounded (2 of those stayed with the troops)

1 man missing

- Oberschütz Otto Fichtner; PGR21 (Missing in action)

4th November 1942:

Daily, the Russians at least pushed forward with reconnaissance probes which could only be repelled in hand-to-hand fighting. Support by artillery close in front of the convoluted fighting line was barely possible, especially when Russian patrols were within hand-grenade distance. The probes caused Gruppe Below small – but persistent – casualties. Among the dead on this day was Obergefreiter Udo Moeller, part of the Abteilung staff of II./Panzergrenadier-Regiment 21.
In the morning, the command of Gruppe Below changed. Oberst von Scheele, Commander of Panzergrenadier-Regiment 26, assumed command of the combat group which now became known as Gruppe Scheele. Oberst von Below, freed up from this command position, headed to the rear area for a rest. Large portions of his Panzergrenadier-Regiment 21 were also in the rear area, integrating replacements and reforming shattered units.

At 1415 hours, the Division issued Divisionsbefehl Nr. 83 which ordered the formation of Gruppe Schwerin and the detachment of a schwadron as a Sturmkompanie. The troops were informed that on the anniversary of the Soviet Union's October Revolution, 7th November, large-scale Russian attacks could be reckoned on. Plied with copious amounts of vodka, the assaults were expected to be determined and fierce.
The Division's main objective stated in Divisionsbefehl Nr. 83 was to hold the current position. The divisional boundary on the right to 100. Jäger-Division was as follows: north-east edge of the farmstead in 53c2 – junction of the wide street from centre of grid square 52 to the west corner of the Steel Factory with the front-line – railway fork south-east of the Chemical Factory. The divisional boundary on the left was set to shift: in the night of 4th/5th November, it would be pushed to the north to take in Hall 10. From 0800 hours the next morning, the newly formed Gruppe Schwerin, headed by the commander of 79. Infanterie-Division, Generalmajor Richard von Schwerin, would assume tactical control over 24. Panzer-Division. Through this, the staff of the Division would be excluded for about a week and freed up for

other tasks. All tactical orders and reports from Gruppe Scheele would immediately go to Gruppe Schwerin. Independently of that command channel, Oberst von Scheele would also report daily to the staff of 24. Panzer-Division about the situation and future objectives.

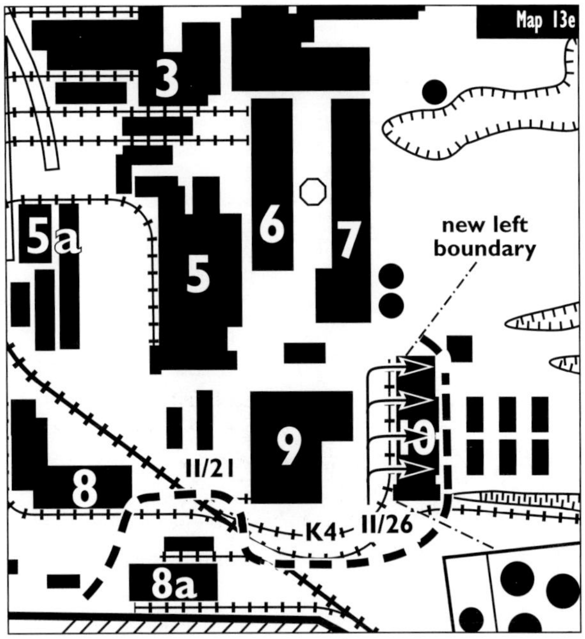

II./PGR26 takes over new positions in Hall 10

Gruppe Scheele, whose mission was unchanged, was made up of the following units:

- the combat-ready elements of Panzergrenadier-Regiment 21 and 26, and Kradschützen-Abteilung 4;
- Panzerartillerie-Regiment 89;
- Division-Reserve 'Schultze' (Alarm unit Panzer-Regiment 24, 3./Panzerpionier-Bataillon 40 without Panzerpionier-Zug); and
- a panzer schwadron of 10 panzers from Panzer Abteilung Winterfeld. This schwadron remained in the vicinity of Oberst von Scheele's command post.

All units not named above remained subordinated to and under the direct command of 24. Panzer-Division.

The sun dropped below the horizon in mid-afternoon and the dreadful darkness once again enveloped the gaunt framework of the Steel Factory's workhalls. Every now and then, a flare would spiral into the air, burst and gently swing to the ground under its parachute. The hollow rattle of a machine-gun would sound in the distance, sometimes followed by the dry crack of rifles and the thud of a hand-grenade. Then silence. To the grenadiers, this was just the normal nocturnal symphony of Stalingrad. And they hoped it stayed that way. They did not want any heavy enemy attacks – they never wanted any – but particularly not on this night. By 2300 hours, the grenadiers of Panzergrenadier-Regiment 26 were scheduled to leave their foxholes and move north, occupying defensive positions actually inside Workhall 10. Details of the takeover had been worked out by their superiors at the command post of Grenadier-Regiment 212 (in grid square 53a South). The unit of 79. Infanterie-Division due to be relieved in Hall 10 was Kampfgruppe Sobottka, with a strength of 2 officers, 14 NCO's and 91 men.

The quarter moon was waning and did not cast a lot of light, so all movements were carried out in darkness. Once the veil of darkness had fully covered the factory, preparations for the relief commenced, the beginning for it being reported to 24. Panzer-Division with the codeword 'Metall'. Almost all the front-line forces of Gruppe Scheele were affected by the lengthening of the Gruppe's sector. Panzergrenadier-Regiment 26 had the biggest task but the other two units were forced to spread out to fill the vacuum created by the shifting of Panzergrenadier-Regiment 26. An orderly timetable had been worked out for when a particular squad or platoon would leave its trenches and trudge north-east through the rubble. Panzerartillerie-Regiment 89 once again placed a defensive barrage in front of Panzergrenadier-Regiment 26 up to the new left divisional boundary. Covered by the noise of the bombardment, the men of Panzergrenadier-Regiment 26 moved through the smashed edifice of Hall 10, forewarned by 79. Infanterie-Division that any loud noise would immediately bring down a hail of Russian mortar fire. Once they reached the allotted position, the bone-weary men of Kampfgruppe Sobottka – relieved to see their replacements – hoisted themselves out of the defensive positions and headed for a rendezvous point further west in the factory grounds. By 2300 hours, the relief had been successfully carried out without a single casualty. It had been a complete success. The codeword 'Metall' was once again sent to Division HQ to report the favourable conclusion of the operation.

Together with the order for the relief, Gruppe Scheele had also been ordered to form a Sturmkompanie. This would be accomplished by relieving a schwadron of II./Panzergrenadier-Regiment 26, and the details of its formation were contained in an appendix to Divisionsbefehl Nr. 83. It stated that before 7th November, Panzergrenadier-Regiment 26 would form a reinforced Sturmkompanie with a strength of about 150 combatants (including a squad of pioneers), equipped with heavy machine-guns and heavy mortars. At the same time, 14. Panzer-Division and 79. Infanterie-Division would be forming Sturmkompanien of their own. It was foreseen that these three heavily equipped units would be subordinated to 100 Jäger-Division for an attack in about a weeks time.

The composition of the Sturmkompanie was as follows:

- a Kompanietrupp (command troop) with the Commander (Offz.), Kompanietruppführer (Uffz.), 8 messengers and a medic.
- three Stoßzug (assault platoons), each consisting of:
  a platoon commander (Uffz.), Zugtruppführer (Uffz.), 3 messengers and a medic
  three Gruppen (squads), each of 1 Unteroffizier and 7 men.

This equals 1 officer, 17 Unteroffiziere and 83 men. There was also a heavy machine-gun squad, a heavy mortar platoon, an anti-tank gun and a 10 man pioneer squad. All up, around 150 men. The core of the Sturmkompanie came from the originating schwadron, together with older soldiers that had not yet been supplied to boost combat strengths and young replacements. To get the headcount up to 150, it was thought possible to hold back people, possibly from schwadrons that were no longer being refreshed and still had a strong core. In addition to that, there was the pioneer squad of 10 men.

The formation was planned to be in assault squads. For each squad, there would be 1 light machine-gun, the rest of the squad carrying rifles, submachine-guns, hand-grenades, explosives, Russian trench periscopes, smoke pots and smoke grenades. The squads of the Sturmkompanie were equipped as follows:

squad commander:	submachine-gun, 2 hand grenades
rifleman 1:	machine-gun, 1 50-round drum magazine, pistol, 2 hand grenades
rifleman 2:	pistol, 4 drum magazines, 1 300-round ammunition can, 2 hand grenades
rifleman 3:	rifle, 2 300-round ammunition cans, 2 hand grenades
riflemen 4-5:	rifle, each with one bag of 8 hand grenades
rifleman 6:	rifle, 1 concentrated charge, 2 hand grenades
rifleman 7:	rifle, 1 bag with 6 smoke grenades, 1 smoke pot, 2 hand grenades

Ammunition was distributed as follows:

for each rifle:	100 rounds
for each submachine-gun:	6 magazines
for each pistol:	2 magazines
for each light machine-gun:	10 50-round drums and 2 300-round ammunition cans
for each heavy machine-gun:	12 300-round ammunition cans
for each soldier:	2 hand grenades

A 3.7cm anti-tank gun was assigned, in addition to heavy mortars and heavy machine-guns, and two rifle grenade launchers would be supplied to this Sturmkompanie by Panzerpionier-Bataillon 40. Missing equipment would be gathered from the Regiment but requests for ammunition would be expedited by submitting them directly to Division. The squad of pioneers would be supplied as an intact unit from Panzerpionier-Bataillon 40, kitted out with specialist equipment for house-to-house fighting, including flamethrowers. This squad would be supplied to the Sturmkompanie early on 6th November and there were strict instructions for its use: it was only to be employed as an intact unit. The pioneers would not be dispersed amongst the grenadiers.

The man chosen to lead this formidably armed and equipped unit was Oberleutnant Eberhard Beyersdorff, Schwadron Commander of 6./Panzergrenadier-Regiment 26. He'd arrived as a replacement on 8th September and in the following two months had earned a reputation as a tough fighter and an excellent leader, precisely the qualities needed for an assignment of this type.

Casualties:

2 men killed

- Obergefreiter Udo Moeller; PGR21 (Killed)

5 men wounded (3 of those stayed with the troops)

5th November 1942:

In the morning, the Schwadron of II./Panzergrenadier-Regiment 26 that had been designated as the framework of the Sturmkompanie was extracted from the Steel Factory and sent back to a forming-up area. Throughout the morning, men that had been assigned to this new company arrived in dribs and drabs, other larger groups arriving in lorries from the rear areas far to the west. There was not much time for the unit to train and bond together: the deadline for completion of training was the evening of 7th November. The focal point of the training was 'Assault troop combat in cities', practiced in ruined villages in the training area. General von Lenski said: "The reinforced Sturmkompanie will be oriented about their forthcoming assignment in house-to-house fighting and the importance of their gallant task will be made to clear to them..."

On this day, in accordance with an order from 6. Armee, a directive was issued for the disbandment of Panzergrenadier-Brigade 24 staff which would take place on 8th November 1942. Officers of Brigade staff freed up by the disbandment would be placed at Division's disposal with the exception of Oberleutnant Erwin Bernhardt, whose future employment was still being decided. A list detailing the ranks, names, functions and units of the men of Brigade staff was sent to Division and upon this basis, a decision would be made as to where each individual would be transferred within the Division. The men would take their personal weapons with them. The centrepiece of the Brigade's vehicles, the Sdkfz. 251/6, a halftrack equipped with powerful communications equipment including radios and an Enigma machine, would be handed over to Panzer-Nachrichten-Abteilung 86. All vehicles and motorcycles would go to Werkstatt-Kompanie 3/40 for repairs and an inspection, and a list with each vehicle's description, its condition, license plate, engine and chassis numbers would be passed on to Division, who would then reassign the vehicles. All vehicular replacement parts, spares and accessories would be given to the workshop companies. It was a sad day for the 70 men of Brigade staff. Since the summer offensive began on 28 June 1942, they had performed well. Their commander, Oberst Freiherr von Broich, had commanded various Kampfgruppen and always emerged victorious from the toughest battles. He received the Knight's Cross at the end of August and this proved the worth of the Brigade staff. Now, with the panzergrenadier regiments reduced to a few men, the days of large-scale attacks gone and Oberst von Broich transferred to another assignment, the Brigade staff no longer served a useful function. And the men knew it. It was only a matter of time before they were reassigned to other duties but they did not expect it when it happened. When Oberst von Broich left on 1st November, a replacement had been announced. Oberst Hans-Joachim von Horn[2] from 7. Panzer-Division had been ordered to report to Stalingrad to take over the Brigade. Why transfer a new commander if they were to be disbanded? An order from 6. Armee, however, ordered 24. Panzer-Division to disband the Brigade. No records exist to confirm whether Oberst von Horn actually arrived in Stalingrad, but it is doubtful that he ever set foot on the tortured soil of the city.

Casualties:

None

6th November 1942:

The battle units of the Division fighting in the Krasny Oktyabr Steel Factory, now known as Kampfgruppe Scheele, had a quiet night and morning. Artillery and mortar fire fell sporadically on the Kampfgruppe's sector, occasionally rising to a heavy barrage but as long as the Russians did not launch a ground attack, the night was referred to as 'quiet'.

At 0940 hours, however, the Russians renewed their attacks on Hall 10 with an initial assault by a large stormgroup. Directly east of Hall 10 was a group of six small buildings[3] and a gully on the right that led directly down to the Volga. Skirting the southern edge of this gully was a small spur railway that branched off the line supplying Hall 10. The Russian assault squad emerged out of this gully and the southernmost house, charging toward the eastern façade of Hall 10, concentrating on entering the three-storey section on its southern end. In the pale morning light and the milky haze that hung over the entire city, the grenadiers saw dozens of

2. See appendix for full career details.

3. Called 'Häuschen' or small houses by the German troops.

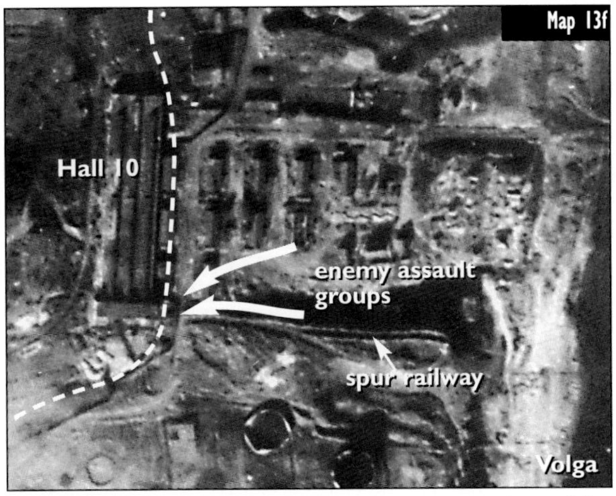

Russian assault on Hall 10. The enemy stormgroups emerged out of the gully to attack the southern end of the hall.

shadowy figures moving towards them and there was no mistaking what their intentions were. Hall 10 had been a focal point for enemy attacks over the past week. The grenadiers aimed their machine-guns and rifles at the murky silhouettes. Ammunition cans were opened next to the machine-guns and stick-grenades were primed, leaving the porcelain knob hanging out of the hollow handle. A gentle command to fire was given and the machine-guns ripped into the attackers. The Russian stormgroup returned fire and lobbed grenades which exploded harmlessly along the face of the building. The grenadiers retaliated with their own volley of grenades, causing more injury to the Russians already caught in the open. One or two courageous Russians tried to restart the stalled assault but as soon as they stood up, they were nailed by eagle-eyed riflemen. With this, the attack faltered and the Russian stormtroop, dragging their dead and wounded, withdrew into the gully. The attack had been successfully repulsed in 15 minutes. The size of the enemy group was estimated to be no more than 30 men. The enemy stayed quiet for the rest of the morning.
Preliminary casualties were as follows:

PGR21: 1 man wounded
PGR26: 2 men wounded
1 Hiwi killed

Mid-afternoon, the clouds broke over Stalingrad and a heavy rain fell on the city. The grenadiers crouched in their miserable foxholes and strongpoints as the heavy drops drummed on their helmets, ran in rivulets down the mangled steelwork and masonry of the workhall, and soaked into the tortured soil. Water dripping from the twisted corrugated iron roof fell into puddles far below on the concrete floor, creating loud watery plopping sounds that echoed eerily through the dead building. Tarpaulins were hastily draped over foxholes or around bodies but the water still managed to find its way in. To make things worse, enemy mortar shells started crashing on the roof or slipping through the many holes in the roof to explode within the building. The grenadiers were forced to keep watch for stealthy Russian assault groups. And the rain continued to pour down. It was miserable.
Shortly after 1500 hours, a T-34 was spotted moving on the high Volga edge east of Hall 10. The report was quickly passed to one of Panzerjäger-Abteilung 40's anti-tank guns that were supporting the grenadiers. A swift change of position for the anti-tank gun put it in excellent position to cover the Russian tank if it continued to move on its presumed course. Sure enough, the tank appeared, the gun crew calmly went into action and shortly thereafter, the tank withdrew after absorbing a couple of rounds. No smoke was seen so it could not be reported as being totally destroyed.

At 1900 hours, an enemy attack in a strength of about one squad, again on Hall 10, was repulsed. Five minutes later, strong ferry traffic on the Volga was reported. Besides that, lively harassment fire by enemy artillery still fell on the Kampfgruppe's sector. At 2200 hours, another enemy probe against Hall 10 was repulsed. The Russians seemed determined to seize the workhall. It was only a matter of time before they gathered sufficient forces to oust the grenadiers.

Strengths:	PGR21:	5 Offz.	34 Uffz.	150 men
	PGR26:	3 Offz.	21 Uffz.	115 men
	K4:	3 Offz.	24 Uffz.	98 men
	Pz.Jg. 40:	5 Offz.	25 Uffz.	148 men
	Alarm Schultze	5 Offz.	14 Uffz.	104 men
	Pz.Pi. 40:	2 Offz.	3 Uffz.	25 men

Casualties:

1 Hiwi killed

10 men wounded (2 of those stayed with the troops)

2 men missing

- Obergefreiter Franz Ihling; PGR21 (Missing in action)
- Panzergrenadier August Lukrafka; PGR21 (Missing in action)

7th November 1942:

In the morning, Panzergrenadier-Regiment 21 reported that the enemy in front of Hall 8 was unchanged. In this right part of the sector, the enemy appeared to be relatively weak. Leutnant Walter Wroblewski, who'd arrived the previous day with the latest contingent of officer replacements from Insterburg, was immediately assigned to the Sturmkompanie on account of his experience, front-line knowledge and courage. He had been wounded in the early days of the summer offensive but now, after his complete recovery and some home leave, he was ready to rejoin his comrades in the front-line.

During the morning, General von Lenski paid a visit to his Sturmkompanie training in the rear area. The General stood next to his Kübelwagen and watched the squads practice assault troop tactics amongst the ruins of a small village. It seemed that within two days, the men from disparate units had bonded together effectively and General von Lenski was pleased with what he saw. He climbed back into his vehicle and headed back to the command post, passing numerous graveyards constructed alongside the roads. This set the General thinking. Once back at his command post, he dictated a message to a clerk for inclusion in the Division's daily order. In it, General von Lenski made special mention of a service that was rarely talked about: the burial of men killed in combat. He said: "I offer special recognition to the burial kommando of our Division, in particular the Division's catholic minister Göttke, for recently carrying out the burial of the fallen of the Division. In the shortest time, they have registered widely scattered individual graves, at times under difficult conditions, and buried the fallen at the Divisions' Heroes Cemetery.

"After burials have taken place, units are advised to ensure that every grave at the Heroes Cemetery is supplied with a wooden cross and, if possible, every individual grave will receive a wooden enclosure."
It was also announced in this Tagesbefehl that Rittmeister Gerhard Thiel would assume command of III./Panzer-Regiment 24 after the transfer of Major von der Lancken on 1st November 1942.

BUNDESARCHIV, BILD 146/78/92/15 / PHOTO: UNKNOWN

Rittmeister Gerhard Thiel

Throughout the early afternoon, observers in Hall 10 noted the gathering of substantial enemy forces (in 71a4 and 71c2) on the high cliff above the Volga directly east of their observation posts. The information was passed to an artillery liaison officer who transmitted the targets to his guns. At 1540 hours, the enemy of 180-200 men and 2 tanks were combatted and smashed by the artillery.

At 2130 hours, the Division issued Divisionsbefehl Nr. 84 concerning further intentions from 8th November. A list of LI. Armeekorps' upcoming operations were listed, as follows:

- the first was set for 11th November in front and north of the Gun Factory with 389. Infanterie-Division.
- the second was an assault on the Martin Furnace Hall (Hall 4) in the north-east sector of the Steel Factory, scheduled to start some time after 14th November.
- the third was an attack on the Volga shore east of the Steel Factory with Gruppe Schwerin, to which Gruppe Scheele belonged.

Gruppe Scheele would remain subordinated to Gruppe Schwerin for the time being but it would support the attack east of the Gun Factory on 11th November. The Sturmkompanie was allocated to 389. Infanterie-Division, being brought forward to the Division's command post in Gorodischche on 8th November. It would be formally subordinated upon its arrival when Oberleutnant Eberhard Beyersdorff, Sturmkompanie Commander, reported himself. The Sturmkompanie was only tactically subordinated to 389. Infanterie-Division: it would still draw supplies from its parent division.

Casualties:

2 men wounded

8th November 1942:

Apart from artillery harassing fire, nothing special happened in the morning. On the right wing of the sector, held by Panzergrenadier-Regiment 21, lively rifle fire descended on the defensive line and whipped into the strongpoints located in Halls 8 and 8a but it was not followed by an enemy attack. Bombing attacks fell on the forward line and rear area. Casualties suffered by Panzergrenadier-Regiment 21 due to the bombing were 1 killed and 3 wounded. One deserter came over to the Regiment. Panzergrenadier-Regiment 21 also lost one of its most capable and bravest Schwadron Commanders courtesy of a shell in one of these bombing attacks. Oberleutnant Dittmar, Commander of 6. Schwadron, known as the 'Bunker King', was wounded. His loss struck the Regiment particularly bitterly because 6. Schwadron was scheduled for a main role in a forthcoming attack to capture the 'Tennis Racket'.

At 1345 hours, an enemy spoiling attack (20 men) on Hall 10 was repulsed. One tank (type not identified) was shot into immobility by a s.I.G.[4] of 10./Panzergrenadier-Regiment 26.
Final casualties for Gruppe Scheele on 8th November:
Panzergrenadier-Regiment 21 = 1 man dead, 1 officer and 3 men wounded
Panzergrenadier-Regiment 26 = 3 men wounded

Casualties:

1 man killed

- Obergefreiter Alfred Drosdzewski; PGR21 (Killed)

1 officer wounded

- Oberleutnant Ludwig Dittmar (Schwadron Kdr); 6./PGR21 (Wounded)

6 men wounded

- Obergefreiter Kurt Goldacker; PGR21 (Wounded but died later in the day)

Decorations bestowed from 2nd November to 8th November:

33 Iron Cross First Class
135 Iron Cross Second Class

Prisoners and booty taken from 2nd November to 8th November:

17 prisoners (of those, 6 were deserters)
1 airplane
2 anti-tank rifles

4. Schwere Infanterie-Geschütz, or heavy infantry gun, a short-barrel 150mm gun assigned directly to a heavy support company in the grenadier regiments.

9th November 1942:

Hauptwachtmeister Rubbel of 7./Panzergrenadier-Regiment 21 reports: "It began to dawn. The Stalin Organs had already played their last verse. This time, it was only three. Punctually, as always, appearing from the east shore of the Volga came the obligatory Russian 'sewing-machine' aircraft, also know as U.v.D. (Unteroffizier vom Dienst – Duty Sergeant), and employed several flares suspended under parachutes over the 80 metre width of no-mans-land. The wind drove them to the Russian side and a few jokers over there fired at them with tracer ammunition. The 'U.v.D' probably deduced: 'Whoever does not want the light must be the correct recipient' and threw his bombs on the Russian positions, apparently with success because to our profound amusement, awful swearing sounded from there."

The enemy was quiet on the right wing. On the left wing, however, an enemy attack in a strength of about 200 men began at around 1215 hours against Hall 10. A small group of the enemy assault force succeeded in penetrating the building. A couple of grenadiers were overwhelmed in the positions but the bulk of the men in that sector were able to abandon their strongpoints, pull back and maintain an elastic defence around the enemy intrusion while the other men of II./Panzergrenadier-Regiment 26 repelled the rest of the enemy stormgroup. A shoot-out developed at close range. Amongst the piles of corrugated iron, girders, bricks, machinery and shattered concrete, both sides lobbed grenades and sprayed each other with machine-guns. The Russians were numerically weaker and managed to put up stiff resistance. A counterattack headed by a couple of experienced Unteroffiziere, however, pushed into the small enemy bridgehead, blasted the Russians with a flurry of grenades and overwhelmed them. A few enemy survivors jumped out of the windows and fled to the east, under cover-fire from their heavy weapons. The old front-line was re-established and the grenadiers occupied their old strongpoints. II./Panzergrenadier-Regiment 26's casualties were 1 man killed, 1 Uffz. and 1 man wounded, and one medium anti-tank gun lost to a direct hit from a bomb.

At 1545 hours, another weak enemy attack on Hall 10 – not carried out with the same gusto as the midday attack – was also repulsed. A menacing spectre was spotted by observers high up in Hall 10: four Russian tanks[5] were moving up the gully east of Hall 10, no doubt for offensive actions against Gruppe Scheele. One of the Russian tanks got itself into trouble when it slipped into a gigantic crater, and despite all its exertions, there it remained.
Exactly 112 Russian flights were counted during the night alone. The thermometer sank to minus 15° and from this night on, remained below freezing point. An ice-cold wind whistled over the steppe and through the ruins of the city.

Casualties:

1 man killed

4 men wounded

-5. Reported as KV's but more likely to have been T-34's

THE CLOUDS GATHER

CHAPTER FOURTEEN

10th November 1942:

The course of the night passed quietly for the infantry with the exception of heavy air activity. The temperature during the night was absolutely freezing and in the morning, the piles of iron and rubble – in fact everything – glistened under a thin layer of frost. The deep blue sky heralded a sunny and clear day. Since the previous night, the enemy had been strengthening himself on the entire sector in front of Panzergrenadier-Regiment 26. Increased ferry traffic was heard.

At 0730 hours, a violent barrage dropped on Hall 10 and its surrounds, placing a curtain of fire between Panzergrenadier-Regiment 26's sector and the rest of the factory. Five minutes later, out of the fuel installation area and along the railway line, several enemy assault groups rushed toward the southern end of Hall 10. There were at least several hundred Russians. The barrage lifted as soon as the assault groups left their starting areas. The grenadiers hardly had time to raise their weapons over the parapets or poke them through loopholes before the tide of Russians washed over the defensive line. A couple of bursts from machine-guns toppled a few Russians but the fighting quickly degenerated into vicious hand-to-hand combat. Groups of grenadiers, cut off by the advancing enemy, held out until their ammunition was depleted, some fighting to the death with their bayonets and spades while others hid amongst the rubble, waiting for the immediate danger to pass before they found their way back to their comrades. The attack was directed on Hall 10 and also simultaneously towards the south-east front from out of the oil tanks along the railway line. Forced back by the pressure of the attackers, the grenadiers around the southern end of Hall 10 scampered back to reserve

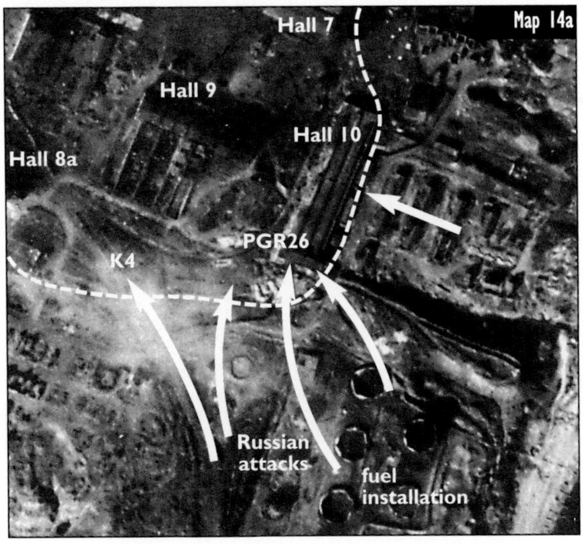

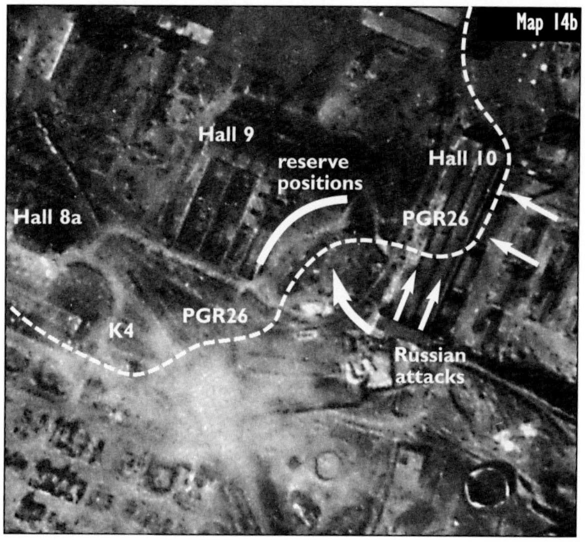

positions between Halls 9 and 10, fighting all the way, and the Russians penetrated into the southern three-storey end of Hall 10, occupying the vital stairwells within. After an hour of gruelling combat, around 0845 hours, the enemy attack was finally halted. The defensive line south-west of Hall 10, in the open ground between Halls 10 and 8a, was held by a few determined squads from II./Panzergrenadier-Regiment 26 and Kradschützen-Abteilung 4, successfully repelling all attacks. In the northern part of Hall 10, the remainder of II./Panzergrenadier-Regiment 26 continued to repel enemy assaults from the east but they had been forced to bend their southern defensive line to the west, out of the western façade of the workhall to join up with the reserve positions that now formed the front-line. They now defended against enemy stormgroups entering the shambles of the factory floor through the two doors coming from the three-storey southern wing. All these assaults were fought off. At 0945 hours, the enemy renewed his attack just as II./Panzergrenadier-Regiment 26 was preparing a counterattack to retake the southern end of Hall 10. The counterattack groups were forced to repel the enemy attack, which they successfully did, but at the expense of the planned counterattack.

While the attack on the previous day was only reconnaissance without substantial enemy artillery support, the enemy artillery support on this day was strong. As a result of the simultaneous attacks from the east and south-east, it was necessary to bring assault groups into action but for all that, the southern stairwell of Hall 10 was still lost. The enemy garrison was estimated to be 30-40 men. Since particularly high casualties arose, no assault groups could be employed during the enemy attack to retake the stairwell. The front-line generally remained in German hands but the enemy lay in front of Panzergrenadier-Regiment 26 within hand-grenade distance. Throughout the day, as forces were gathered for a conclusive counterattack, repeated enemy attacks forced these reserves to be used to defend against the attacks rather than straightening out the enemy penetration. Six times this day, the enemy threw in attacks with 200 and 300 men, the last one at 1800 hours. The Germans were incapable of launching the counterattack. Because of the rigorous German defence with its assault groups, the enemy was unable to expand his initial success. The recapture of the stairwell was scheduled for 0340 hours on the next day.

In the fighting on this day, an assault group assembled under the command of Oberwachtmeister Hans Krafzik[1], who returned to Panzergrenadier-Regiment 21 on 29th

1. Oberwachtmeister Hans Krafzik survived Stalingrad and eventually won the German Cross in Gold on 28th April 1945 while commanding Reiter Schwadron 16./40.

October with a transport of convalescents[2] from Panzergrenadier-Ersatz-Abteilung 413, particularly distinguished itself as a fire-brigade.

Despite all adversity, a healthy sense of humour still existed in the rubble of Stalingrad. With effect from 1st November 1942, Unteroffizier Raaf in 7./Panzergrenadier-Regiment 21 was promoted to Wachtmeister. In addition to two Wachtmeister stars, Hauptwachtmeister Rubbel sent him the following letter:

> "10.11.42
>
> Dear Raaf![3]
> First of all, my sincere congratulations for your promotion to Vize[4]. Until the procurement of Swabian stars, I send you two Prussian ones for now. I also enclose a couple of cigars for you.
> To close, I wish you all the best. Please give your squad[5] my kindest regards, and to you again.
>
> Yours, L.R."

At the end of the day, Gruppe Scheele had the following operational panzers: 1 Panzer III kz, 6 Panzer III lg and 1 Befehlswagen. It also had 15 Pak 5cm and 7 heavy self-propelled anti-tank guns.

Casualties for Panzergrenadier-Regiment 26:
- 1 officer killed, 2 officers wounded
- 3 Uffz and men killed, 19 Uffz. and men wounded
- 2 men sick

Casualties for Panzergrenadier-Regiment 21:
- 1 man killed, 6 Uffz. and men wounded

Casualties:

1 officer killed
- Leutnant Alwin Festerling (Abt OO); II./PGR26 (Killed)

11 men killed
- Gefreiter Bruno Glusinski; PGR26 (Killed)

3 officers wounded (1 of those stayed with the troops)
- Leutnant Eichler (Schwadron Kdr); 8./PGR26 (Wounded)
- Leutnant Reinhard (Zug Kdr); PGR26 (Wounded)
- Oberleutnant Rost (Schwadron Kdr); 3./Pz.Pi.40 (Wounded but stayed with troops)

---

2. Krafzik was wounded on 6th July 1942 while trying to take a bridge outside Voronesh, suffering serious wounds after being struck in the right shoulder by three bullets. While waiting to be transported to hospital, Oberst Lengerke took an Iron Cross First Class from the chest of Oberleutnant Pachnio and awarded it to Krafzik for his courage and daring while trying to seize the bridge.
3. Wachtmeister Friedrich Raaf. Born 25th May 1920 in Urach bei Reutlingen. He won the Iron Cross First Class on 2nd October 1942, Knight's Cross on 18th January 1945 and German Cross in Gold on 20th January 1945, the last two while commanding 7./Pz.Gren-Rgt. 21.Survived the war. Died 14th March 2002 in Bad Urach.
4. Short for Vizefeldwebel, a term used in the Imperial German Army from the First World War. It is used here as slang for Wachtmeister.
5. The original German says 'das ganzer Gewehr', literally meaning 'the entire rifle', an old-fashioned term for 'Gruppe', a squad of 10 men.

23 men wounded (10 of those stayed with troops)

11th November 1942:

Gruppe Scheele's northern neighbour, 79. Infanterie-Division, had been ordered to prepare an attack for the final suppression of the Krasny Oktyabr by taking the keystone of its defence, the Martin Furnace Hall (Workhall 4). Pionier-Bataillon 179, reinforced by the experienced pioneers of 24. Panzer-Division's 3./Panzerpionier-Bataillon 40, would conduct the assault and was employed in the following structure: 3./Pz.Pi.40 was on the right, 1./Pi.179 was in the middle and 2./Pi.179 was on the left, while 3./Pi. 179 followed up behind the centre. All together, the total strength of this assault group amounted to 120 men divided into 4 Keilen (wedges). Hauptmann Helmut Welz, Commander of Pionier-Bataillon 179, had overall command of this operation. Leading the panzerpioniers temporarily detached from 24. Panzer-Division was Oberleutnant Rost, complete with bandages after being wounded the previous day. His group had been designated Keil 1 (Wedge 1) and, as with all Keilen in this attack, had one assault group with 1 Unteroffizier and 8 men closely followed by a securing group with 1 Unteroffizier and 5 men. Following behind each Keil at a distance of about 50 metres was another assault group and securing group in the same strengths. The attack spearhead of each Keil therefore contained 4 Unteroffizier and 26 men. The squads were equipped with explosives, hand grenades, smoke-pots, flamethrowers, concentrated charges as well as submachine-guns, pistols and rifles. Directly supporting Oberleutnant Rost and his men were two 150mm infantry guns from 13./Infanterie-Regiment 208, controlled by a forward observer attached to the Keil and connected to the guns by telephone. Behind the 4 Keilen were the previous defensive troops who would wheel around and occupy any ground won by the pioneer assault squads. Between 0100 and 0200 hours, the assault groups reached the preparation areas, Keil 1 behind Workhall 3 and the other three Keilen along the railway line west of Workhall 4. Before 0250 hours, all assault groups had completed their preparations and moved forward to the actual starting positions for the attack. The tension mounted. The forbidding workhall looked menacing in the darkness and gloom of the destroyed factory. The initial barrage by German weapons was set to fall at 0355 hours but at 0340 hours, shells howled in and started exploding west of Workhall 4, on and behind the German lines. Unteroffizier Sepp Lanz, on the staff of Pionier-Bataillon 179, wrote: "Detonations trembled

Diagram of the distribution of the companies:

Keil 4	Keil 3	Keil 2	Keil 1
2./Pi.Abt. 179	**1./Pi.Abt. 179**		**3./ Pz.Pi. 40**
1/8	1/8	1/8	1/8
1/5	1/5	1/5	1/5

↕ 50 metres

2./Pi.Abt. 179	**3./Pi.Abt. 179**		**3./ Pz.Pi. 40**
1/8	1/8	1/8	1/8
1/5	1/5	1/5	1/5

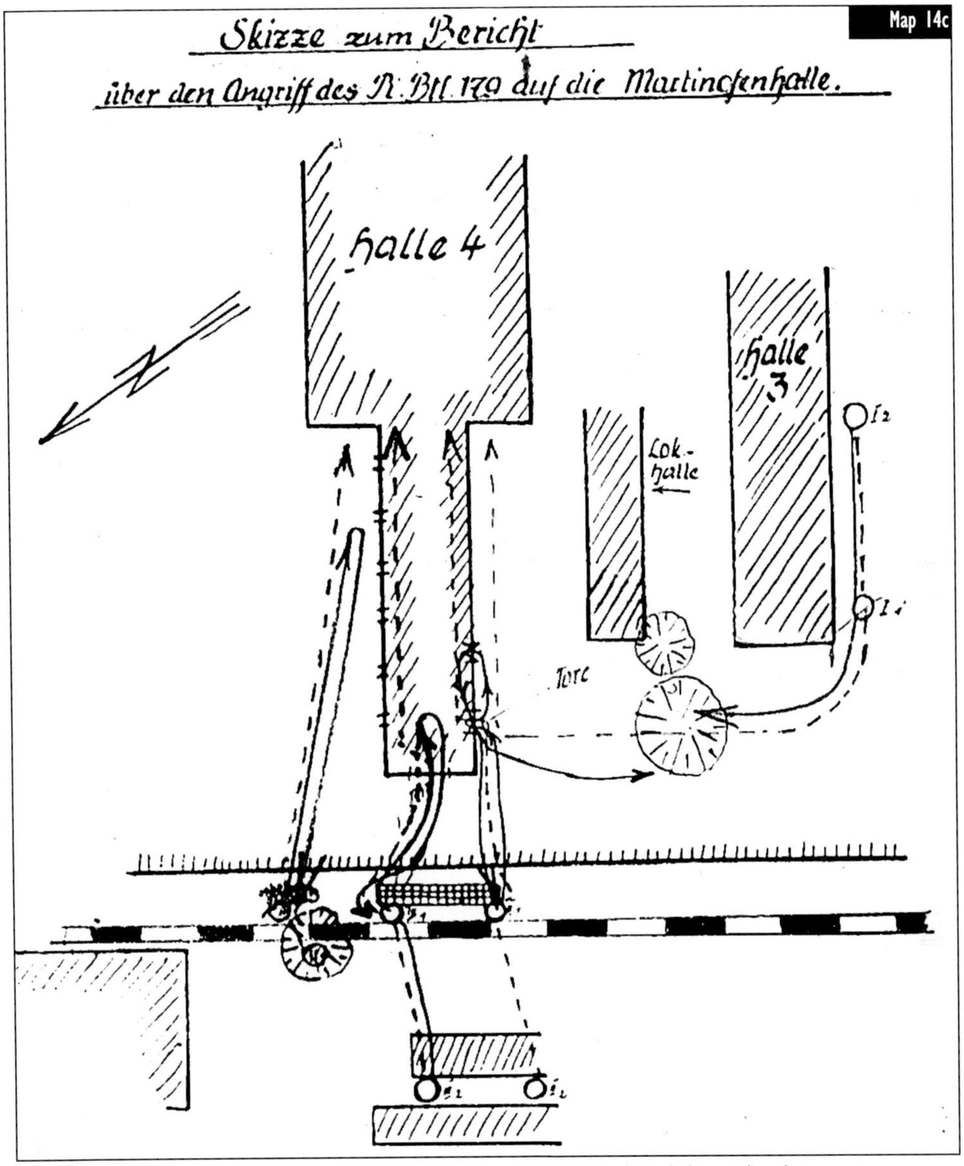

Attack on Hall 4. Dashed lines show proposed routes of Keilen. Solid lines show their actual path.

through the cellar. We looked at our watches. That couldn't be our barrage. No, thundering from the other shore of the Volga were the Russian guns. Heavy shells gurgled past us, on to the railway embankment. Ripping between them were mortar impacts. We were unable to discern their effect in the darkness. Had the Russians detected our preparations?"

Some of the enemy artillery shells impacted on the assault groups' starting positions. The spearhead of Keil 3 received a direct hit, one man being killed and four being severely wounded, while the back-up assault group of Keil 2 lost five men. With the primary spearheads weakened of men and equipment, the assault spearheads moved off.

At precisely 0355 hours, regardless of the Russian artillery fire, the German guns began their preliminary barrage. All infantry artillery guns assigned to support the attack – 14 in all – were scheduled to fire three shells. Once these had been fired, the troops moved forward. A Mörserabteilung (mortar battalion) equipped with the formidable 210mm guns placed heavy fire on the rear sections of Workhall 4 in an attempt to delay the arrival of Russian reinforcements. The barrage of German and Russian weapons raged to a hellish crescendo. To eliminate any Russian snipers, the guns of a 2cm flak platoon hammered the roof girders of the hall, their tracers whizzing over the heads of the advancing pioneers. The fearsome sound of large bullets rapidly striking steel plate cut through the din of the barrage and some of the troops could see the small flashes and sparks of the impacts as the hail of 2cm shells spattered amongst the roof struts. Oberleutnant Rost watched from the safety of a command post as his assault group moved off. Their starting position was in the shadows of Workhall 3, a comparatively safe position where they had avoided the Russian barrage. Now, however, they rounded the corner and headed toward Workhall 4, a sinister edifice of jagged girders and mangled ironwork. A road and railway ran along the southern edge of the hall and a Russian machine-gun nest was positioned where the road passed into the broad covered section of Workhall 4. Beneath a pile of red sand lying near this entrance was another enemy defence position and in a breach about 20 metres from the western corner of Workhall 4 was yet another enemy machine-gun post. Snipers were also perched in the remaining smokestacks. The assault group would have to expose its right flank to all of this but so far, their advance had not been noticed. Of the four Keilen, they had the largest distance to cover before they reached their objective. On their right was the ruins of the Locomotive Shed, a small building halfway between Halls 3 and 4, and in front of this building, a railway passed directly into the main section of Hall 4. On their left they could make out the dark shadows of the neighbouring pioneers struggling forward under thick enemy small-arms fire. Brief flashes from hand grenades briefly lit up the murky haze hanging over the factory. Suddenly, enemy machine-guns opened up on Rost's men, everyone immediately going to ground. Spurred on by the assault group commander, an Unteroffizier, they leapt up and sprinted forward a dozen metres before being forced to the ground. In these leaps and bounds, they managed to reach a giant crater at the western end of the Locomotive Shed, all 9 men of the assault group piling into it. The commanding Unteroffizier and two men were wounded. Every attempt to look over the crater rim was met by a burst of machine-gun fire. A volley of hand grenades landed just in front of the crater. The men could hear the furious fighting a few dozen metres ahead of them as grenades burst, concentrated charges exploded and flamethrowers – and men – screamed. The securing group was also stopped dead by the fire and took cover amongst the rubble at the head of Hall 3. A messenger was quickly sent to Oberleutnant Rost to report the impasse, who in turn sent a message to the commander of this operation, Hauptmann Welz. It simply said: "Assault group has not yet broken in!" The advance of Keil 1 bogged down in the crater and there it remained for the duration of the attack. It was simply not possible to advance into the violent machine-gun fire and expect to have any unwounded men, so the squads set up defensive positions.

The three other Keilen experienced initial success but once the enemy had overcome their initial surprise, they reacted with swift and ferocious resistance. Workhall 4 was a natural defensive position with numerous thick-walled casting containers, endless quantities of steel plate and a secure supply line back to the Volga, and it was also a nightmare for any attacker with a confusion of iron parts, remnants of walls, destroyed machinery, twisted girders and metal as well as general rubble that covered the entire area. The attackers were bewildered by the tangled mess in front of their eyes. The pioneer assault squads were simply not able to overpower the

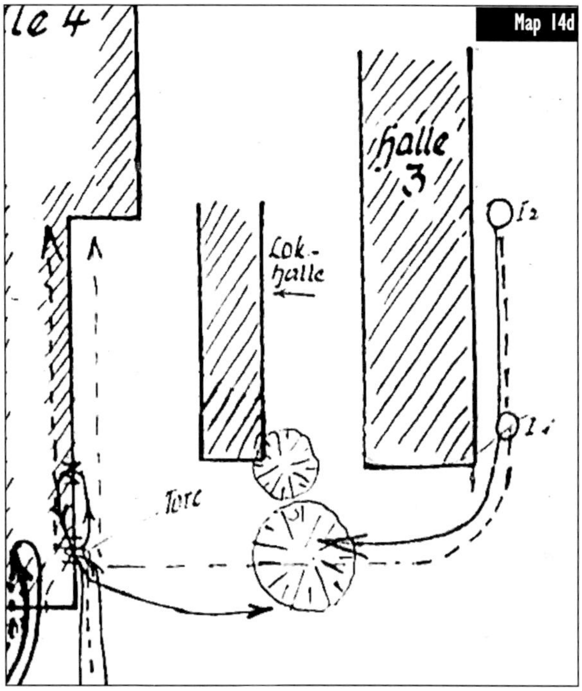

Gruppe Rost was supposed to reach the wall of Hall 4, then push along the wall to the east, parallel to the main attack. Due to intensive enemy defensive fire, however, they were forced to take cover in a large crater.

defenders but they tried and suffered serious casualties in trying to do so. Once the attack failed and the assault groups pulled back, the final tally was calculated: 1 Unteroffizier and 6 men dead, 12 Unteroffiziere and 26 men wounded, most of them seriously, 4 men missing and 5 men disabled with frostbite. Total casualties were 13 Unteroffiziere and 41 men. Oberleutnant Rost and his men considered themselves fortunate to come out of it with only 3 wounded men.

While Rost's pioneers were participating in this doomed assault, routine life in the Krasny Oktyabr continued for the men of 24. Panzer-Division. At 0230 hours, under deep cover of night, a weak enemy probe advanced from the southern corner of Hall 10 to the southern corner of Hall 9. The grenadiers spotted shadowy figures creeping across the shell-pocked no-mans-land, sent up a few flares and caught the enemy group in the open. A couple of machine-guns were sufficient to repel the Russians. It was quiet for the infantry, apart from the customary strong air activity. An artilleryman from Panzerartillerie-Regiment 89 was killed in one of these raids.

Having easily repulsed the enemy probe, the grenadiers formed themselves into assault groups in preparation for the recapture of Hall 10, safe under the barrels of a few panzers drawn forward in the morning hours to provide some solid support. The massive bulk of Hall 9 provided excellent cover for the pre-operation briefing and preparations for the assault, and observers installed in the roof and upper storey of Hall 9 kept the Russian-occupied Hall 10 under close scrutiny. The pale pre-dawn sky silhouetted the menacing squat figure of the hall. The left end of Gruppe Scheele's defensive line was still anchored in the northern end of Hall 10 and would provide a vital launching-pad for re-occupying the remainder of the hall. Listening posts strung through the workhall strained their eyes and ears, trying to peer and hear through the gloom and fog in the dim interior of the hall. The jumble of shattered machinery and intertwined girders provided dozens of hiding places and covered approaches and during the long night, excellent hearing was the best detection system. A spray with the machine-guns and the Russian intruders would scuttle off.

Just after 0630 hours, a flurry of mortar shells exploded in and around the southern end of Hall 10 and at exactly 0635 hours, the German assault groups, toting grenades, spades and submachine-guns, charged toward the hall. An assault group starting inside Hall 10 threaded through the wreckage, clearing a path with grenades and lashing any enemy movement with

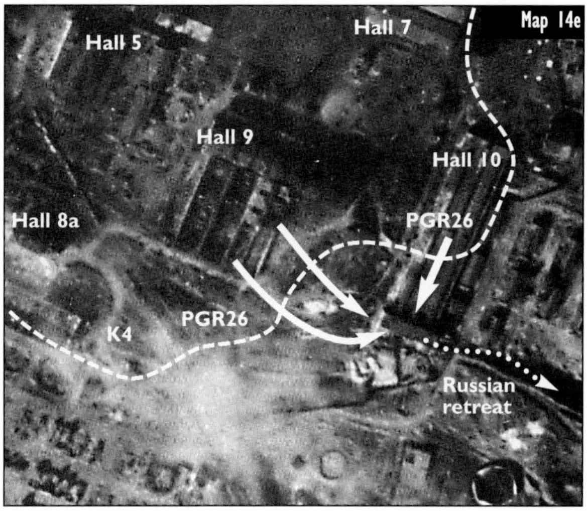

A German counterattack recovers Hall 10, captured the previous day by the Russians.

heavy fire. The Russian garrison was caught off guard, recoiled in surprise and withdrew into the three-storey section. The assault groups departing from Hall 9 quickly covered the scarred ground between the buildings and leapt into the windows of the three-storey section, taking the Russians in the flank and overwhelming them. The tough grenadiers swept through the devastated offices, suppressing the enemy with grenade and bayonet. The Russians knew they were beat and retreated at 0700 hours through the eastern windows into the gully east of the hall. The assault squads were triumphant!
There was no complacency amongst the victorious grenadiers, for they knew the Russians would launch immediate and vicious counterattacks. And they were right. Not long after they established hasty defensive positions, a group of Russians surged out of the gully and charged towards the hall. After the German recapture of the hall, a couple of panzers had driven forward and sited themselves on the flanks of the building. They were in an excellent position and commenced firing on the enemy, pumping high-explosive shells into the mass of yelling enemy soldiers. Muzzle flashes rippled along the defensive line. The counterattack faltered and the Russians pulled back into the gully. Continuous enemy counterthrusts were repulsed with panzer support and all points of penetration were straightened out, ending at 1400 hours with the old forward line firmly in the hands of Panzergrenadier-Regiment 26. New strong enemy counterthrusts were reckoned on. Heavy movements and prisoner statements confirmed an enemy concentration east of Hall 10 and the oil tanks.

In the afternoon hours, the enemy flew over the rear area with several machines and dropped bombs. Apart from a blockading barrage on the railway line west of the Steel Factory, strengthening enemy harassment fire with Stalin Organs was placed up to the edge of the city. Günter Koschorrek, still training with other newly-arrived replacements, recalls the conditions in the rear area: "It had become cold but it stayed dry. Overnight, frost formed on the grass, looking like fine filigree. There was movement in the air every day. Our bombers flew to Stalingrad. We recognised the belt of Russian anti-aircraft fire by the many small explosion clouds in the sky. I climbed out of the bunker for sentry duty with a pal. Like every night, a supply lorry returned from Stalingrad. They unloaded two dead and three wounded. An Oberwachtmeister was severely wounded. They loaded the wounded into an ambulance that took them to the main dressing station.
"We had never had to face the dead. They were always buried at a pre-determined place. I'd already seen the many wooden crosses a few days ago when we drove past for combat training…
"When I went back to my bunker after sentry duty, my spot on the straw was taken. A Landser from Stalingrad lay there. I could barely see his face. It was covered by a stubbly beard, his cap

almost covered his eyes and the ear flaps were pulled down. He slept deeply, without snoring. Occasionally, he jumped as if in a bad dream. I lay down on Kurat's spot, who had relieved me."[6]

Casualties: PGR26: 1 Uffz. and 4 men killed, 16 men wounded
PGR21: 2 men killed
K4: 1 Uffz and 3 men killed, 3 men wounded
PAR89: 1 man killed

Casualties:

12 men killed

- Unteroffizier Joachim Schulke; PGR26 (Killed)
- Stabsgefreiter Gerhard Lüdecke; PGR26 (Killed)

26 men wounded (3 of those stayed with the troops)

12th November 1942:

The stable enemy situation allowed the night to pass peacefully for the infantry, but there was continuous lively air activity and well-placed enemy artillery harassment fire. During the course of the morning, individual enemy probes were repulsed with hand grenades. Further continuing strong movement was observed on the Volga shore from posts perched high in the roofs of the workhalls. The rear area lay under constant heavy enemy artillery fire, mostly medium calibre.

Enemy attacks at 1000 hours and 1348 hours on the southern point of Hall 10 with strengths of 40 to 50 men were repulsed in close combat. Heavy enemy movement between Hall 10, the west shore of the Volga and the oil tanks suggested a new concentration of reinforcements, which was confirmed through prisoner statements, the enemy opposite the right wing of Gruppe Scheele also being reinforced by an anti-tank rifle battalion which was distributed to the single battalion of 117th Rifle Regiment.

The reported enemy artillery harassment fire strengthened towards 1420 hours and concentrated on the supply roads on the city edge. There was no enemy air activity during the day. Despite the suspension of the repeated strong enemy attacks on the left wing of Gruppe Scheele, it seemed that future enemy attacks would be concentrated on this sector, so continued assaults were reckoned on. In general, the sector was quiet. For the time being, no attack intentions were discernible. The forward line was firmly in German hands. Enemy dead amounted to about 45 men.
An example of the depleted manpower of the units is shown by the trench strength of Panzergrenadier-Regiment 21 submitted on this day to Division. Figures in brackets are the authorised strengths: 6 Offz. (70), 47 Uffz. (433), 168 men (1934).

Far away in the homeland, a member of the Division, recovered from his wounds and leading a training course, received a letter from the desk of General von Lenski located deep in

6. From the book 'Vergiß die Zeit der Dornen nicht' by Günter K. Koschorrek; v. Hase & Koehler Verlag 1998.

Stalingrad. Rittmeister Heinz Kolczyk, severely wounded by an anti-tank rifle bullet exploding in his back on 29th August, was teaching tactics at the Schule für schnelle Truppen in Krampnitz, Berlin. A week earlier – on 5th November – he'd received the German Cross in Gold for deeds performed during the summer campaign. His Division back in Stalingrad also heard about the award and that was what prompted General von Lenski to send a note to Kolczyk on his personal letterhead. It said:

> "Dear Kolczyk!
> "The news reached us today saying that you've been awarded the German Cross in Gold by the Führer. In the name of the Division and in my name, I express acknowledgment and the highest thanks to you for this high award. Hoping this news contributes significantly to your recovery, we wholeheartedly wish you all the best. We would be delighted if we could welcome you here again one day.
> "With best wishes, Yours sincerely,
> v. Lenski"

Unknown to General von Lenski, Rittmeister Kolczyk had already recovered from his serious wounds and he never did delight the General by turning up at his command post in Stalingrad.

Casualties:

7 men killed

- Obergefreiter Heinz Ferber; PGR26 (Killed)

36 men wounded (18 of those stayed with the troops)

1 man missing

- Obergefreiter Otto Konetzki; PGR21 (Missing in action)

13th November 1942:

Apart from combat with hand grenades, strong artillery harassment fire on the positions and supply roads and slackening of air activity, the course of the night passed quietly on the entire sector.

The course of the day also passed quietly, apart from the following minor incidents: several probes with hand grenades near Hall 10 were repulsed with minimal casualties; a weak enemy probe near Hall 10 at 1100 hours was repelled with artillery fire; twelve enemy fighter-bombers bombed the rear area at 1130 hours and strafed the approach roads with onboard weapons; artillery harassment fire lay on the forward line only during the morning; an enemy attack with 60 men on Hall 10 at 1530 hours was repulsed. Casualties were comparatively light: Panzergrenadier-Regiment 21 had two men wounded, Panzergrenadier-Regiment 26 had six while Panzerjäger-Abteilung 40 had one.

Unteroffizier Ketelsen, the gun commander from 4./Panzergrenadier-Regiment 26, noted in his diary: "13.11. The night was quiet. Overnight, severe cold set in, we are forced to heat through the night. In the morning, the enemy used his strengthened Organs and artillery. Toward midday, 6 bombers and 4 fighters arrived and dropped bombs about 100 metres from us, so that the bunker shook. Our heavy bombers drew over the Volga and bombed continually. Only individual Stukas bombed ahead of our line."

Perhaps at this point it would be interesting to delve into the nightly routine of bringing rations to the front-line troops, an important but underrated function. And often a dangerous one, as shown in the following report by Günter Koschorrek.

> "From our Schwadron, there are only eighteen men still located at the front. The entire Regiment was concentrated into a Kampfgruppe and was always employed where it was necessary. Still, as far as possible, the daily supply of rations and ammunition took place. In addition to the cookhouse chap, Unteroffizier Winter, the medic and two drivers always went with the vehicle. As carriers for the food pails, two volunteers were sought each time. Küpper and I had already appointed ourselves yesterday because it went by bunkers and our bunker was next in line.
> When it was already dark, we left in a Steyr 70 personnel vehicle with a roof and in a 1 1/2 tonne Opel Blitz with four-wheel drive, equipped with a tarpaulin. We drove into the darkness with weak march lighting. The cookhouse chap knew the way but he said that in Stalingrad, he was not sure of the front-line because the front, amongst the ruins of the city, changed from hour to hour. Since yesterday, our men should lay in the sector of the so-called Tennis Racket. The Russians defended a chemical factory there and had formed a bridgehead.
> 'We must ask our way through', Unteroffizier Winter said to us.
> Well, come on! – We can only hope that we find it as quickly as possible.
> We now drove on a highway guided only by moonlight. Vehicles came towards us or overtook us. On the right side was the railway that ran from Kalach to Stalingrad. A bit behind Voroponovo railway station we turned to the left and after a few kilometres, were already between the first ruins of the city. We drove through flattened craters, over broken stones, dodged rubble and collapsed telephone poles. Thick, acrid smoke from smouldering fires took our breath, to the left and right of us lay burnt-out wrecks of various war equipment. Our driver drove slowly and always zig-zagged up to a small forest or park.
> We stood on a small elevation and surveyed a section of the city. Black smoke and smouldering fires. We felt the hot breath of Stalingrad in the air. A frightful spectacle! Rome must have looked the same when Nero let it burn. Only the howling shells and death-bringing explosions here were still infernally getting stronger. The further we pressed into the city, the closer the shells burst near us.
> 'The usual evening blessing from Ivan', said the medic.
> It was meant to sound amusing but it didn't succeed. He sat, like me, crouched down on several ammunition crates. I felt like my heart was pounding in my neck – anxiety mounted in me. There was a new noise in the air – it sounded like the rushing of a thousand birds. It intensified and came right down on us.
> 'Out! Stalin Organs!' yelled the medic.
> We leapt out of the vehicle under a burnt-out towing tractor. The roaring swelled and then the explosions crackled in front and around us, like fireworks. A fist-sized piece that looked like a bent piece of metal whizzed past my head and smacked into the ground near Küpper.
> 'Lucky', said the medic.
> Behind us, we heard screams and calls for a medic.
> 'A few from the flak position that we passed must have got it', said Unteroffizier Winter, leaping into a hole. "Let's go, we must continue on." We mounted up again.
> The Sanitäts-Gefreiter (medic) said that the Stalin Organ was a primitive rocket-

launcher mounted on an open lorry. The rockets were simply stuck on to rails and electrically ignited. They were not accurate…

We now drove very carefully… We met vehicles whose crews had the same purpose as us. Many loaded dead and wounded. They could only do this during night-time when Ivan had no view…

From below, tracers rose up and in front of us machine-guns rattled. I heard from the sound that they were Russian. A few hand-grenades exploded, we heard cries and stopped somewhere in the ruins. Unteroffizier Winter disappeared between remnants of walls and returned a few minutes later.

'Our people should still be in the same sector as yesterday', he said. The vehicles moved slowly and carefully. I saw two burnt-out Russian T-34 tanks. We rumbled past a large half-destroyed building, apparently a factory building. Against the background of fire, towering out of the ruins was the silhouette of a chimney, like a menacing finger in the sky. We stopped. While we unloaded, Russian artillery fired with heavy calibres precisely where we wanted to go. They also exploded near us. A tongue of flame behind us indicated that a vehicle had been hit…

We set off during a break in the fire. With Küpper, we carried three food containers whose covers were screwed down. In each hand a smaller one, the heavier one we carried together by the handle. We followed Winter, the medic and a driver, who was also laden with ammunition crates and cold rations. The other driver waited with the vehicles.

Ahead of us were craters, broken masonry, heaps of rubble. In the air was the howling of shells and the din of explosions. The skin on my head and back tightened with each impact. We moved in zig-zags, climbed over stones and beams, stumbled, lay on the ground, stood up and hurried on.

'Stay close together', croaked Winter.

He sat on an overturned steel pole and breathed heavily. We suppressed every coughing spasm in the throat. The wind blew cement dust from an explosion into our faces. Thick smoke from a half-extinguished fire made our eyes water.

In the blazing light of the fire, I saw figures running – several hand-grenades detonated. We pressed ourselves closely to the ground and waited. My nerves vibrated – anxiety mounted in my neck and tied up my throat. Küpper lay next to me and breathed deeply. In the flickering light of the fire, I saw his face like a jerking caricature. From the left came the gentle rattling of metal. Several crouching figures ran past us. Winter stood up and spoke to them. I recognised an officers uniform.

'We must go further to the right', he said after that.

We carefully crawled forward – then came an empty expanse. Churned up earth, blocks of concrete into which railway beams were inserted. Perhaps a former bunker destroyed by our aerial bombs. A long wall loomed out of the field of rubble at the other end. Three pillars still stood upright.

'They should be there somewhere', said Winter and pointed to the wall.

We didn't advance. Ivan fired like crazy on the churned up ground over which we had to go. Had he noticed us? We lay behind lumps of stone but the impacts came so close that I could feel the hot fire on my face and the muscles in my back were contracting together in convulsions. In front of us, flares hissed up, salvoes of rifle and machine-gun fire. Was Ivan attacking?

The banging slowly ebbed away. "Let's go, up to the wall!" called Winter quietly. We dashed through the confusion of stone, wire and iron parts. No-one was to be seen.

> We crawled along the wall – arriving at a cellar entrance.
> 'Who goes there?' came a voice out of the darkness.
> 'Supplies and ammunition', said Winter, kneeling in front of us.
> 'Fantastic pal, we already have a mighty hunger. Come in!' Winter disappeared down below but came straight back up.
> 'They're not ours. We must return and go back to the other end of the wall', he said angrily.
> 'Shit!' Küpper squeezed out, and I agreed with him.
> We met a few Landser at the end of the wall. Again, they weren't our people. We crawled on. Out of a hole came a bearded head with a pulled-down cap.
> 'Who are you looking for?' – 'Regiment 21', said the medic this time.
> 'Since this morning, they lie further forward in the ruins', said the bearded one and showed us the point with his hand.
> 'How far?' – "About two hundred metres', he said.
> We continued in this direction over rubble and charred beams... Küpper almost ripped my arm off when he dashed behind a block of rubble. I held the pail tightly and rushed behind him. The heavy burdens slowly hurt, the sweat already running into my eyes and sticking my shirt to my skin, even though it was so cold."

Koschorrek and the ration party continued forward, wondering where the front-line and their own men were located. It was a dangerous period. At any moment they could stumble through the porous front-line straight into the hands of the Russians. Koschorrek again reports:

> "Then suddenly, a call from somewhere, as if from the grave: 'Man, beat it from here! Do you want Ivan rushing for your throats?' I saw a helmet raise itself out of the rubble.
> 'We're looking for our unit', I heard Winter say.
> 'Which?' – Winter told him.
> 'No idea, we don't belong to that mob. But if it is them, the ones who got Ivan out this morning, then they lay no more than 50 metres further to the right in the large factory building. Make sure that you move off here, we're glad that it's still quiet here.'
> The head with the steel helmet disappeared again."

With a new direction, the ration party stumbled through the rubble but were forced to go into cover when heavy Russian artillery fire started falling.

> "... In a short break in the fire, we stumbled on, broken glass crunching under our feet, shadows leaping up. Flares immediately hissed up, sheafs of machine-gun fire pattered into the wall of rubble. We dashed on, the food canisters rattling against blocks of stone. Near us, a shadow stood up.
> 'Are you the food-carriers of 1. Schwadron?' came the question out of the darkness.
> 'Is that you, Domscheid?' asked Winter back.
> 'Of course, I've been waiting here for you for over two hours to guide you.'
> We felt a stone fall from our hearts. Domscheid was an Obergefreiter. He told us that this morning, a counterthrust was carried out and that they were now located a bit further forward in the factory."
> Winter told Domscheid of the trouble we had finding him and that he was extremely worried we would pass through the German lines into enemy hands.

'It's already happened', said Domscheid. 'Last night, four people from 79. Infanterie-Division landed directly near Ivan with rations and ammunition. During our counterthrust this morning, we only found empty containers in the rubble – no trace of the Landser.'

We crawled behind Domscheid, flares occasionally going up from both sides. I stumbled and smashed the canister against a metal rail – a loud noise. A Russian machine-gun started rattling nearby, several flares illuminated the night. Ivan was right nearby! – We lay flat, the shots scorching over my head and crashing into a concrete block. The plaster trickled into my collar and mixed itself with sweat. I rolled forward and pulled both pails behind the block. Küpper had also let go of his pail and pulled it into cover. He lay a couple of paces forward behind a protective wall. I wanted to go to him and make a movement forwards – until I fell into an empty space, into a black hole. Hands reached for me and helped me up.

'Not so hasty', said a deep voice. And then: 'Where did you come from all of a sudden? We wanted to wallop you, so you were lucky.' Domscheid told him.

'My goodness, you had to use this street here? Ivan keeps bothering us here.'

'Two hours ago, I passed by here and Ivan was further forward', said Domscheid.

'Of course, but not since an hour ago. Max, do you have your sprayer ready?' asked the deep voice.

'Sure, like always', came the answer.

'Good, then we can give you cover fire. You can get through over the street behind us. – Now, let's go!'

With the first burst of fire, we dashed off. Küpper was quicker and pulled me along by the arm which held the other handle of the food-pail. Ivan fired back like crazy. Then his artillery also fired with their heavy pieces. Every now and then, I heard the 'plop' of mortar shells. The shells rushed down and exploded around us. The spell of fire suddenly attacked us like a rapacious animal and we hid ourselves in a half-destroyed cellar. I ducked with every impact and thought that the cellar would collapse and bury us. The earth vibrated over us. This must be what an earthquake is like, I thought. My nerves fluttered. Never had I imagined at any time that I could have so much anxiety in my life.

Near me sat the driver and the medic, on the other side Unteroffizier Winter and Küpper. Küpper was deathly pale and all of us stared at the ceiling which already had a little crack in it. Domscheid had the best nerves, standing near the entrance and scouting up to look outside. For Küpper and myself, these few hours in Stalingrad definitely dampened our concept of war, besides which we still had not once had our own contact with the enemy, as someone already said. My thoughts now only circled around how and when we could get out uninjured. We'd already been en route here in the disastrous city of rubble for hours and still hadn't reached our unit.

I heard, as Domscheid said from the entrance, that Ivan was firing on the smallest movements with heavy pieces. When our machine-guns started to rattle, they surely believed that it was an attack that ought to be nipped in the bud.

Then at last, a break in the fire – it seemed like an eternity to me. We jumped up, Domscheid knew the way. He steered us to a factory ruin knowing that there, someone lay in cover and observed everything. He already gently called out the password from afar and called his name. We moved up to a half-blocked cellar entrance. Domscheid led us through an entrance into a room, in front of whose entrance leaned a loose iron plate. Through the wide gap, I saw two Hindenburg lamps that roughly illuminated the room.

Domscheid made a comical gesture: 'Won't you come into our new command post.' On the ground lay a lot of sacks and rags on which lay two coiled-up Landsers, another sitting on a couple of stacked up ammunition crates. Frightened by the noises, both Landser stood up and helped us to carry the pail into the room. They looked damned tired, who knew when they actually got their sleep, I thought. I could barely recognise their faces under the dirt and stubble...
Then a Wachtmeister came in, greeted us and shook hands with Winter... He told Winter that this morning, the last officer of the Kampfgruppe had fallen and he'd taken command of this sector. The men here lay in the ruins to the front and to the sides. It went back and forth, and no-one knew exactly where the actual front-line was. Also today, there was again one dead man and two wounded that were already on the way to the dressing station.
The sheer insanity was here. 'Still only hand-to-hand combat in the ruins and Ivan often sits only 20 or 30 metres, hand-grenade throwing range, in front of us. Barely 300 metres in front of us is a deep gully that leads to the Volga shore. From there, he brings up new reserves every night. For days, we've all waited feverishly on relief or reinforcement and we slowly no longer believe in that.' He'd spoken the last sentence quietly to Winter but I could still understand it with my fine hearing. They therefore had their doubts. It made me pensive. The warm food and the coffee had become frozen in the meantime, even though the pails were double-walled and insulated. Nevertheless, Winter had brought a few solid alcohol and Esbit cookers to warm them up. The food was ice-cold but still not frozen hard. It was a beautiful thick noodle soup with a lot of tinned beef in it. Far better than we received in the bunker positions. The men here had more than earned it.
From outside, several Landser came in with mess-kits. They warmed the soup in the mess-tins and carried them out to the others. We were lucky at that moment. It was relatively quiet outside. I only heard an impact from time to time.
'Ivan also needs rest', a Landser said to me when I was wondering about it. 'But you can rest assured that like an 'Amen' in a church that the spectacle will begin again at daybreak. Then, you can't stick your head out a centimetre...'
Gralla was an Obergefreiter and surely an experienced Landser... As a former horseman, he'd already been in France and also in Russia for a long time. His chest was decorated with the Iron Cross Second Class, but still no wound badge. 'I've been lucky so far', he answered to my question. 'Hopefully, it'll stay that way', and then he added somewhat quieter: 'But here, I have a funny feeling that I will only get out with a Heimatschuß.[2]' He then gave me three letters with the request to give them over to the Spieß[3] for forwarding. Outside, the artillery again fired violently. Sometimes we felt the shuddering of the impacts in the cellar. Despite that, several Landser went in and out. I wondered why they were not disturbed by it.

2. Literally a 'home wound', an injury severe enough for the wounded man to be sent back to Germany for treatment.
3. Spieß, or 'spear', was the term German soldiers gave to the non-commissioned officer, usually a Hauptfeldwebel, who looked after the rifle schwadrons' rear area and relieved the company commander of matters not directly concerning combat. Also called the 'mother of the company', he was in charge of all paperwork, such as reports, orders, promotions etc., but also sent the sympathy letters written by the schwadron commander to the families of fallen soldiers. He also took care of the mail, maintained a fair schedule for furlough passes, oversaw the distribution of food supplies and looked after the front-line soldiers sent to the train for some rest by providing sleeping arrangements and bathing facilities. If it became necessary, he could also be called to the front to take over a command position, as was the case with Hauptwachtmeister Rubbel of 7./Panzergrenadier-Regiment 21.

'What's new?' the Wachtmeister asked one of them when he came in with a handful of empty mess-kits.

The Landser shook his head: 'Only the usual, Herr Wachtmeister. The artillery kicked up a fuss again. But Unteroffizier Seifert from the third asked if someone can bring his two packets of tobacco and a new pipe tomorrow. Everything should be in his backpack in the vehicle.'

Unteroffizier Winter nodded. 'You can tell him everything's in order. Say hello to Seifert for me.' Winter already had his book in hand and made a note.

In a corner of the cellar sat a Landser on a crate, sipping his noodle soup out of the mess-kit that he'd warmed up on one of the Esbit cookers. His face was half in the dark but I saw that it was sooty and covered with stubble. He wore a cap on his head that had the side flaps pulled deep over both ears. His hand trembled when he guided the spoon to his mouth and he stuck his chin out a bit so as not to spill anything.

I was wondering how old he could possibly be. He could not be older than thirty but he already looked like an old man. Every time a shell detonated with a hard crack on the concrete above us, he jumped so sharply that he spilled the contents of the spoon over his stubbly beard on to his filthy uniform jacket. With tired hand movements, he wiped it off, passed over his mouth with the back of his hand and wiped his sticky hand on his pants.

He had no sense for his surroundings. After he'd eaten, he began to roll a cigarette with shaky fingers. He did not succeed, ripping the thin paper again and again. I offered him one of my readies. He took it wordlessly and nodded a little with his head, without looking at me. While he blew out the smoke, his glance went up to the ceiling, again came down and brushed my face. For a moment, I saw in those dull, reddened eyes that he was staring through me into space.

Once, those eyes must have had lustre – once, but for this Landser, that must surely date back an eternity. One required no great knowledge of man to recognise that this fellow was a hollow wreck, a nervous, jittery creature that could collapse at any moment. The war had finished him and eaten away his nerves. I'd already heard that it happened. Here, I could see it with my own eyes. – What use was he at the front? Was he actually still capable of fighting? He belonged in the bunker position where one could employ him another way, I thought. Or at the same time in hospital for recuperation.

We talked about it with the driver. He agreed with me but told me that he had already been near the supply train a few weeks ago until his leave but because of a new Divisionsbefehl, he returned ten days ago with many others to Stalingrad. He was one of the oldest members of the Schwadron who'd been there from the beginning. He'd already received his Iron Cross in France when they were still riding. His name was Petsch and at the moment, he would be the oldest Obergefreiter on operations at the front."

The ration party safely returned from their night-time visit to the Krasny Oktyabr Steel Factory but it had been a shattering first impression of front-line conditions to young Günter Koschorrek.

Casualties:

1 man killed

10 men wounded (5 of those stayed with the troops)

14th November 1942:

The course of the night passed quietly for the infantry apart from enemy artillery harassment fire on the positions and approach roads. There was also weak air activity. Unteroffizier Ketelsen reports: "14.11. The night was quiet, there were no planes. In the morning, he got us with his Organs and artillery. He had us out of the positions, shooting in front and behind us with his mortars. You could barely raise your head during the day. In the evening, a lot of wood was chopped for the day. The Stukas and destroyers continuously bombed until evening."
An enemy probe conducted at 0450 hours in a strength of 40-50 men on Hall 10 was repulsed in hand-to-hand fighting. Casualties: Panzergrenadier-Regiment 26; 4 men wounded, Panzergrenadier-Regiment 21; 1 man wounded. Heavy movement and new tanks, three of which were detected, were reported eastwards of Hall 10 and the oil tanks. Four enemy aircraft flew through anti-aircraft fire at 1000 hours without dropping any bombs. Panzerartillerie-Regiment 89 suppressed four enemy batteries and a strongly occupied bunker near 61b1 (Hall 8), whose garrison wore German overcoats. The remaining course of the day passed quietly.

Casualties:

2 men killed

26 men wounded (13 of those stayed with the troops)

15th November 1942:

For the bone-weary grenadiers, the night passed quietly on the entire sector apart from negligible enemy harassment fire. As long as there were no Russian reconnaissance patrols, the men would bear the occasional, widely-scattered impacts from the enemy artillery. Even the Red airforce was behaving itself: no enemy bomber sorties were reported. Unteroffizier Ketelsen wrote in his diary: "15.11. The night was very quiet, there was nothing to be heard of the planes. Only sporadic rattling of machine-guns."
The previous day, three enemy tanks had been detected by forward observers. On this day, their presence was reconfirmed by the ominous sound of their engines being revved. They were apparently being driven back and forth along the shoreline but their exact location could not be aurally pinpointed because the echoes from their growling diesel engines bounced up the gullies, reflected off the Volga cliff and were moved about by the stiff breeze. To some of the grenadiers, it sounded like an entire tank brigade was warming up below the cliffs. A message was sent to all forward posts and observers to keep out a keen eye for any appearance of the tanks. Several probes in squad strength against Hall 10 were repulsed during the course of the morning but at 1530 hours, a strong enemy attack of 60-80 men was directed towards Hall 10. The Russians struggled forward under the withering small-arms fire and managed to get within hand-grenade distance, and once the attack stalled there, heavy German artillery fire was called down to completely smash the attackers. The large 105mm and 150mm howitzers of Panzerartillerie-Regiment 89 were not accurate enough for this precision work so the grenadiers own organic heavy weapons were used. Unteroffizier Ketelsen, commanding one of these heavy guns, jotted in his diary: "Within a quarter of an hour, we hammered him with 70 shells. His attack was repulsed. He also had no luck this time throwing us out." Caught in the open, the Russian assault force was totally smashed by the barrage, only a few of them managing to crawl back to the safety of a gully. It had not been a one-sided affair: Gruppe

Scheele had suffered its own casualties. Panzerartillerie-Regiment 89 fired on enemy movement near the oil tanks and the railway line, as well as suppressing two enemy batteries and one Stalin Organ. On the remaining sectors of Gruppe Scheele, the rest of the day passed quietly apart from enemy artillery harassment fire and infantry fire. The enemy had reinforced himself in front of the sector with newly arrived machine-guns. Unteroffizier Ketelsen's recollection for the rest of the day: "The artillery boomed the entire day until it was dark. But the Russians answered again. Our bombers and Stukas bombed continuously."

Casualties: PGR26: 2 men killed, 12 men wounded
PGR21: 1 Uffz killed, 1 man wounded, 3 men missing
Alarmein: 2 Uffz sick

Casualties:

7 men killed

- Gefreiter Paul Dörr; Pz.Pi. 40 (Killed)

30 men wounded (1 of those stayed with the troops)

3 men missing

- Grenadier Johannes Petersen; PGR21 (Missing in action)
- Gefreiter Josef Wagner; PGR21 (Missing in action)
- Panzergrenadier Otto Skwar; PGR21 (Missing in action)

Decorations bestowed from 9th November to 15th November:

17 Iron Cross First Class
108 Iron Cross Second Class

16th November 1942:

Unteroffizier Ketelsen of 4./Panzergrenadier-Regiment 26 wrote in his diary: "16.11. The night was quiet, there were no Russian bombers here. In the morning, around 0400 hours, he employed his Organs and artillery. The banging scarcely came to an end. Our bombers and Stukas bombed the artillery positions over the Volga. One could accurately observe his discharges. Have used up 160 rounds during the day, the entire night we had harassing fire."
Apart from this lively artillery fire and infantry fire from light and heavy weapons along the entire sector, there was no enemy ground activity, and enemy air activity remained weak. Casualties were light: Regiment 21 had four men wounded and Regiment 26 had two wounded. Five enemy deserters crossed into Gruppe Scheele's line. Panzerartillerie-Regiment 89 combatted two enemy rocket-launchers with great success, destroying one of them. The artillery also smothered a small enemy attack in 71a4 (east of Hall 10).

During the day, another ominous factor was added to the deteriorating German situation: the first snow fell. Not a heavy snowfall, only a light fall that dusted the mangled ruins and made life just a touch more miserable for the front-line fighters. What it represented was much more frightening: the first icy breath of the dreaded Russian winter, a harbinger to many months of bone-aching cold, knee-deep snow and renewed enemy resistance. And the most painful fact for the Germans was that the Russians had not been finished off and were still stubbornly holding their tiny bridgeheads in devastated Stalingrad. To the men on the ground, and particularly to the grenadiers of Gruppe Scheele holed up in the demolished workshops of Krasny Oktyabr, they knew this was where they would spend their winter.

During the course of the day, the Division issued Divisionsbefehl Nr. 86 for the requisition of another panzer schwadron. On 15th November, the enemy launched a heavy attack against 371. Infanterie-Division, located south of Stalingrad in the area of Kuperossnoye. Reconnaissance indicated that further attacks should be expected, so reinforcements were being garnered as a heavy-punching reserve, and 24. Panzer-Division was ordered to provide a panzer schwadron. The unit selected was Panzer Schwadron von Götz, commanded by the reliable and experienced Rittmeister von Götz, who'd only returned to the Division on 7th September after recovering from severe wounds suffered a year earlier as a regiment adjutant in 1. Kavallerie-Division. Rittmeister von Götz's orders were to report early on 17th November at the command post of Infanterie-Regiment 211 near the Brickworks in the southern Stalingrad suburb of Minina. He would immediately reconnoitre for counterattack possibilities and report his results on 18th November. Even though it was at the other end of the city, the Schwadron remained subordinated to 24. Panzer-Division and would report to it daily. The provision of the schwadron to another sector was just part of the continued misuse and weakening of the Division, provoking further grumblings amongst some of the Divisions higher officers.
At 2200 hours, the Division issued Divisionsbefehl Nr. 87 for the establishment of quick march readiness. The German command was preparing for an inevitable large-scale Russian counterattack and after the first snowfalls, they were pushed to move more quickly. Therefore, the armoured and motorised units of 6. Armee were ordered to prepare themselves for quick extraction from their current positions and be ready to be shifted for counterattacks and mobile defence.

Casualties:

1 man killed
- Unteroffizier Fritz Schröder; PGR21 (Killed)

7 men wounded (1 of those stayed with the troops)

3 men missing
- Obergefreiter Engelbrecht Schuhmacher; PGR21 (Missing in action)
- Panzerobergrenadier Ewald Adamy; PGR21 (Missing in action)
- Panzergrenadier Max Naumann; PGR21 (Missing in action)

17th November 1942:

Besides the usual enemy artillery harassment fire and infantry fire, the night passed quietly on the entire sector. Unteroffizier Ketelsen reports: "17.11. The Russian pilots had a good rest because they did not visit us last night. In return for that, however, he caught us early in the morning with his Organs and artillery. At 0800 hours, he placed a drumfire of artillery on us. Roughly half an hour long. After this had passed, however, one could accurately see where his batteries stood. We fired 50 shots of harassing fire during the night. Two Russian batteries were knocked out of the battle."
The course of the day passed quietly. The enemy placed strengthening artillery and mortar fire on the positions of Scheele's sector and the approach roads. Strengthening operations by Stalin

Organs were particularly noticeable.
Casualties during the day: PGR26: 1 man killed, 2 men wounded
PGR21: 1 man wounded

At 2200 hours, the Division issued Divisionsbefehl Nr. 88 for detachments for the assault of Gruppe Schwerin. This attack had been in the planning stages for some time. It was named Unternehmen Schwerin (Operation Schwerin) and its basic outline was for the northern half of Gruppe Schwerin to attack through to the Volga shore and hold a defensive line there. It was composed of three assault groups but 24. Panzer-Division would only play a minor role by supplying a panzer schwadron as a reserve for Gruppe Schwerin, its main task being to supply 3./Panzerpionier-Bataillon 40 to the southern attack group. Commanded by Major Schuchardt of Grenadier-Regiment 226, this Gruppe consisted of a Sturmkompanie each from Grenadier-Regiments 212 and 226, each with a platoon of pioneers from Pionier-Bataillon 179, and 3./Panzerpionier-Bataillon 40 with two platoons for bunker fighting expected on the steep Volga shore. The commander, Oberleutnant Rost, would report to Major Schuchardt at the latter's bunker in a gully in 63d1 early on 19th November. The assault was scheduled to begin on 20th November.

Casualties:

1 man killed

- Obergefreiter Franz Brix; PGR21 (Killed)

4 men wounded

18th November 1942:

Once again, the course of the night passed relatively quietly on the entire sector apart from artillery harassment fire and infantry fire. There was also no air activity. The grenadiers were becoming unnerved: why were the Russians so quiet?

The day was tolerably calm for the infantry. An enemy reconnaissance troop (strength 10-15 men) pushing along the factory railway from the south out of the oil tanks was easily repulsed in the morning hours. Strengthening enemy artillery harassment and interdiction fire lay on the positions, particularly on the right wing and on the approach roads up to the western edge of the city. New heavy calibre enemy guns were established. Panzerartillerie-Regiment 89 suppressed five known enemy batteries and one rocket-launcher on the east Volga shore, and also detected five new medium enemy guns. The anti-tank gun and panzer situation of Gruppe Scheele was unchanged. It still had 7 Panzer III longs, 2 Panzer III shorts and 1 Befehlswagen. Apart from the repulsion of the enemy reconnaissance probe on the right corner of Hall 10, the day passed quietly on the entire sector. The war diary of the Division remarked concisely about 18th November: "The day passed quietly. Further assault preparations to destroy the enemy north-east and east of the Steel Factory were carried out." On this 'quiet day', the crew of one of the two heavy infantry guns of 4./Panzergrenadier-Regiment 21 still employed close behind the forward line were knocked out by a direct artillery hit. With severe head injuries from shrapnel and burns, Gefreiter Steege reached the overcrowded dressing station outside the city with the other wounded men, survived a bombing the following day by low-level Soviet aircraft and about three weeks later, in intense snow flurries, flew out on a Ju-52 from the Kessel formed by the encircling enemy. Almost none of his companions in misfortune had this luck.

The corresponding schwadron in the other panzergrenadier regiment also had some bad luck. Unteroffizier Karl Ketelsen, commander of a gun in 4./Panzergrenadier-Regiment 26, wrote the following in his diary: "18.11. Planes were not there. He only fired strengthening harassing fire during the night with his artillery. But we also answered our enemy not badly this night. Toward 0600 hours, we received ammunition and 120 rounds. Toward 1300 hours, enemy scored 2 direct hits on our bunker so that half the bunker collapsed. Obergefreiter Lücke and Mülligens lightly wounded. We must leave our beautiful bunker. He fired with oil shells. A black day in the fire emplacements!"

Casualties: PGR26: 2 men wounded
PGR21: 1 man killed, 4 men wounded

Casualties:

1 man killed

7 men wounded (4 of those stayed with the troops)

- Gefreiter Steege; PGR21 (Wounded)
- Obergefreiter Lücke; PGR26 (Wounded but stayed with the troops)
- Obergefreiter Mülligens; PGR26 (Wounded but stayed with the troops)

19th November 1942:

During the night, enemy artillery and mortar harassment fire lay on the positions and approach roads but enemy air activity was negligible. Unteroffizier Ketelsen: "19.11. The planes left us in peace. We fired strongly the entire night. But his artillery answered us again. In the morning, he caught us with strengthening Organs and artillery."

On Scheele's entire sector, the day passed quietly for the infantry. A strengthening increase of artillery harassing fire was generally recognised. One light infantry gun (75mm) was totally destroyed by an artillery strike. Above all, the arrival of the heaviest calibre guns was noticed. Around noon, an enemy reconnaissance troop (20-30 men) that thrust against the southern corner of Hall 10 was repulsed. With the sheet ice on the Volga breaking up, boat traffic was observed during the course of the day. Increasing artillery harassment fire and Stalin Organs were further confirmed despite Panzerartillerie-Regiment 89's efforts in suppressing three enemy batteries. A forward observer from Artillerie-Regiment 179 called in fire from Panzerartillerie-Regiment 89 to plaster an enemy rocket-launcher, and succeeded in setting it on fire. Grenadier-Regiment 212 was warned by a deserter about an enemy attack at 1750 hours on Halls 10 and 7, to be carried out by 400-500 men that had been ferried over. Near darkness, ferry traffic was again able to be perceived by noises in strengthening proportions. At 1800 hours, Panzergrenadier-Regiment 21 reported an enemy attack in their sector to Oberst Scheele. Strength and details were sketchy to begin with but that attack, once again focusing on Hall 10 and the right wing of Gruppe Scheele, was repulsed. In the further course of the night, the enemy didn't repeat the attack and there was no air activity.

Casualties: 2 men wounded (PGR26)
1 man killed (PGR21)
5 men wounded (PGR21)
2 men wounded (Schultze)
1 man killed, 1 man wounded (K4)

20th November 1942:

At daybreak on the previous day, 19th November, 3500 massed enemy guns pounded the Romanian positions far to the west of Stalingrad. This was the beginning of the massive and much feared Russian counteroffensive. Aimed against the vulnerable flanks held by Germany's Romanian allies, the Russians gave themselves a great chance for success because with ten divisions lodged in the rubble of Stalingrad and half a dozen more strung back along the flanks from there, the German command had been forced to utilise their allies to hold the extended northern and southern flanks so that they could withdraw German units for participation in the assault on Stalingrad itself. Now, these Romanian soldiers were dying in their hundreds as their bunkers collapsed under the hammerblows of enemy artillery and then, at 0850 hours, Soviet forces attacked out of the Serafimovich bridgehead, aiming to the south-east, toward Kalach, where they would join hands with another army advancing from the south. It was the beginning of the end for 6. Armee in Stalingrad.

The men in Stalingrad were unaware of the momentous events unfolding around them. In his diary, Unteroffizier Ketelsen only noted the usual occurrences: "20.11. During the night, the highway U.v.D. was above us. Over the entire day, lively artillery and Organ activity. We fired over 200 shells during the day. Have knocked an observation post in a chimney out of the battle."

There is no mention in his diary of the sounds of distant gunfire but to the men who heard it, it was a disturbing sign that the situation had changed and the stakes were now higher than ever. Orders soon arrived throughout 6. Armee's units that they were to discontinue all offensive operations and be prepared to move out at short notice. If the rumbling in the distance did not set alarm bells ringing, this order certainly did.

For the men of 24. Panzer-Division, the battle now entered a gruelling and remorseless phase that eventually ended in an icy hell from which few of them would survive.

Officer Biographies

Appendix One

Achmann, Stabszahlmeister Gerhard; born 18 December 1904 Dettelbach/Main. Abteilung Zahlmeister I./Panzergrenadier-Regiment 26. Wounded on 16 September 1942. Died from these wounds on 17 September 1942 in Novi Rogachik. Posthumous promotion to Oberstabszahlmeister. Now buried in Rossoshka Sammelfriedhof (collective cemetery) in Block 26, Row 13, Grave 485.

Adamheit, Sonderführer (Z) Alfred; born 18 February 1901 Moscow. Dolmetscher (translator) on Stab 24. Panzer-Division. Transferred on 15 September 1942 from 24.Pz.Div. to Stab/4 Pz.AOK. Later became Dolmetscher in 297.Inf.Div. Listed as MIA 22 January 1943 in Stalingrad. Still listed as MIA. His name is on Cube 1, Panel 5 at Rossoshka Sammelfriedhof.

Ahollinger, Hauptmann Siegfried; born 10 February 1915 Dresden. Assigned as General Staff trainee to 24. Panzer-Division Stab. Transferred on 3 October 1942 from Artillerie-Regiment 377 to 24.Pz.Div. In hospital outside the Kessel but flown in early January 1943. Commander of Abteilung Kannegiesser from 8–20 January 1943, then Ib of the Division. Flown out of the Stalingrad pocket on 23 January 1943. Attended General Staff course in Berlin from 15 March–28 May 1943. Attached to General Staff on 1 June 1943. Became Ib of 83.Inf.Div. on 20 June 1943. Major i.G. RDA 01.12.43 (40). Also assigned to General Staff on 1 December 1943. Then Ia XXXVIII. Armeekorps on 20 March 1944. Appointed Ia 218.Inf.Div. on 25 August 1944. Survived the war. Died 4 March 2003 Köln-Weiß.

von Amsberg, Oberleutnant Helmut; Regiment Adjutant Panzerartillerie-Regiment 89. Wounded on 2 September 1942 but stayed with the troops. Again wounded on 3 September 1942 while in Oberst von Nostitz-Wallwitz's command vehicle. Survived Stalingrad. Promoted to Hauptmann RDA 01.01.44. In Division at the end of the war. Still alive in 2001.

Andreesen, Leutnant Hans-Helmut; born 15 March 1923, Mannheim. In IV./Panzerartillerie-Regiment 89. Peacetime unit was I./Artillerie-Regiment 20. Leutnant RDA 01.2.42 (1043a). Transferred on 20 October 1942 from Artillerie-Ausbilding-Abteilung 280 to IV./Pz.Art.Rgt.89. When Leutnant Geissler did not end up being transferred, his place was taken by Andreesen. Listed as MIA 23 January 1943 in Stalingrad. Still listed as MIA. His name is on Cube 2, Panel 5 at Rossoshka Sammelfriedhof.

Anstett, Oberarzt d.R. Dr. Claus; born 3 August 1914 Pirmasens. Abteilung Hilfsarzt I./Panzergrenadier-Regiment 21. Became I. Abteilung Arzt on 27 September 1942. Iron Cross First Class on 2 October 1942. Killed 13 December 1942 near Rychov.

Arndt, Pfarrer Erich; born 11 October 1912 Parchim. Kriegspfarrer IVd (ev.) Stab 24. Panzer-Division at establishment of Division. Wounded 1 August 1942. Sent back to a hospital in Parchim to recover but returned to the division shortly before the Soviet counteroffensive. Captured at Stalingrad. Founding member of all the Soviet-backed anti-fascist groups. Survived captivity and returned home in September 1948. Died 11 May 2012 Rostock, just 5 months short of his 100th birthday.

Arneth, Kriegstechniker Georg Friedrich; born 6 July 1908 Bamberg. Regiment Technischer Beamter; I./Panzergrenadier-Regiment 26. Wounded on 5 June 1942 but stayed with the troops. Missing in action January 1943 in Stalingrad. Still listed as MIA. His name is on Cube 2, Panel 12 at Rossoshka Sammelfriedhof.

Graf von Arnim-Boitzenburg, Leutnant d.R. Alard; born 25 February 1921 Boitzenburg. Zugführer in 6./Panzergrenadier-Regiment 26. Killed 27 July 1942 in Nizhne Chirskaya. Posthumous promotion to Oberleutnant d.R. Iron Cross Second Class on 12 August 1942. Today, probably buried as an unknown soldier in Rossoshka.

SPANNOCCHI

Oberleutnant Sigurd von Arnim in Rennes, France in April 1942

von Arnim, Oberleutnant d.R. Sigurd Alvo; born 16 November 1914 Schloß Kriebstein. Zugführer 1. Zug in 1./Panzer-Regiment 24. Killed 7–8 August 1942 northeast of Chir. Posthumous promotion to Rittmeister d.R. His body has not been recovered for burial in Rossoshka Sammelfriedhof. His brother Oblt.d.R. Allard was killed in an accident in Holland on 29 March 1945, while his 71-year-old father, Rittmeister (ret.) Erik, died in Soviet captivity on 10 November 1945.

von Aulock, Rittmeister Johannes Heini Maria; born 6 December 1915 Breslau; Regiment Adjutant; Panzer-Regiment 24; Regiment Adjutant at establishment of Division. Peacetime unit was Panzer-Regiment 2. Zugführer in 8./Pz.Rgt.2 on 03.01.1939. Applied to marry Eva-Ursula (or Ulla) Lancelle in early 1939 but request was turned down by the OKH. Permission was granted on 27 September 1939 and marriage took place on 2 October 1939 in Eger, Hungary. In May 1944 he is listed as married with two sons. Leutnant RDA 01.04.37 (392). Oberleutnant RDA 01.08.39 (380). Nennung im Ehrenblatt 28 July 1941 as Oblt. in Pz.Rgt.2. Wounded 14–15 October 1941. In hospital until 17 December 1941. On 30 December 1941 detached from Pz.Ers.Abt.1 to Pz.Rgt.24 with effect from 15 December 1941. Hauptmann RDA 01.02.42 (517). On 25 March 1942 this detachment was made permanent with effect from 18 February 1942. Chef 12./Panzer-Regiment 24 from 18 February 1942 until 1 April 1942. Became regimental adjutant 2 May 1942. Wounded 23 August 1942 in the attack that killed Oberst Riebel. In hospital until 5 January 1943. Detached from Pz.Ers.Abt.15 to Pi.Schule as an instructor of panzer tactics for an officer's course (Pz.Lehr.f.Offz.Lehrg.). Adjutant of Panzer-Brigade 100 with effect from 10 March 1943. General Staff training from 1 June 1943. Major RDA 01.02.44 (70a). Assigned to 118.Jäger-Division as Ib on 25 June 1944. Ic of 5. Panzer-Division from 27 June 1944 to 20 December 1944. Admitted to the General Staff on 1 August 1944. Appointed Ia VII. Panzerkorps on 20 December 1944. Survived the war. Died 9 June 1993 Johannesburg, South Africa.

Austinat, Stabszahlmeister Franz; born 10 February 1901. Regiment Zahlmeister Panzergrenadier-Regiment 21. Oberzahlmeister RDA 01.09.36. Regiment Zahlmeister Reiter-Regiment 1 from 1939–1941. Still with Pz.Gr.Rgt.21 on 23 January 1943, so probably captured at Stalingrad. Not known if he survived captivity.

Baaden, Oberleutnant d.R. Alois; born 27 June 1918. In III./Panzerartillerie-Regiment 89. Wounded on 25 August 1942. On 15 December 1942 he took over Alarmeinheit Heemsoth, which became known as Alarmeinheit Baaden. Listed as MIA 11 January 1943 in Stalingrad but he was in fact captured at Stalingrad. Survived captivity and returned home.

Baatz, Oberarzt d.R. Dr. Georg; born 5 June 1912 Naumburg. Abteilung Hilfsarzt III./Panzer-Regiment 24. Promoted to Oberarzt d.R. on 25 May 1942. Wounded 27 July 1942 but stayed with the troops. Missing in action 19 September 1942 when he drove into Russian lines while transporting wounded back to a rear-area hospital. Contemporary sources list him as MIA 22 August 1942 near Tsatsa. Regardless, he was in Soviet captivity, and died 5 January 1943 while being transported from Kamyshin to Oranki. He was buried in Kamyshin and his remains have not been recovered.

Bach, Leutnant, transferred from Panzerpionier-Bataillon 16 to Panzerpionier-Bataillon 40.

Bachler, Leutnant Willi; born 6 December 1916 Gr. Baitschen. Panzerartillerie-Regiment 89. Wounded on 2 September 1942 but stayed with the troops. Iron Cross First Class on 18 October 1942. Survived Stalingrad. Wound Badge in Silver. Promoted to Oberleutnant in early 1944. In II./Panzerartillerie-Regiment 89 on 1 August 1944.

Bade, Leutnant d.R. Gerhard; born 26 July 1915. Beobachtungsbatterie (Pz) 89 in Panzerartillerie-Regiment 89. Transferred on 30 September 1942 from Beobachtung-Ersatz-Abteilung 31 to Pz.Art.Rgt.89. Listed as MIA 1 January 1943 in Stalingrad. Not known if he survived captivity.

Balser, Leutnant d.R. Johannes; born 18 April 1922. Student. Leutnant RDA 01.02.42. Transferred on 14 September 1942 from Führerreserve OKH to Pz.Gr.Rgt.21 as a Zugführer in 5. Schwadron. Wounded on 27 September 1942. Survived Stalingrad. In August 1943 was a Zugführer in 8./Führer-Grenadier-Regiment. Transferred to the Führerreserve OKH on 8 December 1944.

Banser, Oberleutnant d.R. Edgar; born 23 July 1912. Führer Gr.Betr.Stoff.Kol.9/40. Listed as MIA 2 January 1943 Stalingrad. Not known if he survived captivity.

von Barner, Leutnant Claus Heinrich; born 2 October 1918 Trams. Dinafü 40. Killed 29 August 1942 30km north of Aksai. Now possibly buried as an unknown soldier in Rossoshka.

von Bassewitz, Oberstleutnant Barthold; born 19 August 1902 Jasnitz, Mecklenburg-Vorpommern. Kommandeur Panzer-Regiment 24. Married Hedwig Schroeder in 1929 and had one child. On 24 April 1942 left 24. Panzer-Division to attend the Panzertruppschule from 27 April–3 May 1942. While in OKH (Ag P1 – 3.Abt.), detached to Panzertruppenschule Wünsdorf, he was transferred to Pz.Rgt.2 for deployment as a battalion commander with effect from 1 June 1942. Took command of II./Pz.Rgt.2 (16. Panzer-Division) and assumed temporary command of Pz.Rgt.2 on 17 July 1942 when its commander, Oberst Sieckenius, was on sick leave. Left 16.Pz.Div. at beginning of October to take command of Pz.Rgt.24. Fell ill with severe jaundice in

December 1942 but refused to be flown out. Finally flown out on 18–19 January 1943. Promoted to Oberst 01.03.1943. Never promoted to General. Rest of the war spent as officer in OKH headquarters in Berlin. In French captivity from 1945–46. Died in 1992.

Bauchspiess, Oberleutnant d.R. Kurt; born 12 December 1906 Gumbinnen. Führer Kl.Kw.Kol. 3/40 (Kleine Kraftwagen Kolonne 3/40). Wounded on 26 September 1942 but stayed with the troops. Listed as MIA 1 January 1943 in Stalingrad. Not known if he survived captivity.

von Baum, Oberleutnant Manfred; born 20 December 1911 W.-Elberfeld. Regiment Ordonnanzoffizier Panzerartillerie-Regiment 89. Iron Cross First Class on 12 August 1942.

Bayer-Eynck, Leutnant d.R. Friedrich (Fritz) Ernst; born 8 January 1915 Osterwick. Abteilung Adjutant Kradschützen-Abteilung 4. Iron Cross First Class on 18 October 1942. Transferred to II./Panzergrenadier-Regiment 26 on 12 December 1942. Listed as MIA 4 January 1943 in Stalingrad but was in fact killed. Now possibly buried as an unknown soldier in Rossoshka.

Becker, Leutnant; Abteilung Ordonnanzoffizier III./Panzerartillerie-Regiment 89. Survived Stalingrad. Promoted to Hauptmann in early 1944. In mid-1944, he was transferred to a battalion commanders training course.

Becker, Leutnant d.R. Paul; Panzer-Regiment 24; Promoted to Oberleutnant on 24 August 1942. Survived Stalingrad. Chef Stabsschwadron Panzer-Regiment 24 on 15 July 1944.

Becker, Hauptmann d.R. Heinrich (Heinz); born 3 January 1898 Berlin. Transferred from Kraftfahrung-Ersatz-Abteilung 1 to 24.P.Div. as Führer Kraftwagen-Werkstatt-Kompanie 3/40. Listed as MIA 16 January 1943 in Stalingrad but was in fact captured. Died 4 June 1946 in Selenodolsk near Kazan.

Becker, Hauptmann d.R.z.V. Walter; born 11 July 1895 München. Führer Gr.Kw.Kol.f.Betr.Stoff 40. Became Führer gr.Kw.Kol.10/40 on 12 December 1942. Listed as MIA 24 January 1943 in Stalingrad. Not known if he survived captivity.

Beder, Leutnant d.R. Kurt; born 29 December 1919. Zugführer 2./Panzerpionier-Bataillon 40. Transferred from Pi.Btl.194 to 24. Panzer-Division in December 1942 when 94. Infanterie-Division was disbanded. Listed as MIA 23 January 1943 in Stalingrad. Still listed as MIA. His name is on Cube 5, Panel 6 at Rossoshka Sammelfriedhof.

Behrens, Leutnant d.R. Otto; born 1 August 1921 Braunschweig. Leutnant RDA 01.12.42. Zugführer 6./Panzergrenadier-Regiment 26. In June 1943 was a Zugführer in 9.(Flak)/Pz.Gr.Rgt.26. Killed 31 October 1943 near Ternovatka as and Oberleutnant d.R. His remains were unable to be recovered by the Volksbund.

Beischall, Leutnant d.R. Kurt; born 17 February 1917 Braunschweig. Chef Beobachtungsbatterie (Pz) 89 in Panzerartillerie-Regiment 89. Transferred on 15 June 1942 from Beobachtung-Ersatz-Abteilung 31 to Panzerartillerie-Regiment 89. Iron Cross First Class on 2 October 1942. Listed as MIA 10 January 1943 in Stalingrad but was in fact captured. Survived captivity and returned home. Still alive in 2013.

Belli von Pino, Leutnant Erhard Dietrich Anton Maria; born 9 January 1920 Hof. Abteilung Adjutant II./Panzergrenadier-Regiment 21 from 25 August 1942 and held this position until the end of the battle. Wounded on 27 September 1942. Promoted to Oberleutnant in January 1943. Listed as MIA January 1943 in Stalingrad but was in fact captured. Died 20 April 1943 in Frolov POW Camp from spotted fever.

MACARTHUR

Oberst Fritz von Below, Commander of Panzergrenadier-Regiment 21

von Below, Oberst Fritz Reinhold; born 16 December 1896 Serpenten. Kommandeur Panzergrenadier-Regiment 21. Volunteered as a private on 4 August 1915 with Jäger-Regiment 9, which went to the front in February 1915. Fought on the Eastern Front. He was commissioned as a Leutnant on 18 August 1915. Returned home from the Ukraine in February 1919. Remained in the Reichswehr. Rittmeister in 1931 and served with Reiter-Regiment 1 in 1932. Promoted to Major in 1936 and Oberstleutnant in 1939. Promoted to Oberst on 18 January 1942 with RDA 01.02.42 (6) while serving as IIa of 4. Panzerarmee. Held this position until April 1942. After several employments in higher staffs, he returned to his old regiment, being transferred on 11 October 1942 from Führerreserve OKH to Panzergrenadier-Regiment 21 (formerly Reiter-Regiment 1). Listed as MIA 23 January 1943 in Stalingrad but was in fact captured on 2 February 1943. Died 14 June 1951 in Brianka POW Camp (Lager 6101) hospital from a liver ailment. Today, probably buried as an unknown soldier in Rossoshka.

Bernhardt, Oberleutnant d.R. Heinz Joachim; born 15 November 1911 Särichen. Stab Schützen-Brigade 24. Promoted to Oberleutnant on 8 June 1942. Freed for employment after the Brigade Stab was disbanded on 8 November 1942. Took role as Ordonnanzoffizier to Division Ib. Transferred to Ausbildung-Einheit Weiss on 7 January 1943 for training as an infantry officer. Listed as MIA 20 January 1943 in Stalingrad but was in fact captured. Died April 1943 in Frolov POW Camp. Now possibly buried as an unknown soldier at Rossoshka.

Graf von Bernstorff, Rittmeister Bechtold; born 10 December 1912 Beseritz. Peacetime unit was Reiter-Regiment 1. Abteilung Commander I./Panzergrenadier-Regiment 21 at establishment of Division. Rittmeister RDA 01.08.41 (38). Severely wounded on 4 September 1942 in Krutenkiy, dying the same day from these wounds. Awarded a posthumous German Cross in Gold on 7 October 1942.

SPANNOCCHI

The grave of Bechtold Graf von Bernstorff in the Division's Heroes Cemetery near Schafzucht, on the outskirts of Stalingrad.

Besenbeck, Hauptmann; Dinafü 40.

Beyersdorff, Oberleutnant Eberhard Rudolf; born 27 March 1918 Greifenhagen. Führer 6./Panzergrenadier-Regiment 26. Peacetime unit was Kavallerie-Regiment 5. Iron Cross First Class in 1941. Transferred on 8 September 1942 from Panzergrenadier-Ersatz-Abteilung 413 to Pz.Gr.Rgt.26 as Führer 6. Schwadron. Appointed leader of the Sturmkompanie formed by 24.Pz.Div. for the 11 November offensive. Subordinated to 389.Inf.Div. for this operation. Severely wounded on 11 November 1942 when struck in the left elbow by an anti-tank bullet. Promoted to Oberleutnant RDA 01.12.42. German Cross in Gold on 10 January 1943. Recommended for the Knight's Cross but not awarded. Survived Stalingrad and the war. Died of a heart attack 15 September 1974 in Oldenburg.

Binkow, Leutnant d.R. Fritz; born 18 August 1920 Schanzenort. Zugführer 5./Panzergrenadier-Regiment 26. Fought in the Polish, Western and Russian campaigns. Leutnant RDA 01.06.42. Wounded on 23 August 1942. Again wounded on 10 September 1942. Iron Cross Second Class on 27 September 1942. Survived Stalingrad. On 15 June 1943 was a Zugführer in the Stabsschwadron of the reformed Panzergrenadier-Regiment 26. Transferred on 25 February 1944 to Pz.Gr.Ers.Btl.413 as replacement personnel. On 17 April 1944 transferred back to 24. Panzer-Division.

Birkner, Leutnant Heinrich; born 8 October 1916 Gronitten. Panzerartillerie-Regiment 89. Iron Cross Second Class on 12 August 1942.

Birth, Leutnant d.R. Günther; born 3 June 1920 Langfuhr near Danzig. Kommandant Stabsquartier 24. Panzer-Division. Iron Cross First Class on 12 August 1942 while in Panzergrenadier-Regiment 26. Transferred to Division Stab. Listed as MIA 24 January 1943 but was in fact captured at Stalingrad. Survived captivity and returned home. Died 31 December 1998.

Biskupek, Leutnant d.R. Gerhard; born 18 September 1915 Gleiwitz. Führer 11./Art.Rgt. 194. Transferred to Pz.Gr.Rgt.21 on 7 January 1943 when 94.Inf.Div. was disbanded. Then transferred to Krad.Abt.4. Listed as MIA 23 January 1943 in Stalingrad. Post-MIA promotion to Oberleutnant. Not known if he survived captivity.

von Bittenfeld, Oberleutnant d.R. Hans-Heinrich Herwarth; born 14 July 1904. Panzergrenadier-Regiment 21. Volunteered for Reiter-Regiment 4 in 1924. Went to London in 1926 where he learned English. In 1927, after persuading a diplomatic uncle, he moved into foreign affairs. From Paris in 1931, he went to the German Embassy in Moscow. After almost a decade in the Russian capital, he returned to Germany in 1940. He immediately chose to go to the front and was transferred to Reiter-Regiment 1 where, because he had a Jewish grandmother, he was safe from pursuers in the National Socialist regime. Promoted to Oberleutnant on 22 June 1942. Survived Stalingrad. Because of his excellent knowledge of the Russian language and mentality, he became Adjutant to General Köstring, Commander of the Russian volunteer units in the Wehrmacht. Survived the war. After the war, he was in the Adenauer government and transferred to the Rome Embassy on 1 April 1965. He was later Secretary of State in the London and Vatican embassies. President of the Goethe-Instituts from 1971–1977. He was internationally known as 'Johnnie'. Died 21 August 1999.

Blessing, Leutnant d.R. Helmut; born 12 March 1918 Balingen. Transferred from Pz.Ers.Abt.33 to Pz.Rgt.24 on 25 May 1942. While in Pz.Abt.508, died after wounding 15 May 1944 in Roma Armeelazarett 677. Today, buried in Pomezia, Block P, Grave 731.

Blume, Leutnant Hermann; born 26 March 1909. Ia Abteilung, Stab 24. Panzer-Division Stab. German Cross in Gold on 2 November 1941 as a Stabswachtmeister in 2./Reiter-Regiment 1. In October 1942 he was given the responsibility of training and commanding an Alarmeinheiten formed from elements of the Division Stab. Promoted to Leutnant in December 1942 due to exceptional performance and exemplary bravery. Survived Stalingrad. Knight's Cross on 11 March 1945 as Rittmeister and Commander of Panzer-Aufklärungs-Abteilung 24. He survived eight (mostly severe) wounds, the last being the loss of his right arm in the Balga/Heiligenbeil pocket in 1945. Survived the war. Died 17 October 1998.

Bock, Leutnant Alfred; born 16 July 1915 Sommerfeld. IV./Panzerartillerie-Regiment 89. Wounded on 2 September 1942. Iron Cross First Class on 22 October 1942.

Böcker, Leutnant d.R.; Transferred on 28 September 1942 from Flak-Ersatz-Abteilung 31 to IV./Panzerartillerie-Regiment 89. Later became a Zugführer in 3./Pz.Jg.Abt.40.

de Boer, Hauptmann James; born 24 June 1912 Laar. Kommandeur Panzerpionier-Bataillon 40. Took command of Abteilung in July 1942. Became Divisionspionierführer on 7 January 1943. Captured at Stalingrad. Died 28 February 1943 near Orlovka as a POW.

Boese, Oberarzt d.R. Dr. Otto; born 11 June 1910 Diesdorf. Pre-war member of the SS with SS Nr. 254178. Promoted to SS-Obersturmführer 09.11.1938. Leader of Sanitäts-Kompanie (mot.) 1/40. Iron Cross Second Class on 4 September 1942. Listed as MIA 23 January 1943 in Stalingrad but was in fact captured. Promoted to Stabsarzt d.R. Survived captivity and returned home. Still alive in 2001.

Böhlhoff, Leutnant d.R. Hugo; born 17 February 1918. Civilian career: Reichsbahn Inspecktor. Leutnant RDA 01.02.42. Panzergrenadier-Regiment 26. Transferred 1 November 1942 from Dinafü 40 back to Panzergrenadier-Regiment 26. Survived Stalingrad. Awarded the Iron Cross Second Class and Wound Badge in Black. Rejoined Pz.Gr.Ers.Btl.413 as replacement personnel on 25 February 1943. On 1 April 1944 transferred to the Panzertruppenschule at Ohrdruf as a Zugführer for an Unteroffizier training course.

Böke, Oberleutnant August Gustav Heinrich; born 13 December 1914 Elisenhof near Posen, Kreis Koschmin. Adjutant III./Panzer-Regiment 24. Peacetime unit was Kavallerie-Regiment 8. Leutnant RDA 01.10.39 (9). Zugführer in 4. (MG)/Reiter-Rgt. 21 from 5 December 1939 until he took over the Schwadron from 25 June 1941 to 2 November 1941. Iron Cross Second Class on 13 June 1940. Iron Cross First Class on 2 August 1941. General Assault Badge on 1 October 1941. Adjutant III./Panzer-Regiment 24 at establishment of 24. Panzer-Division on 3 November 1941. Oberleutnant RDA 01.02.42 (418). Lightly wounded 26 August 1942 when his face was grazed by a bullet but stayed with the troops. Wound Badge in Black on 26 August 1942. Lightly wounded 27 August 1942 by a shell fragment in his right knee but stayed with the troops. Heavily wounded 25 December 1942 by shell fragments in his head, right bicep, and left calf. Flown out of the Stalingrad pocket on 27 December 1942. In hospital until the end of March 1943 and although not completely healed, returned to his unit. Führer 6./Pz.Rgt.24 from 1 April 1943, appointed Chef of this unit a month later. Recommended for the German Cross in Gold on 21 June 1943 but not awarded. Chef 2./Pz.Rgt.24 from 25 June 1943. Rittmeister RDA 01.04.44 (114). Detached to Panzertruppen Schule Bergen for an Abteilungsführer training course on 8 August 1944. Returned to I./Pz.Rgt.24 (attached to 116. Panzer-Division) on 10 September and appointed Kommandeur. Transferred to Führerreserve on 5 December 1944, and then to the Kriegsakademie (war academy) from 6 January to 13 February 1945. German Cross in Gold 13 January 1945. Survived the war. Died in 2000–2001 Vlotho.

Bömcke, Oberleutnant Dieter; born 28 November 1918 Iserlohn. Führer Stabsschwadron/Panzergrenadier-Regiment 21. Peacetime unit was Reiter-Regiment 1. Oberleutnant RDA 01.11.41 (2). Regiment Nachrichtenoffizier at the establishment of the Division. Took command of Stabsschwadron on 21 July 1942. Killed 3 September 1942 near Alexeyevka. Buried in Gavrilovka. His remains have not yet been recovered by the Volksbund.

von Borcke, Oberleutnant d.R. Jürgen; born 18 December 1913 Stettin. Chef Stabsschw. I./Panzer-Regiment 24. Peacetime unit was Reiter-Regiment 2. In January 1939 was in the Stabsschwadron of Reiter-Regiment 2. Leutnant d.R. RDA 01.01.38 (109). Outside the pocket when it was formed. Flown into the pocket and took command of 1./Panzer-Regiment 24. Promoted to Rittmeister d.R. 2 January 1943 with RDA 01.12.42. Division history says he won the German Cross in Gold but there is no record of this. Listed as MIA 23 January 1943 in Stalingrad. Suffered two frozen feet while trying to escape the Kessel on 1 February 1943. Captured and died of his wounds on 4 February 1943 in the "white house" in Dubovka POW Camp.

Borufka, Leutnant d.R. Helmut; born 26 October 1918 Tannwald. Regiment Nachrichtenoffizier Panzergrenadier-Regiment 21. Pre-war service in the Czechoslavakian Army. Volunteered for Wehrmacht service in 1939. Transferred on 29 October 1942 from Kradschützen-Ersatz-Abteilung 24 to Panzergrenadier-Regiment 21, becoming Regiment Nachrichten Offizier. Listed as MIA 18 January 1943 in Stalingrad but was in fact captured on 2 February 1943. Translated for Oberst von Below during negotiations. Joined the Nationalkomitee "Freies Deutschland" in 1943. Released from captivity in 1949. Eventually attained the rank of Generalleutnant in the East German Nationalen Volksarmee. Retired on 31 December 1982. Died prior to 2010 in Berlin-Köpenick.

Both, Kriegs Ingenieur; IV./Panzerartillerie-Regiment 89. Wounded on 2 October 1942 but stayed with the troops.

Brandtner, Leutnant Hans; born 7 January 1910 in East Prussia. Batterie Offizier 8./Panzerartillerie-Regiment 89. In reiter-Artillerie-Regiment 1 since 1936, thus making him one of the longest-serving members of the Regiment. Iron Cross Second Class on 23 June 1940 as Batterie-Offizier in 6./r.A.R.1. Took temporary command of 8./Pz.Art.Rgt.89 in June 1942 when von Raison went to Führerreserve. Wound Badge in Black in 1944. Sent to battalion commanders training course in mid-1944. Promoted to Hauptmann in early 1944. Ended up as an Abteilung Commander in Pz.Art.Rgt.89. Became a protestant priest after the war. Killed on 2 June 1964 in Lüneburg while heading to a church function when a speeding car crashed into him.

Braun, Leutnant d.R. Hans; born 30 September 1905 in Königsberg. On Stab 24. Panzer-Division. Listed as MIA 3 February 1943 in Stalingrad.

Braun, Sekretar; Division Registrar on Stab 24. Panzer-Division Stab at establishment of Division. Captured at Stalingrad. Not known if he survived captivity.

Braunheim, Leutnant Paul; born 19 June 1915 Hattingen. Abteilung Adjutant II./Panzerartillerie-Regiment 89. Peacetime unit was reiter-Artillerire-Regiment 1. Promoted to Leutnant on 25 May 1942 with RDA 01.01.42 (13). Iron Cross First Class on 4 September 1942. Killed 4 January 1943 by a direct mortar hit near Karpovka, west of Stalingrad.

Baron von Brockdorff, Leutnant Cay-Lorenz Friedrich; born 25 August 1923 Berlin-Charlottenburg. Zugführer 3. Zug of 1./Panzer-Regiment 24. Entered service on 25 October 1940. Panzer Assault Badge 11 September 1941 as Gefreiter in 4./Pz.Rgt.15. Transferred to 24. Panzer-Division. Iron Cross Second Class 18 July 1942. Wounded 22 August 1942 but stayed with the troops. Again wounded 25 August 1942. Wound Badge in Black 28 August 1942. Iron Cross First Class 22.02.1943. Knight's Cross 14 April 1945 while in 11. Panzer-Division. Survived the war. Died 11 September 1997 in Coburg.

Freiherr von Broich, Oberst Friedrich (Fritz); born 1 January 1896 Strassburg/Elsass. Kommandeur Schützen-Brigade 24. Entered service on 2 July 1914 as Fahnenjunker. Promoted to Leutnant on 24 December 1914 while in Ulan-Regiment 9. Stayed in this unit until the end of World War 1. Remained in the Reichswehr with regular promotions. Promoted to Oberstleutnant on 1 October 1937. Transferred to II./Reiter-Regiment 6 on 12 November 1938. Spange to Iron Cross Second Class on 17 September 1939. Commander of Reiter-Regiment 21 on 6 December 1939, and Reiter-Regiment 22 on 25 September 1940. Spange to Iron Cross First Class on 14 June 1940. Oberst on 1 September 1940. Commanded 1. Reiter-Brigade in August 1941. German Cross in Gold on 2 November 1941. Commander of Schützen-Brigade 24 at establishment of 24. Panzer-Division in December 1941. Knight's Cross on 29 August 1942 for his daring actions on 21 August 1942. Took temporary command of the Division on 8 September 1942 after General von Hauenschild was severely wounded. Handed command to General von Lenski on 14 September 1942. Took immediate command on 24 October 1942 of the training service of the march battalions in the reforming area. Transferred on 30 October 1942 from 24.Pz.Div. to Führerreserve of Pz. AOK Afrika. Promoted to Generalmajor on 1 January 1943. Commander of Division von Broich from 10 November 1942. Commander 10. Panzer-Division in Tunisia from 5 February 1943 to 12 May 1943. His Ia was Oberstleutnant Graf Stauffenberg, best remembered for placing the bomb that almost killed Hitler in June 1944. Promoted to Generalleutnant RDA 01.07.43 (5b). Captured on 12 May 1943 near Gambalia in Tunisia. In British captivity until 7 November 1947. Returned to Germany. Died 24 September 1974 in Leoni am Starnberger See.

Broscheit, Leutnant; Beobachtungsbatterie (Pz) 89 in Panzerartillerie-Regiment 89. Promoted to Leutnant on 14 September 1942. Transferred on 10 November 1942 from Panzerartillerie-Regiment 89 to Panzerartillerie-Regiment 4 of 14. Panzer-Division.

Brosig, Oberleutnant Horst; born 15 December 1919 Friedland. Chef 7./Panzergrenadier-Regiment 26. Wounded on 28 July 1942 but stayed with the troops. Again wounded on 7 August 1942. Iron Cross First Class on 10 September 1942.

Buchholz, Oberleutnant Aloisius; born 26 August 1916 Mondtken. Abteilung Nachrichtenoffizier Kradschützen-Abteilung 4. Peacetime unit was Radfahr-Abteilung 1. Oberleutnant RDA 01.03.42 (31). Wounded on 28 July 1942 but stayed with the troops. Again wounded on 25 August 1942. Survived Stalingrad. Later commanded 3. Schwadron in reformed Kradschützen-Abteilung 4. Died 25 October 1943 in Novo-Starodub, Ukraine, by a head shot. Posthumous promotion to Hauptmann RDA 01.10.43.

Buchholz, Leutnant Werner; born 7 July 1916 Balkenwalde. Panzerpionier-Bataillon 40. Iron Cross First Class on 12 October 1942.

Budde, Leutnant d.R. Karl-Friedrich; born 29 June 1915 Brünn (Brno), Czechoslovakia. Zugführer in 2./Panzergrenadier-Regiment 21. Wounded on 1 August 1942 but stayed with troops. Killed 10 August 1942 1km north of Skity.

Buhse, Oberzahlmeister; Abteilung Zahlmeister I./Panzergrenadier-Regiment 21.

Burandt, Leutnant d.R. Fritz; born 8 August 1922 Magdeburg. In Panzergrenadier-Regiment 26. Peacetime unit was Kavallerie-Regiment 3. Killed 4 July 1942 in Malyshevo on the Don River south of Voronezh. Posthumous promotion to Leutnant with backdated RDA 01.07.42 (11). Buried in Malyshevo. His remains have not yet been recovered by the Volksbund.

Burgsthaler, Major Hugo; born 11 January 1908 Austria. Kommandeur II./Panzer-Regiment 24. In Austrian Panzertruppe prior to Anschluß. Married Austrian opera singer, Gertrud in 1938. The marriage produced two sons. Chef 2./Pz.Rgt.11 (6.Pz.Div.) during invasion of France. Received Iron Cross Second Class there. As a Hauptmann, he commanded this same panzer company during Operation Barbarossa. Transferred late 1941 to command II./Panzer-Regiment 24 in the new 24. Panzer-Division. Major RDA 01.01.42 (158a). Abteilung Commander at establishment of Division. Wounded 30 June 1942 in the arm by shell splinters when Stukas attacked his panzer spearhead. German Cross in Gold 20 September 1942. Fell ill shortly before the encirclement and was therefore outside the Kessel. He led an ad hoc Kampfgruppe made up of sick men and men returning from leave. On 3 March 1943 he arrived at 22. Panzer-Division. He took over command of 'Kampfgruppe 22. Panzer-Division' from Oberst Roth by order of Heeresgruppe Don. His job was not intended as a combat command but only to take care of the disbandment of this Kampfgruppe. It was placed in reserve on 10 March 1943 but was called upon again a few days later to contain a Russian breakthrough. After this, the Kampfgruppe was moved to Chistyakovo and Burgsthaler finally finished the disbandment by 6 April 1943. In October 1943, he was transferred to OB West as a General Staff officer. Killed 10 June 1944 near La Caine as Major i.G. and Ia of Panzergruppe West during an Allied bombing raid on the Panzergruppe's HQ. On 09 June 1944 posthumously promoted to Oberstleutnant with an RDA 01.07.1944 (48). Today, buried in La Cambe, Block 30, Grave 399.

von Burkersroda, Oberleutnant Curt Hubertus; born 14 September 1918 Soltau. Regiment Adjutant Panzergrenadier-Regiment 21. His twin brother, Albrecht, an infantry officer, was killed on 25 October 1941 in Russia. Peacetime unit was Reiter-Regiment 1. Oberleutnant RDA 01.04.42 (2848). Commanded 2./Panzergrenadier-Regiment 21 from 5–8 July 1942. Became II. Abteilung Adjutant on 21 July 1942. Iron Cross First Class on 12 August 1942. Wounded on 25 August 1942. Became Regiment Adjutant on 25 October 1942. Held this position until the end of the battle. Listed as MIA 16 January 1943 in Stalingrad but he was in fact captured. Survived captivity and returned home. Still alive in 2001.

Buschinsky, Leutnant d.R. Friedrich; born 19 April 1918 Wölmsdorf. Zugführer in 5./Panzergrenadier-Regiment 26. Transferred on 14 September 1942 from Führerreserve OKH to Pz.Gr.Rgt.26. Wounded on 24 September 1942 but stayed with the troops. Iron Cross Second Class on 27 September 1942. Killed 29 September 1942 in Stalingrad.

Busse, Leutnant Hans-Georg; Batterie Offizier 8./Panzerartillerie-Regiment 89. Survived Stalingrad. Iron Cross Second Class and Wound Badge in Black in 1944.

Butz, Oberleutnant Albertus Hermann; born 27 January 1921 Hagen. Zugführer in 10. (Flak)/Panzergrenadier-Regiment 21. Peacetime unit was Reiter-Regiment 1. Transferred in September 1942 from Flak-Ersatz-Abteilung 55 to Panzergrenadier-Regiment 21. Became Regiment Ordonnanzoffizier on 9 September 1942, holding this position until the end of the battle. Listed as MIA 23 January 1943 but he was in fact captured at Stalingrad. Died 16 April

1943 in Oranki POW Camp from spotted fever. Post-MIA promotion to Oberleutnant with RDA 01.09.43 (37). Buried in Oranki's Waldfriedhof. His remains have not yet been recovered by the Volksbund.

Christiansen, Leutnant Martin; born 4 February 1914. In IV./Panzerartillerie-Regiment 89, formerly Heeresflak-Artillerie-Abteilung 283. Peacetime unit was Artillerie-Regiment 20. Listed as MIA 18 January 1943 in Stalingrad. Post-MIA promotion to Leutnant with RDA 01.01.43 (371).

Constein, Oberleutnant d.R. Heinrich; born 10 March 1912 Sondershausen. Dinafü 40; Transferred on 25 November 1942 from Dinafü 40 to Panzerpionier-Bataillon 40. Survived Stalingrad. Died 13 January 1945 in Komoron, Slovakia.

Cornelius, Leutnant Herbert; Zugführer 1. Zug of 5./Panzer-Regiment 24. Began the war as a Zugführer in 1./Reiter-Rgt. 21. Zugführer at establishment of Division. Wounded 29 June 1942 in the Division's first tank combat near Bykovo. He was so severely wounded that he was only able to perform garrison duties. Survived Stalingrad. Was in reformed Panzer Regiment. Survived the war. Died 1994 in Braunschweig.

Cramer von Laue, Oberleutnant d.R. Adalbert; born 30 March 1904 Rheydt. O3 (Assistant to Ic) Stab 24. Panzer-Division at establishment of Division. Oberleutnant RDA 01.12.41. Killed 1 August 1942 south of Ssurovikino, Russia. He expressed a wish to be sent to one of the rifle regiments to participate in combat and was killed on his first day. Posthumous promotion to Rittmeister. Now buried in Rossoshka, Block 17, as an unknown soldier.

Dahle, Oberleutnant Heinz; born 14 August 1917 Stedorf. Zugführer in 1./Panzerjäger-Abteilung 40. Peacetime unit was Panzerjäger-Abteilung 22. Oberleutnant RDA 01.04.42 (2819). Transferred on 6 November 1942 from Marsch-Bataillon to Panzerjäger-Abteilung 40. Listed as MIA 24 January 1943 in Stalingrad but was in fact killed 20 January 1943 in Gorodishche, west of Stalingrad. His remains were unable to be recovered by the Volksbund.

Dannebaum, Oberleutnant Alfred; born 6 February 1918 Danzig. Abteilung Adjutant Kradschützen-Abteilung 4 at establishment of Division. Oberleutnant RDA 01.06.40 (692). Wounded on 15 September 1942 but stayed with the troops. Again wounded on 3 October 1942 but stayed with the troops. Required hospital treatment for jaundice in early October 1942. Promoted to Rittmeister on 17 November 1942. Survived Stalingrad. Later commanded 4. Schwadron in the reformed Abteilung. Knight's Cross on 17 September 1944. Survived the war. Joined the Bundeswehr, retiring as an Oberst. Died 21 October 1999.

Daschkey, Leutnant Fritz; born 15 December 1911 Neuendorf. Zugführer Aufklärung Zug/Panzer-Regiment 24. Peacetime unit was Panzer-Regiment 15. Received confirmation of his rank 21.09.1942. Oberleutnant RDA 01.12.41 (1062). Survived Stalingrad. Died 22 September 1944 in Zawadka Rymanovska, Poland, as an Oberleutnant in Panzer-Regiment 24. Posthumous promotion to Rittmeister RDA 01.09.44.

Klaus von der Decken before the beginning of Operation Blau in the summer of 1942.

von der Decken, Leutnant d.R. Klaus; born 7 March 1916 Chemnitz. Zugführer 2./Panzer-Regiment 24. Transferred on 25 May 1942 from Panzer-Ersatz-Abteilung 15 to Pz.Rgt.24. Later became Regiment Ordonnanzoffizier. Wounded on 23 August 1942 in the attack that killed Oberst Riebel. Returned to the Regiment, acting as Regiment Ordonnanzoffizier to Oberstleutnant von Bassewitz. Took brief command of 2./Pz.Rgt.24 after Oberleutnant Kühn was flown out. Captured at Stalingrad. Survived captivity and returned home. Survived the war. Died in 1993 in Freiburg/Elbe.

von der Decken, Leutnant Volkmar; born 7 February 1922 Doese. Panzer-Regiment 24. Peacetime unit was Kavallerie-Regiment 13. Leutnant RDA 01.02.42 (392). Listed as MIA 22 January 1943 in Stalingrad. Survived captivity. Died 21 January 1987 Doese.

Dellingshausen, Leutnant Karl August Freiherr von; born 19.08.1923 Groß-Barthen, East Prussia. Chef 10./Panzer-Regiment 24 Transferred to Ausbildung-Einheit Weiss 07.01.1943 for training as an infantry officer. Wounded in January 1943. Missing in action January 1943 at Stalingrad.

Dettmer, Major (Ing.); Regiment V (Ingenieur) Offizier Panzergrenadier-Regiment 21; Regiment V Offizier at the establishment of the Division. Survived Stalingrad. Transferred on 1 March 1943 to Artillerie-Lehr-Regiment 3.

Deuer, Oberleutnant d.R. Wilhelm; born 16 March 1916 Bartenstein. Führer 12./Panzerartillerie-Regiment 89. Iron Cross Second Class on 4 August 1942. Wounded on 2 October 1942 but stayed with the troops. Promoted to Oberleutnant d.R. on 10 November 1942. Commanded 4./Panzerjäger-Abteilung 40 (formed from IV./Pz.Art.Rgt.89) in January 1943. Listed as MIA 18 January 1943 in Stalingrad. Reported to have died in 1943 in Oranki POW Camp.

d'Heureuse, Oberleutnant Gerhard, *see* **Heureuse**.

Diederichs, Major d.R. Dr. jur. Richard; born 17 December 1895 Dinslaken. Divisionsnachschubführer. Promoted to Major d.R. on 1 October 1940. Attached to 24. Panzer-Division in July 1942 after Kursk. Listed as MIA 4 January 1943 in Stalingrad but was in fact captured. Survived captivity and returned home in December 1949 in very poor health. He later died in his home town of Dinslaken.

von Dietmann, Rittmeister Valentin; born 11 March 1913. Chef 7./Panzergrenadier-Regiment 21. Peacetime unit was Reiter-Regiment 1. Rittmeister RDA 01.04.42 (164). Commanded Schwadron from establishment of Division. Wounded on 26 July 1942 near Solonovski but died the same day.

von Dietze, Oberleutnant Gottfried; born 16 April 1921 Breslau. Pz.Rgt.24. Began the war in Reiter-Regiment 2. Wounded 3 September 1942. Promoted to Rittmeister. Severely wounded in the leg in late 1942 and flown out of the Kessel. Survived Stalingrad. He spent the next 15 months in plaster and had to be pushed around in a wheelchair. During his recovery he immersed himself in theology, no doubt influenced by his father, a priest. Survived the war. After the war, he become a protestant priest. Even today, his right leg is still affected by his wounds but he still rides his beloved horses. Still alive in 2012.

MACARTHUR

Oberleutnant Ludwig Dittmar, Commander of 6./Panzergrenadier-Regiment 21

Dinse, Leutnant; Wounded on 2 September 1942 but stayed with the troops.

Dittmar, Oberleutnant d.R. Ludwig; born 10 July 1916 Schweinfurt. Chef 6./Panzergrenadier-Regiment 21. Promoted to Oberleutnant d.R. on 25 May 1942. Took command of Schwadron on 17 July 1942. German Cross in Gold on 9 October 1942. Wounded on 8 November 1942 but stayed with the troops. Nevertheless, gave up command of his Schwadron. Ehrenblattspange on 7 January 1943 for actions on 28 September 1942 in Stalingrad. Survived Stalingrad. Commanded I./Pz.Gr.Rgt.26 on 8 June 1943. Died 30 May 1944 in Stanca, Rumania while a Rittmeister d.R. in Pz.Aufkl.Abt.24.

Donner, Oberarzt d.R. Dr. Kurt; born 8 October 1907 Gumbinnen. Abteilung Arzt II./Panzergrenadier-Regiment 21 from establishment of Division. Iron Cross First Class on 12 August 1942. Wounded on 1 October 1942 but stayed with the troops. Wounded in November 1942.

Dornbach, Leutnant Hans Ebbo Götz; born 11 June 1919. Zugführer 2. Zug of 10./Panzer-Regiment 24. Pecetime unit was Panzer-Regiment 15. Wounded 30 July 1942 but stayed with the troops. Returned to III./Panzer-Regiment 24 as deputy Abteilung Adjutant. Commander of the last Panzer IV at the Tractor Factory. Listed as MIA 23 January 1943 in Stalingrad but he was in fact captured at Stalingrad. Post-MIA promotion to Oberleutnant with RDA 01.04.43 (174). Survived captivity and returned home. Died in 2000 Gräfelfing.

von Dressler, Oberleutnant Arnold; born 12 October 1914. Regiment Adjutant Panzergrenadier-Regiment 26 at establishment of Division. Peacetime unit was Kavallerie-Regiment 3. Oberleutnant RDA 01.11.41 (171). Took command of I./Pz.Gr.Rgt.26 on 28 July 1942 when Schulz-Fademrecht was killed. Wounded on 12 September 1942 but stayed with the troops. Again wounded on 14 October 1942. Promoted to Rittmeister. German Cross in Gold on 6 November 1942. Flown in to the Kessel on 12 January 1943. Listed as MIA January 1943 in Stalingrad. Post-MIA promotion to Major with RDA 01.02.43 (144f). Not listed on Volksbund so may have survived captivity.

von Dressler, Rittmeister; Adjutant Schützen-Brigade 24 at establishment of Division. Rittmeister RDA 01.04.42 (742). With effect from 6 May 1942, his temporary attachment to Stab Schützen-Brigade 24 was made a permanent transfer. His role upon the disbandment of the brigade staff in October 1942 is unknown.

Drews, Rittmeister Otto Johann; born 17 January 1916 Banaskeim. Peacetime unit was Reiter-Regiment 1. Rittmeister RDA 01.03.42 (183a). Chef 8./Pz.Gr.Rgt.21 at establishment of Division. Took command of 7./Pz.Gr.Rgt.21 on 20 August 1942. He then took command of II./Pz.Gr.Rgt.21 on 21 September 1942. Killed 5 October 1942 in northern Stalingrad. His remains were unable to be recovered by the Volksbund.

Dröscher, Leutnant d.R. Günther; born 20 November 1919. Führer 8./Panzergrenadier-Regiment 21. Leutnant RDA 01.02.42. Took command of Schwadron on 5 October 1942. Fell ill with jaundice and on 17 November 1942 was sent to hospital. Survived Stalingrad. On 15 June 1943 was a Zugführer in Stabsschwadron of reformed Panzergrenadier-Regiment 21. Survived the war. Died 30 October 1996.

Düker, Pfarrer Franz; born 15 February 1898 Greven-Ems. Kriegspfarrer IVd (kath.) Stab 24. Panzer-Division. Transferred to 24. Panzer-Division on 2 January 1943 after the disbandment of 94. Infanterie-Division. Missing in action January 1943 in Stalingrad. Reported to have died 20 March 1943 in Russian captivity.

Dura, Kriegs-Ingenieur; Werkstatt-Kompanie 2/40; Transferred on 14 October 1942 from Panzergrenadier-Ersatz-Abteilung 413 to Werkstatt-Kompanie 2/40.

Düran, Leutnant d.R. Eberhard; born 16 June 1922 Lichtenberg. Zugführer 4. Zug of 4./Kradschützen-Abteilung 4. Transferred on 9 October 1942 from Führerreserve Heeresgruppe B to Kradschützen-Abteilung 4. Wounded, command going to Oberwachtmeister Pack. Later commanded 4./Kradschützen-Abteilung 4 in January 1943. Listed as MIA 2 January 1943 in Stalingrad but he was in fact captured. Died February 1943 in Dubovka. Now possibly buried as an unknown soldier at Rossoshka.

Dyckerhoff, KV-Rat Dipl.Ing. Wilhelm Hugo; born 6 February 1908 Amöneburg. Abteilung Technische Beamter Kradschützen-Abteilung 4. Survived Stalingrad, later becoming Technische Beamter of the reformed Abteilung. Survived the war. Resumed control of his family company, a fourth generation of a cement dynasty in Amöneburg. Served a ten-year term on Wiesbaden's city council. President of the Wiesbaden Riding and Driving Club. Recognised for his achievements many times. Died 26 October 1987 Wiesbaden-Biebrich.

Eck, Leutnant Dr. Otto; born 3 April 1911 Kiel. Kl.Kw.Kol 40, 2. Trupp. With divisonal supply services at establishment of Division. Survived Stalingrad. Killed 30 March 1945 in Sanitäts-Kompanie 409 near Seeheilstätte Lochstädt near Pillau.

Eckhardt, Rittmeister Hans; born 18 June 1915. Chef 8./Panzer-Regiment 24. Peacetime unit was Panzer-Abteilung 66. Leutnant RDA 01.04.37 (743). Zugführer 2./Pz.Abt.66 in January 1939 transferred from Pz.Lehrabt. Oberleutnant RDA 01.09.39 (111). In May 1940 transferred to Pz.Abt.101 (the Abt. was set up by the Panzertruppenschule as a Flamm-Abteilung). Wounded in June 1941 and sent to Pz.Ers.Abt.15 after recovery. On 08.12.41 Pz.Abt.101 was dissolved and incorporated into Pz.Rgt.24, and with it went Eckhardt. Rittmeister RDA 01.04.42 (275). Chef 8./Panzer-Regiment 24. Transferred from Pz.Rgt.24 to Stab 24. Panzer-Division on 5 November 1942, temporarily taking command of Ib while Rosenberg-Lipinski was on a training course. Later became IIa (Division Adjutant). Flown out of the pocket 23 January 1943 on one of the last planes. Survived Stalingrad. Sent to Putlos. On 22 June 1943 with Führerreserve OKH but detailed to Abwicklungsstab 6. Armee. On 15 September 1943 detached to OKH/Chef H.Rüst.u.B.d.E./IIa Hilfsoffizier. A note on his card reads: "Gen.Insp.d.Pz.Tr. asks for acceptance into the Waffen-SS, application from there." Eckhardt was "detached" from the Oberkommando des Heeres to the SS-FHA In. 6 with effect 28 September 1943. His SS number was 474314. Effective 1 November 1943 he was formally transferred to the SS-Pz.Ausb.u.Ers.Rgt. with the rank of Hauptsturmführer der Waffen-SS. Per order of 23 March 1944, he was attached to the SS-Tr.Üb.Pl. Seelager. Promoted to SS Sturmbannführer on 21 June 1944. With effect from 8 September 1944 he was reassigned to the SS-FHA/Führerreserve and at the same time "detached" to the staff of the 2. SS-Panzer-Division "Das Reich" for General Staff training for the period 8 September to 7 December 44. In early December 1944 the "detachment" was extended until 8 March 1945.

Edelmann, Leutnant d.R. Hans; born 18 January 1920. In Panzerartillerie-Regiment 89. Wounded on 25 August 1942. Listed as MIA 2 January 1943 in Stalingrad.

Reichsfreiherr von Edelsheim, Oberst Maximilian; born 6 July 1897 Berlin. Regiment Kommandeur Panzergrenadier-Regiment 26. Son of a cavalry officer who won the Pour le Mérite in the First World War. Entered the service in August 1914 as an officer candidate in Garde-Ulan-Regiment 2 in Berlin. As a Leutnant, he transferred to the infantry in 1917. He won the Iron Cross First and Second Class. He remained in the Reichswehr, returning to the cavalry, this time to Prussian-Reiter-Rgt. 4 which continued the tradition of his old regiment. Promoted to Oberleutnant on 1 April 1925. Promoted to Major on 1 March 1936. Took command of Radfahr-Abt. 1 in Tilsit on 10 November 1938. He led this battalion into Poland in September 1939, France in 1940 and Russia on 22 June 1941. Promoted to Oberstleutnant. Wounded on the chin by a grazing shot. Knight's Cross on 30 July 1941. Promoted to Oberst on 1 October 1941, shortly thereafter taking command of Reiter-Rgt. 22. This was converted to Pz.Gr.Rgt.26. Regiment Commander at establishment of Division. Transferred on 10 October 1942 from Pz.Gr.Rgt.26 to Pz.Gren.Brig. 20. Command of Regiment went to Oberst von Scheele. Oakleaves (162) on 22 December 1942. Survived Stalingrad. Commander of 24.Pz.Div. from 1 March 1943 to 20 September 1944. Promoted to Generalmajor on 1 June 1943. Promoted to Generalleutnant on 1 March 1944. Swords (105) on 23 October 1944. Commander of XXXXVIII. Pz.-Korps from 21 September 1944 to late March 1945. Promoted to General der Panzertruppe on 1 December 1944. Survived the war. In captivity in a Generals camp in Garmisch-Partenkirchen until 31 March 1947. Died 26 April 1994 Konstanz.

Eichhorn, Oberleutnant Ernst-Georg; born 14 June 1912. Chef Stabsschw. III./Panzer-Regiment 24. Peacetime unit was Kavallerie-Regiment 8. Leutnant RDA 01.01.38 (1362). In January 1939 was a Zugführer in 11./Kav.Rgt.8. Began the war as Nachrichtenoffizier of Reiter-Rgt. 21. Schwadronschef at establishment of Division. Took command of 9./Panzer-Regiment 24 on 22.08.1942 when von Meyer was wounded. Promoted to Rittmeister 17.11.1942 with RDA 01.11.42 (87). Handed Schwadron back to von Meyer 19.11.1942 but took command again 30.12.1942 when von Meyer became Regiment Adjutant. Listed as MIA 23 January 1943 in Stalingrad but was in fact captured and survived captivity.

Eichler, Leutnant d.R.; Zugführer 8./Panzergrenadier-Regiment 26. Transferred on 9 October 1942 from Führerreserve Heeresgruppe B to Pz.Gr.Rgt.26. Wounded on 10 November 1942 while commanding 8./Panzergrenadier-Regiment 26.

Eickes, Oberleutnant d.R Wilhelm; born 19 July 1915. Zugführer 3. Zug of 1./Kradschützen-Abteilung 4. Peacetime unit was Kavallerie-Regiment 18. Promoted to Oberleutnant d.R. on 10 November 1942, but another source gives his Oberleutnant RDA as 01.09.41 (463). Commanded 2. Schwadron in January 1943. Wounded on 16 January 1943. Listed as MIA 23 January 1943 in Stalingrad. Not known if he survived captivity.

Freiherr von Eickstedt, Leutnant d.R. Hubertus; born 3 January 1917 Breslau. O4 zugl. Ia/Gabo Stab 24. Panzer-Division. Assigned to 1. Kavallerie-Division in April 1940. O4 at establishment of Division. Leutnant RDA 01.07.40 (3324). Sent to hospital in November 1942 with jaundice. Survived Stalingrad. After recovering from his illness, served for a short time with OKH. Rejoined 24. Pz.Div. upon its reactivation. As the 'last son', he did no more front-line duty. His younger brother had been killed in Russia in 1941. Survived the war. Died in 1980 in München.

von Einem, Major Hans-Egon Max Gustav Kurt Oskar; born 26 September 1907 Hannover. Kommandeur Feldersatz-Abteilung 40. Entered service on 8 April 1929 in Reiter-Regiment 3. In Kavallerie-Regiment 3 prior to the outbreak of war. Iron Cross Second Class on 23 September 1939. Abteilung Commander at establishment of Division. Major RDA 01.04.42 (102). Transferred on 24 August 1942 from 24. Panzer-Division to Führerreserve OKH. Survived Stalingrad. Iron Cross First Class on 31 January 1943. Wound Badge in Black on 25 February 1943. Panzer Assault Badge on 21 March 1943. Wound Badge in Silver on 1 September 1943. German Cross in Gold on 11 December 1943 as Commander Panzer-Aufklärungs-Abteilung 23. Promoted to Oberstleutnant on 1 May 1944. Ehrenblattspange on 27 August 1944. Took command of Pz.Gr.Rgt.21 on 25 February 1944. Promoted to Oberst on 1 January 1945. Wounded on 26 March 1945 near Balga. Died on 8 May 1945 in Freiburg. With his wife Edelgard and his four children (9-year old Volkmar, 6-year old Mechthild, 4-year old Ehrengard and 2-year old Sigurd), von Einem was gunned down by the Russians.

Elias, Leutnant d.R. Gerhard; born 1 September 1916 Allenstein, East Prussia. Abteilung Ordonnanzoffizier II./Panzerartillerie-Regiment 89. Listed as MIA 5 January 1943 in Stalingrad.

Freiherr von Eller-Eberstein, Leutnant Hans-Heino; born 6 August 1921 Brockhagen, Haus Patthorst. Zugführer 7./Panzergrenadier-Regiment 21. Peacetime unit was Reiter-Regiment 1. Leutnant RDA 01.02.42 (211). Took command of 7. Schwadron on 21 September 1942. Survived Stalingrad. In reformed regiment as a Zugführer in 6./Pz.Gr.Rgt.21. Oberleutnant RDA 01.12.44. Killed 21 March 1945 near Gerlachsdorf while in II./Panzergrenadier-Regiment 21.

Endruweit, Oberleutnant d.R. Heinz; born 24 January 1918 Belgard. Nachrichtenoffizier Panzer-Regiment 24. Promoted to Oberleutnant 7 September 1942. Transferred to Ausbildung-Einheit Weiss 7 January 1943 for training as an infantry officer. Committed suicide 16 January1943 in Stalingrad. His body has not been recovered for reburial in Rossoshka Sammelfriedhof.

Enge, Leutnant; Zugführer 3./Panzerpionier-Bataillon 40. In Pi.Btl. 194 on 10 December 1942. Transferred from Pz.Pi.Btl. 16 (16.Pz.Div.). Wounded on 22 December 1942.

von Engel, Hauptmann Hans-David Kurt; born 7 February 1915 Dudinghausen. Chef 6./Panzerartillerie-Regiment 89. Peacetime unit was Artillerie-Regiment 12. Wounded on 8 June 1940 as commander 6./r.A.R.1. Iron Cross Second Class on 23 June 1940. Iron Cross First Class on 24 June 1940. Chef 6./Pz.Art.Rgt.89 at establishment of Division. Wounded on 25 July 1942 but stayed with the troops. Again wounded on 27 August 1942 but stayed with the troops. German Cross in Gold on 21 August 1942. Listed as MIA 24 January 1943 in Stalingrad. Once source states he was captured and died in captivity. Post-MIA promotion to Major RDA 01.04.43 (18f). Still listed as MIA. His name is on Cube 125, Panel 6 at Rossoshka Sammelfriedhof.

Engelke, Leutnant d.R. Horst; born 19 November 1912 in East Prussia. Führer 8./Panzergrenadier-Regiment 21. Took command of Schwadron on 17 November 1942. Listed as MIA 2 January 1943, although a contemporary source gives the date as 21 November 1942. Died April 1943 in Oranki POW Camp.

Engels, Leutnant (W) Willi; born 17 February 1915 Euskirchen. Dinafü 40; Promoted to Leutnant on 15 July 1942. Missing in action February 1943 at Stalingrad.

Erdmann, Leutnant Horst; Batterie Offizier 5./Panzerartillerie-Regiment 89. Wounded on 20 August 1942 but stayed with the troops. Again wounded on 24 September 1942 but stayed with the troops. Outside Kessel. Survived the war. Died in July 1963.

Freiherr von Erffa, Oberleutnant Friedrich Wilhelm; born 2 October 1914 Naumburg, Thüringia. Chef 10./Panzerartillerie-Regiment 89. Peacetime unit was Artillerie-Regiment 14. Transferred on 15 September 1942 from Heeres-Flak-Ersatz-Abteilung 272 to 10./Pz.Art.Rgt.89. Transferred to Ausbildung-Einheit Weiss on 7 January 1943 for training as an infantry officer. Listed as MIA 18 January 1943 in Stalingrad. Post-MIA promotion to Hauptmann RDA 01.12.43 (6). Still listed as MIA. His name is on Cube 16, Panel 7 at Rossoshka Sammelfriedhof.

Ernst, Assistenzarzt d.R. Dr. Arnulf; born 30 May 1909 Marxloh. In Panzerartillerie-Regiment 89. Died 23–24 November 1942 near Stalingrad. His body has not been recovered for reburial in Rossoshka.

Erzberger, Leutnant d.R. Heinz; born 28 October 1919 in East Prussia. Leutnant RDA 01.02.42. Zugführer Panzergrenadier-Regiment 21. Transferred on 9 October 1942 from Führerreserve Heeresgruppe B to Pz.Gr.Rgt.21. Fought in Russia and received the Iron Cross Second Class. Survived Stalingrad. Returned to Pz.Gren.Ausb.u.Ers.Btl.413 on 25 May 1943, where he remained until December 1944. On the 7th of that month he was transferred to Pz.Gr.Rgt.21 as a Schwadronführer.

Ewers, Leutnant d.R. Klaus Ernst; born 26 September 1907 Kiel. Ordonnanzoffizier II./Panzer-Regiment 24. Transferred from Pz.Ers.Abt.15 to Pz.Rgt.24 on 29 April 1942. Iron Cross Second Class 26 August 1942. Later became Abteilung Adjutant. Transferred to Ausbildung-Einheit Weiss 7 January 1943 for training as an infantry officer. Listed as MIA 23 January 1943 Stalingrad. Still listed as MIA. His name is on Cube 16, Panel 14 at Rossoshka Sammelfriedhof.

Exner, Leutnant d.R. Dr. Helmut; born 27 August 1914. Zugführer 2./Panzer-Nachrichten-Abteilung 86. Wounded on 27 September 1942. Iron Cross Second Class on 27 September 1942. Survived Stalingrad. Killed 12–13 July 1944 in Le Hommet, Normandy as an Oberleutnant d.R. in Pz.Aufkl.Lehrabt.130. Posthumous promotion to Hauptmann d.R.

Fähnrich, Leutnant d.R. Werner; born 20 March 1909 Riesa. Abteilung Ordonnanzoffizier I./Panzerartillerie-Regiment 89. Iron Cross First Class on 12 August 1942. Became Abteilung Adjutant when Nesslinger took command of 3. Batterie. Wounded on 21 September 1942 but stayed with the troops. Listed as MIA 24 December 1942 but was in fact captured at Stalingrad. Survived captivity and returned home. Died 19 January 1993 in Olsberg.

Freiherr von Falkenhausen, Leutnant d.R. Alexander; born 14 October 1919 Baumgarten, Strehlen. Zugführer 2. Zug of 8./Panzer-Regiment 24. Peacetime unit was Reiter-Regiment 8. Began the war as a Zugführer in 3./Reiter-Rgt. 21. Iron Cross First Class 02.08.1942. Wounded 08.09.1942 but stayed with the troops. Commanded a Schwadron in November 1942. Promoted to Oberleutnant 30.11.1942. Killed 15–16 January 1943 west of Orlovka. Posthumous promotion to Rittmeister d.R. His body has not been recovered for burial in Rossoshka Sammelfriedhof.

Fassbender, Leutnant d.B. Karl; born 20 November 1911 Linden. Führer 4./Kradschützen-Abteilung 4. Leutnant RDA 01.08.41. Wounded on 3 October 1942. Iron Cross Second Class on 12 October 1942. Survived Stalingrad. In reformed battalion June 1943 as a Zugführer in 5./Pz.Aufkl.Abt.24. Earned the Iron Cross First Class. Oberleutnant RDA 01.02.44. Wounded 27 October 1944. Released from hospital on Christmas Day and joined Pz.Aufkl.Ers.Abt.3. Returned to 24. Panzer-Division on 20 January 1945. Employed as an adjutant in a Festungs-Regiment on 4 March 1945.

Fehre, Leutnant Erich; born 23 August 1904. Zugführer 7./Panzergrenadier-Regiment 26. Missing in action January 1943 in Stalingrad.

Feldt, Oberleutnant Alexander (Axel); born 29 December 1918 Sulzbach. Chef 7./Panzergrenadier-Regiment 26. Iron Cross First Class on 12 August 1942. Wounded on 15 October 1942 but stayed with the troops. Survived Stalingrad. German Cross in Gold on 26 December 1943 while commanding 7./Pz.Gr.Rgt.26.

Feller, Zahlmeister; Abteilung Zahlmeister III./Panzer-Regiment 24; Captured at Stalingrad.

Ferno, Oberleutnant Artur; born 8 October 1920 Medow. Peacetime unit was Reiter-Regiment 1. Oberleutnant RDA 01.04.42 (2170). Appointed Regiment Ordonnanzoffizier Panzergrenadier-Regiment 21 on 30 July 1942. Killed 8 September 1942 near Stalingrad. Today, probably buried as an unknown soldier at Rossoshka Sammelfriedhof.

Festerling, Leutnant d.R. Alwin; born 6 June 1914 Langeln. Abteilung Ordonnanzoffizier II./Panzergrenadier-Regiment 26. Transferred on 9 October 1942 from Führerreserve Heeresgruppe B to Pz.Gr.Rgt.26. Took command of a Zug, then became Abteilung Ordonnanzoffizier. Killed 10–11 November 1942 in Stalingrad. Posthumous promotion to Oberleutnant. Buried in Businovka. His remains have not yet been recovered by the Volksbund.

Fey, Leutnant Heinrich; born 23.10.1913 Wanne-Eickel. Führer der Trosse III./Panzer-Regiment 24. Peacetime unit was Kavallerie-Regiment 8. Began the war as Führer of Pz.Jäg.Zug of Reiter-Rgt. 21. Rittmeister RDA 01.03.43 (149a2). Outside of Kessel. Survived Stalingrad. Promoted to Oberleutnant. In reformed Panzer Regiment. Wounded 4 May 1944 in Turzysk south of Kovel while in 3./Panzer-Abteilung 505. Died 15–17 May 1944 in Feldlazarett 4/582 at Cholm. Today, buried in Pulavy, Poland, Block 4, Row 12, Grave 744.

Feyler, Hauptmann d.R.z.V. Wilhelm; born 19 February 1896 Sonnefeld. Zugführer Krankenkraftwagen Zug, Sanitäts-Kompanie 2/40 (mot.). Killed 18 January 1943 in Stalingrad. Posthumous promotion to Major.

Fichtenau, Oberleutnant d.R.; Führer 1./Panzerjäger-Abteilung 40. Wounded on 22 September 1942.

Ficus, Oberarzt d.R. Dr. Adolf Hans-Richard; born 6 February 1915 Steinförde. Dinafü 40. With 24. Panzer-Division at the beginning of Operation Blau. At some point in mid-1942 he was transferred to another assignment but on 29 October 1942 he was transferred from 5. Armee Gef. Sammelstelle (his previous assignment) back to Dinafü 40. Listed as MIA 5 January 1943 in Stalingrad. Died February 1944 in captivity in Stalingrad.

Fink, Leutnant d.R. Hans; born 2 April 1912. Zugführer 8./Panzergrenadier-Regiment 26. SA-Führer. Peacetime unit was Kavallerie-Regiment 3. Leutnant RDA 01.04.42. Oberleutnant RDA 01.12.43. Zugführer 8./Panzergrenadier-Regiment 26 from 15 June 1943. Attended the 23rd Abteilungsführer-Lehrgang from 7 November to 13 December 1944. Result: not yet suitable. Attached to the Panzertruppenschule at Bergen for further training. Attended 24th Abteilungsführer-Lehrgang and deemed suitable. Returned to 24. Panzer-Division on 6 March 1945. Probably survived the war.

Fischer, Hauptmann; Abteilung Commander IV./Panzerartillerie-Regiment 89. In Stalingrad on 6 November 1942.

Fischer, Leutnant Hermann; Zugführer 2. Zug in 2./Panzer-Regiment 24. Führer 2./Panzer-Regiment 24 on 30 September 1942. Survived Stalingrad. Was in reformed Panzer Regiment, where he stayed until the end of the war. German Cross in Gold 4 October 1944 as Oberleutnant in 11./Panzer-Regiment 24. Survived the war. Died 11 July 1974.

Fittkau, Leutnant Hans; born 22 May 1913 Braunsberg. In 6./Panzergrenadier-Regiment 26. Iron Cross First Class on 2 August 1942. Promoted to Leutnant on 14 October 1942. Survived Stalingrad. Survived the war. Still alive in December 1997.

Fleischhauer, Stabsveterinär d.R. Dr. Ernst; born 15 February 1902 Rodgen, Hessen. Chef Schlachterei-Kompanie (mot.) 40. Stabsveterinär RDA 01.02.42. Became IVc on 26 December 1942. Listed as MIA 2 January 1943 in Stalingrad but was in fact captured on 2 February 1943. Survived captivity and returned home in 1953. Moved to Wiesbaden in 1955. Died 25 September 1973 in Wiesbaden.

Flemming, Oberleutnant d.R. Bruno; born 4 January 1912. Beobachtungsbatterie (Pz) 89 in Panzerartillerie-Regiment 89. Promoted to Oberleutnant on 24 August 1942. Killed 13 September 1943 in Italy as Hauptmann.

Fötsch, Oberleutnant d.R. Werner; born 28 July 1908. On Stab 24. Panzer-Division. Listed as MIA 5 January 1943 in Stalingrad.

Franke, Rittmeister d.R. Walter; born 3 January 1908 Dittersbach. Chef 1./Panzer-Nachrichten-Abteilung 86. Promoted to Hauptmann on 25 May 1942. Iron Cross First Class on 12 October 1942. Transferred on 7 December 1942 from Pz.Nachr.Abt.86 to Nachrichten-Abteilung 384. Listed as MIA late January 1943 in Stalingrad but was in fact captured at Stalingrad. Not known if he survived captivity.

Frantzius, Leutnant Karl Eberhard von; born 2 August 1920 Podollen. Peacetime unit was Reiter-Regiment 2. Transferred on 6 November 1942 from Panzergrenadier-Ersatz-Abteilung 413 to Panzergrenadier-Regiment 21. A contemporary source lists him as MIA 21 November 1942 but he was in fact killed 23 November 1942 near Jarki Rubeschni, west of Stalingrad. Now buried in Rossoshka Sammelfriedhof: Block 11, Row 25, Grave 990–1000.

Freise, Leutnant Hans; born 1 August 1922 Potsdam. Peacetime unit was Reiter-Regiment 1. Leutnant RDA 01.02.42 (642). Zugführer 7./Panzergrenadier-Regiment 21. Commanded Schwadron from 26–28 July 1942. Killed 25 August 1942 2.5km south of Solyanka. Now buried in Rossoshka Sammelfriedhof: Block 32, Row 2, Grave 32–50.

Frey, Hauptmann d.R.; Dinafü 40. Captured at Stalingrad. Survived captivity.

Baron von Freytag-Loringhoven, Oberleutnant Klaus; born 18 December 1913 Riga. Chef 6./Panzergrenadier-Regiment 26. Transferred from Division in May or June 1942. Killed 4 December 1943 near Nikolayev as a Major.

Fritz, Oberleutnant d.R. Alfred; born 9 October 1911 Reinickendorf. Panzerpionier-Bataillon 40. Promoted to Oberleutnant on 24 August 1942. Iron Cross First Class on 27 September 1942.

Fröhlich, Kriegs-Ingenieur; Werkstatt-Kompanie 2/40. Transferred on 14 October 1942 from Werkstatt-Kompanie 2/40 to Kraftfahr-Ersatz-Abteilung 4.

Fuchs, Leutnant d.R. Gerhard; born 7 May 1913 Berlin-Charlottenburg. Panzerartillerie-Regiment 89. Iron Cross First Class on 4 August 1942. Listed as MIA 3 January 1943 in Stalingrad. Not known if he survived captivity.

Fuchs, Oberveterinär Julius; born 23 November 1914 Schnappach. Schlachterei-Kompanie 40. Iron Cross Second Class on 4 September 1942. Commanded Alarmeinheiten formed from the Schlachterei Kompanie.

Funk, Sonderführer; Dolmetscher on Stab 24. Panzer-Division. Transferred on 15 September 1942 to 24. Panzer- Division as Dolmetscher.

Gach, Hauptmann Georg; born 2 May 1903. Chef in Panzerpionier-Bataillon 40. Transferred on 10 October 1942 from Panzerpionier-Bataillon 40 to Pionier-Bataillon 60 as its commander. Listed as MIA 16 January 1943 Stalingrad but was in fact captured. A Hauptmann Georg Gach died 22 November 1944 in Jelabuga POW Camp but his date of birth was 2 March 1899 Roswadze, so it is uncertain if it is the same man with an administrative error in his details.

Gebhardt, Leutnant d.R. Harry Dietrich; born 14 March 1921 Tautschken, East Prussia. Chef 5./Panzer-Regiment 24. Transferred from Pz.Ers.Abt.15 to Pz.Rgt.24 on 2 October 1942. Listed as MIA 19 January 1943 Stalingrad. His name is on Cube 21, Panel 4 at Rossoshka Sammelfriedhof.

Geissler, Leutnant; IV./Panzerartillerie-Regiment 89. Scheduled for transfer on 20 October 1942 from Artillerie-Ausbilding-Abteilung 280 to IV./Panzerartillerie-Regiment 89. Did not end up being transferred, his place being taken by Leutnant Andreesen.

Gembus, Leutnant Erich; born 10 September 1912. Oberwachtmeister on Stab II/Panzer-Regiment 24. Peacetime unit was Kavallerie-Regiment 8. Killed 30 June 1942 near Bykovo in a mistaken attack by German Stukas. Posthumous promotion to Leutnant RDA 01.06.42 (93).

Genheimer, Leutnant Kurt; born 24 October 1913. In Panzernachrichten-Abteilung 86. Peacetime unit was Nachrichten-Abteilung 49. Listed as MIA January 1943 in Stalingrad. Post-MIA promotion to Leutnant with backdated RDA 01.01.43 (374). Not known if he survived captivity.

Gensel, Oberleutnant d.R. Joachim Helmuth; born 8 August 1914 Leipzig. Transferred on 20 October 1942 from Artillerie-Ausbilding-Abteilung 280 to IV./Panzerartillerie-Regiment 89. Died 25 December 1942 in Feldlazarett 608 in Lichoj. Buried in Lichoj. The Volksbund has not yet recovered his body for reburial.

Gentzen, Hauptmann Felix-Heinrich; born 19 May 1914. Chef Beobachtungsbatterie (Pz) 89 in Panzerartillerie-Regiment 89. Hauptmann RDA 01.04.40 (117). Peacetime unit was Beobachtung-Abteilung 1. Wounded on 1 July 1942 and gave up command for four weeks. Transferred on 24 August 1942 from Panzerartillerie-Regiment 89 to leichte Beobachtung-Abteilung 28. Listed as MIA 3 February 1943 in Stalingrad but was in fact captured. Not known if he survived captivity.

Gerlach, Oberleutnant d.R. Heinz Karl; born 4 June 1915 Harzgerode. Killed 8 September 1942 west of Stalingrad. Posthumous promotion to Rittmeister d.R. His remains were unable to be recovered for reburial by the Volksbund.

Glemann, Major d.R. Hans Joachim; born 22 April 1914 Alt Negentin. Chef 2./Panzerartillerie-Regiment 89. In reiter-Artillerie-Regiment 1 since 1935. Survived Stalingrad. German Cross in Gold on 26 December 1943 as Hauptmann and Commander of 2./Panzerartillerie-Rgt. 89. Wound Badge in Silver. Died 14 August 1944 in Wojeczka, Poland.

Goder, Rittmeister Wolfdietrich; born 6 March 1909 Lissa. Abteilung Commander; II./Panzergrenadier-Regiment 21; Began war in Aufklärungs-Regiment 8. Commander of Krad.-Ersatz-Abt. 24 in April 1942. Took command of I./Pz.Gr.Rgt.21 at the beginning of November when it was in C-Raum. He then took command of II./Pz.Gr.Rgt.21 on 12 November 1942. Wounded on 23 November 1942. Flown out of the Kessel. Survived Stalingrad. Promoted to Major on 1 March 1943. Died 16 April 1945. Currently buried in a single grave in Jahnsfelde-Kirchlicher Friedhof.

Gollob, Leutnant; Panzerpionier-Bataillon 40; Promoted to Leutnant on 8 June 1942.

Freiherr von der Goltz, Major d.R. Oskar; born 16 August 1898 Kallen. Ia/Stomü Stab 24. Panzer-Division at establishment of Division. Rittmeister RDA 01.08.39 (210). Iron Cross First Class on 2 August 1942. Promoted to Major on 21 September 1942. Later Panzergrenadier-Regiment 21. Transferred on 1 October 1942 from 24. Panzer-Division to Führerreserve OKH. In June 1944, he was IIa in the precinct of South-west France, his Commander-in-Chief was General der Kavallerie Feldt.

Gornth, Leutnant; Panzerartillerie-Regiment 89. Wounded on 20 August 1942.

Gorny, Oberzahlmeister Alfred; born 24 November 1907 Schwentainen. Abteilung Zahlmeister II./Panzergrenadier-Regiment 21. Career soldier. Survived Stalingrad. In reformed Division as Regiment Zahlmeister of Panzergrenadier-Regiment 21. Was seen in Hammerstein officers POW camp at the end of the war by other division members but his fate is unknown.

Gorny, Leutnant d.R. Ernst; born 10 November 1920 Groß Maransen, Osterode. Zugführer in Panzergrenadier-Regiment 26. In Panzerabwehr-Abteilung 11 from 1940 to 1942. Iron Cross Second Class on 15 July 1941. Assault Badge on 27 August 1941. Attended the 10th officer candidates training course at Panzertruppenschule Wünsdorf from 20 June to 28 September 1942. Ostmedaille on 2 September 1942. Temporarily assigned to his reserve unit (Pz.Gren.u.Ausb.Btl. 413) on 29 September before being sent to Führerreserve Heeresgruppe Süd on 21 October 1942. Outside the Stalingrad pocket. Attached to Kampfgruppe Sauerbruch (14. Panzer-Division) on 3 December 1942 and then to Panzergrenadier-Regiment 26 on 5 January 1943. Transferred to the reformed Pz.Aufkl.Abt. 24 on 21 February 1943. Back to his reserve unit (Pz.Gren.u.Ausb.Btl. 413) on 11 May 1943 for almost six months. Transferred to Feld-Ers.Btl. 24 on 6 November 1943 and Panzergrenadier-Regiment 26 on 2 March 1944. Iron Cross First Class on 7 April 1944. Transferred to Armee Waffenschule AOK 8 on 10 June 1944. Wound Badge in Silver on 10 January 1945. Close Combat Clasp in Silver on 30 January 1945. Back to Res.Pz.Gren.Btl. 413 on 13 February before being sent back to front on 27 March (II/Pz.Gren.Rgt. 42). Survived the war.

Göttke, Pfarrer Franz-Josef; born in 1910. Kriegspfarrer IVd (kath.) Stab 24. Panzer-Division. He became Divisionspfarrer in 1940. At the time of the Russian encirclement of Stalingrad he was west of Kalach with the rear area services and therefore avoided the pocket. Survived Stalingrad and survived the war. Died 17 April 1996 in Cloppenburg.

von Götz, Rittmeister Friedrich Albrecht; born 23 August 1915 Charlottenburg. Chef in Panzer-Regiment 24. Married Elisabeth Kelm on 3 April 1942 Meppen. Peacetime unit was Kriegsschule Hannover. Leutnant RDA 01.04.37 (272). In January 1939 he was a Zugführer in 4./Reiter-Regiment 2. Adjutant of Reiter-Regiment 2 in 1941. Rittmeister RDA 01.04.41 (94a). Severely wounded 5 September 1941 during an attack on Starodub and sent back to Germany for hospital treatment. After recovery, he was transferred from Pz.Ers.Abt.15 to Pz.Rgt.24 on 7 September 1942. Transferred 12 December 1942 to Pz.Gr.Rgt.26 to take command of II. Abteilung. Took command of Krad.Abt.4 on 16 December 1942, as well as retaining command of II./Pz.Gr.Rgt.26. Listed as MIA Stalingrad but was in fact captured. Survived captivity and returned home in 1950. Died 22 October 1960 Frankfurt am Main.

SPANNOCCHI

Friedrich von Götz, shown here in 1941 as an Oberleutnant in Reiter-Regiment 2.

Graeve, Leutnant Erdmann; born 20 May 1922 Liegnitz. 3. (Flak)/Panzerjäger-Abteilung 40. Former Zugführer in IV./Pz.Art.Rgt.89, transferred to Panzerjäger-Abteilung 40. Wounded on 9 August 1942 but stayed with the troops. Wounded on 4 September 1942 but stayed with the troops. Again wounded on 15 September 1942 but stayed with the troops. German Cross in Gold on 16 October 1942. Survived Stalingrad. Died 16 July 1944 in Sanitäts-Kompanie 1./359 Hospital Lemberg-Brzezany, Lvov area as a Hauptmann.

Griebenow, Leutnant Gerhard; born 19 September 1921 Helmstadt. Beobachtungsbatterie (Pz) 89 in Panzerartillerie-Regiment 89. Iron Cross First Class on 12 August 1942. Listed as MIA 3 January 1943 in Stalingrad. Still listed as MIA. His name is on Cube 24, Panel 2 at Rossoshka Sammelfriedhof.

Griese, Kriegstechniker; II./Panzergrenadier-Regiment 21. Transferred on 30 October 1942 from Artillerie-Ersatz-Abteilung 4 to Panzergrenadier-Regiment 21.

von der Groeben, Rittmeister Otto-Friedrich; born 25 April 1913 Juckstein. Kommandeur Kradschützen-Abteilung 4. Son of Ann von Le Tanneux von Saint-Paul, who was aunt of Rittmeister von Saint-Paul in 12./Panzer-Regiment 24. Took command of Abteilung on 28 August 1942 when Hellermann took over Pz.Gr.Rgt.21. Killed 8 September 1942 on Hill 151.7 west of Stalingrad in the same attack that severely wounded Generalmajor von Hauenschild.

SPANNOCCHI

The grave of Otto von der Groeben in the Division's Heroes Cemetery

Grübner, Stabsarzt Dr. Ernst Eduard; born 13 October 1911 Fieragen. Abteilung Arzt Panzerjäger-Abteilung 40. Fought in France as Oberarzt and Abteilung Arzt of II./r.A.R.1. Abteilung Arzt of Panzerjäger-Abteilung 40 at establishment of Division. Iron Cross First Class on 2 August 1942. Wounded on 4 October 1942. Stayed with the troops. Died 25 March 1945 in Leysuhnen near Balga, East Prussia, as an Oberstabsarzt.

Grunau, Oberleutnant; Panzergrenadier-Regiment 26. Wounded on 20 August 1942 but stayed with the troops.

Guercke, Oberleutnant Hartwig; born 29 June 1914. Führer 5./Panzergrenadier-Regiment 21. Took command of 8. Schwadron on 20 August 1942. Wounded on 5 September 1942 but stayed with the troops. Took command of 5. Schwadron on 5 October 1942, commanding 7. Schwadron at the same time. On 10 October 1942 he had to enter hospital because he was ill with jaundice. Survived Stalingrad. Commanded a Schwadron in reformed Panzergrenadier-Regiment 21. Wounded on 17 April 1945. Survived the war. Died 13 July 1997.

Gulbin, Oberarzt; Wounded on 2 September 1942.

Gumbert, Leutnant d.R.; Transferred on 20 October 1942 from Artillerie-Ausbilding-Abteilung 280 to IV./Panzerartillerie-Regiment 89.

Gündel, Leutnant d.R. Richard; born 30 December 1918 Johanngeorgenstadt. Zugführer 4./Panzergrenadier-Regiment 21. Wounded on 27 September 1942 but stayed with the troops. Captured at Stalingrad. Died 17 March 1943 in Frolov POW Camp near Stalingrad. Today, probably buried as an unknown soldier in Rossoshka.

Günther, Leutnant; Zugführer 7./Panzergrenadier-Regiment 26.

von Günther, Rittmeister d.R. Arnold-Viktor; born 3 January 1916 Hanau. Pz.Rgt.24. Wounded 04.09.1942 during the battle for Barracks Hill. Promoted to Rittmeister 21 September 1942 with an RDA 01.06.1942. Iron Cross First Class 22 October 1942. Survived Stalingrad. In reformed Panzer Regiment. Took command of I./Panzer-Regiment 24 on 7 August 1944. Killed 9 August 1944 at Sourdeval, south of the Vire near Avranches, France. Posthumous promotion to Major d.R. Today, buried in Champigny-St.Andre: Block 9, Row 25, Grave 1732.

von Gusovius, Rittmeister Hans-Georg; born 27 October 1913 in Pommerania. IIa (Division Adjutant) Stab 24. Panzer-Division at establishment of Division. Entered service on 1 April 1933 as an officer candidate in Reiter-Regiment 5 in Stolp. Oberleutnant RDA 01.10.38 (17). In 1938 he was Adjutant of the newly formed Kavallerieschule in Krampnitz. Chef 1./Aufkl.Abt.175 before being assigned to Stab 24. Panzer-Division on 24 November 1941. Rittmeister RDA 01.10.41 (16). Hauenschild described him as a "personality who knows what he wants. Very good divisional adjutant. A good support in difficult circumstances." Recommended for advancement, either as a battalion commander or corps adjutant. As a result, transferred on 4 September 1942 from 24. Panzer-Division to Führerreserve OKH and attached to Panzertruppenschule Wünsdorf on 21 September 1942. Attended an Abteilungsführer training course in Paris from 23 November to 12 December 1942. Transferred to II./Panzer-Regiment 4 as its Kommandeur on 25 January 1943. Received the German Cross in Gold on 1 June 1944 for his actions. Transferred to the Führerreserve on 1 February 1944. Short stint on the staff of 13. Panzer-Division. Promoted to Major with RDA 01.03.44 (5t). Various training courses and front-line positions for the duration of the war, including another tenure as adjutant of 13.Pz.Div. in August-September 1944, during which he was captured by the Soviets. Survived captivity and returned home in 1949. After a few years as a business, he joined the Bundeswehr in 1955, was promoted to Oberstleutnant in 1956 and took command of Panzer-Bataillon 2 in Hemer. Held various other positions before retiring in 1970. Died 19 May 2006 Hamburg.

von Gyldenfeldt, Oberleutnant Georg; born 30 November 1918 Fuhlsminde. Abteilung Adjutant II./Panzerartillerie-Regiment 89. Fought in France as a Leutnant and Batterie Offizier in 6./r.A.R.1. Abteilung Adjutant at establishment of Division. Oberleutnant RDA 01.04.42 (52). Commanded Alarmeinheiten formed from the Regiment supply trains. Regiment Adjutant in January 1943. Died 26–27 January 1943 in Stalingrad. His remains were unable to be recovered by the Volksbund.

Graf vom Hagen, Rittmeister d.R. Adalbert; born 3 December 1900 Möckern/Magdeburg. Ic (Enemy Intelligence Officer) Stab 24. Panzer-Division at establishment of Division. Promoted to Rittmeister on 25 May 1942 with RDA 01.05.42. Flown out of the Stalingrad pocket late 1942 because he was severely ill with jaundice and transported back to Germany for treatment. When almost recovered, he wanted to return to the Division trapped in the pocket but that was no longer possible. Ic of reformed 24.Pz.Div. in 1944. Survived the war but two of his brothers did not: Hauptmann Hilmar Graf vom Hagen was killed in 1944 and Major Hubertus Graf vom Hagen in 1941. Died 10 September 1961 in Shannon, Ireland when the plane he was on crashed during a flight from Germany to the United States.

Hahn, Oberleutnant d.R. Ernst; born 21 February 1915 Düsseldorf. Panzerjäger-Abteilung 40. Promoted to Oberleutnant on 22 June 1942. Iron Cross First Class on 10 September 1942. Survived Stalingrad. German Cross in Gold on 18 December 1944 as Oberleutnant in Division Begleits Schwadron. Died 11 February 1945 Zinten, East Prussia, as a Rittmeister.

Hammer, Oberleutnant; Panzer-Nachrichten-Abteilung 86. Wounded on 23 August 1942 on Hill 118, south of Krassnoarmeisk.

von Hanstein, Leutnant Karl-Ludwig von; born 27 July 1922 Halle, Salle. Zugführer 2. Zug in 4./Kradschützen-Abteilung 4. Wounded on 7 September 1942 but stayed with the troops. Survived Stalingrad. Killed 26 July 1944 in Russia as an Oberleutnant and schwadron commander in Panzer-Regiment 24.

Hantschke, Leutnant; Zugführer 2./Panzergrenadier-Regiment 26. Killed 31 July 1942.

Hardt, Oberleutnant; Chef 2./Panzer-Nachrichten-Abteilung 86. Wounded on 28 July 1942 but stayed with the troops. Again wounded on 7 August 1942 but stayed with the troops. Surrounded at Stalingrad. Promoted to Hauptmann in January 1943. Captured and shot by the Russians, together with Major Henrici, during a break out attempt in late January 1943.

Haring, Oberleutnant; Dinafü 40.

Haseroth, Oberleutnant; Wounded on 8 September 1942 but stayed with the troops.

Prinz von Hatzfeld zu Trachenberg, Oberleutnant d.R. Hermann Krafft; born 24 November 1912 Brüssel. Stab Schützen-Brigade 24. Promoted to Oberleutnant on 8 June 1942. Killed on 4 July 1942 near Voronesh.

SPANNOCCHI

Generalmajor Bruno von Hauenschild near Bykovo in June 1942. On the left is Oberst Riebel, on the right is Major von Winterfeld.

Ritter von Hauenschild, Generalmajor Bruno; born 9 June 1896 Würzburg, Bavaria. Kommander 24. Panzer-Division. Iron Cross Second Class on 21 May 1915. Iron Cross First Class on 6 December 1917. Won the Bavarian Militär-Max-Josef-Medal on 2 September 1918. Clasp to Iron Cross Second Class on 24 September 1939. Clasp to Iron Cross First Class on 19 October 1939. After the Polish campaign, he took command of Panzer-Regiment 7 when it was incorporated into the newly formed 10. Panzer-Division. He led this Regiment in France under the control of Guderian's XIX. Panzerkorps. Promoted to Oberst on 1 November 1940. He took command of Panzer-Brigade 4 in April 1941, spearheading XXXVI. Panzerkorps' advance during Operation Barbarossa. Received the Knight's Cross on 25 August 1941 as Commander of 4. Panzer Brigade. Transferred to Führerreserve OKH on 20 November 1941 and transferred to the newly formed 24. Panzer-Division a month later. Division Commander at establishment of Division. Promoted to Generalmajor on 1 April 1942 to reflect his new role as Division Commander. Lightly wounded on 3 September 1942. Stayed with the troops. Seriously wounded on 8 September 1942. Command of Division temporarily went to Broich. Wounded on 8 September 1942 for the seventh time. Oakleaves (129) on 27 September 1942. Survived Stalingrad. His wounds were so severe that he remained in Führerreserve OKH for almost a year. He became Commander of the Panzertruppenschule in Krampnitz on 20 November 1943. Promoted to Generalleutnant on 1 January 1944. In January 1945, he became Commander of Wehrkreis III (Berlin) and then also Kampfkommandant of Greater Berlin until evacuated to hospital on 20 March 1945. Survived the war. Died 10 March 1953 München.

Hauschild, Leutnant d.R. Reinhard; born 1921 Koblenz. Panzerartillerie-Regiment 89. Became sick during the Stalingrad battle, saving him from the fate of the Division. In reformed Panzerartillerie-Regiment 89, where he remained until the end of the war. After his return from captivity he worked as a journalist for Frankfurter Zeitung and the Hessischen Rundfunk. In 1955 he joined the Bundeswehr, mainly in the Ministry for Defence. In 1978, as an Oberst, he commanded the Bundeswehr's School for Psychiatric Defence. Author of division's pictorial history and several other books. Died 25 May 2005.

Hecht, Oberleutnant Walter Robert; born 25 June 1919 Kütten. In Panzerartillerie-Regiment 89. Peacetime unit was Artillerie-Regiment 21. Oberleutnant RDA 01.04.42 (111). Killed 13 June 1942 near Propoisk. Buried in Slavgorod/Mogilev. The Volksbund has not yet recovered his body for reburial.

Heemsoth, Major Hermann; born 29 February 1912 Wittlohn. Chef 7./Panzerartillerie-Regiment 89. Peacetime unit was Artillerie-Regiment 1. Fought in France as a Leutnant and Batterie Offizier in 5./r.A.R.1. Hauptmann RDA 01.04.42 (1090). Chef 7./Panzerartillerie-Regiment 89 at establishment of Division. Wounded on 28 September 1942 but stayed with the troops. Again wounded on 4 October 1942 but stayed with the troops. Took command of III./Pz.Art.Rgt.89 on 25 October 1942 when Hauptmann von Raison fell ill. Flown out of the pocket with severe jaundice but died of this illness on 21 December 1942 in Tatsinskaya. Posthumous promotion to Major RDA 01.12.42. Buried in Tatsinskaya. The Volksbund has not yet recovered his body for reburial.

Heffler, Oberveterinär Dr. Dinafü 40. Transfer from IV./Art.Rgt.194 to Schlächterei-Kompanie 40.

Heibel, Hauptmann Erich; born 29 July 1916. Chef Beobachtungsbatterie (Pz) 89 in Panzerartillerie-Regiment 89. Peacetime unit was Beobachtung-Abteilung 6. Hauptmann RDA 01.04.42 (346). Transferred on 21 September 1942 from Führerreserve OKH to command Beobachtungsbatterie (Pz) 89, replacing Hauptmann Gentzen. Listed as MIA 10 January 1943 in Stalingrad. Not known if he survived captivity.

von Heimann, Leutnant Einar; born 28 August 1918 Hamburg. In 1./Panzerartillerie-Regiment 89. Wounded on 20 June 1942 but stayed with the troops. Transferred to Jüterbog on 6 September 1942. Iron Cross First Class on 10 September 1942. Survived Stalingrad. Survived the war. Still alive in 2001.

Heindel, Oberleutnant d.R. Zugführer 6./Panzer-Regiment 24. Promoted to Oberleutnant 15 June 1942. Wounded 1 August 1942. Again wounded 8 August 1942.

Heinemann, Oberarzt d.R. Dr. Alois; born 11 January 1915 München. Abteilung Arzt III./Panzerartillerie-Regiment 89. Wounded on 30 September 1942 but stayed with the troops. Listed as MIA 4 January 1943 in Stalingrad but he was in fact captured. Died 4 April 1943 in Frolovo POW Camp. Now possibly buried as an unknown soldier at Rossoshka Sammelfriedhof.

Helff, Oberfeldarzt Dr. Georg; born 6 September 1898 Frankfurt/Oder. IVb (Divisionsarzt) Stab 24. Panzer-Division. Transferred from Feldlazarett 646 to 24.Pz.Div. His fate isn't known.

SPANNOCCHI

Heinrich von Helldorff takes a captured Willy's jeep for a test drive. In the back (in black uniforms) are Leutnant Sylla and Leutnant Schweißing.

von Helldorff, Oberleutnant Heinrich; born 20 December 1918 Baumersroda or Querfurt. Zugführer 1. Zug in 4./Panzer-Regiment 24. Peacetime unit was Reiter-Regiment 2. Leutnant RDA 01.09.38 (1363). In January 1939 was a Zugführer in 1./Reit-Rgt.2. Iron Cross First Class 02.08.1942. Wounded 22.08.1942 but stayed with the troops. Survived Stalingrad. In reformed Panzer Regiment. Rittmeister RDA 01.10.43 (5). Took command of I./Panzer-Regiment 24 (Panther). Wounded by an artillery burst 07.08.1944 near Le Mesnil-Adelée, near Avranches, France, dying the same day from these wounds. One source states that he was heavily wounded and MIA. Today, he is buried in Marigny: Block 5, Row 21, Grave 1005.

von Hellermann, Oberstleutnant Vollrath; born 18 May 1900 Ratzeburg. Kommandeur Kradschützen-Abteilung 4; Entered the service on 1 March 1924 as an officer candidate, becoming a Leutnant on 1 December 1927 while in Reiter-Regiment 6. Began the war as IIa of 5. Armee but was transferred a month later to become IIa of 18. Armee. On 18 December 1939, he took command of Aufklärungs-Abteilung 158. Promoted to Major on 1 February 1940. Transferred to 1. Kavallerie-Division on 6 October 1940 to become IIa of the Division. Received a combat role on 3 November 1941 when he took command of I./Reiter-Regiment 22. Was given command of Kradschützen-Abteilung 4 in newly created 24. Panzer-Division on 13 March 1942 and was promoted to Oberstleutnant on 1 April 1942. Abteilung Commander at establishment of Division. Wounded on 29 August 1942. Stayed with the troops. Took command of Panzergrenadier-Regiment 21 on 26 August 1942 after Lengerke's death but only received it officially two days later. German Cross in Gold on 20 September 1942. Transferred on 11 October 1942 from Panzergrenadier-Regiment 21 to Führerreserve OKH (Heerespersonalamt). Knight's Cross on 21 November 1942. Survived Stalingrad. Promoted to Oberst on 1 February 1943. Promoted to Generalmajor on 1 October 1944 as General Inspector for the Führernachwuchs. Survived the war. In captivity for two years in a Generals Camp in Garmisch-Partenkirchen, until 1947. Died 25 August 1971 München.

Hellmer, Oberarzt d.R. Dr. Herbert; born 8 September 1911. Chef Sanitäts-Kompanie 1/40. Transferred on 28 September 1942 from Reserve-Kriegs-Lazarett-Gruppe B to Sanitäts-Kompanie 1/40. Listed as MIA 21 January 1943 in Stalingrad. Post-MIA promotion to Stabsarzt d.R. Not known if he survived captivity.

Henning, Leutnant d.R. Konrad; born 16 May 1921 Tübingen. Transferred on 6 November 1942 from Panzergrenadier-Ersatz-Abteilung 413 to I./Panzergrenadier-Regiment 21. Outside of the pocket. Confusion in sources about his fate: one lists him as MIA 15 January 1943 west of Stalingrad, another near Rostov, and a third near Smolensk on the Dnepr River. Whatever the case, he is still listed as MIA.

Henrici, Major Horst; born 20 February 1908 Hagenau. Kommandeur Panzer-Nachrichten-Abteilung 86. Attended the Kriegsakademie (war academy) in 1939. Major RDA 01.01.42 (189). Abteilung Commander at establishment of Division. Iron Cross First Class on 12 October 1942. Listed as MIA 28–30 January 1943 in Stalingrad but reported to have been captured and shot by the Russians during a break out attempt from the city. Still listed as MIA today. His name is on Cube 30, Panel 8 at Rossoshka Sammelfriedhof.

Hentschel, Hauptmann Siegfried Hermann Helmut; born 19 February 1911. Panzer-Regiment 24. Transferred 28.09.1942 from XIII. Armeekorps to Pz.Rgt.24 to serve out his Waffenkommando for the period from 01.–30.10.1942. Major RDA 01.08.1943 (51).

Heppe, Leutnant d.R. Joachim; born 26 February 1906. In Panzerartillerie-Regiment 89. Listed as MIA 18 January 1943 in Stalingrad. Not known if he survived captivity.

Herberg, Leutnant d.R.; Transferred on 9 October 1942 from Führerreserve Heeresgruppe B to Panzergrenadier-Regiment 21 as a Zugführer.

Hermanns, Oberleutnant Johann (Johnny); Abteilung Ordonnanzoffizier Panzer-Nachrichten-Abteilung 86. Iron Cross Second Class before August 1940. In the Stalingrad pocket. Iron Cross First Class on 28 January 1943. Wounded. Captured at Stalingrad. Died in captivity in June 1943.

Hermenau, Leutnant d.R. Siegfried; born 17 July 1915 Wissewatten. Panzerjäger-Abteilung 40. Transferred on 24 August 1942 from Panzerjäger-Ersatz-Abteilung 1 to 24. Panzer-Division. Iron Cross Second Class on 10 September 1942.

Hermes, Oberleutnant d.R. Norbert; born 24 May 1916. Zugführer Pionier Zug of II./Panzer-Regiment 24 Acquitted of a grievous bodily harm charge 08.06.1942. His penalty had been 6 weeks confinement to quarters. Wounded 25.09 1942. Survived the battle. Was in reformed Panzer Regiment. Killed 31.10.1944 in France. Today, buried in Andilly: Block 36, Row 10, Grave 455.

Herold, KV-Rat Otto; born 14 January 1915 Berlin. Stab Pz.Rgt.24 Wounded 22.08.1942 but stayed with the troops. Iron Cross Second Class 26.08.1942. Survived Stalingrad. In reformed Panzer Regiment. With the Werkstattkompanie of Pz.Rgt.24 in October 1944.

d'Heureuse, Oberleutnant Gerhard; born 23 October 1919 Lissa. Chef 7./Panzerartillerie-Regiment 89. Peacetime unit was Artillerie-Regiment 21. Fought in France as Batterie-Offizier with 5./r.A.R.1. Oberleutnant RDA 01.04.42 (1417). Wounded on 25 August 1942 but stayed with the troops. Listed as MIA 30 December 1942 in Stalingrad but he was in fact captured. Died March 1943 in Dubovka POW Camp. Now possibly buried as an unknown soldier at Rossoshka.

von Heydebrand und der Lasa, Leutnant d.R. Rudolf-Dietrich; born 18 August 1920 Jeschütz. Zugführer 3./Kradschützen-Abteilung 4. Began the war as a Zugführer in 4. (MG)/Reiter-Rgt. 21. Severely wounded on 27 or 28 June 1942, dying from these wounds later in the day in Armee-Feldlazarett 3/562 in Schschigry. Now possibly buried as an unknown soldier at Kursk-Besedino.

von Heyden, Major Hans-Wilhelm; born 5 September 1909 Demmin. Kommandeur II./Panzergrenadier-Regiment 26 at establishment of Division. Peacetime unit was Kavallerie-Regiment. Promoted to Major on 8 June 1942. Wounded on 21 September 1942 but stayed with the troops. Again wounded on 27 September 1942. German Cross in Gold on 5 November 1942. Flown out of Kessel. Took command of the part of the Division that was outside the Kessel. Later led the reformed Kradschützen-Abteilung 4. Promoted to Oberstleutnant RDA 01.02.44. Killed 20 February 1944 3km north-east Kriwaja Batka, near Nikopol.

Baron von Heyking, Oberleutnant Ernst-Georg; born 2 April 1915 Berlin. Chef 4./Panzergrenadier-Regiment 21. Entered the service in 1936 as an officer candidate in Reiter-Regiment 1 in Insterburg. This was his peacetime unit. Promoted to Leutnant on 1 January 1938. Zugführer in 2./Reiter-Regiment 1 in Poland. Became Ordonnanzoffizier and later Adjutant of I. Abteilung in France. Wounded on 1 September 1941. Chef 4./Pz.Gr.Rgt.21 at establishment of 24. Panzer-Division. Promoted to Rittmeister on 17 November 1942. Commanded a Kampfgruppe outside of Kessel. German Cross in Gold on 12 February 1943. Commanded 1./Panzergrenadier-Regiment 21 in reformed Division. Transferred on 17 September 1943 to 29.Pz.Gr.Div. Severely wounded on 19 February 1944 and listed as MIA on this date, but he was in fact captured at Anzio by the Americans. Knight's Cross on 6 April 1944 as Kommandeur III./Grenadier-Regiment 15 of 29.MD. Post-MIA promotion to Major RDA 01.02.44 (46). Returned to Germany in 1946. Joined the Bundeswehr in 1956 as a Major, retired in September 1971 as an Oberstleutnant. Died 25 October 2007 Göttingen.

Heyl, Leutnant; Wounded on 13 September 1942.

Hicketier, Hauptmann Erich; born 27 April 1913 Liebwalde. Chef 2./Panzerartillerie-Regiment 89. Peacetime unit was reiter-Artillerie-Regiment 1. Wounded on 26 September 1942. Stayed with the troops. German Cross in Gold on 10 January 1943. Listed as MIA 23 January 1943 in Stalingrad but he was in fact captured at Stalingrad. Died 26 March 1943 in Oranki Lager of spotted fever. Post-MIA promotion to Major RDA 01.07.43 (38a). A grave was not registered, so recovery of his body has not been possible.

Hildebrandt, Leutnant d.R; Transferred on 7 November 1942 from Nachrichten-Abteilung 128 to Panzer-Nachrichten-Abteilung 86.

Hilgenberg, Leutnant Hans-Wilhelm; born 15 November 1920 Essen. Führer 2./Panzergrenadier-Regiment 21. Peacetime unit was Kavallerie-Regiment 13. Transferred on 8 September 1942 from Panzergrenadier-Ersatz-Abteilung 413 to Panzergrenadier-Regiment 21. Wounded on 28 September 1942 but stayed with the troops. Survived Stalingrad. Oberleutnant RDA 01.06.44 (29). Killed 18 September 1944 near Lysa Gora, Poland. German Cross in Gold on 21 October 1944 as Führer 6./Panzergrenadier-Regiment 21.

Baron von Hobe, Major i.G. Heinrich (Heinz) Siegfried; born 25 April 1911 Gut Ohrfeld. Ib (Quartermaster) Stab 24. Panzer-Division. Promoted to Hauptmann on 1 March 1938. Ic of 1. Kavallerie-Division on 1 February 1941. Ib of 1. Kavallerie-Division on 1 September 1941. Ib at establishment of 24. Panzer-Division. Wounded on 2 September 1942 but stayed with the troops.

Promoted to Major on 14 September 1942. Lightly wounded and fell severely ill with jaundice on 30 October 1942, his place as Ib being taken by Rittmeister Weiss. Flown out of Stalingrad on 3 November 1942 for treatment. Scheduled for transfer on 13 November 1942 from 24.Pz.Div. to Stab of 6 Armee as Id but this did not happen because of his illness. After his recovery, he was not flown into the Kessel to take over as Id of 6.Armee but instead transferred to the Stab of XXXXI. Panzerkorps as its Ia. Here, he participated in the anti-partisan operations around Nikitinka and Vyasma and later Operation Büffel, the withdrawal from the Rzhev–Vyasma area. Transferred to 340. Infanterie-Division, which was later surrounded on 18–20 July 1944 near Lvov. Hobe was severely wounded, and captured on 21 July 1944. Survived captivity and returned home on 2 January 1954 and took up a career with the Bundeswehr, finally retiring as an Oberst. Died 24 February 2003 Gelting. His older brother, Knight's Cross winner Cord, attained the rank of Oberst during the war and Generalleutnant in the Bundeswehr.

Hofmann, Oberleutnant Bruno; born 31 December 1914. Adjutant II./Panzer-Regiment 24. Peacetime unit was Reiter-Regiment 1. Leutnant RDA 01.09.38 (1638). In January 1939 was a Zugführer in 5./Reit.Rgt.1. Oberleutnant RDA 01.10.40 (389). Killed 30 June 1942 near Bykovo in a mistaken attack by Stukas.

SPANNOCCHI

Oberleutnant Hofmann as Ordonanzoffizier of Reiter-Regiment 2 in 1941, soon after the beginning of Operation Barbarossa.

Hoffmann, Leutnant d.R. Hubert; born 23 December 1919. Zugführer in 1./Panzergrenadier-Regiment 21. Leutnant RDA 01.04.41 (1488). Fought in the Western and Russian campaigns. Wounded on 28 June 1942. Awarded Wound Badge in Black. In November 1943 was a Zugführer in Pz.Gr.Ers.u.Aus.Btl.413. Promoted to Oberleutnant d.R. RDA 01.02.44.

Hoffmann, Oberleutnant Kurt; born 1 March 1898 Posen. Chef 5./Panzergrenadier-Regiment 26. Promoted to Oberleutnant on 25 May 1942. Wounded on 25 September 1942 but stayed with the troops. Again wounded on 29 September 1942 but stayed with the troops. Survived Stalingrad. In reformed Pz.Gr.Rgt.26. German Cross in Gold on 9 April 1943. Commander of I./Pz.Gr.Rgt.26 on 19 February 1944. Ehrenblattspange on 25 May 1944. Died 8 August 1944 in Angers, France.

Höger, Hauptmann Carl Hans Andreas; born 16 September 1911 Glückstadt. Adjutant Divisions-Nachschubführer 40 at establishment of Division. Peacetime unit was Kraftfahr-Abteilung 10. Hauptmann RDA 01.05.42 (236). Recognised as Offizier z.b.V and gave up adjutancy to Oberleutnant Luber on 1 September 1942. Wounded. Listed as MIA 5 January 1943 in Stalingrad but he was in fact captured at Stalingrad. Died 1943 in Dubovka POW Camp. Today, probably buried as an unknown soldier in Rossoshka.

Höhne, Leutnant Dietrich; born 12 March 1922 Gut Kalenzig. Zugführer 2. Zug in 5./Panzer-Regiment 24. Iron Cross First Class 26.08.1942. Survived the battle. Was in reformed Panzer Regiment. In January 1945 was Rittmeister and Chef 12./Panzer-Regiment 24. Killed 17.02.1945 in East Prussia. Buried in Lipovina, Poland, but his remains have not yet been recovered.

Höhne, Rittmeister Georg; born 22 April 1912 Alterwasch. In Panzergrenadier-Regiment 26. Transferred to the active officers list on 25 May 1942. Took command of Kradschützen-Ersatz-Abteilung 24 on 25 September 1942. Abteilung Commander in reformed Pz.Gr.Rgt.26. Promoted to Major on 1 January 1944. German Cross in Gold on 20 January 1944. Commander of Pz.Gr.Rgt.26 as a Major on 23 January 1945. Killed 19 February 1945 north-west of Zinten, East Prussia.

Holtz, Oberleutnant Udo; born 7 May 1915 Danzig-Langfuhr. Chef 3./Panzerartillerie-Regiment 89. Peacetime unit was reiter-Artillerie-Regiment 1. Oberleutnant RDA 01.09.41 (1). Severely wounded on 4 October 1942 in Stalingrad. Died as a result of these wounds on 16 October 1942 in Kriegslazarett V/528 in Poltava. Posthumous promotion to Hauptmann with RDA 01.10.42. Now buried as an unknown soldier in Kharkov Friedhof: Block 14.

von Horn, Oberst Hans-Joachim; born 23 October 1896 Königsberg. Kommandeur Schützen-Brigade 24. Entered military service on 1 August 1914 as a Fahnenjunker. Promoted to Leutnant on 22 March 1915. Remained in the Reichswehr. Oberstleutnant RDA 01.08.37. Military attaché in Paris on 1 December 1938. Chief-of-Staff of XII. Armeekorps on 10 September 1939. Oberst RDA 01.02.40. Chief-of-Staff of X. Armeekorps from 1 June 1940 to 1 January 1942. On the staff of 7. Panzer-Division on 21 September 1942. Scheduled for transfer on 1 November 1942 from Führerreserve OKH to 24.Pz.Div. to take command of Schützen-Brigade 24. No evidence that this transfer happened and perhaps unlikely because Schützen-Brigade 24 was disbanded on 8 November 1942. Therefore, he was neither in Stalingrad nor served with 24. Panzer-Division, instead, he remained in the Führerreserve of Heeresgruppe Don until early January 1943 awaiting deployment as a division commander. Commanded 198. Infanterie-Division from 5 February 1943 to 31 May 1944. German Cross in Gold on 1 December 1943. Promoted to Generalmajor RDA 01.04.43, and to Generalleutnant 01.10.43. Military attaché in Bern on 17 July 1944. Survived the war. Generalmajor in the Bundeswehr since May 1956, first of all as Commander-in-Chief of Wehrbereich 11 and since autumn 1957 as Commander-in-Chief of the territorial defence. Retired 30 September 1961. Died 10 January 1994 Wiesbaden.

Hornung, Major (Ing.) Adolf; born 23 August 1903 Offenburg. Regiment Ingenieur Offizier Panzergrenadier-Regiment 26. Peacetime unit was Panzerjäger-Abteilung 14. Promoted to Oberstleutnant on 1 November 1942 with backdated RDA 01.10.42 (20a). Listed as MIA 1 January 1943 in Stalingrad but he was in fact captured. Died 28 February 1943 in Beketovka POW Camp. Today, probably buried as an unknown soldier in Rossoshka.

Horst, Leutnant Karl-Heinz; born 26 July 1922 Wilhelmsbad. Panzerpionier-Bataillon 40. Peacetime unit was Pionier-Bataillon 26. Leutnant RDA 01.2.42 (634a). Transferred on 14 September 1942 from Führerreserve OKH to Panzerpionier-Bataillon 40. Iron Cross Second Class on 27 September 1942. Killed 28 September 1942 in northern Stalingrad. Today, probably buried as an unknown soldier in Rossoshka.

Hövel, Leutnant d.R. Heinz; born 13 June 1919. Zugführer 1. Zug in 9./Panzer-Regiment 24. Transferred from Pz.Ers.Abt.11 to Pz.Rgt.24 on 25.05.1942. Wounded 08.09.1942 but stayed with the troops. Iron Cross First Class 22.10.1942. Promoted to Oberleutnant d.R. 10.11.1942. Survived the battle. Was in reformed Panzer Regiment. Listed as MIA 04.05.1944 Mailly le Camp, France while in Pz.Rgt.24.

Huber, Oberarzt d.R. Dr. Max; born 31 August 1906. Abteilung Arzt Panzerjäger-Abteilung 40. Transferred on 26 October 1942 from Sanitäts-Ersatz-Abteilung 1 to Panzerjäger-Abteilung 40. Listed as MIA 6 January 1943 in Stalingrad. Post-MIA promotion to Stabsarzt d.R. Not known if he survived captivity.

Huck, Oberleutnant d.R. Joachim; Zugführer 2. Zug in 1./Kradschützen-Abteilung 4. Promoted to Oberleutnant on 21 September 1942. Outside Kessel. Later commanded 1. Schwadron of the reformed Abteilung. Wounded on 3 June 1944. Commander of II./Pz.Gr.Rgt.26 on 30 May 1944. German Cross in Gold on 7 December 1944 as Rittmeister in I./Pz.Gr.Rgt.21.

Hugenroth, Leutnant d.R. Josef; born 20 May 1917 Stadtlohn. On 28 April 1942 transferred from Panzerjäger-Ersatz-Abteilung 1 to Panzerjäger-Abteilung 40 as a Zugführer. Iron Cross Second Class on 4 September 1942. Survived Stalingrad. Later commanded the Stabsschwadron in the reformed Abteilung. Later in reserve after becoming ill. Survived the war. Ordained as a priest in 1947, subsequently serving as a chaplain in Duisburg and Münster, then various roles in churches and youth groups until his death in 1994.

Humbert, Rittmeister Philipp Karl von; born 21 October 1913 Hohenkränig/Königsberg. Attached to 24. Panzer-Division with effect from 6 January 1943. Before that he was Führer of the D.V.K. (German liaison staff) with 1. Romanian Kavallerie-Division, and prior to the encirclement was a member of the liaison staff of Romanian 3. Armee. Took command of Kradschützen-Abteilung 4 from Rittmeister von Götz. Later commanded II./Panzergrenadier-Regiment 26. Captured at Stalingrad. Died 7 April 1943 in Oranki POW Camp.

Hunger, Leutnant d.R. Hans; born 5 September 1919 Menden. In Panzerjäger-Abteilung 40. Listed as MIA 1 January 1943 near Gorodishsche, Stalingrad. Post-MIA promotion from Feldwebel to Leutnant d.R. Still listed as MIA today. His name is on Cube 35, Panel 8 at Rossoshka Sammelfriedhof.

Freiherr von Imhoff, Oberleutnant; Abteilung Adjutant III./Panzerartillerie-Regiment 89 at establishment of Division. Oberleutnant RDA 01.10.41 (34). Survived Stalingrad. In reformed Pz.Art.Rgt.89 as Chef 8./Pz.Art.Rgt.89. Promoted to Hauptmann RDA 01.01.44. Remained with 24. Panzer-Division until the end of the war. Survived the war.

Ingerfurth, Oberarzt d.R. Dr. Heinrich; born 2 August 1906 Schmidtlorst. Transferred on 7 January 1943 from Panzerjäger-Abteilung 194 to Panzergrenadier-Regiment 26. Listed as MIA 25 December 1942 in Stalingrad but was in fact captured. Died February 1943 in a POW hospital in Stalingrad. His remains were unable to be recovered by the Volksbund.

Jacobi, Oberleutnant d.R.z.V Karl Herbert; born 27 December 1898 Weimar. Chef Stabsbatterie IV./Panzerartillerie-Regiment 89. Took command of IV./Pz.Art.Rgt.89 on 8 September 1942 when something happened to Oberstleutnant Melchers. Clasp to the Iron Cross Second Class on 10 September 1942. Severe concussion. Probably flown out of the Stalingrad pocket. Died 18 March 1945 in Heubude near Danzig as a Hauptmann.

Jahnson, Sonderführer; Dolmetscher to Ic on Stab 24. Panzer-Division. Transferred on 17 August 1942 from Posen Dolmetscher Ersatz Abteilung to 24.Pz.Div.

Jankowski, Rittmeister Hans O.; Chef Stabsschwadron/ Kradschützen-Abteilung 4. Began the war as a Leutnant and Pakzug Kdr. in Radfahr-Abt. 1. Took command of 4./Radfahr-Abt. 1 in 1941 as an Oberleutnant. Stabsschwadron Commander at establishment of Division. Temporary commander of II./Pz.Gr.Rgt.26 in May 1942, then back to Stab/Krad.Abt.4. Took command of 6./Pz.Gr.Rgt.26 on 9 August 1942. Wounded on 27 September 1942. Survived Stalingrad. Took command of reformed I./Pz.Gr.Rgt.21 on 17 September 1943. Wounded on 6 November 1943. Survived the war. Became an Oberstleutnant in the Bundeswehr (Luftwaffe).

Jansen, Leutnant Helmut; born 6 October 1912 Peterswalde. Panzerjäger-Abteilung 40. Iron Cross First Class on 4 August 1942.

Kanschat, Oberleutnant Kurt; born 12 June 1910 Tilsit, East Prussia. Peacetime unit was Radfahr-Abteilung 1. Zugführer in 6./Panzergrenadier-Regiment 26 when wounded on 26 July 1942. Promoted to Rittmeister RDA 01.08.43 (157). Killed 1 November 1943 Korsoanovka, near Nikopol while in Panzergrenadier-Regiment 26. Posthumous promotion to Major RDA 01.11.43. Probably buried as an unknown soldier in Kirovograd Sammelfriedhof.

Karpinski, Hauptmann

Karrasch, Leutnant d.R.; Zugführer in 1./Panzerpionier-Bataillon 40. Wounded on 20 September 1942.

Karsten, Leutnant d.R. Friedrich; born 3 September 1922 Danzig-Langfuhr. In Panzergrenadier-Regiment 26. Killed 4 September 1942 south-west of Stalingrad.

Kastens, Oberleutnant Georg; born 15 April 1915 Schmalförden. Chef 9./Panzerartillerie-Regiment 89. Peacetime unit was reiter-Artillerie-Abteilung 1. Promoted to Hauptmann RDA 01.12.42 (371) and took command of 9. Batterie. Listed as MIA 16 January 1943 in Stalingrad. Still listed as MIA. His name is on Cube 38, Panel 19 at Rossoshka Sammelfriedhof.

Kaul, Oberzahlmeister; 2. Mitarbeiter to IVa on Stab 24. Panzer-Division at establishment of Division. 1. Mitarbeiter from 15 November 1942. Wounded and captured at Stalingrad.

Keiler, Oberleutnant d.R. Christian; born 10 September 1913. Führer 6./Panzergrenadier-Regiment 26. Wounded on 13 September 1942 but stayed with the troops. Again wounded on 15 September 1942. German Cross in Gold on 8 December 1942. Listed as MIA 22 January 1943 in Stalingrad but was in fact captured. Survived captivity and returned home. Still alive in 2001.

Kelz, Oberleutnant Werner; born 30 June 1916. Peacetime unit was Infanterie-Regiment 31. Chef 5./Panzergrenadier-Regiment 26. Transferred to Infanterie-Regiment 276 in December 1942. Hauptmann RDA 01.01.43 (326). Listed as MIA 3 January 1943 in Stalingrad. Not listed on Volksbund so may have survived captivity.

Kerscher, Leutnant d.R. Ludwig; born 12 August 1912. Führer 3./Panzergrenadier-Regiment 26. Killed 1 October 1942 in an accident. Another source reports that he was missing in action October 1942 in Stalingrad.

von Keudell, Oberleutnant Dietrich Otto Hubertus Wilhelm Georg; born 21 September 1918 Berlin. Zugführer 1. Zug in 2./Panzer-Regiment 24. Married Luise von Below and fathered four children, three of them after the war. Leutnant RDA 01.09.38 (1422). In January 1939 was Zugführer in 2./Reit.Rgt.2. Transferred from Pz.Rgt.24 to Führerreserve OKH on 25 May 1942. Survived the war. Died 18 May 1951 Kahlesand-an-der-Elbe.

Freiherr von Keyserlingk, Oberleutnant Werner; born 21 November 1914 Zernikow. In Panzergrenadier-Regiment 21. Iron Cross First Class on 12 August 1942. Survived Stalingrad. In reformed Division. Survived the war. Died 2 June 1997.

Kiehlnecker, Oberleutnant Wilhelm Christian; born 11 March 1910 Ulm. Chef 8./Panzergrenadier-Regiment 26. Died 25 April 1945 in a POW hospital in Neudamm, Poland as a Rittmeister. His remains were unable to be recovered by the Volksbund.

Kirchner, Hauptmann d.R.z.V. Bernhard; born 20 August 1895. Führer Gr.Kw.Kol.f.Betr.Stoff 40. Surrounded at Stalingrad. Appointed Kolonneführer on 12 December 1942. Listed as MIA 30 December 1942 in Stalingrad. Not known if he survived captivity.

Kleeberg, Oberarzt Dr.; Transferred on 29 October 1942 from Dinafü 40 to 5. Armee Gef. Sammelstelle.

Klein, Oberleutnant Werner; born 10 May 1914 Königsberg. Peacetime unit was Pionier-Bataillon 1. Chef 3./Panzerpionier-Bataillon 40. Oberleutnant RDA 01.06.40 (571). Killed 3 July 1942 north of Yatebnoye, near Voronesh, when the barrel of a mortar exploded. Buried in Gremyachye near Voronezh. His remains were unable to be recovered by the Volksbund.

Kleinjohann, Assistenarzt d.R. Dr.; II./Panzergrenadier-Regiment 26. Wounded on 10 September 1942 but stayed with the troops. Temporarily transferred to Kradschützen-Abteilung 4. Transferred on 7 November 1942 from Kradschützen-Abteilung 4 back to Pz.Gr.Rgt.26. Survived Stalingrad. In reformed Kradschützen-Abteilung 4. Regimentsarzt Panzergrenadier-Regiment 26 on 1 May 1944.

Klinge, Oberleutnant; Zugführer 2./Panzer-Nachrichten-Abteilung 86. Transferred on 31 October 1942 from Panzer-Nachrichten-Ersatz-Abteilung 26 to Panzer-Nachrichten-Abteilung 86. Wounded in December 1942 while on operations near Infanterie-Regiment 276 of 94. Infanterie-Division. Transferred to Ausbildung-Einheit Weiss on 7 January 1943 for training as an infantry officer.

von Klot-Heydenfeld, Sonderführer Nikolai Wolfgang August; born 30 June 1894 Riga. Dolmetscher for Ic on Stab 24. Panzer-Division at establishment of Division. Killed 4 July 1942 near Yunevka-on-Don, Voronesh. Now buried in Kursk-Besedino.

von Knebel Doeberitz, Rittmeister Rudolf; born 19 October 1913 Pasewalk. Adjutant Schützen-Brigade 24. Entered the service in 1934 as an officer candidate in Reiter-Regiment 6 in Pasewalk. Promoted to Leutnant in 1936. In 1938, he became Adjutant of I./Kavallerie-Regiment 6 in Darmstadt and Adjutant to Aufklärungs-Abteilung 36 in 1939. Iron Cross Second Class in 1939. Commanded the cavalry training squadron in Krampnitz in 1940. Iron Cross First Class in 1940. Commander of Reiter Schwadron in Aufklärungs-Abteilung 129 in 1941. Transferred to Reiter-Regiment 1 in 1941 to command 3. Schwadron. Commanded 3./Panzergrenadier-Regiment 21 upon the conversion of the Division. Led this Schwadron until

30 July 1942 when he became Adjutant of Schützen-Brigade 24. German Cross in Gold on 29 August 1942. Wounded 3 September 1942. Survived Stalingrad. General Staff training in 1943. Promoted to Major i.G. RDA 01.01.44., Ib of 24. Panzer-Division from 1 February 1944. Transferred to the General Staff on 1 June 1944. Later transferred back to 24. Panzer-Division, becoming Ia in September 1944. Commanded 24.Pz.Div. from 26 March 1945 until the end of the war. He took command after General von Nostitz-Wallwitz was severely wounded. Knight's Cross on 9 May 1945. Survived the war. Died 5 July 1994 Reinbek/Hamburg.

von Knobloch, Oberleutnant d.R. Gerhard; born 2 May 1907 Friedrichsburg. Führer 5./Kradschützen-Abteilung 4. Wounded on 28 July 1942 as a Zugführer but stayed with the troops. Again wounded on 8 September 1942 but died the same day from these wounds.

Koch, Hauptmann Hermann; born 16 March 1914. Chef 3./Panzerartillerie-Regiment 89. Peacetime unit was reiter-Artillerie-Abteilung 1. Fought in France as Oberleutnant and Chef 5./r.A.R.1. Wounded on 9 June 1940. Iron Cross First Class on 25 July 1940. Took command of I./Pz.Art.Rgt.89 on 3 September when von Pawel replaced von Nostitz as Regiment Commander. German Cross in Gold on 6 November 1942. Listed as MIA 15 January 1943 in Stalingrad but was in fact captured. Post-MIA promotion to Major RDA 01.04.43 (16a4). Died in Oranki POW Camp in 1943.

Koch, Oberleutnant Horst; Zugführer 1. Zug in 12./Panzer-Regiment 24. Promoted to Oberleutnant 15 June 1942. Wounded 8 September 1942. Survived Stalingrad. Survived the war.

Köhler, Leutnant Georg; born 24 July 1917 Nizhne-Petropavlovsk/ Chelyabinsk in Siberia. Führer 3./Panzergrenadier-Regiment 26. Peacetime unit was Kavallerie-Regiment 3. Wounded 27 November 1942. German Cross in Gold on 8 December 1942. Knight's Cross on 3 January 1943. Became Adjutant of I./Panzergrenadier-Regiment 26. Listed as MIA 13 January 1943 in Stalingrad but was in fact captured at Stalingrad. Post-MIA promotion to Oberleutnat RDA 01.02.42 (1693), later improved to RDA 01.12.42 (150). Survived captivity and returned home. Recorded his experiences in a book titled "Die Zeit fliegt hin in Windeseile: Erinnerungen (1917–1997)". Died April 2006 Stein bei Nürnberg.

Köhler, Oberleutnant; Regiment Waffen und Gerät Offizier Panzerartillerie-Rgt. 89.

Köhne, Leutnant d.R. Hans-Albrecht; born 23 November 1920 Glöthe. Zugführer in 2./Panzergrenadier-Regiment 26. Iron Cross First Class on 2 August 1942. Wounded on 17 September 1942. Died as a result of wounds 30 November 1942 in a homeland hospital. Buried in a single grave in his home town of Glöthe.

Kohrs, Leutnant der Feldgendarmerie; Feldgendarmerie Trupp 40. Promoted to Leutnant der Fg. on 1 August 1942. Attended a three week training course. In Feldgendarmerie Trupp 40 from 10 October 1942. Transferred to Ausbildung-Einheit Weiss on 7 January 1943 for training as an infantry officer. Attached to Kampfgruppe von Below on 8 January 1943.

Kolbe, Oberleutnant Hans-Joachim; born 30 August 1906. Zugführer 3. Zug Werkstatt-Kompanie 40; Wounded on 25 September 1942. German Cross in Gold on 21 January 1943 while on Division Stab. Listed as MIA 6 January 1943 in Stalingrad. Still listed as MIA. His name is on Cube 44, Panel 7 at Rossoshka Sammelfriedhof.

Kolczyk, Rittmeister Heinz; born 20 November 1912 Breitenbach/Harz. Schwadron Commander; 2./Kradschützen-Abteilung 4; In Police School in Brandenburg/Havel from 7 April 1931 to 8 May 1932. He wanted to become a detective. Member of Police from 3 May 1932 to 30 September 1933. In Berlin State Police from 1 October 1933 to 10 February 1934. All young squads of policemen had been transferred to the State Police with the aim of establishing new Army units. From 11 February 1934 to 2 October 1935, in the Insterburg State Police where they only received military training. Transferred on 2 October 1935 to Radfahr-Abteilung 1 which was being established in Tilsit, East Prussia. His rank of Oberwachtmeister der Landespolizei was changed to Unteroffizier. His role was the training of recruits. Promoted to Wachtmeister on 1 April 1938. Promoted to Oberwachtmeister on 1 October 1938. Promoted to Leutnant on 1 October 1939, backdated to the Polish Campaign. Iron Cross Second Class in September 1939. Promoted to Oberleutnant on 1 July 1940. Commanded a Schwadron in Reiter-Regiment 1. Iron Cross First Class in October 1941. Promoted to Rittmeister on 1 May 1942. Wounded on 20 August 1942. Stayed with the troops. Severely wounded on 29 August 1942. German Cross in Gold on 5 November 1942. Survived Stalingrad. During his recovery, he taught tactics at the Schule für schnelle Truppen in Krampnitz, Berlin. On 3 February 1944, commanded Panzer-Aufklärungs-Abteilung 7 (7.PD). Knight's Cross on 6 April 1944. Promoted to Major RDA 01.08.44. From 10 December 1944 until the end of the war, trained officer candidates at the Schule in Krampnitz. Survived the war. Died 10 November 2008 Hamburg.

von Köller und von Stuckrad, Major Otto; born 28 October 1903 Potsdam. Kommandeur Panzerpionier-Bataillon 40. Entered military service on 1 April 1924 as a cavalryman. Leutnant RDA 01.04.29 while in Reiter-Regiment 5. Oberleutnant RDA 01.04.33. Transferred to Pionier-Bataillon 3 in October 1934. Appointed Chef 1./Pi.Btl.3. a year later. Hauptmann RDA 01.04.36. Transferred to Pionier-Bataillon 23 in October 1936. Discharged May 1937. Recalled to Pionier-Bataillon 3 in January 1939 and began the war in this unit. Appointed Chef 2./Pi.Btl.258 in early 1939. Residence in 1939–1940 was Küstrin-Neustadt. Promoted to Major RDA 01.10.41 (22). Commander Pz.Pi.Btl.40 at establishment of 24. Panzer-Division. Wounded in July 1942.

König, Leutnant d.R. Gustav Adolf; born 1 November 1913 Hemer. Führer 9./Panzergrenadier-Regiment 26. Killed 29 September 1942 in Stalingrad. Posthumous promotion to Oberleutnant. His remains were unable to be recovered by the Volksbund.

Köppel, Leutnant Thilo; born 14 May 1920. Führer 3./Panzerartillerie-Regiment 89. Peacetime unit was Artillerie-Regiment 19. Took command of Batterie on 3 September. Listed as MIA 22 January 1943 in Stalingrad but was in fact captured. Post-MIA promotion to Oberleutnant RDA 01.07.43 (31). Not known if he survived captivity.

Korb, Oberleutnant; Wounded on 29 August 1942 but stayed with the troops. Again wounded on 8 September 1942.

Korbeslühr, Major (Ing.) Karl; born 21 May 1908. Regiment Ingenieur Offizier Pz.Rgt.24. Peacetime unit was Panzer-Regiment 2. Major (Ing.) RDA 01.01.42 (220b). Listed as MIA 22 January 1943 in Stalingrad.

Korte, Leutnant der Feldgendarmerie; Feldgendarmerie Trupp 40; Promoted to Leutnant der Fg. on 1 August 1942. Attended a three week training course. In Feldgendarmerie Trupp 40 from 10 October 1942. Transferred to Ausbildung-Einheit Weiss on 7 January 1943 for training as an infantry officer. On 8 January 1943, was attached to Kampfgruppe von Below.

Krage, Leutnant Heinz Wolfgang; born 15 May 1920 Königsberg. Stab III./Panzerartillerie-Regiment 89; Missing in action January 1943 in Stalingrad.

Krämer, Leutnant d.R. Erwin; born 20 August 1914 Königsberg, East Prussia. Abteilung Ordonnanzoffizier II./Panzergrenadier-Regiment 26. Wounded on 21 September 1942 but stayed with the troops. Iron Cross First Class on 15 October 1942.

Krebs, Oberleutnant d.R. Karl Heinrich Otto; born 9 May 1914 Frankfurt am Main. Chef 3./Panzerjäger-Abteilung 40. Wounded on 4 September 1942 but stayed with the troops. Iron Cross First Class on 4 September 1942. Listed as MIA 6 January 1943 in Stalingrad but was in fact captured. Died 1 April 1943 in Dubovka POW Camp. Probably buried as an unknown soldier in Rossoshka Sammelfriedhof.

Kreke, Oberarzt d.R. Dr. Bernhard; born 8 February 1907 Neuenkirchen in Oldenburg. Completed his medical degree at Göttingen University in 1929. Sanitäts-Kompanie (mot.) 1/40. Iron Cross Second Class on 2 August 1942. Listed as MIA 21 January 1943 in Stalingrad. Not known if he survived captivity.

Krieger, Leutnant d.R. Artur; born 3 July 1907 in East Prussia. Transferred on 6 October 1942 from Bäckerei-Kompanie 40 to Dinafü 40. Listed as MIA 29 December 1942 in Stalingrad. Not known if he survived captivity.

Krinn, Oberzahlmeister Friedrich Hans; born 13 May 1907 Mohrungen. Abteilung Zahlmeister I./Panzer-Regiment 24. Missing in action January 1943 in Stalingrad. Still listed as MIA. His name is on Cube 46, Panel 10 at Rossoshka Sammelfriedhof.

von der Wickerau Graf von Krockow, Leutnant Ulrich; born 5 May 1921 Kleinschlatau. Zugführer 3./Panzergrenadier-Regiment 21. Wounded on 4 July 1942. Survived Stalingrad. In reformed I./Pz.Gr.Rgt.21 as Abteilung Adjutant. Transferred on 17 September 1943 to 29. Infanterie-Division. Died 17 December 1943 in Cassino, Italy.

Kroeger, Oberleutnant d.R.z.V.; Führer Kartenstelle on Stab 24. Panzer-Division.

Kroher, Leutnant d.R. Walter; born 17 January 1920 München. Zugführer in 1./Panzer-Regiment 24. Transferred from the Führerreserve to Pz.Rgt.24 on 9 October 1942. Severely wounded 19 January 1943 west of Orlovka. Died of wounds 21 January 1943 in a field-hospital. His remains have not yet been recovered.

Krüger, Oberleutnant d.R. Horst Hermann; born 21 March 1917. Zugführer 4./Panzergrenadier-Regiment 21. Promoted to Oberleutnant on 22 June 1942. Severely wounded on 4 July 1942. Survived the war. Died 6 September 1997.

Kugler, Oberarzt d.R. Dr. Johann (Hans); born 21 April 1906 München. Regiment Arzt Pz.Rgt.24. In 1939 was living in Arnsdorf. Transferred 07.01.1943 from II./Art.Rgt. 194 to Pz.Art.Rgt.89. Transferred from Pz.Art.Rgt.89 to Pz.Rgt. 24. Listed as MIA 02.01.1943 Stalingrad. Posthumous promotion to Stabsarzt d.R. His name is on Cube 47, Panel 17 at Rossoshka Sammelfriedhof.

Kühl, Leutnant Paul Adolf; born 7 November 1923. Zugführer 6./Panzergrenadier-Regiment 26. Peacetime unit was Reiter-Regiment 2. Leutnant RDA 01.12.42 (1875). Fought in Russia. Awarded the Wound Badge. In June 1943 was a Zugführer in 6./Pz.Gr.Rgt.26. On 21 February 1944 was a Zugführer in Pz.Gr.Ers.Btl.413. Transferred back to Pz.Gr.Rgt.26 on 17 April 1944. Oberleutnant RDA 01.10.44 (124). Wounded 11 November 1944.

Kuhn, Leutnant d.R. Erich; born 8 June 1912 in CSR. Stab II./Panzerartillerie-Regiment 89. Transferred on 6 November 1942 from leichte-Artillerie-Ersatz-Abteilung 228 to Pz.Art.Rgt.89. Listed as MIA 1 January 1943 in Stalingrad. Still listed as MIA. His name is on Cube 47, Panel 19 at Rossoshka Sammelfriedhof.

Kühn, Oberleutnant; Zugführer 2./Panzer-Regiment 24. Promoted to Oberleutnant on 15 June 1942. Later became Schwadroführer. Flown out of the Kessel.

SPANNOCCHI

Oberleutnant Kühn in Rennes, France

Kuls, Assistenarzt d.R. Dr. Martin; born 26.12.1915 Königsberg. Abteilung Hilfsarzt III./Panzer-Regiment 24. Wounded 04.09.1942. Again wounded 27.09.1942. Iron Cross First Class 09.10.1942. Promoted to Oberarzt d.R. 01.11.1942. Flown out of Kessel in January 1943 because of swollen legs and fast-approaching starvation. In reformed Panzer Regiment. Wounded between 30.07.–06.08.1944 in France. German Cross in Gold 30.12.1944 as Stabsarzt d.R. in I./Panzer-Regiment 24. Survived the war.

Kuls, Leutnant Wolfgang; born 27.02.1920 Königsberg. Nachrichtenoffizier II./Panzer-Regiment 24. Entered service 03.11.1937. Iron Cross Second Class 25.07.1940. Iron Cross First Class 23.11.1941. Wounded 30.06.1942. In reformed Panzer Regiment. Promoted to Rittmeister 01.10.1944. Knight's Cross 24.02.1945 as Kdr. III./Panzer-Regiment 24. Survived the war. Died 8 August 2002.

SPANNOCCHI

The much-loved doctor of III./Panzer-Regiment 24, Dr. Martin Kuls

Kumminger, Kriegsgerichtsrat Dr.; III (Division Judge Advocate) Stab 24. Panzer- Division. Transferred on 22 June 1942 from Division Nr. 188 to 24.Pz.Div. Transferred on 28 September 1942 from 24.Pz.Div. to IV. Armeekorps.

Kuse, Oblt. d.R. Batterie Commander Panzerartillerie-Regiment 89; Transferred on 8 November 1942 from Art.-Ersatz-Abt. 54 to Pz.Art.Rgt.89.

Lackner, Oberleutnant Fritz; born 16 June 1911. Chef Stabsbatterie I. Abteilung/Panzerartillerie-Regiment 89. Passionate and successful horseman prior to the war. Fought in France with II./r.A.R.1. Iron Cross Second Class on 21 May 1940. Survived Stalingrad. In mid-1944, as a Hauptmann, he was transferred to a battalion commanders training course. Survived the war. Died 2 March 1990 in Groß-Twülpstedt.

Lakenbrink, Leutnant d.R. Heinz Joseph; born 17 June 1920 Duisburg. Zugführer 3./Panzergrenadier-Regiment 21. Wounded on 28 August 1942 but stayed with the troops. Again wounded on 5 September 1942 but stayed with the troops. Again wounded on 6 September 1942 but stayed with the troops. Iron Cross First Class on 10 September 1942. Killed 12 September 1942 in Stalingrad. Probably buried as an unknown soldier in Rossoshka Sammelfriedhof.

von der Lancken, Major Dietrich; born 13 June 1911 Roschinnow. Kommandeur III./Panzer-Regiment 24. Entered service 01.04.1930. Peacetime unit was Panzer-Regiment 15. Oberleutnant RDA 01.10.35 (60). In January 1939 was Chef 5./Pz.Rgt.15. Iron Cross Second Class 18 September 1939. Iron Cross First Class 28 May 1940. Major RDA 01.04.42 (35). An experienced and battle-hardened leader of panzers, von der Lancken was transferred in early 1942 to take command of the newly formed III./Panzer-Regiment 24. Knight's Cross 29 October 1942. Transferred from Pz.Rgt.24 to Führerreserve OKH on 1 November 1942. Killed 29 December 1942 by the first mortar impacts preceding a Soviet attack in Donskoi-Krassnovka, near Millerovo, as commander of Pz.Abt.138. Also killed in the same strike were his adjutant and communications officer. Lancken's remains have not been recovered.

Lang, Assistenarzt; Wounded on 30 August 1942.

von Langenn-Steinkeller, Oberleutnant Jürgen; Chef Stabsschwadron III./Panzer-Regiment 24. Took command of Schwadron 22.08.1942. Transferred to Division staff as Verbindungs-Offizier (liaison officer). Commander of an Alarmeinheit on 14 January 1943. Wounded 16 January 1943 in right knee and right foot. Flown out 23 January 1943 and sent to Stalino hospital.

von Langenn-Steinkeller, Rittmeister Ernst-Hasse; born 7 December 1916 Matschdorf, Neumark. Chef 3./Kradschützen-Abteilung 4. Entered service on 1 April 1936 as an officer candidate in Reiter-Regiment 10. Promoted to Leutnant on 1 January 1938. In the Polish campaign, he was Abteilung Adjutant in the Aufklärungs-Abteilung of 14. Infanterie-Division. He was then transferred to 1. Kavallerie-Division, participating in the French and Russian campaigns. Won the Iron Cross First and Second Class in France. Commander of 3./Krad.Abt.4 at the establishment of 24. Panzer-Division. Promoted to Rittmeister on 8 June 1942. Took command of Abteilung on 8 September 1942 when von der Groeben was killed. Fell sick with dyptheria and because of this, handed command of Krad.Abt.4 to Rittmeister Wrede on 13 October 1942. German Cross in Gold on 25 January 1943. Survived Stalingrad and later led the reformed Abteilung. Later commanded Pz.Gr.Rgt.26 from 27 March 1944 to 4 April 1944. Wounded on 4 April 1944. He held the Wound Badge in Gold. Promoted to Major on 1 June 1944. Knight's Cross on 9 June 1944. Survived the war. Married Anna Therese von Alvensleben on 30 January 1947. Joined the Bundeswehr and commanded Panzer-Aufklärungs-Bataillon 3 until 1959. Retired as an Oberst. Died 5 September 2004 Sassenberg.

Langermann und Erlencamp, Oberleutnant; Chef 5./Panzergrenadier-Regiment 26. Wounded on 25 July 1942.

Lechtenberg, Major (Ing) Wilhelm; born 30 January 1905.V (Division Ingenieur) Stab 24. Panzer-Division at establishment of Division. Peacetime unit was Pionier-Bataillon 50. Major RDA 01.12.41 (90a). Listed as MIA 24 January 1943 in Stalingrad but was in fact captured at Stalingrad. Survived captivity and returned home. Died 23 March 1966 in Dusseldorf.

von Lederer, Oberst Hans-Wolfgang; Proposed Regiment Commander for Pz.Rgt.24. Peacetime unit was Panzer-Abwehr-Abteilung 6. In January 1939 was Kommandeur Pz.Abw.Abt.6. His name was put forward to take command of Pz.Rgt.24 but the Division did not want him because he was unknown to them. Major RDA 01.01.1937. Commander of Panzerjäger-Abteilung 6 of 6. Inf.-Div. at the outbreak of the war. Oberst RDA 01.03.1942 (9).

Legat, Rittmeister Karl; born 15 August 1908 Jorlen. Chef 1./Panzergrenadier-Regiment 26. Peacetime unit was Radfahr-Abteilung 1. Rittmeister RDA 01.04.42 (1167) C. Killed 26 July 1942 near Nizhne-Chirskaya. Awarded posthumous German Cross in Gold on 4 September 1942.

Leitreuter, Major Kurt Paul Benjamin; born 29 July 1906 Königsberg. Kommandeur III./Panzerartillerie-Regiment 89. Began the war in Panzerartillerie-Regiment 13. Abteilung Commander at establishment of Division. Major RDA 01.01.42 (89). Wounded on 5 July 1942. Survived Stalingrad. Died 28 April 1945 in Sandrovac, Yugoslavia.

SPANNOCCHI

Oberleutnant von Schmidt-Pauli and Oberst von Lengerke near Voronesh

von Lengerke, Oberst Wilhelm; born 17 June 1894 Salchow. Kommandeur Panzergrenadier-Regiment 21. Entered the service on 1 October 1913 as an officer candidate. Promoted to Leutnant on 6 August 1914. Became part of the Reichswehr after the First World War, commanding II./Kavallerie-Regiment 13 until 1937. Promoted to Oberstleutnant on 1 June 1940 and Oberst on 1 February 1942. Commanded I./Reiter-Regiment 1 in 1940 before becoming part of the Mission to Romania until November 1940. Knight's Cross on 31 August 1941 for deeds as Commander of I./Reiter-Regiment 1. Called back to active duty in 1941 to lead Panzergrenadier-Regiment 21. Regiment Commander at establishment of Division. Killed 26 August 1942 near Krassnoarmeisk, south of Stalingrad. Posthumous promotion to Generalmajor backdated to 1 August 1942.

von Lenski, Generalleutnant Arno; born 20 July 1893 Czymochen, East Prussia. Division Commander; 24. Panzer-Division Stab; Entered the service on 23 March 1912 as an officer candidate. Promoted to Leutnant on 16 June 1913. Became part of the Reichswehr after the First World War, commanding Kavallerie-Regiment 6. Promoted to Oberstleutnant on 1 March 1936 and Oberst on 1 August 1938. Took brief command of Schützen-Brigade 2 in 1939 and Schützen-Brigade 11 in 1941, these periods being broken up by his tenure as Commander of the Schule für Schnelle Truppen. Temporarily commanded 2. Panzer-Division from 1 June 1942 to 4 September 1942. Promoted to Generalmajor on 1 June 1942. Took command of Division from Oberst von Broich at midday on 14 September 1942. Division Commander from 14 September

1942 to 2 February 1942. Confirmed as Division Commander on 15 November 1942. Wounded on 31 October 1942. Stayed with the troops. German Cross in Gold on 21 January 1943. Promoted to Generalleutnant on 1 January 1943. Captured 2 February 1943, remained POW until 1949. He was one of the founding members of the 'Nationalkomitee Freies Deutschland'. In Soviet-occupied East Germany, von Lenski eventually became the commander of the 'Panzerschule für die Nationalen Volksarmee'. Died 4 October 1986 in Eichwalde, East Germany.

Leopold, Oberleutnant Gerhard; born 26 November 1911. Führer der Trosse, Stab II./Panzer-Regiment 24. Peacetime unit was Reiter-Regiment 2. Oberleutnant RDA 01.12.41 (834). Wounded 05.09.1942 but stayed with the troops. Transferred from Pz.Rgt.24 to Ib Abteilung of Divisionsstab as Pferdemusterungs Offizier on 01.10.1942. Transferred from Ib back to Pz.Rgt.24 on 15.11.1942. Listed as MIA 23 January 1943 Stalingrad. Captured at Stalingrad.

von Le Tanneux von Saint-Paul, Oberleutnant Guy-Bernhard; born 15 December 1916 Königsberg. Chef 12./Panzer-Regiment 24. Peacetime unit was Reiter-Regiment 2. Leutnant RDA 01.09.38 (147). In January 1939 was a Zugführer in 3./Reit.Rgt.2. Wounded 30.07.1942 but stayed with the troops. Again wounded 29.08.1942. German Cross in Gold 29.08.1942. Rittmeister RDA 01.12.42 (389). Listed as MIA 23.01.1943 Stalingrad. Severely wounded in late January 1943 by a mortar burst: both thighs were smashed and his skull was split open, exposing his brain. Brought into a makeshift hospital in the Bread Factory cellar. Euthanised with morphine by Stabsarzt Dr. Rocholl on 02.02.1943. His remains have not been recovered.

von Le Tanneux von Saint-Paul, Oberleutnant d.R. Ulrich; born 28 July 1911 Otten. Assigned to 24. Panzer-Division. Brother of Guy-Bernhard. Promoted to Oberleutnant on 1 August 1940. Transferred on 25 December 1942 from 24. Panzer-Division to XXXXVIII. Panzerkorps where he became Korps O2. Survived Stalingrad. Rittmeister at end of the war. Apart from Guy, two other brothers—Harry and Julius—were killed during the war. After the war, he returned to his pre-war profession as a farmer.

Lichte, Oberleutnant Karl; born 15 July 1913. Führer 1./Panzergrenadier-Regiment 26. Promoted to Leutnant on 14 October 1942. German Cross in Gold on 10 January 1943. Listed as MIA 14 January 1943 in Stalingrad but was in fact captured. Post-MIA promotion to Oberleutnant RDA 01.12.42 (132). Survived captivity and returned home. Died 19 August 1999.

Liebe, Oberleutnant Günther Hans-Jürgen; born 04.02.1920 Göttingen. Nachrichtenoffizier I./Panzer-Regiment 24. Peacetime unit was Panzer-Regiment 6. Oberleutnant RDA 01.04.42 (1679). Wounded 29 August 1942. Killed 8 October 1942 in northern Stalingrad. Iron Cross First Class 15 October 1942. Probably buried as an unknown soldier in Rossoshka Sammelfriedhof.

Lilienthal, T.K.V. Inspektor Erich; Abteilung Techniker Inspektor III./Panzer-Regiment 24. Captured at Stalingrad. Survived captivity and returned home.

Lindemann, Oberleutnant; Kradschützen-Abteilung 4; Promoted to Oberleutnant on 15 June 1942.

SPANNOCCHI

Oberleutnant Liebe (right) poses in front of a destroyed T-34 with Rittmeister von Mirbach (sitting) and Major von Winterfeld (left).

Lindemann, Leutnant Werner; born 12 December 1918 Insterburg, East Prussia. Peacetime unit was II./Artillerie-Regiment 57. Transferred on 20 October 1942 from Artillerie-Ausbilding-Abteilung 280 to IV./Pz.Art.Rgt.89. Listed as MIA 23 January 1943 in Stalingrad. Post-MIA promotion to Oberleutnant RDA 01.04.43 (100). Still listed as MIA. His name is on Cube 51, Panel 14 at Rossoshka Sammelfriedhof.

Lindenberg, Leutnant; Batterie Offizier 1./Panzerartillerie-Regiment 89.

von Loesch, Oberleutnant Christian; born 1917 in Silesia. Zugführer Erkundung Zug of I./Panzer-Regiment 24. Began the war as a Zugführer in 1./Reiter-Rgt. 21. Erkundung Zugführer at establishment of Division. Survived Stalingrad. Promoted to Major 01.01.1944. During the Red Army advance in 1944–1945, he fled with his wife and child to Lower Saxony. Survived the war. Died prior to 2005.

von Loesch, Oberleutnant Gerhard; born 2 April 1915 Langhelwigsdorf, Kreis Bolkenhain. Zugführer 1. Zug in 10./Panzer-Regiment 24. Began the war as a Zugführer in 2./Reiter-Rgt. 21. Wounded in July 1942. Wounded 3 September 1942. Survived Stalingrad. Was in reformed Panzer Regiment. Wounded 27 January 1945 in Gardony, Hungary, but died while being transported to Sanko 1/81 HVP in Stuhlweißenburg. Today, buried in Szekesfehervar, Hungary: Block 1, Row 12, Grave 480.

Longére, Oberleutnant d.R. Heinz; born 20 April 1914 Berlin-Steglitz. Adjutant Feldersatz-Abteilung 40 at establishment of Division. Oberleutnant RDA 01.12.41. Took command of 7./Panzergrenadier-Regiment 21 on 28 July 1942. Wounded on 20 August 1942. Again wounded on 2 September 1942. Iron Cross Second Class on 10 September 1942. Survived Stalingrad. Died 23 January 1945 in Luxemburg as a Rittmeister.

Lorenz, Oberinspektor Werner; born 17 May 1905 Rothental, Thüringia. Technisches Beamter on Stab 24. Panzer-Division at establishment of Division. Captured at Stalingrad in January 1943.

Edler von Löw, Hauptmann d.R. Hans Ernst Bernhard Agydius; born 8 April 1911 Prag, Czechoslovakia. Chef 2./Panzerjäger-Abteilung 40. German Cross in Gold on 10 January 1943. Listed as MIA 23 January 1943 in Stalingrad but actually died in February 1943 in Stalingrad. His remains were unable to be recovered by the Volksbund.

Luber, Oberleutnant Heinz; born 17 October 1917; Adjutant Dinafü 40. Peacetime unit was Kraftfahr-Abteilung 7. Oberleutnant RDA 01.04.42 (14). Given adjutancy on 1 September 1942 when Hauptmann Hoger was promoted. Listed as MIA 31 December 1942 in Stalingrad. Not known if he survived captivity.

Lücke, Oberarzt Dr.; Wounded on 11 September 1942 but stayed with the troops. An Oberarzt d.R. Dr. Adolf Lücke, born 30 June 1915 in Austria, was MIA 12 July 1944 near Wilna while in Feldlazarett (mot.) 182.

Lüpschen, Pfarrer; Kriegspfarrer IVd (kath.) on Stab 24. Panzer-Division at establishment of Division. Wounded on 28 July 1942. Survived Stalingrad. Survived the war. Died September 1963 in Holzheim.

Luz, Leutnant Helwig; born 25 June 1921 Straubing. Zugführer 3. Zug in 10./Panzer-Regiment 24. Peacetime unit was Kavallerie-Regiment 17. Leutnant RDA 01.04.41 (1060). Wounded 30 July 1942. Again wounded 12 September 1942 but stayed with the troops. Killed 16 September 1942 in southern Stalingrad. Today, buried in Rossoshka Sammelfriedhof: Block 2, Row 6, Grave 222.

Mack, Oberleutnant Wolfgang Dietrich; born 12 October 1916 Danzig. Zugführer 5./Kradschützen-Abteilung 4. Peacetime unit was Kavallerie-Regiment 4. Oberleutnant RDA 01.04.42 (596). Wounded on 28 July 1942 but stayed with the troops. Again wounded on 25 September 1942 but stayed with the troops. Killed 14 October 1942 in northern Stalingrad.

Magens, Leutnant d.R. Hobe; born 4 December 1921 Kollmar, Hamburg. In Panzerartillerie-Regiment 89. Wounded on 28 July 1942 but stayed with the troops. Iron Cross First Class on 17 August 1942. Listed as MIA 31 December 1942 in Stalingrad. Post-MIA promotion to Oberleutnant d.R. Still listed as MIA. His name is on Cube 53, Panel 19 at Rossoshka Sammelfriedhof.

Maier, Oberleutnant Fritz, born 22 June 1918 Nitzwalde. Abteilung Adjutant II./Panzergrenadier-Regiment 26 at establishment of Division. Peacetime unit was Kavallerie-Regiment 4. Oberleutnant RDA 01.04.42 (781). Killed 6 July 1942 4km north-east of Malyshevo. Buried in Malyshevo. His remains have not yet been recovered by the Volksbund.

SPANNOCCHI

Leutnant von Maltzan proudly poses next to the same destroyed T-34

Freiherr von Maltzan zu Wartenberg und Penzlin, Oberleutnant d.R. Falk-Eberhard; born 9 June 1920 Kontopp/Mecklenburg. Abteilung Ordonnanzoffizier I./Panzer-Regiment 24. Grew up in the manor house "Ganschendorf". Joined the army in 1939 and was placed with the cavalry. Began the war as a Zugführer in 3./Reiter-Rgt. 21. Promoted to Oberleutnant 24 August 1942. Transferred 20 October 1942 from Pz.Rgt. 24 to Panzertruppenschule in Wunsdorf for a training course. In reformed Panzer Regiment. German Cross in Gold 26 December 1943 as an Oberleutnant in 11./Panzer-Regiment 24. Survived the war. After the war he moved to Bavaria and married Elisabeth Gräfin von Zech on 12 July 1945, a widow with three children. They had a daughter together. Divorced 12 May 1966. On 30 June 1966 he married Sigrid von Wietersheim, with whom he had a son. Died 6 August 1994 Gauting, Bavaria.

Mangels, Leutnant d.R. Ludwig; born 20 June 1912 Hainmühlen. Wounded on 12 September 1942. Survived Stalingrad. Killed 22 October 1944 near Nemmersdorf, East Prussia, while in Pz.Gr.Ers.u.Ausb.Btl.413. Posthumous promotion to Oberleutnant.

Manzel, Oberleutnant d.R.; Panzer-Nachrichten-Abteilung 86. Promoted to Oberleutnant on 31 August 1942.

Markgraf, Oberleutnant Paul; born 17 July 1910 Berlin. Adjutant Panzerjäger-Abteilung 40. Peacetime unit was Panzerjäger-Abteilung 16 in Hamm, Westphalia. Abteilung Adjutant at establishment of Division. Oberleutnant RDA 01.02.42 (197) C. Iron Cross First Class on 4 August 1942. Took command of Abteilung when Sälzer went on leave in September 1942. Promoted to Hauptmann RDA 01.12.42 (335). Given command of the Abteilung on 30 December 1942, backdated to 1 December 1942. Knight's Cross on 3 January 1943. Listed as MIA 6 January 1943 in Stalingrad but was in fact captured. Joined the anti-fascist groups in captivity. Released in 1945 and became the Communist-appointed chief of Berlin's 'Stadtpolizei'. He was suspended by the Magistrate on 26 July 1948 for his refusal to hand over the position to a new chief. The Soviets refused to recognise the suspension, so the new chief set up an alternate headquarters in the US sector. The 'Stadtpolizei' was Berlin's first city department to split. Rose to the rank of Oberst in the East German Nationalen Volksarmee. Retired in 1958. Died 7 April 1993.

Graf von Marogna-Redwitz, Rittmeister Rudolf; born 23 October 1914 München. Chef 6./Panzergrenadier-Regiment 21. Peacetime unit was Kavallerie-Regiment 17, a good posting for this passionate hunter and horseman. Transferred to Reiter-Regiment 1 in February 1940. Took command of its 6. Schwadron in May 1940. Commanded Schwadron from establishment of Division. Rittmeister RDA 01.03.42 (387a). Wounded on 7 July 1942 during an attack on the barracks in Voronesh. Earlier in the day, he had received an order to report to the Armee's Führerreserve because on 13 May his only brother, 22-year-old Hubert, an Oberleutnant in Aufkl.Abt.113, had been killed near Kharkov. This was in accordance with Germany's last son policy. He ignored this order because he wanted to lead his Schwadron during the attack but sadly, he died of his wounds on 9 July 1942 after being flown to Kriegslazarett 4/509 in Kursk. Because of his great personal bravery, he was awarded a posthumous German Cross in Gold on 26 August 1942. Buried in Kursk. His remains have not yet been recovered by the Volksbund.

Marschner, Leutnant d.R.; Zugführer 6./Panzergrenadier-Regiment 21. Wounded on 4 August 1942 but stayed with the troops. Wounded on 2 September 1942.

Martius, Leutnant Hans-Joachim; born 23 May 1920 Bonn. Abteilung Adjutant II./Panzergrenadier-Regiment 26. Führer of Sturmschwadron 24 from 18 November 1942 until its disbandment on 21–22 November 1942. Killed 25 December 1942 near Marinovka by a direct mortar hit. Posthumous promotion to Oberleutnant. Today, probably buried as an unknown soldier at Rossoshka Sammelfriedhof.

Marx, Kriegstechniker; Abteilung V Offizier I./Panzergrenadier-Regiment 21.

Masuhr, Leutnant d.R. Kurt; born 7 August 1920 Königsberg. Panzergrenadier-Regiment 26. Wounded on 29 August 1942. Iron Cross Second Class on 10 September 1942. Died as a result of wounds 11 September 1942 in Kriegslazarett 2/607 in Stalino. Buried in Donetsk. His remains have not yet been recovered by the Volksbund.

Matzke, Oberleutnant Heinz; born 25 March 1918 Breslau. Kompaniechef in Panzer-Nachrichten-Abteilung 86. Iron Cross Second Class on 14 September 1942. Survived Stalingrad. Survived the war. Still alive in 1997.

Matzke, Oberst Maximilian; born 15 October 1892 Tetschen, Südentland. Kommandeur Panzerartillerie-Regiment 89. Last peacetime assignment Artillerie-Regiment 4 in Naumburg. Promoted to Oberst RDA 01.04.42. Commander of Artillerie-Regiment 194. German Cross in Gold on 5 November 1942. On 14 December 1942 he assumed the role as Artillerieführer of

24.Pz.Div. He also acted as caretaker of 94.Inf.Div. after its disbandment until the last divisional unit had been reassigned to either 24.Pz.Div. or 16. Pz.Div. He was to retain command of Pz.Art.Rgt. 89 only until the return of Oberst von Nostitz-Wallwitz who, in fact, never returned to Stalingrad. Listed as MIA 23 January 1943 in Stalingrad. Still listed as MIA. His name is on Cube 55, Panel 9 at Rossoshka Sammelfriedhof.

Mayer, Hauptmann d.R.z.V. Ferdinand; born 10 May 1900 Oberplan. Chef 2./Panzerpionier-Bataillon 40. Killed 4 September 1942 in a forest 1km north-east of Hill 147.5 2km north-north-east of Minina suburb in Stalingrad. German Cross in Gold on 9 October 1942. His remains were unable to be recovered by the Volksbund.

Melchers, Oberstleutnant Fritz; born 13 January 1899 Bremen. Kommandeur IV./Panzerartillerie-Regiment 89. Peacetime unit was Artillerie-Regiment 70. Abteilung Commander at establishment of Division. Promoted to Oberstleutnant RDA 01.04.42 (715). Iron Cross First Class on 4 August 1942. Wounded on 8 September 1942 but stayed with the troops. Seems to have given up command of Abteilung on 8 September 1942 but retained an unknown role within the Division. Possibly took command of Abteilung again in November. Listed as MIA 23 January 1943 in Stalingrad but was in fact captured. Died 9 April 1943 in Oranki POW Camp near Gorki. A grave was not registered, so recovery of his body has not been possible.

Freiherr von Melville, Leutnant Percy; born 16 December 1921 Riga. Führer 3./Kradschützen-Abteilung 4. Born to a Scottish/Baltic family, raised and educated in an English manner. Peacetime unit was Kavallerie-Regiment 8. Leutnant RDA 01.02.42 (1277). Transferred on 29 October 1942 from Kradschützen-Ersatz-Abteilung 24 to Kradschützen-Abteilung 4. Took command of 3./Krad.Abt.4 when the previous commander fell ill with jaundice. Killed 26–27 November 1942 near Orlovka, Stalingrad. Buried in Alexeyevka. His remains have not yet been recovered by the Volksbund.

von Menges, Major i.G. Otto-Wilhelm Kurt; born 9 January 1908 Rastatt. Ia (Chief-of-Staff) Stab 24. Panzer-Division. A cavalry officer who could speak English. Promoted to Hauptmann in 1937. On 5 October 1937 entered the war academy for a three year course. Attached to General Staff on 1 August 1939. On 26 August 1939 attached to 1. Kavallerie-Brigade in Insterburg as O1. Ib of the Division from 5–20 November 1939. On 20 April 1940 again assigned to General Staff. On 20 November 1941 he became Ia of 1. Kavallerie-Division and retained this position upon conversion to 24. Panzer-Division. German Cross in Gold on 13 October 1942. Wounded on 31 October 1942 but stayed with the troops. Surrounded at Stalingrad. Promoted to Oberstleutnant RDA 01.12.42 (94). Listed as MIA 24 January 1943 but in fact he died on 2 February 1943 in northern Stalingrad. One source says he committed suicide, shooting himself when Russian parliamentaries arrived. A Russian medic in the parliamentary group was called to give aid, but he was already dead. Two sources say that he was struck in the chest by shrapnel while leaving the division command post but that is where the similarities end. One of them says that his dying words were "do not let me go into Russian captivity" and died shortly after. The other says that after he was wounded, a Russian doctor tried to save him, but it was too late. In any case, Menges was killed in Stalingrad on 2 February 1943. His remains were unable to be recovered by the Volksbund.

Mergens, Leutnant d.R.; Batterie Beobachtung Offizier 4./Panzerartillerie-Regiment 89. Wounded on 28 July 1942 but stayed with the troops.

Merseburger, Kriegstechniker; II./Panzergrenadier-Regiment 21. Transferred on 30 October 1942 from Pz.Gr.Rgt.21 to Schule für H. Mot. in Wunsdorf.

Meseck-Selchow, Leutnant d.R. Siegfried; Zugführer in Panzerpionier-Bataillon 40. Transferred on 3 October 1942 from Führerreserve Heeresgruppe B to Panzerpionier-Bataillon 40. Outside of the pocket. Survived Stalingrad and the war. Anerkennungsurkunde des Oberbefehlhabers des Heeres (Commendation Certificate of the Commander-in-Chief of the Army) on 27 December 1944 as Führer 1./Pz.Pi.Btl.40. Still alive in 1986.

Messerschmidt, Oberleutnant Hans Walter; born 27 July 1919 Beerendorf. Zugführer 2. Zug in 4./Panzer-Regiment 24. Iron Cross Second Class on 3 October 1939 while with Aufkl.Abt.14. Leutnant RDA 01.04.40 (2399). Promoted to Oberleutnant 15 June 1942 with RDA 01.04.42. Panzer Assault Badge on 12 July 1942. Iron Cross First Class 2 August 1942. Wounded 23 October 1942 by a shell fragment in the thigh, but stayed with the troops. Wound Badge in Black on 28 October 1942. Later Chef 4./Panzer-Regiment 24. Wounded 13 January 1943 by a shell fragment in the head but stayed with the troops. Wounded 20 January 1943 by a bullet in the thigh and flown out of the Stalingrad pocket on 23 January 1943. Wound Badge in Silver on 23 February 1943. Returned to the reformed Panzer-Regiment 24 on 6 July 1943 and took command of 6. Schwadron. Appointed Chef 12./Pz.Rgt.24 on 24 July 1943. Wounded 28 November 1943 south-west of Konstantinovka by shell fragments in the head. Panzer Assault Badge II. Stufe (for 25 engagements) on 8 December 1943. Promoted to Rittmeister d.R. RDA 01.05.44. Injured in an accident January 1945. In hospital until 6 March. Returned to Panzer-Regiment 24 and fought in Hungary and Austria from 26 March until 8 May 1945. Survived the war. Died 16 May 2012 Göttingen.

Metz, Oberveterinär; Transferred on 2 January 1943 from Pionier-Abteilung 194 to Panzerpionier-Bataillon 40.

von Metzsch, Leutnant d.R. Thuisko; born 10 April 1918 Dresden. Führer 3./Kradschützen-Abteilung 4. Transferred on 1 May 1942 from MG-Bataillon 7 to Kradschützen-Abteilung 4. Iron Cross Second Class on 20 August 1942. Wounded on 1 September 1942 but stayed with the troops. Again wounded on 4 September 1942 but stayed with the troops. Iron Cross First Class on 20 September 1942. Again wounded on 28 September 1942, command going to Fahnenjunker-Unteroffizier von Cramm. Promoted to Oberleutnant on 28 September 1942. Staff officer of Generalfeldmarschall Model in late 1944. Survived the war. Wealthy entrepreneur. Assumed chairmanship of his father-in-law's large fuel trading and shipping company. Resigned in 1988. Died 12 July 1994.

Meya, Leutnant Walter; Zugführer 5./Panzer-Regiment 24. Stammtruppenteil 5.(MG)/Reit.Rgt.2. Wounded 9 August 1942 but stayed with the troops. Received confirmation of his rank on 21 September 1942. Wounded 2 October 1942 but stayed with the troops. Transferred to Stabsschwadron I./Panzer-Regiment 24. Survived Stalingrad and the war. Died 26 October 1980.

Meyer, Leutnant; Stab II./Panzer-Regiment 24. Wounded 22 January 1943. Captured at Stalingrad.

von Meyer, Rittmeister Kuno; born 27 December 1913 Arnswalde in der Neumark. Chef 9./Panzer-Regiment 24. Entered service on 1 June 1936. Two officers called "von Meyer" in Kav.Rgt.6 in January 1939, so I am not sure which is the correct man. Began the war as Adjutant of Reiter-Rgt. 21. Iron Cross Second Class 19 October 1939. Iron Cross First Class 1 July 1940. In November 1941 appointed Chef 9./Panzer-Regiment 24. Wounded 22 August 1942. After release from hospital, he became Ordonnanzoffizier of XXXXVIII. Panzerkorps. He was also suffering from jaundice. On 19 November 1942 he returned to his Schwadron. Later became Regiment Adjutant. German Cross in Gold 10 January 1943. Flown out 23 January 1943 by order of 6.Armee to take command of Pz.Ers.Abt.500. Survived Stalingrad. Was in reformed Panzer Regiment. Knight's Cross 26 November 1944 as Major and Commander of I./Panzer-Regiment 24. Oakleaves (795) 23 March 1945 as Oberstleutnant and Commander of Panzer-Regiment 'Coburg' in Panzer-Brigade 103. Survived the war. His mother, 66-year old Eva von Meyer, died in September 1945 while being transported out of Polish-occupied East Prussia. Two of his brothers were also killed during the war, 25-year old Eberhard dying in captivity after being captured at Stalingrad, and 20-year old Heinz in June 1941, five days after the beginning of Barbarossa. Died 25 January 2010 Argentina.

Meyer, Sonderführer Werner Julius Karl; born 14 June 1892 Goldfingen. Dolmetscher on Stab 24. Panzer-Division. Transferred on 15 September 1942 to 24.Pz.Div. as Dolmetscher. Transferred on 3 October 1942 to Pz.Gr.Rgt.21. Killed 8 October 1942 6km west of Stalingrad. Now buried in Rossoshka Sammelfriedhof: Block 2, Row 15, Grave 588.

Michael, Oberleutnant Georg Roland Burchard; born 10 February 1917 Hamburg. Chef 6./Panzergrenadier-Regiment 26. Began the war as a Wachtmeister in 6./Reiter-Rgt. 22. Promoted to Leutnant on 1 March 1940. Iron Cross Second Class on 25 May 1940. Iron Cross First Class on 27 June 1940. Knight's Cross on 19 January 1941. Chef 6./Pz.Gr.Rgt.26 at establishment of Division. Severely wounded on 8 July 1942. Went to hospital in Germany and returned to Division after recovery. Wounded on 27 July 1942 but stayed with the troops. Again wounded on 7 August 1942. Surrounded at Stalingrad. Earned his third Tank Destruction Badge on 28 November 1942 when he destroyed a T-34 with a Haftladung (magnetic anti-tank mine). Flown out on 23 January 1943. Oakleaves (187) on 25 January 1943. Wounded on 18 January 1944 near Nikopol for the eighth time, dying on 19 January 1944 in a Luftwaffe hospital in Odessa.

SPANNOCCHI

Oberleutnant von Mirbach in 1941

Micke, Oberleutnant d.R. Dietrich; born 27 June 1908 Eberswalde. Ordonnanzoffizier I./Panzergrenadier-Regiment 21 at establishment of Division. Promoted to Oberleutnant on 22 June 1942. Became Adjutant I./Pz.Gr.Rgt.21 on 31 July 1942. Iron Cross First Class on 12 August 1942. Wounded on 5 September 1942 but stayed with the troops. Became Regiment Adjutant on 8 September 1942. Admitted to hospital on 24 October 1942 because of severe jaundice. Survived Stalingrad. Commanded a Schwadron in reformed Pz.Gr.Rgt.21. Survived the war. Died in 1986.

SPANNOCCHI

Oberleutnant von Mirbach as Commander of 3./Reiter-Regiment 2

Freiherr von Mirbach, Rittmeister Emmerich Hanno Ulrich; born 4 March 1914 Tilsit, East Prussia. Chef 1./Panzer-Regiment 24. In 1941 he married Antonie-Ferdinande August Viktoria Gräfin zu Stolberg-Wernigerode. They eventually had 7 children. Abteilung Adjutant of I./Reiter-Regiment 2 at outbreak of war. Transferred to Reiter-Regiment 21 where he became Abteilung Adjutant of II.

Abteilung. Schwadron Commander at establishment of Pz.Rgt.24. Survived Stalingrad. German Cross in Gold 7 February 1945 in Panzer-Brigade 104. Survived the war. Died 15 July 2004 Mölln.

Mollen, Leutnant d.R. Ludwig; born 27 August 1917 Angerburg, East Prussia. In 12./Panzer-Regiment 24. Transferred from Pz.Ers.Abt.15 to Pz.Rgt.24 on 2 October 1942. Wounded in January 1943. Listed as MIA 23 January 1943 at Stalingrad. Still listed as MIA. His name is on Cube 58, Panel 17 at Rossoshka Sammelfriedhof.

Mollon, Leutnant Rolf; born 27 May 1920 Graudenz. Panzerartillerie-Regiment 89. Iron Cross Second Class on 12 August 1942.

Morff, Leutnant Jürgen; born 9 September 1921 Wannsee. IV./Panzerartillerie-Regiment 89; Iron Cross First Class on 10 September 1942.

Moritz, Hauptmann d.R. Georg; born 9 February 1899. Chef Bäckerei Kompanie (mot.) 40 at establishment of Division. Hauptmann RDA 01.06.41. Listed as MIA 7 January 1943 in Stalingrad. Not known if he survived captivity.

Müller, Leutnant d.R.; Zugführer in 1./Panzergrenadier-Regiment 26. Wounded on 26 July 1942 but stayed with the troops. Again wounded on 12 August 1942 but stayed with the troops.

Müller, Leutnant d.R. Franz; born 14 September 1920 Biberach. Transferred on 6 November 1942 from Panzergrenadier-Ersatz-Abteilung 413 to I./Panzergrenadier-Regiment 21. Survived Stalingrad. Listed as MIA 23 July 1944 east of Wolka Pelkinska, Poland.

Müller, Leutnant Oswald; born 5 April 1924. Zugführer 7./Panzergrenadier-Regiment 26. Peacetime unit was Reiter-Regiment 2. Leutnant RDA 01.12.42 (2123). Died 9 November 1943 as a result of wounds.

Müller, Oberleutnant; Panzernachrichten-Abteilung 86. Promoted to Oberleutnant on 17 November 1942.

MÜLLER, Leutnant Walter; born 8 January 1920 in East Prussia. Zugführer 5./Panzergrenadier-Regiment 26; Iron Cross Second Class on 12 August 1942.

Müller-Röhlich, Oberleutnant Gerhardt; born 5 June 1920 Berlin. Zugführer 4. Zug in 3./Kradschützen-Abteilung 4. Peacetime unit was Schützen-Regiment 9. Oberleutnant RDA 01.04.42 (1491). Died 7 July 1942 near Voronezh as a result of wounds. Strangely, a contemporary source gives his date of death as 11 March 1942. Now buried in Kursk-Besedino.

Munker, Oberstabsintendant Dr. Ludwig; born 12 August 1909 Nürnberg. IVa (Division Intendant) on Stab 24. Panzer-Division at establishment of Division. Listed as MIA 24 January 1943 in Stalingrad but he was in fact captured. Died 24 June 1943 in Dubovka POW Camp. Today, probably buried as an unknown soldier at Rossoshka Sammelfriedhof.

Mutschler, Sonderführer Alexander; born 13 May 1900 Pavlovka. Division Dolmetscher on Stab 24. Panzer-Division. Captured at Stalingrad. Died 10 February 1943 in Panchinov POW Camp on the Don River.

Nagel, Stabsveterinär Dr. Franz; born 29 September 1910 St. Marien, Austria. IVc (Division Veterinär) Stab 24. Panzer-Division. Transferred from Artillerie-Regiment 194 (94. Infanterie-Division) to 24. Panzer-Division on 1 January 1943. Captured at Stalingrad. Survived captivity and returned home.

Nahler, Hauptmann; Kommandeur II./Panzerartillerie-Regiment 89. Began the war in Panzerartillerie-Regiment 103 of 4. Panzer-Division. Hauptmann RDA 01.02.40 (3). Abteilung Commander at establishment of Division. Wounded on 25 August 1942 but stayed with the troops. Again wounded on 2 September 1942 but stayed with the troops. Promoted to Major RDA 01.12.42. Survived Stalingrad. Promoted to Oberstleutnant RDA 01.08.44.

Nesslinger, Oberleutnant Martin; born 7 August 1920 Dommelkeim. Abteilung Adjutant I./Panzerartillerie-Regiment 89 at establishment of Division. Peacetime unit was Artillerie-Regiment 21. Oberleutnant RDA 01.04.42 (2104). Later commanded 3. Batterie. Wounded on 22 August 1942 but stayed with the troops. Again wounded on 25 September 1942, dying of these wounds on 28 September 1942 in Feldlazarett (mot.) 613 in Novy Rogachik. Posthumous promotion to Hauptmann.

Neumann, Leutnant; Panzerartillerie-Regiment 89; Outside Kessel. Survived Stalingrad. In reformed Pz.Art.Rgt.89. Chef 5./Pz.Art.Rgt.89 on 1 August 1944.

Neutard, Leutnant d.R. Hans; born 25 January 1920 Heddesheim. Zugführer in 8./Panzergrenadier-Regiment 26. Killed 22 November 1943 Snomenka. Now buried as an unknown soldier in Kirovograd Sammelfriedhof: Block 13.

Nielsch, Leutnant d.R. Hans; born 28 March 1912 Breslau. Messtrupp Offizier (Artillery Surveyor); 10./Panzerartillerie-Regiment 89. Killed 9 August 1942 in Nizhne-Chirskaya near Kalach on the Don River. Posthumous promotion to Oberleutnant d.R. His remains were unable to be recovered by the Volksbund.

Nitschke, Kriegsgerichtsrat Dr. Kurt; III (Division Judge Advocate) Stab 24. Panzer-Division. In May 1938, he transferred to Kavallerie-Brigade 1 in Insterburg as Gerichtsrat. He remained with the Division for six years, from its development from a cavalry brigade to a division and then finally a panzer division. III at establishment of 24. Panzer-Division. Fell ill in October 1942. During his illness, his position was occupied by Dr. Schweinbach. Survived Stalingrad and the war. Died 2 September 1973 Bad Godesberg, Bonn, after a long illness.

Nordmann, Oberleutnant Klaus; born 14 June 1919. Abteilung Adjutant I./Panzer-Regiment 24 at establishment of Division. Peacetime unit was Kavallerie-Regiment 17. Oberleutnant RDA 01.10.41 (28). Wounded 9 August 1942 but stayed with the troops. Listed as MIA 1 January in 1943 at Stalingrad. Still listed as MIA. His name is on Cube 62, Panel 18 at Rossoshka Sammelfriedhof.

SPANNOCCHI

Oberleutnant Nordmann and Major von Winterfeld take it easy

Oberst Gustav von Nostitz-Wallwitz in 1944

von Nostitz-Wallwitz, Oberst Gustav Adolf; born 11 July 1898 Oschatz. Regiment Commander Panzerartillerie-Regiment 89; Entered service as an officer candidate in 1917. Commissioned as a Leutnant in the artillery in 1918. Remained in the Reichsheer and at the beginning of 1939, took command of the III./Reiter und Fahrschule. Commander of an Abteilung in Artillerie-Regiment 12 in Schwerin at the outbreak of war. Promoted to Oberstleutnant on 1 August 1940. On 5 November 1940, became Commander of Artillerie-Regiment 117. Commander of Artillerie-Regiment 89 on 1 January 1941 and promoted to Oberst a month later. Regiment Commander at establishment of Division. Wounded on 3 September 1942. Was on convalescence leave when Stalingrad was encircled but he was still in command of Pz.Art.Rgt.89. Tried to fly into the Kessel in late November 1942 but was denied permission. Survived Stalingrad. Even though he had not commanded his Regiment since 3 September 1942, he was not relieved of this command until 8 February 1943. Resumed command of the Regiment with the reformation of the Division. Commanded Pz.Art.Rgt.89 from 1 January 1941 to 20 February 1944. Commanded Pz.Gr.Rgt.21 from 28 December 1943 to 17 January 1944. Commanded Pz.Gr.Rgt.26 from 20 February 1944 to 27 March 1944. Knight's Cross on 12 June 1944. Transferred to Führerreserve OKH in April. Commanded 2.Pz.Div. from 1 September 1944 to 20 September 1944. Transferred back to 24.Pz.Div., commanding the Division from 21 September 1944 to 25 March 1945. Promoted to Generalmajor on 9 November 1944, backdated to 1 October 1944. Severely wounded on 25 March 1945 by shrapnel in the abdomen during fighting on Belga peninsula. Transported to Eckenförde hospital where he died of these wounds on 31 May 1945. Buried with full military honours by an English general. General von Nostitz-Wallwitz's youngest son (born in January 1945) was christened on the lid of the coffin.

Nueske, Leutnant Ernst-Wilhelm; born 1 August 1920 Tilsit. Führer 1./Panzerartillerie-Regiment 89. Lightly wounded on 9 July by shrapnel in the shoulder and thigh. Iron Cross First Class on 4 August 1942. Took command of 1. Batterie on 4 September after Willenberg was wounded. Lightly wounded on 26 September 1942 but stayed with the troops. Fell ill with jaundice and left Stalingrad on 18 November for hospital treatment in Krakow. Survived Stalingrad. In reformed Panzerartillerie-Regiment 89. Promoted to Hauptmann in early 1944. Received the Anerkennungsurkunde and Wound Badge in Silver in 1944. Survived the war. Died 19 June 1997 Kaarst.

Oberbeck, Oberleutnant Herbert; born 11 October 1909 Edenstedt. Führer 8./Panzergrenadier-Regiment 26. Iron Cross First Class on 12 August 1942. Wounded on 4 September 1942. Again wounded on 20 September 1942 but stayed with the troops. Again wounded on 29 September 1942 but stayed with the troops. Survived Stalingrad. German Cross in Gold on 9 April 1943 as Rittmeister and Chef 8./Pz.Gr.Rgt.26. Survived the war. Still alive in 1979.

Prinz zu Oettingen-Spielberg, Leutnant Josef Emil; born 3 August 1917 Oettingen. Zugführer 6./Panzergrenadier-Regiment 21. Took temporary command of Schwadron 7–17 July 1942. Wounded on 4 August 1942 but stayed with the troops. Again wounded on 9 September 1942 but stayed with the troops. Survived Stalingrad. Killed 27 July 1944 in Dabrowki north of Landshut, Poland.

Prinz zu Oettingen-Wallerstein, Leutnant Moritz; born 18 February 1922 München. Zugführer 5./Panzergrenadier-Regiment 21. Promoted to Leutnant on 31 August 1942. Took command of 5. Schwadron on 10 October 1942. Wounded on 23 November 1942. Survived Stalingrad. In reformed Division. Commanded various Schwadronen in Panzergrenadier-Regiment 21. Wounded on 17 January 1944. Returned to Panzergrenadier-Regiment 21 at the end of February 1944. Wounded on 29 April 1944. Died of these wounds on 3 May 1944. Posthumous German Cross in Gold on 16 June 1944.

Ölkrug, Leutnant Arnulf; born 2 September 1912 Zuffenhausen. In Panzerartillerie-Regiment 89. Peacetime unit was Artillerie-Regiment 5. Killed 30 December 1942 at Stalingrad, but outside the pocket. Posthumous promotion to Leutnant with RDA 01.01.43 (367). His remains were unable to be recovered by the Volksbund.

Otte, Leutnant d.R. Hans-Jürgen; born 11 May 1914 Strassburg. Zugführer 3. Zug in 4./Kradschützen-Abteilung 4. Promoted to Leutnant d.R. on 8 June 1942. Wounded on 2 September 1942. Transported to hospital in Germany. After his recovery, he returned to Kradschützen-Ersatz-Abteilung 24 in Insterburg, East Prussia. On 29 October 1942 transferred from Kradschützen-Ersatz-Abteilung 24 to 1./Panzergrenadier-Regiment 21. Killed 6 January 1943 in Kar Belyanksi. Buried in Kar Belyanski. Posthumous promotion to Oberleutnant. His remains have not yet been recovered by the Volksbund.

Otto, Heeresjustizinspektor; Division Mitarbeiter on Stab 24. Panzer-Division. Transferred on 2 January 1943 from 94. Infanterie-Division to 24. Panzer-Division.

Otto, Leutnant d.R.; Zugführer in 10. (Flak)/Panzergrenadier-Regiment 26. Transferred on 7 September 1942 from Führerreserve Heeresgruppe B to Pz.Gr.Rgt.26. Wounded on 28 September 1942 but stayed with the troops.

Otto, Oberleutnant d.R. Eberhard; born 23 March 1917 Bromberg. Zugführer Aufklärung Zug in I./Panzer-Regiment 24. Began the war as a Zugführer in 3./Reiter-Rgt. 21. Later commanded Stabsschwadron of I. Abteilung. Killed 19 January 1943 Orlovka, west of Stalingrad. Posthumous promotion to Rittmeister d.R. Buried in Orlovka. His remains have not yet been recovered by the Volksbund.

Overhoff, Leutnant Hans-Walter; born 15 November 1921. Zugführer in 2./Panzer-Nachrichten-Abteilung 86. Peacetime unit was Nachrichten-Abteilung 50. Leutnant RDA 01.04.41. Committed suicide on 10 June 1942.

Pachnio, Oberleutnant Jürgen; born 28 September 1917 Berlin. Abteilung Adjutant I./Panzergrenadier-Regiment 21 at establishment of Division. Peacetime unit was Reiter-Regiment 1. Oberleutnant RDA 01.11.41 (563). Took command of 3./Panzergrenadier-Regiment 21 on 31 July 1942. Wounded on 25 August 1942 but stayed with the troops. Again wounded on 28 August 1942 but stayed with the troops. Again wounded on 27 September 1942. German Cross in Gold on 24 November 1942. Died from his wounds on 5 March 1943 in Reserve-Lazarett VI in Leipzig. Buried in Barciary, Poland. His remains have not yet been recovered by the Volksbund.

Pack, Leutnant Franz; born 26 July 1914. Abteilung Ordonnanzoffizier Kradschützen-Abteilung 4. Peacetime unit was Radfahr-Abteilung 1. As an Oberwachtmeister he commanded a platoon in 3. Schwadron and later temporarily commanded 4. Schwadron. He took over the position of Ordonnanzoffizier on 8 September after Leutnant von Ulrici was wounded. Promoted to Leutnant on 30 December 1942 with RDA 01.01.43 (209). Listed as MIA 5 January 1943 in Stalingrad but he was in fact captured on 2 February 1943 and held in Dubovka POW Camp. Not known if he survived captivity.

Pallentin, Oberleutnant d.R. Walter; born 29 August 1910 in East Prussia. Promoted to Oberleutnant on 24 August 1942 while a member of Panzerpionier-Bataillon 40. Survived Stalingrad. Killed 8 September 1943 near Zinkiv while in Panzerpionier-Bataillon 19.

Pampel, Leutnant Heinz; born 19 April 1920. Pz.Rgt.24 Transferred from Pz.Ers.Abt.15 to Pz.Rgt.24 on 02.10.1942. Survived Stalingrad. Killed 19.12.1944 in Luxembourg as a Hauptmann.

Pareik, Kriegstechniker Anton; Technische Beamter of Kradschützen-Abteilung 4 at the end of the battle. Captured at Stalingrad. Survived captivity and returned home. Still alive in 2001.

von Pawel, Major Hans-Walter; born 27 July 1908. Kommandeur I./Panzerartillerie-Regiment 89 at establishment of Division. Peacetime unit was reiter-Artillerie-Regiment 1. Took command of Regiment on 3 September 1942 when Oberst von Nostitz was wounded. German Cross in Gold on 12 November 1942. Promoted to Oberstleutnant on 1 December 1942. Took command of I./Pz.Art.Rgt.89 after Matzke took command of Panzerartillerie-Regiment 89. Listed as MIA 22 January 1943 in Stalingrad but he was in fact captured. Post-MIA promotion to Oberstleutnant with backdated RDA 01.12.42 (97a). Died in captivity on 30 December 1953.

von Pawel-Rammingen, Oberleutnant; Führer 2./Panzergrenadier-Regiment 21. Transferred from Panzergrenadier-Regiment 21 to Werkstatt-Kompanie 40. Commanded the Alarmeinheiten formed from the Werkstatt Kompanie. Transferred on 10 November 1942 back to Panzergrenadier-Regiment 21. Wounded on 24 November 1942. Survived Stalingrad.

Pehl, Leutnant Paul-Heinz; born 30 April 1920 Bonn. Nachrichtenoffizier III./Panzer-Regiment 24. Iron Cross First Class 02.10.1942. Survived Stalingrad. Was in reformed Panzer Regiment. In January 1945 he was the Nachrichtenoffizier of Pz.Rgt.24. Died 17.04.1945 in Peyse, Russia as an Oberleutnant. Today, buried in Germau / Russkoe as an unknown soldier.

Peine, Assistenarzt d.R. Dr.; Abteilung Hilfsarzt I./Panzergrenadier-Regiment 26. Wounded on 9 August 1942 but stayed with the troops. Transferred on 2 October 1942 from Panzergrenadier-Regiment 26 to Panzergrenadier-Regiment 21 to become Hilfsarzt for I. Abteilung. Survived Stalingrad and the war.

Pelzner, Oberleutnant d.R. Curt Otto Gustav; born 26 February 1916 Eydtkau. Promoted to Oberleutnant on 24 August 1942 while a member of Nachschub-Abteilung 40. Survived Stalingrad. Commander of 4./Auf.Abt. 24 on 1 May 1944. Killed 22 December 1944 in Szerzeny, Hungary.

Penners, Leutnant d.R. Dr. Theodor; born 30 December 1912 Kiel. Ordonnanzoffizier Panzergrenadier-Regiment 21 at establishment of Division. Became Abteilung Ordonnanzoffizier (I./Pz.Gr.Rgt.21) on 30 July 1942. Held this position until about 28th August, when he took command of 2. Schwadron. He then became I./Pz.Gr.Rgt.21 Abteilung Adjutant on 8 September 1942. Wounded on 27 September 1942. Iron Cross First Class on 2 October 1942. Survived Stalingrad. Survived the war. On 1 April 1965 he became Direktor des Staatsarchivs Osnabrück. Died 5 March 1994 Kiel.

von Perbandt, Leutnant Sklode; born 22 February 1920 Nahmgeiss, Kreis Preußisch-Holland. Panzer-Regiment 24. Peacetime unit was Reiter-Regiment 2. Leutnant RDA 01.02.41 (611). Died as a result of wounds 5 January 1942 Jüterbog. Volksbund lists him as dying 28 August 1941 in Reservelazarett Jüterbog while another source gives his date of death as 2 January 1942.

Pernutz, Inspektor Hans; born 19 September 1910. Regiment Techniker Inspektor Stab Pz.Rgt.24 Stab. In 1939 was living in Sachsen-Anhalt. MIA January 1943 in Stalingrad. His name is on Cube 65, Panel 13 at Rossoshka Sammelfriedhof.

Peschken, Oberleutnant d.R.; Führer Gepäck-Tross, Ib Abteilung Stab 24. Panzer-Division at establishment of Division. Oberleutnant RDA 01.07.40 (1042).

Peters, Hauptmann Harald; born 30 November 1912. Panzer-Regiment 24. Transferred 5 October 1942 from Führerreserve OKH to VIII. Armeekorps. Sent to Pz.Rgt.24 for the period 15 October - 15 November 1942 to serve his Waffenkommando. Major RDA 01.08.43 (40).

Peters, Leutnant d.R. Hans; born 24 April 1912 Wilhelmshaven. Panzerpionier-Bataillon 40. Iron Cross First Class on 3 August 1942. Promoted to Oberleutnant on 24 August 1942. Wounded on 8 September 1942.

Pfautsch, Oberleutnant Werner; born 30 May 1918 Barsinghausen. In Panzerartillerie-Regiment 89. Peacetime unit was Artillerie-Regiment 19. Iron Cross First Class on 2 August 1942. Promoted to Oberleutnant on 17 October 1942 with RDA 01.10.42 (43). Listed as MIA 23 January 1943 in the Stalingrad area. Still listed as MIA. His name is on Cube 66, Panel 3 at Rossoshka Sammelfriedhof.

Pfeiffer, Feldjustizinspektor; Justizinspektor for III on Stab 24. Panzer-Division at establishment of Division.

Pickert, Leutnant; Wounded on 30 August 1942.

Pietsch, Pfarrer; Kriegspfarrer IVd (ev.) Stab 24. Panzer-Division. Transferred from XXXXVIII. Armeekorps to 24. Panzer-Division on 31 August 1942 to take over from the wounded Arndt.

Pisselhoy, Stabsarzt d.R. Dr. Kurt; born 25 September 1907 Würzburg. Abteilung Arzt Kradschützen-Abteilung 4. In Radfahr-Abteilung 1 from 14 December 1939 until its conversion to Krad.Btl.4 in November 1941. Wounded on 3 September 1942 but stayed with the troops.

Iron Cross First Class on 20 September 1942. Again wounded on 2 October 1942. Spent the next 16 months in various hospitals and replacement units before being discharged from the military in March 1944.

Platz, Hauptmann Hubert; born 5 July 1911 Pachutken, West Prussia. Chef 9./Panzerartillerie-Regiment 89. Iron Cross Second Class on 22 September 1939. Assault Badge on 24 February 1941. Iron Cross First Class on 16 July 1941. Took command of Abteilung on 5 July (his birthday) when Leitreuter was wounded. Wounded on 25 August 1942. Stayed with the troops. Severely wounded on 8 September 1942 on both elbows. German Cross in Gold on 18 January 1943. Promoted to Major RDA 01.03.43. Wound Badge in Silver on 20 December 1943. In reformed Panzerartillerie-Regiment 89 as Kommandeur III./Pz.Art.Rgt.89. Remained with the Division for the rest of the war. Knight's Cross on 9 May 1945 as Commander of Panzerartillerie-Regiment 89. Survived the war. He was known to his comrades as 'Platzmajor'. Died 21 May 1988 in Hamburg from a lung embolism following a hip operation.

von Poser und Groß-Naedlitz, Leutnant Horst; born 30 April 1920 Breslau. Zugführer 3. Zug in 4./Panzer-Regiment 24. Killed 20 August 1942 near Plodovitoye, south of Stalingrad. Today, probably buried as an unknown soldier in Rossoshka Sammelfriedhof.

Proll, Oberleutnant Gotthard Ernst; born 14 November 1913 Bunzelwitz. Zugführer 3. Zug in 9./Panzer-Regiment 24. Married Elfriede Franz in 1938. The marriage produced two children. Leutnant RDA 01.04.39 (94). Iron Cross Second Class on 23 July 1940. Iron Cross First Class on 20 July 1941. Panzer Assault Badge on 21 July 1941. Promoted to Oberleutnant on 2 May 1942 with RDA 01.03.42 (321) C. Wounded 2 August 1942 but stayed with the troops. Wound Badge in Silver on 24 November 1942. Survived Stalingrad. In reformed Panzer Regiment. German Cross in Gold 8 May 1945 as Rittmeister and Chef 9./Panzer-Regiment 24. Died in 1987. [See his award file from Oliver Loerscher for more info]

Punge, Leutnant Friedrich; born 22 December 1921 Herford. Batterie Offizier 1./Panzerartillerie-Regiment 89. Promoted to Leutnant on 31 August 1942. Iron Cross Second Class on 4 September 1942. Wounded on 6 October 1942. Survived Stalingrad. Commanded 4./Panzerartillerie-Regiment 89 in August 1944 as an Oberleutnant. Iron Cross First Class and Wound Badge in Silver in 1944.

von Puttkamer, Oberleutnant Jesco Carl Eugen; born 20 February 1919 Neustrelitz. O2 (Assistant to Ib) Stab 24. Panzer-Division. Peacetime unit was Kavallerie-Regiment 5. Oberleutnant RDA 01.12.41 (227). Transferred on 1 November 1942 from Panzer-Ersatz-Abteilung 10 to Pz.Rgt.24. Transferred on 27 November 1942 from III./Panzer-Regiment 24 to Stab 24. Panzer-Division. Listed as MIA 23 January 1943 in Stalingrad but was in fact captured. Survived captivity and returned home. His education was sufficient for a diplomatic career in 1971. He first served as West German ambassador to Israel, then Bulgaria, Portugal and Sweden. He retired in 1984 to reside in southern Germany. Died in January 1987 in Oberaudorf.

Freiherr von Quadt-Wyckradt-Hüchtenbruck, Leutnant Horst; born 8 October 1920. Zugführer Aufklärung Zug in II./Panzer-Regiment 24. Began the war in Reiter-Rgt. 2. Wounded 11 September 1942 but stayed with the troops. Survived Stalingrad. In reformed Panzer Regiment, where he remained for the rest of the war. Promoted to Oberleutnant RDA 01.08.43. Survived the war. Died in 1986.

von Quast-Vichel, Leutnant Otto-Henning; born 1913. Zugführer 6./Panzergrenadier-Regiment 26. Survived Stalingrad and the war. Died 14 November 1986 Hamburg.

SPANNOCCHI

Oberleutnant Raben in Rennes, France

SPANNOCCHI

Raben hams it up for the camera in Rennes. From left: von Arnim, von Maltzan, von Winterfeld, Otto, Liebe, Raben and von Brockdorff.

SPANNOCCHI

Raben consults with Major von Winterfeld near Bykovo, June 1942

Raben, Oberleutnant Jürgen; born 30 March 1919 Naumburg/Saale. Stab I./Panzer-Regiment 24. Peacetime unit was Kavallerie-Regiment 8. Began the war as Leutnant and Zugführer in 2./Reiter-Rgt. 21. Ordonnanzoffizier of Reiter-Regiment 21 on 30.09.1940. Oberleutnant RDA 01.04.42 (36). Severely wounded 19.01.1943 west of Orlovka. Listed as MIA 20.01.1943 Stalingrad. Still listed as MIA. His name is on Cube 69, Panel 6 at Rossoshka Sammelfriedhof.

Radtke, Oberleutnant d.R.; 9./Panzerartillerie-Regiment 89. Wounded on 28 July 1942. Promoted to Oberleutnant on 24 August 1942. Survived Stalingrad. Chef 9./Panzerartillerie-Regiment 89 in August 1944.

Raeschke, Leutnant d.R. Heinrich; born 30 December 1918 Göttingen. Zugführer 6./Panzergrenadier-Regiment 26. Wounded on 26 July 1942. Sent to hospital in Germany and transferred to Panzergrenadier-Ersatz-Abteilung 413 after recovery. Transferred on 8 September 1942 from Panzergrenadier-Ersatz-Abteilung 413 to Pz.Gr.Rgt.26. Became Abteilung Adjutant of II./Pz.Gr.Rgt.26. Killed 22 September 1942 in Stalingrad. Today, probably buried as an unknown soldier at Rossoshka Sammelfriedhof.

von Raison, Hauptmann Georg-Wilhelm; born 23 May 1914. Chef 8./Panzerartillerie-Regiment 89. Entered the service in 1935 as an officer candidate in Artillerie-Regiment 30 in Rendsburg. In 1936, attended the Kriegsschule in Potsdam, where Rommel was the course leader. Promoted to Leutnant on 1 April 1937. Participated in the Polish campaign as an Abteilung Adjutant in Artillerie-Regiment 30. Promoted to Oberleutnant on 2 October 1939. When the French campaign started, he was heading to a battery commanders training course in Jüterbog. He was surprised when he heard of the invasion and immediately phoned the personnel office, wanting to return to his troops. This was refused and he continued on to the course. Fourteen days later, having completed the course, he was offered a position as Chef 7./reiter-Art.-Rgt.1, which he accepted. Fought in France and Russia with this battery. Batteriechef in Stalingrad with his heavy 15cm howitzers. Took command of III. Abteilung on 8 September 1942 when Platz was wounded. Fell severely ill with jaundice and on 25 October 1942 left Stalingrad for hospital treatment in Reservelazarett 137 in Berlin, arriving there on 3 November 1942. Survived Stalingrad. In reformed Pz.Art.Rgt.89. Major and Kommandeur II./Pz.Art.Rgt.89 in 1943–44. Promoted to Major on 1 January 1944. Became IIa of 15. Panzergrenadier-Division on 8 September 1944. Survived the war. Died 21 August 2000 Lamspringe.

Rauch, Oberleutnant Rupprecht; born 4 December 1917 Allstedt. Zugführer 3. Zug in 5./Kradschützen-Abteilung 4. Commanded 5. Peacetime unit was Kavallerie-Regiment 4. Oberleutnant RDA 01.11.41 (434). Schwadron at the end of the battle. Listed as MIA 24 January 1943 in Stalingrad. Still listed as MIA. His name is on Cube 70, Panel 1 at Rossoshka Sammelfriedhof.

Rautenstrauch, Oberleutnant Alexander Karl Ernst; born 19 September 1914 Trier. Führer 5./Panzergrenadier-Regiment 21. Peacetime unit was Kavallerie-Regiment 8. Severely injured in an accident on 22 July 1942 when a towing tractor ran into him. He was hospitalised. Rittmeister RDA 01.10.42 (77). Died 10 August 1944 in a hospital in Radwan, 25km north of Tarnow. Now buried in Laurahütte / Siemianowice Sammelfriedhof in Poland: Block 1 Row 17 Grave 1039.

Reble, Oberleutnant; Pz.Rgt.24. Transferred from Pz.Ers.Abt.15 to Pz.Rgt.24 on 17 November 1942.

Rees, Leutnant d.R. Dietrich; born 6 March 1919 Bielefeld. IV./Panzerartillerie-Regiment 89. Iron Cross Second Class on 4 September 1942. Transferred on 9 November 1942 from Panzerartillerie-Regiment 89 to Fz. Kdo.VII.

Reifner, Leutnant Egon; born 5 March 1916. Zugführer 3./Panzerpionier-Bataillon 40. Entered the service in 1937 as a conscript in Pionier-Bataillon 1 in Königsberg. After a year he was promoted to Gefreiter. Promoted to Unteroffizier in 1940 and later that same year, transferred to 3./Pionier-Battalion 40 as a Feldwebel. Promoted to Leutnant in 1942. Wounded on 23 August 1942 but stayed with the troops. Again wounded on 8 September 1942 but stayed with the troops. German Cross in Gold on 9 October 1942. In the five months from July to November 1942, he won the Iron Cross First Class, Assault Badge, Wound Badges in Black and Silver, two Tank Destruction Badges and the German Cross in Gold. That was something special for a young Leutnant. Survived Stalingrad. Promoted to Oberleutnant in 1943 and received the Wound Badge in Gold. 1944 was another special year for him: he won both the Close Combat Badges in Bronze and Silver, and the Knight's Cross on 16 November 1944 as Chef 3./Panzerpionier-Bataillon 40. He was also promoted to Hauptmann. In 1945, transferred to Grossdeutschland to take command of its Pionier-Bataillon. Promoted to Major near the end of the war. Survived the war. Died 26 June 1980 Neukirchen-Vluyn.

Reimann, Technischer Inspektor; Panzer-Regiment 24 Stab. Transferred from Pz.Rgt.24 to Schule für H. Mot. on 1 November 1942.

Reinberg, Sonderführer Johannes; Dolmetscher for Ic on Stab 24. Panzer-Division at establishment of Division. Killed 4 July 1942.

Reinhard, Leutnant d.R. Karl-Heinrich; born 28 June 1918. Fought in the Polish and Western campaigns. Leutnant RDA 01.10.42. Transferred on 6 November 1942 from Panzergrenadier-Ersatz-Abteilung 413 to Pz.Gr.Rgt.26 as a platoon leader. Wounded on 10 November 1942. Survived Stalingrad. Returned to Pz.Gren.Ausb.u.Ers.Btl.413 on 25 May 1943, where he remained a platoon leader for the rest of the year. Probably survived the war.

Reinhardt, Sonderführer; Stab 24. Panzer-Division.

Reininghaus, Leutnant Fritz; born 8 August 1919 Wernigerode. IV./Panzerartillerie-Rgt. 89. Wounded on 2 September 1942. Iron Cross Second Class on 4 September 1942.

Remberg, Leutnant d.R. Hermann; born 16 April 1910. Adjutant Panzerpionier-Bataillon 40 at establishment of Division. Leutnant RDA 01.01.41 (908). Promoted to Oberleutnant d.R. Listed as MIA 3 February 1943 in Stalingrad. Still listed as MIA. His name is on Cube 71, Panel 9 at Rossoshka Sammelfriedhof.

Renner, Leutnant Hubertus; born 26 October 1921 Karlsburg, Oels. Zugführer Pionier Zug in Stab III./Panzer-Regiment 24. Peacetime unit was Kavallerie-Regiment 8. Began the war as a Zugführer in 4. (MG)/Reiter-Rgt. 21. Leutnant RDA 01.02.41 (1648a). Killed in an accident 31 July 1942 in Novo Siolonovsky, near Nizhne-Chirskaya. Today, probably buried as an unknown soldier in Rossoshka Sammelfriedhof.

HEITZER

The grave of Hubertus Renner

von Renvers, Oberleutnant Klaus-Ernst; born 9 January 1922 Berlin-Steglitz. Zugführer 2./Panzergrenadier-Regiment 21. Peacetime unit was Reiter-Regiment 1. Leutnant RDA 01.04.41 (1571). Wounded on 5 July 1942 near Schilovo. Died 6 July 1942 in a hospital from these wounds. Buried in Gorshechnoye. His remains have not yet been recovered by the Volksbund.

von Restorff, Oberleutnant; Panzer-Regiment 24. Leutnant RDA 01.01.38 (1072). In January 1939 was a Zugführer in 4./Reit.Rgt.2. Became Adjutant of Reiter-Regiment 2 on 5 September 1941. Unknown role when Reiter-Regiment 2 became Pz.Rgt.24. Transferred 7 May 1942 from Pz.Rgt.24 to Stab Anton in Zossen.

SPANNOCCHI

Oberleutnant von Restorff in 1941

Prinz Reuss, Oberleutnant; Abteilung Adjutant I./Panzergrenadier-Regiment 26 at establishment of Division. Oberleutnant RDA 01.10.41 (538). Wounded on 20 August 1942 but stayed with the troops. Again wounded on 11 September 1942.

Reymann, Leutnant Hellmuth; born 11 January 1922 Breslau. Zugführer 3./Panzergrenadier-Regiment 26. Peacetime unit was Kavallerie-Regiment 10. Entered the service on 25 October 1940 as an officer candidate in Kavallerie-Ersatz-Abteilung 8 in Oels. Leutnant RDA 01.02.42 (362). Wounded on 12 September 1942 but stayed with the troops. Again wounded on 27 September 1942 but died of these wounds the next day in Kriegslazarett (mot.) 4./591 in Tazinskaya. Iron Cross First Class on 5 October 1942.

Richter, Leutnant d.R. Gerhard; born 1921. Student. Leutnant RDA 01.10.42. Transferred on 17 November 1942 from Heeresgruppe B Führerreserve to Panzergrenadier-Regiment 26. Survived Stalingrad. Zugführer 10 (s.I.G.)/Pz.Gr.Rgt.26 from 15 June 1943. In Geschütz-Ersatz-Kompanie (mot). 2 in February 1944. On 13 March 1944 appointed platoon leader in the schwere-Geschütz-Kompanie of Pz.Gr.Lehr-Rgt.902.

von Richthofen, Leutnant d.R. Manfred Otto Freiherr; born 2 September 1922 Riemberg. In 10./Panzer-Regiment 24. Listed as MIA 18 January 1943 in Stalingrad. Still listed as MIA. His name is on Cube 72, Panel 4 at Rossoshka Sammelfriedhof.

Riebel, Oberst Gustav Adolf; born 13 March 1896 Burglehn-Muskau. Kommandeur Pz.Rgt.24. Entered the service as an officer candidate in August 1914 and promoted to Leutnant in January 1916 while in Ulan-Regiment 4. Remained in the Reichsheer after the First World War. Major RDA 01.03.36 (91). Transferred from the staff of XVI. Armeekorps to became adjutant to Guderian in his role as Commander der Schnelle Truppen in November 1938. Peacetime unit was OKH (Chef der Schnelle Truppen). Promoted to Oberstleutnant RDA 01.06.1939. Participated in the Polish campaign as Adjutant in XXII. Armeekorps before being transferred on 15 October 1939 to Guderian's XIX. Armeekorps, staying in this position until 14 October 1940. Took command of Pz.Rgt.15 on 23 February 1941 and led it through the Balkan and Russian campaigns before being transferred to the newly created Pz.Rgt.24. German Cross in Gold 24 December 1941. Oberst RDA 01.02.42 (28a). Killed 23 August 1942 on Hill 118 north of Morosov. Posthumous promotion to Generalmajor RDA 01.08.42. Buried in Pryvolzhki State Farm but his remains have not yet been recovered by the Volksbund.

Major von Winterfeld and Oberst Riebel discuss tactics near Bykovo.

Freiherr Riedesel zu Eisenbach, Oberleutnant d.R. Hubert Kurt; born 17 August 1917 Marburg. Abteilung Adjutant II./Panzergrenadier-Regiment 21. Abteilung Ordonnanzoffizier from establishment of Division. Promoted to Oberleutnant on 8 June 1942. Became Abteilung Adjutant on 28 June 1942. Transferred on 25 August 1942 from Panzergrenadier-Regiment 21 to staff of 4. Panzerarmee as O2, taking a rear area duty because of the Wehrmacht's "last son" policy.

This did not save him. He died 27 February 1943 in Dnepropetrovsk as a result of wounds. Posthumous promotion to Hauptmann. Now buried in Kharkov Sammelfriedhof: Block 12 Row 6 Grave 1034.

Rieger, Leutnant d.R. Karl; born 30 January 1915 Warburg. Abteilung Adjutant Panzer-Nachrichten-Abteilung 86. Iron Cross Second Class on 2 August 1942. Listed as MIA 28 January 1943 in Stalingrad but was in fact captured. Died 24 May 1943 in Arsk POW Camp in Tatarstan. A grave was not registered, so recovery of his body has not been possible.

Rieks, Oberarzt Dr. Franz Joachim; Sanitäts-Kompanie 2/40 (mot.). Began the war in Sanitäts-Abteilung 1. Promoted to Oberarzt on 25 May 1942 with RDA 01.02.42 (53b). Transferred 24 August 1942 from 2/40 to Adjutant Korpsarzt XXIV. Armeekorps.

Rinke, Oberleutnant Hanno Hubertus; born 26 April 1918 Erfurt. Chef Stabsschwadron/Panzer-Regiment 24. Leutnant RDA 01.09.38 (963). Peacetime unit was Reiter-Regiment 2. Zugführer 3./Reiter-Regiment 2 from 1 September 1939 until 1 January 1940. Iron Cross Second Class on 22 October 1939. Oberleutnant RDA 01.09.40 (334). Zugführer 9.(Gesch.)/Reiter-Regiment 2 until 10 June 1941. Ordonnanzoffizier 1. Kavallerie-Division from 11 June to 31 July 1941. Chef 6./Reiter-Regiment 2 until 30 November 1941. Wound Badge in Black on 22 November 1941, Iron Cross First Class on 27 November 1941. Appointed Chef Stabsschwadron/Panzer-Regiment 24 at establishment of 24. Panzer-Division on 1 December 1941. General Assault Badge on 9 January 1942. Took command of 6. Schwadron when Rittmeister v. Sivers was wounded on 8 August 1942. Wounded 22 August 1942. In hospital until February 1943. Returned to the reformed Panzer Regiment as adjutant and held this position until 28 March 1944. Wound Badge in Silver on 24 November 1943. Rittmeister RDA 01.07.43 (35). Attended an Abteilungsführer-Lehrgang in Paris from 7 February to 4 March 1944. Deemed suitable as a battalion commander. Appointed Chef 9./Pz.Rgt.24 on 28 March 1944 and Führer III./Panzer-Regiment 24 in April 1944. Survived the war. Still alive in 2001.

SPANNOCCHI

Oberleutnant Rinke (left) prior to Operation Blau. Rittmeister Spannocchi gets a haircut.

Rocholl, Oberarzt d.R. Dr. Horst; born 23 February 1908 Kassel. Abteilung Arzt I./Panzer-Regiment 24. Eight weeks basic training in autumn 1938 as a Sanitäts-Unteroffizier. Became an Unterarzt after a months training in a hospital and another month as a Truppenarzt. Entered Lazarettzug 643 on 28 August 1939 as a Hilfsarzt. Transferred to Bau-Bataillon 221 in June 1940. Requested and received a transfer to front-line duty in February 1941, going to I./Reiter-Regiment 2 in Poland

SPANNOCCHI

Oberarzt Dr. Rocholl in 1941 as a doctor in Reiter-Regiment 2 as its Abteilung Arzt. Wound Badge in Black and Iron Cross Second Class 22 June 1941 for carrying 20 wounded men out of a forest firefight. Iron Cross First Class in August 1941. Rocholl told the author these medals have nothing to do with heroic acts. Wounded 30 September 1942. Listed as MIA 23 January 1943 in Stalingrad as a Stabsarzt d.R. but was in fact captured on 2 February 1943. During his captivity, he became a member of the anti-fascist groups. Returned to Germany at Fürstenwalde 30 December 1953. Became a doctor in the Soviet zone, living in the town of Neuenhagen near Berlin. He was the only one of seven men in his family to survive the war. Died 1 January 2004 Eberswalde.

Rogge, Rittmeister Wilhelm; born 9 September 1912 Reesen. Chef 11./Panzergrenadier-Regiment 26. Transferred to the active officers list on 25 May 1942. Wounded on 1 August 1942. Iron Cross First Class on 12 August 1942. Again wounded on 15 September 1942. Wounded mid-November and transported to the rear the evening before the Russian counteroffensive. Transported to a hospital in Germany. Survived Stalingrad. Rejoined the reforming Division in France. Became Abteilung Commander in Pz.Gr.Rgt.21 in December 1943. Wounded on 19 December 1943. Wounded on 20 December 1943. German Cross in Gold on 20 May 1944 as Kommandeur II./Pz.Gr.Rgt.21. Survived the war. Died in 1992 in Gifhorn-Winkel.

Rohde, Oberleutnant d.R. August-Karl; born 9 October 1909 Kurtwitz/Strehlen. Kommandant des Stabsquartier on Stab 24. Panzer-Division at establishment of Division. Began the war as Verpflegungsoffizier of Reiter-Rgt. 21. Oberleutnant RDA 01.08.40 (449). Promoted to Rittmeister. Survived the war. Joined the Bundeswehr. In 1957 he was a Major and Standortkommandantur of Rendsburg.

Rohde, Leutnant d.R. Heinrich; born 31 December 1913. Abteilung Ordonnanzoffizier I./Panzerartillerie-Regiment 89. Wounded on 14 October 1942 but stayed with the troops. Listed as MIA 4 January 1943 in Stalingrad. Not known if he survived captivity.

Rose, Leutnant Henner; born 13 March 1920. Peacetime unit was Reiter-Regiment 2. Leutnant RDA 01.10.42 (172). Transferred on 6 November 1942 from Pz.Gr.Ersatz-Abteilung 413 to Panzergrenadier-Regiment 26 and assigned Führer 2. Schwadron. Listed as MIA 13 January 1943 in Stalingrad but was in fact captured. Not known if he survived captivity.

von Rosenberg-Lipinski, Hauptmann Horst; born 4 April 1914 Breslau. Chef 4./Panzerartillerie-Regiment 89. Fought in France as an Oberleutnant and Chef 4./reiter-Artillerie-Regiment 1. Wounded on 9 June 1940. Iron Cross First Class on 17 June 1940. Asked to safekeep the position of IIa on 30 August 1942. This was supposed to be temporary assignment. German Cross in Gold on 20 September 1942. Officially transferred on 10 October 1942 from Pz.Art.Rgt.89 to Division Stab to become permanent IIa. Also temporary O1 from 13–17 November 1942 due to Hauptmann Roth (O1) being transferred. Transferred on 17 November 1942 from 24. Panzer-Division to Berlin for a higher adjutant training course between 17 November 1942 and 15 December 1942. His place as IIa was filled by Rittmeister Eckhardt from Panzer-Regiment 24. Survived Stalingrad. On 1 March 1943, he became IIa of the reforming Division. Promoted to Major on 1 March 1944. Returned to the Division late in the war, assuming command of Panzerartillerie-Regiment 89. Killed on 27 March 1945 near Rosenberg when he was hit by a shell or Stalin Organ salvo. No remains were found.

von Rosenberg-Lipinsky, Oberleutnant Kraft-Viktor Hermann; born 20 April 1917 Braunschweig. Zugführer Erkundung Zug in II./Panzer-Regiment 24. Peacetime unit was Kavallerie-Regiment 8. Began the war as a Zugführer in 4. (MG)/Reiter-Rgt. 21. Oberleutnant

RDA 01.04.42 (627). Listed as MIA 1 January 1943 Stalingrad but in fact tried to break out of the Kessel on 1 February 1943 with Rittmeister von Götz but captured by the Russians. Did not survive captivity. Still listed as MIA. His name is on Cube 74, Panel 2 at Rossoshka Sammelfriedhof.

Rost, Oberleutnant d.R.z.V. Dipl.Ing. Günther; born 12 August 1910. Führer 3./Panzerpionier-Bataillon 40. Residence in 1939 was Zeitz, Saxony-Anhalt. Wounded on 29 September 1942 but stayed with the troops. Again wounded on 10 November 1942 but stayed with the troops. Listed as MIA December 1942 in Stalingrad. Post-MIA promotion to Hauptmann. Still listed as MIA. His name is on Cube 74, Panel 6 at Rossoshka Sammelfriedhof.

Roth, Hauptmann Georg; born 3 August 1915. O1 (Assistant to Ia) Stab 24. Panzer-Division at establishment of Division. Peacetime unit was Panzer-Regiment 7. Hauptmann RDA 01.02.42 (341a). Transferred on 17 November 1942 from 24. Panzer-Division to OKH for General Staff training. Assigned to 370. Inf.Div. to complete his training. Died 20 November 1942 when the plane he was on crashed near Stalino.

Rother, Kriegsingenieur; Abteilung V Offizier II./Panzergrenadier-Regiment 21. Missing in action November 1942 in Stalingrad.

Rudolf, Leutnant der Feldgendarmerie Karl; born 5 February 1903 Altkrautheim. Feldgendarmerie Trupp 40. Iron Cross Second Class on 18 August 1942.

Rühle, Sonderführer Rolf; born 10 January 1921. Panzer-Regiment 24 Iron Cross Second Class 22 October1942. Missing in action January 1943 in Stalingrad. His name is on Cube 74, Panel 18 at Rossoshka Sammelfriedhof.

Rust, Leutnant d.R. Hermann; born 24 January 1916 Rablinghausen near Bremen. IV./Panzerartillerie-Regiment 89; Promoted to Oberleutnant on 31 August 1942. Iron Cross First Class on 10 September 1942. Surrounded at Stalingrad. Transferred to Ausbildung-Einheit Weiss on 7 January 1943 for training as an infantry officer. Listed as MIA January 1943 in Stalingrad. Post-MIA promotion to Oberleutnant d.R. Still listed as MIA. His name is on Cube 75, Panel 6 at Rossoshka Sammelfriedhof.

Saint-Paul, *see* **Le Tanneux von Saint-Paul**

Salamon, Oberarzt d.R. Dr. med. Friedrich; born 10 May 1912 Waldau, West Prussia. Bataillonsarzt II./Panzergrenadier-Regiment 26. Survived Stalingrad. Knight's Cross on 20 July 1944 as Stabsarzt d.R. Survived the war. Died 17 April 1985.

Saltzer, Oberleutnant (W) Heinrich; born 22 July 1912 Gaunrsheim. Regiment Waffen und Gerät Offizier Panzerartillerie-Regiment 89; Iron Cross Second Class on 27 September 1942. Wounded on 14 January 1943 by a splinter. Captured at Stalingrad. Not known if he survived captivity.

Sälzer, Oberstleutnant Rudolf; born 20 June 1896. Kommandeur Panzerjäger-Abteilung 40. Left military service in April 1920, returned November 1936. Ergänzungs-Offizier from March 1937 to March 1941. Major RDA 01.04.40 (182d). Commander of Pz.Jg.Ersatz-Abt. 9 until 2 October 1940 (assessed as a "very good instructor and educator of his Abteilung). Commanded

Panzerjäger-Abteilung 40 in 1. Kavallerie-Division from January 1941. Abteilung Commander at establishment of Division. Promoted to Oberstleutnant on 1 April 1942. Took leave in September-October 1942. Transferred to OKH Führerreserve of Wehrkreis IX on 5 January 1943. Survived Stalingrad. Participated in a Regimentsführer-Lehrgang, which included retraining from panzerjäger to panzers. Assessed as not suitable. On the staff of Armee-Abteilung Narwa as Stopak from 1 June 1944. On the staff of Heeregruppe H as Stopak from 20 January 1945. Promoted to Oberst on 20 April 1945 (98).

Sanden, Oberzahlmeister; Dinafü 40

Sartor, Stabszahlmeister; IVz (Division Zahlmeister) Stab 24. Panzer-Division at establishment of Division. Flown out of the Stalingrad pocket on 14 January 1943 because of severe rheumatism.

von Schack, Hauptmann Axel; Regiment Adjutant Panzerartillerie-Regiment 89 at establishment of Division. Adjutant of reiter-Artillerie-Regiment 1 from 1940 until its conversion to Pz.Art.Rgt.89. Hauptmann RDA 01.04.42 (596). Wounded on 26 July 1942 but stayed with the troops. Again wounded on 2 October 1942 while Chef 4. Batterie but stayed with the troops. Survived Stalingrad. In reformed Pz.Art.Rgt.89 as Kommandeur I. Abteilung. Promoted to Major RDA 01.01.44. German Cross in Gold on 4 February 1944. Transferred to Artillerieschule Groß-Born in May 1944. Part of the territorial defence of Berlin in 1945 and then transferred to OKH, where he ended the war. Survived the war.

Schäfer, Sonderführer; Dolmetscher I./Panzergrenadier-Regiment 26. Transferred on 22 June 1942 from Stab 24. Panzer-Division to Panzergrenadier-Regiment 26.

von Scheele, Oberst Alexander Wilhelm; born 19 March 1894 Berlin. Kommandeur Panzergrenadier-Regiment 26. Commanded Aufklärungs-Abteilung 13 from 12 October 1937 to 1 October 1939 as a Major. Oberst RDA 01.04.42 (303). Transferred on 10 October 1942 from Fahrtruppenschule Hannover to Panzergrenadier-Regiment 26. Severely wounded on 25 November 1942 during the withdrawal of 94.Inf.Div. from the north-east corner of the Kessel. Flown out but died on 26 November 1942 at Flugplatz Morosovskaya. One source says his plane crashed, another that he was killed in an accident.

Schenk, Leutnant; Panzergrenadier-Regiment 26. Wounded on 21 August 1942. Promoted to active officers list on 9 October 1942.

Schiemann, Assistenarzt d.R. Dr. Gerd-Wolfgang; born 21 April 1910. Assistenarzt Kradschützen-Abteilung 4. Transferred on 25 October 1942 from H.Betr. Abteilung 1 to Kradschützen-Abteilung 4. Transferred on 30 November 1942 from Kradschützen-Abteilung 4 to become Abteilung Arzt II./Panzergrenadier-Regiment 21. Listed as MIA 17 January 1943 in Stalingrad but was in fact captured. Promotion to Oberarzt d.R. Not known if he survived captivity.

von Schinckel, Leutnant d.R. Eckart Heinrich Andreas; born 23 November 1917 Hamburg. Abteilung Ordonnanzoffizier in Panzerartillerie-Regiment 89. Killed 8 September 1942 15km west of Point 147.5, 6km west of Stalingrad. Today, probably buried as an unknown soldier at Rossoshka Sammelfriedhof.

Heinz Schlaefereit in December 1942.

Heinz Schlaefereit in 1945

Schlaefereit, Oberleutnant Heinz; Zugführer 1. Zug in 4./Kradschützen-Abteilung 4; Zugführer in Edelsheim's Radfahr-Abteilung 1 at the onset of war and remained with this unit through the Polish, French and Russian campaigns. Radfahr-Abt. 1 was converted to Krad.Abt.4 in the winter of 1941/42. Zugführer at establishment of Division. Wounded on 28 July 1942. Survived Stalingrad. Later commanded 4. Schwadron in the reformed Abteilung. German Cross in Gold on 6 January 1945 as Oberleutnant and Chef 4./Panzer-Auf.-Abt. 24. Ehrenblattspange on 15 March 1945 as a Rittmeister. Survived the war. Still alive in 2001.

Schlenther, Rittmeister Hans-Heinrich; born 28 July 1914 Tilsit. Chef 2./Panzergrenadier-Regiment 21. Peacetime unit was Reiter-Regiment 1. Chef 9./Pz.Gr.Rgt.21 at establishment of Division. Rittmeister RDA 01.03.42 (111a). Took command of 2. Schwadron on 8 July 1942. Wounded on 22 August 1942 near Tsatsa. Died 7 November 1942 as a result of wounds in Reservelazarett 10 in Breslau. Buried in Insterburg.

Freiherr von Schlichting, Oberleutnant d.R.; Zugführer 2. Zug in 9./Panzer-Regiment 24. Promoted to Oberleutnant 22 June 1942. Wounded 22 August 1942.

Schlieter, Major Walter; born 25 April 1911. Divisions-Nachschubführer 40. Began the war in Geb.-Kraftfahr-Abt. 18. Major RDA 01.01.42 (427). Abteilung Commander at establishment of Division. Missing in action January 1943 in Stalingrad. Still listed as MIA. His name is on Cube 78, Panel 19 at Rossoshka Sammelfriedhof.

Freiherr von Schlotheim, Leutnant Heinrich; Zugführer Erkundung Zug in Stab III./Panzer-Regiment 24. Began the war as a Zugführer in 3./Reiter-Rgt. 21. Survived Stalingrad. In reformed Panzer Regiment. Promoted to Oberleutnant on 1 December 1943. Severely wounded July/August 1944 in France. Survived the war.

Graf von Schmettow, Oberleutnant Mathias; Abteilung Adjutant II./Panzergrenadier-Regiment 21 at establishment of Division. Oberleutnant RDA 01.12.41 (10). Wounded on 28 June 1942. Survived Stalingrad. Survived the war. Died 21 August 1986 Bergisch-Gladbach.

Schmidt, Rittmeister Ernst; born 19 August 1914 Neu Polhna. Chef Stabsschwadron/Panzergrenadier-Regiment 21 at establishment of the Division. Peacetime unit was Reiter-Regiment 1. Rittmeister RDA 01.04.42 (1740). Wounded on 20 July 1942 when a bomb shredded the empty tent of Oberst Lengerke. Took command of I./Panzergrenadier-

Regiment 26 on 12 November 1942. With the remnants of his unit, he took command of the Kradschützen-Abteilung 4 from Rittmeister von Humbert. Commander of Kradschützen-Abteilung 4 at the end of the battle. Listed as MIA 15 January 1943 in Stalingrad but he was in fact captured at Stalingrad. Died 11 April 1943 in Oranki POW Camp near Gorki. A grave was not registered, so recovery of his body has not been possible.

Schmidt, Oberleutnant Peter; born 28 December 1914 Raumbach. Chef 9. (s.I.G)/Panzergrenadier-Regiment 21. Peacetime unit was Infanterie-Regiment 118. Promoted to Oberleutnant on 22 June 1942. Took command of 9. Schwadron middle of July 1942. Iron Cross First Class on 12 August 1942. Wounded on 29 August 1942. Promoted to active officers list on 9 October 1942. On 22 November 1942 he commanded a Kampfgruppe on the Chir, outside the Kessel. German Cross in Gold on 10 January 1943. Survived Stalingrad. Hauptmann RDA 01.04.43 (130 gg). Killed 27 December 1944 near Bravuri, north-west of Dobeln in the first near Duki, in the Kurland pocket while in Pz.Gr.Rgt.5. Posthumous promotion to Major RDA 01.12.44. Today, probably buried as an unknown soldier in Saldus (Frauenburg) Sammelfriedhof.

von Schmidt-Pauli, Oberleutnant Egbert; born 24 August 1917 Potsdam. Regiment Adjutant Panzergrenadier-Regiment 21 Stab. He has a passion for horses and horse racing. He secured a name for himself as a horseman and winner of many large races before the war. On 1 December 1936 he entered the service as an officer candidate in 2./Reiter-Regiment 1 in Insterburg. Promoted to Leutnant RDA 01.09.38. Oberleutnant RDA 01.08.40 (535). Regiment Adjutant at establishment of Division. Wounded on 28 August 1942 but stayed with the troops. Wounded on 8 September 1942. After recovery, he was transferred to the General Staff for training. On 17 November 1942 he was notified of his new role as Division O1. Until his arrival however, the Division Ordonnanzoffizier assumed a caretaker role as O1. Von Schmidt-Pauli never assumed his new role. After fully recovering from his wounds, he returned to the reforming I./Pz.Gr.Rgt.21 in April 1943 and became its commander. Ehrenblattspange on 17 December 1943. Wounded on 21 December 1943. Returned to the Division in March 1944. As Major i.G., he rescued the severely wounded General von Nostitz-Wallwitz and took him to hospital on 26 March 1945. Captured by the British at the end of the war and released very soon after. At the beginning of 1946 he became manager of the Cologne Racing Club. His passion for horses continues to this day. Still alive in 2001.

Schneider, Stabszahlmeister Hans-Georg; born 7 October 1911 Königsberg. 1. Mitarbeiter to IVa on Stab 24. Panzer-Division at establishment of Division. One source says he was killed on 31 August 1942 in Varvarovka, another on 1 September 1942. His remains were unable to be recovered by the Volksbund.

Schniewind, Leutnant Werner; born 13 April 1923. Abteilung Ordonnanzoffizier II./Panzergrenadier-Regiment 26. Peacetime unit was Kavallerie-Regiment 2. Leutnant RDA 01.12.42 (1553). Survived Stalingrad. Abteilung Ordonnanzoffizier II./Panzergrenadier-Regiment 26 from 15 June 1943. Wounded in November 1943 and admitted to Luftwaffe-Reservelazarett 9/III. Promoted to Oberleutnant 30 January 1945.

Scholz, Stabszahlmeister Erwin; Abteilung Zahlmeister Kradschützen-Abteilung 4. Began the war as Zahlmeister of Reiter-Rgt. 21. Transferred from Panzergrenadier-Regiment 26 to Krad.Abt.4. Zahlmeister at the end of the battle. Captured at Stalingrad. Survived captivity and returned home.

Scholz, Leutnant Fritz; born 19 September 1909 St. Hartenburg. Panzer-Regiment 24. Peacetime unit was Kavallerie-Regiment 8. Wounded 31 August 1942. Promoted to Leutnant on 9 October 1942. Iron Cross First Class 22 October 1942. Survived Stalingrad. Chef Stabsschwadron I./Panzer-Regiment 24 in August 1943. Promoted to Rittmeister 01.04.44 (99). Listed as MIA 20 August 1944 Argentan, France while in I./Panzer-Regiment 24, but was in fact captured. Returned from captivity.

Scholz, Oberarzt d.R. Dr. Werner; born 17 September 1912. In Sanitäts-Kompanie 40. Listed as MIA 9 January 1943 in Stalingrad. Not known if he survived captivity.

Schönbeck, Leutnant Hans-Erdmann; born 9 September 1922 Breslau. Chef 6./Panzer-Regiment 24. Wounded 22 August 1942 but stayed with the troops. Iron Cross First Class 2 October 1942. Transferred to Ausbildung-Einheit Weiss 07.01.1943 for training as an infantry officer. Wounded 19 January 1943. Flown out of the pocket on 22–23 January 1943. Survived Stalingrad and the war. Still alive in 2013.

Schönberger, Technische Kriegsverwaltungsrat Reinhold; born 26 March 1912 München. Chef Werkstatt-Kompanie Pz.Rgt.24. Wounded 22 August 1942 but stayed with the troops. Iron Cross Second Class on 2 October 1939 while serving with Inf.Rgt.488. Panzer Assault Badge in Silver on 17 September 1940. Wound Badge in Gold on 15 August 1942. Iron Cross First Class 2 October 1942.

Schöneberger, Leutnant d.R. Erwin; born 28 June 1915 Schiffweiler. Beobachtungsbatterie (Pz) 89 in Panzerartillerie-Regiment 89. Transferred on 9 October 1942 from Führerreserve Heeresgruppe B to Panzerartillerie-Regiment 89. Listed as MIA 2 January 1943 in Stalingrad but he was in fact captured. Post-MIA promotion to Oberleutnant d.R. Died April 1943 in Stalingrad-North. His remains were unable to be recovered by the Volksbund.

Schönfeld, Oberleutnant Gerhard; born 27 March 1919 Königsberg, East Prussia. Chef 3./Panzerpionier-Bataillon 40. Student, entered the service on 1 October 1938. Peacetime unit was Pionier-Bataillon 11. Leutnant RDA 01.04.40 (965). Iron Cross Second Class 21 May 1940. Iron Cross First Class 23 June 1940. Also awarded the Assault Badge and Tank Destruction Badge. Chef 3./Pz.Pi.Btl.40 from 1 July 1942. Wounded on 20 August 1942. Knight's Cross on 25 August 1942 for his actions in June 1942. When the Tim River was reached in a swift advance, the bridge over the river was still standing. Schönfeld raced up to the bridge and pulled the burning fuse out of the explosives. This ensured the continued advance of the entire Division. Severely wounded by a head shot on 20 August 1942. Promoted to Oberleutnant 01.11.42. Spent years undergoing medical treatment and never returned to active service. In January 1943 the head physician of the Breslau hospital treating Schönfeld described his condition: "Leutnant Schönfeld is suffering from an aneurysm of the left carotid artery, as well as paralysis of the vocal cord nerves. The attempt to ligate the carotid artery on 4 November 1942 failed because of consecutive symptoms resulting from anemia of the brain, which forced the ligature to be re-opened. His condition is now virtually unchanged." Another by-product of his wounding was almost constant vertigo. He suffered from his head wound for the rest of his life. Died 9 November 1996.

Schriewer, Rittmeister d.R. Fritz; born 11 May 1911 Woldegk. Chef 5./Panzergrenadier-Regiment 21. Studied medicine at Marburg University commencing 1932. Took command of 5. Schwadron in the middle of July 1942. Wounded on 5 September 1942 but stayed with the troops. Iron Cross First Class on 10 September 1942. Took command of II. Abteilung on 5

October 1942. He then took command of I. Abteilung on 12 November 1942. Fell ill in the middle of December 1942. Flown out of the Kessel. Survived Stalingrad. German Cross in Gold on 18 March 1945 in I./Panzergrenadier-Regiment 1. Probably survived the war.

Schröder, Oberleutnant Friedrich; born 26 March 1921 Hückeswagen. Zugführer in 3./Panzerpionier-Bataillon 40; Wounded on 5 August 1942. Wounded on 6 September 1942 but stayed with the troops. Again wounded on 20 September 1942 but stayed with the troops. Iron Cross First Class on 27 September 1942. Promoted to active officers list on 9 October 1942.

Schuh, Assistenarzt d.R. Dr. Hans; born 14 August 1911 Trier. Sanitäts-Kompanie 2/40 (mot.). Promoted to active officers list on 25 May 1942. Iron Cross Second Class on 16 September 1942.

Schulte, Oberleutnant d.R. Paul August; born 14 March 1915 Lüdenscheid. Zugführer in 8./Panzer-Regiment 24. Promoted to Oberleutnant 15 June 1942. Temporarily subordinated to Inf.Rgt.577 with 10 panzers on 13 October 1942. Temporarily subordinated to Jäg.Rgt.54 with 10 panzers on 21 October 1942. Killed 21 October 1942 in Stalingrad. Possibly buried as an unknown soldier in Rossoshka Sammelfriedhof.

Schulz, Leutnant d.R. Hubertus; born 19 October 1920. Zugführer Nachrichten Zug/Kradschützen-Abteilung 4. Leutnant RDA 01.04.41 (177a). Wounded on 22 September 1942. Survived Stalingrad. From 25 July 1943 was a company officer in the Stammkompanie (cadre company) of Pz.Aufkl.Aus.u.Ers.Abt.24. Transferred on 14 June 1944 as leader of the SPW-Kompanie (half-track company) of Pz.Aufkl.Abt.7. Wounded 6 October 1944. Transferred on 15 February 1945 to a training school as an instructor. Survived the war. Still alive in 2001.

Schulz, Leutnant Otto; Zugführer 1./Kradschützen-Abteilung 4. Survived Stalingrad. Later commanded a Zug in 1. Schwadron in reformed Kradschützen-Abteilung 4.

Schulz, Oberstabsarzt Dr.; Chef Sanitäts-Kompanie 2/40 (mot.). Oberstabsarzt RDA 01.01.42. Transferred to Kradschützen-Abteilung 4.

Schultze, Oberleutnant Herbert; born 6 December 1910 Sensburg. Panzer-Regiment 24. Peacetime unit was Reiter-Regiment 2. Oberleutnant RDA 01.12.1941 (497). Listed as MIA 17 January 1943 in Stalingrad. Still listed as MIA. His name is on Cube 84, Panel 15 at Rossoshka Sammelfriedhof.

Schulz-Fademrecht, Rittmeister Peter; born 19 November 1912. Kommandeur I./Panzergrenadier-Regiment 26 at establishment of Division. Peacetime unit was Reiter-Regiment 2. Rittmeister RDA 01.09.40 (19). Killed 27 July 1942 near Nizhne Chirskaya. Awarded posthumous German Cross in Gold on 4 September 1942. Posthumous promotion to Major with RDA 01.07.42.

SPANNOCCHI

The grave of Rittmeister Peter Schulz-Fademrecht

Schulze, Oberleutnant d.R. Alarmeinheit Commander Pz.Rgt.24. Transferred from Führerreserve 24 to Pz.Rgt.24. Wounded 27 October 1942. Captured at Stalingrad.

Schulze, Oberfeldarzt Dr. Martin; IVb (Division Arzt) Stab 24. Panzer-Division at establishment of Division. Oberfeldarzt RDA 01.03.41. Promoted to Oberstarzt on 21 September 1942. Division Arzt until 10 January 1943 when he was buried alive by a bomb, suffering bruises and severe concussion. Against his wishes, he was flown out of the Kessel on 20 January 1943. Survived Stalingrad. Korpsarzt of XI. Armeekorps from 22 July 1943 until 6 March 1944. Died 26 June 1961.

Schumacher, Stabsarzt Dr. Ernst Wilhelm Heinrich; born 26 March 1913 Albisheim. Regimentsarzt Panzer-Regiment 24. Peacetime unit was Sanitäts-Abteilung 28. Began the war as Sanitätsoffizier of Reiter-Regiment 21. Stabsarzt RDA 01.10.41 (5). Wounded 22 August 1942 but stayed with the troops. Severely wounded in the lungs 25 August 1942. Iron Cross First Class 26 August 1942. Also had the Panzer Assault Badge. Died as a result of his wounds on 27 August 1942 in Kriegslazarett 2/607 (mot) in Stalino. Buried in Donetsk but his remains have not yet been recovered.

Schumann, Oberleutnant d.R. Dr. Alfred; born 31 July 1898 Hamburg. Dinafü 40. Dentist in civilian life. Listed as MIA 6 January 1943 in Stalingrad. Still listed as MIA. His name is on Cube 84, Panel 18 at Rossoshka Sammelfriedhof.

Schütz, Oberleutnant Kurt Richard Heinrich von; born 10 July 1919 Mecklenburg. Chef 1./Panzerartillerie-Regiment 89; Promoted to Oberleutnant on 24 August 1942. Wounded on 17 October 1942. Survived Stalingrad. Promoted to Hauptmann in early 1944. Wound Badge in Silver in 1944. German Cross in Gold on 15 April 1945 as a Hauptmann in I./Panzerartillerie-Regiment 89. Killed 8 March 1945 near Kurischen Nehrung.

Schwanenberg, Leutnant d.R. Dr. IV./Panzerartillerie-Regiment 89; Promoted to Leutnant on 14 September 1942.

Schwanke, Major d.R. Wilhelm; Abteilung Kommandeur II./Panzergrenadier-Regiment 21 at establishment of Division. Major RDA 01.01.42. Wounded on 25 August 1942 but stayed with the troops. Sent back to Germany on 28 August 1942 because of exhaustion. German Cross in Gold on 4 September 1942.

Schwarz, Leutnant; Zugführer 3. Zug in 2./Panzer-Regiment 24.

Schwarz, Leutnant Karl; born 24 February 1901 Velgast, Pommerania. Verpflegungsamt 40; Wounded on 22 July 1942 but stayed with the troops. Surrounded at Stalingrad. Transferred to Ausbildung-Einheit Weiss on 7 January 1943 for training as an infantry officer. Wounded on 17 January 1943 west of Orlovka near Stalingrad. Missing in action January 1943 in Stalingrad.

Schwarz, Oberleutnant d.R. Ullrich; born 5 June 1902 Palermo, Italy. Zugführer 2. Zug in 12./Panzer-Regiment 24. Began the war as a Zugführer in 4. (MG)/Reiter-Rgt. 21. Wounded 5 September 1942 but stayed with the troops. Killed 8 September 1942 south of Verkhne Yelshanka, Stalingrad. Posthumous promotion to Hauptmann d.R. Buried in Alexeyevka but his remains have not yet been recovered.

Schwartzkopff, Leutnant d.R. Eckert; born 8 March 1919 Halle. Abteilung Adjutant IV./Panzerartillerie-Regiment 89 at establishment of Division. Leutnant RDA 01.10.40 (2640). Iron Cross Second Class on 4 September 1942. Surrounded at Stalingrad. Promoted to Oberleutnant on 18 December 1942.

Schweinbach, Feldkriegsgerichtsrat d.R. Dr. Otto; born 5 June 1899. III (Division Judge Advocate) Stab 24. Panzer-Division. Became Division Judge Advocate when Dr. Nitschke fell ill. Kriegsgerichter since 25 November 1942. Missing in action January 1943 in Stalingrad.

Schweissing, Leutnant Paul; born 24 January 1914 Argeninken. In I./Panzer-Regiment 24. Peacetime unit was Reiter-Regiment 1. Received confirmation of his rank on 21 September 1942. Survived Stalingrad. Oberleutnant RDA 01.05.43 (129). Killed 28 November 1943 12km south-west of Konstantinovka. Posthumous promotion to Rittmeister. Today, buried in Kirovograd: Block 13, Row 48, Grave 3387.

Graf von Schwerin, Leutnant d.R. Roderich; born 16 January 1920 Wolfshagen, Kreis Prenzlau. Führer 4./Panzer-Regiment 24. Transferred from Pz.Ers.Abt.15 to Pz.Rgt.24 on 2 October 1942. Took command of 4./Panzer-Regiment 24 in January 1943 after Oberleutnant Messerschmidt was wounded and flown out. Wounded in January 1943. Listed as MIA 22 January 1943 in Stalingrad. Still listed as MIA. His name is on Cube 85, Panel 18 at Rossoshka Sammelfriedhof.

Scott, Leutnant d.R. Rudolf; born 3 December 1916 Gronden. 3./Panzerartillerie-Regiment 89. Known to all as Rudi, he was severely wounded on 3 August 1942. Survived Stalingrad. In reformed Panzerartillerie-Regiment 89. Wound Badge in Gold in 1944. Died 5 August 1944 in Mielec, Poland as a Hauptmann d.R. Buried in Wadowice Gorne, Poland. His remains have not yet been recovered by the Volksbund.

Segger, Leutnant d.R. Horst-Herbert; born 1916. Zugführer 10./Panzergrenadier-Regiment 21. Wounded on 12 September 1942 but stayed with the troops. Promoted to Oberleutnant on 21 September 1942 with RDA 01.07.42. Again wounded on 28 September 1942. Survived Stalingrad. Leader of 9.(Flak) Schwadron in reformed Panzergrenadier-Regiment 21 from 15 June 1943. Wounded on 31 October 1943. Survived the war.

von Senger und Etterlin, Leutnant Ferdinand Maria; born 7 June 1923 Tübingen. Zugführer 1. Zug in 2./Kradschützen-Abteilung 4. Entered service in October 1940 in Ersatz-Abteilung of Reiter-Regiment 3. Promoted to Leutnant on 24 August 1942. Wounded on 16 September 1942. Iron Cross First Class on 20 September 1942. Survived Stalingrad. In reformed Kradschützen-Abteilung 4. Later became Adjutant of Kradschützen-Abteilung 4. German Cross in Gold on 4 September 1944 as Oberleutnant in 3./Panzer-Aufklärungs-Abteilung 24. Wound Badge in Silver. Survived the war. Wrote the divisional history. Later became the Supreme Commander of NATO on 1 October 1979, replacing the American General Bernard Rogers. He held this position until 1983. Died 10 January 1987.

Seroka, Oberleutnant d.R. Klaus; born 3 May 1912. Chef 1./Panzerjäger-Abteilung 40. Listed as MIA 29 December 1942 in Stalingrad. Not known if he survived captivity.

Seufferheld, Oberleutnant Karl-Heinz; born 11 March 1917 Grünhaus/Trier. Peacetime unit was Beobachtung-Abteilung 24. Oberleutnant RDA 01.12.41 (413). Took temporary command of Beobachtungsbatterie (Pz) 89 in Panzerartillerie-Regiment 89 on 1 July 1942. Wounded on 12

August 1942. Iron Cross First Class on 12 August 1942. Listed as MIA 9 January 1943 in Stalingrad while in leichte-Beobachtung-Abteilung 43. Still listed as MIA. His name is on Cube 86, Panel 19 at Rossoshka Sammelfriedhof.

von Siegfried, Leutnant d.R. Burkard; born 11 October 1921 Voerderwalde, Kreis Heiligenbeil. Zugführer 3. Zug in 1./Panzer-Regiment 24. Wounded 1 August 1942. Died 27 September 1942 in Stalino Kriegslazarett (mot.) 2/607. Posthumous promotion to Oberleutnant d.R. Buried in Donetsk but his remains have not yet been recovered.

SPANNOCCHI

Leutnant von Siegfried in Rennes, France

Sindermann, Leutnant d.R. Hubert; born 16 January 1920 Liegendorf. Transferred on 24 August 1942 from Panzerjäger-Ersatz-Abteilung 1 to Panzerjäger-Abteilung 40. Iron Cross Second Class on 12 October 1942.

von Sivers, Rittmeister Karl; born 8 February 1912 Heimthal, Livland (Estonia). Chef 6./Panzer-Regiment 24. Spoke fluent German, Russian, English and French. On 01.10.1932 he joined Reiter-Regiment 2 in Osterode, East Prussia. Promoted to Oberleutnant 01.10.1937. Peacetime unit was Reiter-Regiment 2. Iron Cross Second Class 20.09.1939. Iron Cross First Class 15.10.1939. Promoted to Rittmeister 01.08.1940 and held this rank after the conversion into Pz.Rgt.24. He belonged to II./Panzer-Regiment 24 from 12.10.1941 to 09.09.1942. Wounded 08.08.1942 when his tank was shot up. Replaced by Oberleutnant Rinke. Transferred from Pz.Rgt.24 to command II./Pz.Gr.Rgt.21 on 28.08.1942. Transferred 21.09.1942 from Pz.Gr.Rgt.21 to Führerreserve OKH for training as a Panzer Abteilung Commander. Survived Stalingrad. Transferred to Pz.Rgt.15 (11. Panzer-Division) 28.12.1942 and took command of I. Abteilung from 28.02.–15.03.1943 . He then took command of Panzer-Abteilung 52 from 16.03.–04.07.1943. In Grafenwöhr this battalion was equipped with the newly developed Panther. He fell ill and remained in Grafenwöhr, temporarily giving up command of his battalion which participated in the Kursk offensive on 05.07.1943. It suffered heavy casualties, mainly technical losses. After recovering, he commanded Panzer-Abteilung 52 again from 22.07.1943 until 23.01.1944. Major 01.10.43 (9). German Cross in Gold 10.01.1944. From 24.01.–09.04.1944, he commanded Pz.Rgt.15. Knight's Cross 06.03.1944. Killed 10.04.1944 near Buchach in the Proskurov area. Posthumous promotion to Oberstleutnant with RDA 01.04.44. His former Ordonnanzoffizier, Walter Rahn, remembers: "In conversations with former comrades, the name Sivers has a particularly good ring with examples of his personal bravery, care and comradeship." Buried in Buchach, Ukraine, but his remains have not yet been recovered.

RAHN

Karl v. Sivers in 1944

Sodemann, Leutnant Friedrich Karl; Panzerartillerie-Regiment 89; born 9 May 1921 Schwerin. Peacetime unit was Artillerie-Regiment 19. Leutnant RDA 01.04.41 (961). Iron Cross First Class on 2 August 1942. Wounded on 29 August 1942 near Tebektenrovo and died then same day in Feldlazarett (mot.) 1/522 in Aksai. Now buried in Rossoshka Sammelfriedhof: Block 22, Row 14, Grave 538.

Graf zu Solms-Wildenfels, Rittmeister Friedrich Ernst Magnus; born 2 June 1911 Reval. Chef 1./Panzergrenadier-Regiment 21 at establishment of Division. Peacetime unit was Reiter-Regiment 1. Rittmeister RDA 01.01.42 (165a). German Cross in Gold on 21 August 1942. Took command of I. Abteilung on 4 September 1942. Went on leave in November, avoiding the encirclement. He was flown into the pocket in December 1942. Listed as MIA 3 January 1943 but he was in fact captured at Stalingrad on 2 February 1943. Survived captivity and returned home. Married Renata von Schmidt-Pauli on 13 December 1952. Divorced in 1960. Married Maria Theresia Hermanns on 27 December 1962, which produced two children. Died 12 December 1997.

Soltau, Leutnant d.R. Wolfgang Elmar Bernhard; born 20 February 1918 Kiel. Führer 12./Panzerartillerie-Regiment 89. Wounded on 10 August 1942. Died of wounds 27 August 1944 in Feldlazarett 168 in Kielce, Poland as an Oberleutnant d.R. in Fla-Panzerjäger-Abteilung 97. His remains were unable to be recovered by the Volksbund.

Spannocchi, Rittmeister Emil; born 1 September 1916 Aigen bei Salzburg, Austria. Chef 2./Panzer-Regiment 24. Completed school in 1934 and immediately entered the Austrian Bundesheer which was incorporated into the Wehrmacht in 1938. Commander of 6./Reiter-Regiment 2 at outbreak of war. Headed into Russia as Commander of 9. Schwadron. Schwadronschef 2./Panzer-Regiment 24 at establishment of Division. Rittmeister RDA 01.08.42 (7a). Wounded 11 September 1942. Outside of Kessel during Russian encirclement. Survived Stalingrad. Attended General Staff training later in the war, and was promoted to Major RDA 01.11.44 (48). Became IIb of 2. Panzer-Division on 10 December 1944. Survived the war. In 1954, he re-entered the Austrian armed forces as a Rittmeister and in 1957, became Kommandant der Panzertruppenschule, holding this position for four years. In 1960 he took command of 9. Panzergrenadier-brigade. From 1963–1973, he was Kommandant der Stabsakademie des Bundesheeres in Vienna, Austria, receiving a promotion to Generalmajor in 1973 and becoming Supreme Commander of the Austrian Army. He retained this post until 1981, when he retired. Died 29 August 1992 Wiener Neustadt, Austria.

SPANNOCCHI

Oblt. Spannocchi enjoys his pipe on a fresh Russian morning, July 1941.

von Sperber, Oberleutnant; Wounded on 4 September 1942 but stayed with the troops.

Spode, Oberarzt d.R. Dr. Günter; born 23 December 1911 Hamborn. Panzerartillerie-Regiment 89; Wounded on 21 August 1942 but stayed with the troops. Again wounded on 1 September 1942. Iron Cross First Class on 4 September 1942. Promoted to Stabsarzt d.R. Listed as MIA 29 January 1943 in Stalingrad. Not known if he survived captivity.

Graf von Sponeck, Rittmeister Hans-Wilhelm; born 21 February 1913 Spandau. Chef 2./Panzergrenadier-Regiment 21 at establishment of Division. Peacetime unit was Kavallerie-Regiment 3. Rittmeister RDA 01.03.42 (74a). Killed 5 July 1942 during hand-to-hand combat near Shilovo. Buried in Shilovo, near Voronesh. His remains have not yet been recovered by the Volksbund.

Staba, Leutnant Erich; born 3 October 1920 Groß Stamm, East Prussia. Zugführer 6./Panzergrenadier-Regiment 26. Survived Stalingrad. Knight's Cross on 21 September 1944 as Leutnant and Führer 1./Feldersatz-Btl. 89 of 24. Panzer-Division. Ended the war as an Oberleutnant. Survived the war. Died 3 August 1990.

Stach von Goltzheim, Leutnant Ruprecht; born 10 January 1922 Hamburg. Zugführer 1. Zug in 3./Kradschützen-Abteilung 4. Peacetime unit was Kavallerie-Regiment 5. Leutnant RDA 01.04.41 (1575). Died 1 July 1942 from wounds suffered in Russia.

Stählin, Leutnant d.R. Leonhard; born 29 April 1911 Nürnberg. Zugführer 4./Panzergrenadier-Regiment 21. Killed 20 August 1942 in Semkin. Posthumous promotion to Oberleutnant.

Stallechner, K.V. Rat Dr. Karl; born 7 January 1913 Ebendrusen. Panzer-Nachrichten-Abteilung 86; Transferred on 24 August 1942 from PNA86 to Werkstatt-Kompanie 3/40. Iron Cross Second Class on 7 October 1942.

von Steegen, Oberleutnant d.R. Hubertus; born 19 November 1907 Klein Steegen. O3 (Assistant to Enemy Intelligence Officer) Stab 24. Panzer-Division. Could speak fluent Russian. Transferred on 15 August 1942 from Panzerartillerie-Regiment 89 to Division Stab as O3. Promoted to Hauptmann d.R. Killed 25 January 1943 in Stalingrad while attempting to break out.

Stegel, Leutnant d.R. Fritz Martin; born 28 September 1909 Elsterwerda. Zugführer 3. (Fla)/Panzerjäger-Abteilung 40. Wounded on 7 August 1942. Transferred from IV./Panzerartillerie-Regiment 89. Iron Cross First Class on 17 August 1942. Wounded on 4 October 1942 but stayed with the troops. Again wounded on 15 October 1942 but stayed with the troops. Listed as MIA 6 January 1943 in Stalingrad but he was in fact killed 5 January 1943 in Stalingrad. Posthumous promotion to Oberleutnant. His remains were unable to be recovered by the Volksbund.

Steinbach, Technischer Inspektor; Abteilung Inspektor Dinafü 40; Captured at Stalingrad. Survived captivity and returned home.

Steiner, Oberzahlmeister; Abteilung Zahlmeister III./Panzerartillerie-Regiment 89. Fought in France as Abteilung Zahlmeister of II./reiter-Artillerie-Regiment 1. Abteilung Zahlmeister at establishment of Division.

Steinhardt, Leutnant d.R. Hans Friedrich; born 16.12.1914 Ulm/Donau. Zugführer 2./Panzerpionier-Bataillon 40. Killed 15 June 1942 8km east of Shchigry. Posthumous promotion to Oberleutnant.

Stemmler, Kriegsingenieur II./Panzergrenadier-Regiment 26.

Stetzkowski, Leutnant; Zugführer 5./Panzergrenadier-Regiment 26. Wounded on 1 September 1942.

VON STOCKHAUSEN

Hans-Ludwig von Stockhausen in 1980.

von Stockhausen, Leutnant Hans-Ludwig; born 12 May 1920 Trendelburg, one of a pair of twin boys (his brother was Hans-Gottfried). Ordonnanzoffizier Kradschützen-Abteilung 4 at establishment of Division. Peacetime unit was Kavallerie-Regiment 3. Wounded in the jaw on 31 August 1942 near Gavrilovka. After four weeks in a jaw specialists clinic, on 30 September 1942 he was ordered back to the Division. Due to a lack of officers in Kradschützen-Abteilung 4, he became Abteilung Adjutant and took over the Nachrichten Zug. Abteilung Adjutant at the end of the battle. Listed as MIA 10 January 1943 in Stalingrad but was in fact captured on 2 February 1943. Post-MIA promotion to Oberleutnant RDA 01.02.43 (992). Survived captivity and returned home in 1948. Survived the war. Still alive in 2013.

Stockinger, Oberleutnant Ludwig; born 17 June 1908 Waldkirchen. Zugführer 4./Panzerjäger-Abteilung 40. Peacetime unit was Artillerie-Regiment 20. Iron Cross Second Class on 10 September 1942. Iron Cross First Class on 19 September 1942. Wounded on 9 October 1942. He was also commander of 11./Pz.Art.Rgt.89 and at some point, elements of IV./Pz.Art.Rgt.89 were used to make 4. Kompanie of Panzerjäger-Abteilung 40. Listed as MIA 18 January 1943 in Stalingrad but was in fact captured. Post-MIA promotion to Hauptmann RDA 01.01.43 (319b1). Died 19 March 1943 on the transport from Stalingrad to Oranki POW Camp. His remains were unable to be recovered by the Volksbund.

Stockmeier, Oberleutnant d.R. Lange von; Chef Werkstatt-Kompanie 3/40. Transferred from Kraftfahrung-Ersatz-Abteilung 1 to 3/40 on 31 August 1942.

Stratmann, Hauptmann der Feldgendarmerie Johann; born 9 July 1914 Hamm. Führer Feldgendarmerietrupp 40 at establishment of Division. Hauptmann RDA 01.01.42. Iron Cross First Class on 5 October 1942. One source says he became Ia of the Division in January 1943. Listed as MIA 25 January 1943 in Stalingrad but was in fact captured. Not known if he survived captivity.

Strunck, Leutnant d.R.; Transferred on 8 September 1942 from Panzergrenadier-Ersatz-Abteilung 413 to Panzergrenadier-Regiment 21.

von Studnitz, Leutnant d.R. Ernst-Felix; born 12 May 1919 Jeroltschütz. Führer 5./Panzergrenadier-Regiment 21. Transferred on 6 November 1942 from Dinafü 40 back to Panzergrenadier-Regiment 21. He was later in Stab I. Abteilung. Wounded 18 January 1943. Died of these wounds on 24 January 1943.

Stuhlmann, Stabsarzt Dr. Herbert; born 22 August 1920. Adjutant to IVb (Division Arzt) Stab 24. Panzer-Division at establishment of Division. Peacetime unit was Sanitäts-Abteilung 1. Stabsarzt RDA 01.02.42 (45). Listed as MIA 24 January 1943 in Stalingrad. Survived captivity and returned home. Died 30 March 1979 Hamburg.

Suchowski, Oberzahlmeister Franz-Johann; born 5 August 1905. Oberzahlmeister RDA 01.10.1938. On 1 May 1939 was in H.Verpfl.Hpt.A. Insterburg. Dinafü 40. Survived Stalingrad and the war. Still alive in 2001.

Sylla, Oberleutnant Herbert; born 29 September 1914 Kalliss/Kreis Arnswalde. Zugführer 1./Panzer-Regiment 24. Peacetime unit was Panzer-Regiment 15. Oberleutnant RDA 01.04.42 (2956). Received confirmation of his rank 21 September 1942. Wounded 2 October 1942 but stayed with the troops. German Cross in Gold 6 November 1942. Commanded one of the last panzers. He was known as the "Lion of Stalingrad" to his comrades. Listed as MIA 18 January 1943 in Stalingrad but was in fact captured. Died in captivity in March 1943.

Tapfer, Oberzahlmeister Heinz; born 7 November 1912. Abteilung Zahlmeister II./Panzergrenadier-Regiment 26. Missing in action January 1943 in the Stalingrad area.

Teut, Oberleutnant (W) Heinrich Fritz Paul Ernst; born 22 February 1919 Hamburg. Waffenoffizier Panzer-Regiment 24 from 11 March to 2 November 1942. Iron Cross Second Class 22 October 1942. Survived Stalingrad. Survived the war.

Theilig, Leutnant d.R. Alfred Franz Emil; born 28 March 1916 Crimmitschau. Zugführer 1./Panzer-Regiment 24. Killed 28 September 1942 in Stalingrad. Posthumous promotion to Oberleutnant. Possibly buried as an unknown soldier in Rossoshka Sammelfriedhof.

Thiel, Rittmeister Ernst Hans; born 17 November 1908 Tilsit. Chef 4./Panzer-Regiment 24. Peacetime unit was Reiter-Regiment 2. Was with Reiter-Regiment 2 from the beginning of the war. Rittmeister RDA 01.01.42 (275) C. Chef of 4./Panzer-Regiment 24 at establishment of Division. Killed 3 September 1942 by a sniper 2km south-east of Kolyakovka, 5km west of Stalingrad. His remains could not be recovered.

SPANNOCCHI

Rittmeister Ernst Thiel, Commander of 4. Panzer Schwadron, shown here as an Oberleutnant in Reiter-Regiment 2 in 1941.

Thiel, Rittmeister Gerhard; born 9 February 1907 Haynau. Chef 10./Panzer-Regiment 24. Peacetime unit was Kavallerie-Regiment 8. Commander of 3./Reiter-Rgt. 21 from 1 February 1940. Iron Cross Second Class 23 November 1939. Iron Cross First Class 26 August 1941. Schwadronschef at establishment of Division. German Cross in Gold 29 August 1942. Ehrenblattspange 15 October 1942 for actions on 26–27 July 1942 near Nizhne-Chirskaya. Took command of III./Panzer-Regiment 24 on 1 November 1942. Major RDA 01.12.42 (27a). Took command of Pz.Rgt.24 on 19 January 1943 after von Bassewitz was flown out. Knight's Cross 20 January 1943. Listed as MIA 17 January 1943 in Stalingrad but was in fact captured on 2 February 1943 after destroying the last serviceable panzer of the Division. Died 10 April 1943 of typhus in Oranki POW Camp.

SPANNOCCHI

Rittmeister Gerhard Thiel, Commander of 10. Panzer Schwadron, attending a conference on the outskirts of Stalingrad in September 1942.

Thol, Leutnant d.R.; Zugführer 1./Panzer-Nachrichten-Abteilung 86. Wounded on 9 August 1942.

Thom, Hauptmann d.R. Dr. jur. Walter; Chef Stabsbatterie/Panzerartillerie-Regiment 89. Promoted to Hauptmann on 25 May 1942. Wounded on 20 August 1942. Survived Stalingrad. Survived the war. Died 27 October 1982 in Meinhard-Grebdendorf.

Thönessen, Assistenarzt d.R. Dr.; Transferred on 28 September 1942 from Sanitäts-Kompanie 1/40 to Heeres-Sanitäts-Staffel-Lindenberg.

Thylmann, Oberleutnant d.R Hans; born 13 January 1917 Hanau/Main. Chef 2./Panzergrenadier-Regiment 26. Promoted to Oberleutnant on 8 June 1942. Wounded on 31 August 1942. German Cross in Gold on 25 January 1943. Survived Stalingrad. In reformed I./Pz.Gr.Rgt.26. Ehrenblattspange on 5 October 1944. Knight's Cross on 18 February 1945 as Major and Commander I./Pz.Gr.Rgt.26. Survived the war. Died 21 September 1968.

von Tiedemann, Leutnant Hans-Georg; born 11 July 1923 Russoschin, Danzig. Abteilung Adjutant I./Panzergrenadier-Regiment 21. Entered service in September 1940 as an officer candidate in Reiter-Ersatz-Regiment 1 in Insterburg. Transferred on 15 July 1942 from Kradschützen-Ersatz-Abteilung 24 to Panzergrenadier-Regiment 21, becoming I. Abteilung Ordonnanzoffizier. On 25 August 1942, he was transferred to 2. Schwadron. Became I. Abteilung Adjutant on 10 October 1942. Flown out of Kessel to hospital on 19 December 1942. Survived Stalingrad. In reformed Division. In 1945, he attained the rank of Rittmeister. He must surely have been one of the youngest captains in the entire German Army. He was only 21. He had also suffered five wounds and been decorated with the Iron Cross First and Second Class, General Assault Badge, Wound Badge in Gold and Close Combat Clasp in Silver. Captured by the British at the end of the war. Released from captivity in July 1945. Died 21 June 2011 Hannover.

Tiemann, Leutnant d.R. Friedrich Wilhelm; born 6 May 1915 Bochum. Panzerpionier-Bataillon 40; Transferred on 14 September 1942 from Führerreserve OKH to Panzerpionier-Bataillon 40. Iron Cross Second Class on 27 September 1942. Survived Stalingrad. German Cross in Gold on 4 September 1944 as an Oberleutnant in Panzerpionier-Bataillon 40. Died 23 September 1944 in H.V.Pl. Sanko 175 Mestisko, Slovakian Republic as an Oberleutnant.

Tönges, Oberstabsarzt Dr.; Chef Sanitäts-Kompanie 1/40 at establishment of Division. Oberstabsarzt RDA 01.01.42 (41).

Tonsgoke, Leutnant d.R.; Batterie Offizier 11./Panzerartillerie-Regiment 89. Promoted to Leutnant on 7 September 1942. Wounded on 9 October 1942.

von der Trenck, Leutnant Wilhelm Karl Robert Martin; born 10 November 1919 Königsberg, East Prussia. Zugführer 2. Zug in 6./Panzer-Regiment 24. Entered service 1 December 1939 in Reiter-Regiment 2 in Angerburg. Promoted to Leutnant in 1941. Wounded 26 August 1942. Again wounded 29 August 1942 when a shell fragment almost sliced off his nose. Survived Stalingrad. In reformed Panzer Regiment, where he remained for the rest of the war. As a Rittmeister, he was captured by the Americans and released from captivity in 1945. Married Thea Springmann on 20 May 1947. The marriage produced three children. Joined the Bundeswehr in 1956 as a Hauptmann, retiring in 1976 as an Oberstleutnant. Died 30 March 2007 Weinheim.

Treptau, Oberleutnant; V.-Offizier Stab II./Panzer-Regiment 24. Survived Stalingrad. Was in reformed Panzer Regiment.

von Treuenfels, Leutnant Gebhardt; born 24 July 1920 Herzberg. Abteilung Ordonnanzoffizier II./Panzergrenadier-Regiment 21. Peacetime unit was Reiter-Regiment 1. Became Abteilung Ordonnanzoffizier on 28 June 1942. Wounded on 1 August 1942 but stayed with the troops. Again wounded on 25 August 1942. Survived Stalingrad. Promoted to Oberleutnant RDA 01.02.43 (1075). In reformed Division. Transferred on 17 September 1943 to command a Kompanie in Inf.Rgt. 15 at Anzio. Killed 15–16 December 1943 on Monte Lungo, not far from Monte Cassino, Italy. Posthumous promotion to Hauptmann RDA 01.12.43.

Tummescheit-Balzershöfen, Oberleutnant d.R. Arno; born 16 November 1901 Ragnit, East Prussia. Regiment Ordonnanzoffizier Panzergrenadier-Regiment 26. Survived Stalingrad. In 1945, Rittmeister d.R. and Adjutant in Festungs-Regiment 'Königsberg'. Survived the war. Died 1 May 1990 Köthel. His death notice reads: "He died far from his beloved East Prussian homeland."

Türke, Leutnant d.R. Martin; born 11 July 1900 Leipzig. Transferred on 7 January 1943 from IV./Artillerie-Regiment 194 to Panzerpionier-Bataillon 40. Promoted to Oberleutnant d.R. Listed as MIA 8 January 1943 in Stalingrad while in Pi.Btl.194. Still listed as MIA. His name is on Cube 95, Panel 5 at Rossoshka Sammelfriedhof.

Turowski, Oberarzt d.R. Dr. Hans; born 19 August 1908. Abteilung Arzt Kradschützen-Abteilung 4. Transferred on 28 June 1942 from Kradschützen-Abteilung 4 to Pz.Art.Rgt.89. Transferred on 7 November 1942 from Pz.Art.Rgt.89 back to Kradschützen-Abteilung 4. Listed as MIA January 1943 in Stalingrad while a Stabsarzt d.R on Stab 24. Panzer-Division. Not known if he survived captivity.

Tutein, Leutnant d.R. Werner Richard; born 9 February 1919 Augsburg. Zugführer 1./Panzergrenadier-Regiment 21. Promoted to Leutnant on 22 June 1942. Wounded on 25 August 1942 but stayed with the troops. Took command of 1. Schwadron on 4 September 1942. Iron Cross First Class on 10 September 1942. Again wounded on 19 September 1942 but stayed with the troops. Fell ill with jaundice in October 1942 and was sent to a rear area hospital and avoided the encirclement. Survived Stalingrad. In reformed I./Pz.Gr.Rgt.21. Ehrenblattspange on 15 August 1944. Killed 25 July 1944 in Wolka Pelkinska, Poland as an Oberleutnant.

Twardy, Oberarzt Dr. Helmut; Abteilung Arzt II./Panzerartillerie-Regiment 89. Wrote his doctoral thesis on appendicitis at Königsberg University in 1936. Abteilung Hilsarzt in I./Reiter-Regiment 22 in May 1940. Wounded on 16 August 1942 but stayed with the troops. Later became Regiment Arzt. Survived Stalingrad and the war.

von Uechtritz und Steinkirch, Leutnant Heinrich Sigismund; born 24 February 1923 Pomehnen. Transferred on 8 September 1942 from Panzergrenadier-Ersatz-Abteilung 413 to Panzergrenadier-Regiment 26. Survived Stalingrad. In Panzergrenadier-Regiment 26 in May 1944. Died 25 March 1945 near Heiligenbeil.

Uhlig, Leutnant d.R. Manfred; born 1919. Panzergrenadier-Regiment 26. Leutnant RDA 01.06.42. Transferred on 14 September 1942 from Führerreserve OKH to Panzergrenadier-Regiment 26. In June 1943 with Pz.Gren.Ausb.u.Ers.Btl.413.

von Ulrici, Leutnant Gert; born 6 March 1923 Liegnitz. Ordonnanzoffizier Kradschützen-Abteilung 4. Peacetime unit was Kavallerie-Regiment 8. Leutnant RDA 01.02.42 (1030). Wounded on 8 September 1942. Died as a result of these wounds on 9 September 1942.

Urbahn, Leutnant; II./Panzergrenadier-Regiment 26. Surrounded at Stalingrad. Transferred on 7 January 1943 from Nachrichten-Abteilung 194 to Pz.Gr.Rgt.26. Transferred to Ausbildung-Einheit Weiss on 7 January 1943 for training as an infantry officer.

Urbassek, Assistenarzt d.R. Dr. Leo; born 25 August 1914 Prag, Czechoslovakia. Abteilung Hilfsarzt II./Panzergrenadier-Regiment 21. Killed 21 July 1942 near Morosovskaya.

Urbons, Oberleutnant d.R. Wilhelm; born 11 December 1911 Marunen. Chef Stabsschwadron/Kradschützen-Abteilung 4. Died 28 September 1942 in Sanitäts-Kompanie 1/40. Posthumous promotion to Rittmeister. Today, probably buried as an unknown soldier in Rossoshka.

Uszkureit, Leutnant d.R.; Zugführer Werkstatt-Kompanie 40, Kr.Kw.Zug 1. Transferred on 14 October 1942 from Panzerjäger-Ausbildungs-Abt. 1 to Kr.Kf.Zug 1/40.

von Veltheim, Leutnant d.R. Lorenz; born 28 August 1922 Bremlingen. Zugführer 6./Panzergrenadier-Regiment 21. Transferred on 8 September 1942 from Pz.Gren.Ersatz-Abt. 413 to Pz.Gr.Rgt.21. Took command of Schwadron on 8 November 1942. Listed as MIA 24 January 1943 in Stalingrad but was in fact captured. Died May 1943 in Soviet captivity. His remains were unable to be recovered for reburial by the Volksbund.

von Vieregge-Randow, Leutnant Konrad Waldemar; born 18 August 1921 Frankfurt/Oder. Zugführer 6./Panzergrenadier-Regiment 26. Married Baroness Margot von Brandenstein and had three children. Survived Stalingrad. Fled as refugees from the Mecklenburg area in 1945. Survived the war. Privately published his 125-page "Lebenserinnerungen" in 1996. Died 16 June 2003 Elmshorn. Buried in the family grave in Neuburg/Mecklenburg.

Viertel, Oberleutnant Reinhard; born 20 October 1918 Königsberg. Führer 2./Panzerpionier-Bataillon 40. Peacetime unit was Grenz-Pionier-Bataillon 71. Oberleutnant RDA 01.10.40 (90). Transferred on 14 September 1942 from Führerreserve OKH to Panzerpionier-Bataillon 40. Killed 27 September 1942 in Stalingrad. Iron Cross First Class on 5 October 1942. His remains were unable to be recovered for reburial by the Volksbund.

Vitzthum von Eckstädt, Rittmeister Heinrich (Heino) Philipp Arthur Woldmar Paul Fritz Graf; born 13 August 1914 Leipzig. Married Rosemarie Edelmann and had two children. Chef 1./Kradschützen-Abteilung 4. Prior to the war, he was a member of 4./Reiter-Regiment 4 in Allenstein, becoming adjutant of its I. Abteilung on 10 November 1938. On 7 December 1940, he was O1 of AOK2. Fought in the Balkans in 1941. Returned to Germany for a short spell of garrison duty before taking part in the opening stages of Barbarossa. Transferred to newly-formed Krad.Abt.4 on 29 November 1941. Transferred on 28 September 1942 from Krad.Abt.4 to Generalstabsdienst of 60.Inf.Div. for training. Flown out of the Kessel on 23 January 1943. Took part in General Staff training from 15 March to 28 May 1943. Promoted to Major on 1 August 1943. Remainder of war spent in various General Staff and division staff positions, including Ib of 20. Pz.-Gren.-Div. from 5 July 1943 to 15 May 1944, and 62.Volksgrenadier-Division in 1945. Survived the war. Joined Bundeswehr after the war. Assignments at NATO office in Rome. Retired as an Oberst. Still alive in 2001.

Vogel, Assistenarzt d.R. Dr. Wilhelm; born 11 April 1913 Emmendingen. Abteilung Hilfsarzt Kradschützen-Abteilung 4. Wounded on 28 July 1942. Promoted to Oberarzt. Iron Cross First Class on 9 October 1942. Transferred to Sanitäts-Kompanie 2/40. Listed as MIA 17 January 1943 in Stalingrad. Post-MIA promotion to Oberarzt d.R. Not known if he survived captivity.

Vogt, Leutnant Wolfgang; born 18 September 1923 Posen. Abteilung Ordonnanzoffizier I./Panzerartillerie-Regiment 89. Peacetime unit was reiter-Artillerie-Abteilung 1. Leutnant RDA 01.02.42 (1216a). Listed as MIA 4 January 1943 in Stalingrad but was in fact captured. Died June 1943 in Dubovka POW Camp. Probably buried as an unknown soldier in Rossoshka Sammelfriedhof.

Wachter, Oberzahlmeister Franz; born 16 September 1914. Abteilung Zahlmeister II./Panzer-Regiment 24. In 1939 lived in Regensburg/Opf. Occupation: career soldier. Listed as MIA January 1943 Stalingrad. Still listed as MIA. His name is on Cube 97, Panel 8 at Rossoshka Sammelfriedhof.

Wagner, Leutnant Wofram; born 15 February 1915 Schönbeck. IV./Panzerartillerie-Regiment 89. Wounded on 2 September 1942. Iron Cross Second Class on 10 September 1942.

Walsdorfer, Stabsarzt d.R. Dr. Franz; Regiment Arzt Panzergrenadier-Regiment 21. Promoted to Stabsarzt d.R. on 25 May 1942. Was also I. Abteilung Arzt at the same time he was Regiment Arzt. Wounded on 27 September 1942.

Wanger, Assistenarzt Helmut; born 14 February 1915 Marchegg. Sanitäts-Kompanie 2/40. Iron Cross Second Class on 16 September 1942.

Warlimont, Leutnant d.R. Hans; born 18 September 1922 Hamburg. Zugführer 3./Kradschützen-Abteilung 4. Leutnant RDA 01.02.42. Iron Cross Second Class on 20 September 1942. Wounded on 24 September 1942. From 25 July 1943 was a company officer in the Stammkompanie (cadre company) of Pz.Aufkl.Aus.u.Ers.Abt.24. In September 1943 was a Zugführer in this battalion's 1. Panzerspäh-Kompanie (armoured car company). On 20 October 1943 attached to OKH, before being assigned to the staff of LXXXI. Armeekorps on 5 November 1943 as a Zugführer.

Wätjen, Oberleutnant Klaus; born 13 December 1917 Petrikau. Chef Stabsbatterie III./Panzerartillerie-Regiment 89. Peacetime unit was reiter-Artillerie-Abteilung 1. Wounded on 25 August 1942. Survived Stalingrad. In reformed regiment. Promoted to Hauptmann RDA 01.06.43 (68a1). Killed 27 November 1943 10km south of Dneprovka. Now buried as an unknown soldier in Kirovograd Sammelfriedhof: Block 13.

Weckesser, Oberleutnant d.R. Eugen; born 22 September 1903 Warsaw, Poland. Chef 4./Panzergrenadier-Regiment 26. Wounded on 12 September 1942 but stayed with the troops. Killed 20 January 1943 west of Orlovka. Posthumous promotion to Rittmeister. Buried in Orlovka. His body has not been recovered for burial in Rossoshka Sammelfriedhof.

Wehrmann, Leutnant d.R. Walter; born 20 November 1917. Panzer-Nachrichten-Abteilung 86. Transferred on 12 October 1942 from Führerreserve Heeresgruppe B to Panzer-Nachrichten-Abteilung 86. Outside the Kessel Survived Stalingrad. Survived the war. Still alive in 1997, living in Herne.

Weidemann, Oberleutnant Gert-Axel Kurt Louis; born 10 February 1917 Berlin-Charlottenburg. Regiment Ordonnanzoffizier Panzer-Regiment 24. Entered service 4 December 1936 with Reiter-Regiment 4. Peacetime unit was Reiter-Regiment 2. Leutnant RDA 01.09.39 (1131). Transferred in August 1939 as an Oberfähnrich to Reiter-Regiment 2. As a Leutnant and Zugführer, he rode through Poland, Holland, France and Russia. Iron Cross Second Class on 8 August 1940. Lightly wounded 30 July 1941 by a shell fragment in the right ear. Stayed with the troops. Ordonnanzoffizier Reiter-Regiment 2 from 2 September 1941. Wound Badge in Black on 15 September 1941. Iron Cross First Class on 30 September 1941. Promoted to Oberleutnant RDA 01.11.1941 (327). Took command of 5./Panzer-Regiment 24 on 15 August 1942. Panzer Assault Badge on 2 August 1942. Heavily wounded 23 September 1942 by a shell fragment in the right buttock during a Russian night-time air attack. In hospital for almost two months. While returning to his unit, he was appointed adjutant of an ad hoc defensive group on 22 November 1942. On 10 December 1942 he was tasked with assembling the remnants of the division for reformation. In reformed Panzer Regiment, first as adjutant of Panzer-Regiment 24 from 5 March until 7 July 1943, followed by Chef 8./Panzer-Regiment 24 for three weeks, and then Chef 4./Panzer-Regiment 24 for over a year. Rittmeister RDA 01.04.44. Fought in Normandy and the Western Front until the end of 1944. Survived the war. Joined the Bundeswehr, had various roles as battalion and regiment commander, as well as an exchange officer in the US. Ended his military career with the rank of Oberstleutnant. Wrote the regimental history "Unser Regiment". Died 29 March 1983 Köln.

Weiss, Oberleutnant d.R. Josef; born 12 August 1907 Polkheim. Chef Stabsschwadron II./Panzer-Regiment 24. Wounded 8 September 1942 but stayed with the troops. Promoted to Rittmeister d.R. 21 September 1942. Commanded an Alarmeinheiten formed from the battalion supply trains. Later commanded II./Panzer-Regiment 24. Listed as MIA 22 January 1943 in Stalingrad but he was in fact captured at Stalingrad. Died 8 April 1943 Oranki POW camp. A grave was not registered, so recovery of his body has not been possible.

Weiss, Rittmeister d.R. Josef; born 6 November 1893 München. O2 (Assistant to Ib) Stab 24. Panzer-Division at establishment of Division. Rittmeister RDA 01.01.42. Conflicting reports about his fate. One source says he died in captivity, another that he was killed on 28 January 1943 in the Tractor Factory. Listed as MIA 23 January 1943 in Stalingrad but he was in fact killed on 23 January 1943 in Stalingrad-North. His remains were unable to be recovered by the Volksbund.

Weissenborn, Leutnant d.R. Gerhard; born 18 March 1918 Tilsit. Zugführer 1. Zug in 1./Kradschützen-Abteilung 4. Iron Cross First Class on 4 August 1942. Commanded 1. Schwadron at the end of the battle. Listed as MIA 5 January 1943 in Stalingrad but he was in fact captured at Stalingrad. Survived captivity and returned home.

Well, Oberleutnant Herbert; born 23 April 1915 Rogonnen/Kreis Treuburg. Kradschützen-Abteilung 4. Peacetime unit was Radfahr-Abteilung 1. Oberleutnant RDA 01.03.42 (698). Received confirmation of his rank on 21 September 1942. In July 1943 was adminstratively part of Pz.Aufkl.Aus.u.Ers.Abt.24 but was actually in Reservelazarett Tilsit, possibly from wounds suffered at Stalingrad. Transferred to Pz.Aufkl.Aus.u.Ers.Abt.3 on 10 March 1944. Then assigned to various schools over the following months. Assessed as ab "above average" officer and suitable as a company commander. Survived the war. Died 3 May 2005 Tübingen after a serious illness.

Werther, Leutnant d.R. Edgar; born 31 December 1920 Rodebusch. Zugführer 8./Panzergrenadier-Regiment 21. Killed 3 September 1942 south of Yezovka. Posthumous promotion to Oberleutnant. Iron Cross Second Class on 10 September 1942. His remains were unable to be recovered by the Volksbund.

Weyer, Hauptmann Rolf; born 21 February 1913 Königsberg. IV./Panzerartillerie-Regiment 89. Peacetime unit was Beobachtung-Abteilung 1. Began the war in Panzerjäger-Abteilung 12. Hauptmann RDA 01.04.41 (95). Iron Cross First Class on 4 August 1942. Wounded on 12 September 1942. Survived Stalingrad. Killed 30 August 1943 north-east of Kotlomin on the Mius River while in Heeres-Flak-Artillerie-Abteilung 271. Posthumous promotion to Major with backdated RDA 01.06.43.

Wicus, Oberarzt Dr. Hans; Dinafü 40. His surname has been misspelt in several sources. *See* **Ficus** for full information.

Oberarzt Dr. Hans Wicus administers some 'medication' to his patients.

Wieczorek, Leutnant d.R. Horst; born 19 October 1907 Schönlanke. IV./Panzerartillerie-Regiment 89. Promoted to Oberleutnant d.R. on 31 August 1942. Outside the Stalingrad pocket. Killed 3 December 1942 in the Don bend west of Stalingrad while serving with Regiment Erdmann of 384. Infanterie-Division.

Wiemann, Hauptmann Friedrich-August; born 13 December 1916. Peacetime unit was Panzerartillerie-Regiment 73. Hauptmann RDA 01.07.42 (115). Transferred on 20 October 1942 from Heeres-Flak-Art.Abt. 272 to IV./Pz.Art.Rgt.89 as Chef 10. (schwere) Batterie, equipped with 88mm Flak guns. Later commanded IV./Pz.Art.Rgt.89. Listed as MIA 24 January 1943 in Stalingrad. Not known if he survived captivity.

Wien, Rittmeister Friedrich-Wilhelm; born 15 January 1913 Königsberg. Chef 10. (Flak)/Panzergrenadier-Regiment 21 at establishment of Division. Peacetime unit was MG-Bataillon 31. Hauptmann RDA 01.10.41 (58). Wounded on 18 January 1943. Listed as MIA 24 January 1943 in Stalingrad but was in fact captured. Died 24 April 1943 in Oranki POW Camp. Buried in Novo. His remains have not yet been recovered by the Volksbund.

Wiktorin, Oberleutnant d.R. Walter; born 16 October 1913 Wien. Ordonnanzoffizier III./Panzer-Regiment 24. Promoted to Oberleutnant d.R. on 15 June 1942. Wounded 22 August 1942 by shrapnel while in his panzer. Died of these wounds two days later in Feldlazarett (mot.) 1/522 in Aksai. Iron Cross First Class 4 September 1942. Now buried in Rossoshka Sammelfriedhof: Block 22, Row 13, Grave 502.

Wildeus, Leutnant d.R. Günter; born 16 September 1920. Zugführer 3./Kradschützen-Abteilung 4. Promoted to Leutnant on 15 September 1942 while at Schule for Schnelltruppen in Krampnitz. Transferred on 29 October 1942 from Kradschützen-Ersatz-Abteilung 24 to Kradschützen-Abteilung 4. Took command of 3. Schwadron after Leutnant Melville was killed on 26 November 1942. Commanded 3. Schwadron until the end of the battle. Wounded on 20 January 1943. Listed as MIA 24 January 1943 in Stalingrad but was in fact captured. Survived captivity and returned home. Died 10 December 1990 Wiesbaden.

Wilke, Hauptmann (W) Erwin; born 15 March 1913. Ib/WuG, Ib Abteilung 24. Panzer-Division at establishment of Division. Promoted to Hauptmann on 8 June 1942 with RDA 01.06.42 (35). Listed as MIA in Stalingrad but was in fact captured. Survived captivity and returned home. Died in 1985.

Wilking, Leutnant d.R. Heino; born 21 November 1920 Ahnebergen. Zugführer in Kradschützen-Abteilung 4. Transferred on 9 October 1942 from Führerreserve Heeresgruppe B to Kradschützen-Abteilung 4. Survived Stalingrad. In reformed Division. Killed 25 October 1943 near Novo Starodub by a direct hit on his half-track. Buried in Starodub. His remains have not yet been recovered by the Volksbund.

Willenberg, Oberleutnant Hans Wilhelm; born 6 May 1915 Kandewitz. Chef 1./Panzerartillerie-Regiment 89. Peacetime unit was Artillerie-Regiment 18. Severely wounded on 4 September 1942. Promoted to Hauptmann on 17 November 1942 with RDA 01.11.42 (18). Died 23 October 1944 in Kiskallo, Hungary while in Heeres-Artillerie-Abteilung 127. Posthumous promotion to Major.

Windemuth, Hauptmann d.L.z.V. Ernst; Werkstattkp./Panzer-Regiment 24. Began the war in Panzerjäger-Abteilung 30. Hauptmann RDA 01.07.42. Transferred from Werkstattkompanie/Panzer-Regiment 24 to XXXXVIII. Pz.Korps as IIb on 17 June 42. Survived Stalingrad. Promoted to Major RDA 01.01.44.

von Winterfeld, Major Hans Joachim Alexander Georg Wilhelm Friedrich (Hild-Wilfried); born 17 April 1903 Frankfurt/Oder, only son of Generalmajor Georg von Winterfeld. Kommandeur I./Panzer-Regiment 24. Peacetime unit was Panzer-Regiment 6. In the cavalry prior to the war but at the beginning of the war, he belonged to Pz.Rgt.6 of 3. Panzer-Division. As a

SPANNOCCHI

Major von Winterfeld on the beach at Rennes, France in April 1942.

SPANNOCCHI

Major von Winterfeld completes paperwork in Verkhniakovsk, early August 1942.

Hauptmann, he commanded its 6. Panzer Kompanie, leading it through the Polish and French campaigns. Iron Cross Second Class 21 September 1939. Iron Cross First Class 21 May 1941. Transferred early 1942 to take command of the newly formed I./Panzer-Regiment 24. Took temporary command of Pz.Rgt.24 on 23 August 1942 after Riebel was killed. German Cross in Gold 5 November 1942. Promoted to Oberstleutnant RDA 01.11.42 (19). Lightly wounded 17 January 1943 by mortar fragments. Tried to get flown out. Knight's Cross in 22 January 1943.

SPANNOCCHI

Oberst Freiherr von Broich, Major von Winterfeld and Rittmeister von Mirbach discuss details of an upcoming attack.

SPANNOCCHI

A quiet moment allows Major von Winterfeld to have a shave.

SPANNOCCHI

Major von Winterfeld prepares a battle plan with one of his staff members.

SPANNOCCHI

Major von Winterfeld conducts the wedding ceremony of Unteroffizier Denda. The bride was being married at the same time in Germany.

SPANNOCCHI

Major von Winterfeld bestows the Iron Cross Second Class to several men from his battalion. Verkhniakovsk, August 1942.

SPANNOCCHI

Major von Winterfeld hangs out his washing. He was obviously not expecting a visit from his superior officers.

Listed as MIA 23 January 1943 in Stalingrad but was in fact captured. Died 3 April 1943 in Beketovka POW Camp south of Stalingrad. Probably buried as an unknown soldier in Rossoshka Sammelfriedhof.

Wippern, Oberleutnant Erich; born 14 September 1918 Kiel. Chef 5./Panzerartillerie-Regiment 89. Peacetime unit was Artillerie-Regiment 22. Fought in France as Abteilung Adjutant of II./reiter-Artillerie-Regiment 1. Iron Cross Second Class on 25 June 1940. Oberleutnant RDA 01.08.40 (95). He became Regiment Ordonnanzoffizier. Killed 9 August 1942 in Kunovka. Posthumous promotion to Hauptmann RDA 01.08.42. Probably buried as an unknown soldier in Rossoshka Sammelfriedhof.

Wittkowski, Oberleutnant; Abteilung Adjutant Panzer-Nachrichten-Abteilung 86 at establishment of Division. Oberleutnant RDA 01.11.41 (66). Survived Stalingrad. In reformed Abteilung as a Kompanieschef.

Wochnik, Leutnant d.R. Alois; born 6 March 1914. Ia/Mess Stab 24. Panzer-Division. Transferred to Ausbildung-Einheit Weiss on 7 January 1943 for training as an infantry officer. Listed as MIA 23 January 1943 in Stalingrad. Not known if he survived captivity.

Woelki, Leutnant Gert-Dietrich; born 8 May 1922 Georgenhorst near Insterburg, East Prussia. Batterie Offizier 2./Panzerartillerie-Regiment 89. Severely wounded on 22 August 1942. Iron Cross First Class on 4 September 1942. Survived Stalingrad. Survived the war. In 1964, he became counsellor in the West German Embassy in Washington D.C. Died in October 1974.

Freiherr von Woellwarth-Lauterburg, Rittmeister Konrad Maximilian Robert Richard Wilhelm; born 27 March 1916 Ludwigsburg, Baden-Württemberg. Chef 5./Panzer-Regiment 24. Abteilung Adjutant of II./Reiter-Regiment 2 at outbreak of war. Schwadron Commander at establishment of Division. Transferred from Pz.Rgt.24 into the Führerreserve OKH on 15.08.1942 for training for the Generalstabsdienst of 75. Inf.-Div. Survived Stalingrad. IIb of 26. Panzer-Division from 20.06.43–15.02.1944. Major RDA 01.08.43 (34e). Deputy Leader for Training of Inspector General der Panzertruppe in 1945. Survived the war. Died 12 July 2003.

Woesch, Hauptmann Rudolf; born 17 May 1915 Nürnberg. II./Panzerartillerie-Regiment 89. Hauptmann RDA 01.03.42 (9). Killed 15 January 1943 near Karpovka in Stalingrad. Posthumous promotion to Major RDA 01.01.43. His remains were unable to be recovered for reburial by the Volksbund.

Wohlers, Leutnant Franz; born 17 March 1921 Friedrichstadt. IV./Panzerartillerie-Regiment 89. Peacetime unit was II./Artillerie-Regiment 58. Iron Cross Second Class on 27 September 1942. Survived Stalingrad. Oberleutnant RDA 01.09.43 (120). Killed in an accident 15 July 1944 in Denmark while in Heeres-Flak-Art.Ers.u.Ausb.Abt.280. Now buried in Esbjerg: Block O1 Row 5 Grave 19.

Wolf, Leutnant d.R. Karl Alfred; born 6 January 1916 Frankenhausen. Zugführer 6./Panzergrenadier-Regiment 21. Wounded on 16 September 1942 in Stalingrad, later dying in Sanitäts-Kompanie 2/40 hospital.

Freiherr von Wolff-Metternich, Leutnant Wilhelm; Panzergrenadier-Regiment 26. Promoted to Leutnant on 28 September 1942. Later 24. Panzer-Division Stab, Ib Abteilung. Survived Stalingrad and the war. Died in 1996 in Frankfurt.

Wollenschläger, Oberleutnant Gerhard; born 11 March 1913 Insterburg. Panzerjäger-Abteilung 40. Iron Cross First Class on 10 September 1942.

Wolter, Oberleutnant d.R.; IV./Panzerartillerie-Regiment 89; Transferred on 22 June 1942 from Panzerartillerie-Regiment 89 to II./Artillerie-Regiment 72.

Wolter, Oberleutnant d.R. Dr. Johannes; born 22 February 1899 Rosengarten. Chef 10. (Flak)/ Panzergrenadier-Regiment 26. Iron Cross Second Class on 18 October 1942. Transferred on 7 November 1942 from Flak-Bataillon 619 to Panzergrenadier-Regiment 26. Died 25 November 1942 in Spartakovka near Stalingrad. Posthumous promotion to Hauptmann d.R.

Wrede, Rittmeister Walter; born 5 November 1912 Hadersleben. Chef 5./Kradschützen-Abteilung 4. Peacetime unit was Radfahr-Abteilung 1. Rittmeister RDA 01.04.42 (1317). Took command of Kradschützen-Abteilung 4 on 13 October 1942. Survived Stalingrad. In reformed Division. Killed 27–28 October 1943 in Novo Starodub, Ukraine when a salvo of Stalin Organs landed on his command post. He was commanding II./Panzergrenadier-Regiment 21. Posthumous promotion to Major RDA 01.10.43. Buried in Kirovograd: Block 12 Row 14 Grave 996.

Wroblewski, Leutnant d.R. Walter Herbert Fritz; born 30 March 1917 Stettin. Zugführer 7./Panzergrenadier-Regiment 26. Entered the service in 1938 in Kavallerie-Regiment 14 in Mecklenburg. In 7./Reiter-Regiment 22 from 1940. Iron Cross Second Class 28 October 1941. Assault Badge 30 November 1941. Zugführer at establishment of Division. Wounded in June or July 1942. Promoted to Leutnant RDA 01.10.42. Transferred on 6 November 1942 from Panzergrenadier-Ersatz-Abteilung 413 to Panzergrenadier-Regiment 26 as a Zugführer in 7. Schwadron but immediately took charge of a Stosszug in Sturmschwadron 24. Took command of the Sturmschwadron on 11 November 1942. Wounded 18 November 1942. Survived Stalingrad. Wound Badge 7 January 1943. Spent the rest of the war as a Zugführer and Schwadronsführer in Pz.Gr.Rgt.26. Severely wounded in 1945, but recovered in Lübz Lazarett in Mecklenburg. All together, he suffered 7 wounds during the war, the last being an amputation of a leg. Survived the war. Joined the Bundeswehr in 1956 and finally retired with the rank of Oberstleutnant. Died 26 December 1994 Isernhagen.

Wulf, Stabsarzt Dr.; Chef Sanitäts-Kompanie 1/40 Transferred on 24 August 1942 from Stab of XXIV. Armeekorps to 24. Panzer-Division.

Wünsche-Steude, Hauptmann Joachim Richard Ernst; born 28 January 1914 Bautzen. Peacetime unit was Artillerie-Regiment 4. Ib (Division Quartermaster) Stab 24. Panzer-Division. Transferred on 13 November 1942 from 6. Armee to 24. Panzer-Division as Ib. Division Ib since 25 November 1942. Listed as MIA 23 January 1943 in Stalingrad but was in fact killed 21 January 1943. Posthumous promotion to Major i.G RDA 01.08.43 (4). His remains were unable to be recovered by the Volksbund.

Wust, Oberleutnant d.R.; Transferred on 6 November 1942 from Marsch Bataillon to Panzergrenadier-Regiment 26.

von Zawadzky-Polanka, Rittmeister d.R. Erwin; born 27 August 1900 Kaltennordheim. Führer Verpflegung-Tross, Ib Abteilung 24. Panzer-Division. As a Leutnant, he was Ordonnanzoffizier of Reiter-Regiment 21 from 7 June 1940 to 30 September 1940. Führer Verpflegung-Tross at establishment of Division. Rittmeister RDA 01.03.42. Transferred on 21 September 1942 from Verpflegung Trupp to 24. Panzer-Division Stomü. Found himself outside the Stalingrad pocket. Killed 19 October 1944 in Mezötur, Hungary.

Zieher, Assistenarzt Dr. Wilhelm; born 29 April 1916 Oberndorf. Abteilung Assistenarzt III./Panzer-Regiment 24. Wounded 05.09.1942 but stayed with the troops. Promoted to Oberarzt. Iron Cross Second Class 22.10.1942. Survived Stalingrad. Oberarzt in III./Panzer-Regiment 24 in April 1944. Later became Divisionsarzt. Survived the war. After the war, he became a neurological specialist. Died in 1997.

Zieke, Hauptmann Erhardt; born 4 July 1910 Malitzschkendorf. Chef 1./Panzerjäger-Abteilung 40. Peacetime unit was Kavallerie-Regiment 10. Oberleutnant RDA 01.12.39 (36). Hauptmann RDA 01.05.42 (122) C. Awarded Iron Cross Second Class and Assault Badge. In May 1941 he was described as "coldblooded in action" and possessed the "outstanding nature of a leader." Killed 28 July 1942 south of Chir railway station. Buried in the middle of Yerotskoye village, Grave 1. His remains have not yet been recovered by the Volksbund.

Zimmermann, Hauptmann Hans; born 23 September 1915 Mainz. Chef 8./Panzergrenadier-Regiment 26. On 3 December 1942 he fended off a large Russian attack with only his supply train people. Wounded and flown out of the Kessel. Knight's Cross on 22 January 1943. Survived the war. Joined the Bundeswehr and retired with the rank of Oberstleutnant. Died 29 June 1993 München.

Zyznewski, Unterarzt d.R. Dr. Alexander; born 28 January 1910. Transferred on 17 November 1942 from Allenstein-Sanitäts-Abteilung to I./Panzergrenadier-Regiment 26. Later transferred to Dinafü 40 as Assistenarzt d.R. Listed as MIA in Stalingrad but was in fact captured. Survived captivity and returned home. Moved to the United States. Died May 1984.

KNIGHT'S CROSS

APPENDIX TWO

Knight's Cross

- Oberleutnant Georg Michael (Abteilung Commander of II./Panzergrenadier-Regiment 26) Knight's Cross on 19th January 1941 as Zug Commander in 6./Reiter-Regiment 6.

- Unteroffizier Otto Brakat (Gruppenführer 2./Radfahr-Abteilung 1) Knight's Cross on 27th July 1941.

- Oberst Reichsfreiherr Maximilian von Edelsheim (Regiment Commander of Panzergrenadier-Regiment 26) Knight's Cross on 30th July 1941 as Commander of Radfahr-Abteilung 1.

- Generalmajor Bruno Ritter von Hauenschild (Division Commander) Knight's Cross on 25th August 1941 as Commander of Panzer-Brigade 4.

- Oberst Wilhelm von Lengerke (Regiment Commander of Panzergrenadier-Regiment 21) Knight's Cross on 31st August 1941 as Commander of I./Reiter-Regiment 1.

- Wachtmeister Siegfried Freyer (Panzer Commander in 4./Panzer-Regiment 24) Knight's Cross on 23rd July 1942.

- Oberleutnant Gerhard Schönfeld (Schwadron Commander of 3./Panzerpionier-Bataillon 40) Knight's Cross on 25th August 1942.

- Oberst Friedrich Freiherr von Broich (Brigade Commander of Schützen Brigade 24) Knight's Cross on 29th August 1942.

- Major Dietrich von der Lancken (Abteilung Commander of III./Panzer-Regiment 24) Knight's Cross on 29th October 1942.

- Oberstleutnant Vollrath von Hellermann (Regiment Commander of Panzergrenadier-Regiment 21) Knight's Cross on 21st November 1942.

- Leutnant Georg Köhler (Schwadron Commander in 3./Panzergrenadier-Regiment 26) Knight's Cross on 3rd January 1943.

- Oberleutnant Paul Markgraf (Abteilung Commander of Panzerjäger-Abteilung 40) Knight's Cross on 3rd January 1943.
- Oberwachtmeister Ernst Neufeld (Zug Commander in 2./Kradschützen-Abteilung 4) Knight's Cross on 3rd January 1943.
- Rittmeister Gerhard Thiel (Abteilung Commander of III./Panzer-Regiment 24) Knight's Cross on 20th January 1943.
- Oberstleutnant Hild-Wilfried von Winterfeld (Abteilung Commander of I./Panzer-Regiment 24) Knight's Cross on 22nd January 1943.
- Hauptmann Hans Zimmermann (Schwadron Commander of 8./Panzergrenadier-Regiment 26) Knight's Cross on 22nd January 1943.

Oakleaves

- Generalmajor Bruno Ritter von Hauenschild (Division Commander) Oakleaves (129) on 27th September 1942.
- Oberst Reichsfreiherr Maximilian von Edelsheim (Regiment Commander of Panzergrenadier-Regiment 26) Oakleaves (162) on 22nd December 1942.
- Oberleutnant Georg Michael (Abteilung Commander of II./Panzergrenadier-Regiment 26) Oakleaves (187) on 25th January 1943.

GERMAN CROSS IN GOLD

APPENDIX THREE

German Cross in Gold

- Oberst Friedrich Freiherr von Broich (Brigade Commander of Schützen-Brigade 24) German Cross in Gold on 2nd November 1941 while commanding Reiter-Regiment 22.

- Oberst Gustav Adolf Riebel (Regiment Commander of Panzer-Regiment 24) German Cross in Gold on 24th December 1941 as Commander of Panzer-Regiment 15.

- Hauptmann Hans-David von Engel (Batterie Commander of 6./Panzerartillerie-Regiment 89) German Cross in Gold on 21st August 1942.

- Oberwachtmeister Richard Juckel (7./Panzergrenadier-Regiment 21) German Cross in Gold on 21st August 1942.

- Oberwachtmeister Karl Misch (2./Panzergrenadier-Regiment 21) German Cross in Gold on 21st August 1942.

- Rittmeister Friedrich Graf zu Solms-Wildenfels (Abteilung Adjutant of II./Panzergrenadier-Regiment 21) German Cross in Gold on 21st August 1942.

- Rittmeister Rudolf Graf von Marogna-Redwitz (Schwadron Commander of 6./Panzergrenadier-Regiment 21) German Cross in Gold on 26th August 1942.

- Rittmeister Rudolf von Knebel Doeberitz (Brigade Adjutant of Schützen-Brigade 24) German Cross in Gold on 29th August 1942.

- Rittmeister Guy von Saint-Paul (Schwadron Commander of 12./Panzer-Regiment 24) German Cross in Gold on 29th August 1942.

- Rittmeister Gerhard Thiel (Schwadron Commander of 10./Panzer-Regiment 24) German Cross in Gold on 29th August 1942.

- Oberwachtmeister Gerhard Baldauf (7./Panzergrenadier-Regiment 26) German Cross in Gold on 4th September 1942.

- Rittmeister Karl Legat (Schwadron Commander of 1./Panzergrenadier-Regiment 26) German Cross in Gold on 4th September 1942.
- Rittmeister Peter Schulz-Fademrecht (Abteilung Commander of I./Panzergrenadier-Regiment 26) German Cross in Gold on 4th September 1942.
- Major d.R. Wilhelm Schwanke (Abteilung Commander of II./Panzergrenadier-Regiment 21) German Cross in Gold on 4th September 1942.
- Wachtmeister Walter Rathjens (7./Panzergrenadier-Regiment 26) German Cross in Gold on 13th September 1942.
- Major Hugo Burgsthaler (Abteilung Commander of II./Panzer-Regiment 24) German Cross in Gold on 20th September 1942.
- Oberstleutnant Vollrath von Hellermann (Abteilung Commander of Kradschützen-Abteilung 4) German Cross in Gold on 20th September 1942.
- Hauptmann Horst von Rosenberg-Lipinski (Batterie Commander of 4./Panzerartillerie-Regiment 89) German Cross in Gold on 20th September 1942
- Rittmeister Graf Bechtold von Bernstorff (Abteilung Commander of I./Panzergrenadier-Regiment 21) German Cross in Gold on 7th October 1942.
- Oberleutnant Ludwig Dittmar (Schwadron Commander of 6./Panzergrenadier-Regiment 21) German Cross in Gold on 9th October 1942.
- Hauptmann d.R.z.V. Ferdinand Mayer (Schwadron Commander of 2./Panzerpionier-Bataillon 40) German Cross in Gold on 9th October 1942.
- Leutnant Egon Reifner (Zug Commander in 3./Panzerpionier-Bataillon 40) German Cross in Gold on 9th October 1942.
- Oberwachtmeister Johann Schwarzer (1./Panzerartillerie-Regiment 89) German Cross in Gold on 9th October 1942.
- Major i.G. Otto-Wilhelm von Menges (Division Ia – Chief-of-Staff) German Cross in Gold on 13th October 1942.
- Leutnant Erdmann Graeve (3./Panzerjäger-Abteilung 40) German Cross in Gold on 16th October 1942.
- Major Hans-Wilhelm von Heyden (Abteilung Commander of II./Panzergrenadier-Regiment 26) German Cross in Gold on 5th November 1942.
- Major Hild-Wilfried von Winterfeld (Abteilung Commander of I./Panzer-Regiment 24) German Cross in Gold on 5th November 1942.

- Rittmeister Heinz Kolczyk (Schwadron Commander of 2./Kradschützen-Abteilung 4) German Cross in Gold on 5th November 1942.

- Rittmeister Arnold von Dressler (Abteilung Commander of I./Panzergrenadier-Regiment 26) German Cross in Gold on 6th November 1942.

- Hauptmann Hermann Koch (Abteilung Commander of I./Panzerartillerie-Regiment 89) German Cross in Gold on 6th November 1942.

- Leutnant Herbert Sylla (Zug Commander in 1./Panzer-Regiment 24) German Cross in Gold on 6th November 1942.

- Major Hans-Walter von Pawel (Regiment Commander of Panzerartillerie-Regiment 89) German Cross in Gold on 12th November 1942.

- Oberleutnant Jürgen Pachnio (Schwadron Commander of 3./Panzergrenadier-Regiment 21) German Cross in Gold on 24th November 1942.

- Oberleutnant Christian Keiler (Schwadron Commander of 6./Panzergrenadier-Regiment 26) German Cross in Gold on 8th December 1942.

- Leutnant Georg Köhler (Schwadron Commander of 3./Panzergrenadier-Regiment 26) German Cross in Gold on 8th December 1942.

- Oberleutnant Eberhard Beyersdorff (Schwadron Commander of 1./Panzergrenadier-Regiment 26) German Cross in Gold on 10th January 1943.

- Wachtmeister Fritz Enderweit (4./Panzerartillerie-Regiment 89) German Cross in Gold on 10th January 1943.

- Obergefreiter Willy Gillmeister (Gruppe Commander in 6./Panzergrenadier-Regiment 26) German Cross in Gold on 10th January 1943.

- Hauptmann Erich Hicketier (Batterie Commander of 2./Panzerartillerie-Regiment 89) German Cross in Gold on 10th January 1943.

- Leutnant Karl Lichte (Schwadron Commander of 1./Panzergrenadier-Regiment 26) German Cross in Gold on 10th January 1943.

- Hauptmann Hans von Löw (Schwadron Commander of 2./Panzerjäger-Abteilung 40) German Cross in Gold on 10th January 1943.

- Rittmeister Kuno von Meyer (Schwadron Commander of 9./Panzer-Regiment 24) German Cross in Gold on 10th January 1943.

- Oberleutnant Peter Schmidt (Panzergrenadier-Regiment 21) German Cross in Gold on 10th January 1943.

- Oberwachtmeister Bruno Stelzer (1./Panzergrenadier-Regiment 26) German Cross in Gold on 10th January 1943.
- Oberwachtmeister Walter Thimm (1./Panzer-Regiment 24) German Cross in Gold on 10th January 1943.
- Hauptmann Hubert Platz (Abteilung Commander of III./Panzerartillerie-Regiment 89) German Cross in Gold on 18th January 1943.
- Oberleutnant Hans-Jochen Kolbe (24. Panzer-Division Stab) German Cross in Gold on 21st January 1943.
- Generalleutnant Arno von Lenski (Division Commander) German Cross in Gold on 21st January 1943.
- Oberwachtmeister Walter Jordan (5./Panzergrenadier-Regiment 26) German Cross in Gold on 25th January 1943.
- Rittmeister Ernst-Hasse von Langenn-Steinkeller (Abteilung Commander of Kradschützen-Abteilung 4) German Cross in Gold on 25th January 1943.
- Oberleutnant d.R Hans Thylmann (Schwadron Commander of 2./Panzergrenadier-Regiment 26) German Cross in Gold on 25th January 1943.
- Rittmeister Ernst-Georg Baron von Heyking (Schwadron Commander of 4./Panzergrenadier-Regiment 21) German Cross in Gold on 12th February 1943.

Iron Cross

Appendix Four

Iron Cross

Iron Cross First Class on 2nd August 1942

Unteroffizier Hans Böhnlein	Panzergrenadier-Regiment 21
Rittmeister d.R. Oskar Freiherr von der Goltz	Panzergrenadier-Regiment 21
Unteroffizier Wilhelm Grosse-Maesstrup	Panzergrenadier-Regiment 21
Wachtmeister Paul Plemert	Panzergrenadier-Regiment 21
Wachtmeister Fritz Reiter	Panzergrenadier-Regiment 21
Obergefreiter Josef Zauner	Panzergrenadier-Regiment 21
Unteroffizier Johann Bahlig	Panzer-Regiment 24
Leutnant d.R. Alex Frhr. von Falkenhausen	8./Panzer-Regiment 24
Unteroffizier Alfons Fischer	4./Panzer-Regiment 24
Gefreiter Arnold Groll	4./Panzer-Regiment 24
Oberleutnant Heinrich von Helldorff	4./Panzer-Regiment 24
Unteroffizier Kurt Herrmann	Panzer-Regiment 24
Leutnant Hans Messerschmidt	4./Panzer-Regiment 24
Gefreiter Heinrich Müller	4./Panzer-Regiment 24
Unteroffizier Wilhelm Sanir	Panzer-Regiment 24
Unteroffizier Wilhelm Schmidt	4./Panzer-Regiment 24
Unteroffizier Heinrich Warzun	1./Panzer-Regiment 24
Oberwachtmeister Hans Fittkau	6./Panzergrenadier-Regiment 26
Unteroffizier Walter Gieplow	Panzergrenadier-Regiment 26
Leutnant Albrecht Köhne	2./Panzergrenadier-Regiment 26
Unteroffizier Günter Szostakowski	Panzergrenadier-Regiment 26
Unteroffizier Günter Wilke	Panzergrenadier-Regiment 26
Oberwachtmeister Alfred Tausendfreund	3./Kradschützen-Abteilung 4
Oberwachtmeister Horst Reinert	Panzer-Nachrichten-Abteilung 86
Unteroffizier Herbert Engel	Panzerartillerie-Regiment 89
Unteroffizier Adolf Fischer	Panzerartillerie-Regiment 89

Leutnant Werner Pfautsch	Panzerartillerie-Regiment 89
Oberwachtmeister Friedrich Rüpke	Panzerartillerie-Regiment 89
Leutnant Friedrich Sodemann	Panzerartillerie-Regiment 89
Stabsarzt Dr. Ernst Grübner	Stab/Panzerjäger-Abteilung 40

Iron Cross First Class on 3rd August 1942

Sanitäts-Unteroffizier Josef Heimbrock	Panzerpionier-Bataillon 40
Unteroffizier Karl Leon	Panzerpionier-Bataillon 40
Leutnant d.R. Hans Peters	Panzerpionier-Bataillon 40

Iron Cross First Class on 4th August 1942

Leutnant Helmut Jansen	Panzerjäger-Abteilung 40
Wachtmeister August Diendel	II./Artillerie Regiment 72
Wachtmeister Paul Müller	II./Artillerie Regiment 72
Wachtmeister Josef Schaller	II./Artillerie Regiment 72
Unteroffizier Willi Wanneck	II./Artillerie Regiment 72
Wachtmeister Heinrich Wannheller	II./Artillerie Regiment 72
Leutnant Gerhard Fuchs	Panzerartillerie-Regiment 89
Unteroffizier Karl Hammer	Panzerartillerie-Regiment 89
Wachtmeister Siegfried Jungblut	Panzerartillerie-Regiment 89
Oberstleutnant Fritz von Melchers	IV./Panzerartillerie-Regiment 89
Leutnant Ernst Nueske	1./Panzerartillerie-Regiment 89
Oberwachtmeister Herbert Rohde	Panzerartillerie-Regiment 89
Oberwachtmeister Karl Schmeichel	Panzerartillerie-Regiment 89
Hauptmann Rolf Weyer	IV./Panzerartillerie-Regiment 89
Oberleutnant Paul Markgraf	Panzerjäger-Abteilung 40
Leutnant d.R. Gerhard Weissenborn	1./Kradschützen-Abteilung 4

Iron Cross First Class on 12th August 1942

Oberleutnant Kurt von Burkersroda	Panzergrenadier-Regiment 21
Oberarzt d.R. Dr. Kurt Donner	II./Panzergrenadier-Regiment 21
Obergefreiter Erich Edinger	Panzergrenadier-Regiment 21
Unteroffizier Fritz Kabbeck	Panzergrenadier-Regiment 21
Oberleutnant Werner Freiherr von Keyserlingk	Panzergrenadier-Regiment 21
Oberleutnant d.R. Dietrich Micke	Panzergrenadier-Regiment 21
Obergefreiter Hans Oehler	Panzergrenadier-Regiment 21
Sanitäts-Feldwebel Heinz Palkus	Panzergrenadier-Regiment 21
Oberleutnant Peter Schmidt	Panzergrenadier-Regiment 21
Stabswachtmeister Herbert Sommer	Panzergrenadier-Regiment 21
Unteroffizier Wilhelm Wichmann	Panzergrenadier-Regiment 21

Oberwachtmeister Rudiger Zimmermann	Panzergrenadier-Regiment 21
Leutnant Günther Birth	Panzergrenadier-Regiment 26
Oberleutnant Axel Feldt	7./Panzergrenadier-Regiment 26
Wachtmeister Gustav Fromm	Panzergrenadier-Regiment 26
Obergefreiter August Lange	Panzergrenadier-Regiment 26
Unteroffizier Richard Letzenberger	Panzergrenadier-Regiment 26
Sanitäts-Oberfeldwebel Heinz Müller	Panzergrenadier-Regiment 26
Unteroffizier Alfred Nadolny	Panzergrenadier-Regiment 26
Oberleutnant Herbert Oberbeck	8./Panzergrenadier-Regiment 26
Rittmeister Wilhelm Rogge	10./Panzergrenadier-Regiment 26
Unteroffizier Kurt Wachtel	Panzergrenadier-Regiment 26
Unteroffizier Erich Noreike	Panzerpionier-Bataillon 40
Oberleutnant Manfred von Baum	Panzerartillerie-Regiment 89
Leutnant d.R. Werner Fähnrich	I./Panzerartillerie-Regiment 89
Leutnant Gerhard Griebenow	Panzerartillerie-Regiment 89
Unteroffizier Otto Neumann	Panzerartillerie-Regiment 89
Oberleutnant Karl-Heinz Seufferheld	Panzerartillerie-Regiment 89

Iron Cross First Class on 16th August 1942

Unteroffizier Heinrich Forsthöfel	Panzerjäger-Abteilung 40

Iron Cross First Class on 17th August 1942

Unteroffizier Arnold Erpenbach	Panzerartillerie-Regiment 89
Unteroffizier Franz Gross	Panzerartillerie-Regiment 89
Leutnant Hobe Magens	Panzerartillerie-Regiment 89
Leutnant Fritz Stegel	3./Panzerjäger-Abteilung 40

Iron Cross First Class on 18th August 1942

Wachtmeister Ewald Kniephoff	Panzergrenadier-Regiment 21
Wachtmeister Martin Backebusch	Panzergrenadier-Regiment 26
Stabswachtmeister Hans Brakebusch	6./Panzergrenadier-Regiment 26
Oberwachtmeister Erich Bredfeldt	Panzergrenadier-Regiment 26
Unteroffizier Fritz Krüger	Panzergrenadier-Regiment 26
Obergefreiter Walter Kubinski	Panzergrenadier-Regiment 26
Obergefreiter Otto Mai	Panzergrenadier-Regiment 26
Unteroffizier Walter Nordmann	Panzergrenadier-Regiment 26
Obergefreiter Willi Tewes	Panzergrenadier-Regiment 26
Obergefreiter Fritz Wöbse	Panzergrenadier-Regiment 26

Iron Cross First Class on 20th August 1942

Unteroffizier Walter Budweg	Kradschützen-Abteilung 4
Unteroffizier Hans König	Kradschützen-Abteilung 4
Obergefreiter Bernhard Lüken	Kradschützen-Abteilung 4
Unteroffizier Hans Magdsack	Kradschützen-Abteilung 4
Oberwachtmeister Erich Paetsch	3./Kradschützen-Abteilung 4
Wachtmeister Otto Prädel	Kradschützen-Abteilung 4
Oberwachtmeister Fritz Ruddat	Kradschützen-Abteilung 4
Wachtmeister Walter Ruff	3./Kradschützen-Abteilung 4
Unteroffizier Willi Wiehmeier	Kradschützen-Abteilung 4

Iron Cross First Class on 22nd August 1942

Obergefreiter Hermann Fleischer	Panzergrenadier-Regiment 21
Unteroffizier Willi Krause	Panzergrenadier-Regiment 21
Gefreiter Fritz Lakaschus	Panzergrenadier-Regiment 21
Wachtmeister Wilhelm Mäck	Panzergrenadier-Regiment 21
Obergefreiter Franz Schmitt	Panzergrenadier-Regiment 21
Gefreiter Hermann Weiss	Panzergrenadier-Regiment 21
Obergefreiter Rufus Risenbarth	Panzerpionier-Bataillon 40

Iron Cross First Class on 24th August 1942

Wachtmeister Bruno Hammer	Panzer-Nachrichten-Abteilung 86

Iron Cross First Class on 26th August 1942

Oberwachtmeister Rudi Bastisch	Panzer-Regiment 24
Obergefreiter Hans Dohany	Panzer-Regiment 24
Leutnant Dietrich Höhne	5./Panzer-Regiment 24
Oberwachtmeister Gerhard Konopke	12./Panzer-Regiment 24
Unteroffizier Erich Meier	Panzer-Regiment 24
Wachtmeister Wilhelm Merta	Panzer-Regiment 24
Wachtmeister Paul Nowak	Panzer-Regiment 24
Stabsarzt Dr. Ernst Schumacher	Panzer-Regiment 24
Feldwebel Christopher Friedrichs	Panzerjäger-Abteilung 40

Iron Cross First Class on 4th September 1942

Oberleutnant Walter Wiktorin	III./Panzer-Regiment 24
Leutnant Paul Braunheim	II./Panzerartillerie-Regiment 89
Oberwachtmeister Heinz Meyer	Panzerartillerie-Regiment 89
Unteroffizier Alfons Sombrutzki	Panzerartillerie-Regiment 89
Oberarzt Dr. Günter Spode	Panzerartillerie-Regiment 89
Leutnant Gert Woelki	Panzerartillerie-Regiment 89

Iron Cross First Class on 10th September 1942

Wachtmeister Otto Burgschat	Panzergrenadier-Regiment 21
Unteroffizier Franz Endres	Panzergrenadier-Regiment 21
Obergefreiter Theobald Gall	Panzergrenadier-Regiment 21
Obergefreiter Josef Huter	Panzergrenadier-Regiment 21
Unteroffizier Erich Kindl	Panzergrenadier-Regiment 21
Leutnant Heinz Lakenbrink	Panzergrenadier-Regiment 21
Unteroffizier Herbert Raudßus	Panzergrenadier-Regiment 21
Obergefreiter Heinrich Rempe	Panzergrenadier-Regiment 21
Gefreiter Eduard Scheibner	Panzergrenadier-Regiment 21
Rittmeister Fritz Schriewer	Panzergrenadier-Regiment 21
Leutnant d.R. Werner Tutein	1./Panzergrenadier-Regiment 21
Wachtmeister Edmund Wiederer	Panzergrenadier-Regiment 21
Unteroffizier Kurt Bartholomes	Panzergrenadier-Regiment 26
Oberleutnant Horst Brosig	7./Panzergrenadier-Regiment 26
Obergefreiter Willi Donsei	Panzergrenadier-Regiment 26
Unteroffizier Johann Eiden	Panzergrenadier-Regiment 26
Unteroffizier Wilhelm Elbl	Panzergrenadier-Regiment 26
Wachtmeister Karl Füllekrug	Panzergrenadier-Regiment 26
Unteroffizier Robert Karst	Panzergrenadier-Regiment 26
Unteroffizier Heinrich Logemann	Panzergrenadier-Regiment 26
Wachtmeister Richard Möck	Panzergrenadier-Regiment 26
Obergefreiter Theo Müller	Panzergrenadier-Regiment 26
Unteroffizier Johann Paulsen	Panzergrenadier-Regiment 26
Wachtmeister Heinz Röger	Panzergrenadier-Regiment 26
Unteroffizier Horst Schalla	Panzergrenadier-Regiment 26
Obergefreiter Fritz Stahnke	Panzergrenadier-Regiment 26
Unteroffizier Kurt Brethauer	Panzerjäger-Abteilung 40
Oberleutnant d.R. Ernst Hahn	Panzerjäger-Abteilung 40
Oberleutnant Heinrich Krebs	3./Panzerjäger-Abteilung 40
Oberleutnant Gerhard Wollenschläger	Panzerjäger-Abteilung 40
Unteroffizier Gerhard Pfeiffer	Panzerpionier-Bataillon 40
Unteroffizier Willibald Weber	Panzerpionier-Bataillon 40
Leutnant Einar von Heimann	1./Panzerartillerie-Regiment 89
Leutnant Jürgen Morff	IV./Panzerartillerie-Regiment 89
Wachtmeister Anton Riehe	IV./Panzerartillerie-Regiment 89
Leutnant d.R. Hermann Rust	IV./Panzerartillerie-Regiment 89
Obergefreiter Walter Schorning	Panzerartillerie-Regiment 89

Iron Cross First Class on 16th September 1942

Oberwachtmeister Fritz Pfannkuchen	Panzerartillerie-Regiment 89
Unteroffizier Fritz Wallert	Panzerartillerie-Regiment 89

Iron Cross First Class on 19th September 1942

Oberleutnant Ludwig Stockinger	IV./Panzerartillerie-Regiment 89

Iron Cross First Class on 20th September 1942

Obergefreiter Otto Allissat	Kradschützen-Abteilung 4
Obergefreiter Bernhard Birrewitz	Kradschützen-Abteilung 4
Unteroffizier Gerhard Dahlke	Kradschützen-Abteilung 4
Oberwachtmeister Oskar Gaschk	Kradschützen-Abteilung 4
Obergefreiter Rudiger Gümmer	Kradschützen-Abteilung 4
Obergefreiter Herbert Jewko	Kradschützen-Abteilung 4
Obergefreiter Wilhelm Krzyzanowski	Kradschützen-Abteilung 4
Obergefreiter Leo Kühnapfel	Kradschützen-Abteilung 4
Unteroffizier Hans Meinig	Kradschützen-Abteilung 4
Leutnant d.R. Thuiske von Metzsch	3./Kradschützen-Abteilung 4
Unteroffizier Helmut Neumann	Kradschützen-Abteilung 4
Oberarzt d.R. Dr. Kurt Pisselhoy	Stab/Kradschützen-Abteilung 4
Leutnant Ferdinand v. Senger und Etterlin	2./Kradschützen-Abteilung 4
Unteroffizier Albert Warstat	Kradschützen-Abteilung 4
Obergefreiter Wilhelm Westermann	2./Kradschützen-Abteilung 4

Iron Cross First Class on 22nd September 1942

Wachtmeister Willi Hartkopf	Panzergrenadier-Regiment 21
Obergefreiter August Ostermann	Panzerartillerie-Regiment 89

Iron Cross First Class on 27th September 1942

Unteroffizier Karl Weidemann	Panzergrenadier-Regiment 21
Wachtmeister Wilhelm Biermann	Panzergrenadier-Regiment 26
Unteroffizier Albert Fischer	Panzergrenadier-Regiment 26
Wachtmeister Franz Karl Glenz	Panzergrenadier-Regiment 26
Obergefreiter Stanislaus Florian Glomb	Panzergrenadier-Regiment 26
Obergefreiter Gerd Heine	Panzergrenadier-Regiment 26
Unteroffizier Artur Henriksen	Panzergrenadier-Regiment 26
Obergefreiter Friedrich Nordhusen	Panzergrenadier-Regiment 26
Oberwachtmeister Helmut Schalow	Panzergrenadier-Regiment 26
Obergefreiter Werner Schulz	Panzergrenadier-Regiment 26
Obergefreiter Werner Storbeck	Panzergrenadier-Regiment 26
Unteroffizier Fritz Uruck	Panzergrenadier-Regiment 26

Unteroffizier Alfred Werner	Panzergrenadier-Regiment 26
Oberleutnant d.R. Alfred Fritz	Panzerpionier-Bataillon 40
Feldwebel Oskar Mirwald	Panzerpionier-Bataillon 40
Leutnant d.R. Friedrich Schröder	3./Panzerpionier-Bataillon 40
Oberfeldwebel Alex Wuttke	1./Panzerpionier-Bataillon 40

Iron Cross First Class on 2nd October 1942

Assistenarzt Dr. Claus Anstett	Panzergrenadier-Regiment 21
Hauptwachtmeister Hans Fendrich	Panzergrenadier-Regiment 21
Obergefreiter Anton Fischl	Panzergrenadier-Regiment 21
Unteroffizier Walter Herrmann	Panzergrenadier-Regiment 21
Obergefreiter August Mienelmann	Panzergrenadier-Regiment 21
Wachtmeister Wilhelm Müller	Panzergrenadier-Regiment 21
Leutnant d.R. Dr. Theo Penners	I./Panzergrenadier-Regiment 21
Unteroffizier Fritz Raaf	Panzergrenadier-Regiment 21
Unteroffizier Josef Ehrl	Panzer-Regiment 24
Wachtmeister Hans Kasparek	Panzer-Regiment 24
Unteroffizier Karl Kätz	Panzer-Regiment 24
Wachtmeister Richard Link	Panzer-Regiment 24
Wachtmeister Alfred Myrczek	Panzer-Regiment 24
Leutnant Paul Pehl	III./Panzer-Regiment 24
Wachtmeister Herbert Quell	Panzer-Regiment 24
Unteroffizier Werner Reutner	Panzer-Regiment 24
Leutnant Hans-Erdmann Schönbeck	6./Panzer-Regiment 24
Unteroffizier Karl Wehring	Panzer-Regiment 24
Oberwachtmeister Franz Rams	Panzer-Regiment 24
KV-Rat Reinhard Schönberger	Panzer-Regiment 24
Obergefreiter Helmut Wydra	Panzer-Regiment 24
Obergefreiter Richard Hilz	Panzerartillerie-Regiment 89
Oberwachtmeister Fritz Kieck	Panzerartillerie-Regiment 89
Oberwachtmeister Richard Ollnow	Panzerartillerie-Regiment 89
Wachtmeister Gustav Palfner	Panzerartillerie-Regiment 89
Leutnant Kurt Beischall	Panzerartillerie-Regiment 89
Oberwachtmeister Emil Pfeiffer	Panzerartillerie-Regiment 89
Obergefreiter Herbert Toll	Panzerartillerie-Regiment 89

Iron Cross First Class on 5th October 1942

Wachtmeister Walter Becker	Panzergrenadier-Regiment 26
Unteroffizier Gerhard Bergmann	Panzergrenadier-Regiment 26
Unteroffizier Oskar Brecht	Panzergrenadier-Regiment 26
Wachtmeister Otto Fischer	Panzergrenadier-Regiment 26
Obergefreiter Adolf Hempel	Panzergrenadier-Regiment 26
Stabsfeldwebel Heinz Heyermann	Panzergrenadier-Regiment 26

Oberwachtmeister Richard Löhrke	6./Panzergrenadier-Regiment 26
Obergefreiter Hermann Prüßner	Panzergrenadier-Regiment 26
Leutnant Hellmuth Reymann	3./Panzergrenadier-Regiment 26
Wachtmeister Ernst Schick	Panzergrenadier-Regiment 26
Gefreiter Edmund Ulbrich	Panzergrenadier-Regiment 26
Obergefreiter Paul Schütz	Panzerjäger-Abteilung 40
Hauptmann d. Fg. Johann Stratmann	Feldgendarmerie-Trupp 40
Oberleutnant Reinhard Viertel	2./Panzerpionier-Bataillon 40

Iron Cross First Class on 9th October 1942

Wachtmeister Alfred Czelck	Panzer-Regiment 24
Assistenarzt d.R. Dr. Martin Kuls	III./Panzer-Regiment 24
Wachtmeister Ernst Zimmermann	Panzer-Regiment 24
Assistenarzt d.R. Dr. Wilhelm Vogel	2./Sanitäts-Kompanie 40

Iron Cross First Class on 12th October 1942

Obergefreiter Erno Boettcher	Kradschützen-Abteilung 4
Fahnenjunker-Wachtmeister Dr. Thedel Freiherr von Cramm	3./Kradschützen-Abteilung 4
Unteroffizier Heinrich Declair	Kradschützen-Abteilung 4
Wachtmeister Walter Koitzsch	Kradschützen-Abteilung 4
Sanitäts-Unteroffizier Wilhelm Kommer	Kradschützen-Abteilung 4
Gefreiter Willi Langhans	Kradschützen-Abteilung 4
Unteroffizier Heinz Pirl	Kradschützen-Abteilung 4
Unteroffizier Ernst Raeder	Kradschützen-Abteilung 4
Wachtmeister Ernst Schulz	Kradschützen-Abteilung 4
Wachtmeister Max Schulz	Kradschützen-Abteilung 4
Oberwachtmeister Erwin Sehlmacher	Kradschützen-Abteilung 4
Unteroffizier Alfred Stahlfeld	Kradschützen-Abteilung 4
Unteroffizier Otto Ullmann	Kradschützen-Abteilung 4
Obergefreiter Bernhard Dettmeyer	Panzerjäger-Abteilung 40
Sanitäts-Feldwebel Wilhelm Grenkler	Panzerjäger-Abteilung 40
Obergefreiter Heinrich Hartmann	Panzerjäger-Abteilung 40
Oberfeldwebel Otto Koebe	Panzerjäger-Abteilung 40
Unteroffizier Otto Plumberg	Panzerjäger-Abteilung 40
Leutnant Werner Buchholz	Panzerpionier-Bataillon 40
Unteroffizier Josef Lange	Panzerpionier-Bataillon 40
Wachtmeister Horst Beier	Panzerartillerie-Regiment 89
Unteroffizier Wilhelm Biebers	Panzerartillerie-Regiment 89
Unteroffizier Urban Kombüchen	Panzerartillerie-Regiment 89
Stabswachtmeister Ernst Pätzold	Panzerartillerie-Regiment 89

Hauptmann Walter Franke	1./Panzer-Nachrichten-Abteilung 86
Major Horst Henrici	Panzer-Nachrichten-Abteilung 86

Iron Cross First Class on 15th October 1942

Sanitäts-Unteroffizier Johann Büttner	Panzergrenadier-Regiment 21
Unteroffizier Walter Koch	Panzergrenadier-Regiment 21
Wachtmeister Wilhelm Sekula	Panzergrenadier-Regiment 21
Unteroffizier Otto Stieme	Panzergrenadier-Regiment 21
Obergefreiter Ludwig Thomann	Panzergrenadier-Regiment 21
Unteroffizier Walter Todtenhaupt	Panzergrenadier-Regiment 21
Oberleutnant Günther Hans-Jürgen Liebe	I./Panzer-Regiment 24
Oberwachtmeister Gebhardt Wessely	5./Panzer-Regiment 24
Oberwachtmeister Gerhard Galonska	Panzergrenadier-Regiment 26
Obergefreiter Rikus Klüver	6./Panzergrenadier-Regiment 26
Leutnant d.R. Erwin Krämer	III./Panzergrenadier-Regiment 26
Wachtmeister Fritz Paschke	Panzergrenadier-Regiment 26
Unteroffizier Paul Scheminski	Panzergrenadier-Regiment 26
Unteroffizier Ewald Stein	Panzergrenadier-Regiment 26

Iron Cross First Class on 18th October 1942

Leutnant Ernst Bayer-Eynck	Panzergrenadier-Regiment 26
Obergefreiter Hermann Koch	Panzergrenadier-Regiment 26
Sanitäts-Oberfeldwebel Bruno Kordowitzki	II./Panzergrenadier-Regiment 26
Unteroffizier Emil Ranyemann	Panzergrenadier-Regiment 26
Gefreiter Hermann Staberow	Panzergrenadier-Regiment 26
Gefreiter Kurt Lupat	Panzerpionier-Bataillon 40
Unteroffizier Fritz Niedermeier	Panzerpionier-Bataillon 40
Oberfeldwebel Willi Ruhnau	Panzerpionier-Bataillon 40
Leutnant Willi Bachler	Panzerartillerie-Regiment 89
Wachtmeister Emil Stender	Panzerartillerie-Regiment 89
Unteroffizier Paul Wilmes-Bäcker	Panzerartillerie-Regiment 89

Iron Cross First Class on 22nd October 1942

Obergefreiter Gustav Busch	Panzergrenadier-Regiment 21
Wachtmeister Hubert Große-Holz	Panzergrenadier-Regiment 21
Unteroffizier Otto Hasselburg	Panzergrenadier-Regiment 21
Unteroffizier Herbert Pede	Panzergrenadier-Regiment 21
Rittmeister d.R. Arnold von Günther	Panzer-Regiment 24
Leutnant d.R. Heinz Hövel	9./Panzer-Regiment 24
Wachtmeister Friedrich Schirrweit	2./Panzer-Regiment 24

Leutnant Fritz Scholz	Panzer-Regiment 24
Oberfeldwebel Georg Stamlach	Panzer-Regiment 24
Unteroffizier Franz Berges	Panzer-Nachrichten-Abteilung 86
Obergefreiter Sühl Scheff	Panzer-Nachrichten-Abteilung 86
Unteroffizier Helmut Beyer	Panzerartillerie-Regiment 89
Leutnant Alfred Bock	IV./Panzerartillerie-Regiment 89
Unteroffizier Heinrich Friedrich	Panzerartillerie-Regiment 89
Unteroffizier Heinrich Meinen	Panzerartillerie-Regiment 89
Unteroffizier Kurt Stawitzki	Panzerartillerie-Regiment 89
Obergefreiter Josef Weishaupt	Panzerartillerie-Regiment 89

EHRENBLATTSPANGE

APPENDIX FIVE

Ehrenblattspange

- Rittmeister Gerhard Thiel (Schwadron Commander of 10./Panzer-Regiment 24) Ehrenblattspange on 15th October 1942 for actions on 26th/27th July 1942 near Nizhne-Chirskaya.

- Oberleutnant Ludwig Dittmar (Schwadron Commander of 3./Panzergrenadier-Regiment 21) Ehrenblattspange on 7th January 1943 for actions on 28th September 1942 in Stalingrad.

Panzer IV Long-Barrel '434'

Appendix Six

Crew of Panzer IV long-barrel '434'

FISCHER, Unteroffizier Alfons Gunner Born 24th December 1915 in Reichenberg. Iron Cross First Class on 2nd August 1942.

FREYER, Wachtmeister Siegfried Commander Born 11th February 1917. Iron Cross Second Class on 12th June 1940. Iron Cross First Class on 26th October 1941. Awarded the Knight's Cross on 23rd July 1942 for his actions in Voronesh on 7th July 1942. Survived Stalingrad and survived the war.

GROLL, Gefreiter Arnold Loader Born 13th June 1921 in Oberhausen. Iron Cross First Class on 2nd August 1942. Wounded in the head on 7th July 1942.

MÜLLER, Gefreiter Heinrich Radio Operator Born 24th May 1921 in Kätalingen, Anhalt. Iron Cross First Class on 2nd August 1942. Missing in action at Stalingrad in January 1943.

SCHMIDT, Unteroffizier Wilhelm Driver Born 13th June 1915 in Riedermähren, Westfalen. Iron Cross First Class on 2nd August 1942. Missing in action at Stalingrad in January 1943.

Actions of Panzer IV long-barrel '434'

Wachtmeister Siegfried Freyer was the first winner of the Knight's Cross in the newly formed 24. Panzer-Division. On 7th July, the second day of 24. Panzer-Division's assault on Voronesh, heavy house-to-house fighting raged throughout the city and by the afternoon, with the sun low in the horizon, the Russian defenders had not been crushed and still offered stubborn resistance. The tanks that formed the backbone of their defence tried to break through the German encircling forces, developing into a close-range tank duel that was decided by the skill of the German panzer crews and, in particular, the valour of the crew of Panzer '434'. Here is a report of that encounter by the commander of that panzer, Wachtmeister Siegfried Freyer:

> "On 7th July, I took up position with my Panzer IV long-barrel at an important crossroads in Voronesh, well camouflaged, we stood next to a house in a garden. In front of the panzer was a wooden fence, covering us from view from the street. Our orders were to support our panzergrenadiers who were attempting to clear the town,

MICHAEL J. PRUETT

Wachtmeister Freyer and his crew pose for the cameras in the hatches of Panzer IV '434'.

and to protect them from enemy tanks. During the day, our only problems came from scattered Russian troops, but the actions between friend and foe in the town kept us on our toes. It was a hot day but we didn't realise that the evening was going to be even hotter. At about 2000 hours, a T-34 appeared from a side street to out left and attempted to get past us at high speed. He was followed by a column of some 30 more tanks and we had to prevent this breakout. In quick succession we engaged and knocked out the first three T-34's, then our gunner Unteroffizier Fischer reported: 'The gun is jammed!'. Our gun was new and had had some teething troubles because every second or third round, the empty shellcase got stuck in the breech. Our driver, Unteroffizier Schmidt, and I jumped out of the panzer, screwed together the barrel cleaner and with it pushed the empty shell out of the breech. The next Russian tank fired wildly round about and wounded our loader Gefreiter Groll in the head. We pulled him out of the panzer and our radioman took his place to help operate our weapon. We fired time and time again and kept on hitting targets. A few more times we had to grab the barrel cleaner and push out the jammed shells and then take cover quickly. The Russians cut the fence in front of us to pieces with their fire, but didn't hit our panzer. We, however, hit 11 enemy tanks, the only time they got past us was when our gun jammed again. The fight took about 20 minutes, by then, 11 enemy tanks were on fire in front of us, the flames and explosions giving the place an eerie appearance. That is how the rest of our Schwadron found us, despite the dark, and brought us back to the regimental laager on the southern edge of Voronesh. We could not sleep, the day had been too hot. Oberst Riebel expressed his appreciation of this brave action in the following Regiment Order:

REGIMENT ORDER
The Führer and High Command is decorating Wachtmeister Freyer 4. Schwadron with the Knight's Cross of the Iron Cross. Wachtmeister Freyer destroyed nine heavy T-34's and two light T-60's with his Panzer IV at Voronesh. When the enemy tanks which remained in the town tried to break out with over 30 tanks, Wachtmeister Freyer remained with exemplary bravery at his post. He let the far superior enemy approach him and then destroyed them. The hard fighting Russian tank brigade was scattered and to a large part destroyed. Our infantry managed to occupy the town after heavy fighting.
In the name of the Regiment, I wish to express my congratulations to Wachtmeister Freyer for his high war decoration. The Regiment views with pride and pleasure our Knight's Cross bearer and wishes him further success and best wishes for the future.
At the same time, I take the opportunity to thank the brave crew of the vehicle:

the gunner	Unteroffizier Fischer
the driver	Unteroffizier Schmidt
the loader	Gefreiter Groll
the radio operator	Gefreiter Müller

and to express my thanks and admiration for the action of this panzer on 7th July 1942. It will go down in the Honour Roll of our glorious Regiment."

On 23rd July 1942, during a break in the fighting, Wachtmeister Freyer was awarded the Knight's Cross by his Regiment Commander – Oberst Riebel – and his Abteilung Commander – Major von Winterfeld – in a small ceremony in Krassnaya Svesda, while the rest of the crew were recognised for their bravery by each being awarded the Iron Cross First Class. It was quite a rare feat for an entire crew to be wearing such a valued decoration.

SPANNOCCHI

From left: Major von Winterfeld, Wachtmeister Freyer, Gefreiter Groll, Unteroffizier Fischer and Gefreiter Müller. Unteroffizier Schmidt, driver of Panzer 434, missed the ceremony because he was in hospital having his wounds treated.

SPANNOCCHI

SPANNOCCHI

The reason for Wachtmeister Freyer's Knight's Cross: a street full of destroyed Russian tanks, 11 in total (nine T-34's and two T-60's). The confusion and devastation caused by Freyer's steadfast defence is evident in the photos. Desperately trying to avoid the accurate German fire, the Russian tanks raced through the darkened streets at high speed, cannons pointed in the direction of Panzer 434. Most of the Russian tanks were stopped dead in their tracks but one T-34 rammed the rear of another and immediately burst into flames.
The visual impact of so many destroyed tanks in such a small area prompted many photographers to capture the scene on film, and the successful destruction of the tanks has been attributed to several units, most notably the Grossdeutschland Division. There is no doubt, however, that this was the work of Wachtmeister Siegfried Freyer and the crew of Panzer IV 434.

SPANNOCCHI

SPANNOCCHI

BÖKE

Bestowal of the Knight's Cross. From left: Wachtmeister Freyer, Gefreiter Groll, Unteroffizier Fischer, Gefreiter Müller and Oberst Riebel, Commander of Panzer-Regiment 24.

Panzerjäger-Abteilung 670

Appendix Seven

After being subordinated to 24. Panzer-Division on 31st August, Panzerjäger-Abteilung 670 had performed excellently and racked up impressive totals of enemy tank kills. Commanded by the experienced Hauptmann Johannes Rohweder[1], bearer of a Knight's Cross awarded to him on 23rd August 1941, the battalion also had a group of highly-decorated company commanders: Oberleutnant Jobst-Joachim Friebe, Commander of 1. Kompanie (German Cross in Gold on 28th February 1942); Oberleutnant Josef Huber, Commander of 2. Kompanie (he would be awarded the German Cross in Gold on 6th January 1943); Oberleutnant Karl-Heinz Reiss, Commander of 3. Kompanie (German Cross in Gold on 8th June 1942). The battalion was equipped with the highly-effective Marder II, a hybrid vehicle created from a Russian 76.2mm anti-tank gun on an ex-Czech chassis. This potent combination of man and machine provided excellent tank-killing abilities to the Division. Its tally of enemy tanks destroyed was as follows:

3rd September:	1 T-34
4th September:	1 KV1, 1 T-34
5th September:	2 T-34, 1 T-60, 1 T-28
6th September:	1 T-60
7th September:	1 KV1, 2 T-34
8th September:	3 T-34
9th September:	1 T-34, 1 T-28
10th September:	1 T-34
12th September:	8 T-34
14th September:	3 T-34, 2 T-70, 1 T-60, 1 KV1 damaged.

That was a total of 22 T-34, 2 KV1, 3 T-60, 2 T-70 and 2 T-28, destroyed, and 1 KV1 damaged. The last tank was shot up in the front-line but was carted away during the night by the enemy.

---

1. Hauptmann Johannes Rohweder. Born 19th August 1903 in Lütjenwestedt, Rendsburg. Survived Stalingrad. Promoted to Oberstleutnant on 1st September 1943. Survived the war. Joined the Bundeswehr in 1956 as Commander of the Panzerjägerschule. Retired in 1962 as an Oberst. Died 6th January 1992 in Bremen.

RANK COMPARISON

APPENDIX EIGHT

Ranks	Translation
Schütze	Rifleman
Soldat	Soldier
Grenadier	Infantryman
Kanonier	Gunner
Panzergrenadier	Armoured Infantryman
Pionier	Engineer
Oberschütz	Chief Rifleman
Obergrenadier	Chief Infantryman
Oberpanzergrenadier	Chief Armoured Infantryman
Oberpionier	Chief Engineer
Oberfunker	Chief Radioman
Gefreiter	Lance Corporal
Obergefreiter	Corporal
Stabsgefreiter	Staff Lance Corporal
Unteroffizier	Junior Sergeant
Wachtmeister	Sergeant
Oberwachtmeister	Sergeant First Class
Hauptwachtmeister	Chief Sergeant
Stabswachtmeister	Staff Sergeant
Leutnant	Second Lieutenant
Oberleutnant	First Lieutenant
Hauptmann	Captain
Rittmeister	Captain
Major	Major
Oberstleutnant	Lieutenant Colonel
Oberst	Colonel
Generalmajor	Major General
Generalleutnant	Lieutenant-General
General der General der Infanterie	General of Infantry
General der Artillerie	General of Artillery
General der Kavallerie	General of Cavalry
General der Panzertruppen	General of Armoured Troops
General der Pioniere	General of Engineers
Generaloberst	Colonel General
Generalfeldmarschall	General Field Marshal

Orders of Battle

Appendix Nine

24. Panzer-Division Stab

Kommandeur:	Generalmajor Ritter von Hauenschild (wounded 8.9.42)
later:	Oberst Freiherr von Broich (temporary)
	Generalmajor von Lenski (from 14.9.42) (captured)
Ia:	Major von Menges (killed 2.2.43)
O1:	Hauptmann Roth (transferred 13.11.42)
later:	Hauptmann von Rosenberg-Lipinski (temporary, transferred 17.11.42)
O4:	Leutnant Freiherr von Eickstedt (fell ill in November 1942)
later:	Oberleutnant von Puttkamer (captured)
Ia/Stomü:	Major von der Goltz (transferred 1.10.42)
later:	Rittmeister v. Zawadzky-Polanka (from 21.9.42) (outside Kessel)
Ia/Mess.:	Leutnant Wochnik (missing in action January 1943)
Ia/Kartenstelle:	Oberleutnant Kroeger
Ic:	Rittmeister Graf vom Hagen (fell ill late 1942 and flown out of Kessel)
later:	Oberleutnant von Steegen
O3:	Oberleutnant Cramer von Laue (killed 1.8.42)
later:	Oberleutnant von Steegen (from 15.8.42)
Dolmetscher:	Sonderführer (Z) von Klot (killed)
	Sonderführer (Z) Reinburg (killed)
	Sonderführer (Z) Mutschler
	Sonderführer (Z) Adamheit (transferred 15.9.42)
	Sonderführer (Z) Funk (from 15.9.42)
	Sonderführer (Z) Jahnson (from 17.9.42)
	Sonderführer (Z) Meyer (from 15.9.42, killed 9.10.42)
	Sonderführer (Z) Reinhardt

Ib:	Major von Hobe (fell ill 30.10.42)
later:	Rittmeister Weiß (until 13.11.42)
	Hauptmann Wünsche-Steude (from 13.11.42) (killed 21.1.43)
	Hauptmann Ahollinger (flown out of Kessel on 23.01.1943)
O2:	Rittmeister Hans-Ulrich Weiß (captured at Stalingrad)
Ib/WuG:	Hauptmann Wilke
Ib/Gepäck:	Oberleutnant Peschken
Ib/Verpflegung:	Rittmeister von Zawadzky-Polanka
IIa:	Rittmeister von Gusovius (transferred 4.9.42)
later:	Hauptmann von Rosenberg-Lipinski (also O1 from 13.11.42, transferred 17.11.42)
	Rittmeister Eckhardt (flown out of Kessel 23.1.43)
III:	Kriegsgerichtsrat Dr. Nitschke (fell ill in October 1942)
later:	Kriegsgerichtsrat Dr. Schweinbach
	Kriegsgerichtsrat Dr. Kumminger (assigned 22.6.42 – 28.9.42)
Justizinspector:	Feldjustizinspektor Pfeiffer
IVa:	Oberstabsintendant Dr. Munker
1. Mitarbeiter:	Stabszahlmeister Schneider (killed 1.9.42)
	Oberzahlmeister Kaul (from 15.11.42)
2. Mitarbeiter:	Oberzahlmeister Kaul
IVb:	Oberfeldarzt Dr. Schulze (wounded 10.1.43, flown out 20.1.43)
later:	Oberfeldarzt Dr. Helff
Adjutant to IVb:	Stabsarzt Dr. Stuhlmann
IVc:	Stabsveterinär Dr. Fleischhauer (from 26.12.42)
later:	Stabsveterinär Dr. Nagel (from 94.ID from 1.1.43)
IVd:	(katholisch) Kriegspfarrer Lüpschen (wounded 28.7.42)
later:	(katholisch) Kriegspfarrer Göttke (outside Kessel on 19.1.42)
	(katholisch) Kriegspfarrer Düker (from 10.1.43)
IVd:	(evangelisch) Kriegspfarrer Arndt (wounded in August 1942)
later:	(evangelisch) Kriegspfarrer Pietsch
IVz:	Stabszahlmeister Sartor (ill, flown out 14.1.43)
V:	Major (Ing.) Lechtenberg
Technisch Beamter:	Oberinspektor Lorenz
Feldgendarmerie:	Hauptmann Straatmann

Feldersatz-Abteilung: Major von Einem (transferred 24.8.42)
Adjutant: Oberleutnant Longere (transferred 28.7.42)

Hauptquartier Kommandant: Oberleutnant Rohde
later: Leutnant Birth

Other officers: Oberleutnant Freiherr von Oppen von Huldenberg
Leutnant Blume

24. Panzer-Division Supply Services

Kommandeur: Major Schlieter
later: Major Dr. jur. Diederichs (from July 1942)

Adjutant: Hauptmann Hoger (until 1.9.42)
later: Oberleutnant Luber

Offizier b. Stabe: Hauptmann Hoger

Arzt: Oberarzt Dr. Wicus

Zahlmeister: Oberzahlmeister Suchowski
Oberzahlmeister Sanden

Inspektor: Technisches Inspektor Steinbach (captured)

San.Ko. 1/40: Oberstabsarzt Dr. Tonges
Stabsarzt Dr. Wulf (from 24.8.42)
Oberarzt Dr. Boese
Oberarzt Dr. Hellmer (from 28.9.42)
Oberarzt Dr. Kreke
Assistenarzt Dr. Thonessen (transferred 28.9.42)

San.Ko. 2/40: Oberstabsarzt Dr. Schulz (transferred to K4)
Oberarzt Dr. Rieks (transferred 24.8.42)
Oberarzt Dr. Kleeburg (transferred 29.10.42)
Oberarzt Dr. Wicus (from 29.10.42)
Assistenarzt Dr. Schuh
Assistenarzt Dr. Wanger

Krankenkraftwagen Zug. 1: Leutnant Uszkureit (from 14.10.42)

Krankenkraftwagen Zug. 2: Hauptmann Feyler

Schlächterei-Ko.:	Stabsveterinär Dr. Fleischhauer (transferred to IVc 26.12.42) Oberveterinär Fuchs Oberveterinär Heffler
Bäckerei-Ko.:	Hauptmann Moritz Leutnant Krieger (Zug Kommandeur)
Verpflegungtrupp:	Rittmeister von Zawadzky-Polanka (transferred 21.9.42)
Werkstatt-Ko. 2/40:	Kriegs-Ingenieur Fröhlich (transferred 14.10.42) Kriegs-Ingenieur Dura (from 14.10.42)
Werkstatt-Ko. 3/40:	Hauptmann Becker (captured) Oberleutnant Stockmeier (from 31.8.42) (Zug Kommandeur) Oberleutnant Kolbe (Zug Kommandeur)
Feldgendarmerie:	Hauptmann d. Fg. Straatmann (captured) Feldwebel Block Stabsfeldwebel Hummel Leutnant d. Fg. Kohrs Leutnant d. Fg. Korte Feldwebel Kühlmann Oberfeldwebel Marquass Leutnant d. Fg. Rudolf Stabsfeldwebel Wahl

Officers whose positions are unknown:

Hauptmann Besenbeck
Oberleutnant von Barner (killed 29.8.42)
Leutnant Bauchspieß (Kdr. Kraftwagen Kolonne 3/40)
Oberleutnant Constein (transferred 25.11.42)
Leutnant Dr. Eck (Kdr. Kraftwagen Kolonne 2/40)
Leutnant (W) Engels
Hauptmann Frey (captured)
Major Gerstung
Oberleutnant Haring
Hauptmann Karpinski
Hauptmann Kirchner (Kolonne Kdr.) (captured)
Oberleutnant Pelzner
Leutnant Schwarz

24.Schützen-Brigade Stab

Kommandeur:	Oberst Freiherr von Broich (transferred 30.10.42) Oberst von Horn (never assumed command due to disbandment of Brigade staff)

Adjutant: Rittmeister von Dressler
Rittmeister von Knebel Doeberitz (wounded 3.9.42)

Other officers: Oberleutnant Bernhardt
Oberleutnant Prinz von Hatzfeldt (killed 4.7.42)

Panzer-Nachrichten-Abteilung 86

Kommandeur: Major Henrici (captured and shot January 1943)

Adjutant: Oberleutnant Wittkowski
Leutnant Rieger

Ordonanzoffizier: Oberleutnant Hermanns

Abteilung-Arzt: Assistenarzt Dr.Urbassek (killed 21.7.42)

V.-Offizier: K.V.Rat Dr. Stallechner (transferred 24.8.42)

Schirrmeister: Oberschirrmeister (K) Zarth (transferred 1.11.42)

1. Kompanie:

Kommandeur: Hauptmann Franke (transferred 7.12.42)

Zug Kommandeur: Leutnant Thol (wounded 9.8.42)

2. Kompanie:

Kommandeur: Oberleutnant Hardt (captured and shot January 1943)

Zug Kommandeur: Leutnant Overhoff (committed suicide 10.6.42)
Zug Kommandeur: Leutnant Dr. Exner (wounded 27.9.42)
Zug Kommandeur: Oberleutnant Klinge (from 31.10.42)

Officers of the Abteilung whose positions are unknown:
Leutnant Hildebrandt (from 7.11.42)
Oberleutnant Hammer (wounded 23.8.42)
Oberleutnant Manzel
Oberleutnant Matzke
Leutnant Müller
Leutnant Wehrmann (from 12.10.42)

Panzer-Regiment 24

Regiment Stab:

Kommandeur: Oberst Riebel (killed 23.8.42)
later: Major von Winterfeld (temporary)
Oberstleutnant von Bassewitz (from October 1942) (flown out 19.1.43)
Major Gerhard Thiel (from 19.1.43)
Major von der Lancken (commanded Rgt. units outside the Kessel)

Adjutant: Rittmeister von Aulock (wounded 23.8.42)
later: Rittmeister von Meyer (from 30.12.42, flown out 23.1.43)

Ordonanzoffizier: Oberleutnant Weidemann (transferred to 5./PR24 15.8.42)
Leutnant von der Decken (wounded 23.8.42, resumed role in October)
Leutnant von der Decken (command of 2./PR24 in January 1943)

Regimentsarzt: Stabsarzt Dr. Schumacher (wounded 25.8.42, died 27.8.42)
later: Oberarzt Dr. Kugler (missing in action January 1943)

Assistenarzt: Assistenarzt Dr. Zieher

Waffen-Offizier: Oberleutnant (W) Teut

Ingenieur: Major (Ing.) Korbeslühr

Kriegsverwaltungsrat: K.V.Rat Herold

Inspektor: T.K.V. Inspektor Reimann (transferred 1.11.42)
later: T.K.V Inspektor Pernutz (missing in action January 1943)
Oberfähnrich (Ing.) Vetter

Dolmetscher: Sonderführer Ruhle

Regiment Stabsschwadron:

Chef: Oberleutnant Rinke (transferred to 6./PR24 on 8.8.42)
later: Leutnant Meya (?)

Nachrichtenoffizier: Leutnant Endruweit (committed suicide 16.1.43)

Aufklärung-Zug: Leutnant Daschkey

Other officers: Oberleutnant Raben (missing in action January 1943)

Panzer Werkstattkompanie:

Chef: Kriegsingenieur Schönberger

I. Abteilung Stab:

Kommandeur: Major von Winterfeld (captured and died in captivity)

Adjutant: Oberleutnant Nordmann (missing in action January 1943)

Ordonanzoffizier: Leutnant Freiherr von Maltzan (transferred 20.10.42)

Abteilung-Arzt: Oberarzt Dr. Rocholl (wounded 30.9.42) (captured)

Zahlmeister: Oberzahlmeister Krinn (missing in action January 1943)

Abteilung Stabsschwadron:

Chef: Oberleutnant von Borcke
later: Oberleutnant Otto (killed 19.1.43)
Oberleutnant Raben (wounded and died 19.1.43)

Nachrichtenoffizier: Oberleutnant Liebe (killed 8.10.42)

Erkundung-Zug: Oberleutnant Christian von Loesch

Aufklärung-Zug: Oberleutnant Otto (took command of Stabsschwadron)

Pionier-Zug: Leutnant Schönfeld

Spieß: Hauptwachtmeister Heese

1. Schwadron:

Chef: Rittmeister Freiherr von Mirbach
later: Oberleutnant von Borcke

Zug Kommandeur: Leutnant von Arnim (killed 8.8.42)
Zug Kommandeur: Leutnant Baron Brockdorf (wounded 9.8.42)
Zug Kommandeur: Leutnant von Siegfried (wounded 1.8.42, died 27.9.42)
later: Leutnant Sylla (captured and died in captivity March 1943)
Leutnant Theilig (killed 28.9.42)
Leutnant Kroher (from 9.10.42) (died 21.1.43)

Spieß: Hauptwachtmeister Palau

2. Schwadron:

Chef:	Rittmeister Spannocchi (wounded 11.9.42)
later:	Oberleutnant Schulte (killed 21.10.42)
	Oberleutnant Kühn (flown out of Kessel in January 1943)
	Leutnant von der Decken (from January 1943)
Zug Kommandeur:	Oberleutnant von Keudell (transferred 25.5.42)
Zug Kommandeur:	Leutnant Fischer
Zug Kommandeur:	Leutnant Schwarz
Spieß:	Hauptwachtmeister Meyer-zur-Heide

4. Schwadron:

Chef:	Rittmeister Ernst Thiel (killed 3.9.42)
later:	Oberleutnant Messerschmidt (wounded and flown out)
	Leutnant Graf von Schwerin (missing in action January 1943)
Zug Kommandeur:	Oberleutnant von Helldorf
Zug Kommandeur:	Oberleutnant Messerschmidt (flown out of Kessel)
Zug Kommandeur:	Leutnant von Poser (killed 20.8.42)
later:	Leutnant Graf von Schwerin (Schwadronschef in January 1943)
Spieß:	Hauptwachtmeister Grossnik

II. Abteilung Stab:

Kommandeur:	Major Burgsthaler (outside Kessel on 19.11.42)
later:	Rittmeister Weiß (captured 1.2.43)
Adjutant:	Oberleutnant Hofmann (killed 30.6.42)
later:	Leutnant Ewers (missing in action January 1943)
Ordonanzoffizier:	Leutnant Ewers (became Abteilung Adjutant)
later:	Leutnant Meyer (wounded 22.1.43)
Zahlmeister:	Oberzahlmeister Wachter
Other officers:	Leutnant Meyer (captured)

Abteilung Stabsschwadron:

Chef:	Rittmeister Weiß (took command of II. Abteilung)
Nachrichtenoffizier:	Leutnant Kuls (wounded 30.6.42)
Erkundung-Zug:	Oberleutnant von Rosenberg-Lipinski (captured 1.2.43)
Aufklärung-Zug:	Leutnant Freiherr von Quadt
Pionier-Zug:	Oberleutnant Hermes (wounded 25.9.42)
F. d. Trosse:	Leutnant Leopold (transferred to Div. Stab 1.10.42)
V.-Offizier:	Oberleutnant Treptau
Spieß:	Hauptwachtmeister Schürbusch

5. Schwadron:

Chef:	Rittmeister Frhr. v. Woellwarth-Lauterberg (transferred 15.8.42)
later:	Oberleutnant Weidemann (wounded 23.9.42)
	Leutnant Gebhardt (from 2.10.42) (outside Kessel)
Zug Kommandeur:	Leutnant Cornelius (wounded 29.6.42)
Zug Kommandeur:	Leutnant Höhne
Zug Kommandeur:	Leutnant Meya (later transferred to Stabschw. I Abt./PR24)
Spieß:	Hauptwachtmeister von Lojewski

6. Schwadron:

Chef:	Rittmeister v. Sivers (wounded 8.8.42 & transferred 28.8.42)
later:	Oberleutnant Rinke (wounded 22.8.42)
	Leutnant Schönbeck (wounded 19.1.43. Flown out 23.1.43)
Zug Kommandeur:	Oberleutnant Heindel (wounded 8.8.42)
Zug Kommandeur:	Leutnant von der Trenck (wounded 29.8.42)
Spieß:	Hauptwachtmeister Bautsch

8. Schwadron:

Chef:	Rittmeister Eckhardt (transferred 5.11.42)
later:	Leutnant Freiherr von Falkenhausen (killed 15.1.43)
Zug Kommandeur:	Oberleutnant Schulte (killed 21.10.42)
Zug Kommandeur:	Leutnant von Falkenhausen (became Schwadronschef 5.11.42)
Schirrmeister:	Schirrmeister Holkenbrink (missing in action January 1943)
Spieß:	Hauptwachtmeister May

III. Abteilung Stab:

Kommandeur:	Major von der Lancken (transferred 1.11.42)
later:	Rittmeister Gerhard Thiel (captured 2.2.43. Died in captivity 10.4.43)
Adjutant:	Oberleutnant Böke (wounded 25.12.42, flown out of Kessel 27.12.42)
later:	Leutnant Dornbach (captured and died in captivity)
Ordonanzoffizier:	Leutnant Wiktorin (wounded 22.8.42, died 24.8.42)
Abteilung-Arzt:	Oberarzt Dr. Baatz (missing in action 19.9.42)
later:	Oberarzt Dr. Kuls (wounded 27.9.42, flown out of Kessel in January 43)
Zahlmeister:	Zahlmeister Feller (captured 1.2.43)
Inspektor:	T.K.V Inspektor Lilienthal (captured 1.2.43)
Other officers:	Oberleutnant von Puttkamer (from 1.11.42) (transferred 27.11.42)

Abteilung Stabsschwadron:

Chef:	Oberleutnant Eichhorn (took command of 9. Schwadron)
later:	Oberleutnant von Langenn-Steinkeller (flown out of Kessel)
Nachrichtenoffizier:	Leutnant Pehl
Erkundung-Zug:	Leutnant Freiherr von Schlotheim
Pionier-Zug:	Leutnant Renner (killed 31.7.42)
F. d. Trosse:	Leutnant Fey (outside Kessel)
Spieß:	Hauptwachtmeister Köberlein

9. Schwadron:

Chef:	Rittmeister von Meyer (wounded 22.8.42)
later:	Oberleutnant Eichhorn
	Rittmeister von Meyer (from 19.11.42 to 30.12.42)
	Rittmeister Eichhorn (captured 1.2.43. Survived captivity)
Zug Kommandeur:	Leutnant Hövel (from 25.5.42)
Zug Kommandeur:	Leutnant Freiherr von Schlichting (wounded 22.8.42)
Zug Kommandeur:	Leutnant Proll
later:	Oberwachtmeister Frenzel
Spieß:	Hauptwachtmeister Bodeck

10. Schwadron:

Chef:	Rittmeister Gerhard Thiel (became Abt. Kdr. on 1.11.42)
later:	Leutnant von Dellingshausen (missing in action January 1943)
Zug Kommandeur:	Oberleutnant Gerhard von Loesch (wounded 3.9.42)
Zug Kommandeur:	Leutnant Dornbach (captured 1.2.43. Died in captivity)
Zug Kommandeur:	Leutnant Luz (killed 16.9.42)
later:	Leutnant von Dellingshausen (became Schwadronschef)
	Leutnant Freiherr von Richthofen (missing in action or killed)
Spieß:	Hauptwachtmeister Schoch

12. Schwadron:

Chef:	Rittmeister Guy-Bernhard von Saint-Paul (wounded 29.8.42)
later:	Rittmeister von Götz (Schwadron Commander from 7.9.42)
	Rittmeister Guy-Bernhard von Saint-Paul (killed 2.2.43)
Zug Kommandeur:	Oberleutnant Koch (wounded 8.9.42)
Zug Kommandeur:	Leutnant Schwarz (killed 8.9.42)
later:	Leutnant Mollen (from 2.10.42) (missing in action Jan. 1943)
Spieß:	Hauptwachtmeister Deinert

Officers of the Regiment whose positions are unknown:

Oberleutnant Becker
Leutnant Blessing (from 25.5.42)
Oberleutnant von Dietze (wounded late 1942 and flown out of Kessel)
Rittmeister von Günther (wounded 4.9.42)
Hauptmann Hentschel (assigned 1.10 – 30.10.42)

Leutnant Pampel (from 2.10.42)
Hauptmann Peters (assigned 15.10 – 15.11.42)
Oberleutnant Reble (from 17.11.42)
Oberleutnant von Restorff (transferred 7.5.42)
Oberleutnant Ulrich von Saint-Paul (transferred 25.12.42)
Oberleutnant Schulze (captured)
Leutnant Schweissing
Hauptmann Windemuth (assigned from 1.11.42)

Panzergrenadier-Regiment 21

Regiment Stab:

Kommandeur:	Oberst von Lengerke (killed 26.8.42)
later:	Oberstleutnant von Hellermann (transferred 11.10.42)
	Oberst von Below (captured and died in captivity)
Adjutant:	Oberleutnant von Schmidt-Pauli (wounded 8.9.42)
later:	Oberleutnant Micke (fell ill 24.10.42)
	Oberleutnant von Burkersroda (captured)
Ordonanzoffizier:	Oberleutnant Ferno (killed 8.9.42)
later:	Leutnant Dr. Penners (from 28.6. – 30.7.42, then transfer to I. Abteilung)
	Leutnant Butz (from 9.9.42) (captured and died in captivity)
Nachrichtenoffizier:	Oberleutnant Bömcke (killed 3.9.42)
later:	Leutnant Borufka (from 29.10.42) (captured)
Regiment-Arzt:	Stabsarzt Dr. Walsdorfer (wounded 26.9.42)
V.-Offizier:	Major (Ing.) Dettmer (transferred)
Zahlmeister:	Stabszahlmeister Austinat

Regiment Stabsschwadron:

Chef:	Rittmeister Schmidt (wounded 20.7.42)
later:	Oberleutnant Bömcke (killed 3.9.42)
Spieß:	Hauptwachtmeister Nieß
Schirrmeister:	Schirrmeister Röhr

I. Abteilung Stab:

Kommandeur: Rittmeister Graf von Bernstorff (killed 4.9.42)
later: Rittmeister Graf zu Solms-Wildenfels (went on leave 1.11.42)
Rittmeister Goder (until 12.11.42)
Rittmeister Schriewer (from 12.11.42, fell ill middle of December 1942)

Adjutant: Oberleutnant Pachnio (took over 3. Schwadron 31.7.42)
later: Oberleutnant Micke (took over Regiment adjutancy 8.9.42)
Leutnant Dr. Penners (wounded 26.9.42)
Leutnant von Tiedemann (from 10.10.42) (fell ill 19.12.42)

Ordonanzoffizier: Oberleutnant Micke (took over Abteilung adjutancy 31.7.42)
later: Leutnant Dr. Penners (from 30.7. – 28.8.42)
Leutnant von Tiedemann (from 15.7. – 25.8.42, transfer to 2. Schw.)

Adjutant-Arzt: Stabsarzt Dr. Walsdorfer (Regiment-Arzt at the same time)
later: Oberarzt Dr. Anstett (killed 13.12.42)

V.-Offizier: Kriegstechniker (K) Marx

Zahlmeister: Oberzahlmeister Buhse

Spieß: Hauptwachtmeister Eder (killed 21.2.43)

Schirrmeister: Oberschirrmeister Brobeil

1. Schwadron:

Chef: Rittmeister Graf zu Solms-Wildenfels (until 4.9.42)
later: Leutnant Tutein (fell ill with jaundice in October 1942)
Oberleutnant von Pawel-Rammingen (wounded 24.11.42)

Zug Kommandeur: Leutnant Otte (from 29.10.42) (killed 6.1.43)
Zug Kommandeur: Leutnant Tutein (took command of Schwadron 4.9.42)

Spieß: Hauptwachtmeister Grahl (killed 26.11.42)

Schirrmeister: Schirrmeister Fischer (captured)

2. Schwadron:

Chef:	Rittmeister Graf von Sponeck (killed 5.7.42)
later:	Oberleutnant von Burkersroda (until 8.7.42)
	Rittmeister Schlenther (wounded 22.8.42, died 7.11.42)
	Leutnant Dr. Penners (until 8.9.42)
	Leutnant Hilgenberg (from 8.9.42)
	Leutnant von Tiedemann (from 30.9. until 10.10.42)
	Leutnant Hilgenberg (until 10.11.42)
	Oberleutnant von Pawel-Rammingen (wounded 24.11.42)
Zug Kommandeur:	Oberleutnant von Renvers (wounded 5.7.42, died 6.7.42)
Zug Kommandeur:	Leutnant Budde (killed 10.8.42)
Zug Kommandeur:	Leutnant Hilgenberg
Spieß:	Hauptwachtmeister Lagies (killed 8.9.42)

3. Schwadron:

Chef:	Rittmeister von Knebel Doeberitz (transferred 30.7.42)
later:	Oberleutnant Pachnio (wounded 27.9.42, died 5.3.43)
Zug Kommandeur:	Leutnant Lakenbrink (killed 12.9.42)
Spieß:	Hauptwachtmeister Fendrich (wounded 12.9.42)
later:	Oberwachtmeister Ruddat
Schirrmeister:	Wachtmeister Pallapies

4. Schwadron:

Chef:	Oberleutnant Baron von Heyking
Zug Kommandeur:	Leutnant Gündel (captured and died in captivity)
Zug Kommandeur:	Leutnant Stählin (killed 20.8.42)
Spieß:	Hauptwachtmeister Ast (wounded 25.11.42)
Schirrmeister:	Schirrmeister Schulz

II. Abteilung Stab:

Kommandeur:	Major Schwanke (fell ill on 28.8.42)
later:	Rittmeister v. Sivers (transferred on 21.9.42)
	Rittmeister Drews (killed 5.10.42)
	Rittmeister Schriewer (until 12.11.42, took command of I./PGR26)
	Rittmeister Goder (wounded 23.11.42)
Adjutant:	Oberleutnant Graf von Schmettow (wounded 28.6.42)
later:	Oberleutnant Freiherr Riediesel zu Eisenbach (transferred 21.7.42)
	Oberleutnant von Burkersroda (wounded 25.8.42)
	Oberleutnant Belli von Pino (captured and died in captivity)
Ordonanzoffizier:	Oberleutnant Freiherr Riediesel zu Eichenbach (adjutant on 28.6.42)
later:	Oberleutnant von Treuenfels (wounded 25.8.42)
Abteilung-Arzt:	Stabsarzt Dr. Donner (wounded in November 1942)
later:	Oberarzt Dr. Schiemann (captured 18.1.43)
Hilfsarzt:	Unterarzt Dr. Urbassek (killed 21.7.42)
later:	Assistenarzt Dr. Peine (transferred 2.10.42 to I./PGR26)
V.-Offizier:	Kriegsingenieur (K) Rother (missing in action November 1942)
later:	Kriegstechniker Merseburger (transferred 30.10.42)
	Kriegstechniker Griese (from 30.10.42)
Zahlmeister:	Oberzahlmeister Gorny
Spieß:	Hauptwachtmeister Stasch

5. Schwadron:

Chef:	Oberleutnant Rautenstrauch (wounded in July 1942)
later:	Rittmeister Schriewer (until 5.10.42)
	Oberleutnant Guercke (until 10.10.42)
	Leutnant Prinz zu Oettingen-Wallerstein (wounded 23.11.42)
	Leutnant von Studnitz (wounded 18.1.43, died 24.1.43)
Zug Kommandeur:	Leutnant Balser (from 14.9.42) (wounded 27.9.42)
Zug Kommandeur:	Leutnant Prinz zu Oettingen-Wallerstein
later:	Leutnant von Studnitz (from 6.11.42)
Spieß:	Hauptwachtmeister Erwied

6. Schwadron:

Chef:	Rittmeister Graf von Marogna-Redwitz (killed 7.7.42)
later:	Leutnant Prinz zu Oettingen-Spielberg (until 17.7.42)
	Oberleutnant Dittmar (wounded 8.11.42)
	Leutnant von Veltheim (captured and died in captivity)
Zug Kommandeur:	Leutnant Dittmar (took command of Schwadron 17.7.42)
Zug Kommandeur:	Leutnant Marschner (wounded 2.9.42)
Zug Kommandeur:	Leutnant Prinz zu Oettingen-Spielberg
Spieß:	Stabswachtmeister Aurnhammer
Schirrmeister:	Schirrmeister Morowecz (until 1.9.42)
later:	Schirrmeister Profus

7. Schwadron:

Chef:	Rittmeister von Dietmann (killed 26.7.42)
later:	Leutnant Freise (until 28.7.42)
	Oberleutnant Longere (until 20.8.42)
	Rittmeister Drews (command of Abt. on 21.9.)
	Leutnant Freiherr von Eller-Eberstein (until 5.10.42)
	Oberleutnant Guercke (until 10.10.42, together with 5. Schw.)
	Hauptwachtmeister Rubbel (until 9.11.42)
Zug Kommandeur:	Leutnant Freise (temp. command Schwadron) (killed 25.8.42)
Spieß:	Hauptwachtmeister Rubbel
later:	Oberwachtmeister Bruderhus (captured)
Schirrmeister:	Unteroffizier Tangermann (transferred 20.11.42)

8. Schwadron:

Chef:	Rittmeister Drews (until 20.8.42, took over 7. Schwadron)
later:	Oberleutnant Guercke (until 5.10.42)
	Leutnant Dröscher (fell ill on 17.11.42)
	Leutnant Engelke (captured and died in captivity)
Zug Kommandeur:	Leutnant Werther (killed 8.9.42)
Zug Kommandeur:	Leutnant Dröscher
Spieß:	Oberwachtmeister Bruderhus (transferred to 7. Schwadron)
later:	Stabswachtmeister Pumpa (missing in action 22.11.42)

9. Schwadron:

Chef:	Rittmeister Schlenther (until 8.7.42)
later:	Oberleutnant Peter Schmidt
Spieß:	Hauptwachtmeister Abraham (killed 5.8.42)

10. Schwadron:

Chef:	Rittmeister Wien
Zug Kommandeur:	Leutnant Butz (became Regiment Ordonanzoffizier)
Zug Kommandeur:	Oberleutnant Segger (wounded 28.9.42)
Spieß:	Hauptwachtmeister Buhk
Schirrmeister:	Schirrmeister Hartel

Officers of the Regiment whose positions are unknown:

Oberleutnant von Bittenfeld
Leutnant Erzberger (Zug Kommandeur) (from 9.10.42)
Leutnant von Frantzius (from 6.11.42) (killed 23.11.42)
Leutnant Fritz Henning (from 6.11.42) (missing in action Dec. 1942)
Leutnant Konrad Henning (missing in action 15.1.43)
Leutnant Herberg (Zug Kommandeur) (from 9.10.42)
Oberleutnant Freiherr von Keyserlingk
Oberleutnant Krüger
Leutnant Franz Müller (from 6.11.42)
Leutnant Strunck (from 8.9.42)

Panzergrenadier-Regiment 26

Regiment Stab:

Kommandeur:	Oberst Reichsfreiherr von Edelsheim (transferred 10.10.42)
later:	Oberst von Scheele (wounded 25.11.42, died 26.11.42)
Adjutant:	Oberleutnant von Dressler
later:	Rittmeister Michael (from 1.12.42) (flown out of Kessel 23.1.42)
Ordonanzoffizier:	Oberleutnant Tummescheit-Balzershöfen
V.-Offizier:	Oberstleutnant (Ing.) Hornung (captured and died in captivity)

I. Abteilung Stab:

Kommandeur:	Rittmeister Schulz-Fademrecht (killed 27.7.42)
later:	Oberleutnant von Dressler (wounded 14.10.42)
	Rittmeister Ernst Schmidt (took command on 12.11.42)
	Rittmeister von Dressler (flown into Kessel 12.1.43)
Adjutant:	Oberleutnant Prinz Reuß (wounded 11.9.42)
later:	Leutnant Martius (killed 6.1.43)
V.-Offizier:	Kriegstechniker Arneth (missing in action January 1943)
Hilfsarzt:	Unterarzt Dr. Zyznewski (from 17.11.42)
Zahlmeister:	Stabszahlmeister Achmann (wounded 16.9.42, died 17.9.42)
later:	Stabszahlmeister Scholz (transferred to K4)
Dolmetscher:	Sonderführer Schäfer (from 22.6.42)

1. Schwadron:

Chef:	Rittmeister Legat (killed 26.7.42)
later:	Oberleutnant Lichte (captured)
Zug Kommandeur:	Leutnant Müller
later:	Oberwachtmeister Stelzer

2. Schwadron:

Chef:	Oberleutnant Thylmann (wounded 31.8.42)
later:	Leutnant Rose (from 6.11.42)
Zug Kommandeur:	Leutnant Hantschke (killed 31.7.42)
Zug Kommandeur:	Leutnant Köhne (wounded 17.9.42)

3. Schwadron:

Chef:	Leutnant Kerscher (killed 1.10.42)
Zug Kommandeur:	Leutnant Reymann (wounded 27.9.42, died 28.9.42)

4. Schwadron:

Chef:	Oberleutnant Weckesser

II. Abteilung Stab:

Kommandeur:	Major von Heyden
later:	Rittmeister Jankowski (temporarily in May 1942)
	Major von Heyden (wounded 27.9.42)
	Rittmeister Michael (became Regiment adjutant on 1.12.42)
	Rittmeister von Götz (from 12.12.42, also command of K4 on 16.12.42)
	Rittmeister von Humbert (captured and died in captivity)
Adjutant:	Leutnant Raeschke (transferred to 6./PGR26 in May 1942)
later:	Oberleutnant Maier (Killed 6.7.42)
	Leutnant Raeschke (from 8.9.42) (killed 22.9.42)
	Leutnant Bayer-Eynck (transferred from K4 on 12.12.42)
	Oberleutnant Köhler (captured)
Ordonanzoffizier:	Leutnant Schniewind
later:	Leutnant Krämer
	Leutnant Festerling (from 9.10.42) (killed 10.11.42)
Abteilung-Arzt:	Oberarzt Dr. Salamon
Hilfsarzt:	Assistenarzt Dr. Peine (transferred to PGR21 on 2.10.42)
later:	Unterarzt Dr. Hurtienne
V.-Offizier:	Kriegsingenieur Stemmler
Schirrmeister:	Oberschirrmeister Kurrat
Zahlmeister:	Oberzahlmeister Tapfer (missing in action January 1943)

5. Schwadron:

Chef:	Oberleutnant Hoffmann (until June 1942)
later:	Oblt. Frhr. v. Langermann-Erlencamp (wounded 25.7.42)
	Oberleutnant Hoffmann
	Hauptmann Keltz (from 94.ID on 8.1.43)
Zug Kommandeur:	Leutnant Walter Müller
Zug Kommandeur:	Leutnant Binkow (wounded 10.9.42)
Zug Kommandeur:	Leutnant Stetzkowski (wounded 1.9.42)
later:	Leutnant Buschinksi (from 14.9.42) (killed 29.9.42)
Spieß:	Hauptwachtmeister Jordan

6. Schwadron:

Chef: Oberleutnant Baron von Freytag-Loringhoven (killed 7.7.42)
later: Oberleutnant Michael (wounded 8.7.42)
Stabswachtmeister Brakebusch (until 9.7.42)
Rittmeister Michael (wounded 27.7.42)
Rittmeister Jankowski (wounded 27.9.42)
Oberleutnant Beyersdorff (wounded 11.11.42)
Oberleutnant Keiler (captured)

Zug Kommandeur: Leutnant Raeschke (wounded 26.7.42)
Zug Kommandeur: Leutnant von Vieregge
Zug Kommandeur: Leutnant Staba
Zug Kommandeur: Leutnant Behrens
later: Leutnant Kühl
Leutnant Kanschat (wounded 26.7.42)
Leutnant Graf von Arnim-Boitzenburg (killed 27.7.42)
Leutnant von Quast-Vichel
Leutnant Fittkau
Oberwachtmeister Löhrke
Wachtmeister Rasch (wounded 26.6.42)

Spieß: Stabswachtmeister Stegemann

7. Schwadron:

Chef: Oberleutnant Feldt
later: Oberleutnant Brosig (wounded 7.8.42)

Zug Kommandeur: Leutnant Günther
Zug Kommandeur: Leutnant Oswald Müller
Zug Kommandeur: Leutnant Fehre (missing in action January 1943)
later: Oberwachtmeister Baldauf

Spieß: Hauptwachtmeister Koth

8. Schwadron:

Chef: Oberleutnant Kiehlnecker
later: Oberleutnant Oberbeck (wounded 29.9.42)
Leutnant Eichler (wounded 10.11.42)
Hauptmann Zimmermann

Zug Kommandeur: Leutnant Neutard
Zug Kommandeur: Leutnant Fink
Zug Kommandeur: Leutnant Wroblewski (wounded, returned on 6.11.42)
later: Leutnant Eichler (took command of Schwadron)

Spieß: Wachtmeister Niehaus

9. Schwadron:

Chef: Leutnant König (killed 29.9.42)

10. Schwadron:

Chef: Rittmeister Rogge (wounded 15.9.42)
later: Oberleutnant Dr. Wolter (from 7.11.42)

Zug Kommandeur: Leutnant Otto (from 7.9.42)

Officers of the Regiment whose positions are unknown:

Leutnant Birth (transferred to Div. Stab)
Leutnant Bohlhoff (from 1.11.42)
Oberleutnant Grunau
Rittmeister Höhne
Leutnant Masuhr
Leutnant Reinhard (from 6.11.42) (wounded 10.11.42)
Leutnant Richter (from 17.11.42)
Leutnant Schenk (wounded 21.8.42)
Oberleutnant Seufferheld (missing in action 9.1.43)
Leutnant von Uechtritz und Steinkirch (from 8.9.42)
Leutnant Uhlig (from 14.9.42)
Leutnant Freiherr von Wolff-Metternich
Oberleutnant Wust (from 6.11.42)

Panzerartillerie-Regiment 89

Regiment Stab:

Kommandeur: Oberst von Nostitz-Wallwitz (wounded 3.9.42)
later: Major von Pawel (gave up command to Matzke)
Oberst Matzke (from 31.12.42) (missing in action 23.1.43)

Adjutant: Hauptmann von Schack (took command of 4. Batterie 30.8.42)
later: Oberleutnant von Amsberg (wounded 3.9.42)
Oberleutnant von Gyldenfeldt (killed 26.1.43)

Ordonanzoffizier: Leutnant von Baum
later: Oberleutnant Wippern (killed 9.8.42)
Leutnant Schuffenhauer (from 8.1.43)
Stabsmusikmeister Pehl

Regiment-Arzt:	Oberarzt Dr. Spode (wounded 1.9.42)
later:	Oberarzt Dr. Kugler (transferred to PR24)
Waffen-Offizier:	Oberleutnant (W) Köhler
later:	Oberleutnant (W) Saltzer (captured)
Ingenieur:	Kriegs-Ingenieur Both

Regiment Stabsbatterie:

Kommandeur:	Hauptmann Dr. Thom (wounded 20.8.42)

Panzer-Beobachtung-Batterie:

Kommandeur:	Hauptmann Gentzen (wounded 1.7.42)
later:	Oberleutnant Seufferheld (from 1.7.42 to 31.7.42)
	Hauptmann Gentzen (transferred 24.8.42)
	Hauptmann Heibel (from 21.9.42) (killed 14.11.42)
	Leutnant Beischall (captured)
Batterie Offizier:	Oberleutnant Flemming
	Leutnant Beischall (from 15.6.42)
	Leutnant Bade (from 30.9.42)
	Leutnant Broscheit (transferred 10.11.42)
	Leutnant Schoneberger (from 9.10.42)

I. Abteilung Stab:

Kommandeur:	Major von Pawel (until 3.9.42)
later:	Hauptmann Koch (captured and died in captivity)
	Oberstleutnant von Pawel (captured and died in captivity)
Adjutant:	Oberleutnant Neßlinger (took command of 3. Batterie on 3.9.42)
later:	Leutnant Fähnrich (captured)
Ordonanzoffizier:	Leutnant Fähnrich (took over adjutancy on 3.9.42) (captured)
later:	Leutnant Rohde
	Leutnant Vogt (captured)
Abteilung-Arzt:	Oberarzt Dr. Spode

Abteilung Stabsbatterie:

Kommandeur:	Oberleutnant Lackner

1. Batterie:

Kommandeur:	Oberleutnant Willenberg (wounded 4.9.42)
	Oberleutnant von Schütz (wounded 17.10.42)
	Leutnant Nueske (fell ill and left Stalingrad on 18.11.42)
Batterie Offizier:	Leutnant von Heimann
later:	Leutnant Lindenberg
	Leutnant Punge (wounded 6.10.42)

2. Batterie:

Kommandeur:	Hauptmann Hicketier (captured and died in captivity)
Batterie Offizier:	Leutnant Woelki (wounded 22.8.42)

3. Batterie:

Kommandeur:	Hauptmann Koch (until 3.9.42)
later:	Leutnant Köppel (temporary)
	Oberleutnant Neßlinger (wounded 25.9.42, died 28.9.42)
	Oberleutnant Holtz (wounded 4.10.42)
Batterie Offizier:	Leutnant Scott (wounded 3.8.42)
	Leutnant Köppel (captured)

II. Abteilung Stab:

Kommandeur:	Hauptmann Nahler
Adjutant:	Oberleutnant von Gyldenfeldt (became Regiment adjutant on 3.9.42)
later:	Leutnant Braunheim (killed 4.1.43)
Ordonanzoffizier:	Leutnant Elias (missing in action December 1942)
Abteilung-Arzt:	Oberarzt Dr. Twardy

Abteilung Stabsbatterie:

Kommandeur:	Hauptmann Woesch (killed 15.1.43)

4. Batterie:

Kommandeur:	Hauptmann v. Rosenberg-Lipinski (transferred 30.8.42 to IIa) Hauptmann von Schack
Beobachtung Offizier:	Leutnant Mergens

5. Batterie:

Kommandeur:	Oberleutnant Wippern (became Regiment Ordonanzoffizier)
Batterie Offizier:	Leutnant Erdmann (outside Kessel)

6. Batterie:

Kommandeur:	Hauptmann von Engel

III. Abteilung Stab:

Kommandeur: later:	Major Leitreuter (wounded 5.7.42) Hauptmann Platz (wounded 8.9.42) Hauptmann von Raison (fell ill 25.10.42) Hauptmann Heemsoth (flown out of Kessel in January 1943)
Adjutant:	Oberleutnant von Imhoff
Ordonanzoffizier:	Leutnant Becker
Abteilung-Arzt: later:	Assistenarzt Dr. Heinemann Oberarzt Dr. Turowski (from 28.6. – 7.11.)
Zahlmeister:	Oberzahlmeister Steiner

Abteilung Stabsbatterie:

Kommandeur:	Oberleutnant Waetjen (wounded 25.8.42)

7. Batterie:

Kommandeur: later:	Hauptmann Heemsoth (until 25.10.42) Oberleutnant d'Heureuse (captured and died in captivity)

8. Batterie:

Kommandeur: Hauptmann von Raison (until 8.9.42)

Batterie Offizier: Leutnant Busse

9. Batterie:

Kommandeur: Hauptmann Platz (until 5.7.42)
later: Oberleutnant Radtke
Hauptmann Kastens (missing in action January 1943)

Batterie Offizier: Leutnant Radtke (wounded 28.7.42)

IV. Abteilung Stab:

Kommandeur: Oberstleutnant von Melchers (wounded 8.9.42)
later: Oberleutnant Jacobi
Hauptmann Fischer
Hauptmann Wiemann (from 20.10.42)

Adjutant: Leutnant Schwartzkopff

Waffen Offizier: Leutnant (W) Rees (wounded 2.9.42)

Abteilung Stabsbatterie:

Kommandeur: Oberleutnant Jacobi

10. Batterie:

Kommandeur: Oberleutnant Freiherr von Erffa
Hauptmann Wiemann (from 20.10.42)

Messtrupp-Offizier: Leutnant Nielsche (killed 9.8.42)

11. Batterie:

Kommandeur: Oberleutnant Stockinger (transferred to Pz.Jg.40)
later: Oberleutnant Tonsgoke (wounded 9.10.42)

Batterie Offizier: Leutnant Radtke (wounded 28.7.42)

12. Batterie:

Kommandeur: Leutnant Soltau (wounded 10.8.42)
later: Leutnant Deuer (captured and died in captivity)

Officers of the Regiment whose positions are unknown:

Leutnant Andreesen (IV.) (from 20.10.42)
Oberleutnant Baaden (III.) (captured)
Leutnant Bachler
Leutnant Birkner
Leutnant Bock (IV.)
Leutnant Boecker (IV.) (from 28.9.42)
Leutnant Fuchs
Oberleutnant Gensel (IV.) (from 20.10.42)
Hauptmann Glemann
Leutnant Gornth (wounded 20.8.42)
Leutnant Graeve (IV.)
Leutnant Griebenow
Leutnant Gumbert (from 20.10.42)
Leutnant Hauschild
Leutnant Karsten (killed 4.9.42)
Oberleutnant Kuse (Batterie Kommandeur)
Leutnant Lindemann (IV.) (from 20.10.42) (missing in action 12.42)
Leutnant Magens (missing in action January 1943)
Leutnant Masuhr (wounded 29.8.42)
Leutnant Mollon
Leutnant Morff (IV.)
Leutnant Pfautsch (missing in action January 1943)
Leutnant Reininghaus (wounded 2.9.42)
Leutnant Rust (IV.)
Leutnant von Schinckel (killed 8.9.42)
Leutnant Dr. Schwanenberg
Oberleutnant Seufferheld (transferred to PGR26)
Leutnant Sodemann (wounded 29.8.42)
Oberleutnant von Steegen (transferred to Div. Stab 15.8.42)
Leutnant Stegel (wounded 7.8.42 and transferred to Pz.Jg.40)
Leutnant Wagner (IV.) (wounded 2.9.42)
Hauptmann Weyer (IV.) (wounded 12.9.42)
Leutnant Wieczorek (IV.) (outside Kessel) (killed 3.12.42)
Leutnant Wohlers (IV.)
Oberleutnant Wolter (transferred 22.6.42)

Kradschützen-Abteilung 4

Abteilung Stab:

Kommandeur:	Oberstleutnant von Hellermann (transferred 26.8.42 to PGR21)
later:	Rittmeister von der Groeben (killed 8.9.42)
	Rittmeister von Langenn-Steinkeller (fell ill 13.10.42)
	Rittmeister Wrede
	Oberleutnant Rauch
	Rittmeister von Götz (took command on 16.12.42)
	Rittmeister von Humbert (took command of II./PGR26)
	Rittmeister Ernst Schmidt (captured and died in captivity)
Adjutant:	Oberleutnant Dannebaum (fell ill in early October)
later:	Leutnant von Stockhausen (from 28.9.42)
	Leutnant Bayer-Eynck (transferred to II./PGR26 12.12.42)
Ordonanzoffizier:	Leutnant von Stockhausen (wounded 31.8.42)
later:	Leutnant von Ulrici (wounded 8.9.42)
	Leutnant Pack (captured)
Nachrichtenoffizier:	Oberleutnant Buchholz (wounded 25.8.42)
later:	Leutnant Hubertus Schulz (wounded 22.9.42)
	Leutnant von Stockhausen (from 28.9.42) (captured)
	Oberwachtmeister Schumacher
Abteilung-Arzt:	Stabsarzt Dr. Pisselhoy (wounded 2.10.42)
later:	Oberarzt Dr. Turowski (from 7.11.42)
Hilfsarzt:	Assistenarzt Dr. Vogel (wounded 28.7.42)
later:	Assistenarzt Dr. Kleinjohann (transferred back to PGR26 7.11.42)
V.-Offizier:	Kriegsverwaltungsrat Dyckerhoff
later:	Kriegstechniker Pareik (captured)
Zahlmeister:	Stabszahlmeister Scholz (transferred from PG26) (captured)

Abteilung Stabsschwadron:

Chef:	Rittmeister Jankowski (transferred 9.8.42 to PGR26)
later:	Leutnant Urbons (killed 28.9.42)
	Leutnant von Stockhausen (from 28.9.42)

1. Schwadron:

Chef:	Rittmeister Graf Vitzthum von Eckstadt (transferred 28.9.42)
later:	Oberleutnant Huck (outside Kessel)
	Leutnant Weissenborn (from 22.11.42) (captured)
1. Zug Kommandeur:	Leutnant Weissenborn (took command of Schw. on 22.11.42)
2. Zug Kommandeur:	Leutnant Huck (took command of Schw. on 28.9.42)
3. Zug Kommandeur:	Leutnant Eickes (transferred to 2. Schw. 29.8.42)
later:	Leutnant Otto Schulz
	Oberwachtmeister Sehlmacher
Spieß:	Hauptwachtmeister Mende
later:	Oberwachtmeister Balnus

2. Schwadron:

Chef:	Rittmeister Kolczyk (wounded 29.8.42)
later:	Leutnant von Senger und Etterlin (temporary)
	Oberleutnant Eickes (missing in action February 1943)
1. Zug Kommandeur:	Leutnant von Stockhausen (became Abt. OO)
2. Zug Kommandeur:	Leutnant Hubertus Schulz (became Abt. NO)
3. Zug Kommandeur:	Oberwachtmeister Neubacher
4. Zug Kommandeur:	Oberwachtmeister Peschel
later:	Fahnenjunker-Wachtmeister von Senger und Etterlin (1. Zug)
	Oberwachtmeister Neufeld
Spieß:	Hauptwachtmeister Wiechert

3. Schwadron:

Chef:	Rittmeister von Langenn-Steinkeller (until 8.9.42)
later:	Leutnant von Metzsch (wounded 28.9.42)
	Leutnant Fassbender (wounded 3.10.42)
	Fahnenjunker-Wachtmeister von Cramm (temporary)
	Leutnant Melville (from 29.10.42, killed 26.11.42)
	Leutnant Wildeus (captured)
1. Zug Kommandeur:	Leutnant Stach von Golzheim
2. Zug Kommandeur:	Oberwachtmeister Sendkow
3. Zug Kommandeur:	Leutnant von Heydebrand und der Lasa (killed 27.7.42)

4. Zug Kommandeur: Leutnant Müller-Röhlich
later: Leutnant Fassbender (took command of Schwadron 28.9.42)
Leutnant von Metzsch (took command of Schwadron 8.9.42)
Fahnenjunker-Wachtmeister von Cramm
Leutnant Warlimont (wounded 24.9.42)
Oberwachtmeister Paetsch
Oberwachtmeister Tausendfreund
Wachtmeister Ruff

Spieß: Hauptwachtmeister Well
later: Oberwachtmeister Pack
Oberwachtmeister Scharnoian
Oberwachtmeister E. Schulz

4. Schwadron:

Chef: Rittmeister von der Groeben (until 26.8.42)
later: Leutnant Duran (from 9.10.42 until wounded)
Oberwachtmeister Pack

1. Zug Kommandeur: Oberleutnant Schlaefereit (wounded 28.7.42)
2. Zug Kommandeur: Leutnant von Hanstein
3. Zug Kommandeur: Leutnant Otte (wounded 2.9.42)
4. Zug Kommandeur: Leutnant Düran (took command of Schw. 26.8.42)

Spieß: Hauptwachtmeister Rieder

5. Schwadron:

Chef: Rittmeister Wrede (until 13.10.42)
later: Oberleutnant Rauch (missing in action 2.2.43)

Zug Kommandeur: Oberleutnant Mack (killed 14.10.42)
Zug Kommandeur: Oberleutnant von Knobloch (wounded 8.9.42)
Zug Kommandeur: Oberleutnant Rauch (took command of Schw. 13.10.42)
later: Oberwachtmeister Nettekoven

Spieß: Oberwachtmeister Broszies

Officers of the Abteilung whose positions are unknown:

Leutnant Biskupeck (from 94.ID)
Leutnant Meckel
Leutnant Well
Leutnant Wilking (from 9.10.42) (Zug Kommandeur)

Panzerpionier-Bataillon 40

Abteilung Stab:

Kommandeur: Major von Koller und von Stockrad (wounded in July 1942)
later: Hauptmann de Boer (captured and died in captivity)

Adjutant: Leutnant Remberg (missing in action January 1943)

1. Kompanie:

Kommandeur: Hauptmann de Boer
later: Hauptmann Gach (transferred on 10.10.42)

Zug Kommandeur: Leutnant Karrasch (wounded 20.9.42)
later: Oberfeldwebel Wuttke

2. Kompanie:

Kommandeur: Hauptmann Mayer (killed 4.9.42)
later: Oberleutnant Viertel (from 14.9.42, killed 27.9.42)
Oberleutnant Fotsch

Zug Kommandeur: Leutnant Beder
Zug Kommandeur: Leutnant Steinhardt (killed 15.6.42)

3. Kompanie:

Kommandeur: Oberleutnant Schönfeld (wounded 20.8.42)
later: Oberleutnant Rost

Zug Kommandeur: Oberleutnant Rost (became Kompanie Kommandeur)
Zug Kommandeur: Oberleutnant Schröder
Zug Kommandeur: Leutnant Reifner
later: Leutnant Enge (wounded 22.12.42)
Feldwebel Wasch (killed 16.12.42)

Officers of the Bataillon whose positions are unknown:

Leutnant Bach
Leutnant Buchholz
Oberleutnant Constein (from 25.11.42)
Oberleutnant Fritz
Leutnant Gollob
Leutnant Horst (from 14.9.42, killed 28.9.42)
Leutnant Meseck-Selchow (from 3.10.42)
Oberleutnant Pallentin
Oberleutnant Peters (wounded 8.9.42)
Leutnant Tiemann (from 14.9.42)

Panzerjäger-Bataillon 40

Abteilung Stab:

Kommandeur:	Oberstleutnant Sälzer (transferred in September 1942)
later:	Oberleutnant Markgraf (captured)
Adjutant:	Oberleutnant Markgraf (assumed command of Abteilung)
later:	Leutnant Martin (from 94.ID)
Abteilung Arzt:	Stabsarzt Dr. Grübner
later:	Oberarzt Dr. Huber (from 26.10.42)
Assistenarzt:	Unterarzt Dr. Schindler (from 9.11.42)

1. Kompanie:

Kommandeur:	Hauptmann Zieke (killed 28.7.42)
later:	Oberleutnant Fichtenau (wounded 22.9.42)
	Oberleutnant Seroka (captured)
Zug Kommandeur:	
later:	Oberleutnant Dahle (from 6.11.42)

2. Kompanie:

Kommandeur:	Hauptmann von Löw

3. Kompanie:

Kommandeur:	Oberleutnant Krebs
Zug Kommandeur:	Leutnant Graeve
later:	Leutnant Böcker (transferred from IV./PAR89)
	Leutnant Stegel (transferred from IV./PAR89)

4. Kompanie:

Kommandeur:	Oberleutnant Stockinger
later:	Oberleutnant Deuer (captured and died in captivity)

Officers of the Bataillon whose positions are unknown:

Oberleutnant Wollenschlager
Oberleutnant Hahn
Leutnant Hermanau (from 24.8.42)
Leutnant Hugenroth (Zug Kommandeur)
Leutnant Jansen
Leutnant Sindermann (from 24.8.42)

Panzer, Vehicle & Equipment Losses

Appendix Ten

Strengths at beginning of campaign on 28th June 1942:

32	Panzer II
112	Panzer III
32	Panzer IV
7	Panzerbefehlswagen
36	Armoured reconnaissance vehicle (Panzerspähwagen)
112	Armoured personnel carriers (Schützenpanzerwagen)
1250	Motorcycles
909	Personenkraftwagen (Passenger vehicles)
1852	Lorries (Lastkraftwagen)
29	Kom.
250	Zugkraftwagen (Towing-tractors)

Losses from 8th July – 30th July 1942:

64	motorcycles
34	PKW
41	lorries
3	Kr.Kw.
7	towing-tractors
1	Kom.
1	Panzer III kz
5	Panzer III lg
1	light armoured reconnaissance vehicle
1	armoured observation vehicle (Sdkfz. 253)
12	MG34
2	2cm anti-aircraft guns (Flak 38)
1	5cm anti-tank gun (Pak 38)
1	barrel on a heavy mortar (schwere Granatwerfer 34)
1	barrel on a light infantry gun (leichte Infanteriegeschütz)
1	7.5cm anti-tank gun (Kwk. 40)
4	large inflatable boats (große Floßsäcke)
5	pontoons

From 28th June – 1st September 1942.

Total losses:

2 Panzer II (6.2% of total Panzer II's)
19 Panzer III (17.1% of total Panzer III's)
4 Panzer IV (12.4% of total Panzer IV's)
2 Panzerspähwagen (5.6% of total armoured reconnaissance vehicles)
7 Schützenpanzerwagen (6.3% of total armoured personnel carriers)
98 Motorcycles (7.8% of total motorcycles)
53 PKW (5.8% of total PKW)
67 Lorries (3.6% of total lorries)
2 Kom. (6.8% of total Kom.)
8 Towing-tractors (3.1% of total towing-tractors)

Damaged but still operational:

140 Motorcycles
106 PKW
103 Lorries
2 Kom.
11 Towing-tractors

Vehicles being repaired. (Percentages are when combined with total losses shown above):

19 Panzer II (21 lost or being repaired– 65.1% of total Panzer II's)
79 Panzer III (96 lost or being repaired– 86.4% of total Panzer III's)
27 Panzer IV (31 lost or being repaired– 96.9% of total Panzer IV's)
5 Panzerbefehlswagen (5 being repaired– 71% of total Panzerbefehlswagen)
9 Panzerspähwagen (11 lost or being repaired– 30.8% of total reconnaissance vehicles)
12 Schützenpanzerwagen (19 lost or being repaired– 17.1% of total personnel carriers)
164 Motorcycles (402 lost or being repaired– 32.1% of total motorcycles)
101 PKW (260 lost or being repaired– 28.6% of total PKW)
106 Lorries (276 lost or being repaired– 14.9% of total lorries)
1 Kom. (5 lost or being repaired– 17.2% of total Kom.)
11 Towing-tractors (30 lost or being repaired– 11.7% of total towing-tractors)

Vehicles knocked out between 28th June – 20th September:

3 Panzer II (total loss)
24 Panzer III (total loss)
4 Panzer IV (total loss)
11 Schützenpanzerwagen (total loss)
2 Panzerspähwagen (total loss)
122 motorcycles
73 PKW
86 lorries
2 Kom.
17 Zugkraftwagen

Strength report on the evening of 1st October:

Operational panzers:

8	Panzer II
12	Panzer III lg
2	Panzer III kz
3	Panzer IV lg
2	Panzer IV kz
2	Panzerbefehlswagen

Non-operational due to shortages of starter motors and replacement parts:

20	Panzer II
27	Panzer III lg
43	Panzer III kz
6	Panzer IV lg
17	Panzer IV kz
5	Panzerbefehlswagen

Losses:

3	Panzer II
17	Panzer III lg
9	Panzer III kz
3	Panzer IV lg
1	Panzer IV kz
9	Schützenpanzerwagen (Sdkfz. 251/1 and /2)
6	light Schützenpanzerwagen (Sdkfz. 250/1/3/5/7 and /10)
2	Panzerspähwagen
15	Zugkraftwagen 1 tonne
2	Zugkraftwagen 3 tonne
3	Zugkraftwagen 8 tonne
1	Zugkraftwagen 12 tonne
4	Zugkraftwagen 18 tonne
139	Motorcycles
79	PKW
127	Lorries
2	88mm Flak guns
2	heavy howitzers (schwere Feldhaubitze)
2	10cm Kanone 18
2	light infantry guns (leichte Infanteriegeschütz 18)
3	light howitzers (leichte Feldhaubitze)
2	heavy mortars (schwere Granatwerfer 34)
7	2cm Flak

Strength report on the evening of 10th October:

Operational panzers:

7	Panzer II
15	Panzer III lg
5	Panzer III kz
4	Panzer IV lg
3	Panzer IV kz
2	Panzerbefehlswagen

Non-operational due to shortages of starter motors and replacement parts:

22	Panzer II
23	Panzer III lg
40	Panzer III kz
5	Panzer IV lg
15	Panzer IV kz
5	Panzerbefehlswagen

Losses:

3	Panzer II
18	Panzer III lg
9	Panzer III kz
3	Panzer IV lg
2	Panzer IV kz
9	Schützenpanzerwagen (Sdkfz. 251/1 and /2)
6	light Schützenpanzerwagen (Sdkfz. 250/1/3/5/7 and /10)
2	Panzerspähwagen
15	Zugkraftwagen 1 tonne
2	Zugkraftwagen 3 tonne
3	Zugkraftwagen 8 tonne
1	Zugkraftwagen 12 tonne
4	Zugkraftwagen 18 tonne
139	Motorcycles
79	PKW
127	Lorries
2	88mm Flak guns
2	heavy howitzers (schwere Feldhaubitze)
1	10cm Kanone 18
2	light infantry guns (leichte Infanteriegeschütz 18)
2	light howitzers (leichte Feldhaubitze)
3	heavy mortars (schwere Granatwerfer 34)
7	2cm Flak

Strength report on the evening of 17th October:

Operational panzers:

8	Panzer II
15	Panzer III lg
5	Panzer III kz
3	Panzer IV lg
3	Panzer IV kz
2	Panzerbefehlswagen

Non-operational due to shortages of starter motors and replacement parts:

21	Panzer II
23	Panzer III lg
40	Panzer III kz
6	Panzer IV lg
15	Panzer IV kz
4	Panzerbefehlswagen

Losses:

3	Panzer II
18	Panzer III lg
9	Panzer III kz
3	Panzer IV lg
2	Panzer IV kz
1	Panzerbefehlswagen
7	Schützenpanzerwagen (Sdkfz. 251/1 and /2)
7	light Schützenpanzerwagen (Sdkfz. 250/1/3/5/7 and /10)
2	Panzerspähwagen
22	Zugkraftwagen 1 tonne
2	Zugkraftwagen 3 tonne
3	Zugkraftwagen 8 tonne
1	Zugkraftwagen 12 tonne
4	Zugkraftwagen 18 tonne
144	Motorcycles
90	PKW
132	Lorries
2	88mm Flak guns
2	heavy howitzers (schwere Feldhaubitze)
1	10cm Kanone 18
3	light infantry guns (leichte Infanteriegeschütz 18)
2	light howitzers (leichte Feldhaubitze)
3	heavy mortars (schwere Granatwerfer 34)
8	2cm Flak
2	anti-tank rifles (schwere Panzerbuchse 41)

Strength report on the evening of 24th October:

Operational panzers:

2	Panzer II
8	Panzer III lg
2	Panzer III kz
1	Panzer IV lg
0	Panzer IV kz
2	Panzerbefehlswagen

Non-operational due to shortages of starter motors and replacement parts:

27	Panzer II
29	Panzer III lg
43	Panzer III kz
8	Panzer IV lg
18	Panzer IV kz
4	Panzerbefehlswagen

Losses:

3	Panzer II
19	Panzer III lg
9	Panzer III kz
3	Panzer IV lg
2	Panzer IV kz
1	Panzerbefehlswagen
6	Schützenpanzerwagen (Sdkfz. 251/1 and /2)
7	light Schützenpanzerwagen (Sdkfz. 250/1/3/5/7 and /10)
2	Panzerspähwagen
23	Zugkraftwagen 1 tonne
2	Zugkraftwagen 3 tonne
3	Zugkraftwagen 8 tonne
1	Zugkraftwagen 12 tonne
4	Zugkraftwagen 18 tonne
148	Motorcycles
94	PKW
135	Lorries
2	88mm Flak guns
2	heavy howitzers (schwere Feldhaubitze)
1	10cm Kanone 18
5	light infantry guns (leichte Infanteriegeschütz 18)
2	light howitzers (leichte Feldhaubitze)
5	heavy mortars (schwere Granatwerfer 34)
9	2cm Flak
3	anti-tank rifles (schwere Panzerbuchse 41)

Strength report on the evening of 31st October:

Operational panzers:

2	Panzer II
8	Panzer III lg
2	Panzer III kz
1	Panzer IV lg
1	Panzer IV kz
2	Panzerbefehlswagen

Non-operational due to shortages of starter motors and replacement parts:

27	Panzer II
30	Panzer III lg
43	Panzer III kz
8	Panzer IV lg
16	Panzer IV kz
4	Panzerbefehlswagen

Losses:

3	Panzer II
19	Panzer III lg
9	Panzer III kz
3	Panzer IV lg
3	Panzer IV kz
1	Panzerbefehlswagen
6	Schützenpanzerwagen (Sdkfz. 251/1 and /2)
7	light Schützenpanzerwagen (Sdkfz. 250/1/3/5/7 and /10)
2	Panzerspähwagen
23	Zugkraftwagen 1 tonne
2	Zugkraftwagen 3 tonne
3	Zugkraftwagen 8 tonne
1	Zugkraftwagen 12 tonne
4	Zugkraftwagen 18 tonne
148	Motorcycles
94	PKW
135	Lorries
2	88mm Flak guns
2	heavy howitzers (schwere Feldhaubitze)
1	10cm Kanone 18
5	light infantry guns (leichte Infanteriegeschütz 18)
1	light howitzers (leichte Feldhaubitze)
6	heavy mortars (schwere Granatwerfer 34)
10	2cm Flak
3	anti-tank rifles (schwere Panzerbuchse 41)

Glossary and Abbreviations

Abt.: *see* Abteilung

Abteilung: This term could mean "detachment", "department" or "battalion", but most of the time Abteilung meant "battalion". In 24. Panzer-Division, the sub-units of any Abteilung were called Schwadron rather than Kompanie.

Alarmeinheiten: Alarm units were ad hoc units assembled by rear area support units, training units and surplus personnel to respond to local emergencies.

Angriff: Attack

AOK: Armeeoberkommando

Arko: Artilleriekommandeur – Artillery Commander. An Arko was a numbered headquarters used to control artillery assets at Korps level.

Armee: A term meaning "army". An organisational formation made up of Korps units.

Armeekorps: Infanterie-Korps

Armeenachrichtenführer: Army Signals Officer

Armeepionierführer: Army Engineer Officer

Artillerie: Artillery

Artilleriekommandeur: *see* Arko

Arzt: Doctor

Assistenarzt: Military doctor with a rank equivalent to Leutnant

Aufklärer: Reconnaissance soldier

Aufklärung: Combat reconnaissance. *See also* Erkundung

Ausbildungs: Training

Bataillon: A term meaning "battalion". An organisational formation composed of companies and usually attached to a regiment. In 24. Panzer-Division, the sub-units of a Bataillon were called Kompanie rather than Schwadron.

Batl.: *see* Bataillon

Batterie: A term meaning "battery". A company-sized element of artillery. An Artillerie-Abteilung was made up of 1 staff battery and 3 artillery batteries.

Beamte: Official

Befehlspanzer: Command tank

Befehlswagen: Command vehicle

Beobachtung: Observation

Brigade: Means the same in German as in English. An organisational unit usually made up of 2 or more regiments. Brigade-sized units served either as independent units or as an organic part of a Division. Sometimes they served as an organic part of a Korps in place of a Division.

Btl.: *see* Bataillon

Chef: Company commander

Dienstgrad: Rank

Dinafü.: Division Nachschubführer, Division Supplies Officer.

Div.: *see* Division

Division: Means the same in German as in English. An organisational unit made up of regiments and usually controlled by a Korps.

DKiG.: Deutsches Kreuz in Gold, German Cross in Gold

d.L.: der Landwehr. Reserve officers may be transferred to the Landwehr (land defence) list because of age or relative unfitness.

Doktor: Doctor. Often an academic title rather than a medical one, except in the cases of the Division's medical personnel.

d.R.: der Reserve. Retired officers may be transferred to the reserve list and suitable candidates were sometimes commissioned directly.

d.R.z.V.: der Reserve zur Verfügung (available). Over-age officers who had passed the age limit for their rank and classification – but who remained fit and willing to serve – were transferred to the z.V. (available) list.

Dr.: *see* Doktor

Ehrenblattspange: Honour Roll Clasp. When a soldier had performed a meritorious or brave act, he was sometimes recognised by having his name added to the Wehrmacht's Honour Roll. The Clasp was a medal signifying that the holder was on the Honour Roll and was worn through a buttonhole, on top of the Iron Cross Second Class ribbon.

Eichenlaub: Oakleaves

Einheit: Detachment or unit

Einsatz: Operation

Eisernes Kreuz: Iron Cross

EK.: *see* Eisernes Kreuz

EKI: Eisernes Kreuz I. Klasse, Iron Cross First Class

EKII: Eisernes Kreuz II. Klasse, Iron Cross Second Class

Erkundung: Route reconnaissance. *See also* Aufklärung

Ersatz: Replacement

Ersatz Abteilung: Replacement battalion

Evangelischer Kriegspfarrer: Evangelical priest

Fahnenjunker-Wachtmeister: Officer candidate with the equivalent rank of a Wachtmeister.

Fahrer: Driver

Feldgendarmerie: Field police.

Feldhaubitze: Field howitzer

Feldlazarett: Field hospital.

Feldpost: Field post office

Feldpostnummer: Field post number

Flak: Fliegerabwehrkanone, anti-aircraft gun

Flak-Zug: Anti-aircraft platoon

Flieger: Flyer or pilot

Fliegerabwehrkanone: Anti-aircraft gun

FPN.: *see* Feldpostnummer

Freiherr: A German hereditary title, corresponding approximately to Baron

Frhr.: *see* Freiherr

Führer: A temporary commander. Also the commonly-used term for Hitler.

Führerreserve: A reserve of officers maintained by larger units, such as Division, Korps and Armee. Officers would be called upon from the Führerreserve to replace active officers that had become casualties.
Funk: Radio
Funker: Radio operator
Gefreiter: Lance-Corporal
Gegenstoß: Counterthrust
Generalkommando: General Headquarters
Generalleutnant: Lieutenant-General
Generalmajor: Major-General
Generaloberst: Colonel-General
Generalstabsoffizier: General Staff officer
Gen.Lt.: *see* Generalleutnant
Gen.Maj.: *see* Generalmajor
Gen.Oberst: *see* Generaloberst
Geschütz: Gun or artillery piece
Graf: A German hereditary title, corresponding approximately to Earl
Granatwerfer: Mortar (literally "grenade thrower")
Grenadier: In 1942, the Germans needed to reinforce their field forces in some way. Since they didn't have the men or equipment to send out in quantity, they decided to reinforce the morale of their field forces by resurrecting traditional military terms and thereby recalling Germany's glorious military past. The most significant resurrection was Grenadier, a traditional term for a type of infantryman.
Gruppe: Typically a group or squad but also used to denote a large combat-group (also called a Kampfgruppe). A Gruppe would consist of various arms, such as panzers, flak and pioneers. These formations were widely and successfully used by the German Army.
Hauptmann: Captain
Hauptwachtmeister: Master-Sergeant. *See also* Spieß
Heer: This term means "Army" but in general referred to the regular German Army.
Heeresgruppe: Literally, "Army Group". An organisational formation made up of a number of armies and was the largest single German organisational formation during the war, usually consisting of hundreds of various units and upwards of a few hundred thousand men.
Hilfsfreiwillige (Hiwi): Auxiliary volunteers. After the invasion of the Soviet Union, thousands of citizens and prisoners-of-war volunteered to fight Stalin's regime. At first, Hitler refused to use them but, in the face of mounting casualties, he eventually relented and allowed the German Army to use them in non-combat roles. Hiwis served as auxiliaries to the front-line troops with roles such as ammunition- and food-carriers, stretcher-bearers and various construction and road-building projects, but in some cases, these men were issued with weapons and participated in combat.
Hiwi: *see* Hilfsfreiwillige
H.Pers.A.: Heerespersonalamt, army personnel office
Infanterie: Infantry
i.G.: im Generalstab (applied to General Staff officers in the service of the General Staff)
Ia: Division Chief-of-Staff. 1st General Staff Officer of the Division – Leiter der Führungsabteilung. The Ia dealt with everything that involved individual units in command and tactical terms, including troop leadership, training, organisation etc. He presented possibilities of battle conduct to the Division Commander, worked out orders and represented the Commander in his absence.

Ib: Division Quartermaster. 2nd General Staff Officer of the Division – Leiter der Versorgungabteilung. The Ib was responsible for supplying the whole Division, as well as sending forward supplies such as ammunition, rations and sending prisoners, wounded men etc. to the rear.
Ib/WuG: (Waffen und Geräte = weapons and equipment) This officer was responsible for the replacement, supply and maintenance of weapons and ammunition.
Ib/Kfz: (Kraftfahrzeug = vehicles) This officer was responsible for the replacement, supply and maintenance of motor vehicles, spare parts, repairs and fuel.
Ic: Division Enemy Intelligence Officer. 3rd General Staff Officer of the Division. The Ic handled all matters that concerned the enemy, such as interrogations, surveillance and interception of enemy communications and, after evaluation, presenting it to the Commander.
I.D.: Infanterie-Division
IIa: Division Adjutant. Functions included handling of replacements, personnel matters of the officers (such as promotions, decorations, leave, punishment) as well as casualty lists.
IIb: Had the same functions as IIa but relating to non-commissioned officers and enlisted men.
III: Division Judge Advocate. Headed courts-martial within the division and presided over court cases and matters of discipline.
Inf.: Infanterie
Inf.Div.: Infanterie Division
Inf.Rgt.: Infanterie-Regiment
Infanteriegeschütz: Infantry howitzer
Ing.: *see* Ingenieur
Ingenieur: Technical engineer
Instandsetzung: Maintenance and repair
IR: Infanterie-Regiment
I-Trupp: Instandsetzungstrupp, repair troop
IVa: Division Assistant Adjutant was the superior officer of all the administrative and supply services, such as rations, clothing, equipment, canteen goods etc.
IVb: Division Surgeon was simultaneously the troop commander of the medical services and superior officer of all medical personnel in the division.
IVc: Division Veterinarian was the commander of the veterinary services and superior officer of all the divisions veterinary and blacksmith personnel.
IVd: Division Chaplains. Both Catholicism and Protestantism were represented within the divisions.
IVz: Division Paymaster
JR: Jäger-Regiment
Kampfgruppe: Battlegroup
Kampfwagen: Fighting vehicle
Kaserne: Barracks
Katholischer Kriegspfarrer: Catholic priest
Kav.: *see* Kavallerie
Kavallerie: Cavalry
Kdr.: *see* Kommandeur
Kdr.Gen.: *see* Kommandierender General
KG: *see* Kommandierender General
Inf.: Infanterie
Ko.: *see* Kompanie

Kommandeur: Usually the person commanding a unit (Divisionskommandeur: divisional commander). A temporary commander was called "Führer" (Abteilungsführer: temporary battalion commander).
Kommandierender General: General of an Armeekorps, Panzerkorps etc.
Kommando: A "detail" or some small ad hoc formation (e.g., Bootykommando was a term for a detail sent out to collect enemy weapons).
Kompanie: Company
Korps: Corps
Kradschützen: Motorcycle soldier
Kriegsgefangen: Prisoner of war. The Germans used, or at least attempted to use, some POW construction units.
Kriegslazarett: Military hospital
Kriegstagebuch: War diary
KTB: *see* Kriegstagebuch
KV1: Klimenti Voroshilov 1, a heavy Russian tank weighing 52 tonnes, equipped with a 76.2mm cannon, 3 machine-guns and thick armour.
KV Rat: Kriegsverwaltungsrat, an administration official with the equivalent rank of Major.
Kwk: Kampfwagenkanone, the main gun of a panzer
Leutnant: Second-lieutenant
LKW: Lastkraftwagen, lorry
Lt.: *see* Leutnant
Mannschaften: Enlisted personnel
Marschbataillon: Personnel replacement transfer battalion
Maschinengewehr: Machine-gun.
MG: *see* Maschinengewehr
motorisiert: Motorised
Nachschub: Supply
Nachrichten: Signals and communications
Nebelgranate: Smoke shells
Nebelwerfer: Rocket-launcher. "Nebelwerfer" was originally a term for a chemical smoke mortar.
O1: 1st Assistant Adjutant and assistant to Ia, whose duties including preparing maps, maintaining the war diary and liaising with neighbouring units.
O2: 2nd Assistant Adjutant and assistant to Ib, handling the organisation of rear-area services.
O3: 3rd Assistant Adjutant and assistant to Ic.
O4: 4th Assistant Adjutant and personal aide to the division commander.
OB: *see* Oberbefehlshaber
Oberbefehlshaber: Commander-in-Chief, commander of an army-sized grouping.
Oberfeldarzt: Military doctor with a rank equivalent to Oberstleutnant
Obergefreiter: Corporal
Oberleutnant: First-lieutenant
Oberst: Colonel
Oberstabsarzt: Military doctor with a rank equivalent to Major
Oberstarzt: Military doctor with a rank equivalent to Oberst
Oberstleutnant: Lieutenant-Colonel
Oberwachtmeister: Sergeant First Class
Oblt.: *see* Oberleutnant
Obstlt.: *see* Oberstleutnant
Offizier: Officer

Ogf.: *see* Obergefreiter
OKH: Oberkommando des Heeres
OKW: Oberkommando der Wehrmacht
OO: *see* Ordonanzoffizier
Ord.Offz.: *see* Ordonanzoffizier
Ordonanzoffizier: Orderly officer
Ostpreußen: East Prussia
Pak: *see* Panzerabwehrkanone
Panzer: Armour/armoured. The word "Panzer" was assimilated into English when referring to German tanks and tank units.
Panzerabwehrkanone: Anti-tank gun. The term was mostly used at the tactical level.
Panzerbefehlswagen: Command tank
Panzergrenadier: "Armoured infantrymen". Panzergrenadier units were not necessarily armoured. While they ideally should have been equipped with armoured personnel carriers, most used trucks.
Panzergranate: Armour-piercing shells. Some of the varieties are as follows:
Panzergranate 38 – capped armour-piercing shell
Panzergranate 39 – capped armour-piercing shell without ballistic cap
Panzergranate 40 – solid high-density core armour-piercing shell
Panzerjäger: Anti-tank (person or vehicle). Literally "tank hunter". Also used to denote a private in an anti-tank unit.
Panzerkorps: Armoured corps
Panzernachrichten: Armoured signals
Panzerpionier: Armoured combat engineers. Also used to denote a private in a Panzerpionier unit.
Panzerspähwagen: Armoured reconnaissance vehicle
Panzertruppe: Armoured troops
Panzer-Zug: Tank platoon
Pi.: *see* Pionier
Pionier: Engineer
PKW: Personenkraftwagen, passenger vehicle
Pz.: *see* Panzer
Pz.Div.: Panzer-Division
Pz.Gren.: *see* Panzergrenadier
Pz.Gren.Rgt.: Panzergrenadier-Regiment
Pz.Jg.: *see* Panzerjäger
Pz.Jg.Abt.: Panzerjäger-Abteilung
Pz.Korps: *see* Panzerkorps
Pz.Pi.: *see* Panzerpionier
Pz.Zug: *see* Panzer-Zug
Regiment: Regiment
Reiter: Literally "rider" or cavalryman
Rgt.: *see* Regiment
Ritter: German hereditary title meaning Knight. A Ritter whose title is hereditary owns a Rittergut – or Knight's estate – and thus takes his name from it. In other cases, the title is derived from a grant made to an officer for heroism in action or for distinguished service to the state. In Bavaria until 1919, the Military Order of Max Joseph carried with it a knighthood which was not hereditary. This was the case with Bruno Ritter von Hauenschild.
Ritterkreuz: Knight's Cross

Ritterkreuzträger: Bearer of the Knight's Cross
Rittm.: *see* Rittmeister
Rittmeister: Captain, a rank used in the cavalry but carried over to 24. Panzer-Division.
RK: *see* Ritterkreuz
Rotkopf: An anti-tank shell – Kern Granate rot, used by 7.5cm L/24 guns, used on Stug. III Ausf. A–E and Pz IV Ausf. A – F1. KGr rot: 41mm @ 100m, 38mm @ 500m, 35mm @ 1000m, 32mm @ 1500m.
Sanitäter: Medic

Sanitäts: Medical
Schirrmeister: Motor Sergeant
Schnell: "Fast" or mobile. The term "schnelltruppen" usually meant motorised troops.
Schützenpanzerwagen: Armoured personnel carrier
Schw.: *see* Schwadron
Schwadron: A company in a cavalry unit but also the term for a company-level unit in 24. Panzer-Division.
schwere: Heavy
Sdfhr.: *see* Sonderführer
Selbstfahrlafette: Self-propelled gun mount
Sfl.: *see* Selbstfahrlafette
Soldbuch: Military paybook
Sonderführer: A language-specialist attached to headquarter units and used for translating captured material and interrogations.
Sonderkraftfahrzeug: Special purpose vehicle
Spieß: Literally "spear" but also called "mother of the company". A Spieß was a senior Unteroffizier, usually a Hauptwachtmeister or Hauptfeldwebel, that looked after the non-combat operations of a unit.
SPW: *see* Schützenpanzerwagen
Stab: Staff
Stabsarzt: Military doctor with a rank equivalent to Hauptmann or Rittmeister
Stabsbtr.: *see* Stabsbatterie
Stabsbatterie: Headquarters battery
Stabsgefreiter: Staff Lance Corporal
Stabsko.: *see* Stabskompanie
Stabskompanie: Headquarters company
Stabsschw.: *see* Stabsschwadron
Stabsschwadron: Headquarters company
Stabswachtmeister: Staff Sergeant
Stgfr.: *see* Stabsgefreiter
Stomü.: Stabsoffizier für Marschüberwachung, a staff officer responsible for march and traffic control.
Stoßgruppe: Assault group or raiding party
Stug.: *see* Sturmgeschütz
Stuka: Sturzkampfbomber, dive-bomber
Sturmartillerie: Literally means "assault artillery" but usually referred to assault guns. The assault guns were part of the artillery branch and not the panzer troops.

Sturmgeschütz: Assault gun. Not all assault guns were in assault gun units, as this weapon was so useful that it was used in various anti-tank units and as replacements for tanks in Panzer units.

Stwm.: *see* Stabswachtmeister

T-34: A medium Russian tank equipped with a 76.2mm cannon, 2 machine-guns, thick sloping armour and a powerful engine.

Teile: A part or portion of a unit.

Uffz.: *see* Unteroffizier

Unteroffizier: This has two meanings: "Junior Sergeant" when referring to a specific rank, and "non-commissioned officer" when referring to one of the three rank classes, eg. Mannschaften, Unteroffiziere und Offiziere (men, non-commissioned officers and officers).

Verb.Offz.: Verbindungsoffizier, liaison officer

Veterinär: Veterinarian

Vorstoß: Assault

w.: Wounded

Wachtmeister: Sergeant in a cavalry unit but used extensively in 24. Panzer-Division.

Waffenfarbe: Branch colour. 24. Panzer-Division's Waffenfarbe was golden yellow, a tradition carried over from the cavalry. It was the only Panzer-Division to wear this colour (all other Panzer-Divisions wore the standard pink Waffenfarbe).

Werfer: Literally "launcher" or "thrower". Rocket artillery units. *See* Nebelwerfer.

Werkstattkompanie: Maintenance company

Westpreußen: West Prussia

Wm.: *see* Wachtmeister

Zahlmeister: Paymaster

z.b.V.: zur besonderen Verwendung, "for special use" or "at special employment".

Zeltbahn: Tent quarter

Zm.: *see* Zahlmeister

Zug: Platoon

Bibliography

Unpublished Archival Material:

War Diaries of 24. Panzer Division
War Diaries of XXXXVIII. Panzerkorps
War Diaries of 6. Armee (Armee Oberkommando, Ia Kriegstagebuch)
War Diaries of 79. Infanterie-Division
War Diaries of 4. Panzerarmee

Published Works about 24. Panzer-Division:

Böttger, Armin. *Überstehen war alles. Stationen und Impressionen eines Lebensweges vom Soldaten im Panzer zum Professor der Zahnmedizin*. Berg am See 1993, VGB–Verlagsgesellschaft Berg. ISBN 3-86118-028-6

Erinnerungsblätter r.AR1/Pz.AR89 (Collective Authorship). Published by Regiments-Kameradenschaft der r.AR1/Pz.AR89. No date or place of publication, and no ISBN.

Erinnerungsblätter über den Einsatz der II./r.AR1 vom 10.Mai 1940 bis 25.Juni 1940. (Collective Authorship). Königsberg 1940.

Hauschild, Reinhard. *Der Springende Reiter: 1. Kavallerie-Division – 24. Panzer-Division im Bild.* Groß Umstadt 1984, Ernst J. Dohany Verlag. ISBN 3-924434-00-X

Jeffke, G.W. *Geschichte des Reiter-Regiment 21 (1. Kavallerie-Division) Vom 15. Dezember 1939 bis 10. Dezember 1941.* Goslar 1973, published by Kameradenschaft 8. Reiter. No ISBN

Koschorrek, Günter K. *Vergiß die Zeit der Dornen nicht.* Mainz 1998, v. Kase & Koehler Verlag. ISBN 3-7758-1375-6

Kuehn, Dietrich & Behrens, Wilhelm. *Geschichte des Reiter-Regiment 1. Teil I Friedensjahre 1919-1939.* Köln-Weidenpesch 1962, published by Regiments-Kameradenschaft. No ISBN

Kuehn, Dietrich. *Geschichte des Reiter-Regiment 1 & Panzergrenadier-Regiment 21. Teil III 1942-45.* Köln, published by Kameradenschaft Reiter-Rgt.1 & Pz.Gr.Rgt.21. No ISBN

Kuehn, Dietrich. *Bilder und Skizzen zur Geschichte des Reiter-Regiment 1 & Panzergrenadier-Regiment 21. Teil III 1942-45.* Köln, published by Kameradenschaft Reiter-Rgt.1 & Pz.Gr.Rgt.21. No ISBN

Kusterer, Ferdinand. *In den Händen der Zeit. Von Stalingrad nach Amerika.* Karlsruhe 1994, INFO Verlag GmbH. ISBN 3-88-190-124-8

Rinke, Hanno. *Unser Regiment im Bild. Das Panzer-Regiment 24 und seine Stammtruppenteile.* Groß Umstadt 1990, Ernst J. Dohany Verlag. ISBN 3-924434-06-9

Schulz, Hubertus. *Die Aufklärer der 1. Kavallerie-Division/24. Panzer-Division.* Groß Umstadt 1993, Ernst J. Dohany Verlag. ISBN 3-924434-07-7
Senger und Etterlin, Dr. Ferdinand Maria von. *Die 24. Panzer-Division vormals 1. Kavallerie-Division 1939-1945.* Friedberg 1986, Podzun Pallas Verlag. ISBN 3-7909-0203-9
Unser General (Collective Authorship). Hemmingen 1977, published by Divisions-Kameradenschaft der 1. Kavallerie-Division/24. Panzer-Division. No ISBN
Weidemann, Gert-Axel. *Unser Regiment. Reiter-Regiment 2 – Panzer-Regiment 24.* Groß Umstadt 1984, Ernst J. Dohany. ISBN 3-924434-01-8

Privately Published Works about 24. Panzer-Division:

Rocholl, Dr. Horst. *Briefe aus einem Bunker.* Selbstverlag 1995. No ISBN
Rocholl, Dr. Horst. *Ende und Anfang.* Selbstverlag 1995. No ISBN
Rocholl, Dr. Horst. *Klosterlager Dubowka.* Selbstverlag 1998. No ISBN
Rocholl, Dr. Horst. *Stalingrad - Katastrophe und Besinnung.* Selbstverlag 1996. No ISBN
Wildeus, Günter. *Meine Erinnerungen an Stalingrad.* Selbstverlag. No ISBN

Other Published Works:

Bender, Roger James & Odegard, Warren W. *Uniforms, Organization and History of the Panzertruppe.* San Jose 1980, R. James Bender Publishing. ISBN 0-912138-18-1
Chuikov, Vasili I. *The Beginning of the Road.* London 1963, MacGibbon & Kee. No ISBN
Doerr, Hans. *Der Feldzug nach Stalingrad.* Darmstadt 1955, E.S.Mittler & Sohn GmbH. No ISBN
Düfel, Andreas & Range, Clemens. *Die Ritterkreuzträger in der Bundeswehr.* Selbstverlag 2000. No ISBN
Fellgiebel, Walther-Peer. *Die Träger des Ritterkreuzes des Eisernen Kreuzes 1939-1945.* Wölfersheim-Berstadt 1996, Podzun Pallas Verlag. ISBN 3-7909-0284-5
Gedenkbuch des deutschen Adels. Band 3. Limburg/Lahn 1967, C. S. Starke Verlag. No ISBN
Gedenkbuch des deutschen Adels – Nachtrag. Band 6. Limburg an der Lahn 1980, C. S. Starke Verlag. No ISBN
Grams, Rolf. *Die 14. Panzer-Division.* Friedberg 1986, Podzun Pallas Verlag. ISBN 3-7909-0286-1
Holl, Adalbert. *Als Infanterist in Stalingrad.* Duisburg 1978, Verlag Ludwig Müller Erlangen. No ISBN
Keilig, Wolf. *Rangliste des Deutschen Heeres 1944-45.* Bad Nauheim 1955, Verlag Hans-Henning Podzun. No ISBN
Krylow, Nikolai I. Stalingrad. *Die Entscheidende Schlacht des Zweiten Weltkrieges.* Köln 1981, Pahl-Rugenstein Verlag. ISBN 3-7609-0624-9
Neidhardt, Hanns. *Mit Tanne und Eichenlaub. Kriegschronik der 100. Jäger-Division.* Stuttgart 1981, Leopold Stocker Verlag. ISBN 3-7020-0373-8
Niehorster, Dr. Leo W.G. *German World War II Organizational Series. Volume 4/I. Mechanized Army Divisions (28th June 1942).* Hannover 1994, self-published. No ISBN
Podewils, Clemens. *Don und Wolga.* München 1952, Carl Hanser Verlag. No ISBN
Rotundo, Louis (Ed.). *Battle of Stalingrad: The 1943 Soviet General Staff study.* London 1989, Pergamon-Brassey's International Defense Publications, Inc.
Samsonov, Aleksandr M. *Stalingradskaya Epopeya.* Moscow 1968. No ISBN

Sänger, Hans. *Die 79. Infanterie-Division.* Friedberg, Podzun Pallas Verlag. ISBN 3-7909-0083-4

Scheibert, Horst. *Die Träger des Deutschen Kreuzes in Gold – Das Heer.* Friedberg, Podzun Pallas Verlag. ISBN 3-7909-0207-1

Thomas, Franz. *Die Eichenlaubträger 1940-1945. Band 1: A-K.* Osnabrück 1997, Biblio Verlag. ISBN 3-7648-2299-6

Thomas, Franz. *Die Eichenlaubträger 1940-1945. Band 2: L-Z.* Osnabrück 1998, Biblio Verlag. ISBN 3-7648-2300-3

Periodicals:

Der Springende Reiter: Mitteilungsblatt der Divisionskameradenschaft der 1. Kavallerie-Division/24. Panzer-Division. Various editions from 1952 to the present.

INDEX

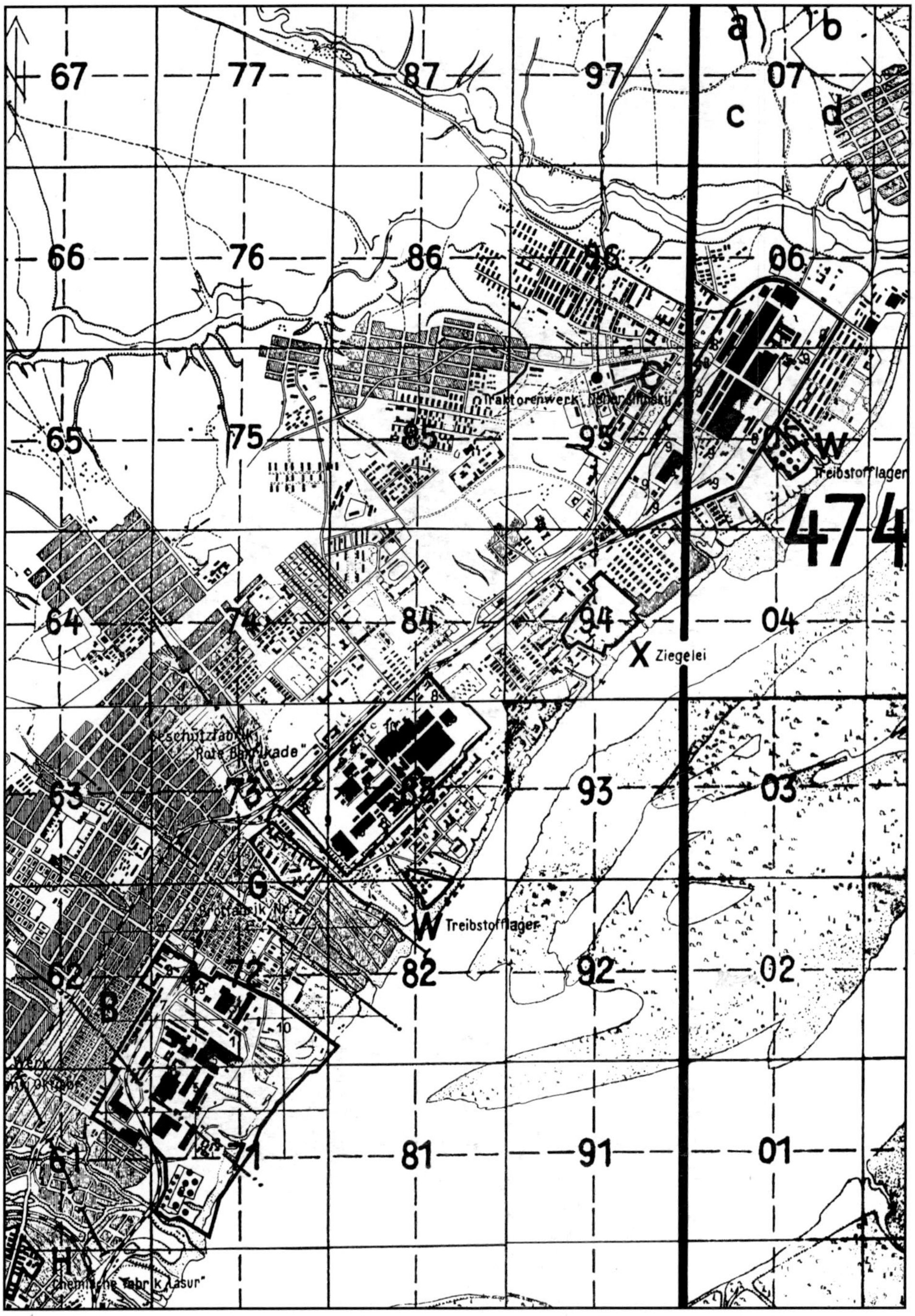
a
b
c
d
67
77
87
97
07
66
76
86
96
06
65
75
85
95
W
Treibstofflager
474
64
74
84
94
04
X Ziegelei
63
73
83
93
03
G
W Treibstofflager
62
72
82
92
02
B
61
71
81
91
01
H